West's
Criminal Justice Series

WEST PUBLISHING COMPANY
St. Paul, Minnesota 55102
March, 1979

CONSTITUTIONAL LAW

Cases and Comments on Constitutional Law 2nd Edition by James L. Maddex, Professor of Criminal Justice, Georgia State University, 486 pages, 1979.

CORRECTIONS

Corrections—Organization and Administration by Henry Burns, Jr., Professor of Criminal Justice, University of Missouri-St. Louis, 578 pages, 1975.

Legal Rights of the Convicted by Hazel B. Kerper, Late Professor of Sociology and Criminal Law, Sam Houston State University and Janeen Kerper, Attorney, San Diego, Calif., 677 pages, 1974.

Selected Readings on Corrections in the Community 2nd Edition by George G. Killinger, Member, Board of Pardons and Paroles, Texas and Paul F. Cromwell, Jr. Director of Juvenile Services, Tarrant County, Texas, 357 pages, 1978.

Readings on Penology—The Evolution of Corrections in America 2nd Edition by George G. Killinger, Paul F. Cromwell, Jr., and Jerry M. Wood, about 350 pages, 1979.

Selected Readings on Introduction to Corrections by George G. Killinger and Paul F. Cromwell, Jr., 417 pages, 1978.

Selected Readings on Issues in Corrections and Administration by George G. Killinger, Paul F. Cromwell, Jr. and Bonnie J. Cromwell, San Antonio College, 644 pages, 1976.

Probation and Parole in the Criminal Justice System by George G. Killinger, Hazel B. Kerper and Paul F. Cromwell, Jr., 374 pages, 1976.

Introduction to Probation and Parole 2nd Edition by Alexander B. Smith, Professor of Sociology, John Jay College of Criminal Justice and Louis Berlin, Formerly Chief of Training Branch, New York City Dept. of Probation, 270 pages, 1979.

CRIMINAL JUSTICE SYSTEM

Introduction to the Criminal Justice System 2nd Edition by Hazel B. Kerper as revised by Jerold H. Israel, 520 pages, 1979.

Introduction to Criminal Justice by Joseph J. Senna and Larry J. Siegel, both Professors of Criminal Justice, Northeastern University, 540 pages, 1978.

Study Guide to accompany Senna and Siegel's Introduction to Criminal Justice by Roy R. Roberg, Professor of Criminal Justice, University of Nebraska-Lincoln, 187 pages, 1978.

Introduction to Law Enforcement and Criminal Justice by Henry M. Wrobleski and Karen M. Hess, both Professors at Normandale Community College, Bloomington, Minnesota, 525 pages, 1979.

CRIMINAL LAW

California Law Manual for the Administration of Justice by Joel Greenfield, Sacramento City College and Rodney Blonien, Executive Director, California State Peace Officer's Association, about 700 pages, 1979.

Cases and Materials on Basic Criminal Law by George E. Dix, Professor of Law, University of Texas, and M. Michael Sharlot, Professor of Law, University of Texas, 649 pages, 1974.

West's Criminal Justice Series

CRIMINAL LAW—Continued

Readings, on Concepts of Criminal Law by Robert W. Ferguson, Administration of Justice Dept. Director, Saddleback College, 560 pages, 1975.

Principles, Cases and Readings on Criminal Law by Thomas J. Gardner, Professor of Criminal Justice, Milwaukee Area Technical College and Victor Manian, Milwaukee County Judge, 782 pages, 1975.

Principles of Criminal Law by Wayne R. LaFave, Professor of Law, University of Illinois, about 600 pages, 1978.

CRIMINAL PROCEDURE

Teaching Materials on Criminal Procedure by Jerry L. Dowling, Professor of Criminal Justice, Sam Houston State University, 544 pages, 1976.

Criminal Procedure for the Law Enforcement Officer 2nd Edition by John N. Ferdico, Assistant Attorney General, State of Maine, 409 pages, 1979.

Cases, Materials and Text on the Elements of Criminal Due Process by Phillip E. Johnson, Professor of Law, University of California, Berkeley, 324 pages, 1975.

Cases, Comments and Questions on Basic Criminal Procedure 4th Edition by Yale Kamisar, Professor of Law, University of Michigan, Wayne R. LaFave, Professor of Law, University of Illinois and Jerold H. Israel, Professor of Law, University of Michigan, 790 pages, 1974. Supplement Annually.

EVIDENCE

Criminal Evidence by Thomas J. Gardner, Professor of Criminal Justice, Milwaukee Area Technical College, 694 pages, 1978.

Criminal Evidence by Edward J. Imwinkelried, Professor of Law, University of San Diego; Paul C. Giannelli, Associate Professor, Case Western Reserve University; Francis A. Gilligan, Adjunct Professor, Jacksonville State University; Fredric I. Lederer, Associate Professor, Judge Advocate General's School, U.S. Army, 425 pages, 1979.

Law of Evidence for Police 2nd Edition by Irving J. Klein, Professor of Law and Police Science, John Jay College of Criminal Justice, 632 pages, 1978.

Criminal Investigation and Presentation of Evidence by Arnold Markle, The State's Attorney, New Haven County, Connecticut, 344 pages, 1976.

INTRODUCTION TO LAW ENFORCEMENT

The American Police—Text and Readings by Harry W. More, Jr., Professor of Administration of Justice, California State University of San Jose, 278 pages, 1976.

Police Tactics in Hazardous Situations by the San Diego, California Police Department, 228 pages, 1976.

Law Enforcement Handbook for Police by Louis B. Schwartz, Professor of Law, University of Pennsylvania and Stephen R. Goldstein, Professor of Law, University of Pennsylvania, 333 pages, 1970

Police Operations—Tactical Approaches to Crimes in Progress by Inspector Andrew Sutor, Philadelphia, Pennsylvania Police Department, 329 pages, 1976.

Introduction to Law Enforcement and Criminal Justice by Henry Wrobleski and Karen M. Hess, both Professors at Normandale Community College, Bloomington, Minnesota, 525 pages, 1979.

JUVENILE JUSTICE

Text and Selected Readings on Introduction to Juvenile Delinquency by Paul F. Cromwell, Jr., George G. Killinger, Rosemary C. Sarri, Professor, School of Social Work, The University of Michigan and H. N. Solomon, Professor of Criminal Justice, Nova University, 502 pages, 1978.

Juvenile Justice Philosophy: Readings, Cases and Comments 2nd Edition by Frederic L. Faust, Professor of Criminology, Florida State University and Paul J. Brantingham, Department of Criminology, Simon Fraser University, 467 pages, 1979.

Introduction to the Juvenile Justice System by Thomas A. Johnson, Professor of Criminal Justice, Washington State University, 492 pages, 1975.

West's Criminal Justice Series

JUVENILE JUSTICE—Continued

Cases and Comments on Juvenile Law by Joseph J. Senna, Professor of Criminal Justice, Northeastern, University and Larry J. Siegel, Professor of Criminal Justice, Northeastern University, 543 pages, 1976.

MANAGEMENT AND SUPERVISION

Selected Readings on Managing the Police Organization by Larry K. Gaines and Truett A. Ricks, both Professors of Criminal Justice, Eastern Kentucky University, 527 pages, 1978.

Criminal Justice Management: Text and Readings by Harry W. More, Jr., 377 pages, 1977.

Effective Police Administration: A Behavioral Approach 2nd Edition by Harry W. More, Jr., Professor, San Jose State University, about 350 pages, 1979.

Police Management and Organizational Behavior: A Contingency Approach by Roy R. Roberg, Professor of Criminal Justice, University of Nebraska at Omaha, 350 pages, 1979.

Police Administration and Management by Sam S. Souryal, Professor of Criminal Justice, Sam Houston State University, 462 pages, 1977.

Law Enforcement Supervision—A Case Study Approach by Robert C. Wadman, Rio Hondo Community College, Monroe J. Paxman, Brigham Young University and Marion T. Bentley, Utah State University, 224 pages, 1975.

POLICE—COMMUNITY RELATIONS

Readings on Police—Community Relations 2nd Edition by Paul F. Cromwell, Jr., and George Keefer, Professor of Criminal Justice, Southwest Texas State University, 506 pages, 1978.

PSYCHOLOGY

Interpersonal Psychology for Law Enforcement and Corrections by L. Craig Parker, Jr., Criminal Justice Dept. Director, University of New Haven and Robert D. Meier, Professor of Criminal Justice, University of New Haven, 290 pages, 1975.

VICE CONTROL

The Nature of Vice Control in the Administration of Justice by Robert W. Ferguson, 509 pages, 1974.

Cases, Text and Materials on Drug Abuse Law by Gerald F. Uelman, Professor of Law, Loyola University, Los Angeles and Victor G. Haddox, Professor of Criminology, California State University at Long Beach and Clinical Professor of Psychiatry, Law and Behavioral Sciences, University of Southern California School of Medicine, 564 pages, 1974.

*

Criminal Evidence

Edward J. Imwinkelried
Professor of Law
University of San Diego

Paul C. Giannelli
Professor of Law
Case Western Reserve University

Francis A. Gilligan
Lieutenant Colonel
Judge Advocate General's Corps
United States Army

Frederic I. Lederer
Major
Judge Advocate General's Corps
United States Army

Criminal Justice Series

West Publishing Co.
St. Paul • New York • Los Angeles • San Francisco
1979

The opinions and conclusions expressed in this book are those of the authors and do not necessarily represent the views of the Department of the Army or any other government agency.

COPYRIGHT © 1979 By WEST PUBLISHING CO.
                 50 West Kellogg Boulevard
                 P.O. Box 3526
                 St. Paul, Minnesota 55165

Printed in the United States of America

Library of Congress Cataloging in Publication Data

Main entry under title.

Criminal evidence.

    (The West criminal justice series)
    1. Evidence, Criminal—United States. I. Imwinkelried, Edward J. II. Series.
KF9660.C75   345'.73'06   78–31954

ISBN 0–8299–0221–x

Dedication and Acknowledgment

Professor Imwinkelried would like to dedicate his work on this text to his parents and Cindy.

Professor Giannelli would like to dedicate his work to his mother and to Sue.

Lieutenant Colonel Gilligan would like to dedicate his work to Barb, Cheryl, Kelly, and the Criminal Law Division of the Judge Advocate General's School.

Major Lederer would like to dedicate his work to Diane.

The authors, especially Professor Imwinkelried, would like to take this opportunity to express their gratitude to Ms. Marilyn Riley, the former Executive Editor of the San Diego Law Review. Ms. Riley helped edit the entire text. Ms. Riley not only gave us invaluable editorial assistance; she gave us additional moral courage by striking the term *arguably* whenever we used the term unnecessarily.

*

Foreword

In the first edition of his work, Dean McCormick commented that "the manifest destiny of evidence law is a progressive lowering of the barriers to truth." Dean McCormick's comment has proven to be a remarkably accurate prediction of the course of Criminal Evidence Law. The past two decades have witnessed a progressive lowering of the barriers to the admission of relevant evidence.

Both the legislatures and the courts have played a significant role in this trend. The 1960s witnessed the adoption of liberal evidence codes in several states, perhaps most notably in California. In the 1970s the trend has gained even more momentum. Despite strong opposition, Congress enacted the Federal Rules of Evidence, liberalizing admissibility standards in federal courts. Congress' action prompted several state legislatures to adopt similar evidence codes.

It is true that in the 1960s the Warren Court created new barriers to admissibility by fashioning exclusionary rules to implement the fourth, fifth, and sixth amendments. However, during the past decade the Burger Court has steadily relaxed those exclusionary rules.

The current course of the evolution of Criminal Evidence Law is unmistakable. It is hoped that this text will document that course. It is also hoped that this text will explain Criminal Evidence Law in clear, understandable terms for practitioners, law students, and other professionals in the criminal justice system. The authors have attempted to explain the rules of Criminal Evidence Law in simple terms and present the rules as an organic whole.

*

Summary of Contents

SUMMARY OF CONTENTS

PART 7. FURTHER CONSTITUTIONAL PROTECTIONS

PART 8. SUFFICIENCY OF THE EVIDENCE

Table of Contents

TABLE OF CONTENTS

PART 2. LOGICAL RELEVANCE

PART 3. LEGAL RELEVANCE

TABLE OF CONTENTS

PART 4. RELIABILITY AND PRIVILEGE

TABLE OF CONTENTS

TABLE OF CONTENTS

TABLE OF CONTENTS

TABLE OF CONTENTS

†

Criminal Evidence

INTRODUCTION

1. General

Although law school curricula devote a tremendous number of hours to the study of substantive law subjects such as crimes, the new practitioner soon discovers that the two most important subjects are procedure and evidence. An attorney is a craftsman, and the rules of procedure and evidence are the tools of the craft, the devices the attorney uses to achieve results for the client. Honesty demands recognition that procedure is the most important subject for the attorney, but, as any trial attorney will attest, evidence is a very close second. Even the office attorney who never sets foot in a courtroom must master evidence law. The attorney advisor must give his or her client a prediction of the legal consequences of historical events. For example, if the client engages in a contemplated course of conduct, the court will or will not say that the conduct amounts to a crime. However, the rules of evidence make counseling surrealistic. An attorney should *not* base his or her advice on the actual events. Rather, the attorney should base the advice on the provable events, the events and facts which can be established under evidence law. In a courtroom, a legal consequence will flow from an event only if evidence law permits proof of that event. Thus, mastery of evidence law is a necessary task for any attorney, regardless of the amount of time the attorney spends in the courtroom. Also, an understanding of evidence law is necessary for the criminal justice professional who must gather and preserve evidence for use in the courtroom.

While conceding the importance of the subject, many students of evidence law have complained about its complexity. Judge Hand, himself an astute student of evidence law, once remarked that character evidence is a "subject [which] seems to gather mist which discussion serves only to thicken."[1] So many exceptions exist to the hearsay rule that one commentator characterized hearsay law as "farcical."[2] The importance of evidence law makes such mystifying complexity

---

1. Nash v. United States, 54 F.2d 1006, 1007 (2d Cir. 1932).

2. Nokes, The English Jury and the Law of Evidence, 31 Tulane L.Rev. 153, 167 (1956).

intolerable, and one of the purposes of this text is to simplify evidence law. The text attempts to accomplish that purpose in two ways. First, within each area of evidence law, the text presents an analytic framework. The chapter on common-law privileges is illustrative.[3] The beginning of the chapter contains a summational statement: "In certain types of proceedings, the holder has certain privileges with respect to certain types of information unless (1) the holder has waived the privilege or (2) there is a special exception to the privilege." The chapter then breaks this statement into component elements and explains the entire law of privilege in terms of those elements. Second, the text develops an analytic framework for all evidence law. Section 3 of this chapter outlines that framework, and the succeeding chapters of the text follow the outline. The authors hope that this structure will enable the student to view the rules of evidence as an organic, rational whole.

2. Sources of the Law of Evidence

Suggested Reading:

Mapp v. Ohio, 367 U.S. 643, 81 S.Ct. 1684, 6 L.Ed. 2d 1081 (1961).

United States v. Jordan, 20 U.S.C.M.A. 614, 44 C.M.R. 44 (1971).

What are the sources of evidence law? Where do the courts find the rules governing presentation of evidence? The answers depend upon the jurisdiction in which the questions arise.

Federal Civilian Courts. The first source of the rules of evidence in federal civilian courts is the Constitution itself, especially the Bill of Rights. One of the most important areas in criminal evidence law is the study of the constitutional exclusionary rules, which exclude evidence seized in violation of the fourth amendment,[4] involuntary[5] and improperly warned[6] confessions obtained in violation of the fifth amendment, and lineup evidence obtained in violation of the sixth amendment.[7] These constitutional rules have an evidentiary impact, for they render the illegally obtained evidence inadmissible.

The second source of federal evidence law is federal statutes. The various titles of the United States Code contain numerous statutes prescribing evidentiary rules. For example, there are statutes creating evidentiary privileges[8] and governing the admissibility of depositions in organized crime prosecutions.[9]

The third and most frequently consulted source is the Federal Rules of Evidence.[10] In 1973 the Supreme Court submitted a draft of the Rules to Congress, and after some debate and amendment, Congress enacted the Rules in 1975. The Rules deal with judicial notice (Article II), presumptions (Article III), relevancy (Article IV), privileges (Article V), witnesses (Article VI), opinion testimony (Article VII), hearsay (Article VIII), authentication (Article IX), and best evidence (Article X).

Finally, where gaps are found in the statutes and Rules, the federal courts turn to the case or decisional law.

---

3. Chapter 14, infra.

4. Weeks v. United States, 232 U.S. 383, 34 S.Ct. 341, 58 L.Ed. 652 (1914).

5. Brown v. Mississippi, 297 U.S. 278, 56 S.Ct. 461, 80 L.Ed. 682 (1936).

6. Miranda v. Arizona, 384 U.S. 436, 86 S.Ct. 1602, 16 L.Ed.2d 694 (1966).

7. United States v. Wade, 388 U.S. 218, 87 S.Ct. 1926, 18 L.Ed.2d 1149 (1967).

8. See, e. g., 21 U.S.C.A. §§ 872, 1175; 42 U.S.C.A. § 242(a).

9. 18 U.S.C.A. § 3503.

10. Fed.Evid.Rules, 28 U.S.C.A.

State Courts. The first source of state evidence law is the federal Constitution. The fourteenth amendment's due process clause incorporates many of the fundamental provisions of the Bill of Rights;[11] and for that reason, the fourth amendment's prohibition of unreasonable searches,[12] the fifth amendment's privilege against self-incrimination,[13] and the sixth amendment's right to counsel[14] apply to the states as well as to the national government.

The second source of state evidence law is federal statutes. At times a state court will have to apply an evidentiary rule supplied by federal statute. Article IV of the federal Constitution requires that each state give full faith and credit to "the public acts, records, and judicial proceedings of every other State."[15] The article further empowers Congress to "prescribe the manner in which such acts, records, and proceedings shall be proved."[16] Exercising that power, Congress has enacted statutes which provide that if state #1 authenticates its records in a prescribed manner, the courts of state #2 must accept those records into evidence.[17]

The third source of state evidence law is the state's own constitution. In a sense, the national Constitution provides only minimum standards; when a Bill of Rights provision applies to the states through the fourteenth amendment, the states must observe at least that minimal restriction on government power. However, a state may adopt a more restrictive constitutional rule. For example, although the United States Supreme Court has held that a voluntary but unwarned confession is admissible for the limited purpose of impeachment,[18] several state courts have held that under their constitutions, unwarned confessions are inadmissible even for that limited purpose.[19]

A fourth source is the state's statutes. Almost all states have some statutes dealing with evidentiary issues such as the admission of business records, and a growing number of states have adopted comprehensive evidence codes. The Uniform Rules of Evidence and the Model Code are commonly used patterns for evidence codes. Recently, a number of states, including Arkansas, Florida, Maine, Nebraska, Nevada, New Mexico, and Wisconsin, have adopted the Federal Rules of Evidence with minor amendments.

Finally, as in the federal courts, the state courts turn to the common law in the absence of a controlling constitutional or statutory provision.

Federal Military Courts. The first source of military rules of evidence is the federal Constitution. The highest military appellate court, the United States Court of Military Appeals,[20] has announced that military personnel are entitled to the protections of the Bill of Rights except those which are expressly or by necessary implication denied them.[21] On that rationale, the court incorporated the *Miranda* warning requirements into military practice.[22]

The second source is federal statutes, notably the Uniform Code of Military Jus-

---

11. See, e. g., Malloy v. Hogan, 378 U.S. 1, 84 S.Ct. 1489, 12 L.Ed.2d 653 (1964).

12. Mapp v. Ohio, 367 U.S. 643, 81 S.Ct. 1684, 6 L.Ed.2d 1081 (1961).

13. Malloy v. Hogan, 378 U.S. 1, 84 S.Ct. 1489, 12 L.Ed.2d 653 (1964).

14. Gideon v. Wainwright, 372 U.S. 335, 83 S.Ct. 792, 9 L.Ed.2d 799 (1963).

15. U.S.C.A.Const. Art. IV § 1.

16. Id.

17. See, e. g., 28 U.S.C.A. §§ 1738–39.

18. Harris v. New York, 401 U.S. 222, 91 S.Ct. 643, 28 L.Ed.2d 1 (1971).

19. See, e. g., People v. Disbrow, 16 Cal.3d 101, 127 Cal.Rptr. 360, 545 P.2d 272 (1976).

20. 10 U.S.C.A. § 867.

21. United States v. Jacoby, 11 U.S.C.M.A. 428, 29 C.M.R. 244 (1960).

22. United States v. Tempia, 16 U.S.C.M.A. 629, 37 C.M.R. 249 (1967).

tice.[23] Article 31(b) of the Code requires warnings similar to those required under *Miranda*,[24] and Article 31(d) expressly provides that involuntary confessions are inadmissible.[25] Article 49(d) lists the situations in which depositions are admissible in courts-martial.[26]

The third source is the Manual for Courts-Martial. Article 36 of the Code authorizes the President to prescribe evidentiary rules for courts-martial.[27] The President has invoked this power and promulgated the Manual by Executive order 11476. Chapter XXVII of the Manual contains a detailed set of evidentiary rules.[28]

The fourth source is the evidence law of federal civilian courts. When a gap exists in federal military evidence law, the military courts look to federal civilian evidence law. The Manual specifically directs courts-martial to follow "so far as not otherwise prescribed in this manual, the rules of evidence generally recognized in the trial of criminal cases in the United States district courts." [29] Thus, the military courts can now consult the Federal Rules of Evidence to supplement the Manual.

Finally the military courts may consider the common law. The same Manual paragraph authorizing consideration of federal civilian evidence law also sanctions resort to the common law.[30] The military courts look to the common law when: (1) the rule stated in the Constitution, Code, or Manual is ambiguous; or (2) the Constitution, Code,

and Manual are silent on an evidentiary question.[31]

Observations About the Sources of Evidence Law. Within each jurisdiction, the list of sources is a hierarchy. The sources listed first have greater legal force and effect than the sources listed subsequently. If a rule based on a higher source conflicts with a rule based on a lower source, the former prevails. The most obvious example is a conflict between a provision of the federal Constitution and a state statute. In the event of such conflict, the Constitution prevails. The result is the same whenever a rule based on a higher source positively conflicts with a rule based on a lower source. In military practice, if a Manual provision conflicts with the Code, the Code prevails.[32]

However, if a rule based on a lower source does not conflict with any higher sources and at the same time grants the defendant more rights than he or she would otherwise be entitled to, the rule is valid. As we previously noted, acting under their own constitutions some state courts have imposed more stringent restrictions on police authority than the federal Constitution mandates.[33] A parallel development has occurred in military courts. The drafters of the Manual incorporated several relatively liberal readings of Warren Court precedents in the Manual. Even though the Burger Court has retreated from the Warren Court positions, the Manual provisions remain binding in courts-martial. Reading *Miranda* broadly, the

---

23.   10 U.S.C.A. §§ 801–934.

24.   Id. at § 831(b).

25.   Id. at § 831(d).

26.   Id. at § 849(d).

27.   Id. at § 836.

28.   Manual for Courts-Martial, United States, 1969 (rev. ed.)

29.   Id. at para. 137.

30.   Id.

31.   See, e. g., United States v. Massey, 15 U.S.C.M.A. 274, 35 C.M.R. 246 (1965).

32.   See United States v. Greer, 3 U.S.C.M.A. 576, 13 C.M.R. 132 (1953). Article 150b of the Manual provided that military law enforcement officials did not have to give a suspect an Article 31 warning before requesting him or her to speak for purpose of voice identification. In *Greer*, the Court of Military Appeals held that Article 31 applied to voice identification. Since paragraph 150b conflicted with Article 31 and the Code was a higher source, Article 31 had to prevail.

33.   See note 19 and accompanying text, supra.

drafters included a Manual provision prohibiting any use of an unwarned statement.[34] Although Harris v. New York[35] limited *Miranda* by permitting impeachment use of a voluntary but unwarned statement, the military courts continue to adhere to a broad reading of *Miranda*.[36]

3. The Conceptual Framework of the Law of Evidence

There are two major divisions of evidence law. The first includes the rules governing the admissibility of items of evidence. These rules address the question of whether the judge should admit an individual item of evidence. The second major division includes the rules governing the sufficiency of all the party's evidence. These rules address other questions. For example, has the party presented sufficient evidence to sustain the burden of going forward and avoid a directed verdict? Has the party presented sufficient evidence to sustain the burden of proof and persuade the jury to find in his or her favor?

The Admissibility of Individual Items of Evidence. Within this major division are two important clusters of rules.

Witnesses. The first cluster relates to witnesses. At the outset, we want to know whether the person is qualified to give any testimony at all in the case; the competency rules determine this issue. If the prospective witness is competent, we can put the witness on the stand. The witness's ascent to the stand triggers another group of rules regulating the witness's examination. The examination rules govern the order, scope, and form of the attorneys' examination of the witness. Moreover, the witness's ascent

to the stand places that person's credibility in issue. There are credibility rules regulating the manner in which the proponent may attempt to increase the witness's believability and the opponent to decrease the believability. Finally, even if the person is generally a competent witness, he or she might not be qualified to give opinion testimony. The law recognizes two types of witnesses, laypersons and experts. Experts may express opinions more liberally than may laypersons. In sum, after a decision that the witness is competent, it becomes necessary to classify the witness as either a layperson or an expert.

The Content of Witnesses's Testimony. The second cluster of rules determines the permissible content of a witness's testimony. In this cluster, there are two central concepts: relevance and competence.

An item of evidence is *logically relevant* if it has any tendency in reason to increase or decrease the probability of the existence of a fact which is of consequence in the case. Logically irrelevant evidence is inadmissible, for it lacks probative value. The courts have developed a companion concept of *legal relevance*. When courts say that to be admissible logically relevant evidence must also be legally relevant, they mean that the evidence's probative worth must outweigh any attendant probative dangers such as the evidence's tendency to inflame the jurors' passions or to distract the jurors from the pivotal issues in the case. In administering the legal relevance requirement, the courts balance probative value (logical relevance) against probative danger. Although this balancing is obviously highly subjective, in several important areas such as character and uncharged misconduct, the courts' rulings have been so standardized that relatively hard and fast rules have emerged. If an item of evidence is both logically and legally relevant, it is presumptively admissible.

The law might nevertheless render the evidence incompetent and inadmissible.

---

34. Para. 153(b)(2)(c), Manual for Courts-Martial, United States, 1969 (rev. ed.).

35. 401 U.S. 222, 91 S.Ct. 643, 28 L.Ed.2d 1 (1971).

36. United States v. Jordan, 20 U.S.C.M.A. 614, 44 C.M.R. 44 (1971).

Competence is a catch-all concept subsuming every doctrine that excludes relevant evidence.

In some cases, the law renders evidence incompetent because of a fear that the evidence is unreliable. The best evidence and hearsay rules illustrate this fear. The best evidence rule is that if a document's contents are in issue, the proponent must produce the original or present an excuse for non-production. Affirmatively, the rule is based on a preference for the original document; negatively, the rule expresses distrust of the reliability of secondary evidence such as copies and oral testimony. The hearsay rule excludes in-court testimony about assertive, out-of-court statements when the truth of the assertion is in issue. This rule reflects a belief that the opponent should have the opportunity to test the assertion's reliability by cross-examination. Simply stated, the rule expresses a fear that in-court testimony about the out-of-court statement might be unreliable.

In other cases, the law renders evidence incompetent in order to promote extrinsic social policies. The constitutional exclusionary rules are excellent illustrations of competence rules based on social policy. The fourth amendment exclusionary rule often operates to exclude relevant and reliable physical evidence; the court excludes the evidence solely to promote an external social policy, the protection of privacy under the fourth amendment. Similarly, the common-law privileges for confidential relations are competence rules based on social policy. Again, the excluded evidence is relevant and often highly reliable. However, the court excludes the privileged conversations in order to protect the confidential relation and encourage free communication within the circle of confidence.

The Sufficiency of the Evidence to Sustain the Burdens. The first major division of evidence law answers the threshold question of whether the judge may admit the individual item of evidence. Even if the judge admits all the evidence the proponent offers, the proponent may never reach the jury, for the judge might rule that even cumulatively, the evidence lacks sufficient probative value to permit a rational jury to find in the proponent's favor. When a judge makes that ruling, the proponent is said to have failed to sustain the burden of going forward; the jury could not rationally find for the proponent, and the judge makes a peremptory ruling for the opponent. Even if the proponent gets over the hurdle of the burden of going forward, the jury might nevertheless find against him or her, for the jury makes its own assessment of the evidence's sufficiency, deciding whether the proponent has sustained the burden of proving that the disputed fact exists. The judge could rule that there is a permissive inference; that is, that a rational jury could find for the proponent. Nevertheless, the jury could simply disbelieve the proponent's evidence and refuse to draw the inference. The judge's decision on the burden of going forward and the jury's decision on the burden of proof are both evaluations of the evidence's sufficiency rather than its mere admissibility.

An individual party may sufficiently establish a fact by formally presenting evidence of the fact's existence. However, when the fact's existence is not subject to reasonable dispute, it would obviously be wasteful of the court's time to require the time-consuming presentation of formal proof. In this situation, the trial judge may judicially note the fact's existence. Judicial notice is an alternative method of establishing the existence of a fact.

PART 1
WITNESSES

CHAPTER 1
THE EXAMINATION OF WITNESSES

1. Introduction

As a practical matter, because of their intimate knowledge of the case, the parties in large part determine the order and method of the witnesses's examination. However, formally, the trial judge regulates the order and method of examining witnesses.[1] In exercising his or her discretion, the trial judge considers the factors of attainment of truth,[2] undue consumption of time,[3] and the protection of the witnesses and parties to the litigation.[4] To attain the truth, the judge may ex-

to decide whether the evidence will be in narrative form or elicited as answers to specific questions. The judge may also control the order of calling witnesses and the use of demonstrative evidence.

3. Fed.Evid.Rule 611(a)(1), 28 U.S.C.A. A companion rule is stated in Fed.Evid.Rule 403(b), 28 U.S.C.A.

4. Fed.Evid.Rule 611(a)(3), 28 U.S.C.A. The judge may protect the witness from examinations that "go beyond the bounds of proper cross-examination merely to harass, annoy, or humiliate." Alford v. United

1. Fed.Evid.Rule 611, 28 U.S.C.A.; West's Ann.Cal. Evid.Code § 320.

2. Fed.Evid.Rule 611(a)(1), 28 U.S.C.A. This provision states the general rule which permits the judge

ercise discretion to permit a witness to modify, correct, or explain his or her testimony if the witness has misspoken or given an erroneous impression.[5] The judge may prevent the undue consumption of time by precluding unnecessarily repetitious testimony.[6] Finally, protecting a witness is necessary when the witness is a child of tender years or when the examiner is unfairly attempting to discredit or intimidate the witness.[7] In exercising discretion, the judge will be reversed only if the appellate court finds a clear abuse of discretion that prejudiced a party's right to a fair trial.[8]

Although the order and method of examination are subject to the trial judge's discretion, customary norms have developed. These norms apply to both the trial as a whole and the examination of each witness. The remaining sections of this chapter discuss these norms.

2. The Macrocosm of the Trial

At the outset of the trial, the judge or attorneys question the prospective jurors concerning their qualifications; this questioning is known as the *voir dire* examination. When the examination is complete, the parties select the jurors. The parties' selection power is essentially negative. The parties may challenge and remove prospective jurors for cause or peremptorily; the trial judge rules on the challenges for cause and decides

whether there is a sufficient showing of cause such as bias, but the parties may exercise the peremptory challenges without stating a reason.

When the jury selection process is complete, the two sides deliver their opening statements. An opening statement is a preview of the evidence the party intends to present to the jury. The prosecutor makes the first opening statement. In many jurisdictions, the defense counsel may make his or her opening immediately after the prosecution opening or defer the defense opening until the beginning of the defense case-in-chief.

The parties now present their evidence. The first major evidentiary presentation is the prosecution case-in-chief. In this case, the prosecution may present any evidence logically relevant to any fact of legal consequence in the case.[9] The prosecution usually devotes this case to evidence establishing the essential elements of the charged crime.

When the prosecution concludes its case-in-chief, the defense may make a motion based on the insufficiency of the evidence. The defense may argue that as a matter of law, the prosecution evidence has insufficient probative value to sustain the prosecution's burden of going forward. The defense presses this argument by making a motion for a directed verdict, finding of not guilty, or judgment of acquittal. If the judge denies the motion, the trial proceeds.

The defense then presents its case-in-chief. Like the prosecution case-in-chief, the defense case includes any evidence logically relevant to any fact of consequence in the trial. During its case, the defense presents evidence (1) rebutting the evidence of the crime's essential elements and (2) establish-

---

States, 282 U.S. 687, 694, 51 S.Ct. 218, 220, 75 L.Ed. 624 (1931). Protection is especially necessary when the opponent is trying to impeach the witness by using acts of uncharged misconduct.

5. Muir v. Grier, 160 Cal.App.2d 671, 325 P.2d 664 (1958).

6. See, e. g., United States v. Stoehr, 100 F.Supp. 143 (M.D.Pa.1951); State v. Jones, 14 N.C.App. 558, 188 S.E.2d 676 (1972).

7. See, e. g., People v. Smith, 164 Cal.App.2d 510, 330 P.2d 678 (1958); Wanzer v. State, 232 Ga. 523, 207 S.E.2d 466 (1974).

8. C. McCormick, Handbook of the Law of Evidence 8 (2d ed. 1972).

9. Federal Rule 401 states: "'Relevant evidence' means evidence having any tendency to make the existence of any fact that is of consequence to the determination of the action more probable or less probable than it would be without the evidence."

ing any affirmative defenses to criminal responsibility.

The third major evidentiary presentation is the prosecution rebuttal. As of right, the prosecutor may now present evidence to refute any new matters raised during the defense case-in-chief. The prosecutor may now present evidence rebutting any affirmative defenses or attacking the credibility of defense witnesses. The trial judge has discretion to widen the scope of rebuttal. The judge may permit the prosecutor to present evidence logically relevant to any fact of consequence. For example, suppose that the prosecutor did not discover an eyewitness until after the prosecution case-in-chief. In his or her discretion, the judge could permit the prosecutor to call the eyewitness in rebuttal.

The fourth and final major evidentiary presentation is the defense rejoinder or surrebuttal. The scope of defense surrebuttal is similar to that of prosecution rebuttal. As of right, the defense may present evidence to rebut any new matters raised during the prosecution rebuttal. In his or her discretion, the judge may permit the defense counsel to present evidence logically relevant to any fact of consequence in the case.

After the parties' evidentiary presentations, the judge may decide to call a witness. The judge may do so on his or her own motion,[10] on the motion of a party,[11] or at the request of a juror. Judges rarely exercise this power. However, judges sometimes do so in the exceptional situation where a witness with relevant knowledge has a rather unsavory background. On the one hand, the judge would want the jury to hear the witness's testimony; the witness may be the only source for that relevant knowledge. On the other hand, if the witness is easily im-

peachable, neither side might be willing to call the witness and thereby run the risk that the witness will taint the calling side.

When both sides have rested and all the evidence has been presented, the judge and parties may now conduct an instructions conference in the judge's chambers or at least in the jury's absence. During the conference, the judge and parties discuss the jury instructions and other matters such as which exhibits will be submitted to the jury during deliberations.

After the conference, the parties deliver their summations or closing arguments to the jury. In many jurisdictions, the prosecution makes the first summation, the defense the second, and the prosecution a third and final summation. During the closing arguments, the attorneys discuss such evidentiary problems as which witnesses the jurors should believe and which inferences the jurors should draw from the evidence.

Before the jury retires to deliberate, the trial judge gives the jurors their final charge or jury instructions. The instructions describe the rules of law governing the charged crime and any affirmative defense. The instructions also address evidentiary matters. The instructions typically list general factors the jurors should consider in evaluating the witnesses' credibility. The final charge may also include limiting and cautionary instructions. A limiting instruction informs the jury that a particular item of evidence is admissible for a certain purpose or against a certain party but inadmissible for other purposes or against other parties. For example, an item of evidence might be admissible to impeach the defendant's credibility but inadmissible as substantive evidence that the defendant committed the charged crime. Or an item might be admissible against one defendant but inadmissible against a co-defendant. Cautionary instructions warn the jury to be especially careful in evaluating a certain type of testimony such as the testimony of an accomplice.

---

10. Fed.Evid.Rule 614(a), 28 U.S.C.A.; West's Ann. Cal.Evid.Code §§ 730, 775.

11. Id.

3. The Order and Scope of the Examination

The Sequestration, Exclusion, or Separation of the Witness. When a judge sequesters a witness, the judge is ordering the witness to remain outside the courtroom while the other witnesses in the case testify. The rationale for sequestration is that if the witness does not hear the other witnesses' testimony, the witness will not ·be tempted to tailor his or her testimony to agree with the other witnesses' testimony. When a judge sequesters a witness, the judge usually places the witness "under the rule"—that is, orders the witness not to discuss his or her testimony with other witnesses in the case.

In some jurisdictions, the trial judge automatically sequesters the witnesses at the beginning of the trial.[12] However, the prevailing practice is that a party must move for an order sequestering the witnesses.[13]

Certain persons cannot be sequestered. It would violate both the confrontation and due process guarantees to sequester the defendant; the judge may exclude the defendant from the courtroom only in extreme circumstances.[14] Many jurisdictions likewise recognize that the prosecuting sovereign has a right to have a representative in the courtroom. Federal Evidence Rule 615 specifically states that the judge may not sequester "an officer or employee of a party which is not a natural person designated as its representative by its attorney."[15] The legislative history indicates that Congress adopted this provision to enable prosecutors to except investigative agents from sequestration orders.[16]

Even if a party does not have a right to have a witness excepted from a sequestration order, the party may ask the judge to invoke his or her discretion to do so. Under Federal Rule 615, the judge should except "a person whose presence is shown by a party to be essential to the presentation of his cause."[17] The accompanying Advisory Committee Note states that "an expert needed to advise counsel in the management of the litigation" would fall within this exception.[18]

Suggested Reading:

Illinois v. Allen, 397 U.S. 337, 90 S.Ct. 1057, 25 L.Ed.2d 353 (1970).

The Administration of the Oath or Affirmation to the Witness. In most jurisdictions the bailiff or clerk administers an oath to every witness except a child witness.[19] The purpose of the oath is to arouse the witness's conscience and motivate the witness to testify truthfully.[20] In addition, the oath subjects the witness to criminal responsibility for perjury if the witness gives willfully false testimony. [21]

The language of the oath is often prescribed by statute.[22] If the witness is willing to swear before God, the bailiff or clerk administers an oath to him or her, invoking God's name. If the witness does not recog-

12. In these jurisdictions many courtroom entrances have signs declaring: "Witnesses Should Remain Outside Until Called."

13. Fed.Evid.Rule 615, 28 U.S.C.A.

14. Illinois v. Allen, 397 U.S. 337, 90 S.Ct. 1057, 25 L.Ed.2d 353 (1970).

15. Fed.Evid.Rule 615(2), 28 U.S.C.A.

16. Report of the Senate Committee on the Judiciary, West's Federal Rules of Evidence for United States Courts and Magistrates 77 (1975).

17. Fed.Evid.Rule 615(3), 28 U.S.C.A.

18. Advisory Committee Note, Fed.Evid.Rule 615, 28 U.S.C.A.

19. Fed.Evid.Rule 603, 28 U.S.C.A.

20. People v. Haeberlin, 272 Cal.App.2d 711, 77 Cal. Rptr. 553 (1969).

21. Chapter 2 points out the evolution of the competency requirement of moral capacity. In many jurisdictions, the modern understanding of that requirement is that the witness must have the cognitive capacity to understand that untruthful testimony will subject him or her to prosecution for perjury.

22. West's Ann.Cal.Code Civ.Proc. § 2094.

nize a deity or has a scruple against oaths, the bailiff asks the witness to affirm under penalty of perjury. The proper time to determine whether to swear or affirm the witness is before the administration of the oath.[23] The attorney calling the witness should alert the bailiff if any question exists as to whether the prospective witness is willing to swear.

Suggested Reading:

Flores v. State, Alaska, 443 P.2d 73 (1968).

Direct Examination. The order of a witness's examination is: direct by the witness's proponent, cross by the opponent, redirect by the proponent, and recross by the opponent. The range of topics on which a witness may be questioned is called the *scope of the examination.*

The first examination by the witness's proponent, the party calling the witness, is the direct examination. On direct examination during his or her case-in-chief, the proponent may question the witness about any fact logically relevant to the facts of legal consequence in the case.[24] All jurisdictions agree that this is the proper scope of direct examination.

---

23. State v. Chyo Chiagh, 92 Mo. 395, 4 S.W. 704 (1887).

24. Again, the expression, *fact of consequence,* is employed in Fed.Evid.Rule 401, 28 U.S.C.A.
There is an interplay between the scope rules for the macrocosm of the whole trial and the microcosm of the examination of a single witness. During the case-in-chief on direct, the proponent may question the witness about any information logically relevant to any fact of consequence. However, during rebuttal or surrebuttal, the scope rules for the macrocosm may limit the scope of the direct examination. During rebuttal or surrebuttal, the dispute may have narrowed to one or some of the facts of consequence. If so, the scope rules for the macrocosm will limit the scope of direct examination.

Cross-Examination. Cross-examination is the first examination by the adversary or opponent. As to the *scope of cross-examination,* the courts are in agreement on two points. First, the courts concur that the scope of cross includes the witness's credibility. The opponent may impeach the witness's credibility during cross. Second, the courts agree that the judge has discretion over the scope of cross. The judge may widen or narrow the normal scope of cross within the jurisdiction. However, there is a marked split of authority over what the normal scope of cross is.

One minority view is that the scope of cross is wide-open; that is, like the scope of direct, the scope of cross includes any fact logically relevant to any fact of consequence in the case.[25] Under this view, the scope of direct examination does not limit the scope of cross. The cross-examiner may question the witness about the opponent's case or the cross-examiner's own case.

A second minority view is the compromise position that the cross-examiner (1) may question the witness about the opponent's case but (2) may not question the witness about the cross-examiner's own affirmative case unless it is mentioned on direct examination.[26] Suppose that the government charges the defendant with murder and that defendant raises the affirmative defense of insanity. The prosecutor calls an eyewitness to the killing. On direct examination, the witness testifies solely about the killing. On cross, the defense counsel could question the witness about the killing. Indeed, the defense counsel could question the witness about any essential element of the charged crime. However, the defense counsel could not inquire about the defendant's

---

25. This is also the English view. See Saxon v. Harvey, 190 So.2d 901 (Miss.1966); Mask v. State, 32 Miss. 405 (1856); State v. West, 349 Mo. 221, 161 S.W.2d 966 (1942).

26. Smith v. State, 125 Ohio St. 137, 180 N.E. 695 (1932).

sanity, since that matter relates to an affirmative defense which was not touched upon during direct. Suppose, however, that on direct, the prosecutor elicited the witness's opinion of the defendant's sanity. Then the defense counsel could probe about the defendant's sanity during cross; although sanity is part of the defense case rather than the prosecution case, the witness mentioned the topic of sanity on direct examination.

The third and majority view is that the scope of cross is restricted to the matters covered on direct examination.[27] Here, the basic problem is definitional: What are the matters covered on direct examination?

It is conceivable that a court could limit the scope of cross to the precise statements made on direct examination. However, that view is so illiberal that it is patently unacceptable, and no court has opted for that view.[28]

Some courts following the restrictive view equate the matters covered on direct examination with the essential elements of the crime or affirmative defense mentioned on direct examination. Suppose that under the substantive Criminal Law in the jurisdiction, the charged crime has two essential legal elements: the criminal act (the taking of the property) and the criminal state of mind (the intent to deprive the owner of the property). The defendant takes the stand but limits his or her testimony to a denial of committing the act. The defendant has testified about only one essential element of the crime. Courts following this so-called *legal test* for the scope of cross would preclude the prosecutor from inquiring about the defendant's state of mind on cross. Although the defendant's state of mind is a fact of consequence under the substantive

law and pleadings, the defendant did not refer to that element of the crime on direct.

Other courts use the so-called *factual test* to define the scope of cross. These courts equate matters covered on direct with historical transactions mentioned during direct examination. Historical transactions are events with dimensions in time and space. Under the factual test, the cross-examiner may question the witness about any aspect of the historical transactions mentioned on direct but may not question the witness about other events. Suppose that prior to the alleged larceny, the defendant committed certain acts which are logically relevant to prove his subsequent commission of the crime. For example, on the day before the alleged larceny, the defendant may have discussed his or her plans for the larceny with an accomplice. Again, the defendant elects to take the stand and testify. Now the defendant carefully limits the direct examination to testimony about his or her conduct at the time and place of the alleged larceny. On cross, the prosecutor could not question the defendant about the defendant's discussion with the accomplice; that discussion is a discrete historical event, and the defendant did not mention that historical transaction on direct.

In addition to the legal and factual tests for the scope of cross, there is a third, *rebuttal test*. Under the rebuttal test, the cross-examiner may question the witness to rebut either the very facts mentioned on direct or any inference from those facts. Assume that the defense theory is that the alleged victim of the larceny had given the defendant consent to take the property. Specifically, the defense theory is that by the terms of a prior contract between the alleged victim and the defendant, the alleged victim agreed to give the property to the defendant to settle a debt.[29] At trial, the pros-

---

27. Fed.Evid.Rule 611(b), 28 U.S.C.A.; West's Ann. Cal.Evid.Code § 773.

28. C. McCormick, Handbook of the Law of Evidence 48–49 (2d ed. 1972).

29. This hypothetical is based on Problem 6–2, K. Broun & R. Meisenholder, Problems in Evidence (1973).

ecutor calls the alleged victim as a witness. On direct the alleged victim testifies that he or she discovered the property missing and reported it to the police. On cross the defense counsel attempts to elicit that witness's admission that a month prior to the alleged theft, the witness and defendant entered into the settlement agreement. On the one hand, the witness did not mention the prior settlement agreement on direct; the settlement discussions amount to a separate historical transaction. However, the obvious inference from the direct examination is that the witness had not consented to the defendant's taking of the property. The question tends to rebut that inference and would hence be permissible in a jurisdiction following the rebuttal test.

Suggested Reading:

State v. West, 349 Mo. 221, 161 S.W.2d 966 (1942).

The Procedural Consequences of the Scope Rules. In most instances, the scope rules regulate only the order of proof. For example, assume that the prosecution calls a witness and that on cross, the judge rules a certain question the defense counsel wants to pose exceeds the proper scope of cross. The ruling does not foreclose posing that question to the witness. Rather, the ruling forces the defense to call the witness during its case-in-chief to pose the question.

There is one exceptional situation in which the scope rules can have a formal foreclosure effect. That exception arises when a witness or a party has a privilege that bars the opposing party from calling him to the stand. Suppose that the defendant testifies and that on cross, the judge rules that a certain question the prosecutor wants to ask exceeds the proper scope of cross. Since the prosecutor may not call the defendant as a witness, the formal effect of the ruling is to

foreclose the possibility of posing the question to the defendant.

Even if the ruling does not formally foreclose posing the question, the ruling can have that practical effect. In the original hypothetical, the defense counsel may decide that the matter is too insignificant to warrant the trouble of recalling the witness. Or the defense counsel may be reluctant to call a hostile prosecution witness during the defense case.

However, apart from the rare situations where the scope rules have a formal or practical foreclosure effect, they generally affect only the sequence in which the jurors hear the evidence.

The first consequence of the scope limitations has already been mentioned. If the question exceeds the proper scope of cross and the cross-examiner wants to ask the question, the cross-examiner may have to call the witness. If a question put to a prosecution witness exceeds the scope, the defense counsel may call the witness during the defense case-in-chief. If a question put to a defense witness exceeds the scope, the prosecutor may call the witness during the prosecution rebuttal.

The second consequence is the problem which arises when there has been a wrongful denial or undue restriction of the opportunity for cross-examination. A denial may occur because the witness dies or otherwise becomes unavailable before cross begins or is completed.[30] An undue restriction may occur if the trial judge erroneously sustains a scope objection. An erroneous curtailment of the defendant's right to cross-examine prosecution witnesses may violate the defendant's sixth amendment right to confrontation. In Alford v. United States,[31] the Supreme Court held that the judge violated the

---

30. For an excellent discussion of the factual variations of this problem, see C. McCormick, Handbook of the Law of Evidence § 19 (2d ed. 1972).

31. 282 U.S. 687, 51 S.Ct. 218, 75 L.Ed. 624 (1931).

defendant's confrontation right when the judge refused to allow cross-examination of a government witness about his residence. In Smith v. Illinois,[32] the Court held that the judge violated the defendant's right by a ruling denying cross-examination about a key prosecution witness's correct name and address. The Court's recent decision in Davis v. Alaska [33] extends the same reasoning to restrictions on attempted impeachment of government witnesses during cross-examination. It is true that the trial judge has discretion in regulating the extent of cross-examination, especially cross-examination relating to credibility rather than the facts on the merits.[34] However, it will ordinarily be constitutional error for the judge to invoke scope rules to completely preclude the defendant from presenting highly impeaching evidence during the cross-examination of a key prosecution witness.[35] If the judge discovers the error before the trial's conclusion, the available remedies include giving cautionary instructions about uncross-examined testimony, striking the direct, and granting a mistrial.

The third procedural consequence arises when the cross-examiner exceeds the proper scope of direct. The early view was that to the extent the cross-examiner exceeds the scope of the direct, the cross-examiner "adopts" the witness. In effect, the courts reasoned that the formal cross-examination was functionally direct examination. Given that premise, the courts naturally concluded that with respect to the new matter outside the scope of the direct, the cross-examiner could neither impeach the witness nor pose leading questions to the witness.[36]

That conclusion is still the prevailing view in the United States.

Suggested Reading:

Smith v. Illinois, 390 U.S. 129, 88 S.Ct. 748, 19 L. Ed.2d 956 (1968).

Alford v. United States, 282 U.S. 687, 51 S.Ct. 218, 75 L.Ed. 624 (1931).

Redirect Examination. Redirect examination includes all subsequent examinations of the witness by the proponent. There is substantial consensus on the scope of redirect examination. As of right, the proponent may question the witness about the witness's credibility and new matters mentioned on cross. Redirect examination about the witness's credibility is quite common. If on cross the opponent elicited the witness's admission of a prior inconsistent statement, on redirect the proponent may give the witness an opportunity to explain away the apparent inconsistency. On cross the prosecutor might have questioned a defense witness about a relationship with the defendant, suggesting that the witness is biased in the defendant's favor. On redirect the defense counsel could elicit the witness's testimony that notwithstanding the relationship, the witness would not lie for the defendant. Thus, redirect serves an important rehabilitation function.

While redirect as of right is limited to credibility and new matters mentioned on cross, the judge has discretion to broaden the scope to any fact logically relevant to the facts of consequence in the case.

Recross-Examination. Recross includes all subsequent examinations of the witness by the opponent. The scope of recross-examination includes the witness's credibility and "new matter . . . brought out on redirect examination." [37] If the judge has

---

32. 390 U.S. 129, 88 S.Ct. 748, 19 L.Ed.2d 956 (1968).

33. 415 U.S. 308, 94 S.Ct. 1105, 39 L.Ed.2d 347 (1974).

34. United States v. Callahan, 551 F.2d 733 (6th Cir. 1977); United States v. Polk, 550 F.2d 1265 (10th Cir. 1977); United States v. Brown, 546 F.2d 166 (5th Cir. 1977).

35. Id.

36. C. McCormick, Handbook of the Law of Evidence § 23 (2d ed. 1972).

37. Hale v. United States, 435 F.2d 737, 749–50 (5th Cir. 1970). See also United States v. Morris, 485 F.2d

properly enforced the rules limiting the scope of redirect, there will rarely be recross-examination as of right on the merits. Of course, here again the judge has discretion to broaden the normal scope of recross.

The Rule of Completeness. The rule of completeness is a corollary of the scope rules. Stated simply, the rule is that if one part of a transaction has been introduced in evidence during one examination, other relevant parts of the same transaction may be admitted during the next examination. An analysis of the rule requires discussion of three questions.

First, what types of evidence does the rule apply to? Federal Evidence Rule 106 applies the federal version of the rule to written or recorded statements.[38] Some state statutes are slightly broader in scope; one such statute encompasses "an act, declaration, conversation or writing."[39]

Second, what is the requisite relation between the part already introduced and the part the party now wishes to introduce? In some jurisdictions, the only requirement is that the two parts be logically relevant to the same subject matter. However, in most jurisdictions, the requirement is more rigorous. The state statute is typical in its requirement that the introduction of the second is "necessary to make (the first part properly) understood."[40] Essentially, the proponent of the second part must persuade the judge that the jury's consideration of the first part, standing alone, would be misleading.

Third, how does the rule operate procedurally? In most jurisdictions, the rule operates to permit the proponent of the second part of the transaction to introduce evidence of that part. For example, if the prosecutor forces the defendant to read one paragraph of a letter on cross, the defense counsel could introduce another paragraph of the same letter on redirect. The rule of completeness thus functions as a particularization of the scope rules.

In a few jurisdictions, including the federal courts, the rule operates in a different fashion. Federal Evidence Rule 106 reads: "When a writing or recorded statement or part thereof is introduced by a party, an adverse party may require him at that time to introduce any other part or any other writing or recorded statement which ought in fairness to be considered contemporaneously with it."[41] In these jurisdictions, the opponent can force the proponent of the first part of the transaction to broaden the scope of his or her examination of the witness. Under this rule, the defense counsel in the previous hypothetical could force the prosecutor to have the defendant read both paragraphs on cross-examination.

Questions by the Trial Judge. Like the attorneys, the trial judge has a right to question the witness.[42] In some circumstances the judge may even have a duty to do so; some courts impose a duty on the judge when a proper foundation has not been laid for an item of evidence and the lack of a proper foundation amounts to constitutional error.

The judge may interrupt an attorney's examination to pose questions to the witness. However, judges usually prefer to wait until the attorneys have completed their examinations. In examining the witness, the judge must refrain from becoming a partisan. The judge errs if the tenor, extent, and tone of his or her questions create the distinct impression that the judge believes the defendant is guilty.[43] There is a division of author-

---

1385 (5th Cir. 1973); United States v. Stoehr, 196 F.2d 276 (3d Cir. 1952).

38. Fed.Evid.Rule 106, 28 U.S.C.A.

39. West's Ann.Cal.Evid.Code § 356.

40. Id.

41. Fed.Evid.Rule 106, 28 U.S.C.A.

42. Griffin v. United States, 164 F.2d 903 (D.C.Cir. 1947); State v. Riley, 28 N.J. 188, 145 A.2d 601 (1958).

43. United States v. Sheldon, 544 F.2d 213 (5th Cir. 1976); United States v. Dotson, 21 U.S.C.M.A. 79, 44 C.M.R. 133 (1971).

ity on the issue, but the majority view seems to be that the judge may pose leading questions to the witness.[44]

Suggested Reading:

United States v. Sheldon, 544 F.2d 213 (5th Cir. 1976).

Questions by the Trial Jurors. In a few jurisdictions, including Kentucky, the petit jurors have a right to ask questions of the witness.[45] However, in most jurisdictions, the jurors may pose questions only at the judge's discretion.[46] The obvious danger is that lay jurors will pose improper and prejudicial questions. To eliminate that danger, many judges use the following procedure. The judge instructs the jurors that if they want to pose a question, they should raise their hand. If a juror does so, the judge directs the juror to reduce the question to writing. The juror hands the slip of paper to the judge, and the judge and attorneys discuss the question's propriety. If the judge concludes that the question is proper, the judge asks the question or permits the juror to do so. The judge may include the slip of paper in the record of trial.

Suggested Reading:

Stamp v. Commonwealth, 200 Ky. 133, 253 S.W. 242 (1923).

Excusal and Recall. After the judge, attorneys, and jurors have examined the witness, the witness is excused from the courtroom. The witness may be excused permanently or subject to recall.

If a witness has been excused subject to recall, a party may recall the witness as of right. However, if the witness has been excused permanently, the judge has discretion whether to grant a party's request to recall the witness;[47] the party must seek leave to recall the witness. The judge will ordinarily deny leave if the stated reason for recalling the witness is to have the witness repeat his or her testimony merely for purpose of emphasis. On the other hand, the judge will ordinarily grant leave if the stated reason is giving the witness an opportunity to deny or explain impeaching evidence introduced by the opposition.

4. Form of Examination

Narrative Testimony. May the proponent ask a general question, inviting the witness to state the relevant facts in narrative form? Or must the proponent ask narrow questions, designed to elicit specific facts? Some commentators have argued that narrative testimony is more likely to be correct and complete. However, there are two dangers in narrative testimony. The first danger is that it is more difficult for the judge, jurors, and opposing counsel to follow the testimony. The second danger is that there is a greater probability that the witness will inject incompetent evidence such as hearsay. The decision whether to permit the witness to give narrative testimony is entrusted to the judge's discretion.[48] Many judges permit narrative testimony at least at the be-

---

44. Commonwealth v. Galavan, 91 Mass. (9 Allen) 271 (1864); C. McCormick, Handbook of the Law of Evidence § 8 (2d ed. 1972).

45. Stamp v. Commonwealth, 200 Ky. 133, 253 S.W. 242 (1923).

46. See, e. g., O'Nellion v. Haynes, 122 Cal.App. 329, 9 P.2d 853 (1932).

47. See, e. g., United States v. Manglona, 414 F.2d 642 (9th Cir. 1969) (proper to allow the prosecution to recall special agent who had forgotten to testify about one element of the *Miranda* warnings).

48. Advisory Committee Note, Fed.Evid.Rule 611, 28 U.S.C.A.

ginning of direct examination. If difficulties develop, that is, if the witness's narrative is disorganized or the witness makes repeated references to irrelevant or incompetent matter, the judge will then direct the proponent to elicit the testimony in response to specific questions.

Suggested Reading:

Deams v. State, 159 Tex.Cr.R. 496, 265 S.W.2d 96 (1954).

Vague or Indefinite Questions. The proponent's questions must be worded clearly. A question is objectionable if it is unduly vague. The question's clarity must be judged from the witness's perspective. Even if the question would be clear to a person with legal training, the question may be improper when posed to a lay witness. Defense counsel must be particularly alert to ambiguous questions which may cause the injection of improper character evidence.[49] For example, a prosecutor might ask a witness whether the defendant had been in any "trouble." The ambiguity of that question might cause the witness to make incompetent references to the defendant's arrests or acts of uncharged misconduct.

Leading Questions. The lay notion of a leading question is a question that can be answered categorically by a Yes or No. Unfortunately, the lay notion is both under-inclusive and overinclusive. The notion is underinclusive, since some questions are leading even though they cannot be answered by a Yes or No response. The notion is overinclusive, for some questions which can be answered Yes or No are not leading.

The following is the most accurate *definition of leading question*: *"A leading question is a question that suggests to the witness the answer that the examining party desires."*[50] To be leading, the question's language must suggest the response the questioning attorney wants.

What types of language will convey such a suggestion to the witness? First, language in effect expressing a preference can convey the suggestion. The prosecutor puts a police officer on the stand and questions the officer about an interrogation of the defendant. The prosecutor asks, "Didn't the defendant admit his pistol was unregistered?" The question is leading. However, the question is not leading simply because it can be answered Yes or No. The question is leading because, given its wording and the probable tone of the prosecutor's voice, the language in effect tells the witness which answer the prosecutor prefers.

Second, the questioning attorney may convey the suggestion by manipulating the detail in the question. The government has charged the defendant with reckless driving. The prosecutor is questioning the arresting officer who pursued the defendant. The prosecutor asks, "Was the defendant's car proceeding slowly, or was it proceeding in a northerly direction at approximately 80 miles per hour?" The question contains two clauses, but the clauses are not evenly balanced. The amount of detail in the second clause suggests to the witness that the second clause contains the desired answer.

As a rule of thumb, many trial judges assume that a question beginning with *who, how, when, where, why, which,* or *what* is not leading. Such questions rarely suggest an answer and will usually survive a leading question objection.

---

49. For an analysis of the restrictions on character evidence, see Chapter 9, infra.

50. West's Ann.Cal.Evid.Code § 764.

Suggested Readings:

United States v. Littlewind, 551 F.2d 244 (8th Cir. 1977).

United States v. Johnson, 495 F.2d 1097 (5th Cir. 1974).

The Propriety of Leading Questions. There are numerous situations in which leading questions are permissible. Trial judges routinely permit leading questions on cross-examination.[51] On cross-examination, the witness is frequently more or less hostile to the cross-examiner, and there is little danger that the witness will accept the cross-examiner's suggestions. In the extraordinary case where the witness is friendly to the cross-examiner, the judge may prohibit leading questions.[52]

Leading questions are often permissible on direct examination. Prosecutors often call witnesses who are the defendant's acquaintances and hostile to the government. An attorney may use leading questions during the direct examination of a hostile witness.[53] Certain types of witnesses—children, elderly persons, ill persons, and people who are not fluent in English—often have communications problems on the witness stand. An attorney may use leading questions during the direct examination of such a witness to assist the witness.[54] Similarly, an attorney may use leading questions to refresh the recollection of a witness whose memory has failed.[55] Finally, judges rou-tinely permit leading questions on direct when the attorney is questioning about preliminary matters rather than the pivotal facts on the merits.[56]

Compound Questions. The prohibition of compound questions is self-explanatory. A compound question poses two questions rather than one. To ensure the clarity of testimony and facilitate objections to improper questions, the law generally insists that the questioner elicit one historical fact at a time. If a question is compound, the opponent may object and demand that the proponent ask the questions one at a time.

Repetitive or "Asked and Answered" Questions. The judge will ordinarily permit a counsel to repeat a question already posed to the witness by the opposing counsel so long as there is any possibility that the witness may change his or her answer. However, the judge will usually prevent a counsel from repeating a question which that counsel already posed to the witness and obtained a definite answer to.

Argumentative Questions. One of the most neglected courtroom objections is the objection to argumentative questions.[57] Perhaps the reason for the oversight of argumentative questions is that few attorneys have a good grasp of the definition of an argumentative question. An argumentative question usually has two characteristics. First, negatively, the questioner is not attempting to elicit a new historical fact from the witness. Second, affirmatively, the questioner is challenging or badgering the witness about an inference from the facts already in evidence.[58] The following questions would be argumentative: "How can you reconcile those two statements?" "Do you

51. Id. at § 767(b).

52. Assembly Committee Comment, Parker's Evidence Code of California 96 (1975); 3 Wigmore, Evidence § 773 (3d ed. 1940).

53. People v. Gallery, 336 Ill. 580, 168 N.E. 650 (1929); Advisory Committee Note, Fed.Evid.Rule 611, 28 U.S.C.A.

54. Id.

55. Id.

56. Id. See also Southern Ry. Co. v. Hall, 209 Ala. 237, 96 So. 73 (1923).

57. Goff, Argumentative Questions, 49 Calif.B.J. 140 (1974).

58. Id.

mean that seriously?" "Do you expect the jury to believe that?" On the pretext of asking a question, the attorney is really arguing about the inferences to be drawn from the evidence. The attorney may do so during closing argument, but the attorney may not do so during the examination of witnesses.

Suggested Reading:

State v. Taggert, 443 S.W.2d 168 (Mo.1969).

State v. Hunter, 183 Wash. 143, 48 P.2d 262 (1935).

Misleading Questions Assuming Facts Not in Evidence. Like the compound question objection, this objection is self-explanatory. In the previous reckless driving hypothetical in the subsection dealing with leading questions, the prosecutor may ask the defendant, "Didn't you see the 50 mile an hour sign when you passed the gas station?" If there has been no evidence to this point that there is such a sign, the question is objectionable; the question is misleading because it assumes facts not in evidence.

The proponent of the question may overcome the objection if there is any evidence in the record to support the facts assumed in the question. It is immaterial that there is contrary evidence in the record. It is also immaterial which side introduced the evidence supporting the assumed fact. The objection will be overruled so long as there is any evidence in the record supporting a finding that the assumed fact exists.

Suggested Reading:

Haithcock v. State, 23 Ala.App. 460, 126 So. 890 (1930).

Non-Responsive Answer. An answer is non-responsive if it does not respond to the very question asked. Suppose that a defense attorney is cross-examining a police officer. The defense attorney asks, "Isn't it true that you didn't see the defendant take any money from the cash register?" If the officer answered, "Yes, but the victim told me that it was the defendant," the reference to the victim's statement would be non-responsive: the question asked only about the officer's own perception, and the police officer improperly volunteered the reference to the victim's statement. An answer may be completely or partially non-responsive. The answer is completely non-responsive if the answer is not at all logically relevant to the question. The answer is partially non-responsive if part of the answer is logically relevant but the remainder exceeds the scope of the question.

If an answer is non-responsive, the proper procedural device for attacking the answer is a motion to strike; the party moves to strike the answer and asks the judge to instruct the jury to disregard the stricken matter.

There are two troublesome questions concerning non-responsive answers. The first question is: Who has standing to move to strike the non-responsive answer? The majority view seems to be that only the attorney posing the question may move to strike the non-responsive answer.[59] The opposing party may move to strike the answer on other grounds if the answer is irrelevant or incompetent, but the theory is that the questioner is the only person injured if the answer is merely non-responsive. Other jurisdictions permit either party to move to strike a non-responsive answer.[60]

The second question is whether the trial judge must grant the motion to strike. The common-law view was that the judge had

---

59. Davidson v. State, 211 Ala. 471, 100 So. 641 (1924); Hester v. Goldsbury, 64 Ill.App.2d 66, 212 N.E.2d 316 (1965).

60. See, e. g., West's Ann.Cal.Evid.Code § 766.

discretion to deny the motion so long as the answer was otherwise relevant and competent. A few jurisdictions have adopted the the view that on a timely motion, the judge must strike a non-responsive answer.[61]

This doctrine has a significant interplay with the scope rules. The proponent of the witness may be attempting to carefully limit the direct's scope to restrict the scope of cross. For example, the defense counsel may be attempting to limit the defendant's direct to preclude the prosecutor from inquiring into certain highly prejudicial matters on cross. A non-responsive answer from the witness on direct may broaden the scope of the direct and thereby undermine the proponent's attempt to limit the scope of

the cross. The proponent must be alert for such non-responsive answers and immediately move to strike the answers.

In addition to being concerned about the form of the questions asked of a witness, the examining attorney must ensure that he or she satisfies all the requirements for the admission of a particular type of evidence before the evidence is offered at trial. For example, before an attorney offers a writing into evidence, the attorney must ordinarily prove that it is authentic, that is, that it was actually written by the person whose signature appears on the writing. Proof of the writing's authenticity is part of the "foundation" for the writing's admission, and the attorney must "lay the foundation" before offering the writing into evidence. The following chapters discuss the foundational requirements which the various evidentiary doctrines impose.

---

61. Id. at §§ 11 and 766.

CHAPTER 2
COMPETENCY OF WITNESSES

1. Introduction

This chapter deals with competency of persons to be witnesses. To be eligible or qualified to serve as a witness, a person must satisfy a minimum standard of credibility. The competency rules address the question of whether the person may give any testimony at all in the case. Even if the person satisfies the threshold competency standards, he or she might nevertheless be unable to give particular types of testimony. For example, the judge might rule that the person is competent as a witness but lacks the necessary qualifications to give expert opinion testimony. Subsequent chapters analyze the restrictions on the content of a competent witness's testimony. Those restrictions can limit the testimony by the witness on the stand. The competency rules can have the more drastic effect of keeping the person off the witness stand.

2. General Rules—The Substantive Standards

Suggested Reading:

Gillars v. United States, 182 F.2d 962 (D.C.Cir. 1950).

The competency standards apply to both in-court witnesses and hearsay declarants. Thus if the proponent offers a hearsay declaration, the opponent may attack the competency of the declarant. As a general proposition, if the opponent can demonstrate the declarant's incompetency, the hearsay declaration is inadmissible.[1] Regardless of whether the person is an in-court witness or a hearsay declarant, he or she must meet substantive competency standards.

Common Law. *The common law insists that the prospective witness possess four capacities or testimonial qualities. The first requirement is moral capacity or the testimonial quality of sincerity.* Historically, this moral sense requirement has evolved through three interpretations. The original was religious; the prospective witness had

---

1. Most courts have made an exception in the case of excited utterances; if a statement otherwise falls within the excited utterance exception to the hearsay rule, the statement is admissible even though the declarant would be incompetent. State v. Breyer, 40 Idaho 324, 232 P. 560 (1925). The reasoning is that the statement's spontaneity is such a strong guarantee of trustworthiness that it compensates for the deficiencies in the declarant's competency. For an analysis of the excited utterance exception to the hearsay rule, see § 8, Chapter 13, infra.

to have a theistic belief that divine punishment would follow perjury. Under this approach atheists and agnostics were incompetent as witnesses. The religious test eventually gave way to an essentially ethical test. Whether or not the prospective witness believed in a diety, the person had to recognize a moral duty to tell the truth. Modernly, the ethical test is yielding to a new test just as the religious yielded to the ethical. Contemporary statutes often frame the requirement in terms of capacity to understand the nature and consequences of an oath or affirmation. For example, one state statute states that the prospective witness must be "capable of understanding the duty of a witness to tell the truth."[2] The statutes uniformly require the administration of an oath or affirmation designed to emphasize the meaning of an oath,[3] and the ability to understand the oath's importance and the possibility of a perjury prosecution is becoming the modern understanding of the moral capacity requirement.

The second requirement is the mental capacity to observe or the testimonial quality of perception. This requirement is relative to the subject matter of the proposed testimony. Although the word *observe* connotes sight, in this context it refers to all sense organs, meaning to gain knowledge by any sense. Thus, a deaf-mute may testify through signs about what he or she saw, and a blind person may testify about what he or she heard. The court tests this capacity as of the time of the relevant event.[4] If the prospective witness possessed the capacity at that time, it is immaterial that the person loses the capacity in the interim between the event and the trial. A person who saw an assault can testify about the assault even if he or she became blind before trial. A

person who heard a threat can testify about the threat even if he or she became deaf prior to trial.

The third requirement is the mental capacity to remember or the testimonial quality of memory. Like the mental capacity to observe, this capacity is relative to the proposed testimony's subject matter. Suppose that the prospective witness is suffering from amnesia but that the amnesia relates to only a limited period in the person's life. The person would be competent to testify about remembered events outside that period but incompetent with respect to events falling within the period.[5] The courts test this capacity as of the time of trial.

The final requirement is mental capacity to relate or the testimonial quality of narration. The prospective witness must be "capable of expressing himself concerning the matter so as to be understood, either directly or through interpretation by one who can understand him."[6] Thus the prospective witness does not need a physical ability to speak, for the individual can communicate through signs or writing. Similarly, although the individual is not fluent in English, he or she can communicate through an interpreter. The court tests the prospective witness's communicative capacity as of the time of trial.

Modern Statutes. The statutory trend, exemplified by the federal statute, is to liberalize the common-law standards.

The starting point for competency analysis under the new Federal Rules is the first sentence of Rule 601,[7] proclaiming that "(e)very person is competent to be a witness except as otherwise provided in these rules."[8] The text does not prescribe any

2. West's Ann.Cal.Evid.Code § 701(b).

3. Fed.Evid.Rule 603, 28 U.S.C.A.; West's Ann.Cal. Evid.Code § 710.

4. People v. Delaney, 52 Cal.App. 765, 199 P. 896 (1921).

5. People v. Curry, 97 Cal.App.2d 537, 218 P.2d 153 (1950).

6. West's Ann.Cal.Evid.Code § 701(a).

7. Fed.Evid.Rule 601, 28 U.S.C.A.

8. Id.

moral or mental qualifications, and the accompanying Advisory Committee Note explains that the omission was purposeful: "No mental or moral qualifications for testifying as a witness are specified. Standards of mental capacity have proved elusive in actual application. Standards of moral qualification in practice consist essentially of evaluating a person's truthfulness in terms of his own answers about it." [9] The only remnant of the moral capacity requirement occurs in Rule 603, mandating that the witness take an oath or affirmation before testifying.[10] The only vestige of the mental capacity requirement is in Rule 602, stating that the witness must testify from personal knowledge.[11] Even here the standard is lax, for the witness may testify so long as the record contains "evidence sufficient to support a finding that he has personal knowledge of the matter." [12]

3. Application to Particular Types of Witnesses

Children. Children must satisfy the normal competency standards in order to qualify as witnesses. However, the courts have applied the standards to children rather laxly. So long as the infant has a basic understanding that it is wrong to lie, he or she possesses the requisite moral capacity.[13] The judge usually personally conducts the child's questioning (referred to as a *voir dire* examination) and inquires whether the child realizes that he or she will be punished for a lie.[14] In fact, the case law on moral capacity for infants anticipated the evolution of the law on moral capacity for adults; when the prospective witness was a child,

the courts routinely held the child competent if the child stated that he or she realized that people would suffer an "earthly evil" for perjury.[15]

The problem of children's mental capacity has divided the courts and legislatures, with some developing presumptions of capacity and incapacity. Using such ages as 7, 10, 12, and 14 as dividing lines, these courts and legislatures take the approach that a child under the specified age is presumed incompetent though a child above the specified age is presumed competent. However, in most jurisdictions, there are no such presumptions; the child's competency is simply a question for the trial judge. At an early date, the Supreme Court set a liberal standard for the case law by holding a five-year-old child competent.[16] Since then lower courts have frequently held five-year-old children competent,[17] and some judges have allowed even four-year-old children to testify.[18] These extreme cases are child molestation prosecutions in which the court often strains to find the child competent, realizing that without his or her testimony, the prosecution will probably suffer a directed verdict. However, at least one court has suggested that it would be unreasonable to place a two- or three-year-old child on the stand.[19]

Suggested Reading:

Wheeler v. United States, 159 U.S. 523, 16 S.Ct. 93, 40 L.Ed. 244 (1895).

---

9. Id. at Advisory Committee Note.

10. Fed.Evid.Rule 603, 28 U.S.C.A.

11. Fed.Evid.Rule 602, 28 U.S.C.A.

12. Id.

13. Beausoliel v. United States, 107 F.2d 292 (D.C. Cir. 1939); People v. Denton, 78 Cal.App.2d 540, 178 P.2d 524 (1947).

14. Id.

15. People v. Lamb, 121 Cal.App.2d 838, 264 P.2d 126 (1954).

16. Wheeler v. United States, 159 U.S. 523, 16 S.Ct. 93, 40 L.Ed. 244 (1895).

17. People v. Pike, 183 Cal.App.2d 729, 7 Cal.Rptr. 188 (1960); People v. Gibbons, 83 Cal.App.2d 504, 189 P.2d 37 (1948).

18. People v. Delaney, 52 Cal.App. 765, 199 P. 896 (1921).

19. Wheeler v. United States 159 U.S. 523, 16 S.Ct. 93, 40 L.Ed. 244 (1895). But see Bradburn v. Peacock,

Insane People. The legal test for mental competency varies with the legal issue. For example, if the issue is criminal responsibility, the test is whether at the time of the crime, the individual knows the nature and quality of the act, can distinguish right from wrong, and can adhere to the right. If the issue is the individual's competency to stand trial, the test is whether the individual understands the nature of the proceedings and can assist his or her counsel. Because the test varies from context to context, other legal determinations of incompetency are not conclusive when the issue is the person's competency as a witness. Thus although a previous commitment to a mental institution is relevant,[20] neither a previous commitment[21] nor an adjudication of criminal insanity[22] requires a finding that the prospective witness is incompetent. Since formal legal determinations of mental incompetency are not dispositive, *a fortiori* chronic alcoholism and drug addition[23] do not automatically render a witness incompetent.

In short, mental diseases and prior adjudications of incompetency are merely evidentiary matters. The court considers the matter in deciding whether the prospective witness's mental disorder negatives one of the requisite elements of competency, such as the capacity to remember. Even under the stricter common-law standards, virtually the only time a court will find a mentally diseased person incompetent is the situation in which the opponent presents expert testimony that the individual suffers from a psychosis which seriously interferes with one of the requisite mental capacities—observation, recollection, or narration.[24] A psychosis is "[a] major mental disorder in which the individual's ability to think, respond emotionally, remember, communicate, interpret reality, and behave appropriately is sufficiently impaired so as to interfere grossly with his capacity to meet the ordinary demands of life."[25] An attorney attempting to exclude a mentally diseased person as incompetent should be prepared to present expert testimony that (1) the prospective witness is laboring under a recognized psychosis such as a schizophrenic reaction and (2) the psychosis grossly, seriously interferes with the individual's capacity to observe, remember or relate.

If the attorney cannot establish the prospective witness's general incompetency, the attorney can alternatively attempt to establish a relevant insane delusion.[26] To be disabling, the delusion must be relevant to the prosecution's subject matter.[27] For instance, if the charged crime is a sex offense, the prospective witness's sexual fantasies would be relevant. Although the courts regard cautiously witnesses with a history of delusion, judges rarely exclude witnesses on this ground alone.[28] As in the case of an attack on general competency, the attacking attorney should marshal expert testimony

---

135 Cal.App.2d 161, 164–65, 286 P.2d 972, 974 (1955) (error for judge to rule a three year old child incompetent without conducting *voir dire* examination).

20. People v. Horowitz, 70 Cal.App.2d 675, 161 P.2d 833 (1945).

21. People v. McCaughan, 49 Cal.2d 409, 317 P.2d 974 (1957).

22. Shibley v. United States, 237 F.2d 327 (9th Cir. 1956), cert. denied 352 U.S. 873, 77 S.Ct. 94, 1 L.Ed. 2d 77; People v. Ives, 17 Cal.2d 459, 110 P.2d 408 (1941).

23. Government of Virgin Islands v. Ventura, 476 F.2d 780 (3d Cir. 1973); State v. Thach, 5 Wash.App. 194, 486 P.2d 1146 (1971); People v. Sorrentini, 26 A.D.2d 827, 273 N.Y.S.2d 981 (1966); People v. Drumwright, 48 Ill.App.2d 392, 199 N.E.2d 282 (1964); State v. Cox, 352 S.W.2d 665 (Mo.1961).

---

24. In Helge v. Carr, 212 Va. 485, 184 S.E.2d 794 (1971), there was expert testimony that the prospective witness suffered from a psychosis, a schizophrenic reaction.

25. American Psychiatric Association, A Psychiatric Glossary 81 (1969).

26. People v. McCaughan, 49 Cal.2d 409, 317 P.2d 974 (1957); People v. Ives, 17 Cal.2d 459, 110 P.2d 408 (1941).

27. People v. Jackson, 273 Cal.App.2d 248, 78 Cal. Rptr. 20 (1969).

28. Id.

that (1) the prospective witness has a delusional history and (2) the particular delusion the prospective witness suffers from will significantly interfere with his or her ability to testify accurately on the proposed subject matter.

Suggested Reading:

Helge v. Carr, 212 Va. 485, 184 S.E.2d 794 (1971).

4. Exceptional Types of Witnesses

The Accused. As Chapter 20 points out, the fifth amendment recognizes two separate privileges: the accused's privilege and the witness's privilege. The witness has a limited privilege to refuse to answer individual incriminating questions. The accused, the named defendant in the proceeding, has a much broader privilege to refuse to testify at all in the prosecution. Because the prosecution may not call the accused as a witness, the accused in effect may render himself or herself incompetent as a witness.

Suggested Reading:

Malloy v. Hogan, 378 U.S. 1, 84 S.Ct. 1489, 12 L.Ed. 2d 653 (1964).

Spouses. At early common law, spouses were absolutely incompetent as witnesses in actions involving the other spouse. Thus, if one spouse was the defendant, the other spouse had *both a disability and a privilege*: The spouse was disabled from testifying as a defense witness and privileged not to testify as a prosecution witness. Eventually, the courts and legislatures relaxed this strict doctrine. Now, in all jurisdictions, the disability has been removed; the witness spouse is competent to testify as a defense witness.[29]

The division of authority concerns the privilege not to testify as a prosecution witness. The two questions dividing the courts and legislatures are: Should they recognize such a privilege? If so, who should be the holder—the defendant spouse or the witness spouse? There are four views.

The first view is that there should be no privilege. Approximately 10 jurisdictions treat the witness spouse as any other witness competent to testify for the prosecution or defense.[30]

However, the prevailing view is that the defendant spouse has a privilege to keep the other spouse off the witness stand.[31] Under this view, the defendant has a privilege if the marriage is valid and existing at the time the prosecution attempts to call the other spouse as a witness.[32] A voidable marriage is sufficient for the privilege. In jurisdictions validating common-law marriages, a ceremonial marriage is unnecessary.[33] A void marriage is insufficient, and authority exists that sham marriages, entered without intent to live together as husband and wife, are also insufficient to support the privilege.[34] If the marriage is dissolved or annulled before the prosecution calls the former spouse, no privilege remains.[35] The privilege is lost even if the divorce becomes final after

29. Funk v. United States, 290 U.S. 371, 54 S.Ct. 212, 78 L.Ed. 369 (1933).

30. Fla.Stat.Ann. 90.04; Burns Ind.Ann.Stat. §§ 2–1713, 2–1714, 9–1602; 15 Me.Rev.Stat.Ann. § 1315; N.H.Rev.Stat.Ann. 516.27; McKinney Consol.Laws of N.Y. CPLR § 4512; S.C.Code 1962 § 26–403; Tenn. Code Ann. § 24–103; Wis.Stat.Ann. 325.18.

31. Hawkins v. United States, 358 U.S. 74, 79 S.Ct. 136, 3 L.Ed.2d 125 (1958).

32. People v. Keller, 165 Cal.App.2d 419, 332 P.2d 174 (1959); People v. Glab, 13 Cal.App.2d 528, 57 P.2d 588 (1936).

33. A void marriage is one which has no legal effect, such as a bigamous marriage. A voidable marriage is one in which there is a legal imperfection, but, although the marriage can be dissolved in an annulment proceeding, it is valid for all other civil purposes.

34. Lutwak v. United States, 344 U.S. 604, 73 S.Ct. 481, 97 L.Ed. 593 (1953).

35. Pereira v. United States, 347 U.S. 1, 74 S.Ct. 358, 98 L.Ed. 435 (1954).

the prosecution begins and only a few days before the prosecution calls the witness.[36]

The third view is that the witness spouse holds a privilege to refuse to testify against the defendant spouse.[37] The witness spouse decides whether to testify. The privilege is personal to the witness spouse; if the witness spouse is willing to testify, the defendant spouse cannot prevent him or her from testifying. The courts and legislatures taking this approach point out that the basic purpose of the privilege is to protect the marital relationship, and they reason that if the witness spouse is willing to voluntarily jeopardize the relationship by giving damaging testimony, the marriage is not viable enough to warrant protection.

The fourth and final view is that both spouses have privileges. The defendant spouse has a privilege to prevent the witness spouse from testifying for the prosecution, and the witness spouse has a privilege to refuse to be called as a prosecution witness. In the jurisdictions following this approach, even if the witness spouse is prepared to waive his or her privilege, the defendant spouse can preclude the witness spouse from testifying.

Although the courts and legislatures disagree sharply over the privilege, the courts recognizing the privilege are in general agreement over one exception to the privilege, the injured spouse exception. If the witness spouse is the victim of the charged offense, the privilege is inapplicable.[38] The offense injuring the witness spouse must be the crime named in the indictment or information.[39] The list of crimes that may be

considered injuries against the witness varies. However, an almost universal agreement exists that an offense against the person of the witness spouse, or a child of either, is an injury to the witness spouse. Thus, there is no privilege in child abuse prosecutions.[40] Many jurisdictions also deny the privilege if the defendant commits a crime against the person of a third party in the course of attacking the witness spouse.[41] In addition the courts and legislatures extend the exception to crimes against the witness spouse's property even if it is community property or held in joint tenancy.[42] Finally, many jurisdictions consider offenses against the marital relation to be injuries to the witness spouse. Depending upon the jurisdiction, bigamy,[43] adultery,[44] Mann Act violations,[45] incest, and sodomy[46] qualify as injuries to the witness spouse.

Some jurisdictions recognize a second exception to the privilege, refusing to apply the privilege when the prosecution desires to elicit the witness spouse's testimony about facts occurring before the marriage.[47] The fact could be any criminal act the defendant spouse committed before the marriage; the fact would not have to be a crime against the person of the witness spouse. The proposed draft of Federal Rule 505(c)(2) would

---

36. People v. Bradford, 70 Cal.2d 333, 74 Cal.Rptr. 726, 450 P.2d 46 (1969), cert. denied 399 U.S. 911, 90 S.Ct. 2204, 26 L.Ed.2d 566 (1970).

37. See, e. g., West's Ann.Cal.Evid.Code § 971.

38. Id. at § 972.

39. People v. Seastone, 3 Cal.App.3d 60, 82 Cal. Rptr. 907 (1969); People v. Green, 236 Cal.App.2d 1, 45 Cal.Rptr. 744 (1965); State v. Woodrow, 58 W. Va. 527, 52 S.E. 545 (1905).

40. United States v. Allery, 526 F.2d 1362 (8th Cir. 1975).

41. People v. Green, 236 Cal.App.2d 1, 45 Cal.Rptr. 744 (1965) (the distinction between a crime committed "in the course" of the crime against the witness spouse and one committed "after" the crime against the witness spouse).

42. People v. Schlette, 139 Cal.App.2d 165, 293 P.2d 79 (1956), cert. denied 352 U.S. 1012, 77 S.Ct. 584, 1 L.Ed.2d 559 (1957).

43. West's Ann.Cal.Evid.Code § 972(e)(3).

44. Id.

45. Draft Fed.Evid.Rule 505(c)(3).

46. People v. Batres, 269 Cal.App.2d 900, 75 Cal.Rptr. 397 (1969).

47. United States v. Van Drunen, 501 F.2d 1393 (7th Cir. 1974).

have recognized this exception.[48] A second group of courts applies the privilege if at the time of marriage, the witness spouse knew of the prior crime. The theory is that the witness spouse can forgive or condone the prior crime; "the proper inference appears to be that any grievance . . . was settled before the (marriage) ceremony," and it would now be improper to permit the witness spouse to testify about the forgiven crime.[49] Of course, condonation assumes knowledge, and these courts deny the privilege if the witness spouse was unaware of the crime at the time of the marriage. A third group of courts simply refuses to recognize the exception.[50]

Suggested Reading:

Hawkins v. United States, 358 U.S. 74, 79 S.Ct. 136, 3 L.Ed.2d 125 (1958).

Judges. A judge is a perfectly competent witness in a case at which he or she is not presiding. For example, judges often testify in habeas corpus proceedings collaterally attacking judgments of conviction they have entered.[51]

The problems arise when a party calls the judge as a witness in a case the judge is presiding over, for the jury might attach undue weight to the judge's testimony, and the opposing counsel will be reluctant to aggressively cross-examine the presiding judge. Nevertheless, the early common-law view was that the judge was competent but had

discretion to decline to testify.[52] Modern courts have taken a more restrictive approach to judges' testimony, some limiting it to formal or undisputed matters.[53]

The legislative reforms are even more restrictive. Federal Rule 605 mandates that "[t]he judge presiding at the trial may not testify in that trial as a witness."[54] The opponent has an automatic objection: "No objection need be made in order to preserve the point."[55] The California procedure is almost as restrictive and far more complex. Before a judge may be called as a witness, the judge must conduct a hearing out of the jury's presence.[56] At the hearing, the judge discloses his or her knowledge about the case.[57] If the proponent reconsiders and decides not to call the judge, the issue is moot.

If the proponent persists and indicates a continuing desire to call the judge, the opponent has a choice. The opponent may consent to the judge's testimony.[58] However, if the opponent objects to the judge's testimony, the judge must declare a mistrial and order the action assigned to another judge.[59]

The statute expressly states that by objecting, the opponent impliedly makes a motion for mistrial.[60] The legislative intent was that if the opponent is a criminal defendant, the defendant is deemed to consent to a mistrial, and thus there is no double jeopardy bar to the second trial.[61]

---

48. Draft Fed.Evid.Rule 505(c)(2).

49. United States v. Williams, 55 F.Supp. 375 (D. Minn.1944).

50. People v. Souleotes, 26 Cal.App. 309, 146 P. 903 (1915).

51. Leighton v. Henderson, 220 Tenn. 91, 414 S.W. 2d 419 (1967).

52. O'Neal v. State, 106 Tex.Cr. 158, 291 S.W. 892 (1927).

53. State ex rel. Smith v. Wilcoxen, 312 P.2d 187 (Okl.Crim.1957).

54. Fed.Evid.Rule 605, 28 U.S.C.A.

55. Id.

56. West's Ann.Cal.Evid.Code § 703(a).

57. Id.

58. Id. at § 703(d).

59. Id. at § 703(b).

60. Id. at § 703(c).

61. Parker's Cal.Evid.Code § 703, Assembly Committee Comment.

Suggested Reading:

State ex rel. Smith v. Wilcoxen, 312 P.2d 187 (Okl. Cr.1957).

Jurors. If the juror is sitting in a different trial, he or she is a competent witness. However, as with a presiding judge, numerous practical problems arise if counsel calls a juror as a witness in a case on which the juror is sitting. Strangely, the common-law view was that the juror is a competent witness even after the juror is impaneled and sworn in that very case. Although few jurisdictions have changed the common-law rule by decisional law, there are numerous statutory reforms. The federal and California statutes on jurors roughly parallel the statutes on judges. The governing federal statute is Rule 606(a),[62] which like Rule 605, begins by announcing an absolute rule: "A member of the jury may not testify as a witness before that jury in the trial of the case in which he is sitting as a juror."[63] However, unlike Rule 605, Rule 606 does not provide for automatic objection; the Rule requires an objection but guarantees the opponent "an opportunity to object out of the presence of the jury."[64] The California statutes prescribe the same complex procedure for jurors that they employ for judges. The judge calls an out-of-court hearing[65] at which the juror discloses his or her knowledge.[66] If the proponent reconsiders, the issue is moot. If the proponent persists, the opponent is once again put to an election. The opponent may elect to permit the juror to testify.[67] However, the opponent may elect to object, and the judge must then declare a mistrial and order the action assigned to another jury.[68] The statute again states that by objecting, the opponent impliedly moves for a mistrial.[69]

Suggested Reading:

State v. Cavanaugh, 98 Iowa 688, 68 N.W. 452 (1896).

Attorneys. If an attorney's firm is not involved in a case, the attorney is a competent witness in that case. If by chance, the attorney witnesses a crime, the attorney should be competent to testify for either side when his or her firm has no connection with the suit. Moreover, despite the ethical restraints on attorneys' testimony, the common law takes the position that an attorney is a competent witness even in a case he or she is trying. One side may call its own attorney as a witness; the prosecution may call the prosecutor,[70] and the defense may call a defense counsel.[71] The courts even permit one side to call the other side's attorney; the defense may call a prosecutor,[72] and the prosecution may call a defense attorney.[73]

The prevailing view continues to be that an attorney is a competent witness even in a

---

62. Fed.Evid.Rule 606(a), 28 U.S.C.A.

63. Id.

64. Id.

65. West's Ann.Cal.Evid.Code § 704(a).

66. Id.

67. Id. at § 704(d).

68. Id. at § 704(b).

69. Id. at § 704(c).

70. People v. Burwell, 44 Cal.2d 16, 279 P.2d 744, cert. denied 349 U.S. 936, 75 S.Ct. 788, 99 L.Ed. 1265 (1955); People v. Hamberg, 84 Cal. 468, 24 P. 298 (1890).

71. State v. Blake, 157 Conn. 99, 249 A.2d 232 (1968); State v. Sullivan, 60 Wash.2d 214, 373 P.2d 474 (1962); State v. Woodville, 161 La. 125, 108 So. 309 (1926); Shannon v. State, 104 Tex.Crim. 483, 284 S.W. 586 (1926).

72. People v. Boford, 117 Cal.App.2d 576, 256 P.2d 334 (1953); State v. Lee, 203 S.C. 536, 28 S.E.2d 402 (1943).

73. State v. Cresto, 130 Wash. 436, 227 P. 856 (1924).

case he or she is trying.[74] However, by case law, the courts are beginning to make changes in this norm, limiting both testimony for the attorney's own side and for the opposing side. They are restricting prosecutors' testimony for the prosecution side [75] by reversing convictions in trials at which prosecutors testified. They are also limiting defense attorneys' testimony for the defense side [76] by sustaining trial court rulings excluding the attorneys as witnesses. In addition the courts are taking a restrictive approach to calling the opposing side's attorney.[77]

With increasing frequency, judges are inquiring at pretrial conferences whether it is foreseeable that either counsel will testify at trial.[78] When an attorney's testimony is foreseeable, the judge conditions the testimony on withdrawal from the case. If an unforeseen development occurs, and an attorney decides during trial to testify, the judge weighs the necessity for the attorney's testimony.[79] How relevant is the proposed testimony? Do any reasonably available alternative sources exist for equivalent testimony? Although the attorney's competency remains the norm, there is substantial movement in the case law away from this norm.

Suggested Reading:

People v. Smith, 13 Cal.App.3d 897, 91 Cal.Rptr. 786 (1970).

---

74. United States v. Buckhanon, 505 F.2d 1079 (8th Cir. 1974).

75. People v. Guerrero, 47 Cal.App.3d 441, 448, 120 Cal.Rptr. 732, 736 n. 8 (1975).

76. United States v. Buckhanon, 505 F.2d 1079 (8th Cir. 1974); United States v. Clancy, 276 F.2d 617 (7th Cir. 1960), rev'd on other grounds 365 U.S. 312, 81 S.Ct. 645, 5 L.Ed.2d 574 (1961); People v. Johnson, 46 Mich.App. 212, 207 N.W.2d 914 (1973); People v. Smith, 13 Cal.App.3d 897, 91 Cal.Rptr. 786 (1970).

77. United States v. Newman, 476 F.2d 733 (3d Cir. 1973); Gajewski v. United States, 321 F.2d 261 (8th Cir. 1963), cert. denied 375 U.S. 968, 84 S.Ct. 486, 11 L.Ed.2d 416 (1964).

78. People v. Smith, 13 Cal.App.3d 897, 91 Cal.Rptr. 786 (1970).

79. United States v. Fiorillo, 376 F.2d 180, 185 (2d Cir. 1967).

CHAPTER 3

TYPES OF WITNESSES—LAY AND EXPERT

1. The Personal or Firsthand Knowledge Rule

Suggested Reading:

United States v. Fernandez, 480 F.2d 726 (2d Cir. 1973).

The requirement that the testimony of a lay witness [1] be based on matters of which he or she has personal, firsthand knowledge has long been recognized.[2] The firsthand knowledge rule requires the proponent of the evidence to establish that the witness "had an opportunity to observe and did observe" [3] the matter about which he or she is testifying. The policy underlying this rule—pro-

viding the trier of fact with the most reliable information—is a theme that runs throughout the law of evidence; a similar justification underlies the best evidence rule,[4] the hearsay rule,[5] and the opinion rule.[6] The firsthand knowledge requirement is typically satisfied by the witness's own testimony, although extrinsic evidence may be used.[7] If the witness is testifying from firsthand knowledge, his or her lack of certainty in observing or recalling affects only the evidence's weight, not its admissibility.[8]

Since it is often difficult to separate what a witness knows from what a witness thinks he or she knows, the jury should be left the responsibility of determining the ex-

---

1. For a discussion of the basis of expert testimony, see § 7, infra.

2. See United States v. Fernandez, 480 F.2d 726, 739 (2d Cir. 1973); United States v. Borelli, 336 F.2d 376, 392 (2d Cir. 1964); Fed.Evid.Rule 602, 28 U.S.C.A.; Uniform Rule of Evidence 19 (1953); Model Code of Evidence Rule 104; 2 Wigmore, Evidence § 650 (3d ed. 1940); C. McCormick, Handbook of the Law of Evidence § 10 (2d ed. 1972).

3. 7 Wigmore, Evidence § 1922 at 20 (3d ed. 1940).

4. See Chapter 11.

5. See Chapter 12.

6. See § 2, infra.

7. "Evidence to prove personal knowledge may, but need not consist of the testimony of the witness himself." Fed.Evid.Rule 602, 28 U.S.C.A.

8. See, e. g., Auerbach v. United States, 136 F.2d 882, 885 (6th Cir. 1943) ("best of his belief" voice was defendant's); People v. Pena, 25 Cal.App.3d 414, 432, 101 Cal.Rptr. 804, 815 (1972) ("want of positiveness goes only to weight of the testimony"); People v. Cahan, 141 Cal.App.2d 891, 897, 297 P.2d 715, 719 (1956) ("I believe" defendant was one of the robbers); 2 Wigmore, Evidence § 658 (3d ed. 1940).

tent of the witness's actual knowledge. The trial judge's role in ruling on an objection based on lack of firsthand knowledge is limited to assuring that the witness's testimony meets a minimum level of credibility.[9] Professor Morgan expressed the rule as follows: "It is only when no reasonable trier of fact could believe that the witness perceived what he claims to have perceived that the court may reject the testimony."[10] Federal Rule of Evidence 602 recognizes the judge's limited role; testimony is inadmissible only if the trial judge determines that the evidence is not "sufficient to support a finding that (the witness) has personal knowledge."[11]

Because the declarant of an admissible hearsay statement is in fact a witness in the case, the reasons underlying the firsthand knowledge rule also apply to hearsay statements. Thus, statements falling within most hearsay exceptions must be based on the declarant's personal knowledge.[12] An important exception, however, is the exception for admissions of party-opponents, typically the defendant's confessions in criminal cases.[13]

In many cases the firsthand knowledge rule and the hearsay rule overlap.[14] For example, if a witness testifies about a bank robbery and the witness's knowledge comes only from a statement of another person, the testimony violates both rules. The witness has no personal knowledge of the bank robbery and he or she is merely repeating an out-of-court declarant's statements. However, the proper objection depends on the form in which the testimony is presented. If the witness indicates that the basis of his or her testimony is an out-of-court declarant's statement, the hearsay objection is proper. If, instead, it appears from the testimony that the witness was not present at the robbery, the lack of firsthand knowledge objection would be appropriate.[15]

2. The Opinion Rule

Suggested Reading:

United States v. Schneiderman, 106 F.Supp. 892 (S.D.Cal.1952).

The firsthand knowledge rule requires that the witness base his or her testimony on observed facts. The opinion rule affirmatively requires that a witness generally limit his or her testimony to recitations of observed fact. The opinion rule negatively prohibits a lay witness from testifying in the form of conclusions, inferences, or opinions. In this

9. "The judge may reject the testimony of a witness that he perceived a matter if he finds that no trier of fact could reasonably believe that the witness did perceive the matter." Uniform Rule of Evidence 19 (1953).

10. E. Morgan, Basic Problems in Evidence 59–60 (1962).

11. Fed.Evid.Rule 602, 28 U.S.C.A. The Advisory Committee Note observes that the Rule is "a specialized application of the provisions of Rule 104(b) on conditional relevancy." If the jury does not believe the witness has firsthand knowledge, it will disregard the testimony.

12. "In a hearsay situation, the declarant is, of course, a witness, and neither rule governing hearsay exceptions dispenses with the requirement of firsthand knowledge. It may appear from his statement or be inferable from circumstances." Advisory Committee Note, Fed.Evid.Rule 803, 28 U.S.C.A.

13. C. McCormick, Handbook of the Law of Evidence § 263 (2d ed. 1972); 4 Wigmore, Evidence § 1053 (Chadbourn rev. 1972). Fed.Evid.Rule 801(d)(2) also dispenses with the firsthand knowledge requirement but does not treat such admissions as hearsay. Advisory Committee Note, Fed.Evid.Rule 801, 28 U.S.

C.A. See 2 Wigmore, Evidence § 670 (3d ed. 1940) for other exceptions.

14. E. g., United States v. Fernandez, 480 F.2d 726, 739 (2d Cir. 1973) (witness "had no personal knowledge and his statements were thus pure hearsay"); Advisory Committee Note, Fed.Evid.Rule 602, 28 U.S. C.A.

15. C. McCormick, Handbook of the Law of Evidence §§ 10, 247 (2d ed. 1972); 2 Wigmore, Evidence § 657 (3d ed. 1940); 5 Wigmore, Evidence § 1361, 1363(3) (Chadbourn rev. 1974).

context opinion refers to "an inference from observed and communicable data" and not to "a guess, a belief without good grounds." [16] The guess would be objectionable under the firsthand knowledge rule. The inference may be objectionable under the opinion rule.

The Merits of the Opinion Rule. A rule encouraging witnesses to state their knowledge in concrete rather than abstract terms, and to relate primary sensory perceptions rather than inferences from the perceptions, has obvious merit. If the witness includes both primary perceptions and inferences in his or her testimony, the latter will often be superfluous; the jury may be just as capable as the witness to draw the inference.[17] If the witness provides only the inference, the jury may be misled, for it might have drawn a different inference had it been presented with the underlying perceptions.

There are, however, several arguments for abolishing the opinion rule. First, the rule is unnecessary in most instances because the adversary system has built-in mechanisms that discourage opinion testimony. Since "the detailed account carries more conviction than the broad assertion, and a lawyer can be expected to display his witness to the best advantage," counsel naturally tend to elicit the more concrete testimony from their witnesses.[18] Moreover, the adversary has an opportunity to expose weaknesses in the opinion testimony during cross-examination.[19]

The second argument concerns the practicalities of applying the opinion rule in the trial setting. Witnesses frequently draw inferences in testifying; it is the natural way to tell a story. "Opinions are constantly given. A case can hardly be tried without them. Their number is so vast, and their use so habitual, that they are not noticed as opinions distinguished from other evidence." [20] A rigid rule prohibiting opinions would stultify the presentation of testimony, "making it impossible for the witness to convey to the jury what he has observed." [21] Furthermore, opinion testimony will be the only feasible evidence in some cases because the witness will be unable to articulate all the primary sensory impressions on which the opinion is based. For example, a witness may be unable to verbalize all the primary sensory data underlying an impression of intoxication.

Finally, the application of the opinion rule in practice tends to turn on an unrealistic fact-opinion dichotomy; witnesses may testify to "facts" but not "opinions." [22] This approach has proved unworkable because "there is no distinction in kind between fact and opinion; the distinction is one of degree." [23] For example, the witness who testi-

---

16. 7 Wigmore, Evidence § 1917 at 10 (3d ed. 1940).

17. Id. at § 1918.

18. Advisory Committee Note, Fed.Evid.Rule 701, 28 U.S.C.A.

19. Id. There may be tactical reasons for not cross-examining the witness. "If a witness answers in terms of opinion rather than facts or if the question calls for such an answer, a wise opponent may choose not to urge the opinion objection because if sustained, a new question would be asked which would cause the witness to speak factually with much more telling effect than the expression of an opinion." Ladd, Expert Testimony, 5 Vand.L.Rev. 414, 415–16 (1952).

20. State v. Pike, 49 N.H. 399, 423 (1870).

21. United States v. Schneiderman, 106 F.Supp. 892, 903 (S.D.Cal.1952). See also Central R. Co. of New Jersey v. Monahan, 11 F.2d 212, 214 (2d Cir. 1926) (L. Hand, J.) ("Every judge of experience in the trial of causes has again and again seen the whole story garbled because of insistence upon a form with which the witness cannot comply, since, like most men, he is unaware of the extent to which inference enters into his perceptions. He is telling the 'facts' in the only way that he knows how, and the result of nagging and checking him is often to choke him altogether.").

22. 7 Wigmore, Evidence § 1919 (3d ed. 1940).

23. E. Morgan, Basic Problems in Evidence 216 (1962). See also J. Maguire, Evidence, Common Sense and Common Law 24 (1947) ("In a way, all human assertions are opinion."); C. McCormick, Handbook of the Law of Evidence 24 (2d ed. 1972); J. Thayer, A Preliminary Treatise on Evidence at Common Law 524 (1898); Advisory Committee Note, Fed.Evid.Rule 701, 28 U.S.C.A. ("The practical im-

fies that the defendant had "slurred speech" and "staggered" is using inferences as much as the witness who testifies that the defendant was "intoxicated;" the difference is "one of degree." Professor Morgan commented that the opinion rule has "invited numberless trivial appeals and (has) caused many indefensible reversals." [24]

The Modern Status of the Opinion Rule. To avoid the untoward results of a strict prohibition against opinions, the courts have carved out exceptions. The shorthand rendition or collective fact exception permits the lay witness to express an opinion if: (1) it involves an inference that lay persons commonly draw; (2) the recitation of the underlying facts would not adequately convey the impression; and (3) providing the underlying facts would be a waste of time.[25] In this situation, the lay witness is competent to form the opinion, and the opinion's admission is relatively necessary because the witness cannot convey all the primary sensory data to the trier of fact. Witnesses may express opinions concerning distance, time, size, speed, and identity.[26] In criminal cases, lay opinions about intoxication [27] are common.

A skilled lay observer may testify about insanity [28] or handwriting style if the witness is sufficiently familiar with the person or style. Although this exception was originally explained in terms of necessity, it is now recognized that convenience is the principal justification.[29]

The modern trend is to view the opinion rule as a rule of preference, rather than a rule of exclusion; [30] primary sensory perceptions are preferred to inferences or conclusions drawn from those perceptions. If, however, an opinion will assist the jury or is the best evidence available, it is admissible. Federal Rule of Evidence 701 follows this approach; when based on personal observation, opinions are admissible if "helpful to a clear understanding of (the witness's) testimony or the determination of a fact in issue." Wigmore advocated the abolition of the opinion rule.[31] While not going that far, the Federal Rule de-emphasizes the prohibition against opinion testimony and leaves the matter to the trial judge's discretion. Testimony that a person was "nervous" [32] or "dis-

---

possibility of determining by rule what is a 'fact,' demonstrated by a century of litigation of the question of what is a fact for purposes of pleading under the Field Code, extends into evidence also.").

24. Morgan, Foreword to Model Code of Evidence at 34 (1942).

25. See Stone v. United States, 385 F.2d 713 (10th Cir. 1967), cert. denied 391 U.S. 966, 88 S.Ct. 2038, 20 L.Ed.2d 880 (1968). See E. Morgan, supra note 23 at 217; C. McCormick, Handbook of the Law of Evidence § 11 at 25 (2d ed. 1972); McCormick, Opinion Evidence in Iowa, 19 Drake L.Rev. 245, 248–50 (1970).

26. E. Morgan, supra note 23 at 28. Fed.Evid.Rules 901(b)(2) & (5) follow the traditional practice of permitting identification of handwriting and speakers, respectively, through lay opinion testimony if the witness has the requisite familiarity. See also West's Ann.Cal.Evid.Code § 1416.

27. E. g., People v. Moore, 70 Cal.App.2d 158, 160 P.2d 857 (1945); Vigil v. People, 160 Colo. 229, 416 P.2d 361 (1966); State v. Fletcher, 279 N.C. 85, 181 S.E.2d 405 (1971) (drugs). See 7 Wigmore, Evidence § 1974 (3d ed. 1940).

28. See, e. g., Breland v. United States, 372 F.2d 629 (5th Cir. 1967); Evalt v. United States, 359 F.2d 534 (9th Cir. 1966); Kaufman v. United States, 350 F.2d 408 (8th Cir. 1965), cert. denied 383 U.S. 951, 86 S.Ct. 1211, 16 L.Ed.2d 212 (1966); State v. Lujan, 87 N.M. 400, 402, 534 P.2d 1112, 1114 (1975); West's Ann.Cal.Evid.Code § 870(a). See 7 Wigmore, Evidence §§ 1933–38 (3d ed. 1940).

29. See C. McCormick, Handbook of the Law of Evidence 24–25 (2d ed. 1972); McCormick, Opinion Evidence in Iowa, 19 Drake L.Rev. 245, 246–47 (1970).

30. See West's Ann.Cal.Evid.Code § 800; Kan.Stat. Ann. 60–456(a); N.J.Evid.Rule 56(1). Fed.Evid.Rule 701 and the state codes which have adopted the Federal Rules also follows this trend. See Ark.Stat.Ann. 28–1001 Rule 701; Me.Evid.Rule 701; Neb.Rev.Stat. § 27–701; Nev.Rev.Stat. § 50.265; N.Mex.1953 Comp. Laws § 20–4–701; Wis.Stat.Ann. § 907.01. See also Model Code of Evidence Rule 401; Uniform Rules of Evidence 56(1) (1953); C. McCormick, Handbook of the Law of Evidence 25 (2d ed. 1972).

31. 7 Wigmore, Evidence § 1929 at 27 (3d ed. 1940).

32. See United States v. Mastberg, 503 F.2d 465, 469–70 (9th Cir. 1974).

traught" [33] would be admissible under the Rule.[34]

3. The Ultimate Issue Rule

Suggested Reading:

United States v. Spaulding, 293 U.S. 498, 55 S.Ct. 273, 79 L.Ed. 617 (1935).

Closely related to the opinion rule is the ultimate issue rule proscribing opinion testimony, lay or expert, on the ultimate issues in the case.[35] The rule precludes opinions that "invade the province of the jury" or "usurp the function of the jury." [36] The rule is objectionable on several grounds.[37] First, difficult questions of application arise in distinguishing ultimate facts from other facts.[38] Second, the witness can never usurp the jury's function.[39] The jury is not bound by even an expert's opinion [40] and will be instructed that it may disregard the opinion of witnesses, including experts.[41] Of course, there is a danger that the jury may be unduly influenced by the opinion of a particular witness, especially an expert, but this problem exists whether the witness is offering an opinion or testifying about observed facts.[42] Third, the jury may have the greatest need for the witness's assistance on an ultimate issue.[43] In a forgery prosecution, the ultimate issue is the identity of the person who executed the document. The witness, a questioned document examiner or a lay person familiar with the defendant's handwriting style, may be capable of identifying the defendant's signature on the forged document. Although the testimony relates to an ultimate issue, all courts would permit the witness to testify.

The trend is to abolish the ultimate issue prohibition. Erosion of the rule began with expert opinions,[44] and it now includes lay witnesses as well.[45] Nevertheless, some opinion testimony is still properly excluded. "No witness should be permitted to give his

---

33. See Cole v. United States, 327 F.2d 360, 361 (9th Cir. 1964).

34. If the opinion rule is viewed as a rule of preference, it makes no sense to apply it to out-of-court statements. Counsel cannot rephrase the question to elicit the underlying facts and the opinion would be excluded, if the rule is applied in such cases. See C. McCormick, Handbook of the Law of Evidence § 18 (2d ed. 1972).

35. See United States v. Spaulding, 293 U.S. 498, 506, 55 S.Ct. 273, 79 L.Ed. 617 (1935) ("the issue is not to be decided by opinion evidence. It was the ultimate issue to be decided by the jury.").

36. See, e. g., United States v. Cairns, 434 F.2d 643, 644 (9th Cir. 1970) (defendant argued that witness's opinion "invades the province of the jury"); Linden v. United States, 254 F.2d 560, 566 (4th Cir. 1958) (defendant argued "province of the fact finder was thus invaded").

37. See 7 Wigmore, Evidence § 1920 at 17 ("usurping function of jury argument is 'a mere bit of empty rhetoric.' ").

38. C. McCormick, Handbook of the Law of Evidence § 12 (2d ed. 1972); Ladd, Expert Testimony, 5 Vand.L.Rev. 414, 423 (1952).

39. 7 Wigmore, Evidence § 1920 (3d ed. 1940); Ladd, supra note 38 at 424–25.

40. Mason v. United States, 402 F.2d 732, 737 (8th Cir. 1968), cert. denied 394 U.S. 950, 89 S.Ct. 1288, 22 L.Ed.2d 484 (1969); McDaniel v. United States, 343 F.2d 785, 789 (5th Cir. 1965), cert. denied 382 U.S. 826, 86 S.Ct. 59, 15 L.Ed.2d 71.

41. See 1 E. Devitt & C. Blackmar, Federal Jury Practice and Instructions § 11.27 (1970) (expert witness instruction).

42. Note, Opinion Testimony "Invading the Province of the Jury," 20 U.Cin.L.Rev. 484, 488 (1951).

43. 7 Wigmore, Evidence § 1921 (3d ed. 1940).

44. See, e. g., Feguer v. United States, 302 F.2d 214, 242 (8th Cir. 1962), cert. denied 371 U.S. 872, 83 S.Ct. 123, 9 L.Ed.2d 110 ("This court has long held generally that an expert, as distinguished from a lay witness, may express his opinion on the ultimate jury question.").

45. Kan.Stat.Ann. 60–456(d); N.J.Evid.Rule 56(3). Fed.Evid.Rule 704, as well as the states that adopted the Federal Rules, have abolished the prohibition. Ark.Stat.Ann. § 28–1001 Rule 704; Me.Evid.Rule 704; Neb.Rev.Stat. § 27–704; Nev.Rev.Stat. § 50.295; Wis.Stat.Ann. § 907.04. See also Uniform Rule of Evidence 56(4) (1953).

opinion directly that a person is guilty or innocent, or is criminally responsible or irresponsible." [46] The reason for exclusion is that the opinion does not assist the jury, not that it violates the ultimate issue prohibition.[47]

A court may also be more concerned about opinion testimony that relates to critical, as opposed to collateral, issues in a case. The more critical the issue, the more important it is to obtain primary sensory perceptions.[48] This situation should be analyzed in terms of helpfulness to the jury rather than by resort to the ultimate issue doctrine.

4. Expert Witnesses

As noted earlier, the opinion rule is designed to encourage witnesses to relate primary sensory perceptions in their testimony. The jury is thought to be as capable as the lay witness to draw inferences and conclusions from the observations. However, there are some subjects about which the average lay juror is incapable of drawing reliable inferences. Experts remedy this deficiency [49] by drawing inferences for the jury or by providing the jury with sufficient information to evaluate the facts.[50] To enable experts to serve this function, the courts relax the application of the firsthand knowledge and opinion rules to expert testimony.[51]

Before permitting a witness to express an expert opinion, the trial judge must determine that: (1) the subject matter is appropriate for expert testimony; (2) the witness possesses the requisite qualifications (expertise) to testify about the subject; and (3) there is a proper basis for the expert's opinion.

5. Subject Matter Appropriate for Expert Opinion

Suggested Reading:

Fineberg v. United States, 393 F.2d 417 (9th Cir. 1968).

State v. Linn, 93 Idaho 430, 462 P.2d 729 (1969).

Expert testimony is admissible if "scientific, technical, or other specialized knowledge will assist the trier of fact to understand the evidence or to determine a fact in issue." [52] Such testimony is used extensively in criminal cases.[53] The nature of some crimes often

---

46. Grismore v. Consolidated Products Co., 232 Iowa 328, 361, 5 N.W.2d 646, 663 (1942) (dictum) (a leading case on ultimate issue doctrine).

47. "If . . . attempts are made to introduce meaningless assertions which amount to little more than choosing up sides, exclusion for lack of helpfulness is called for by the rule." Advisory Committee Note, Fed.Evid.Rule 701, 28 U.S.C.A. Opinions on the interpretation of law are also excluded. See Huff v. United States, 273 F.2d 56, 61 (5th Cir. 1959) (customs inspector's testimony as to "his construction and interpretation of the customs laws, statutes, rules and regulations and his opinion that the jewelry found in the possession of the defendant was of a commercial nature rather than personal effects" excluded). See 7 Wigmore, Evidence § 1952 (3d ed. 1940).

48. C. McCormick, Handbook of the Law of Evidence § 12 at 26 (2d ed. 1972).

49. Experts were originally used to advise the court. Only with the advent of the adversary system of trial did they become witnesses. 7 Wigmore, Evidence § 1917 at 3–4 (3d ed. 1940).

50. "An intelligent evaluation of facts is often difficult or impossible without the application of some scientific, technical, or other specialized knowledge. The most common source of this knowledge is the expert witness although there are other techniques for supplying it. Most of the literature assumes that experts testify only in the form of opinions. The assumption is logically unfounded. Federal Rule 702 accordingly recognizes that an expert on the stand may give a dissertation or exposition of scientific or other principles relevant to the case, leaving the trier of fact to apply them to the facts." Advisory Committee Note, Fed.Evid.Rule 702, 28 U.S.C.A.

51. See § 7, infra.

52. Fed.Evid.Rule 702, 28 U.S.C.A.

53. See generally A. Moenssens, R. Moses & F. Inbau, Scientific Evidence in Criminal Cases (1973).

necessitates the use of experts—forensic chemists in drug cases,[54] pathologists and toxicologists in homicide cases,[55] and questioned document examiners in forgery cases.[56] Similarly, certain defenses such as insanity typically involve expert testimony.[57] Other illustrations of expert testimony include fingerprint comparisons,[58] firearms and toolmark identification,[59] blood typing,[60] and intoxication tests.[61] New techniques, such as neutron activation analysis,[62] voice-print,[63] and bitemark identification [64] are continually being added to this list.

A subject may fall outside the range of expert testimony because (1) it has not been proved sufficiently reliable for admission in criminal cases or (2) it falls within the jurors' common knowledge: "The field of expertness is bounded on one side by the great area of the commonplace, supposedly within the ken of every person of moderate intelligence, and on the other by the even greater area of the speculative and uncertain. Of course, both these boundaries constantly shift."[65]

On the one hand, polygraph [66] and truth serum [67] are examples of techniques that most courts regard as too uncertain; the reliability of these techniques has not been adequately demonstrated. Other techniques, such as firearms identification,[68] have progressed from the uncertain to the expert testimony category. This issue is explored more fully in Chapter 8 on Scientific Evidence.[69]

On the other hand, expert testimony is improper if the subject matter of the testimony falls within the average juror's knowl-

---

54. See, e. g., State v. Carvelle, 290 A.2d 190 (Me. 1972) (marihuana); State v. Baca, 81 N.M. 686, 472 P.2d 651 (1970), cert. denied 81 N.M. 721, 472 P.2d 984 (morphine).

55. E. g., Coppolino v. State, 223 So.2d 68 (Fla.App. 1968), cert. denied 399 U.S. 927, 90 S.Ct. 2242, 26 L.Ed.2d 794 (1969) (poisoning); State v. Hessenius, 165 Iowa 415, 146 N.W. 58 (1914) (strangulation); State v. David, 222 N.C. 242, 22 S.E.2d 633 (1942) (asphyxiation); Ward v. State, 427 S.W.2d 876 (Tex. Cr.App.1968) (gunshot wound).

56. See, e. g., United States v. Galvin, 394 F.2d 228 (3d Cir. 1968); Robles v. United States, 279 F.2d 401, 404 (9th Cir. 1960), cert. denied 365 U.S. 836, 81 S.Ct. 750, 5 L.Ed.2d 745 (1961).

57. See, e. g., United States v. Welp, 446 F.2d 867 (9th Cir. 1971), cert. denied 405 U.S. 933, 92 S.Ct. 991, 30 L.Ed.2d 808 (1972); United States v. Schappel, 445 F.2d 716 (D.C.Cir. 1971); United States v. Bohle, 445 F.2d 54 (7th Cir. 1971).

58. See, e. g., United States v. Braxton, 417 F.2d 878 (5th Cir. 1969). See 2 Wigmore, Evidence § 414 (3d ed. 1940); Moenssens, Admissibility of Fingerprint Evidence and Constitutional Objections to Fingerprinting Raised in Criminal and Civil Cases, 40 Chi.-Kent L.Rev. 85 (1963).

59. E. g., Ignacio v. People of Territory of Guam, 413 F.2d 513 (9th Cir. 1969), cert. denied 397 U.S. 943, 90 S.Ct. 959, 25 L.Ed.2d 124 (1970); Cummings v. State, 226 Ga. 46, 172 S.E.2d 395 (1970); King v. State, 456 P.2d 121 (Okl.Cr.1969). See 2 Wigmore, Evidence § 417a (3d ed. 1940).

60. E. g., Shanks v. State, 185 Md. 437, 45 A.2d 85 (1945); State v. Jacobs, 6 N.C.App. 751, 171 S.E.2d 21 (1969).

61. See Watts, Some Observations on Police-Administered Tests for Intoxication, 45 N.C.L.Rev. 34 (1966).

62. E. g., United States v. Stifel, 433 F.2d 431 (6th Cir. 1970), cert. denied 401 U.S. 994, 91 S.Ct. 1232, 28 L.Ed.2d 531 (1971); State v. Coolidge, 109 N.H. 403, 260 A.2d 547 (1969), rev'd on other grounds 403 U.S. 433, 91 S.Ct. 2022, 29 L.Ed.2d 564 (1971). See Chapter 8, infra.

63. E. g., United States v. Baller, 519 F.2d 463 (4th Cir. 1975), cert. denied 423 U.S. 1019, 96 S.Ct. 456, 46 L.Ed.2d 391; United States v. Franks, 511 F.2d 25 (6th Cir. 1975), cert. denied 422 U.S. 1042, 95 S.Ct. 2654, 45 L.Ed.2d 693; Commonwealth v. Lykes, 367 Mass. 191, 327 N.E.2d 671 (1975). See Chapter 8, infra.

64. E. g., People v. Marx, 54 Cal.App.3d 100, 126 Cal. Rptr. 350 (1976); People v. Milone, 43 Ill.App.3d 385, 2 Ill.Dec. 63, 356 N.E.2d 1350 (1976).

65. J. Maguire, Evidence, Common Sense and Common Law 30 (1947).

66. See Chapter 8, infra.

67. E. g., State v. Linn, 93 Idaho 430, 462 P.2d 729 (1969); Dugan v. Commonwealth, 333 S.W.2d 755 (Ky.1960); State v. Levitt, 36 N.J. 266, 176 A.2d 465 (1961).

68. Compare People v. Berkman, 307 Ill. 492, 139 N.E. 91 (1923) (firearms identification "preposterous"), with People v. Fisher, 340 Ill. 216, 172 N.E. 743 (1930) (firearms identification trustworthy).

69. See Chapter 8, infra.

edge.[70] In such a case, the jury does not need the assistance of the expert. Given the primary sensory data, the lay juror is competent to draw the proper inferences. The test for determining this issue is sometimes phrased as whether the subject is "beyond the comprehension of laymen." [71] If applied literally, this standard is too restrictive a view of the function of expert testimony. Many subjects are not entirely beyond a lay juror's comprehension, and yet expert testimony should be admitted because it will aid the jurors. Handwriting comparisons exemplify this point. Although the jurors may compare handwriting exemplars on their own,[72] the testimony of a questioned document examiner about a comparison of the exemplars is far superior. A more controversial example is expert testimony to inform the jury of the dangers of eyewitness identifications. In United States v. Amaral,[73] such testimony was excluded because according to the court, the jury was capable of evaluating the dangers without expert testimony.[74] A persuasive argument can be made that the jury would be significantly aided by the testimony of an expert witness psychologist who has systematically studied this subject.[75]

The better view,[76] the one adopted by the Federal Rules of Evidence,[77] requires only that the testimony "assist the trier of fact." This standard is similar to the standard for determining the admissibility of lay opinion testimony; [78] the rationale—assisting the jury—is the same for both rules. The overlap between expert and lay testimony is illustrated by the rules governing handwriting [79] and voice identification,[80] as well as insanity.[81] On these subjects both the expert and the lay witness may give opinion testimony, but the basis of their testimony differs: "the lay witness is using his opinion as a composite expression of his observations otherwise difficult to state, whereas the expert is expressing scientific knowledge through his opinion." [82] The lay witness cannot articulate all the underlying primary sensory data, and the expert witness's knowledge and skill enable the expert to draw inferences helpful to the jury in evaluating the primary data.

Since individual judges may disagree on whether proffered testimony will assist the trier of fact, the trial judge has "broad discretion in the matter of the admission or exclusion of expert evidence, and his action is

---

70. See Ladd, Expert Testimony, 5 Vand.L.Rev. 414, 419 (1952) ("Stated in the negative, expert testimony is not admissible to prove or disprove matters within common knowledge as to which facts may be so described that the triers of fact may form a reasonable opinion themselves.").

71. E. g., Fineberg v. United States, 393 F.2d 417, 421 (9th Cir. 1968) ("beyond the knowledge of the average layman"); Jenkins v. United States, 307 F.2d 637, 643 (D.C.Cir. 1962) ("beyond the ken of the average layman," quoting C. McCormick, Handbook of the Law of Evidence § 13 (1954)).

72. See Fed.Evid.Rule 901(b)(3), 28 U.S.C.A.

73. 488 F.2d 1148, 1153 (9th Cir. 1973). In United States v. Collins, 395 F.Supp. 629, 635–37 (M.D.Pa. 1975), the court did not reach the issue of whether such testimony was a proper subject of expert testimony. Instead, the court excluded the testimony because the potential dangers of the evidence outweighed the probative value.

74. "Certainly effective cross-examination is adequate to reveal any inconsistencies or deficiencies in the eyewitness testimony." 488 F.2d at 1153.

75. See Chapter 26, infra.

76. See C. McCormick, Handbook of the Law of Evidence § 13 (2d ed. 1972); 7 Wigmore, Evidence § 1923 at 2 (3d ed. 1940) ("On this subject can a jury from this person receive appreciable help? ").

77. Fed.Evid.Rule 702, 28 U.S.C.A.

78. Fed.Evid.Rule 701 permits the use of lay opinion testimony when "helpful to a clear understanding of his testimony or the determination of a fact in issue."

79. 3 Wigmore, Evidence §§ 693, 708 (Chadbourn rev. 1970); 7 Id. § 1996 (3d ed. 1940).

80. 2 Id. §§ 660, 667 (3d ed. 1940).

81. 7 Id. §§ 1933–38.

82. Ladd, Expert Testimony, 5 Vand.L.Rev. 414, 419 (1952).

to be sustained unless manifestly errone-ous." [83]

6. Qualification of the Expert

Suggested Reading:

United States v. Snow, 552 F.2d 165 (6th Cir. 1977).

A witness who testifies about a proper sub-ject of expert testimony must have expertise in that subject matter; he or she must be "qualified as an expert by knowledge, skill, experience, training, or education." [84] The qualification requirement follows from the subject matter requirement. If the witness is not qualified, he or she is incapable of as-sisting the jury.

An expert may acquire the necessary knowledge or skill through education, experi-ence, or a combination of both. [85] A patholo-gist or chemist, for example, usually will have practical experience in addition to for-mal academic education. Firearms and fin-gerprint experts typically become specialists through crime laboratory training programs which include on-the-job training. In some cases experience alone suffices. For exam-ple, police officers have testified as experts about the modus operandi of certain crimes such as pickpocketing,[86] gambling,[87] till-tap-ping,[88] and larceny by means of the "creeper" technique.[89] The witness's title is not deter-minative of his or her qualifications; be-cause of their training and experience, some psychologists are qualified to testify on the issue of insanity, while others are not.[90]

The proponent of the evidence has the burden of establishing the witness's qualifi-cations.[91] Before the witness is accepted as an expert, opposing counsel has an opportu-nity to question or *voir dire* the witness on his or her qualifications. Although counsel commonly offer to stipulate to the qualifica-tions of an expert, it may be a tactical mis-take to accept such a stipulation because the witness's qualifications are "as important to the weight of his testimony as (they are) to its admissibility." [92] The trial judge decides as a preliminary matter [93] whether the wit-ness is qualified. The decision lies within the judge's discretion and will rarely be reversed on appeal.[94] As a practical matter, the requi-site level of expertise is a variable function of the complexity of the subject matter. On-the-job training may qualify a laboratory technician to conduct a simple chemical color test to identify suspected contraband drugs. However, a cause-of-death determination of-ten involves such subtle, evaluative analysis

---

83. Salem v. United States Lines Co., 370 U.S. 31, 35, 82 S.Ct. 1119, 1122, 8 L.Ed.2d 313 (1962).

84. Fed.Evid.Rule 702, 28 U.S.C.A.

85. 2 Wigmore, Evidence § 556 (3d ed. 1940) (The witness's expertise "may have been attained, so far as legal rules go, in any way whatever; all the law requires is that it should have been attained.").

86. See United States v. Jackson, 425 F.2d 574 (D. C.Cir. 1970).

87. See Moore v. United States, 394 F.2d 818 (5th Cir. 1968), cert. denied 393 U.S. 1030, 89 S.Ct. 641, 21 L.Ed.2d 573 (1969).

88. See People v. Clay, 227 Cal.App.2d 87, 38 Cal. Rptr. 431 (1964).

89. See People v. Crooks, 250 Cal.App.2d 788, 59 Cal.Rptr. 39 (1967).

90. See United States v. Riggleman, 411 F.2d 1190 (4th Cir. 1969); Jenkins v. United States, 307 F.2d 637 (D.C.Cir. 1962) (rehearing en banc).

91. 2 Wigmore, Evidence § 559 (3d ed. 1940) ("The possession of the required qualifications by a particu-lar person offered as a witness must be expressly shown by the party offering him.").

92. Ladd, Expert Testimony, 5 Vand.L.Rev. 414, 422 (1952).

93. See Fed.Evid.Rule 104(a), 28 U.S.C.A.

94. See, e. g., United States v. Lopez, 543 F.2d 1156 (5th Cir. 1976). Wigmore goes further and states that the decision "will not be reviewed on appeal." 2 Wigmore, Evidence § 561 at 643 (3d ed. 1940).

that the witness must qualify as a forensic pathologist.

7.   Proper Bases for Expert Opinion

Opinion testimony of an expert may be based on three different sources: (1) the expert's personal knowledge; (2) assumed facts supported by evidence in the record; or (3) information supplied to the expert outside the record.

Personal Knowledge. Virtually all jurisdictions permit experts to testify on the basis of their own personal observations. The chemist who analyzes a substance suspected of being an illicit drug and offers an opinion about the substance's identity, or the pathologist who conducts an autopsy and offers an opinion about the cause of death, base their respective opinions on firsthand knowledge. In effect, the expert is both a fact and an opinion witness in this situation.

Assumed Facts. An expert may also offer an opinion on the basis of assumed facts. This method of presenting evidence capitalizes on the expert's skill in drawing inferences in cases in which the expert has no personal knowledge of the underlying facts. In some jurisdictions an expert who attends the trial may be requested to assume that the testimony he or she has heard is true and to give an opinion based on this testimony.[95] The major problem with this method is that it may be unclear to the jury which facts the expert is assuming to be true; this is a danger in trials that are long, complicated, or involve conflicts in the evidence. Recognizing the trial judge's discretion to require prior disclosure to the jury of the facts on which the opinion is based would solve this problem.[96]

Expert opinion testimony may also be based on assumed facts stated in a hypothetical question. Suppose that the arresting officer has already testified that the defendant was staggering and had a breathalyzer reading of 0.16. The prosecution could then call an expert doctor and question the doctor hypothetically. "Doctor, please assume hypothetically that a person was staggering and had a breathalyzer reading of 0.16. Given those assumptions, could you form an opinion of the person's sobriety or intoxication?" Or the prosecutor might ask, "Doctor, please assume that Officer Merideth's testimony about the defendant's staggering and breathalyzer reading is accurate. Given those assumptions, would you have an opinion about the defendant's intoxication?"

All jurisdictions allow hypothetical questions;[97] some require it.[98] The facts assumed must be supported by evidence in the record[99] although the evidence need not be uncontroverted. Moreover, the trial judge has discretion to permit hypothetical questions based on facts not yet introduced into evidence if counsel provides assurance that the evidence will be forthcoming.

The hypothetical question technique has several advantages. Because the assumed facts are stated in the question, the jury knows the factual assumptions underlying the expert's opinion. In addition, opposing counsel has an opportunity to object before the expert offers an opinion.[1]

However, the hypothetical technique has been criticized as a cumbersome and unwield-

---

95.   2 Wigmore, Evidence § 681 (3d ed. 1940); C. McCormick, Handbook of the Law of Evidence § 14 (2d ed. 1972).

96.   See Fed.Evid.Rule 705, 28 U.S.C.A.

97.   2 Wigmore, Evidence § 674 at 796 (3d ed. 1940) ("This general principle is now universally accepted.").

98.   In some cases the expert's opinion may be based partly on his or her own observations and partly on assumed facts. Id. at § 678.

99.   Id. at § 682. However, the cross-examiner is not limited by this restriction in propounding hypothetical questions to the expert. Id. at § 684.

1.   Hearsay and lack of supporting evidence for an assumed fact are typical objections.

ly procedure that gives a one-sided presentation of the facts and deprives the jury of the full benefit of the expert's skill and knowledge.[2] "Rather than inducing a clear expression of expert opinion and the basis for it, the hypothetical question inhibits the expert and forecloses him from explaining his reasoning in a manner that is intelligible to a jury."[3] The technique has also been faulted because it permits counsel to present a summary of his or her case in the middle of the trial.[4] Nevertheless, in some cases the hypothetical question offers an excellent vehicle to present expert testimony. The trend is not to abolish this device, but rather to give counsel the option of presenting expert testimony through other methods.

Following the view of a minority of jurisdictions,[5] Federal Rule of Evidence 703 permits an expert to give an opinion without resort to a hypothetical question even if the expert does not have personal knowledge of the underlying facts.[6] Rule 703 must be read in conjunction with Rule 705 permitting an expert to offer an opinion without prior disclosure of the opinion's basis.[7]

However, the trial judge has discretion to require prior disclosure, and on cross-examination opposing counsel may elicit the basis on which the opinion rests.[8] From a tactical perspective, it is often advisable for the proponent to establish the opinion's basis on direct examination. Doing this will buttress the expert's conclusions against the cross-examiner, who can be expected to elicit only unfavorable material.

Suggested Reading:

Rabata v. Dohner, 45 Wis.2d 111, 172 N.W.2d 409 (1969).

Hearsay Reports from Third Parties. The expert's opinion will often be based on information received from third parties outside the courtroom. For example, an expert medical witness might have relied on hospital reports, the patient's statements, and consultation with other physicians. Out-of-court statements are generally excluded from evidence by the hearsay rule. Thus, the expert's opinion may be based on statements which are inadmissible hearsay. Federal Rule 703 allows the expert to base his or her opinion on information that may otherwise be inadmissible hearsay.[9] The Rule

---

2. See C. McCormick, Handbook of the Law of Evidence § 16 (1954); 2 Wigmore, Evidence § 686 (3d ed. 1940); Diamond & Louisell, The Psychiatrist as an Expert Witness: Some Ruminations and Speculations, 63 Mich.L.Rev. 1335, 1346–48 (1965); Ladd, Expert Testimony, 5 Vand.L.Rev. 414, 427 (1952).

3. Rabata v. Dohner, 45 Wis.2d 111, 129, 172 N.W. 2d 409, 417 (1969).

4. Advisory Committee Note, Fed.Evid.Rule 705, 28 U.S.C.A.

5. See, e. g., West's Ann.Cal.Evid.Code § 801(b); Kan.Stat.Ann. 60–456(b), 60–457; N.J.Evid.Rules 57 and 58; McKinney's Consol.Laws of N.Y. CPLR 7.242; Mich.Gen.Court Rule 605.

6. The following states have adopted provisions identical to the federal rule: Ark.Stat.Ann. § 28–1001 Rule 703; Neb.Rev.Stat. § 27–703; Nev.Rev.Stat. § 50.285; N.Mex.1953 Comp.Laws § 20–4–703; Wis. Stat.Ann. § 907.03.

7. This procedure would not be acceptable in a jurisdiction that required hypothetical questions. However, Rule 705 is also applicable to opinions based on personal observation.

8. The Advisory Committee noted that the Rule "assumes that the cross-examiner has the advance knowledge which is essential for effective cross-examination." Advisory Committee Note, Fed.Evid. Rule 705, 28 U.S.C.A. This may present a problem in criminal cases because of the limited scope of pretrial discovery, especially for the prosecution.

9. "If of a type reasonably relied upon by experts in the particular field in forming opinions or inferences upon the subject, the facts or data need not be admissible in evidence." Fed.Evid.Rule 703, 28 U.S. C.A. Many commentators have advocated this position. C. McCormick, Handbook of the Law of Evidence § 15 (1954); 3 Wigmore, Evidence § 688 (Chadbourn rev.1970) (physicians). See also Maguire & Hahesy, Requisite Proof of Basis of Expert Opinion, 5 Vand.L.Rev. 432 (1952).

assumes that unreliable information—the principal concern underlying the hearsay rule—will be "winnowed through the mental processes of the expert" [10] and rejected. As the Ninth Circuit states in United States v. Sims: [11] "the rationale in favor of the admissibility of expert testimony based on hearsay is that the expert is fully capable of judging for himself what is, or is not, a reliable basis for his opinion. This relates directly to one of the functions of the expert witness, namely, to lend his special expertise to the issues before him." [12] In many cases involving psychiatric testimony the expert relies on such information.[13] The Rule is not limited, however, to this type of testimony. In United States v. Golden,[14] for example, an expert was permitted to offer an opinion on the market value of heroin based,

in part, on information supplied by other narcotics agents. "Such information was of the type reasonably relied upon by experts determining prevailing prices in clandestine markets." [15] The Federal Rule does limit the type of outside sources on which an expert may base an opinion to those "reasonably relied upon by experts in the particular field." Reliability, therefore, is predicated on customary acceptance by a profession as a whole, not merely on acceptance by one individual in that profession.

The use of hearsay sources as the basis of expert testimony has been challenged as violative of the sixth amendment right to confrontation. In United States, v. Williams,[16] the Fifth Circuit rejected this argument because the expert was available for cross-examination about "the authenticity and accuracy of the sources relied upon." [17]

In one sense all expert testimony is based, at least in part, on hearsay information; the extrajudicial statements of colleagues, textwriters and teachers are all used by the expert. See 2 Wigmore, Evidence § 665b (3d ed. 1940).

10. Brown v. United States, 375 F.2d 310, 318 (D.C. Cir. 1966), cert. denied 388 U.S. 915, 87 S.Ct. 2133, 18 L.Ed.2d 1359 (1967).

11. 514 F.2d 147 (9th Cir.), cert. denied 423 U.S. 845, 96 S.Ct. 83, 46 L.Ed.2d 66 (1975).

12. Id. at 149. The Advisory Committee to the Federal Rules pointed out that a physician makes "life-and-death" decisions on the basis of "information from numerous sources and of considerable variety, including statements by patients and relatives, reports and opinions from nurses, technicians and relatives and other doctors, hospital records, and X-rays." Advisory Committee Note, Fed.Evid.Rule 703, 28 U.S.C.A. Much of this information would fall within hearsay exceptions. See Fed.Evid.Rules 803(3), (4) and (6), 28 U.S.C.A.

13. See, e. g., United States v. Sims, 514 F.2d 147, 149 (9th Cir.), cert. denied 423 U.S. 845, 96 S.Ct. 83, 46 L.Ed.2d 66 (1975); Kibert v. Peyton, 383 F.2d 566, 570 (4th Cir. 1967); Brown v. United States, 375 F.2d 310, 318 (D.C.Cir. 1966), cert. denied 388 U.S. 915, 87 S.Ct. 2133, 18 L.Ed.2d 1359 (1967); Birdsell v. United States, 346 F.2d 775, 779–80 (5th Cir. 1965), cert. denied 382 U.S. 963, 86 S.Ct. 449, 15 L.Ed.2d 366; State v. Clark, 112 Ariz. 493, 496, 543 P.2d 1122, 1125 (1975). See also Rheingold, The Basis of Medical Testimony, 15 Vand.L.Rev. 473 (1962).

14. 532 F.2d 1244 (9th Cir. 1976).

Suggested Reading:

United States v. Golden, 532 F.2d 1244 (9th Cir. 1976).

---

8. Cross-Examining the Expert

One of the most effective methods of cross-examining an expert is to use a learned treatise that contradicts the expert's testimony. The opponent confronts the expert with the text and asks the expert to explain

---

15. Id. at 1248. See also State v. Jones, 320 So.2d 182, 184 (La.1975) ("opinion as to cause of death is not inadmissible merely because it is in part based upon other medical or laboratory reports as well as upon personal examination.").

16. 447 F.2d 1285 (5th Cir. 1971), cert. denied 405 U.S. 954, 92 S.Ct. 1168, 31 L.Ed.2d 231 (1972). The court in *Williams* reversed the earlier panel decision which had found a constitutional violation. 424 F.2d 344 (5th Cir.), petition for rehearing denied 431 F.2d 1168 (1970).

17. 447 F.2d at 1289.

the contradiction. Nearly all jurisdictions permit this impeachment technique.[18] However, there are important differences in the foundational requirements in the various jurisdictions. "The most restrictive position is that the witness must have stated expressly on direct examination his reliance upon the treatise. A slightly more liberal approach still insists upon reliance but allows it to be developed on cross-examination. Further relaxation dispenses with reliance but requires recognition as an authority by the witness, developable on cross-examination. The greatest liberality is found in decisions allowing use of the treatise on cross-examination when its status as an authority is established by any means." [19]

The Federal Rules of Evidence [20] follow Wigmore's view.[21] They allow statements from a learned treatise to be used as substantive evidence (evidence of the truth of the matter they contain) in addition to allowing their more limited use as a means of impeachment (evidence used solely to attack a witness's credibility). Suppose that a learned text states that a blow to a certain part of the body cannot cause a heart attack.[22] Under the traditional view, the text could be used merely for impeachment. If a witness testified to the contrary, the cross-examiner could confront the witness with the passage in the text; and the judge would instruct the jury that they could consider the text only to the extent that the contradiction between the text and the testimony impeached the witness's credibility. In contrast, under the Federal Rules, the party relying on the text could use the passage as substantive evidence, that is, as proof that in fact a blow to that part of the body cannot induce a heart attack.

---

18. C. McCormick, Handbook of the Law of Evidence § 321 (2d ed. 1972).

19. Advisory Committee Note, Fed.Evid.Rule 803 (18), 28 U.S.C.A. The last approach is the one followed by the Supreme Court in Reilly v. Pinkus, 338 U.S. 269, 70 S.Ct. 110, 94 L.Ed. 63 (1949). See also 6 Wigmore, Evidence § 1700(b) (Chadbourn rev. 1976).

20. Fed.Evid.Rule 803(18), 28 U.S.C.A.

21. 6 Wigmore, Evidence § 1700(b) (Chadbourn rev. 1976).

---

22. It is questionable whether a jury would appreciate the difference between the substantive and impeachment uses of the evidence in any event.

CHAPTER 4
CREDIBILITY OF WITNESSES

1. Introduction

Three basic stages must be examined when discussing the credibility of competent witnesses. First, at times a witness's testimony may be bolstered before impeachment. Here the proponent of the witness attempts to increase the witness's credibility in the jurors' eyes before the opponent has tried to impeach the witness. The second stage is impeachment. Impeachment, the generic term for all attacks on the witness's credibility, takes place when the opponent attempts to decrease the witness's credibility in the jurors' eyes. The third stage is rehabilitation. During this stage the proponent attempts to increase the witness's credibility in the jurors' eyes after the opponent has attempted impeachment.

2. Bolstering Before Impeachment

Suggested Reading:

People v. Gould, 54 Cal.2d 621, 7 Cal.Rptr. 273, 354 P.2d 865 (1965).

The general rule is that the proponent may not bolster the witness's credibility before the opponent has attempted to impeach the witness.[1] However, the courts have recognized exceptions to this rule. First, the wit-

1. Coltrane v. United States, 418 F.2d 1131 (D.C. Cir. 1969).

ness's testimony may be corroborated before the opponent has attempted to impeach the witness.[2] Corroboration occurs when other witnesses support the testimony of the witness about a fact in issue. Suppose that the witness testifies that he or she saw the defendant enter the building where a murder occurred. The general rule against bolstering would prevent the prosecution from calling another witness to testify that the first witness is a truthful person, but the prosecution could corroborate the first witness by having the second witness testify to the same fact on the merits, namely, that the defendant entered the building. Second, in some jurisdictions the courts recognize the fresh complaint exception.[3] This doctrine holds that if the defendant is charged with a sex offense or with robbery, the victim's complaint to the authorities or to other third parties soon after the alleged crime is admissible to bolster the testimony of the alleged victim. The third method of bolstering a witness's credibility is the pretrial identification exception.[4] Under this exception, if the witness identifies a person in the courtroom—for example, the defendant—evidence of the witness's pretrial identification of that same person is admissible to bolster the witness's credibility provided that the pretrial showup or lineup violated neither due process nor right to counsel.[5] Although a number of courts do not recognize this exception,[6] others admit the pretrial identification as substantive evidence even though no prior in-court identification has been made.[7] This exception is especial-

ly important to the prosecution if the witness is senile, has been intimidated, or is unavailable for trial.

3. Impeachment—Who May Be Impeached

Suggested Reading:

Chambers v. Mississippi, 410 U.S. 284, 93 S.Ct. 1038, 35 L.Ed.2d 297 (1973).

Impeaching the Opponent's Witness. The common law begins with the assumption that a party may impeach any witness other than his or her own. Thus, at common law, a party may ordinarily attack the credibility of any witness called by the opposing party, the judge, or the jurors, but may not attack the credibility of any witness that he or she has called.

Some courts recognized an exception to this norm when the witness called was an ally of the opposing party. Suppose, for example, that the posture of the case forces the prosecution to call the defendant's brother as a witness and that, on the stand, he proves hostile to the prosecution. Although the brother is formally a prosecution witness, he is obviously aligned with the defense. In this circumstance, some courts would preclude the defense from impeaching the witness.

Impeaching One's Own Witness. As previously stated, although the common law permits the opponent to impeach the opposing party's witnesses, it generally prohibits the impeachment of one's own witnesses. At the outset, we must clarify the limited scope of the prohibition: The prohibition prevents

---

2. Laughlin v. United States, 385 F.2d 287 (D.C.Cir. 1967).

3. 4 Wigmore, Evidence §§ 1134–40 (Chadbourn rev. 1972); 6 Wigmore, Evidence §§ 1160, 1171 (3d ed. 1940).

4. People v. Gould, 54 Cal.2d 621, 7 Cal.Rptr. 273, 354 P.2d 865 (1965); Hill v. State, 500 P.2d 1075 (Okl.Cr.1972).

5. Chapter 26, infra.

6. State v. Degraffenreid, 477 S.W.2d 57 (Mo.1972).

7. Virgin Islands v. Petersen, 507 F.2d 898, 902 (3d Cir. 1975); United States v. Puco, 476 F.2d 1099, 1101

(2d Cir. 1973); United States v. Anderson, 406 F.2d 719 (4th Cir. 1969); State v. Draughn, 121 N.J.Super. 64, 296 A.2d 79 (1972); People v. Nival, 33 N.Y.2d 391, 353 N.Y.S.2d 409, 308 N.E.2d 883 (1974); Fed. Evid.Rule 801(d)(1), 28 U.S.C.A.

the party from directly attacking the witness's credibility, but it does not prevent the party from introducing extrinsic evidence to contradict the witness's testimony on the merits.[8] Suppose that to the defense's surprise, defense witness #1 testified that he or she saw the defendant enter the building where the murder occurred. The common-law voucher rule would prohibit the defense from calling witness #2 to testify that witness #1 is an untruthful person; such testimony would be a direct attack on the defense witness's credibility, and the defendant vouches for the credibility of his or her witnesses.[9] However, the defense could specifically contradict witness #1's testimony by eliciting witness #2's testimony that the defendant was in another state at the time of the murder.

In recent years, the courts and legislatures have become dissatisfied with the voucher rule. They have created numerous exceptions to the rule. One exception is that the proponent of a witness could impeach a witness made indispensable, either by law or by the facts.[10] Assume that there is only one eyewitness to a crime. The facts practically compel the prosecution to call that person as a witness. Some courts would permit the prosecution to impeach that witness on the grounds that the witness is factually indispensable and that the prosecution has no choice in calling the witness. A second exception is that the proponent may impeach a witness[11] who, to the proponent's surprise, gives testimony affirmatively damaging the proponent's case.[12] To invoke this exception, the proponent must show that the

witness's testimony is both surprising and affirmatively damaging. If the proponent knew or had good reason to know that the witness would testify in that fashion, the exception is inapplicable. The exception is also inapplicable if the witness simply fails to give expected favorable testimony. Assume that the defense expected the witness to testify to an alibi. The exception would be inapplicable if the witness testified negatively that he or she cannot recall seeing the defendant on the day in question. The exception would apply if the witness gave the affirmatively damaging testimony that he or she saw the defendant near the crime scene. Finally, even when the witness's testimony is surprising and affirmatively damaging, the party calling the witness may impeach the witness only to the extent necessary to repair the party's case. In the hypothetical, the defense could impeach the witness with a prior inconsistent statement tending to establish the alibi, but most courts would not permit the defense to generally attack the witness's truthfulness.

The modern trend is to abolish the voucher rule and generally permit a party to impeach his or her own witnesses.[13] Federal Rule of Evidence 607 is illustrative. That Rule states that "(t)he credibility of a witness may be attacked by any party, including the party calling him."

4. Methods of Impeachment

The second stage to be examined in the discussion of witness credibility is impeachment and the methods or techniques of impeaching witnesses. The first four methods are generalized attacks on the witness himself or herself. The remaining techniques attack the witness's specific testimony in the case.

Character Trait for Untruthfulness. As soon as a witness testifies, his or her credi-

---

8. 3A Wigmore, Evidence §§ 902–05 (Chadbourn rev. 1970).

9. See Chambers v. Mississippi, 410 U.S. 284, 93 S.Ct. 1038, 35 L.Ed.2d 297 (1973). C. McCormick, Handbook of the Law of Evidence § 38 (2d ed. 1972).

10. Mich.Comp.Laws Ann. § 767.40a.

11. St. Clair v. United States, 154 U.S. 134, 150, 14 S.Ct. 1002, 1008, 38 L.Ed. 936 (1893).

12. Fed.Evid.Rule 607, 28 U.S.C.A.; West's Ann. Cal.Evid.Code § 607. But cf. N.J.Evid.Code 20.

13. Chambers v. Mississippi, 410 U.S. 284, 93 S.Ct. 1038, 35 L.Ed.2d 297 (1973).

bility becomes an issue in the case. One method of impeachment is an attack on the witness's character trait of truthfulness. The rules governing this impeachment technique parallel the character evidence rules discussed in Chapter 9. In brief, *the opponent may introduce timely reputation or opinion evidence about the witness's character trait of untruthfulness.*

"Reputation or Opinion Evidence." There are two types of character evidence. Evidence of an individual's reputation among members of the community is called reputation evidence. Evidence consisting of a witness's personal opinion is called opinion evidence.

At common law and under the majority view today, only reputation evidence is admissible to impeach credibility.[14] The character witness is not permitted to give a personal opinion despite the fact that opinion evidence may be more persuasive.[15] The modern trend, however, is to permit both opinion and reputation evidence. The Federal Rules allow both. Even traditional courts that have a rule barring opinion evidence often admit it disguised as reputation evidence.[16]

To lay a proper foundation for reputation evidence, the proponent must show that the character witness is (1) ordinarily a resident of the same community as the witness and (2) has lived in that community long enough to have become familiar with the witness's reputation in that community. While the courts originally insisted that the community be residential, the modern trend is to admit a reputation arising within any large social group likely to be familiar with the witness. In the minority of jurisdictions admitting opinion evidence, a proper founda-

tion requires the character witness to (1) know the witness personally and (2) be well enough acquainted to have had an opportunity to form a reliable opinion of the witness's character trait for truthfulness.

"About the Witness's Character Trait of Untruthfulness." The majority view is that only the witness's specific character trait for truthfulness is in issue.[17] This view has been phrased differently in various jurisdictions without a change in result; some courts refer to the character trait for truthfulness and veracity, others to truth and honesty, and still others to integrity or mendacity. The minority view is that in addition to the specific character trait of truthfulness, the witness's general moral character is in issue.[18] The Federal Rules specifically reject this minority view,[19] for the reason that the minority approach results in unfair surprise, waste of time, and confusion for the fact finders. A few courts have adopted a third view for a special category of cases. In sex offense prosecutions, where consent is an issue, some jurisdictions admit evidence of the lewd character of the prosecuting or complaining witness for impeachment.[20] Recently, legislation has been passed in some states which forbids the impeachment use of evidence about the alleged rape victim's past sexual conduct.[21] The trend seems to be to preclude the defense from impeaching the alleged victim with specific instances of sexual conduct; the argu-

---

14.   C. McCormick, Handbook of the Law of Evidence § 44 (2d ed. 1972).

15.   Id.

16.   Fed.Evid.Rule 608(a), 28 U.S.C.A.; West's Ann. Cal.Evid.Code § 1100.

17.   West's Ann.Cal.Evid.Code § 790.

18.   State v. Teager, 222 Iowa 391, 269 N.W. 348 (1936).

19.   Fed.Evid.Rule 608(a), 28 U.S.C.A. (evidence limited to "truthfulness or untruthfulness"); West's Ann. Cal.Evid.Code § 786 provides that evidence of a witness's character traits other than honesty or veracity or their opposites is inadmissible to attack or support the credibility of a witness.

20.   Coles v. Peyton, 389 F.2d 224 (4th Cir. 1968); Burnley v. Commonwealth, 208 Va. 356, 158 S.E.2d 108 (1967).

21.   17 Crim.L.Rep. 2203 (Ohio 1975); 17 Crim.L.Rep. 2243 (Hawaii 1975).

ment is that it is arbitrary to treat alleged rape victims as a class of persons whose credibility is especially suspect.

"Timely." We are interested in the witness's credibility at the time of trial. The evidence introduced must consist of a reputation arising or an opinion formed near the time of the trial.[22] In the case of reputation evidence, some courts employ a mechanical rule that the reputation must have arisen in the community the witness resides in at the time of trial. However, many jurisdictions admit reputation arising in any community the witness resided in shortly before trial.

Suggested Reading:

United States v. Null, 415 F.2d 1178 (4th Cir. 1969).

Prior Conviction. The common law rule that a person previously convicted of treason, a felony, or a misdemeanor involving dishonesty is incompetent to testify [23] has been modified by the modern courts.[24] However, the idea that a person with a criminal record is less credible remains ingrained in the law in the form of the rule that a witness, including a defendant, may be impeached by showing that he or she has suffered a valid, final conviction for certain types of offenses. Exceptions to this rule are practiced in Kansas and Pennsylvania, where an inquiry into the defendant's criminal record is prohibited unless the defendant has placed his or her character in issue.[25] Because the impeachment use of a prior conviction is to decrease the witness's credibility

in the eyes of the jurors, asking the witness about the defendant's prior criminal record is improper if the defendant has not taken the stand himself or herself.[26]

What May the Opponent Prove? The opponent may prove that *the witness has suffered a valid, final, recent conviction for certain types of offenses.*

"Valid." The requirement that the conviction be valid is especially important if the conviction was obtained in violation of due process of law or the witness's right to counsel under the sixth amendment.[27] However, most courts limit the attack on a prior conviction used for impeachment to evidence of the denial of a right affecting the fairness of the trial, especially the sixth amendment right to counsel. These courts will not sustain collateral attacks based on the fact that reliable evidence supporting the conviction was obtained in violation of the fourth amendment.[28]

"Final." The general view is that so long as the trial court has entered a final judgment, the conviction may be used for impeachment purposes.[29] It is immaterial that a motion for a new trial or an appeal is pending.[30] Although in order to rehabilitate the witness, the proponent may show that the motion for a new trial has been made or that the appeal is pending, this showing does not preclude the use of the conviction. However, if the conviction has been reversed on appeal, it certainly may not be used for im-

---

22. United States v. Null, 415 F.2d 1178 (4th Cir. 1969).

23. C. McCormick, Handbook of the Law of Evidence § 43 (2d ed. 1972).

24. Fed.Evid.Rule 609, 28 U.S.C.A.; Mich.Comp. Laws Ann. § 27A.2158; Minn.Stat.Ann. § 595.07.

25. Kan.Stat.Ann. § 60–421; Pa.Stat.Ann. tit. 19, ch. 9, § 19–711.

26. United States v. Comi, 336 F.2d 856 (4th Cir. 1964); People v. Mays, 48 Ill.2d 164, 269 N.E.2d 281 (1971).

27. See, e. g., Loper v. Beto, 405 U.S. 473, 92 S.Ct. 1014, 31 L.Ed.2d 374 (1972).

28. See, e. g., United States v. Penta, 475 F.2d 92 (1st Cir. 1973).

29. Fed.Evid.Rule 609(e), 28 U.S.C.A.; Vernon's Ann.Tex.Stat. art. 38.29. See also Revuelta v. State, 86 Nev. 224, 467 P.2d 105 (1970).

30. Fed.Evid.Rule 609(e), 28 U.S.C.A.; People v. Scrivens, 276 Cal.App.2d 429, 81 Cal.Rptr. 86 (1969).

peachment.[31] In contrast, a pardon will usually not prevent the conviction's use for impeachment.

In some states the sentence must be imposed in order to have a final conviction. Other courts have indicated that the imposition of probation as a sentence does not preclude the conviction's use for impeachment purposes.[32] However, a conflict exists over whether a judgment based on a plea of *nolo contendere* may be used to impeach a witness.[33]

Rule 410 of the Federal Rules of Evidence provides that a plea of *nolo contendere* which is later withdrawn may not be used; this rule seems to imply that if the plea is not withdrawn, a judgment based on the plea may be used.

"Recent." Generally, admitting the conviction is discretionary with the trial judge, who must weigh the conviction's probative value against its prejudicial effects. In part, the conviction's probative value depends on its recency. Rule 609(b) expressly singles out as discretionary the admissibility of a conviction which occurred more than ten years before the trial in question.[34] The conviction is admissible if the judge determines that its probative value outweighs its prejudicial effect and if advance written notice is given of the intent to use the prior conviction for impeachment. This notice grants the adverse party a better opportunity to ascertain if the conviction is valid and final.

"Conviction." There must be a conviction.[35] An arrest, indictment or information may not be used for impeachment.[36] However, as the next subsection points out, employing a different impeachment technique a minority of jurisdictions allows a witness or defendant to be asked if he or she is actually guilty of a crime that may not have resulted in a conviction. Generally, a juvenile adjudication may not be used for impeachment.[37] Nevertheless, the trial court may permit using a witness's juvenile adjudication to attack the credibility of that witness when necessary for a fair trial.[38] However, the offense must have been of the type that would either affect truthfulness or manifest moral turpitude.[39]

"For Certain Types of Offenses." In most states the admissibility of a conviction for impeachment turns on the potential or actual sentence. Hence, some jurisdictions limit the admissible convictions to felonies.[40] In other jurisdictions, the conviction's admissibility depends on the nature of the underlying offense. For example, impeachment may be limited to convictions of "infamous crimes," of "felonies and misdemeanors involving moral turpitude,[41] or of "felonies and misdemeanors in the 'crimen falsi'."[42] Some courts require that all crimes used to impeach involve dishonesty.[43]

---

31. State v. Spears, 83 Ill.App.2d 18, 226 N.E.2d 67 (1967).

32. Smith v. State, 455 S.W.2d 282 (Tex.Cr.App. 1970); State v. Knott, 6 Wash.App. 436, 493 P.2d 1027 (1972). Contra, State v. Frey, 459 S.W.2d 359 (Mo. 1970).

33. C. McCormick, Handbook of the Law of Evidence § 43 (2d ed.1972); Fed.Evid.Rule 410, 28 U.S.C.A.

34. Fed.Evid.Rule 609(b), 28 U.S.C.A.

35. People v. Peabody, 37 Mich.App. 87, 194 N.W.2d 532 (1971).

36. See, e. g., State v. Tosatto, 107 Ariz. 231, 485 P.2d 556 (1971); Corbin v. State, 259 So.2d 543 (Fla. App.1972).

37. Fed.Evid.Rule 609(d), 28 U.S.C.A.

38. Davis v. Alaska, 415 U.S. 308, 94 S.Ct. 1105, 39 L.Ed.2d 347 (1974).

39. Fed.Evid.Rule 609(d), 28 U.S.C.A.

40. State v. Bowen, 104 Ariz. 138, 449 P.2d 603 (1969); Swan v. State, 245 Ark. 154, 431 S.W.2d 475 (1968); Commonwealth v. Nunes, 351 Mass. 401, 221 N.E.2d 752 (1966).

41. See, e. g., People v. Jackson, 132 Ill.App.2d 464, 270 N.E.2d 498 (1971); Neam v. State, 14 Md.App. 180, 286 A.2d 540 (1972); Holgin v. State, 480 S.W. 2d 405 (Tex.Cr.App.1972).

42. Commonwealth v. Maroney, 423 Pa. 589, 225 A. 2d 236 (1967).

43. See, e. g., State v. Gunzelman, 210 Kan. 481, 502 P.2d 705 (1972); Cotton v. Commonwealth, 454 S.W. 2d 698 (Ky.1970). Contra, People v. Cantrell, 27

The new Federal Rules adopt a compromise position: If the crime is punishable by death or by imprisonment in excess of one year *or* if the crime entails a false statement or dishonesty, regardless of the punishment, the conviction may be used for impeachment.[44] The Advisory Committee Notes indicate that the Rule includes such crimes as fraud, embezzlement, and deceit.[45] The cases construing the Rule have held that crimes such as perjury, subornation of perjury, and income tax evasion involve an element of false statement or dishonesty. The cases split on the question whether offenses such as larceny and robbery entail a sufficient element of dishonesty to qualify under the Rule.

Which Methods May the Opponent Use to Prove the Fact of the Conviction? The minority view today is that the best evidence rule prevents cross-examining the witness about the prior conviction; thus the questioner must introduce a properly authenticated copy of the judgment of conviction into evidence.[46] However, in most jurisdictions the conviction may be shown either by cross-examination or by independent evidence of the conviction.[47] Most jurisdictions have indicated that the application of the best evidence rule is obviated because of the reliability of the witness's answer. Moreover, requiring the introduction of independent evidence is inconvenient. Some jurisdictions allowing either cross-examination or independent evidence hold that when a witness denies a conviction, the cross-examination must be terminated and the impeachment continued only with independent evidence, the introduction of the copy of the judgment.[48] However, in many jurisdictions the cross-examiner may not only continue the questioning; in addition to asking about the prior conviction, the cross-examiner may inquire about the location of the conviction,[49] the general nature of the crime,[50] and the sentence imposed.[51] In contrast, some courts, applying the old common-law rule, limit the examiner to the mere fact of the conviction.[52]

If the Proferred Evidence of a Conviction is Otherwise Proper, Does the Trial Judge Have Discretion to Exclude it? In some jurisdictions no discretion is left to the trial judge.[53] Congress has passed a statute depriving District of Columbia district court judges of discretion to exclude convictions.[54] However, the prevailing rule in the United States is that allowing impeachment by prior conviction is discretionary with the trial judge, who must weigh its probative value against its prejudicial effect on the defendant.[55] In applying this discretionary test, a number of factors must be considered—for example, how remote the conviction is in time; how directly the offense relates to credibility; how similar it is to the crime charged; how crucial the witness's testimony is; how time consuming the impeachment

---

Mich.App. 210, 183 N.W.2d 401 (1970); State v. Hungerford, 54 Wis.2d 744, 196 N.W.2d 647 (1972).

44. Fed.Evid. Rule 609(a), 28 U.S.C.A.

45. Advisory Committee Note, Fed.Evid.Rule 609, 28 U.S.C.A. See United States v. Papia, 560 F.2d 827 n. 14 (7th Cir. 1977).

46. People v. Harter, 4 Ill.App.3d 772, 282 N.E.2d 10 (1972).

47. Fed.Evid.Rule 609(a), 28 U.S.C.A.

48. Graham v. State, 13 Md.App. 171, 282 A.2d 162 (1971); People v. Luoni, 40 Mich.App. 457, 198 N.W.2d 887 (1972).

49. State v. Mendoza, 107 Ariz. 51, 481 P.2d 844 (1971); People v. Boehm, 270 Cal.App.2d 13, 75 Cal. Rptr. 590 (1969).

50. People v. Wynn, 44 Cal.App.2d 723, 112 P.2d 979 (1941); Mays v. People, 177 Colo. 92, 493 P.2d 4 (1972).

51. State v. Bass, 280 N.C. 435, 186 S.E.2d 384 (1972); Brown v. State, 496 P.2d 395 (Okl.Cr.1972).

52. Harmon v. Commonwealth, 212 Va. 442, 185 S.E.2d 48 (1971); State v. Hungerford, 54 Wis.2d 744, 196 N.W.2d 647 (1972).

53. State v. Adams, 50 N.J. 1, 231 A.2d 605 (1967); Howard v. State, 480 S.W.2d 191 (Tex.Cr.App.1972).

54. D.C.Code § 14–305.

55. Fed.Evid.Rule 609(a), 28 U.S.C.A.; West's Ann. Cal.Evid.Code § 788.

will be; and whether the witness will suffer undue humiliation or prejudice.

Suggested Reading:

Loper v. Beto, 405 U.S. 473, 92 S.Ct. 1014, 31 L.Ed. 2d 374 (1972).

Luck v. United States, 348 F.2d 763 (D.C.Cir. 1965).

Misconduct Not Resulting in Conviction. In this area little uniformity exists in the rules of the various jurisdictions. Federal Rule of Evidence 608(b) allows the court discretion in permitting cross-examination concerning misconduct which is "probative of untruthfulness." [56] The cross-examiner may inquire about prior acts of perjury or deceit. However, the opponent is limited to the witness's answer and may not prove the act by extrinsic evidence. If the witness perjuriously denies the act of misconduct, the cross-examiner must "take the answer;" the cross-examiner may not call another witness to prove the prior witness's act of misconduct. On cross-examination some jurisdictions allow the opponent to ask the witness whether he or she has committed any act of misconduct, but only if the opponent has a good-faith belief that the witness committed such an act.[57]

A minority of jurisdictions generally prohibits cross-examination about specific acts of misconduct which have not resulted in a conviction. However, even these jurisdictions recognize at least three exceptions to this prohibition. First, the opponent may prove acts of misconduct directly related to the case—for example, attempted suborna-

tion of perjury by a witness in the case. Second, if on direct-examination the witness makes a sweeping claim disavowing any misconduct, the opponent may question him or her regarding specific acts. Thus, if a defendant on direct examination stated that he or she had never had drugs in his or her possession, the prosecutor could impeach the defendant's statements; the trial judge would permit the prosecutor to conduct cross-examination and introduce independent evidence of the defendant's possession of drugs on prior occasions. Third, in sex offense prosecutions some courts admit evidence that the complainant has made similar false accusations in the past.

Suggested Reading:

People v. Sorge, 301 N.Y. 198, 93 N.E.2d 637 (1950).

Deficiencies in Elements of Competency. As previously stated, at common law, to be a competent witness, a person must possess the testimonial capacities of sincerity, perception, memory, and narration. The opponent may question the witness to impeach his or her capacity for perception, memory, or narration. Certain sensory conditions, such as defects in distance, color, and time perception are the proper subjects of cross-examination or for extrinsic evidence. A number of other factors, such as excitement,[58] fright,[59] physical pain,[60] and infirmities of old age [61] may affect the witness's testimony.[62]

---

56. Fed.Evid.Rule 608(b), 28 U.S.C.A.

57. Wright v. State, 243 Ark. 221, 419 S.W.2d 320 (1967); State v. Stout, 83 N.M. 624, 495 P.2d 802 (1972); State v. Lassiter, 17 N.C.App. 35, 193 S.E. 2d 265 (1972); Wood v. State, 486 S.W.2d 771 (Tex. Cr.App.1972).

58. Roberts v. State, 117 Tex.Cr.R. 418, 35 S.W.2d 175 (1931).

59. Id.

60. Id.

61. State v. Miskell, 161 N.W.2d 732 (Iowa 1968).

62. Martin v. State, 251 Ind. 387, 244 N.E.2d 100 (1969).

Past Mental Condition. The credibility of a witness may be called into question by the present presence of a disease or other condition affecting perception, memory, or narration.[63] The past mental condition of a witness may also be admissible under the principle that the jury should be informed of all matters relevant to the witness's credibility. Some of the first cases permitting impeachment use of evidence of mental disorder were sex offense cases.[64] Next the courts admitted psychiatric evidence to permit impeachment of the principal witness.[65] The testimony was limited to the principal witness in order to avoid confusing the issues. The value of such testimony depends on the ability of the expert to form a reliable opinion: "An opinion based solely upon a hypothetical question seems almost valueless here. Only slightly more reliable is an opinion derived from the subject's demeanor and his testimony in the courtroom. Most psychiatrists would say that a satisfactory opinion can only be formed after the witness has been subjected to a clinical examination."[66] The admission of psychiatric evidence is discretionary with the trial judge and occurs only in unusual cases.[67]

Under some statutes, evidence of a mental condition in existence prior to testifying is incompetent.[68] And the fact that the witness is an epileptic is likewise an improper subject of cross-examination unless a showing is made of the epilepsy's effect on the witness's memory.[69]

Intelligence. Recent studies have shown that the intelligence of a witness has a great bearing on his or her credibility.[70] Therefore, the courts have held that the witness's intelligence is a proper subject for cross-examination,[71] but it generally may not be shown by extrinsic evidence.[72] Intelligence may be considered by the jury in light of the personal appearance and conduct of the witness.[73]

Basis of Knowledge and Recollection. Because knowledge and recollection have an impact on credibility, it is proper to consider the source of the information,[74] how the information was obtained,[75] when the information was obtained,[76] the power and opportunity for accurate observation,[77] and the witness's understanding and comprehension of the facts to which he or she testified. The reason for recalling the facts, the ability of

---

63. State v. Miskell, 161 N.W.2d 732 (Iowa 1968).

64. Miller v. State, 49 Okl.Cr. 133, 295 P. 403 (1930); Rice v. State, 195 Wis. 181, 217 N.W. 697 (1928).

65. United States v. Hiss, 88 F.Supp. 559 (S.D.N.Y. 1950).

66. C. McCormick, Handbook of the Law of Evidence § 45 (2d ed. 1972).

67. United States v. Partin, 493 F.2d 750, 762 (5th Cir. 1974).

68. People v. Tyree, 21 Cal.App. 701, 132 P. 784 (1913); People v. Harrison, 18 Cal.App. 288, 123 P. 200 (1912).

69. State v. Smythe, 148 Wash. 65, 268 P. 133 (1928); Sturdevant v. State, 49 Wis.2d 142, 181 N.W.2d 523, 526 (1970).

70. Levine & Tapp, The Psychology of Criminal Identification: The Gap from *Wade* to *Kirby*, 121 U. Pa.L.Rev. 1079 (1973).

71. Blanchard v. People, 70 Colo. 555, 203 P. 662 (1922). But see State v. Pevear, 110 N.H. 445, 270 A. 2d 598 (1970); Bryant v. State, 4 Md.App. 572, 244 A.2d 446 (1968).

72. People v. Lambersky, 410 Ill. 541, 102 N.E.2d 326 (1951) (feeble mindedness may reflect on credibility); State v. Armstrong, 232 N.C. 727, 62 S.E.2d 50 (1950) (extrinsic evidence admissible to show that state's only witness to homicide was a moron or imbecile); Sturdevant v. State, 49 Wis.2d 142, 181 N.W. 2d 523 (1970).

73. Blanchard v. People, 70 Colo. 555, 203 P. 662 (1922).

74. United States v. Kahaner, 317 F.2d 459 (2d Cir. 1963); Inglis v. State, 13 Ala.App. 184, 68 So. 583 (1915).

75. Cf. Aguilar v. Texas, 378 U.S. 108, 84 S.Ct. 1509, 12 L.Ed.2d 723 (1964).

76. Wright v. Best, 19 Cal.App.2d 368, 121 P.2d 702 (1942).

77. United States v. Foster, 9 F.R.D. 367 (D.C.N.Y. 1949).

the witness to recall them, and the witness's familiarity with the matter in controversy are proper subjects of cross-examination.[78] In addition the witness's interest in observing and remembering is a subject of cross-examination, for if a person was not interested in an event that occurred several years before, this lack of interest may affect credibility.[79]

Intoxication. Evidence that the witness was intoxicated at the time of the event or at the time of testifying is admissible and is a proper subject of cross-examination.[80] Intoxication reflects on the ability to observe, remember, and recall facts. But the fact that a witness is an alcoholic is not, without more, ground for impeachment.[81]

Drug Addiction. Even though there is agreement on intoxication, the courts are split on the effect drugs have on credibility. Those courts favoring a broad range of inquiry say that drug addiction has an inherent tendency to affect the addict's powers of perception, narration and memory, and therefore they permit introducing evidence of drug addiction to impeach the witness.[82] Other courts require expert testimony that the particular addiction in question is likely to affect the witness's mental capacity.[83]

Still other courts hold that the use of narcotics may be a subject of cross-examination only when there is reason to believe that the person being examined was under the influence of drugs at the time of the events in question.[84]

Suggested Reading:

State v. Armstrong, 232 N.C. 727, 62 S.E.2d 50 (1950).

Prior Inconsistent Statement. If prior to trial the witness made a statement inconsistent with his or her testimony, the opponent may cross-examine the witness about the prior inconsistent statement. Some jurisdictions strictly require a flat contradiction between the pretrial statement and the trial testimony.[85] However, the majority view is that any significant variance between the testimony and the previous statement is sufficient. Generally, if the witness's pretrial statement omits a material fact which he or she would not reasonably have done,[86] if the witness's testimony appears to be a recent fabrication,[87] or if the witness alters a material fact in his or her testimony,[88] the pretrial statement is sufficiently inconsistent.

---

78. Id.

79. Cf. Lomax v. State, 248 Ark. 534, 452 S.W.2d 646 (1970).

80. Lomax v. State, 248 Ark. 534, 452 S.W.2d 646, 649 (1970); Simmons v. State, 220 Ga. 881, 142 S.E. 2d 798 (1965); Benge v. Commonwealth, 264 Ky. 28, 94 S.W.2d 38 (1936); Prisk v. State, 137 Conn. 35, 74 A.2d 462 (1950); Newton v. State, 150 Tex.Cr.R. 500, 202 S.W.2d 921 (1947).

81. Indemnity Ins. Co. of North America v. Marshall, 308 S.W.2d 174 (Tex.Civ.App.1957).

82. People v. Strother, 53 Ill.2d 95, 290 N.E.2d 201 (1972); People v. Talaga, 37 Mich.App. 100, 194 N.W. 2d 462 (1971); People v. Perez, 239 Cal.App.2d 1, 48 Cal.Rptr. 596 (1965).

83. Fields v. State, 487 P.2d 831 (Alaska 1971); People v. Smith, 4 Cal.App.3d 403, 84 Cal.Rptr. 412 (1970); People v. Smith, 38 Ill.2d 237, 231 N.E.2d 185 (1967); State v. Belote, 213 Kan. 291, 516 P.2d 159 (1973). Cf. United States v. Gregorio, 497 F.2d 1253,

1261 (4th Cir. 1974) (denial of "addict instructions" not error).

84. See Doe v. State, Alaska, 487 P.2d 47 (1971); State v. Ballesteros, 100 Ariz. 262, 413 P.2d 739 (1966); State v. Goodin, 8 Or.App. 15, 492 P.2d 287 (1971); People v. Ortega, 2 Cal.App.3d 884, 83 Cal. Rptr. 260 (1969).

85. Sanger v. Bacon, 180 Ind. 322, 101 N.E. 1001 (1913); State v. Bowen, 247 Mo. 584, 153 S.W. 1033 (1913).

86. State v. Paul, 83 N.M. 619, 495 P.2d 797 (1972); State v. Mack, 282 N.C. 334, 193 S.E.2d 71 (1972); State v. Brewton, 247 Or. 241, 422 P.2d 581 (1967).

87. Esderts v. Chicago Rock Island & Pacific Railroad Co., 76 Ill.App.2d 210, 222 N.E.2d 117 (1966).

88. People v. Taylor, 8 Cal.3d 174, 104 Cal.Rptr. 350, 501 P.2d 918 (1972).

A stricter standard for inconsistency has been applied by some courts when the person to be impeached is the defendant. Here these courts require outright contradiction.

In addition to cross-examining the witness about the prior inconsistent statement, the opponent may sometimes use extrinsic evidence to prove the statement. For example, the opponent may call another witness to the stand to testify to the prior witness's prior inconsistent statement. *Extrinsic evidence is permissible when the following conditions are satisfied: (1) The opponent has laid a proper foundation on cross-examination; (2) the witness has denied making the inconsistent statement; and (3) the statement relates to a material fact in the case rather than a collateral fact.*

The first condition, the requirement for a proper foundation on cross-examination, relates back to the 1820 English opinion, Queen Caroline's case. The jurisdictions following this case require that the opponent name the place of the statement, the time, and the person to whom the statement was made.[89] The witness is given an opportunity to explain or to deny the statement. A second group of jurisdictions do not require that the witness be told the details of the prior statement as a prerequisite to cross-examination.[90] The courts in this second group permit the opponent to ask general questions about the prior inconsistent statement such as, "Have you ever told anyone that you saw the defendant chamber a round before stepping into the alley?" A third group of jurisdictions completely dispense with the requirement for a foundation in certain circumstances. One state, for example, permits the opponent to omit the foundation on cross so long as the witness to be impeached is excused subject to recall.[91]

The proponent could then recall the witness to explain away or deny the inconsistent statement.

The second condition is that on cross, the witness deny the prior inconsistent statement. This condition is clearly satisfied if the witness makes an outright denial that he or she ever made the inconsistent statement. The condition is also satisfied when the witness claims that he or she cannot remember making such a statement. If the witness admits having made the statement the trial judge will usually not permit extrinsic evidence. The minority view is that even if the witness admits the statement, it is admissible through extrinsic proof.[92]

The third condition of admissibility of extrinsic evidence is that the statement must not relate to a collateral fact. This condition is merely an application of the general collateral fact rule. The rule is discussed in a subsequent subsection.[93] That subsection defines "collateral fact" in detail. Simply stated, a collateral fact is a fact that is not directly related to the ultimate historical questions in the case such as whether the defendant committed the alleged act and whether the defendant had a certain state of mind at the time of the act's commission.

Suggested Reading:

United States v. Bibbs, 564 F.2d 1165 (5th Cir. 1977).

Prior Inconsistent Act. Like prior inconsistent statements, prior inconsistent acts are admissible to impeach. Suppose that in an embezzlement prosecution, the prosecution offers a character witness's testimony that the defendant is an untrustworthy person.

---

89. Edwards v. State, 287 Ala. 588, 253 So.2d 513 (1971); Bullock v. State, 53 Wis.2d 809, 193 N.W.2d 889 (1972).

90. Fed.Evid.Rules 613(a), 28 U.S.C.A.

91. West's Ann.Cal.Evid.Code § 770.

92. People v. Knowles, 91 Ill.App.2d 109, 234 N.E.2d 149 (1968).

93. See the last subsection in this section.

To impeach the character witness, the defense could elicit testimony that the witness had made an unsecured, signature loan to the defendant. A person who truly believed the defendant to be untrustworthy would probably not make such a loan to the defendant. If the defendant testified at trial to exculpatory facts, some courts have treated his or her silence during pretrial interrogation as an inconsistent act. As Section 2 of Chapter 13 points out, the Supreme Court has recently held that the fifth amendment prohibits the prosecution from commenting on the defendant's pretrial silence even for the limited purpose of impeaching exculpatory trial testimony.[94]

Suggested Reading:

United States v. Brown, 436 F.Supp. 998 (E.D.Mich. 1974).

Bias. A witness may also be impeached by showing bias, interest, or hostility, for these qualities have a bearing on the credibility of the witness's testimony. Because bias is never a collateral fact, the courts are quite liberal in accepting testimony that demonstrates bias. Such evidence may be admitted even after the witness's disavowal of partiality toward one side.[95] The courts sometimes say that proof of bias must be direct and positive. However, as a practical matter, the standard is quite lax. Bias in favor of the

defendant may be explored through questions about the witness's family ties,[96] friendship,[97] romantic involvement,[98] employment,[99] financial ties,[1] enmity,[2] or fear.[3] Some courts admit proof that the witness and the defendant have been members of the same criminal conspiracy as evidence of bias in the defendant's favor.[4] Factors evidencing bias against the defendant are a showing that the witness is a paid informer,[5] a material witness in protective custody, a co-indictee, has been granted immunity,[6] or promised a reduced sentence through plea bargaining.[7]

The majority view is that before introducing extrinsic evidence of a witness's bias, the opponent must lay a foundation during the witness's cross-examination. The opponent must afford the witness an opportunity to deny or explain the bias. However,

---

94. Cf. Doyle v. Ohio, 426 U.S. 610, 96 S.Ct. 2240, 48 L.Ed.2d 91 (1976); Baxter v. Palmigiano, 425 U.S. 308, 96 S.Ct. 1551, 47 L.Ed.2d 810 (1976); United States v. Hale, 422 U.S. 171, 95 S.Ct. 2133, 45 L.Ed. 2d 99 (1975).

95. United States v. Haggett, 438 F.2d 396 (2d Cir. 1971) (error not to allow extrinsic evidence to contradict witness's statement that he had not attempted to bribe witnesses to testify falsely); Salgado v. United States, 278 F.2d 830, 831 (1st Cir. 1960) ("Questions of bias and prejudice . . . can be proved by extrinsic evidence, and this evidence is not foreclosed by a prior denial on the part of the witness.").

96. See, e. g., Adams v. State, 280 Ala. 678, 198 So. 2d 255 (1967); People v. Jones, 7 Cal.App.3d 48, 86 Cal.Rptr. 717 (1970); Mich.Comp.Laws Ann. § 27A.-2158; Vernon's Ann.Mo.Stat. § 546.260.

97. People v. Casper, 25 Mich.App. 1, 180 N.W.2d 906 (1970); State v. Franklin, 185 Neb. 62, 173 N.W. 2d 393 (1971); State v. Guerrero, 11 Or.App. 284, 501 P.2d 998 (1972).

98. See, e. g., United States v. Johnson, 426 F.2d 1112 (7th Cir. 1970); People v. Jones, 7 Cal.App.3d 48, 86 Cal.Rptr. 717 (1970).

99. See, e. g., State v. DiNunzio, 5 Conn.Cir. 608, 259 A.2d 768 (1969).

1. See, e. g., United States v. Kerr, 464 F.2d 1367 (6th Cir. 1972); Garcia v. State, 454 S.W.2d 400 (Tex. Cr.App.1970).

2. Wynn v. United States, 397 F.2d 621 (D.C.Cir. 1967).

3. United States v. Cerone, 452 F.2d 274 (7th Cir. 1971).

4. United States v. Robinson, 530 F.2d 1076 (D.C. Cir. 1976).

5. See, e. g., Wheeler v. United States, 351 F.2d 946 (1st Cir. 1965).

6. United States v. Musgrave, 483 F.2d 327, 328 (5th Cir. 1973) (The witness's "prior status as a co-indictee certainly suggested a personal interest in the litigation, a potential lack of complete impartiality"); United States v. Dickens, 417 F.2d 958 (8th Cir. 1969).

7. See, e. g., Gordon v. United States, 344 U.S. 414, 73 S.Ct. 369, 97 L.Ed. 447 (1953).

the statutory trend is to abolish the requirement for a foundation on cross-examination. Numerous state statutes impliedly abolish the requirement by expressly applying the requirement only to impeachment by prior inconsistent statement. Federal Rule of Evidence 613 is in accord with the statutory trend.

Suggested Reading:

Gordon v. United States, 344 U.S. 414, 73 S.Ct. 369, 97 L.Ed. 447 (1953).

Specific Contradiction. Specific contradiction, another method of impeachment, is based on the inference that if a witness makes a mistake about one fact, his or her testimony may be untrustworthy about another fact. The strength of this inference of untrustworthiness varies depending on which specific error is brought to the attention of the trier of fact.

One danger in using this impeachment method is that the jury may be distracted from the main issues by contradictions about extraneous evidence whose explanation consumes a great deal of time.[8] Therefore a limitation is placed in this type of impeachment by applying the collateral fact rule, which states that extrinsic evidence is not admissible to show a specific contradiction that is collateral to the matter in issue.[9] At least two classes of evidence are never considered collateral under this rule: facts which are of consequence to the matter in issue;[10] and,

facts independently admissible to impeach, such as a showing of bias, of untruthfulness, or of deficiencies that go to the witness's competency.[11] The next subsection analyzes the collateral fact rule in detail.

Suggested Reading:

Gaddis v. State, 360 P.2d 522 (Okl.Cr.1961).

The Collateral Fact Rule. As previously stated, credibility evidence relates directly to the witness's believability rather than to the historical, material facts on the merits of the case. To ensure that the jurors maintain perspective and focus primarily on the merits, the courts have imposed numerous limitations on the admissibility of impeaching credibility evidence. The previous discussion of the various impeachment techniques highlighted some of the limitations. A limitation common to several techniques is the collateral fact rule. The collateral fact rule is a confused area of law, but the rule can be understood if we proceed through three steps of analysis.

What Impeachment Techniques Does the Rule Apply To? The primary thrust of the rule is that it bars the use of extrinsic evidence to impeach a witness. If the impeaching evidence relates to a collateral fact, the opponent may cross-examine the witness about the fact but may not introduce extrinsic evidence of the fact. The rule does not apply to any impeachment technique which necessarily involves or usually requires the presentation of extrinsic evidence. For example, the rule is inapplicable to impeachment by proof of the witness's bad character of untruthfulness. To use this technique to impeach witness #1, the op-

8. Fed.Evid.Rule 403, 28 U.S.C.A., directs the court to consider the factors of confusion, prejudice, and waste of time in determining whether the otherwise relevant evidence should be excluded.

9. United States v. Browning, 439 F.2d 813 (1st Cir. 1971); Tinker v. United States, 417 F.2d 542 (D.C. Cir. 1969).

10. United States v. Guinn, 454 F.2d 29 (5th Cir. 1972); State v. Long, 280 N.C. 633, 187 S.E.2d 47 (1972).

11. See, e. g., United States v. Schennault, 429 F.2d 852 (7th Cir. 1970); People v. Pierce, 269 Cal.App.2d 193, 75 Cal.Rptr. 257 (1969).

ponent must call character witness #2 to establish witness #1's bad character. Because this impeachment technique requires extrinsic evidence, the collateral fact rule is inapplicable. On similar reasoning, the courts generally do not apply the rule to the following impeachment techniques: prior conviction (extrinsic evidence in the form of a certified copy of the judgment of conviction), attack on the witness's mental capacity (extrinsic evidence in the form of expert or lay testimony about the witness's mental deficiencies), polygraph (extrinsic evidence in the form of testimony of a polygraph examiner), and bias. Many cases admitting extrinsic evidence of bias contain the expression that bias is "always independently provable;"[12] the expression is simply another way of saying that the collateral fact rule is inapplicable to the bias technique of impeachment. By process of elimination, the rule applies to only three impeachment techniques: specific acts of misconduct which have not resulted in a conviction, prior inconsistent statement, and specific contradiction. Many cases excluding extrinsic evidence of specific acts contain the expression that the opponent must "take the answer" the witness gives on cross;[13] this expression is another way of saying that the rule applies to that impeachment technique.

Does the Impeaching Evidence Relate to a Collateral Fact? If the rule does not apply to the technique the opponent is using, the extrinsic evidence is admissible. However, even if the rule applies to the technique, the extrinsic evidence is not automatically inadmissible. The judge must examine the spe-

cific impeaching evidence offered and decide whether that evidence relates to a collateral fact. This step in analysis presents a definitional problem: What is "a collateral fact"?

The soundest approach to defining "collateral fact" is a negative approach: A fact is *not* collateral if (1) the fact is logically relevant to the historical, material facts in issue; or (2) the witness's testimony about the historical, material facts in issue is necessarily mistaken if the witness is mistaken about the fact.

A hypothetical involving prior inconsistent statement impeachment will illustrate element (1). Assume that on direct examination, a prosecution witness testifies that while he was in a department store to shop for cigarettes, he saw the defendant steal a radio. During the defense case-in-chief, the defense calls an investigator who interviewed the prosecution witness. First, the defense counsel attempts to elicit the investigator's extrinsic testimony that the prosecution witness told her that he was shopping for candy. That testimony would be objectionable; the type of product the witness was shopping for is not logically relevant to the historical facts in issue in a larceny prosecution. Second, the defense counsel attempts to elicit the investigator's testimony that the prosecution witness told her that he did not have a good view of the culprit and has serious doubt that the culprit he saw was the defendant. The judge would admit this extrinsic evidence of the prosecution witness's prior inconsistent statement. This statement does not relate to a collateral fact. Rather, it is logically relevant to the material fact in dispute whether the defendant was the person who stole the radio from the department store.

A hypothetical involving specific contradiction impeachment will illustrate element (2). Suppose that the government charges the defendant with burglarizing Mr. Kerig's house on August 1. The prosecution

---

12. United States v. Harvey, 547 F.2d 720 (2d Cir. 1976); Johnson v. Brewer, 521 F.2d 556 (8th Cir. 1975); Moynahan v. Manson, 419 F.Supp. 1139 (D. Conn.1976).

13. Federal Evidence Rule 608(b) illustrates the operation of the collateral fact rule. The Rule specifically permits cross-examination about specific acts "probative of . . . untruthfulness," but the same Rule states that the act "may not be proved by extrinsic evidence."

calls Ms. Hildreth as a witness.[14] Ms. Hildreth is a door-to-door salesperson. She testifies that on August 1, she was selling wares in the neighborhood where the burglary occurred. She further testifies that she visited Ms. Merton's house, immediately across from Mr. Kerig's house, and sold Ms. Merton some goods. Finally, she testifies that as she was leaving Ms. Merton's house, she saw the defendant emerge from Mr. Kerig's house. During the defense case-in-chief, the defense calls Ms. Merton. Ms. Merton is prepared to testify that she was on vacation between July 1 and September 1 and was not residing at her house on August 1. The prosecutor objects that this extrinsic evidence is collateral. At first glance, the objection seems sound; the timing of Ms. Merton's vacation seems completely irrelevant to the historical facts in issue in the burglary prosecution. However, on closer analysis, the evidence does not relate to a collateral fact. If Ms. Merton was not residing in her house on August 1 and Ms. Hildreth's testimony is correct in every other respect, Ms. Hildreth could not have visited Ms. Merton's house on August 1. If Ms. Hildreth did not visit Ms. Merton's house on August 1, her testimony on the merits is necessarily mistaken; if she visited Ms. Merton's house on another date, she could not have observed a burglary occurring on August 1. Hence, the defense may use this extrinsic evidence to specifically contradict Ms. Hildreth's testimony; although Ms. Merton's testimony does not directly relate to the merits of the burglary prosecution, Ms. Merton's testimony necessarily calls into question Ms. Hildreth's testimony on the merits.[15]

What Is the Procedural Consequence of the Rule's Applicability? Assume that the court concludes that the rule applies to the impeachment technique the opponent is employing and that the specific impeaching evidence offered relates to a collateral fact. What procedural consequence flows from those conclusions?

Notwithstanding those conclusions, the judge may still permit the opponent to cross-examine the witness about the impeaching facts. The defense counsel could ask the prosecution witness whether he had made a prior inconsistent statement that he was shopping for candy rather than cigarettes. If the witness has committed a specific act of misconduct such as perjury which reflects on his or her credibility, the opponent may cross-examine the witness about the act. The opponent may do so even if the witness's prior act of perjury has no historical connection whatsoever with the crime the defendant is charged with. However, in both cases, the opponent must "take the answer" the witness gives on cross; the opponent may not introduce extrinsic evidence to prove the impeaching facts. The defense counsel may not call the investigator to testify to the prior inconsistent statement, and the opponent may not call witness #2 to establish witness #1's perjury. Even if the fact is collateral, the opponent may cross-examine the witness about the fact so long as the fact is logically relevant to impeach the witness's credibility. The procedural significance of the collateral fact rule is that it precludes the opponent from presenting extrinsic evidence of the collateral, impeaching fact.

---

14. This hypothetical is based on Problem 6–3 in K. Broun & R. Meisenholder, Problems in Evidence (1973).

15. C. McCormick, Handbook of the Law of Evidence § 47 (2d ed. 1972) gives the following justification for admitting this type of impeaching evidence: "Suppose a witness has told a story of a transaction critical to the controversy. To prove him wrong in some trivial detail of time, place, or circumstance is 'collateral.' But to prove untrue some fact recited by the witness that if he were really there and saw what he claims to have seen, he could not have been mistaken about, is a convincing kind of impeachment that the courts must make place for. To disprove such a fact is to pull out the linchpin of the story. So we may recognize this . . . type of allowable contradiction, namely, the contradiction of the background and circumstances of a material transaction, which as a matter of human experience he would not have been mistaken about if his story were true."

Suggested Reading:

United States v. Harvey, 547 F.2d 720 (2d Cir. 1976).

5. Rehabilitation After Impeachment

Suggested Reading:

Outlaw v. United States, 81 F.2d 805 (5th Cir. 1936).

People v. Coleman, 71 Cal.2d 1159, 80 Cal.Rptr. 920, 459 P.2d 248 (1969).

The third stage to be examined in the discussion of credibility is the rehabilitation of a witness after impeachment. Except for bolstering which is discussed in section 2 of this chapter, rehabilitation may take place only after the witness's credibility has been attacked. There are four primary methods of rehabilitating an impeached witness: (1) giving the witness an opportunity on redirect to explain or deny the impeaching evidence; (2) corroborating the witness's testimony; (3) introducing evidence of the witness's character trait of truthfulness; and (4) proving that the witness made a prior statement consistent with his or her testimony at trial.

Denial or Explanation on Redirect. The opponent normally attempts to impeach the witness during the witness's cross-examination. After the witness's testimony has been attacked, the proponent usually may give the witness an opportunity on redirect to explain or deny the impeaching evidence. On cross, the prosecutor might attempt to impeach the witness for bias by eliciting the witness's admission of friendship with the defendant. On redirect, the witness could testify that he or she would not lie in court even for a friend. Similarly, after the defense counsel elicited a prosecution witness's

admission of a seemingly inconsistent prior statement, on redirect the witness could attempt to explain away the apparent inconsistency.

Corroboration. Just as the proponent may corroborate before impeachment, he or she may corroborate after impeachment. Corroborating evidence is not directly relevant to credibility but rather is evidence on the merits which incidentally rehabilitates the witness's credibility. Like the next two types of rehabilitating evidence, corroboration is subject to a general norm that rehabilitating evidence must be a response in kind to the impeaching evidence. If the only impeachment technique the opponent employs is specific contradiction, the only permissible method of rehabilitation is corroboration. Specific contradiction impeaches the witness by contradicting the witness's testimony on the merits; and to respond in kind, the proponent must rehabilitate the witness on the merits.

Character Trait of Truthfulness. As in the case of corroborating evidence, evidence of the witness's good character for truthfulness is admissible rehabilitating evidence if it represents a response in kind to the attempted impeachment. Thus, at common law when the opponent uses evidence of a character trait of untruthfulness—for example, bad reputation, prior convictions, specific act of misconduct, or corrupt act showing bias—the proponent may introduce character evidence to rehabilitate the witness.[16] When a witness's credibility has been attacked through the use of prior convictions or acts of misconduct, Federal Evidence Rule 608(b) allows the introduction of opinion or reputation evidence in support of the witness's truthfulness.

When character evidence is not a response in kind, the evidence is inadmissible. If the bias arises from a circumstance other

---

16. Rodriguez v. State, 165 Tex.Cr.R. 179, 305 S.W. 2d 350 (1950).

than a corrupt act, such as family or business ties, character evidence may not be introduced to rehabilitate the witness.[17] When the method of impeachment is specific contradiction or prior inconsistent statement, evidence in support of the witness's truthfulness is generally inadmissible.[18] However, the courts are divided on the question of whether evidence of a prior inconsistent statement amounts to an attack on the witness's truthfulness.[19]

One court has suggested that in each case, the facts should be examined to determine whether the evidence amounts to an attack on the character of the witness. If it does, the introduction of character evidence demonstrating the witness's truthfulness should be permitted.[20]

Prior Consistent Statement. Whether a witness may be supported by a prior consistent statement depends on which method of impeachment is employed. On the one hand, with impeachment by evidence of a witness's character trait of untruthfulness, prior conviction, or act of misconduct not resulting in a conviction, a prior statement may not be introduced to rehabilitate.

On the other hand, the proponent may rehabilitate the witness by showing the prior consistent statement under a number of circumstances. First, if the opponent imputes bias or improper motive to the witness, the proponent may show a prior consistent statement made before the alleged bias or motive arose.[21] Conversely, if the motive arose before the statement, rehabilitation is not permitted.[22] Second, where the opponent suggests that the witness's memory is faulty, the prior consistent statement may be admitted if it was made when the event was fresh in the witness's mind. For example, when the defense attempts to impeach the eyewitness identification by suggesting faulty memory, the prosecutor may introduce evidence that the witness identified the defendant soon after the event.[23] Third, a prior consistent statement may be introduced when the opponent expressly or impliedly charges that the witness fabricated testimony. Such a charge is contradicted if the witness made a statement consistent with his or her testimony before the alleged fabrication occurred.[24] Suppose the defendant testifies to an affirmative defense on direct. During cross, the prosecutor might ask, "Isn't it true that you didn't think of that defense until you consulted your attorney?" The prosecutor's question amounts to a charge of fabrication. To rehabilitate the defendant, the defense counsel could introduce evidence of a prior statement consistent with the defense if the defendant made the statement before consulting the defense counsel. Fourth, a prior consistent statement is permissible rehabilitation when the opponent charges incapacity to remember or observe if the statement was made prior to the alleged incapacity arising.[25]

---

17. Lassiter v. State, 35 Ala.App. 323, 47 So.2d 230 (1950).

18. 4 Wigmore, Evidence §§ 1108–09 (Chadbourn rev. 1972).

19. Outlaw v. United States, 81 F.2d 805 (5th Cir. 1936) sets forth the various views.

20. Id.

21. Copes v. United States, 345 F.2d 723, 725 n. 3 (D.C.Cir. 1964). See also Fed.Evid.Rule 801(d)(1)(B), 28 U.S.C.A.; West's Ann.Cal.Evid.Code § 791.

22. Abernathy v. Emporia Mfg. Co., 122 Va. 406, 95 S.E. 418 (1918).

23. Clemons v. United States, 408 F.2d 1230, 1242–43 (D.C.Cir. 1968); Gill v. State, 479 S.W.2d 289 (Tex.Civ.App.1972); Martin v. Commonwealth, 210 Va. 686, 173 S.E.2d 794 (1970). See also Fed.Evid. Rule 801(d)(1)(C), 28 U.S.C.A.

24. United States v. Fayette, 388 F.2d 728, 734–35 (2d Cir. 1968); United States v. Leggett, 312 F.2d 566, 572 (4th Cir. 1962); People v. Welch, 8 Cal.3d 106, 104 Cal.Rptr. 217, 501 P.2d 225 (1972); Fed.Evid. Rule 801(d)(1)(B), 28 U.S.C.A.; West's Ann.Cal.Evid. Code § 791(b).

25. C. McCormick, Handbook of the Law of Evidence 105 (2d ed. 1972).

PART 2
LOGICAL RELEVANCE
CHAPTER 5
RELEVANCE

1. Materiality and Logical Relevance

Suggested Reading:

United States v. Austin, 532 F.2d 297 (2d Cir. 1976).

United States v. Larson, 526 F.2d 256 (5th Cir. 1976).

As previously stated, two central concepts govern the content of witnesses's testimony: relevance and competence. This chapter begins our analysis of the relevance concept. To understand that concept, we must analyze three distinctions: materiality and logical relevance; logical relevance and legal relevance; and finally direct and circumstantial relevance.

The Definition of Materiality. An item of evidence is immaterial if it tends to prove a fact that is not in issue in the case. Thus, materiality concerns the relationship between the proposition an item is offered to prove and the facts in issue in the case. In

any given case, certain facts will be in dispute. Some of the facts in dispute are procedural, e. g., jurisdiction and venue. The facts on the case's merits are also usually disputed. For instance, the defendant ordinarily disputes the historical question of whether he or she committed the act with the requisite intent. The courts often use the adjectives, "material" and "ultimate," to describe such historical facts alleged in the indictment or information. Finally, the witnesses' credibility will be a disputed fact in the case. All these are facts of consequence in the decision of the case,[1] and are therefore the facts within the range of issues in the case.

An item of evidence is immaterial if its proponent offers it to prove some fact that is not properly in issue in the case. Suppose that the government has charged the defendant with a general intent assault. At the trial the defense attorney attempts to elicit testimony that the defendant was vol-

---

1. West's Ann.Cal.Evid.Code § 210.

untarily intoxicated at the time of the offense. Because voluntary intoxication is a defense to a specific intent crime, but not to a general intent crime,[2] this testimony is objectionable as immaterial. The defense is offering the testimony to establish the defendant's voluntary intoxication, and under the substantive law the defendant's voluntary intoxication is not a fact of consequence in the case. The same analysis applies to evidence of the defendant's good motives for committing a criminal act.[3] If the defendant committed the proscribed act with the necessary state of mind, the fact that the defendant had a commendable motive for the act is no defense. For this reason, the prosecution may object to evidence of defendant's good motives as immaterial.[4] On its face, the evidence of the intoxication or the motives would be inadmissible.

The Definition of Logical Relevance. Pure logical relevance concerns the relation between an item of evidence and the fact which the proponent offers the item to prove. An item of evidence is logically irrelevant if it lacks a tendency in reason to increase or decrease the probability of the fact's existence. Thus, the item is logically relevant to and connected with the fact if the item affects the balance of the probability of the fact's existence. In the preceding hypothetical, the judge could sustain a materiality objection as soon as the defense attorney said, "I am offering this testimony to prove the defendant's voluntary intoxication." Because voluntary intoxication is not in issue in a general intent assault prosecution, the defense's theory of admissibility is patently invalid. However, if the prosecu-

tion were for a specific intent assault, a prosecution materiality objection would be patently incorrect. Here the prosecution would have to resort to a relevance objection, and the judge would have to decide whether the specific evidence proffered had any tendency in reason to increase the probability that the defendant was voluntarily intoxicated when he or she committed the act charged.

Modern Codes' Merger of Materiality into Relevance. The modern evidence codes generally omit any reference to materiality, for they merge materiality into relevancy, requiring that evidence be relevant and then defining relevance as a logical connection with the facts of consequence in the case. Federal Rule of Evidence 401 is typical: " 'Relevant evidence' means evidence having any tendency to make the existence of any fact that is of consequence to the determination of the action more probable or less probable than it would be without the evidence."[5] Under such statutes, the determination of relevance is a two-step process.

The first step is identifying all the consequential facts in the case. In order to identify these facts, the judge must consider the substantive law, the pleadings, and the evidence already admitted. When the prosecution files its pleading, all the essential elements of the alleged crimes come into issue. The defense may (1) remove elements from dispute by admitting that they are true and (2) place additional elements in dispute by raising true affirmative defenses. Finally, the judge must consider the evidence already introduced. If one party has improperly injected either an immaterial issue or irrelevant evidence into the case, the judge may permit the other party to respond on a theory of curative admissibility.[6] Suppose

---

2. R. Perkins, Criminal Law 789 (1957).

3. United States v. Austin, 532 F.2d 297 (2d Cir. 1976).

4. We are assuming that the trial is a bifurcated proceeding with separate stages for findings and sentence. If the proceeding were unitary, the defendant could argue that motive was at least material on sentencing.

5. Fed.Evid.Rule 401, 28 U.S.C.A. See also West's Ann.Cal.Code § 210.

6. United States v. Bolin, 514 F.2d 554 (7th Cir. 1975). For a discussion of curative admissibility, see C. McCormick, Handbook of the Law of Evidence § 58

that the charge is possession of drugs at a specific time. On direct examination, the defendant goes far beyond the scope of the issues in the case; after denying possession at the time in question, the defendant volunteers the technically irrelevant statement, "I have never had drugs in my possession." The judge may then invoke curative admissibility and permit the prosecution to adduce evidence of the defendant's possession of drugs on other occasions.[7] Thus, like the substantive law and pleadings, the evidence already introduced can help to determine the facts of consequence in the case.

After reviewing the substantive law, pleadings, and evidence, the judge can identify the facts of consequence at any given juncture in the case. These can include: (1) jurisdiction; (2) venue; (3) the essential elements of the crimes alleged in the indictment or information; (4) the essential elements of any affirmative defense the defendant has raised; (5) the witnesses's credibility; and (6) a fact which one party improperly injected into the case and which the other party is responding to on a curative admissibility rationale.

The second step is the determination of whether the evidence proffered bears a logical relation to any fact of consequence in the case. McCormick has given us the best formulation of the test for logical connection: "[D]oes the evidence offered render the desired inference more probable than it would be without the evidence?"[8] Thus to be admissible, the item of evidence does not have to make the desired inference more likely than not, for demanding 51% probability of each item is unreasonable. Instead, it needs only to meet the lax standard of affecting the balance of probabilities. For example, judges routinely admit prosecution evidence of the defendant's motive and opportunity to commit the crime. Although neither motive nor opportunity evidence creates a 51% probability that the defendant committed the *actus reus*, the evidence is logically relevant because it ever so slightly increases the probability of the defendant's guilt. The following example should further dramatize the laxity of the standard. Suppose that the defendant in a hit-and-run prosecution is Caucasian. The prosecution offers an eyewitness's testimony that she saw the accident but remembers only that the driver was Caucasian. Despite the fact that it does not create even a 1% probability that the defendant was the driver, this testimony is logically relevant. Although the testimony is certainly inconclusive, a judge could not exclude it as logically irrelevant, for the evidence tends to establish the defendant's guilt by slightly increasing its probability. On its face, the testimony has a logical connection with the facts of consequence in the case.

2. Logical Relevance and Legal Relevance

Suggested Reading:

United States v. Clavey, 565 F.2d 111 (7th Cir. 1977).

Terry v. State, 491 S.W.2d 161 (Tex.Cr.App.1973).

The Distinction. Logical relevance concerns only probative value. The test for logical relevance is whether the item of evidence has any tendency whatsoever in reason to affect the balance of probabilities of the existence of a fact of consequence. Although logical relevance is an absolute re-

---

(2d ed. 1972). In deciding whether to permit the opponent to respond, the judge considers two primary factors: (1) the likelihood that the improper evidence the proponent initially introduced will affect the case's outcome; and (2) whether the opponent attempted to protect himself or herself by objecting.

7. Walder v. United States, 347 U.S. 62, 74 S.Ct. 354, 98 L.Ed. 503 (1954); People v. Westek, 31 Cal. 2d 469, 190 P.2d 9 (1948).

8. C. McCormick, Handbook of the Law of Evidence § 185 (2d ed. 1972).

quirement for admissibility, alone it is not sufficient and thus does not ensure admissibility. Under the rubric of "legal relevance," the courts have imposed an additional requirement that the item's probative value outweigh any attendant probative dangers. In general the courts are concerned about four probative dangers. The first is that the evidence might create a serious risk that the jury will decide the case on an improper basis. Counsel often raise the objection that an opponent's evidence is "unduly prejudicial." In itself the evidence's damning character is not a ground for exclusion; the opponent would not be offering the evidence unless he or she assumed that it would damage the opposing case. Rather the danger is that the jury will misuse the evidence and thus decide the case on an improper basis.

Gruesome photographs of the victim in a homicide case are illustrative. Because the photographs might inflame the jurors and arouse their emotions, they might feel an overpowering urge to convict someone of the heinous crime, and the defendant is of course the most convenient person. This same rationale applies to evidence of the defendant's criminal record. Because recidivism is a common phenomenon, the evidence is certainly logically relevant. Nevertheless, the prosecution's introduction of such evidence creates a serious danger that the jury will convict simply because the defendant seems a threat to society and therefore should be in prison—not because the jurors believe that the prosecution has proved the defendant's commission of the alleged crime beyond a reasonable doubt.

The evidence posing this first probative danger usually has an emotional appeal to prejudice, hostility, or sympathy, but the danger itself is that a decision will be made on an improper basis—ordinarily a conviction for some reason other than the jurors' honest belief in the defendant's guilt of the crime charged.

The second danger is that the evidence will either confuse the jurors or distract them from the main issues in the case. Even though evidence is logically relevant, its probative value might be minimal, and it might focus the jury's attention on matters other than the pivotal facts in the case. For example, as soon as a witness testifies, his or her credibility comes into issue. The opponent may then call a witness to attack the first witness's credibility. However, because as soon as the second witness testifies, his or her credibility also comes into issue, the party calling the first witness might call a third witness to impeach the second; the party calling the second witness could call a fourth to impeach the third, and so on. In this situation the judge may limit credibility evidence to ensure that the jury does not lose sight of the main dispute over the historical events in question.

A third danger is that the presentation of and the opponent's response to the evidence will be unduly time-consuming. The evidence's probative value might be so miniscule that the judge simply does not think that it is worth the expenditure of court time necessary to present it to the jury.

Finally, at common law, the courts recognize a fourth danger of unfair surprise to the opponent. Under this view, if the defense attempts to introduce wholly unexpected evidence, the prosecution may object on legal relevance grounds. In jurisdictions which retain this view and have strictly limited prosecution discovery, a legal relevance objection can be an important prosecution weapon. However, most modern evidence codes do not treat surprise as a ground for excluding evidence. For example, Federal Evidence Rule 403 [9] and some state statutes [10] omit surprise from their listing of probative dangers. The Advisory Commit-

---

9. Fed.Evid.Rule 403, 28 U.S.C.A.

10. West's Ann.Cal.Evid.Code § 352.

tee's Note to Rule 403 explains the omission: "While it can scarcely be doubted that claims of unfair surprise may still be justified despite procedural requirements of notice and instrumentalities of discovery, the granting of a continuance is a more appropriate remedy than exclusion of the evidence." [11]

The Application of the Legal Relevance Requirement to Various Types of Evidence. Like the logical relevance requirement, the legal relevance doctrine applies to all types of evidence. The application of the legal relevance requirement to some types of evidence remains a highly discretionary process, for the judge applies the requirement on an ad hoc, case-by-case basis. The judge must first assess the evidence's probative value or worth. Is the evidence remote in point of time? If the evidence directly relates to an event other than the particular event in dispute, how much time elapsed between the two? Is the evidence cumulative —that is, has the proponent already introduced some evidence on that point? Is other evidence available to prove the same point? [12] After considering all these factors, the judge determines the evidence's affirmative, probative value.

After this initial assessment, the judge must identify the probative danger attending the specific evidence proffered. We have already listed the major probative dangers: the evidence's tendencies to invite a decision on an improper basis; to distract the jurors from the main issues; to unduly consume time; and to unfairly surprise the opponent. In weighing these negative, countervailing factors, the judge must consider how effective a limiting instruction would be. If the judge admits evidence of the defendant's past criminal record, the judge could at the same time give the jurors an instruction specifically directing them to consider the record only for the limited purpose of assessing the defendant's credibility. However, the judge must speculate whether the jurors are sophisticated and conscientious enough to follow the limiting instruction.

Finally, the judge must balance the evidence's probative value against its probative dangers. Because the affirmative value and negative dangers are both intangibles, the balancing process is highly discretionary and subjective. The judge decides whether in his or her opinion, the probative value outweighs the probative danger. Under the Federal Rules, the test is slightly different; it is biased in favor of admissibility, for the judge may exclude evidence on a legal relevance theory only when the probative value is "substantially outweighed" by the accompanying probative dangers. [13]

The application of the legal relevance requirement to photographs illustrates the analytic sequence through which the judge proceeds. No hard and fast rules exist to determine when a photograph is too gruesome to be admissible. The judge first weighs the photograph's probative value. On the one hand in a first degree murder prosecution involving malice aforethought, a photograph depicting the ferocity of the assault would be highly relevant on the malice issue. On the other hand, if the only seriously controverted issue is the defendant's participation in the crime, photographs of the victim's body might have only marginal relevance. [14] The judge then considers the countervailing probative dangers. How shocking are the photographs? How effective would it be to give a jury instruction reminding the jurors to dispassionately weigh the objective evidence? In practice,

---

11. Advisory Committee Note, Fed.Evid.Rule 403, 28 U.S.C.A.

12. Frank v. United States, 262 F.2d 695 (D.C.Cir. 1958).

13. Fed.Evid.Rule 403, 28 U.S.C.A. West's Ann. Cal.Evid.Code § 352 uses the same expression.

14. Commonwealth v. Dankel, 450 Pa. 437, 301 A.2d 365 (1973); Beagles v. State, 273 So.2d 796 (Fla.App. 1973); State v. Waitus, 224 S.C. 12, 77 S.E.2d 256 (1953).

the courts usually balance in favor of the photograph's admissibility.[15]

Although the application of the legal relevance requirement is highly discretionary in such areas as photographs, in other areas the rulings are so standardized that discretion has hardened into relatively definite rules of thumb. Chapters 9 and 10 will discuss the admissibility of character and uncharged misconduct evidence. In the final analysis, both types of evidence pose legal relevance issues; the evidence is logically relevant, but a serious probative danger exists that the jurors will misuse the evidence. Because the norms are fairly clear, the rulings in these areas are much more predictable than in those where the courts have been unable to develop a standardized approach.

3. Direct and Circumstantial Relevance

Suggested Reading:

Holland v. United States, 348 U.S. 121, 75 S.Ct. 127, 99 L.Ed. 150 (1954).

The Distinction. Most laypeople have heard the expressions "direct evidence" and "circumstantial evidence." The distinction between the two types of evidence turns on the manner in which they relate to the facts of consequence in the case.

Evidence is directly relevant if the immediate inference from the evidence is the existence or non-existence of the fact of consequence. Thus, direct evidence "directly proves a fact, without an inference or presumption."[16] Suppose that the defendant is charged with soliciting the felony of murder. A witness testifies that the defendant

asked him to murder the defendant's wife in return for $3,000. The only decision the jury must make is whether to believe the witness. If the jury believes him, the testimony on its face establishes the solicitation; the jury does not have to decide whether to draw any intermediate inference.

In contrast, circumstantial evidence does not immediately supply the answer to the question of whether the fact of consequence exists. Rather, the evidence is circumstantially relevant if it can serve as a step in a reasoning process which leads to establishing the existence or non-existence of the fact of consequence. Even after deciding to believe the witness, the jury must make an additional decision to draw one or more intermediate inferences before determining the existence of the fact of consequence. Suppose that a witness gives the following testimony in a homicide prosecution. The witness was standing outside a room when she heard loud noises in the room and what sounded like a scream. She entered the room and found a large pool of red liquid on the floor. This testimony would be circumstantial evidence of a homicide. Even if the jury decides to believe the witness, the jurors would nevertheless also have to decide whether to draw intermediate inferences before finding that a homicide occurred. Was the red liquid blood? If so, was there so much blood that the person who lost that amount probably died? Thus the testimony could serve as a link in a chain of evidence leading to a finding of fact that a homicide occurred.

The Importance of the Distinction. Some commentators have asserted that the distinction between direct and circumstantial evidence is of purely academic interest. Although there is an element of truth in the assertion, it is nevertheless an overstatement.

In a few jurisdictions, the trial judge must give special cautionary instructions, and the appellate court uses a more stringent standard of review if the prosecution relies

15. See, e. g. United States v. Hoog, 504 F.2d 45 (8th Cir. 1974).

16. West's Ann.Cal.Evid.Code § 410.

wholly or primarily upon circumstantial evidence. In these minority jurisdictions, the trial judge tells the jury that circumstantial evidence must exclude every reasonable hypothesis of innocence; it is not enough that the circumstantial evidence is consistent with the hypothesis of guilt.[17] In some of these jurisdictions, the appellate courts purport to apply a more rigorous standard of review to prosecution cases based on circumstantial evidence.[18]

In the overwhelming majority of jurisdictions, however, the courts do not recognize any formal distinction between direct and circumstantial evidence. In one leading case,[19] the Supreme Court remarked that "[c]ircumstantial evidence . . . is intrinsically no different . . . ." from direct evidence.[20] Many jurisdictions employ the popular jury instruction that "[b]oth direct and circumstantial evidence are acceptable as a means of proof. Neither is entitled to any greater weight than the other."[21] Eight of the federal circuits have explicitly rejected the proposition that a special standard of review must be used for the sufficiency of the evidence in circumstantial evidence cases.[22]

However, even in the majority of jurisdictions, there is one occasion when the distinction between direct and circumstantial evidence can be critical. Section 2 of this chapter pointed out that one of the probative dangers recognized under the legal relevance doctrine is the evidence's tendency to distract the jurors from the central issues in the case. By its very nature, circumstantial evidence has a more pronounced tendency to create this danger than does direct evidence. If the opponent raises a legal relevance objection to evidence, the proponent can often prevail by stressing that the proffered evidence is direct rather than circumstantial. This is not to say that the legal relevance doctrine is inapplicable to direct evidence. In a homicide prosecution, the cadaver would be direct evidence of the death, but it is difficult to believe that any judge would permit a prosecutor to drag the corpse into the courtroom to prove the fact of death. Thus although a legal relevance objection to direct evidence will usually be unsuccessful, such evidence is not immune from the legal relevance doctrine.

The Relative Reliability of Direct and Circumstantial Evidence. In the minds of most laypeople, direct evidence is inherently more reliable than is circumstantial evidence. The typical layperson has probably seen several movies in which the defense attorney disparaged the prosecution's reliance on "mere circumstantial evidence." However, direct evidence does not have any intrinsically superior reliability. In the last decade, witness psychology has begun exposing the weaknesses of direct, eyewitness testimony.[23] Numerous studies indicate that in stressful situations, the eyewitness loses more in accuracy of perception that he or she gains in immediacy of perception.[24] The Supreme

---

17. One of the seminal cases in this line of authority is Sumner v. State, 5 Blackf. 579 (Ind.1841). See Note, 7 Ind.L.Rev. 883, 885 (1974).

18. State v. Fortes, 110 R.I. 406, 293 A.2d 506 (1972); Manlove v. State, 250 Ind. 70, 232 N.E.2d 874 (1968).

19. Holland v. United States, 348 U.S. 121, 75 S.Ct. 127, 99 L.Ed. 150 (1954).

20. Id. at 140.

21. California Jury Instructions—Criminal 2.00 (3d ed. 1970).

22. United States v. Taylor, 482 F.2d 1376, 1377 (4th Cir. 1973); United States v. Currier, 454 F.2d 835, 838 (1st Cir. 1972); United States v. Fench, 470 F.2d 1234, 1242 (D.C.Cir. 1972), cert. denied 410 U.S. 909, 93 S.Ct. 964, 35 L.Ed.2d 271 (1973); United States v. Hamilton, 457 F.2d 95, 98 (3d Cir. 1972); United States v. Henry, 468 F.2d 892, 894 (10th Cir. 1972); United States v. Ordones, 469 F.2d 70, 71 (9th Cir. 1972); United States v. Glasser, 443 F.2d 994, 1006–07 (2d Cir. 1970), cert. denied 404 U.S. 854, 92 S.Ct. 96, 30 L.Ed.2d 95 (1971); United States v. Stroble, 431 F.2d 1273, 1276 (6th Cir. 1970).

23. Levine and Tapp, The Psychology of Criminal Identification: The Gap from *Wade* to *Kirby*, 121 U. Pa.L.Rev. 1079 (1973).

24. Id.

Court itself has stated that "the vagaries of eye-witness identification are well-known; the annals of criminal law are rife with instances of mistaken identification." [25]

In contrast, many types of circumstantial evidence are highly reliable. Chapter 8 discusses the validation of scientific evidence.[26] Although even scientific techniques of criminal investigation are not infallible, some forensic techniques such as neutron activation analysis are amazingly accurate. Most of this scientific evidence is circumstantial, analyzing trace evidence and connecting the defendant with the crime scene. This scientific, circumstantial evidence is certainly entitled to more weight than suspect, eyewitness identification testimony.

The defense bar has attempted to seize the initiative against direct, eyewitness identification testimony. First, defense counsel have attempted to present expert, psychological testimony detailing the weakness of eyewitness testimony. These attempts have been largely unsuccessful, with the courts generally excluding the testimony.[27] Second, defense counsel have sought special cautionary instructions about the weaknesses of eyewitness testimony. The prevailing view

is that at most, the judge has discretion to give such an instruction and appellate courts rarely find a judge's denial of a requested instruction an abuse of discretion.[28] However, a substantial and growing minority of jurisdictions have adopted special cautionary instructions on eyewitness identification testimony.[29] Many of these jurisdictions use a model *Telfaire* instruction patterned after the jury charge the Court of Appeals for the District of Columbia approved.[30]

4. Relevance and Admissibility

Although few propositions of law are absolute enough to qualify as true "rules," one absolute proposition exists in evidence law: Irrelevant evidence is inadmissible. Relevance is a presupposition of admissibility. Chapters 6–10 discuss how the courts have applied the logical and legal relevance requirements to various types of evidence.[31]

---

25. United States v. Wade, 388 U.S. 218, 228–29, 87 S.Ct. 1926, 1932–33, 18 L.Ed.2d 1149 (1967).

26. Chapter 8, infra.

27. See, e. g., United States v. Amaral, 488 F.2d 1148 (9th Cir. 1973).

28. United States v. Masterson, 529 F.2d 30 (9th Cir. 1976); United States v. Sambrano, 505 F.2d 284 (9th Cir. 1974); United States v. Johnson, 386 F.Supp. 1034 (D.Pa.1974); State v. Mazurek, 88 N.M. 56, 537 P.2d 51 (1975); State v. Motes, 264 S.C. 317, 215 S.E.2d 190 (1975).

29. United States ex rel. Kirby v. Sturges, 510 F.2d 397 (7th Cir. 1975); United States v. Holley, 502 F.2d 273 (4th Cir. 1974); United States v. Telfaire, 469 F. 2d 552 (D.C.Cir. 1972); United States v. Barber, 442 F.2d 517 (3d Cir. 1971).

30. See United States v. Holley, 502 F.2d 273, 277–78 (4th Cir. 1974).

31. Chapters 6–10, infra.

CHAPTER 6
AUTHENTICATION

1. General

The law does not ascribe relevance to an item of evidence until the proponent proves that that item is authentic—that is, that the item is what it is claimed to be. An item of evidence such as a writing is conditionally relevant; it is relevant only on the condition that it is authentic. On the writing's face, the writing's contents may appear to be relevant to a fact in issue, but the writing lacks probative value unless the writing is genuine. "Authentication" is the generic term for the process of proving the genuineness of writings, oral statements, photographs, and physical evidence. Evidence has *facial probative value* if on its face, it is material to the facts of consequence. The law also demands *underlying probative value*, authenticity.

2. Writings

Private Writings. The *author* may *expressly acknowledge* authorship. The author becomes a witness at trial, and the proponent elicits the witness's testimony that he or she wrote or signed the writing. The author's express acknowledgment is suffi-

cient authentication.[1] The acknowledgment is direct evidence of the writing's authenticity.

Admission by the Party-Opponent. Suppose that the prosecutor wants to offer a writing into evidence. Outside the courtroom, the defendant made a written or oral admission of the writing's authenticity. Proof of the admission is sufficient authentication of the writing.[2]

Testimony of a Witness to the Writing's Execution. A person who observed a writing's execution may authenticate that writing. The witness simply testifies that: (1) He or she witnessed the writing's execution and (2) he or she recognizes the exhibit as the writing.[3]

Testimony of a Witness Familiar with the Author's Handwriting Style. A layperson familiar with the author's handwriting style may testify that the handwriting is

---

1. C. McCormick, Handbook of the Law of Evidence § 219 (2d ed. 1972).

2. West's Ann.Cal.Evid.Code § 1414.

3. Id. at § 1413.

that of the purported author.[4] The testimony is proper lay opinion if the witness has the requisite familiarity. The witness may acquire the requisite familiarity in numerous manners. The witness can have personally observed the purported author write or sign. The witness can have exchanged correspondence with the purported author. The witness can have seen writings bearing the author's signature under circumstances vouching for the signature's authenticity. For example, a corporate vice-president's secretary may be familiar with the corporate president's signature even though he or she has never personally seen the president sign a document.

Comparison By an Expert. A handwriting expert or questioned document examiner may compare the questioned document with other samples of the author's handwriting. The first step in this authentication technique is to introduce other exemplars of the author's handwriting. These exemplars serve as the standard of comparison. The proponent must authenticate the standards. In most jurisdictions, the judge finally decides the question of the standards' authenticity.[5] The second step is marking the questioned document for identification. Next, the proponent hands the questioned document to the expert and asks the expert to compare that document with the standards of comparison. If the expert opines that the same author prepared all the documents, that opinion is sufficient authentication of the questioned document.[6]

Comparison by the Trier of Fact. This authentication technique is very similar to the previous technique. The only major difference is that the comparison is made by the trier of fact (the jury or, in a non-jury case, the judge) rather than by an expert. The first step again is the authentication of the standards. The proponent then marks the questioned document for identification. The proponent finally hands the standards and questioned document to the trier(s) of fact for comparison.[7]

The Reply Letter Doctrine. Another circumstantial method of authentication is the reply letter doctrine.[8] Generally, the proponent shows that a correspondent mailed letter #1 to the alleged author and in the due course of mail, the correspondent received letter #2 purportedly signed by the author. The first step in authenticating the reply letter is showing that letter #1 was properly stamped, addressed, and mailed. The second step is demonstrating that letter #2 bore the purported author's signature, was received in the due course of mail, and either referred or was responsive to the first letter. If these two standards are met, the reply letter, letter #2, is authenticated. This doctrine applies to replies to telegrams as well as to letters, and a telegram may be admitted into evidence once it is shown that the earlier message was actually sent.[9] The rationale behind the reply letter or telegram doctrine is the assumption that messages are ordinarily delivered to the addressee, and that it would be unlikely for someone else to know of and respond to the original message.

Ancient Documents. A writing which has been in existence for a number of years is difficult to authenticate; over any substantial period of time, memories fade and witnesses disappear. To ease the burden of authentication, Federal Rule 901(b) provides that documents may be authenticated by showing that they (1) have an unsuspicious

4. Inbau, Lay Witness Identification of Handwriting (An Experiment), 34 Ill.L.Rev. 433 (1939).

5. Law Revision Commission Comment, West's Ann. Cal.Evid.Code § 1418.

6. Fed.Evid.Rule 901(b)(3), 28 U.S.C.A.

7. Fed.Evid.Rule 901(b)(3), 28 U.S.C.A.; West's Ann. Cal.Evid.Code § 1417.

8. West's Ann.Cal.Evid.Code § 1420.

9. State v. Rothrock, 45 Nev. 214, 200 P. 525 (1921); Clemons v. State, 17 Ala.App. 533, 86 So. 177 (1920).

physical appearance, (2) were found in a place where if authentic, they would likely be, and (3) have been in existence for 20 or more years at the time they are offered.[10] In most jurisdictions, the minimum period is 30 years.

The first requirement is that the document has an unsuspicious appearance. A number of different facts can create suspicious conditions—for example, erasures, discontinuity in handwriting, or indications of forgery or tampering. The second requirement is that the document was obtained from a place where, if authentic, it would be likely to be found. The appropriateness of custody will often depend on the nature of the document. The fact that it may have changed hands several times does not, by itself, render it inadmissible.[11] Various methods of proof exist that may be used to establish the age of the document. The proponent may use either the witness's direct knowledge or expert testimony. The expert can establish the age of a written instrument by identifying the age of the paper, ink, handwriting, typewriting, or other marks on the paper. Most jurisdictions require extrinsic evidence of the document's age. However, the physical appearance of the document is itself evidence of antiquity. Moreover, several jurisdictions have statutory presumptions that a writing is correctly dated.[12] If the document bears a date 20 or 30 years prior to trial, the presumption supplies the third element of the foundation.

Contents. A writing may be authenticated on the basis of its contents. The writing may refer to matters unlikely to be known by anyone other than the person claimed to be the author. Generally, for this rule to operate, the document must deal with a matter sufficiently obscure or particularly within the knowledge of the person making the writing; the subject matter must not be of common knowledge.[13] In Rice v. United States,[14] the court admitted three telegrams on the basis of the code words they used, for the words could have been known only by an individual familiar with a certain location.

Linguistic Patterns. Another method for authenticating documents is the use of internal linguistic patterns. Some commentators have argued that the internal word or thought patterns in certain documents are so particularly characteristic of a purported writer that they authenticate the document. This science of identification is known as psycholinguistics, that is, studying the relationship between the messages and the characteristics of the person sending the messages.[15]

Acknowledged Writings. State statutes commonly authorize persons executing documents such as deeds to acknowledge the execution before notaries public The notary may then affix a formal acknowledgment to the document: "On this _____ day of _____ in the year of _____ before me _____ personally appeared and acknowledged that (he) (she) had executed the same." The notary signs the certificate and affixes a notarial seal. In many jurisdictions, if the acknowledgment certificate is in proper order, the writing is self-authenticating. The proponent may introduce the acknowledged writing without a live, sponsoring witness.[16]

Private Writings in Official Custody. Although a writing has a private origin, the

---

10. The general rule is 30 years. C. McCormick, Handbook on the Law of Evidence 549 (2d ed. 1972).

11. McGuire v. Blount, 199 U.S. 142, 26 S.Ct. 1, 50 L.Ed. 125 (1905).

12. West's Ann.Cal.Evid.Code § 640.

13. Hartzell v. United States, 72 F.2d 569 (8th Cir. 1934). See also State v. Huffman, 141 W.Va. 55, 87 S.E.2d 541 (1955).

14. 35 F.2d 689 (2d Cir. 1929).

15. Arens & Meadow, Psycholinguistics in the Confession Dilemma, 56 Colum.L.Rev. 19 (1956).

16. See, e. g., West's Ann.Cal.Evid.Code § 1451.

writing may find its way into official custody. For example, a statute may authorize private parties to file and record deeds in a government office. In some jurisdictions, such private writings become official writings for authentication purposes.[17] As we shall see, there are special techniques for authenticating official writings; if an official writing bears a proper attesting or authenticating certificate, the writing will be self-authenticating.[18] In some jurisdictions, these special authentication techniques also apply to private writings in official custody.[19]

Circumstantial Authentication of a Private Writing. Suppose that an attorney prepares a document for a client's signature. The attorney places the document on a table inside an office. The attorney waits outside the office. Before anyone else enters the room, the client appears and enters the room. A few moments later, the client exits the room. There are ink stains on the client's sleeves. The attorney immediately enters the room. The attorney finds the document where he left it, but the document now bears the purported signature of the client in fresh ink.[20] On the one hand, this fact pattern does not fall within any of the well-settled doctrines previously discussed. On the other hand, there is a compelling circumstantial inference that the document is authentic. In the final analysis, the test for authentication is whether the proponent has introduced sufficient evidence to support a finding of fact that the writing is genuine.[21] In the instant hypothetical, there is more than enough evidence to support a finding that the client signed the document.

Suggested Reading:

Lewis v. State, 469 P.2d 689 (Alaska 1970).

Rice v. United States, 35 F.2d 689 (2d Cir. 1929).

State v. Rothrock, 45 Nev. 214, 200 P. 525 (1921).

Business Writings. The techniques for authenticating private writings also apply to business writings. For example, the employee who prepared the document may expressly acknowledge authorship. Moreover, a person who witnessed the writing's execution could testify to that fact. However, there are special additional techniques for authenticating business writings.

Custody. A witness may authenticate a business writing by proving that it comes from proper custody. Simply stated, the witness testifies that he or she removed the writing from the proper file cabinet. The witness must be personally familiar with the business' filing system.[22] The witness must know where the business keeps that type of record. The witness will usually be the business' records custodian or the supervisor of the employee who prepared the record.

Simplified, Statutory Authentication Procedures. Legislatures have come to realize that it is often an inconvenience for a business to bring its records to court. The business often needs the records to operate. For that reason, several legislatures have prescribed special, simplified authentication procedures for banking records, hospital records, or business records generally. The California statute is illustrative.[23] Under California procedure, if a party serves a subpoena duces tecum[24] on a business' records

---

17. See, e. g., West's Ann.Cal.Evid.Code § 1530. § 1530 refers generally to any "writing in the custody of a public entity."

18. See the subsection on official writings, infra.

19. West's Ann.Cal.Evid.Code § 1530.

20. 7 Wigmore, Evidence § 2148 (3d ed. 1940).

21. Fed.Evid.Rule 901(a), 28 U.S.C.A.; West's Ann. Cal.Evid.Code § 1400.

22. C. McCormick, Handbook of the Law of Evidence § 224 (2d ed. 1972).

23. West's Ann.Cal.Evid.Code §§ 1560–66.

24. A court order requiring not only that the witness appear but also that the witness bring with him or her certain documents.

custodian, the custodian must ordinarily personally appear and bring the original records to the hearing. Now, under special California legislation, the custodian may respond in this fashion. First, the custodian need not personally appear; he or she may respond by mailing. Second, the custodian need not mail the originals; the custodian may submit copies. Finally, the custodian attaches a certificate that (1) he or she is the business' records custodian and (2) the attached documents are accurate and complete copies of originals in the business' custody.

Suggested Reading:

State v. Miller, 79 N.M. 117, 440 P.2d 792 (1968).

Reeves v. Warden, 346 F.2d 915 (4th Cir. 1965).

Official Writings. Any technique for authenticating business writings can be applied to official writings. Thus, a witness may testify that he or she removed the writing from the proper official custody. However, the use of live testimony to authenticate official writings has serious drawbacks. If attorneys routinely used live testimony to authenticate official writings, the routine would seriously interfere with government agencies' operations; rather than discharging their normal official duties, officials would spend an inordinate amount of time in court to give authenticating testimony. To eliminate that possible interference, almost all states permit the use of attesting and authenticating certificates attached to copies of the official records.

An attesting certificate is a statement that (1) the signatory is the custodian of the original official writing and (2) the attached document is a true and accurate copy of the original in his or her custody. The following is an example of an attesting certificate: "The foregoing instrument is a full,

true, and correct copy of the original on file in this office. Attest _____, 19__ KAY ZILLMAN, County Clerk and Clerk of the Superior Court of the State of El Dorado, in and for the County of Morena. By _____ Deputy." The custodian or deputy signs the certificate and usually affixes the office seal. State evidence law usually presumes such signatures and seals to be genuine.[25] That presumption authenticates the attesting certificate. In turn, the attesting certificate authenticates the attached copy of the official writing. The net effect is that the attested copy is self-authenticating.

Suggested Reading:

United States v. Rodriguez, 524 F.2d 485 (5th Cir. 1975).

United States v. Wingard, 522 F.2d 796 (4th Cir. 1975).

3. Oral Statements

Suggested Reading:

Durns v. United States, 562 F.2d 542 (8th Cir. 1977).

People v. Kelly, 17 Cal.3d 24, 130 Cal.Rptr. 144, 549 P.2d 1240 (1976).

United States v. Glass, 277 F.2d 566 (7th Cir. 1960).

Like a written statement, an oral statement must be authenticated. The authentication of a written statement necessitates identifying the author. Authentication of an oral statement requires the identification of the speaker. There are numerous authenticating techniques.

25.   See, e. g., West's Ann.Cal.Evid.Code §§ 1452–54.

General. The speaker may become a witness at trial and expressly acknowledge that he or she uttered the oral statement.

Admission by the Party-Opponent. The party-opponent may have made an out-of-court admission of the speaker's identity. The admission is sufficient authentication of the oral statement.

Testimony of a Witness to the Statement. If someone was present when the statement was made, the witness may identify the speaker and thereby authenticate the statement.

Testimony of a Witness Familiar with the Speaker's Voice. The identification of the voice heard is sufficient if the witness is sufficiently familiar with the voice. The decision whether the witness is sufficiently familiar lies within the discretion of the trial court.[26] Generally, the court should give the witness every benefit of the doubt. The identification of the voice may be based on familiarity acquired either before or after the disputed conversation.[27]

Expert Sound Spectographic Analysis. In many jurisdictions, the proponent may use sound spectography to identify the speaker who made an oral statement. Chapter 8 on Scientific Evidence describes this technique in detail.[28]

The Reply Doctrine. This is the counterpart of the reply letter doctrine for writings. The doctrine's basic assumption is the reliability of telephone directories. The basic elements of the foundation are these: (1) The directory listed a certain telephone number for the person; (2) someone called that number and asked for that person; and (3) the person answering identified himself or herself as the person requested.[29] This set of circumstances creates an inference that the speaker was the person whose name appeared in the directory. The courts have applied the doctrine to businesses as well as individuals. If someone phones a business' number and, during the telephone conversation, conducts a transaction normal for that business, there is an inference that the speaker was an authorized agent of the business called.[30]

Contents. Just as a writing's contents may identify the author, a statement's contents may identify the speaker. Suppose that only one person is likely to possess certain information. If the statement discloses that information, the speaker was probably that person.

Tape Recordings. It is now quite common for attorneys to offer tape recordings into evidence. Traditionally, the courts insisted upon a rather strict foundation for tape recordings. The proponent had to establish that: (1) The recording device was in working order; (2) the operator was competent; (3) the tape was in safekeeping between the time of the recording and the time of trial; (4) a person familiar with the speaker's voice identified the speakers; and (5) someone present at the time of the conversation testifies that the recording is a correct, accurate reproduction of the conversation.[31] In recent years, some courts have accepted less extensive showings. For example, in many jurisdictions, the proponent

---

26. United States v. Glass, 277 F.2d 566 (7th Cir. 1960) (identification allowed after a person had listened to the individual during a three-hour conversation).

27. United States v. Carr, 219 F.2d 876 (7th Cir. 1955).

28. Chapter 8, infra.

29. Palos v. United States, 416 F.2d 438 (5th Cir. 1969); United States v. Benjamin, 328 F.2d 854 (2d Cir. 1964); Fed.Evid.Rule 901(b)(6), 28 U.S.C.A.

30. Fed.Evid.Rule 901(b)(6), 28 U.S.C.A.; C. McCormick, Handbook of the Law of Evidence § 226 (2d ed. 1972).

31. United States v. McMillan, 508 F.2d 101 (8th Cir. 1974); Monroe v. United States, 234 F.2d 49 (D.C.Cir. 1956); State v. Williams, 49 Wash.2d 354, 301 P.2d 769 (1956); Steve M. Solomon, Jr., Inc. v. Edgar, 92 Ga.App. 207, 88 S.E.2d 167 (1955); State v. Alleman, 218 La. 821, 51 So.2d 83 (1950); Conrad, Magnetic Recordings in Court, 40 Va.L.Rev. 23 (1954).

may dispense with element (5).[32] The courts reason that elements (1) through (3) prove that the tape is an accurate reproduction of some speaker's statement and that element (4) identifies the speaker. Alternatively, element (5) alone can be sufficient authentication.[33] The testimony of a person who heard the conversation that the tape is an accurate reproduction of the conversation certainly has sufficient probative value to support a finding that the tape is genuine.

In deciding the admissibility of such recordings, the judge should determine authenticity out of the jury's hearing. Recordings may be admitted even though partially inaudible so long as the unintelligible portions are not so substantial "as to render the recording as a whole untrustworthy."[34] The recording may also be admitted even though some of it has been deleted or erased so long as the deleted portions do not render the recording as a whole untrustworthy.[35] If the recording is technically defective, a re-recording to delete the defects without altering the contents is admissible in evidence.[36]

4. Photographs

Suggested Reading:

United States v. McNair, 439 F.Supp. 103 (E.D.Pa. 1977).

Ferguson v. Commonwealth, 212 Va. 745, 187 S.E. 2d 189 (1972).

People v. Doggett, 83 Cal.App.2d 405, 188 P.2d 792 (1948).

32. United States v. Turner, 528 F.2d 143 (9th Cir. 1975).

33. People v. Patton, 63 Cal.App.3d 211, 133 Cal. Rptr. 533 (1976).

34. Monroe v. United States, 234 F.2d 49, 55 (D.C. Cir. 1956).

35. United States v. Knohl, 379 F.2d 427, 440 n. 8 (2d Cir. 1967).

36. United States v. Madda, 345 F.2d 400 (7th Cir. 1965).

Still Photographs. Like a writing or oral statement, a photograph must be authenticated. The process of authenticating photographs is usually described as verification. The proponent can verify a still photograph rather simply. The proponent has the print marked for identification and then hands it to the witness. The witness then identifies the object or scene depicted. The witness describes the basis for his or her familiarity with the object or scene. The proponent then asks whether the photograph is a fair, accurate, or true reproduction of the object or scene. If the witness answers in the affirmative, the foundation is complete. The witness need not be the photographer. The witness does not have to know what type of photographic equipment or procedures were used. The only qualification the witness must possess is familiarity with the object or scene.

Still Photographs Taken by an Automated System. Many commercial establishments now use automated photographic systems. For example, banks use surveillance cameras, and retail stores use check cashing cameras which simultaneously photograph the check and the person cashing the check. A person present during a robbery may certainly authenticate the surveillance films taken. Likewise, the employee who was on duty at the check cashing window may authenticate the check cashing photograph. However, sometimes the witnesses forget, and on other occasions their recollection is so weak that the proponent wants to corroborate their testimony by means of the photograph.

Suppose that there is no witness to the historical event depicted who is prepared to testify that the photograph is accurate. In this circumstance, the proponent must lay the following foundation: (1) The particular automated system is reliable; (2) the camera was in working order at the time the photograph was taken; and (3) the film was in safekeeping from the time it was extracted from the camera to the time of trial.[37] The proponent will need a photographic expert to lay the first element. The system's manufacturer will often supply the expert. The proponent can call maintenance personnel and introduce maintenance records to lay the second element. The third element is proof of a chain of custody. Chapter 7 on Physical Evidence discusses the method of proving a chain of custody.[38]

X-Ray Photographs. X-rays are peculiar in the sense that there is no witness to testify that he or she saw what the plate depicts. The usual foundation for an X-ray photograph includes the following elements: (1) The X-ray machine was in proper working order; (2) the operator of the machine was qualified, i. e., a radiologist or X-ray technician (radiographer); (3) the operator used the proper procedures, e. g., employing a proper contrast medium such as barium; and (4) the plate offered at trial is the same plate the X-ray operator took.[39] Many hospitals and laboratories now use identification assemblies. They use lead letters and numbers to spell out the name or identification number of the patient, the date of the X-ray, the name of the institution, and the name or identification number of the physician. The operator positions the identification assembly just above the film. When the cassette is exposed to X-rays, the lead casts shadows on the film, thereby marking the film with the letters and numbers. The markings identify the plate. In addition, the proponent usually proves that the plate was taken from the proper file of the hospital's or laboratory's X-ray custodian.

Some modern courts accept less extensive showings. Rather than requiring a showing of both markings and custody,

courts often accept a showing of either markings or custody. Some courts have held that the markings convert the plate into a readily identifiable article. Chapter 7 on Physical Evidence discusses the ready identifiability theory of admissibility.[40] Secondly, some courts accept showings of chain of custody, the chain of possession of the plate from the time of the X-ray to its offer at trial. As previously stated, Chapter 7 analyzes the method of establishing a chain of custody.

Motion Pictures. The courts have traditionally been suspicious of motion pictures. As one court warned, "Motion pictures should be received as evidence with caution, because the modern art of photography and the devices of an ingenious director frequently produce results which may be quite deceiving. Telescopic lenses, ingenious settings of the stage, the elimination of unfavorable portions of the film, an angle from which a picture is taken, the ability to speed up the reproduction of the picture and the genius of a director may tend to create misleading impressions."[41] Given the courts' suspicion of motion pictures, it is understandable that the traditional view requires a very strict foundation. The foundation parallels the foundation for tape recordings: (1) The camera was in working order; (2) the operator was competent; (3) the film was in safekeeping from the time the picture was shot until the time of trial; (4) someone familiar with the persons or objects depicted identifies them; and (5) someone present when the activity occurred testifies that the motion picture accurately reproduces the activity.[42] All jurisdictions would treat the above foundation as acceptable.

37. Ferguson v. Commonwealth, 212 Va. 745, 187 S.E.2d 189 (1972); Sisk v. State, 236 Md. 589, 204 A. 2d 684 (1964).

38. Chapter 7, infra.

39. Scott, X-Ray Pictures as Evidence, 44 Mich.L. Rev. 773 (1946).

40. Chapter 7, infra.

41. Harmon v. San Joaquin L. & P. Corp., 37 Cal. App.2d 169, 174, 98 P.2d 1064, 1067 (1940).

42. McGoorty v. Benhart, 305 Ill.App. 458, 27 N.E. 2d 289 (1940); Metropolitan Life Ins. Co. v. Wright, 190 Miss. 53, 199 So. 289 (1940); C. McCormick, Handbook of the Law of Evidence § 214 (2d ed. 1972).

Just as the courts have begun liberalizing admission of tape recordings, the courts are now accepting less extensive foundations for motion pictures. Many jurisdictions permit the proponent to disregard element (5). Elements (1) through (3) establish that the motion picture accurately reproduces some event, and element (4) supplies the identity of the participants. Alternatively, many courts will accept a showing of element (5) standing alone. If a witness testifies that he or she observed a certain event and then adds that the motion picture accurately reproduces the event, there is sufficient probative value to sustain a finding that the motion picture is authentic.

Videotapes. With one exception, a videotape is similar to a motion picture. That exception is that the tape carries aural reproduction as well as visual reproduction. That exception necessitates that the proponent lay an additional element of the foundation. Someone familiar with the speaker's voice must identify the voice. In effect, the proponent must lay two foundations: one to authenticate an oral statement and a second to verify the accompanying motion picture.

The use of videotapes is becoming quite common in criminal practice. In some areas, police routinely make videotapes of the conduct of persons arrested for drunk driving. The police can videotape lineups to show that the lineup was conducted in a fair manner. The police can also videotape confessions to show the confession's voluntariness and the administration of proper *Miranda* warnings.

Circumstantial Verification of Photographs. In every authentication case, the fundamental question is whether the proponent has presented sufficient evidence to create a permissive inference that the evidence is genuine. If proponent can marshall enough circumstantial evidence to create that inference, the photograph is verified even if the evidence does not fall within a well-settled doctrine.

Suppose that the government charges the defendant with committing an act of sodomy on a small child. During the course of a legal search of the defendant's apartment, the police discover a photograph depicting the defendant committing the act on his own child. The defendant refuses to testify, and the prosecutor concludes that the child is too frightened to be a good witness. Must the prosecutor forego using the photograph? In similar cases, prosecutors have verified the photograph circumstantially.[43] The prosecutor first calls the landlord to identify the persons depicted in the photograph. The landlord testifies that he or she knows both the defendant and the child and identifies them as the persons in the photograph. The prosecutor next calls a photography expert. The expert testifies that the photograph is neither fake nor composite. The cumulative value of the landlord's and expert's testimony is sufficient to support a finding that the photograph is genuine and accurately depicts a sodomitical act between the defendant and the child.

---

43. People v. Doggett, 83 Cal.App.2d 405, 188 P.2d 792 (1948).

CHAPTER 7
IDENTIFYING PHYSICAL EVIDENCE

1. Introduction

Chapter 6 discusses the general concept of authentication. As that chapter explains, authentication is the generic term for the process of proving that an item of evidence is what its proponent claims it to be. Like documentary evidence, physical evidence must be authenticated. The cases usually refer to the identification of physical evidence. This chapter discusses the identification of real or original physical evidence. Real or original evidence has historical connection with an incident involved in the prosecution. For example, it is the actual murder weapon or the actual forged check. Some authorities use the terms *real* and *demonstrative* evidence interchangeably.[1] However, this chapter uses the expression *demonstrative* evidence in the narrow sense of items admitted for solely illustrative purposes.[2] Thus, a reproduction or replica of an item of real evidence would be demonstrative evidence. If the police could not find the actual murder weapon, an eyewitness could use a similar weapon during his or her testimony to illustrate what they observed.

There are several methods of identifying physical evidence. First, the proponent may prove that the article is readily identifiable. Second, the proponent may establish a chain of custody for the article.

2. Readily Identifiable Articles

Suggested Reading:

State v. Ross, 275 N.C. 550, 169 S.E.2d 875 (1969).
United States v. Reed, 392 F.2d 865 (7th Cir. 1968).

The ready-identifiability theory is the simplest method of identifying an article of physical evidence. The theory utilizes direct evidence: The issue is the identity of the article, and the witness testifies that he or she recognizes the article exhibited in the courtroom. The identification of a pistol illustrates this method. In the course of his or her testimony, the witness refers to a pistol. At this point, the prosecutor has a pistol marked for identification, hands the pistol to the witness, and asks the witness whether he or she can identify the pistol. The witness answers in the affirmative.

---

1. C. McCormick, Handbook of the Law of Evidence § 212 (2d ed. 1972).

2. Comment, 10 Drake L.J. 44 n. 1 (1960). Suppose that the defendant is charged with an assault with a dangerous weapon—namely a machete knife. The police cannot find the knife used in the assault. The trial judge could permit the victim to use a similar machete knife to illustrate his or her testimony. Depending upon the jurisdiction, the illustrative knife might be formally admitted into evidence. In all jurisdictions, the trial judge would give the jury a limiting instruction that the knife is being used for solely illustrative purposes and is not historically connected with the alleged assault.

The prosecutor then asks how the witness recognizes the pistol. The witness responds that he or she remembers the serial number on the pistol. The prosecutor now formally offers the pistol into evidence. The foundation is complete, and the trial judge will receive the pistol into evidence. The serial number makes the pistol readily identifiable, a one-of-a-kind item, and the witness may rest an identification on the serial number.

The courts have applied the ready-identifiability theory in numerous cases. Like serially numbered objects, items with distinctive natural markings or characteristics are readily identifiable. For example, the courts have treated the following items as readily identifiable: a "very unusual looking hat;"[3] a coin of unusual thinness;[4] a ball and socket assembly with a distinctive abrasion;[5] a peculiarly twisted and battered bullet;[6] and an automobile transmission with special marks.[7] Finally, the courts have applied the theory to items on which the witness has made distinctive markings. Even if the article lacks distinctive natural markings, the witness can convert the object into a readily identifiable article by placing distinctive markings on it. For example, the courts have allowed witnesses to identify the following objects on the basis of marks the witnesses placed on the objects when they first seized them: a pistol grip;[8]

a coin;[9] a dollar bill;[10] a jar;[11] a bullet;[12] a catheter;[13] a crowbar;[14] and a shotgun.[15] In short, whether natural or artificial, a distinctive marking makes the article readily identifiable.

What is the underlying theory of admissibility? The witness's statement that he or she recognizes the article is an expression of opinion, and [16] courts do not accept opinions at face value. Rather they inquire whether the witness has observed facts which adequately support the opinion.[17] To decide whether the opinion on identity has an adequate factual basis, the courts focus on the physical characteristics the witness relies upon as the basis for his or her opinion. The observed characteristics must be so unusual that they make it more likely than not that the item is unique. Wigmore remarked: "In the process of identification of two supposed objects by a common mark, the force of the inference depends on the degree of necessariness of association of that mark with a single object. In practice it rarely occurs that the evidential mark is a single circumstance. The evidencing feature is usually a group of circumstances which as a whole constitute a feature capable of being associated with a single object. Rarely can one circumstance alone be inherently pecu-

---

3. United States v. Reed, 392 F.2d 865 (7th Cir. 1968), cert. denied 393 U.S. 984, 89 S.Ct. 457, 21 L. Ed.2d 445.

4. Jenkins v. United States, 361 F.2d 615 (10th Cir. 1966).

5. Jenkins v. Bierschenk, 333 F.2d 421 (8th Cir. 1964).

6. State v. Shawley, 334 Mo. 352, 67 S.W.2d 74 (1933).

7. State v. Augustine, 1 Or.App. 372, 462 P.2d 693 (1969).

8. United States v. Madril, 445 F.2d 827 (9th Cir. 1971), vacated 404 U.S. 1919, 92 S.Ct. 692, 30 L.Ed. 2d 657.

9. United States v. Bourassa, 411 F.2d 69 (10th Cir. 1969), cert. denied 396 U.S. 915, 90 S.Ct. 235, 24 L.Ed.2d 192.

10. Rosemund v. United States, 386 F.2d 412 (10th Cir. 1967).

11. O'Quinn v. United States, 411 F.2d 78 (10th Cir. 1969).

12. State v. Ross, 275 N.C. 550, 169 S.E.2d 875 (1969).

13. State v. Ball, 1 Ohio App.2d 297, 204 N.E.2d 557, 30 O.O.2d 304 (1964).

14. People v. Horace, 186 Cal.App.2d 560, 9 Cal. Rptr. 43 (1960).

15. Dixon v. State, 243 Ind. 654, 189 N.E.2d 715 (1963).

16. 7 Wigmore, Evidence § 1977 (3d ed. 1940).

17. C. McCormick, Handbook of the Law of Evidence §§ 10 & 11 (2d ed. 1972).

liar to a single object. It is by adding circumstance to circumstance that we obtain a composite feature or mark which as a whole cannot be supposed to be associated with more than a single object. The process of constructing an inference of identity thus consists usually in adding together a number of circumstances, each of which by itself might be a feature of many objects, but all of which together make it more probable that they coexist in a single object only." [18] Thus, in testing the sufficiency of the basis for the opinion of identity, the courts apply a probabilistic test: Is the combination of physical characteristics the witness has testified to sufficiently unusual to make it more likely than not that the item possessing those characteristics is a unique item? [19]

3. Chain of Custody

Suggested Reading:

United States v. Picard, 464 F.2d 215 (1st Cir. 1972).

Commonwealth v. Thomas, 448 Pa. 42, 292 A.2d 352 (1972).

If the article is not readily identifiable, the proponent usually establishes a chain of custody for the article. The chain of custody theory necessitates analysis of four questions.

When Must the Proponent Prove a Chain of Custody? There are four situations in which the proponent will have to prove a chain of custody. The first occurs when the article is not readily identifiable. Although the courts are fairly liberal in treating items as readily identifiable, the articles must nevertheless possess a unique characteristic or combination of characteristics. Among the items that even the most liberal court cannot treat as readily identifiable are: blood specimens; [20] urine specimens; [21] and drugs. [22] The identification of such fungible items ordinarily requires proof of a chain of custody.

The second situation occurs when although by its nature the article is readily identifiable, the witness did not note the article's identifying physical characteristic at the time of seizure. For example, the witness might not have noted the pistol's serial number when the pistol came into the witness's possession. In these circumstances, proof of a chain of custody is "a more than adequate substitute." [23]

The third situation occurs when by its nature the item is readily identifiable but at the time of trial the witness cannot recall the item's unique characteristic. Here again, a chain of custody is necessary. These three situations highlight the elements of the foundation for ready identifiability: (1) The item has a unique physical characteristic; (2) the witness observed the characteristic at the time of seizure; and (3) the witness recognizes the characteristic at the time of trial. If any element of the foundation is missing, proving a chain of custody is necessary.

The fourth situation occurs when the article is delicate and the critical issue is its condition at the time of seizure. The chain of custody establishes both the item's identity and its condition at the time of seizure. Some commentators argue that if the article is "susceptible to alteration by tampering

---

18. 2 Wigmore, Evidence § 412 (3d ed. 1940).

19. Imwinkelried, The Identification of Original, Real Evidence, 61 Mil.L.Rev. 145, 153 (1973).

20. United States v. Martinez, 43 C.M.R. 434 (ACMR 1970).

21. United States v. Spencer, 21 C.M.R. 504 (ABR 1956).

22. United States v. Sears, 248 F.2d 377 (7th Cir. 1957), rev'd on other grounds 355 U.S. 602, 78 S.Ct. 534, 2 L.Ed.2d 525.

23. United States v. Hooks, 23 C.M.R. 750, 754 (AFBR 1956).

or contamination, sound exercise of the trial court's discretion may require" proof of a chain of custody.[24] Illustrative is a delicate part of a crashed aircraft. Suppose that the instrument is serially numbered. Assume further that the setting of the instrument at the time of the crash would establish the existence of a criminal agency; if the instrument had a certain setting, the crash was probably an accident, but if the instrument had another setting, the probable cause is tampering, and the deaths are thus homicidal. At trial, the investigator who seized the instrument at the crash scene could readily identify the instrument, for it is serially numbered. The investigator's testimony establishes the instrument's identity, but the pivotal question is whether the instrument had the same setting at the time of the crash as it has when it is offered at trial. Because the instrument is delicate, the judge would be justified in exercising discretion to require proof of a chain of custody, for careless handling between seizure and trial might have jarred the instrument into a different setting.

What Is the Length of the Chain? If the answer to the threshold question is that a chain of custody is necessary, the next question is the length of the chain: For what period of time must the proponent account? Here we must distinguish between two fact situations.

In the first, the article's logical relevance depends upon a witness's in-court identification. Assume that the article is a common pen knife, allegedly used in an assault. The prosecutor wants to identify the knife by proving a chain of custody. The chain must run from the time of seizure to the time of trial; thus the proponent must establish a chain running to the moment when he or she offers the knife into evidence

at trial.[25] The proponent, who is attempting to prove identity between the item seized and the item offered, must accordingly assume the burden of proving a chain running from the time of seizure to the time of offer.

In the second situation, the proponent is relying upon the real evidence as the basis for expert testimony about the evidence's scientific analysis. Here the chain must run only from the time of seizure to the time of the analysis or test. For example, in United States v. Singer,[26] the court stated that testimony about the scientific analysis is admissible even if the sample analyzed is lost or destroyed after the test.

Who Are the Links in the Chain? After determining the period of time for which he or she must account, the proponent next identifies the links in the chain during that period. The links are the people who handled the article during the relevant period. People who merely had access to the article are not links in the chain, and the proponent need not make any affirmative showing of their conduct with respect to the article.[27] Even though these people had an opportunity to contact the article, they are not links in the chain unless there is an affirmative indication that they actually came into contact with the article.[28]

In contrast, if the evidence indicates that a person physically handled the article, that person is a link, and the proponent must usually account for the person's handling. The most important exception to this norm is that the proponent does not have to make an affirmative showing of postal em-

---

24. C. McCormick, Handbook of the Law of Evidence § 212 (2d ed. 1972).

25. State v. Conley, 32 Ohio App.2d 54, 288 N.W.2d 296, 60 O.O.2d 210 (1971).

26. 43 F.Supp. 863 (E.D.N.Y.1942).

27. United States v. Fletcher, 487 F.2d 22 (5th Cir. 1973); Gallego v. United States, 276 F.2d 914 (9th Cir. 1960); People v. Hines, 131 Ill.App.2d 638, 267 N.E.2d 696 (1971).

28. Wright v. State, 501 P.2d 1360 (Alaska 1972).

ployees' handling of mailed articles.[29]   Although postal employees who handle mailed articles are clearly custodians and links in the chain, the courts realize that if they required the proponent to show the postal employees' handling, the rule would practically preclude evidence custodians from using the mail to transmit articles, for it is virtually impossible to identify all the postal employees who have handled an article.   Thus the courts presume that postal employees discharge their duties and handle the article carefully.[30]

How Does the Proponent Prove the Chain?   The final question is what showing must the proponent make to prove the chain. Affirmatively, the proponent must show that the article offered in evidence is the same item originally seized and that it is in substantially the same condition it was in at the time of seizure.[31]   Negatively, the proponent must show that it is improbable that either substitution or tampering occurred.[32] With respect to each link in the chain, the proponent must show: (1) the link's receipt of the item; (2) the link's ultimate disposition of the item—i. e., transfer, destruction, or retention; and (3) the link's safeguarding of the item between receipt and ultimate disposition.   This third element is the proponent's most difficult problem of proof.

Proof that the article was kept in a secure area is a satisfactory showing of safekeeping.   The courts have held that items kept in the following areas were adequately safeguarded: a secured closet;[33] a locked automobile;[34] an evidence locker;[35] a police safe;[36] a police lock box;[37] a locked evidence cabinet;[38] a locked evidence file;[39] a police department evidence room;[40] and a locked narcotics cabinet.[41]   Similarly, proof that an article was kept in a sealed container in the interim between receipt and disposition is an adequate showing of safekeeping.[42] The very nature of a sealed container makes substitution or tampering improbable.[43]   It is now becoming a common practice of law enforcement agencies to place seized fungibles in locked, sealed envelopes.   United States v. Picard[44] is illustrative.   Agents seized heroin and placed it in a locked, sealed envelope.   An agent delivered the envelope to the chief chemist, who subsequently delivered the envelope with the seal unbroken to the examining chemist.   Although he was clearly a link in the chain, the chief chemist did not testify at trial.   Nevertheless, the court sustained the chain, inferring from the unbroken seal that neither substitution nor tampering had occurred.[45]

---

29. State v. Jordan, 14 N.C.App. 453, 188 S.E.2d 701 (1972); People v. Jamison, 29 App.Div.2d 973, 289 N.Y.S.2d 299 (1968).

30. Rodgers v. Commonwealth, 197 Va. 527, 90 S.E. 2d 257 (1955).

31. United States v. S. B. Penick & Co., 136 F.2d 413 (2d Cir. 1943).

32. Id.

33. Forrester v. United States, 210 F.2d 923 (5th Cir. 1954).

34. State v. Walker, 202 Kan. 475, 449 P.2d 515 (1969).

35. Id.

36. People v. Waller, 260 Cal.App.2d 131, 67 Cal. Rptr. 8 (1968).

37. Robinson v. State, 163 Tex.Cr.R. 499, 293 S.W.2d 781 (1956).

38. State v. Baines, 394 S.W.2d 312 (Mo.1965), cert. denied 384 U.S. 992, 86 S.Ct. 1900, 16 L.Ed.2d 1008 (1966).

39. State v. Tokatlian, 203 N.W.2d 116 (Iowa 1972).

40. State v. Seifried, 84 N.M. 581, 505 P.2d 1257 (1973).

41. Gomez v. State, 486 S.W.2d 338 (Tex.Cr.App. 1972).

42. United States v. Santiago, 534 F.2d 768 (7th Cir. 1976); United States v. Williams, 503 F.2d 50 (6th Cir. 1974).

43. West v. United States, 359 F.2d 50 (8th Cir. 1966), cert. denied 385 U.S. 867, 87 S.Ct. 131, 17 L. Ed.2d 94.

44. 464 F.2d 215 (1st Cir. 1972).

45. See also State v. Simmons, 57 Wis.2d 285, 203 N.W.2d 887 (1973).

As a practical matter, the standard of proof in chain-of-custody cases is rather slight. The Minnesota Supreme Court has declared that it will sustain a chain except if foundational evidence is "entirely absent." [46] Courts have sustained chains even when the agents' handling was "inexcusably lax" [47] or the evidence "weak," [48] and when the article was left unattended [49] or in an insecure area.[50]

In only two types of cases do the courts tend to impose a strict standard of proof. In the first type the evidence raises a strong possibility that the article has been confused with other similar articles.[51] One court ap-

plied this view when the article was a blood sample extracted from a body at the coroner's mortuary.[52] There was no evidence that the body or blood sample had been segregated from other bodies and samples. Thus the court held the chain insufficient.

In the second situation, the article is delicate and malleable. The court may impose a higher standard of proof when the article is easily alterable or "easily susceptible to undetected alteration." [53] Blood samples fall within this category.[54] Like blood samples, suspected drug specimens are easily susceptible to tampering and substitution.[55] The Iowa Supreme Court has stated that a judge trying a marijuana prosecution should require "a more elaborate foundation" than the judge would require in the typical chain-of-custody case.[56]

---

46. State v. Coy, 294 Minn. 281, 200 N.W.2d 407 (1972); State v. Daby, 293 Minn. 179, 197 N.W.2d 670 (1972).

47. Williams v. United States, 381 F.2d 20, 21 (9th Cir. 1967).

48. State v. Belcher, 83 N.M. 130, 132, 489 P.2d 410, 416 (1971).

49. United States v. Von Roeder, 435 F.2d 1004 (10th Cir. 1971); State v. Smith, 222 S.W. 455 (Mo.1920).

50. State v. Huffman, 181 Neb. 356, 148 N.W.2d 321 (1967); Wright v. State, 420 S.W.2d 411 (Tex. Crim.App.1967); State v. Cook, 17 Kan. 392 (1877).

51. In evaluating the sufficiency of the chain of custody, the court must consider the possibility of intermingling or substitution. United States v. Mc-

Dowell, 539 F.2d 435 (5th Cir. 1976); State v. Lunsford, 204 N.W.2d 613 (Iowa 1973). See Casenote, 30 Ark.L.Rev. 344 (1976).

52. Id.

53. State v. Limerick, 169 N.W.2d 538 (Iowa 1969).

54. Bradford, Handling and Preserving Blood Alcohol Test Samples, 41 J.Crim.L. & Criminology 107 (1950).

55. State v. Lunsford, 204 N.W.2d 613 (Iowa 1973).

56. Id. at 616.

CHAPTER 8
VALIDATING SCIENTIFIC EVIDENCE

1. Introduction

Scientific knowledge can be used in two distinct ways in criminal trials.[1] First, data ordinarily unavailable to lay people can be obtained by scientific means. For example, a stain found at a murder scene can be analyzed by a serologist to determine whether the stain is blood and, if human blood, the type.[2] Second, scientific knowledge may supply the general proposition or hypothesis needed to evaluate specific data.[3] Evidence that the defendant's blood type matches the type found at the crime scene is relevant in the trial only because scientific research has demonstrated that the general population can be classified according to blood type—for example, 42% of the population is blood type A. Therefore, evidence that the blood found at the crime scene and defendant's blood are the same type tends to make the existence of a material or consequential fact, the murderer's identity, more probable than it would be without the evidence.[4]

---

1. See Strong, Questions Affecting the Admissibility of Scientific Evidence, 1970 U.Ill.L.F. 1, 2 (1970).

2. E. g., People v. Gillespie, 24 Ill.App.3d 567, 321 N.E.2d 398 (1974).

3. See James, Relevancy, Probability and the Law, 29 Calif.L.Rev. 689, 696 n. 15 & 704 (1941); Korn, Law, Fact, and Science in the Courts, 66 Colum.L. Rev. 1080, 1110 (1966); Strong, supra note 1 at 2–4. General propositions are usually supplied by "logic and general experience." J. Thayer, A Preliminary Treatise on Evidence at the Common Law 265 (1898). Scientific knowledge, however, can also be used for this purpose. In drafting the Federal Rules of Evidence, the Advisory Committee rejected the formulation of relevancy found in the Uniform Rules of Evidence (1953) because it overemphasized the "logical process" to the detriment of "experience or science."

Advisory Committee Note, Fed.Evid.Rule 401, 28 U.S. C.A.

Because scientific knowledge is beyond the ken of most judges and juries, an expert witness is used to supply general scientific propositions. An evolutionary process, however, is involved—at some point much of what is initially classified as "scientific" knowledge is assimilated into general knowledge and an expert is no longer needed to supply these propositions. See J. Maguire, Evidence, Common Sense and Common Law 30 (1947).

4. See Fed.Evid.Rule 401, 28 U.S.C.A. The text analysis assumes that the victim's and defendant's blood types differ.

This chapter deals primarily with the first use of scientific knowledge, the admissibility of specific data derived by scientific means, and the foundational requirements for validating such data.[5] The foundational requirements ensure the reliability of the specific data. If, for example, the data (blood type) presented in court was not derived through reliable means, the probative value of the evidence is questionable. Before data derived from scientific means is admissible, the proponent must authenticate the evidence, establishing that: *(1) The underlying scientific principle is valid;*[6] *(2) the forensic technique successfully applies the principle; (3) any instrumentation employed in the technique was in working order at the time of the test; (4) the proper procedures were used in conducting the test; and (5) the person who conducted the examination and the person who interpreted the results had the requisite qualifications.* Each foundational element is discussed in the following sections.

2. Validity of the Underlying Principle

Suggested Reading:

Coppolino v. State, 223 So.2d 68 (Fla.App.1968).

United States v. Frye, 293 F. 1013 (D.C.Cir. 1923).

Unless the principle which forms the basis of a scientific technique is valid, evidence derived from that technique is irrelevant.[7] For example, uniqueness is the premise underlying voiceprint identification.[8] However, if everyone's voice were not unique, the results of a voiceprint analysis would not tend to establish that the defendant was the person who made the extortion demand, bomb threat, etc. The validity of the underlying scientific principle can be established in several ways: judicial notice, legislative recognition, or expert testimony.

Judicial Notice. Under modern practice[9] judicial notice is permitted of facts that can be accurately and readily verified. Once a scientific principle is accepted, the courts do not hesitate to take judicial notice of the principle.[10] For example, the principles underlying radar, intoxication tests,[11] fingerprints,[12] and magnetometers,[13] firearm,[14]

---

5. Professor Strong has pointed out that although the second use of scientific knowledge is usually treated under the topic of expert testimony, there is an overlap between the two uses. Strong, supra note 1 at 5.

6. Although the courts use the terms *validity* and *reliability* interchangeably, the terms have distinct meanings in scientific jargon. *Validity* refers to the ability of a test procedure to measure what is supposed to measure—its accuracy. *Reliability* refers to whether the same results are obtained each instance the test is conducted—its consistency. Validity includes reliability but the converse is not necessarily true. Barland, The Reliability of Polygraph Chart Evaluations 120, 121, in Legal Admissibility of the Polygraph (N. Ansley ed. 1975).

7. United States v. Ridling, 350 F.Supp. 90, 94–95 (E.D.Mich.1972); United States v. DeBetham, 348 F.Supp. 1377, 1384 (S.D.Cal.1972), aff'd 470 F.2d 1367 (9th Cir.), cert. denied 412 U.S. 907, 93 S.Ct. 2299, 36 L.Ed.2d 972 (1973).

8. See § 7, infra.

9. C. McCormick, Handbook of the Law of Evidence 763 (2d ed. 1972).

10. For a further discussion of judicial notice, see chapter 28, infra.

11. E. g., People v. Stringfield, 37 Ill.App.2d 344, 185 N.E.2d 381 (1962) (breathalyzer); State v. Miller, 64 N.J.Super. 262, 165 A.2d 829 (1960) (drunkometer); State v. Hanrahan, 523 S.W.2d 619 (Mo.App.1975) (breathalyzer); People v. Donaldson, 36 A.D.2d 37, 319 N.Y.S.2d 172 (1971) (breathalyzer).

12. E. g., Piquett v. United States, 81 F.2d 75 (7th Cir. 1936), cert. denied 298 U.S. 664, 56 S.Ct. 749, 80 L.Ed. 1388; People v. Jennings, 252 Ill. 534, 96 N.E. 1077 (1911); Lamble v. State, 96 N.J.Law 231, 114 A. 346 (1921); State v. Rogers, 233 N.C. 390, 64 S.E.2d 572 (1951); Grice v. State, 142 Tex.Cr.R. 4, 151 S.W. 2d 211 (1941); State v. Bolen, 142 Wash. 653, 254 P. 445 (1927).

13. E. g., United States v. Lopez, 328 F.Supp. 1077 (E.D.N.Y.1971).

14. E. g., People v. Fischer, 340 Ill. 216, 172 N.E. 743 (1930); State v. Hackett, 215 S.C. 434, 55 S.E.2d 696 (1949); Cummings v. State, 226 Ga. 46, 172 S.E. 2d 395 (1970); Pickens v. State, Okl.Cr., 450 P.2d 837 (1969).

handwriting, and typewriting identification have been judicially recognized. The availability of judicial notice for certain scientific principles relieves the proponent from the burden of establishing the validity of the principle by expert testimony.

Legislative Recognition. In some jurisdictions the admissibility of scientific evidence, principally radar [15] and intoxication tests,[16] is statutorily sanctioned. Legislative acceptance of the underlying principle is implicit in these statutes.[17] The effect of these statutes is similar to that of judicial notice; they relieve the proponent of the burden of introducing expert testimony to validate the underlying principle.

Expert Testimony. The validity of the underlying principle can also be established by expert testimony. New scientific techniques initially gain admissibility by this means.[18] It might be expected that once a qualified expert testifies to the validity of the underlying principle, this foundational element is satisfied. This, however, has not been the case. Beginning in 1923 with United States v. Frye,[19] a special requirement has been imposed for the admissibility of scientific evidence. In *Frye,* the exclusion of the results of a polygraph examination was upheld by the Court of Appeals for the District

of Columbia because the technique had not gained widespread acceptance. The court, in an oft-quoted passage, stated: "Just when a scientific principle or discovery crosses the line between the experimental and demonstrable stages is difficult to define. Somewhere in this twilight zone the evidential force of the principle must be recognized, and while courts will go a long way in admitting expert testimony deduced from a well-recognized scientific principle or discovery, the thing from which the deduction is made must be sufficiently established to have gained general acceptance in the particular field in which it belongs." [20] Applying this "general acceptance" standard, the court concluded that the polygraph had "not yet gained such standing and scientific recognition among physiological and psychological authorities." [21] *Frye's* general acceptance standard has been applied to evidence of voiceprint identification,[22] neutron activation analysis,[23] the "paraffin test," [24] and other forensic techniques.

The *Frye* standard, however, has not received universal acceptance. The leading case espousing an opposing view is Coppolino v. State.[25] In *Coppolino* the prosecution con-

---

15. See Ohio Rev.Code § 4511.091; Va.Code 1950, § 46.1–198; N.Y.Veh. & Traf.Law § 1180. See Thomas v. City of Norfolk, 207 Va. 12, 147 S.E.2d 727 (1966), upholding the constitutionality of the Virginia statute.

16. See Uniform Chemical Test for Intoxication Act, 9 U.L.A.; Ark.Stats. 75–1031.1; No.Dak.Cent.Code 39–20–07(S); Utah Code Ann. 41–6–44.

17. In some cases a legislature may intervene and prohibit the evidentiary use of certain scientific techniques. See, e. g., Ill.Ann.Stat. Ch. 110, § 54.1 (excluding polygraph evidence).

18. See Tiffin v. Whitmer, 60 Ohio Misc. 169, 170, 290 N.E.2d 198, 199, 61 O.O.2d 291 (1970) ("because the instrument (Vascar) is new, expert testimony as to the scientific principle, construction, operation and accuracy and reliability of the device must be established beyond a reasonable doubt.")

19. 293 F. 1013 (D.C.Cir. 1923).

20. Id. at 1014.

21. Id.

22. E. g., United States v. Franks, 511 F.2d 25 (6th Cir. 1975), cert. denied 422 U.S. 1042, 1048, 95 S.Ct. 2654, 2656, 2667, 45 L.Ed.2d 693; United States v. Addison, 498 F.2d 741 (D.C.Cir. 1974).

23. E. g., United States v. Stifel, 433 F.2d 431 (6th Cir. 1970), cert. denied 401 U.S. 994, 91 S.Ct. 1232, 28 L.Ed.2d 531 (1971); State v. Coolidge, 109 N.H. 403, 260 A.2d 547 (1969), rev'd on other grounds 403 U.S. 433, 91 S.Ct. 2022, 29 L.Ed.2d 564 (1971).

24. E. g., Brooke v. People, 139 Colo. 388, 339 P.2d 993 (1959) (general acceptance); Born v. State, 397 P.2d 924 (Okl.Crim.1964), cert. denied 379 U.S. 1000, 85 S.Ct. 718, 13 L.Ed.2d 701 (1965); Clarke v. State, 218 Tenn. 259, 402 S.W.2d 863 (1964), cert. denied 385 U.S. 942, 87 S.Ct. 303, 17 L.Ed.2d 222 (1965).

25. 223 So.2d 68 (Fla.App.1968). See also People v. Bobczyk, 343 Ill.App. 504, 99 N.E.2d 567 (1951); McKay v. State, 155 Tex.Cr.R. 416, 235 S.W.2d 173 (1951).

tended that the defendant had murdered his wife by administering a toxic dose of succinylcholine chloride. At the time of the offense, the medical community generally agreed that no reliable method existed for detecting succinylcholine chloride or its derivatives in human tissue.[26] However, a prosecution toxicologist developed a method of detection specifically for the *Coppolino* case. His trial testimony concerning the presence of succinic acid, a derivative of succinylcholine chloride, was a crucial link in the prosecution case. In upholding the admissibility of the toxicologist's testimony, the court of appeal cited *Frye* but then ruled "that the trial judge enjoys wide discretion in areas concerning the admission of evidence."[27] The court further held that the judge had not abused his discretion in this case. In effect, *Coppolino* rejected the special requirement-"general-acceptance"-for the admissibility of scientific evidence.

The *Coppolino* approach follows the views of many commentators who have criticized the *Frye* test. Professor McCormick argued that scientific evidence should be admissible if its probative value outweighs the "dangers of prejudicing or misleading the jury, unfair surprise and undue consumption of time."[28] Professor McCormick viewed the *Frye* general-acceptance test as an appropriate standard for judicial notice of scientific facts, but not for establishing the validity of the underlying principle through expert testimony.[29] *Frye* has also been attacked because it introduces an inconsistency into evidence law. Expert opinion testimony about a witness's credibility may be obtained from both a psychiatrist and a polygraph examiner; only the latter, however, is burdened by the *Frye* general-acceptance

test.[30] In addition, *Frye* forces the law to lag behind science, for the courts cannot use a scientific technique until it gains widespread scientific acceptance.[31] During the interim courts are often deprived of valuable and reliable evidence.

In spite of these criticisms, the majority of courts adheres to the general-acceptance standard.[32] In rejecting voiceprint evidence, the Court of Appeals for the District of Columbia in United States v. Addison[33] reiterated its support for the *Frye* test. The court recognized that delay in the reception of possibly valuable evidence is an inevitable consequence of the general-acceptance requirement. However, the court believed that such a delay is not an "unwarranted cost,"[34] for the standard "assure(d) that those most qualified to assess the general validity of a scientific method will have the determinative voice."[35] The court also noted that the *Frye* standard guarantees that a "minimal reserve of experts exists who can critically examine the validity of a scientific determination in a particular case."[36]

The *Frye* test requires a two-step analysis: (1) identifying the discipline in which the underlying principle falls, and (2) establishing that the principle is generally accepted by the members of that discipline. Neither step is free of difficulty. Many techniques arguably fall within the domain of

---

26. Id. at 70 and 75.

27. Id. at 70.

28. C. McCormick, Handbook of the Law of Evidence 363–64 (1954).

29. Id. at 363.

30. Boyce, Judicial Recognition of Scientific Evidence in Criminal Cases, 8 Utah L.Rev. 313 (1963).

31. Maletskos & Spielman, Introduction of New Scientific Methods in Court, in Law Enforcement, Science & Technology (S. Yefsky ed. 1967).

32. United States v. Alexander, 526 F.2d 161, 163 n. 3 (8th Cir. 1975) ("federal courts of appeals continue to subscribe to [the] 'general scientific acceptability' criterion").

33. United States v. Addison, 498 F.2d 741 (D.C.Cir. 1974).

34. Id. at 743.

35. Id. at 744. The California Supreme Court took the same position in People v. Kelly, 17 Cal.3d 24, 130 Cal.Rptr. 144, 549 P.2d 1240 (1976).

36. 498 F.2d at 744.

more than one academic discipline. Voiceprint identification is such a technique.[37] Moreover, the so-called "forensic sciences" could be considered a discrete discipline for the purposes of the *Frye* test.[38] If the forensic sciences were accepted, a court could rely on the opinions of polygraph examiners rather than on those of experts in physiology and psychology to validate the principle underlying polygraph evidence.[39]

Some courts have modified the first step of the *Frye* test. In People v. Williams,[40] the court considered the validity of the Nalline test for detecting narcotic use. Because, according to the prosecution's own experts, the "medical profession generally (was) unfamiliar with the use of Nalline,"[41] the government could not have met its burden under *Frye* if the entire field of medicine was the appropriate field. Nevertheless, the court admitted the evidence because it "has been generally accepted by those who

would be expected to be familiar with its use. In this age of specialization more should not be required."[42]

The second part of the *Frye* test, determining general acceptance, is no more precise than ascertaining the field in which a particular technique belongs. Most courts recognize that "(p)ractically every new scientific discovery has its detractors and unbelievers, but neither unanimity of opinion nor universal infallibility is required for judicial acceptance."[43] However, the percentage of those in the field who must accept the underlying principle has never been clearly defined.[44] For example, one court defined "general acceptance" as "widespread; prevalent; extensive, though not universal."[45]

3. Validity of the Forensic Technique

Although most courts do not distinguish between the validity of the underlying scientific principle and the forensic technique's successful application of the principle, two distinct issues are present. A court, for example, could accept the underlying premise of voiceprint identification (voice uniqueness) but not the voiceprint technique.[46] Similarly, the underlying psychological and physiological principles of the polygraph could be acknowledged without endorsing the proposition that a polygraph examiner can detect deception by means of the polygraph

---

37. See People v. King, 266 Cal.App.2d 437, 72 Cal. Rptr. 478 (1968) ("While Kersta [the developer of the voiceprint technique] has degrees in electrical engineering and physics, his field of knowledge is acoustical and audio engineering; there is no indication either from his educational background or his employment experience that he engaged in any scientific investigation or medical research to substantiate his analysis of the functions of the body which produce speech.") See also Jones, Danger—Voiceprints Ahead, 11 Am.Crim.L.Rev. 549, 564–65 (1973).

38. Forensic science "is as much a discipline in its own right as is medicine, which also is not chemistry, not biology, not physics, but a fusion of all three, modified and adapted to a specific purpose, the treatment of disease in human beings." Kirk, The Interrelationship of Law and Science, 13 Buff.L.Rev. 393 (1964). See also Fong, Criminalistics and the Prosecutor in the Prosecutor's Deskbook 547 (1971).

39. See § 8, infra. In effect, the underlying theory would be validated empirically or inferentially rather than theoretically or deductively. Thus one commentator has argued for the admissibility of polygraph evidence because "it works." Tarlow, Admissibility of Polygraph Evidence in 1975: An Aid in Determining Credibility In a Perjury-Plagued System, 26 Hastings L.J. 917, 922 (1975).

40. 164 Cal.App.2d 858, 331 P.2d 251 (1958).

41. Id. at 862, 331 P.2d at 253.

42. Id., 331 P.2d at 253–54.

43. State v. Johnson, 42 N.J. 146, 171, 199 A.2d 809, 823 (1964).

44. "The resulting standard, something greater than acceptance by the expert himself but less than acceptance by all experts in the field, is obviously somewhat lacking in definiteness." Strong, supra note 1 at 11. See also J. Richardson, Modern Scientific Evidence 164 (2d ed. 1974) (suggesting that a "substantial majority" of a field would constitute "general acceptance").

45. United States v. Zeiger, 350 F.Supp. 685, 688 (D.D.C.1972), rev'd 475 F.2d 1280 (D.C.Cir.).

46. See § 7, infra.

technique.[47]   The distinction becomes important if a court requires scientific evidence to meet a special standard such as *Frye*. If a court applied the *Frye* standard to the validity of the underlying principle, it would probably apply a requirement of general acceptance to the technique.[48]

Because the scientific techniques used in criminal trials vary widely, challenges to the validity of individual techniques differ. Some forensic procedures, such as fingerprints, firearms, and handwriting comparisons, involve straightforward applications of the underlying theory. These techniques consist only of a visual comparison of exemplars.[49]   Other techniques, especially those involving instrumentation, are more complex. The validity of these techniques depends in part on the accuracy of the instrument employed. Radar, for example, is a purely instrumental technique; the device not only measures but also interprets data. Thus, the validity of the technique and the accuracy of the instrument present identical issues. Other techniques, such as the polygraph and voiceprint analysis, involve both the use of instrumentation [50] and the interpretation of data derived from them. In these techniques, the capability of the instrument to produce specific data or the interpretation of that data may be challengeable. In fact, the interpretive aspects of the polygraph and voiceprint procedures, not the instrumentation, have been the principal source of controversy.

4. Condition of the Instrument

Suggested Reading:

State v. Overton, 135 N.J.Super. 443, 343 A.2d 516 (1975).

If a scientific procedure involves instrumentation, the accuracy of the results derived from that procedure depends on the functioning of the instrument at the time of the test.[51]   Evidence of the results of a polygraph or voiceprint examination, for example, will be inadmissible if the machine malfunctioned during the examination.[52] As part of the foundation for admissibility, the proponent should present evidence on the condition of the instrument. However, this position has not always been followed. Thus some courts hold that radar results are admissible notwithstanding the lack of evidence that the equipment was in proper working order at the time of the readings.[53] According to these courts the lack of evidence affects the weight and not the admissibility of the evidence. The better view requires the proponent to establish that the instrument was in working order.[54]   In the case of radar, this requirement could be ful-

---

47. See § 8 infra.

48. The validity of the technique can be established by the same methods used to establish the underlying principle: expert testimony, judicial notice, or legislative recognition. See Strong, supra note 1 at 15.

49. While the expert's interpretation of the exemplars in a particular case may involve a sophisticated analysis, the technique itself—the examination of exemplars with aid of a microscope or other magnification device—is not complex.

50. The polygraph machine and sound spectrometer respectively.

51. A similar issue is presented by forensic procedures that involve the use of reagents or chemicals. The condition of those materials at the time of the test will affect the outcome.

52. See United States v. Ridling, 350 F.Supp. 90, 93 (E.D.Mich.1972) ("the recording device or polygraph [must] be in good operating condition").

53. E. g., People v. Dusing, 5 N.Y.2d 126, 181 N.Y.S. 2d 493, 155 N.E.2d 393 (1959); People v. Abdallah, 82 Ill.App.2d 312, 226 N.E.2d 408 (1967) (dictum). While the New York cases admit the results of untested speedmeter devices, that evidence alone is insufficient to sustain a conviction for speeding. See Fisher, Legal Aspects of Speed Measurement Devices 41–42 (1967).

54. This result is required by statute in some jurisdictions. E. g., Fla.Stat.Ann. § 316.058(1); Pa. Vehicle Code § 1002(d).

filled by testimony that the instrument was tested by a tuning fork [55] or a test run [56] by a vehicle with a calibrated speedometer. Some courts have also accepted evidence of periodic maintenance.[57]

5. Use of Proper Procedures

Suggested Reading:

People v. Meikrantz, 77 Misc.2d 892, 351 N.Y.S.2d 549 (1974).

Most courts require "the proponent of the evidence (to) demonstrate that correct procedures were used in the particular case." [58] In some jurisdictions a showing of the analyst's qualifications raises a presumption that the analyst used the proper procedures.[59] A checklist of the procedure may be introduced to corroborate the analyst's testimony.[60]

6. Qualification of Administrators and Interpreters

Because the typical juror is not familiar with the subject matter, introducing scien-tific evidence invariably requires expert testimony. The rules governing expert testimony are discussed in Chapter 3. Expert testimony may be used in several distinct ways. As previously noted [61] expert testimony is often used to establish the validity of the underlying scientific principle and the forensic technique's successful application of that principle. The availability of either judicial notice or a statute dispenses with the need for expert testimony in many cases. Nevertheless, evidence concerning the test conducted in the particular case would still be required.

In many instances the person who conducts the test also interprets the results. Firearms identification, fingerprint identification, and drug analysis are illustrative techniques. However, some techniques involve two experts. An X-ray technician operates the X-ray machine, but a physician interprets the results.[62] Both must be qualified. Similarly, a police officer could qualify as an expert in operating a breathalyzer but would not have the requisite expertise to interpret the results.[63] A physician or toxicologist would have to testify about the relationship between alcohol content of the breath and the effect on the brain. In many jurisdictions statutes [64] create presumptions eliminating the requirement of two experts. If a statute creates a presumption of intoxication when the alcohol concentration reaches a specified level, the prosecution need not call an expert to establish the nexus between such concentration and intoxication.

---

55. State v. McDonough, 302 Minn. 468, 225 N.W.2d 259 (1975); State v. Overton, 135 N.J.Super. 443, 343 A.2d 516 (1975).

56. Whitehead v. City of Lynchburg, 213 Va. 742, 195 S.E.2d 858 (1973).

57. People ex rel. Katz v. Jones, 10 Misc.2d 1067, 171 N.Y.S.2d 325 (1958).

58. People v. Kelly, 17 Cal.3d 24, 130 Cal.Rptr. 144, 549 P.2d 1240 (1976) (voiceprints); accord, United States v. Ridling, 350 F.Supp. 90, 93 (E.D.Mich.1972) ("For a test to be successful, it is important . . . that appropriate scientific methods be used in connection with the questioning of the [polygraph] subject.").

59. People v. Meikrantz, 77 Misc.2d 892, 351 N.Y.S. 2d 549 (1974). But see People v. Foulger, 26 Cal. App.3d Supp. 1, 103 Cal.Rptr. 156 (1972).

60. State v. Hamaker, 524 S.W.2d 176 (Mo.App. 1975); State v. Sutton, 253 Or. 24, 450 P.2d 748 (1967).

61. See §§ 2 and 3, supra.

62. The interpretation of the X-ray requires medical training the X-ray technician lacks.

63. As in note 62, supra, the police officer lacks the medical training necessary to evaluate the data.

64. The statutes vary in the concentration necessary to raise the presumption. One state uses 0.05%, a few states use 0.15%, but the overwhelming majority uses 0.10%. If a person weighing 140 pounds consumes three martinis within an hour, that person's blood alcohol concentration (BAC) will rise to 0.22%. If the person consumes three beers in that period, the BAC will rise to 0.05%.

A detailed discussion of the various types of scientific evidence currently used in criminal trials is not possible in a work of this scope.[65] Two techniques, however, have been singled out for individual treatment: voiceprints and the polygraph.

7. Voiceprints

Suggested Reading:

People v. Kelly, 17 Cal.3d 24, 130 Cal.Rptr. 144, 549 P.2d 1240 (1976).

United States v. Addison, 498 F.2d 741 (D.C.Cir. 1974).

Speaker identification by voiceprint[66] analysis (sound spectography) is based upon the uniqueness of each human voice. Differences in the vocal anatomy[67] as well as learned differences in the use of the vocal mechanism for speech production[68] apparently cause dissimilarities in the way different people pronounce the same word. This dissimilarity is called interspeaker variability. Speech

scientists also recognize intraspeaker variability—that is, a speaker will not pronounce the same word in exactly the same way twice. Speaker identification by voiceprints depends on the assumption that interspeaker variability is greater than intraspeaker variability.[69]

The voiceprint technique involves using a sound spectrograph[70] to produce a visual display (a spectrogram) of selected words or phrases of a recorded voice.[71] The examiner compares known and unknown spectrograms. Like many other forensic identification procedures, the comparison calls for the examiner's subjective evaluation. Accordingly, the qualifications of the examiner, his or her training and experience, are crucial.[72]

The most extensive and influential research on voiceprints was conducted at Michigan State University under the supervision of Dr. Oscar Tosi.[73] 34,992 experimental trials involving 250 male speakers and 29 examiners were conducted over a two-year period. The false identification rate[74] in

---

65. For a discussion of the various techniques, see C. McCormick, Handbook of the Law of Evidence 491–523 (2d ed. 1972); A. Moenssens, R. Moses & F. Inbau, Scientific Evidence in Criminal Cases (1973); J. Richardson, Modern Scientific Evidence (2d ed. 1974). For an excellent article on drug analysis, see Stein, Laessig & Indriksons, An Evaluation of Drug Testing Procedures Used by Forensic Laboratories and the Qualifications of their Analysts, 1973 Wis.L. Rev. 727.

66. The term "voiceprints" has been criticized by speech scientists and courts because it suggests an unwarranted comparison with fingerprint identification. See United States v. Baller, 519 F.2d 463 (4th Cir. 1975); Bolt et al., Speaker Identification by Speech Spectrograms: A Scientist's View of Its Reliability for Legal Purposes, 47 J.Acoust.Soc'y.Am. 597 (1970).

67. Nasal, oral, and pharyngeal cavities.

68. Articulators (lips, teeth, tongue, soft palate), which play an important role in speech production, are critical to the theory of voice uniqueness.

69. Tosi et al., Experiment on Voice Identification, 51 J.Acoust.Soc'y.Am. 2030, 2031 (1972).

70. The sound spectrograph is widely used by speech specialists for research and therapy. Bolt, supra note 66 at 597. Because it is recognized as an accurate instrument, its reliability has not been a factor in the voiceprint cases.

71. Three parameters of speech are portrayed in a spectrogram—frequency (vertical axis); time (horizontal axis); and relative amplitude (darkness). Tosi, supra note 69 at 2031.

72. The proponents of the technique have continually emphasized this factor. E. g., Tosi, Voice Identification in Scientific and Expert Evidence in Criminal Advocacy 241, 262 (J. Cederbaums & S. Arnold eds. 1975) ("the crucial problem with subjective methods consists in testing the honesty and reliability of the examiner").

73. Voice Identification Research (February 1972) (submitted to L.E.A.A. by Department of Michigan State Police). The results of the research are also reported at Tosi, supra note 69.

74. Errors of false elimination were reported to be approximately 13%. Tosi, supra note 69 at 2041. Proponents argue that false eliminations should not be considered in evaluating the accuracy of the

trials most closely resembling the forensic situation [75] was approximately 6%.[76] This figure is reduced to 2% if the trials in which the examiners expressed "uncertainty" about their conclusions are eliminated.[77] According to Dr. Tosi's court testimony, for several reasons the error rate would be "negligible" [78] in a real-life situation. (1) The professional examiner is thoroughly trained and qualified; the experimenters had only one month's training. (2) The examiner has unlimited time to compare the spectrograms; the experimenters had only 15 minutes in which to reach a decision. (3) The examiner would compare the exemplars aurally as well as visually; the experimenters' conclusions were based on only the visual comparison of spectrograms. (4) The examiner could utilize the complete text of a conversation, while the experimenters considered only a limited number of words. (5) The examiner would not have to render a conclusion if he or she was not positive; the experimenters were required to make a choice. (6) The examiner would be more conscientious in light of the possible consequences of his or her conclusions; no personal consequences followed from the experimenters' conclusions.[79]

Notwithstanding the Tosi study, many speech scientists believe that our current understanding of speaker variability is such that voice identification by sound spectrography has not been adequately demonstrated.[80] However, proponents of the technique

claim that the Tosi study provides the empirical data to inferentially establish the underlying theory of voiceprint identification—that is, even if the "why" and "how" of the technique are not fully understood, the technique "works," [81] and that fact is sufficient validation for legal purposes.[82]

Two factors—the Tosi research and the evidentiary standard adopted for scientific evidence—have affected the admissibility of voiceprint evidence. Until the Tosi research, the validity of the voiceprint technique was supported only by the claims of its developer, Lawrence Kersta. Consequently, two of the three appellate courts that initially considered voiceprint identification rejected the technique for lack of general acceptance.[83]

---

technique inasmuch as the consequence of convicting an innocent person is not raised by such errors.

75. The forensic model involved "open trials" in which the examiner was not informed if the unknown voice was in known recordings, non-contemporary recordings, and clue words in context rather than in isolation. Id.

76. Id.

77. Id. Confidence ratings were required of the experimental examiners.

78. People v. Law, 40 Cal.App.3d 69, 79, 114 Cal. Rptr. 708, 713 (1974).

79. Id. at 79, 114 Cal.Rptr. at 714.

80. Bolt et al., Speaker Identification by Speech Spectograms: Some Further Observations, 54 J.

Acoust.Soc'y.Am. 531 (1973); Thomas, Voiceprint-Myth or Miracle, in Scientific and Expert Evidence in Criminal Advocacy 273, 274 n. 6 (J. Cederbaums & S. Arnold eds. 1975). For a reply, see Black et al., Reply to Speaker Identification by Speech Spectograms: Some Further Observations, 54 J.Acoust. Soc'y.Am. 535 (1973). See generally Jones, Evidence Vel Non, The Nonsense of Voiceprint Identification, 62 Ky.L.J. 301, 319–23 (1974); Comment, The Voiceprint Dilemma: Should Voices Be Seen and Not Heard, 35 Md.L.Rev. 267 (1975); Siegel, Cross-Examination of a "Voiceprint" Expert: A Blueprint for Trial Lawyers, 12 Crim.L.Bull. 509 (1976); Hollien & McGlone, The Effect of Disguise on "Voiceprint" Identification, 2 J.Crim.Def. 117 (1976); Decker & Handler, Voiceprint Identification Evidence—Out of the Frye Pan and Into Admissibility, 26 Amer.U.L. Rev. 314 (1977).

81. Boren, Voiceprint-Staging a Comeback, 3 U.S.F. V.L.Rev. 1, 9 (1974).

82. This aspect of voiceprint identification makes cross-examination difficult because "the spectographic identification of a voice by a trained observer appears to rely on a broad assessment of loosely defined points of similarity rather than on a carefully specified set of objectively defined spectographic attributes." Bolt, supra note 80 at 533.

83. People v. King, 266 Cal.App.2d 437, 72 Cal.Rptr. 478 (1968) (also rejected Kersta as a qualified expert); State v. Cary, 49 N.J. 343, 230 A.2d 384 (1967), on remand 99 N.J.Super. 323, 239 A.2d 680 (1968), appeal granted 53 N.J. 256, 250 A.2d 15 (1969), aff'd 56 N.J. 16, 264 A.2d 209 (1970). Contra, United States v. Wright, 17 U.S.C.M.A. 183, 37 C.M.R. 447 (1967) (general acceptance standard not applied; voiceprints admitted to corroborate aural identification).

This trend was reversed once Dr. Tosi began testifying about the results of his research.[84]

However, some sectors of the scientific community were not as receptive as were the courts to the Tosi research. Although recognizing Dr. Tosi's contribution, these scientists commented that insufficient research had been conducted,[85] and some courts interpreted such comments as a failure of the technique to gain general acceptance. In United States v. Addison,[86] the District of Columbia Circuit, applying a strict *Frye* test, held that "voiceprint identification is not now sufficiently accepted by the scientific community as a whole.[87] In People v. Kelly,[88] the California Supreme Court rejected voiceprint evidence, at least on the basis of the evidence presented in that case. Three grounds were offered by the court. First, the court questioned "whether the testimony of a single witness alone is ever sufficient to represent, or attest to, the views of an entire scientific community regarding the reliability of a new technique." [89] Second, the partiality of the government's expert, a leading proponent of the technique, troubled the

court.[90] Third, the expert's qualification on the issue of "general acceptance of the voiceprint technique in the scientific community" [91] was raised. According to the court, the expert's "qualifications are those of a technician and law enforcement officer, not a scientist." In 1977, in People v. Tobey,[92] Michigan decided to follow the *Kelly* approach.

Other courts, however, responded to the criticism of the Tosi research by either modifying or abandoning *Frye* as the applicable standard. In Commonwealth v. Lykes,[93] the Supreme Judicial Court of Massachusetts limited the "field" in which general acceptance was required to "those who would be expected to be familiar with its use." [94] The court attached "greater weight to those experts who have had direct and empirical experience in the field of spectrography.[95] In United States v. Frank,[96] the Sixth Circuit took the position that general acceptance was nearly synonymous with reliability." [97] In a later voiceprint case the court did not even refer to *Frye*.[98] Finally, in United States v. Baller,[99] the Fourth Circuit rejected *Frye* in

84. E. g., United States v. Raymond, 337 F.Supp. 641 (D.D.C.1972), overruled United States v. Addison, 498 F.2d 741 (D.C.Cir.1974); Hodo v. Superior Court, 30 Cal.App.3d 778, 106 Cal.Rtpr. 547 (1973) (applying modified "general acceptance" test); United States v. Brown, 13 Crim.L.Rep. 2203 (D.C.Super.Ct. May 1, 1973); Worley v. State, 263 So.2d 613 (Fla.App.1972) (as corroborative evidence, citing *Coppolino*); Alea v. State, 265 So.2d 96 (Fla.App.1972); Trimble v. Hedman, 291 Minn. 442, 192 N.W.2d 432 (1971) (as corroborative evidence). In addition, the New Jersey Supreme Court seemed disposed to reconsider its earlier position on voiceprints after the Tosi study. State v. Andretta, 61 N.J. 544, 296 A.2d 644 (1972).

85. See note 80, supra.

86. 498 F.2d 741 (D.C.Cir. 1974).

87. Id. at 745. In a later case, United States v. McDaniel, 538 F.2d 408, 413 (D.C.Cir. 1976), the court indicated a willingness to reexamine *Addison* "in light of the apparently increased reliability and general acceptance in the scientific community."

88. 17 Cal.3d 24, 130 Cal.Rptr. 144, 549 P.2d 1240 (1976).

89. Id. at 37, 30 Cal.Rptr. at 152, 549 P.2d at 1248.

90. Id. at 38, 30 Cal.Rptr. at 153, 549 P.2d at 1249.

91. Id.

92. 257 N.W.2d 537 (Mich.1977). (Mich.Sup.Ct. Sept. 20, 1977).

93. 367 Mass. 191, 327 N.E.2d 671 (1975). See also Commonwealth v. Vitello, 367 Mass. 224, 327 N.E.2d 819 (1975).

94. Id. at 677.

95. Id. at 678 n. 6. Accord, State v. Reed, 18 Crim. L.Rep. 2011 (Montgomery City Cir.Ct. Sept. 9, 1975) ("we are restricting the relevant field of experts to those who are knowledgeable, directly knowledgeable through work, utilization of the techniques, experimentation and so forth, (and) we are not taking the broad general scientific community of speech and hearing science").

96. 511 F.2d 25 (6th Cir. 1975), cert. denied 422 U.S. 1042, 95 S.Ct. 2654, 45 L.Ed.2d 693.

97. Id. at 33 n. 12. Accord, United States v. Brown, 13 Crim.L.Rep. 2203 (D.C.Super.Ct. May 1, 1973).

98. United States v. Jenkins, 525 F.2d 819, 827 (6th Cir. 1975).

99. 519 F.2d 463 (4th Cir.1975), cert. denied 423 U.S. 1019, 96 S.Ct. 456, 46 L.Ed.2d 1391.

favor of *Coppolino*: "Unless an exaggerated popular opinion of the accuracy of a particular technique makes its use prejudicial or likely to mislead the jury, it is better to admit relevant scientific evidence in the same manner as other expert testimony and allow its weight to be attacked by cross-examination and refutation." [1]

Even if the general trend toward admissibility of voiceprint evidence continues,[2] applying the technique under certain circumstances may present problems. Because the Tosi study attempted to establish the validity of the technique inferentially,[3] any significant differences between the test conditions and an actual case may affect the admissibility of the evidence. For example, female [4] and disguised voices [5] were not part of the Tosi research. Additionally, the tapes used in the Tosi study were recorded a month apart, and the Tosi research indicates that the greater the time lapse, the greater the error rate.[6]

Perhaps the most striking aspect of the voiceprint cases is the failure of most defense counsel to adequately contest the validity of the voiceprint evidence. In many cases, no opposing experts were called by the defense to challenge the technique.[7] Even if the validity of the technique is established, the examiner's conclusions in a particular case may be subject to attack. In some cases experts have disagreed on whether a positive identification could be made.[8] In one case, the expert misidentified a spectrogram during an in-court test.[9] Defense challenges are important, especially in light of the number of juries that have acquitted defendants despite the introduction of voiceprint evidence.[10]

The Committee on Evaluation of Sound Spectrograms of the National Academy of Science is currently preparing a report summarizing the state of the scientific research on sound spectrography. Since the Academy is such a prestigious organization, the report will undoubtedly have a dramatic impact on the acceptance of spectrography in both scentific and legal circles.

8. Polygraphs

Suggested Reading:

United States v. Ridling, 350 F.Supp. 90 (E.D.Mich. 1972).

State v. Valdez, 91 Ariz. 274, 371 P.2d 894 (1962).

---

1. Id. at 466.

2. Approximately 50 trial courts have accepted voiceprint evidence. Greene, Voiceprint Identification: The Case in Favor of Admissibility, 13 Am. Crim.L.Rev. 171, 184–85 (1975).

3. Tosi, supra note 69 at 2031.

4. See State v. Reed, 18 Crim.L.Rep. 2011 (Montgomery Cty.Cir.Ct. September 9, 1975) (limited admissibility to male voices). But see Trimble v. Hedman, 291 Minn. 442, 192 N.W.2d 432 (1971) (woman's voice).

5. People v. Law, 40 Cal.App.3d 69, 114 Cal.Rptr. 708 (1974).

6. See State v. Andretta, 61 N.J. 544, 296 A.2d 644 (1972). See Bolt, supra, note 80: "Further studies are needed, with particular attention to the examiner's decision criteria, the selection of speaker population, the time lapse between voice samples, background noise conditions, and the psychological condition of the speaker." Id. at 534. One commentator has argued that all such objections should affect the weight and not admissibility of the evidence. He also notes that such conditions would result in greater "false eliminations" rather than "false identifications." Greene, supra note 2 at 195.

7. People v. Chapter, 13 Crim.L.Rep. 2479 (Marin Cty.Super.Ct. July 23, 1973) (no opposing expert in 80% of cases).

8. Tosi, supra note 72 at 266–67.

9. People v. Chapter, 13 Crim.L.Rep. 2479 (Marin Cty.Super.Ct. July 23, 1973).

10. Greene, supra note 2 at 190–91. In United States v. Goldstein, 532 F.2d 1305 (9th Cir. 1976), the defendant argued that the trial court erred in not requiring voiceprint identification instead of aural identification of a taped voice. The court rejected this argument.

The polygraph technique is based upon the premise that psychological stress caused by fear of detection will be manifested in involuntary physiological responses [11]—changes in blood pressure, pulse, respiration, and galvanic skin resistance.[12] The polygraph machine records these physiological reactions on a chart (polygram), which is evaluated by the examiner to determine the presence or absence of deception.[13]

The polygraph technique involves several steps: a pretest interview, examination of the subject who is attached to the machine,[14] and chart interpretation. The pretest interview serves several functions. First, it acquaints the subject with the effectiveness of the technique, thereby allaying the truthful subject's apprehensions and stimulating the deceptive subject's concern about detection.[15] Second, the subject's suitability for testing is assessed. The examiner may be alerted to some condition, such as a physical ailment [16] or low intelligence,[17] that would affect test results. Third, test questions are formulated with the subject's assistance.[18]

Although several different examination techniques exist,[19] all recognized techniques use "control" or "probable lie" questions designed to stimulate the truthful subject.[20] Generally, the truthful person will respond to the control questions because they represent a greater threat to his or her well-being, whereas the deceptive person will respond to the "relevant questions" for the same reason.[21] For example, a person being investigated who is innocent of a rape could truthfully answer No to questions about the rape but will still probably lie in response to the control question, "Have you ever stolen anything?" A guilty person would lie in response to both the control and relevant questions, and the lies to the relevant questions will probably cause greater anxiety and more marked reactions on the polygram chart. Therefore, the subject's comparative physiological responses to control and relevant questions are the key to chart interpretation.[22]

Both the critics and proponents of the polygraph technique agree that the examiner, and not the machine, is the crucial determinant in arriving at reliable results. If in proper working order, the machine adequately records the relevant physiological responses. The examiner's expertise is critical in (1) determining the suitability of the subject for testing, (2) formulating proper test questions, (3) establishing rapport with

---

11. J. Reid & F. Inbau, Truth and Deception 50 & 168 (1966). For a discussion of other possible theories, see Barland & Raskin, Detection of Deception in Electrodermal Activity in Psychological Research 417, 445–47 (W. Prokasy & D. Raskin eds. 1973).

12. Reid & Inbau, supra note 11 at 4.

13. Because the machine measures only physiological reactions, the term "lie detector" is a misnomer. The examiner, not the machine, makes the deception diagnosis.

14. Respiration is measured by a pneumograph tube which is fastened around the subject's abdomen or chest. Blood pressure is measured by a cardiostigmagraph or blood pressure cuff. Galvanic skin resistance is measured by electrodes attached to the subject's fingertips.

15. Reid & Inbau, supra note 11 at 10–11.

16. Id. at 15.

17. Id. at 196.

18. There are no surprise questions once the examination commences. Id. at 203.

19. For a discussion of the differences in technique between the major polygraph schools, see N. Ansley (ed.), Legal Admissibility of the Polygraph 220–54 (1975).

20. Control questions concern acts of wrongdoing which are of the same general nature as the incident under investigation. Reid & Inbau, supra note 11 at 19 and 125–27.

21. N. Ansley, supra note 19 at 227 and 236. In addition to relevant and control questions, irrelevant questions are used to obtain a subject's normal tracings.

22. Orne, Implications of Laboratory Research for Detection of Deception 94, 96, in N. Ansley, supra note 9.

the subject, (4) detecting attempts to mask or create chart reactions, (5) stimulating the subject to react, and (6) interpreting the charts. This expertise takes on added significance because of the large number of unqualified examiners holding themselves out as experts.[23]

Since 1923, when polygraph evidence was rejected in Frye v. United States,[24] courts in overwhelming numbers have excluded the results of unstipulated polygraph examinations.[25] Although several arguments have been offered to support this rule of exclusion,[26] the validity of the technique is the critical issue.[27] Since Frye, both the technique and instrumentation have improved.[28] In addition, a growing body of research on the technique supports the validity of polygraph examinations conducted by qualified examiners employing proper techniques.[29] The validity question, however, is an extremely complex issue, and some scientists believe additional research is necessary.[30] Moreover, caution must be exercised before relying on the error rates frequently quoted in court decisions and supportive literature. The figures used by field examiners are especially suspect because they are often based on the assumption that polygraph results are correct unless proven otherwise.[31] In many instances no systematic follow-up studies are conducted to verify the examiner's conclusions, verification criteria are not specified, and improper procedures are used to compute the error rate.[32] In addition favorable results from laboratory experimentation cannot automatically be assumed to apply in real-life situation, for important differences exist between the laboratory and forensic environments that may adversely affect the result of these experiments.[33]

In the early 1970's several trial courts broke with nearly 50 years of precedent and admitted the results of unstipulated polygraph examinations.[34] In United States v.

---

23. Reid & Inbau, supra note 1 at 235.

24. For a discussion of Frye, see § 2, supra.

25. For an extensive listing of cases, see 3A Wigmore, Evidence § 999 (Chadbourn ed. 1970). The courts have also excluded evidence concerning a defendant's refusal or willingness to take a polygraph examination as well as the fact that an examination has been administered.

26. In addition to the validity issue and the closely related issue of the examiner's qualifications, several arguments have been raised against the use of polygraph evidence. For a discussion of the objections, see Tarlow, Admissibility of Polygraph Evidence in 1975: An Aid in Determining Credibility in a Perjury-Plagued System, 26 Hastings L.J. 917, 957–69 (1975).

27. E. g., United States v. Alexander, 526 F.2d 161, 166 (8th Cir. 1975) ("We are still unable to conclude that there is sufficient scientific acceptability and reliability to warrant the admission of the results of such tests in evidence"). Accord, United States v. Wilson, 361 F.Supp. 510 (D.Md.1973); United States v. Urquidez, 356 F.Supp. 1363 (C.D.Cal.1973).

28. The instrument used in Frye measured only one physiological response, blood pressure, whereas the modern polygraph also measures respiration and galvanic skin resistance. In addition, the technique has been improved through the development of the control questions, the pretest interview, and stimulation methods.

29. See Abrams, Polygraph Validity and Reliability: A Review, 18 J.For.Sci. 313 (1973).

30. Orne, Thackray, & Paskewitz, On the Detection of Deception, in Handbook of Psychophysiology 743, 751 (W. Greenfield & R. Steimback eds. 1972) ("No fully satisfactory way is available at this time for evaluating the overall effectiveness of the technique, and it is probable that no such answer will be forthcoming in the near future from real life situations."); Barland & Raskin, supra note 11 at 435 ("the question of the validity of the lie detection technique in the field is an extremely complex issue which may never be fully answerable").

31. Orne, supra note 30 at 116; Validity Panel 153, 154, in N. Ansley, supra note 19.

32. Orne, supra note 30 at 98, 103–04; Validity Panel, supra note 19 at 155.

33. Validity Panel, supra note 19 at 160–62; Barland & Raskin, supra note 11 at 436–37.

34. People v. Kenny, 167 Misc. 51, 3 N.Y.S.2d 348 (Sup.Ct.Queens Cty.1938), is an exception to the general rule of exclusion. That case was soon undercut

Ridling,[35] a federal district court found that "the theory of the polygraph is sound" and "directly relevant" to the issue (perjury) before the court.[36] The court held that the results of a polygraph examination by a court-appointed expert would be admissible under certain conditions.[37] Polygraph results were also admitted in United States v. Zeiger.[38] The *Zeiger* court held that the "polygraph has been accepted by authorities in the field as being capable of producing highly probative evidence in a court of law when properly used by competent, experienced examiners."[39] Additionally, a state Superior Court in People v. Cutler[40] admitted polygraph evidence during a suppression hearing after finding that the "polygraph now enjoys general acceptance among authorities, including psychologists and researchers . . . as well as polygraph examiners."[41]

The incipient trend in favor of admissibility which these cases seemed to forecast never developed. *Zeiger* was reversed per curiam,[42] while *Ridling* and *Cutler* were never appealed, thus the opportunity for appellate approval was precluded. Furthermore, subsequent appellate cases have generally declined to follow the approach adopted in these cases.[43] Nevertheless, the polygraph has re-emerged as an important evidentiary issue and will remain one for the foreseeable future. Several noteworthy developments are considered in the following sections.

The Admissibility Standard. The courts adhering to *Frye* for judging the admissibility of polygraph evidence have divided over the interpretation of the general-acceptance test. According to *Frye*, psychology and physiology are the fields in which general acceptance must be achieved.[44] Several recent decisions have expanded the field to include polygraph examiners.[45] Such an expansion is significant, for general acceptance is almost assured if the opinions of examiners are considered. However, in United States v. Alexander,[46] the Eighth Circuit rejected this view: "Experts in neurology, psychiatry and physiology may offer needed enlightenment upon the premises of polygraphy. Polygraphists often lack extensive

---

by People v. Forte, 279 N.Y. 204, 18 N.E.2d 31 (1938), which reaffirmed the New York Court of Appeals' earlier position excluding the results of polygraph examinations. Trial court decisions admitting polygraph evidence have been reported. See Ferguson, Polygraph v. Outdated Precedent, 35 Tex.B.J. 531 (1972).

35. 350 F.Supp. 90 (E.D.Mich.1972).

36. Id. at 95.

37. Admissibility was conditioned on the selection of a court appointed expert and that expert's determination that the results indicated either truth or deception. If the appointed expert testified, the defendant's own expert would also be permitted to render an opinion. Id. at 99.

38. 350 F.Supp. 685 (D.D.C.1972), rev'd 475 F.2d 1280 (D.C.Cir.) (per curiam).

39. Id. at 690.

40. 12 Crim.L.Rep. 2133 (Cal.Super.Ct. November 6, 1972).

41. Id. at 2134. Polygraph evidence was also admitted in United States v. Hart, 344 F.Supp. 522 (E.D. N.Y.1971); State v. Watson, 115 N.J.Super. 213, 278 A.2d 543 (Hudson Cty.Ct.1971) (sentencing); Walther v. O'Connell, 72 Misc.2d 316, 339 N.Y.S.2d 386 (Queens Civ.Ct.1972) (civil case); Matter of Stenzel, 71 Misc.2d 719, 336 N.Y.S.2d 839 (Niagara Fam. Ct.1972) (civil case). In United States v. DeBetham, 348 F.Supp. 1377 (S.D.Cal.1972), aff'd 470 F.2d 1367 (9th Cir.), cert. denied 412 U.S. 907, 93 S.Ct. 2299, 36 L.Ed.2d 972 (1973), the court indicated that polygraph results would have been admitted if the court had not been bound by precedent.

42. 475 F.2d 1280 (D.C.Cir. 1972).

43. E. g., United States v. Alexander, 526 F.2d 161 (8th Cir. 1975); United States v. Cochran, 499 F.2d 380, 393 (5th Cir. 1974), cert. denied 419 U.S. 1124, 95 S.Ct. 810, 42 L.Ed.2d 825 (1975); United States v. Skeens, 494 F.2d 1050, 1053 (D.C.Cir. 1974); United States v. Gloria, 494 F.2d 477 (5th Cir. 1974), cert. denied 419 U.S. 995, 95 S.Ct. 306, 42 L.Ed.2d 267; United States v. Sockel, 478 F.2d 1134, 1136 (8th Cir. 1973).

44. 293 F. at 1014.

45. United States v. Zeiger, 350 F.Supp. 685, 689 (D.D.C.1972), rev'd 475 F.2d 1280 (D.C.Cir.); United States v. DeBetham, 348 F.Supp. 1377, 1388 (S.D. Cal.1972), aff'd 470 F.2d 1367 (9th Cir.), cert. denied 412 U.S. 907, 93 S.Ct. 2299, 36 L.Ed.2d 972 (1973); United States v. Wilson, 361 F.Supp. 510, 511 (D.Md. 1973).

46. 526 F.2d 161 (8th Cir. 1975).

training in these specialized sciences." [47] A related issue is the extent to which the widespread use of the polygraph in law enforcement, security, and industrial activities can be considered evidence of general acceptance. Some courts have accorded such evidence [48] considerable weight, while others have ignored it.[49]

Some cases have held that a trial court has discretion to reject or admit polygraph evidence. The leading case using this approach is Commonwealth v. A. Juvenile.[50] There the Supreme Judicial Court of Massachusetts held polygraph evidence admissible if: (1) The defendant agrees in advance to the admission of test results, irrespective of the outcome of the test; and (2) the trial judge conducts a "close and searching inquiry" into the qualifications of the examiner, the methods employed in the examination and the suitability of the defendant for testing." [51] Several federal courts have also indicated that a trial judge has discretion to admit polygraph evidence.[52] In United

States v. Marshall,[53] for example, the Ninth Circuit stated: "Because the polygraph has yet to gain general judicial recognition, the proponent of such evidence has the burden of laying a proper foundation showing the underlying scientific basis and reliability of the expert's testimony . . . . Even if a proper foundation can be laid, the district court can consider that introduction of polygraph evidence will inject a time-consuming, potentially prejudicial and, perhaps confusing collateral issue into the trial." [54]

Although in most cases trial courts have exercised this discretion by excluding polygraph results,[55] this approach represents a shift away from *Frye*. Under the emerging concept the trial judge performs traditional legal relevancy analysis, weighing the probative value of the evidence against the dangers of jury confusion, time, consumption and undue prejudice.

Admissibility by Stipulation. Courts have divided over the admissibility of polygraph evidence offered pursuant to a stipulation between the parties. Some courts maintain that an agreement to admit polygraph results "does nothing to enhance the reliability of such evidence" [56] and therefore hold that test results are excludable despite the stipulation.[57] An opposing line of authority admits stipulated results.[58] These

---

47. Id. at 164 n. 6. The position advanced in *Alexander* seems inconsistent with an earlier decision of the same court. United States v. Oliver, 525 F.2d 731, 736 (8th Cir. 1975) ("We believe the necessary foundation can be constructed through the testimony showing a sufficient degree of acceptance of the science of polygraphy by experienced practitioners in polygraphy and related experts.").

48. E. g., United States v. Zieger, 350 F.Supp. 685, 688 (D.D.C.1972), rev'd 475 F.2d 1280 (D.C.Cir.); United States v. DeBetham, 348 F.Supp. 1377, 1389 (S. D.Cal.1972), aff'd 470 F.2d 1367 (9th Cir.), cert. denied 412 U.S. 907, 93 S.Ct. 2299, 36 L.Ed.2d 972 (1973); United States v. Ridling, 350 F.Supp. 90 (E.D.Mich. 1972); People v. Cutler, 12 Crim.L.Rep. 2133 (Cal. Super.Ct.1972).

49. E. g., United States v. Alexander, 526 F.2d 161 (8th Cir. 1975).

50. 365 Mass. 421, 313 N.E.2d 120 (1974).

51. Id. at 124.

52. Two federal circuit courts of appeals have a line of cases supporting the position. Seventh Circuit: United States v. Infelice, 506 F.2d 1358, 1365 (7th Cir. 1974), cert. denied 419 U.S. 1107, 95 S.Ct. 778, 42 L.Ed.2d 802 (1975); United States v. Penick, 496 F.2d 1105 (7th Cir. 1974); United States v. Chastain, 435 F.2d 686, 687 (7th Cir. 1970). Ninth Circuit: United States v. Marshall, 526 F.2d 1349, 1360 (9th Cir. 1975); United States v. Watts, 502 F.2d 726

(9th Cir. 1974); United States v. Alvarez, 472 F.2d 111 (9th Cir. 1973), cert. denied 412 U.S. 921, 93 S.Ct. 2742, 37 L.Ed.2d 148; United States v. DeBetham, 470 F.2d 1367 (9th Cir. 1973), cert. denied 412 U.S. 907, 93 S.Ct. 2299, 36 L.Ed.2d 972.

53. 526 F.2d 1349 (9th Cir. 1975).

54. Id. at 1360.

55. For an exception, see United States v. Penick, 496 F.2d 1105 (7th Cir. 1974).

56. Romero v. State, 493 S.W.2d 206, 213 (Tex.Cr. App.1973).

57. Pulakis v. State, 476 P.2d 474 (Alaska 1970); State v. Corbin, 285 So.2d 234 (La.1973); Stone v. Earp, 331 Mich. 606, 50 N.W.2d 172 (1951); Romero v. State, 493 S.W.2d 206 (Tex.Cr.App.1973).

58. State v. Valdez, 91 Ariz. 274, 371 P.2d 894 (1962); People v. Houser, 85 Cal.App.2d 686, 193 P.2d 937 (1948); State v. Brown, 177 So.2d 532 (Fla.

latter cases recognize, at least implicitly, that the technique possesses some degree of validity.[59] Adoption of this approach has increased in recent years, a development which may represent an intermediate step toward full acceptance.

The leading stipulation case is State v. Valdez,[60] in which the Arizona Supreme Court held that stipulated results were admissible if: (1) The prosecutor, defense counsel, and defendant signed a written stipulation; (2) the trial judge accepted the expert's qualifications and test procedures; (3) the opposing party had an opportunity to cross-examine the expert on his or her qualifications, test procedures, and the limitations of the technique; and (4) the jury was instructed that the expert's opinion did not "prove or disprove any element of the crime" but "tends only to indicate that at the time of the examination defendant was not telling the truth," and that the responsibility for determining the weight of polygraph testimony fell within the province of the jury.[61]

Admissibility Under Constitutional Compulsion. Three distinct constitutional grounds have been offered to support the admissibility of polygraph evidence. In United States v. Hart,[62] a federal district court ruled that the results of a polygraph examination of a government witness which indicated deception were admissible under Brady v. Maryland.[63] The court interpreted *Brady* as requiring the disclosure of "any evidence which may tend to exculpate the defendant." [64] Because the government initially thought the polygraph sufficiently reliable to conduct an examination, it had the burden, according to the court, of explaining why the test results should now be excluded. *Hart* was followed in State v. Christopher.[65] *Christopher* held that the government's administration of the test constituted an implied stipulation to admit the test results.

A different constitutional argument was offered in State v. Dorsey.[66] In *Dorsey*, the New Mexico Supreme Court upheld the reversal of a trial court's exclusion of polygraph evidence on the basis of Chambers v. Mississippi; [67] the defendant had a due process right to present critical and reliable defense evidence. The reliability standard demanded under *Chambers* may be lower than a jurisdiction's admissibility standard. If so, the general-acceptance test may be unconstitutional as applied to evidence offered by a criminal defendant.

Finally, in State v. Sims,[68] an Ohio court found an implied right to present defense evidence in the compulsory process guarantee and concluded that that right compelled the admission of defense polygraph evidence when the prosecution case rests on weak eyewitness testimony.

App.1965); Cagle v. State, 132 Ga.App. 227, 207 S.E.2d 703 (1974) (dictum); State v. McNamara, 252 Iowa 19, 104 N.W.2d 568 (1960); State v. Lassley, 218 Kan. 758, 545 P.2d 383 (1976); State v. Fields, 434 S.W.2d 507 (Mo.1968); State v. McDavitt, 62 N.J. 36, 297 A.2d 849 (1972); State v. Lucero, 86 N.M. 686, 526 P.2d 1091 (1974); State v. Steele, 27 N.C. App. 496, 219 S.E.2d 540 (1975); State v. Towns, 35 Ohio App.2d 237, 301 N.E.2d 700, 64 O.O.2d 371 (1973); Jones v. State, 527 P.2d 169 (Okl.Cr.1974); State v. Bennett, 17 Or.App. 197, 521 P.2d 31 (1974); Commonwealth v. McKinley, 181 Pa.Super. 610, 123 A.2d 735 (1956) (dictum); State v. Jenkins, 523 P.2d 1232 (Utah 1974); State v. Ross, 7 Wash.App. 62, 497 P.2d 1343 (1971); State v. Stanislawaki, 62 Wis. 2d 730, 216 N.W.2d 8 (1974).

59. E. g., United States v. Oliver, 525 F.2d 731, 736 (8th Cir. 1975) cert. denied 424 U.S. 973, 96 S.Ct. 1477, 47 L.Ed.2d 743 (1976).

60. 91 Ariz. 274, 371 P.2d 894 (1962).

61. Id. at 900–01.

62. United States v. Hart, 344 F.Supp. 522 (E.D. N.Y.1971).

---

63. 373 U.S. 83, 83 S.Ct. 1194, 10 L.Ed.2d 215 (1963).

64. 344 F.Supp. at 523.

65. 134 N.J.Super. 263, 339 A.2d 239 (1975).

66. 87 N.M. 323, 532 P.2d 912, aff'd 88 N.M. 184, 539 P.2d 204 (1975).

67. 410 U.S. 284, 93 S.Ct. 1038, 35 L.Ed.2d 297 (1973). See also Galloway v. Brewer, 525 F.2d 369 (8th Cir. 1975) (*Chambers* requires that all materials used by a polygraph examiner be provided to defense counsel).

68. 52 Ohio Misc. 31, 369 N.E.2d 24, 6 O.O.3d 124 (1977).

PART 3
LEGAL RELEVANCE

CHAPTER 9
CHARACTER EVIDENCE

1. Introduction

Chapter 5 noted the distinction between logical and legal relevance. Even if evidence is logically relevant, the judge may conclude that the attendant probative dangers outweigh the probative value of the evidence. The primary probative dangers are prejudice, confusion, undue time consumption, and unfair surprise.[1] Evidence of the defendant's character illustrates the problems of legal relevance. To be sure, evidence of the defendant's criminal character is logically relevant. The rate of criminal recidivism in the United States is very high. The fact that the defendant has a criminal disposition, evidenced by past crimes and misdeeds, at least slightly increases the probability that the defendant is guilty of the charged offense. However, evidence of the defendant's bad character can pose all four probative dangers. First, the evidence is prejudicial in the extreme; and its introduction will create a serious risk that the jurors will find the defendant guilty, not because they believe he or she committed the crime charged, but rather because they think

the defendant is an anti-social person who should be in prison. Second, a dispute over the defendant's character can distract the jury from the central, historical question of whether at the time and place alleged, the defendant committed the *actus reus* with the requisite *mens rea*. Third, the dispute may be quite time-consuming if the defense calls numerous character witnesses and the prosecution answers with rebuttal witnesses. Finally, either side may surprise the other with evidence relating to an obscure incident in the defendant's background.

Before analyzing the rules governing character evidence, we must distinguish character evidence from two other types of evidence. The first is credibility evidence. Chapter 4 discusses credibility theories of admissibility. As it points out, the opponent may attack the witness's credibility by introducing character evidence.[2] Credibility character evidence relates to the specific character trait of truthfulness. The character evidence discussed in this chapter relates to either general, law-abiding character or

---

1. C. McCormick, Handbook of the Law of Evidence §§ 185–86 (2d ed. 1972).

2. Chapter 4, § 4, supra.

specific traits relevant to the charged offense, e. g., the character trait of peacefulness in a violent crime prosecution. There is another important distinction between the two types of evidence. Credibility character evidence is admissible for the limited purpose of impeachment; the jury considers the evidence solely to evaluate the witness's truthfulness. The character evidence discussed in this chapter is admitted as substantive evidence. Thus, the jury may consider evidence of the defendant's criminal disposition as proof that the defendant committed the charged offense.

The second type of evidence that must be distinguished is uncharged misconduct evidence. Chapter 10 discusses the uncharged misconduct theory of admissibility. Like credibility evidence, uncharged misconduct evidence differs radically from character evidence. The courts limit character evidence to reputation or opinion methods of proof: The witness testifies about the defendant's reputation as a law-abiding person or expresses his or her opinion whether the defendant is a law-abiding person. Under a character evidence theory, neither the prosecution nor the defense may use specific acts by the defendant to prove the defendant's character. In contrast, the uncharged misconduct theory permits the prosecution to introduce evidence of specific misdeeds by the defendant. Another major distinction is the use of the evidence. Under a character theory, the parties use the reputation and opinion evidence immediately as evidence of character and ultimately as circumstantial evidence of conduct. For example, the defense calls character witnesses to testify that the defendant is reputed to have a law-abiding disposition and, hence, is unlikely to have committed the charged crime. Under the uncharged misconduct theory, the prosecution must demonstrate that the evidence of the misconduct is logically relevant to prove some fact other than the defendant's criminal disposition. Uncharged misconduct evidence thus differs from character evidence in both the methods of proof and the underlying theory of logical relevance.

2. The Defendant's Character

Suggested Reading:

Michelson v. United States, 335 U.S. 469, 69 S.Ct. 213, 93 L.Ed. 168 (1948).

When the Defendant's Character Is In Issue. A person's character may be an ultimate, material fact in a criminal case. Suppose that a jurisdiction has a criminal libel statute but recognizes the affirmative defense of truth. The government may allege that the defendant violated the statute by writing that some third party is a violent person. The defendant raises the defense of truth. In this procedural setting, the third party's character is one of the ultimate, material facts of consequence in the case.

When the courts say that the defendant has placed his or her character in issue, they do not mean that the defendant's character has become one of the ultimate, material facts in issue. The defendant's character comes into issue in the limited sense that both sides may use the defendant's character as circumstantial evidence of his or her conduct at the time of the offense. The defendant asserts that he or she has a law-abiding character and that his or her character decreases the probability of the commission of the crime. In contrast, the prosecution argues that the defendant has a criminal disposition and that that disposition increases the probability of the commission of the crime. The ultimate, material fact in dispute is whether the defendant committed the crime, and both sides use the defendant's character as circumstantial evidence of the fact.

When does the defendant's character come into issue in the sense that the parties may use it as circumstantial evidence of the defendant's conduct? The general rule is that the prosecutor may not introduce evidence of the defendant's character until the defendant places his or her character in issue.[3] The defendant places his or her character in issue when he or she personally testifies about his or her character or when the inference from the testimony is that the defendant is testifying about his or her good character. For example, the defendant may testify about a reputation for peacefulness. A second means of putting the defendant's character in issue is asking a witness to testify concerning the defendant's quality and traits. The courts often refer to such witnesses as character witnesses.

Methods of Proving the Defendant's Character. *What types of character evidence may the defense present?* Simply stated, *the defendant may present timely reputation or opinion evidence about his or her general character or a relevant specific character trait.*

"Timely." When the parties introduce credibility evidence about a witness's truthfulness, the relevant point in time is the time of trial. We are interested in the witness's veracity at trial, and the character evidence offered must relate to the witness's character at that time.

However, when the parties use the defendant's character as circumstantial evidence of his or her conduct under the present theory of admissibility, the relevant point in time is the time when the defendant allegedly committed the crime.[4] We are interested in learning whether the defendant had a criminal or law-abiding disposition at that time.

Thus, reputation or opinion evidence must be confined to circumstances at the time, or at a reasonable time before, the commission of the alleged offense.[5] The evidence cannot relate to opinions formed or reputation acquired long after the commission of the offense. Evidence too remote in time is not logically relevant to the alleged offense.[6] The judge must consider the time element in determining the admissibility of the evidence. The prosecution is not limited to the time period put in issue by the defendant, but may introduce any character evidence having a reasonable relationship to the period the defendant's evidence relates to.[7]

"Reputation or Opinion Evidence." Three basic methods exist of proving the character of a defendant. The first is opinion evidence; the second, reputation evidence; and the third, evidence about specific acts of good or bad conduct. Under the first method the defendant may introduce evidence that acquaintances have formed an opinion that he or she is a law-abiding person or that he or she is an honest or peaceful citizen. To lay a foundation for such testimony, the witness must testify that (1) he or she has been acquainted with the defendant (2) for a sufficient period of time (3) to have formed an opinion about the defendant's character. Although opinion evidence has been described as an "irresponsible product of multiplied guesses and gossip",[8] it has also been lauded as colorful, warm, straightforward, and intimate.[9] In fact opinion evidence may be stronger than reputation evidence because

---

3. Fed.Evid.Rule 404(a)(1), 28 U.S.C.A.; Kan.Stat. Ann. 60–447.

4. Cf. United States v. Webb, 463 F.2d 1324 (5th Cir. 1972); United States v. Joines, 327 F.Supp. 253 (D.Del.1971).

5. Brooks v. State, 52 So.2d 616 (Miss.1951); Flournoy v. State, 34 Ala.App. 23, 37 So.2d 218 (1948).

6. United States v. Null, 415 F.2d 1178 (4th Cir. 1969).

7. People v. Willy, 301 Ill. 307, 133 N.E. 859 (1922); Commonwealth v. White, 271 Pa. 584, 115 A. 870 (1922); United States v. Kindler, 14 U.S.C.M.A. 394, 34 C.M.R. 174 (1964).

8. 7 Wigmore, Evidence § 1986 (3d ed. 1940).

9. Id. at §§ 1983, 1986.

with the former the witness who testifies is personally acquainted with the defendant and thus is probably able to testify about more traits than is a witness who gives reputation evidence. At present, however, only a minority of jurisdictions permits the parties to introduce opinion evidence of the defendant's character. Federal Rule of Evidence 608(a) illustrates the modern trend to admit opinion evidence.

While only a minority of courts permits the parties to use opinion evidence, all courts permit the parties to use the second method. The second method of proving the defendant's character is reputation evidence.[10] The defendant may introduce evidence that within the community, he or she has a reputation as a law-abiding person, or he or she may introduce evidence that the witness has heard nothing unfavorable about the defendant.[11] To lay a proper foundation, the witness must testify that he or she is a member of the community, has lived in the community long enough to know the defendant's reputation, and is acquainted with the defendant's reputation. A person testifying about the reputation of the defendant need not know the defendant personally, for the testimony is not based on personal knowledge but rather on hearsay—that is, on statements of others about the defendant's character within the community. Because reputation evidence is hearsay, it is admitted as an exception to the hearsay rule. Dean Wigmore has described the circumstantial probability of the reliability of reputation evidence: "Where the subject matter is one on which all or many members of the community have an opportunity of acquiring information and have also an interest or motive to obtain such knowledge, there is likely to be a constant, active and intelligent discussion in consequence that the resulting opinion, if a definite opinion does result, is like-

ly to be fairly trustworthy."[12] At first, the courts limited the evidence to reputation in the residential community where the defendant lived. The modern trend is to admit reputation within any large group the defendant is a member of. For example, the courts have admitted evidence of reputation within large business and social groups.

Although the courts unanimously approve of the second method of proving the defendant's character, they unanimously disapprove of the third method. Neither the defense nor the prosecution may use evidence of specific acts by the defendant to prove the defendant's character. The courts have permitted the use of specific acts to prove character only when character is an ultimate, material fact in the case. The courts do not sanction the third method when the parties are using character as circumstantial evidence of conduct.

"His or Her General Character or a Relevant Specific Character Trait." The defendant may place his or her general law-abiding character in issue or may introduce specific character traits if they are relevant to the offense charged.[13] The courts usually reject evidence of general good character, finding it unduly distracting, unnecessarily time consuming, and not pertinent to the offense charged.[14] Although limiting a witness's testimony to a particular relevant trait might be tactically difficult, such evidence has the greatest impact on a jury. In order for evidence about a specific character trait to be admissible, the trait must have a reasonable tendency to show that the defendant is not likely to have committed the specific offense charged. For example whenever a crime of violence is involved, the defendant's character trait for peacefulness

---

10. Fed.Evid.Rule 608(a), 28 U.S.C.A.

11. Michelson v. United States, 335 U.S. 469, 476, 69 S.Ct. 213, 218, 93 L.Ed. 168 (1948).

12. 7 Wigmore, Evidence §§ 1981 and 1986 (3d ed. 1940).

13. Fed.Evid.Rule 405(b), 28 U.S.C.A.

14. C. McCormick, Handbook of the Law of Evidence § 191 (2d ed. 1972). Some states have the contrary view. Id.

is relevant.[15] If the defendant is charged with larceny, the defendant's character traits for honesty and trustworthiness are relevant. In rare cases, character and credibility theories of admissibility can overlap; in a perjury prosecution, the defendant's character trait for truthfulness and veracity would be logically relevant.

Prosecution Rebuttal. After the defense places the defendant's character in issue, the prosecution may attack the defendant's character. The prosecution may cross-examine defense character witnesses and call prosecution character witnesses during its rebuttal.

It is well-settled that the prosecutor may ask a defense reputation witness whether he or she has heard negative rumors about the defendant's character.[16] What is the relevance of such a question? On the one hand, if the witness answers that he or she has not heard about the defendant's prior arrests and convictions, it is questionable whether that witness is familiar with the defendant's community reputation. On the other hand, if the witness testifies he or she has heard about prior arrests, convictions, and or misconduct, and nevertheless thinks that the defendant has a good reputation, the witness's standard of reputation is faulty. In either event, the answer is logically relevant to impeach the defense witness.

In many jurisdictions, the courts insist that when cross-examining the defense witness, the prosecutor use the formula, "Have you heard?" In Michelson v. United States,[17] the Supreme Court stated that that is the proper form of the question. Because of *Michelson*'s widespread influence, a number of cases have indicated that the question "Do you know?" is impermissible. However,

opposition to the "Do you know?" form of cross-examination is weakening. Under the Federal Rules of Evidence the form of the question is immaterial,[18] and several states have specifically approved that form.[19] Certainly, if the jurisdiction admits opinion evidence to prove the defendant's character and the defense witness testifies to his or her opinion, the judge should permit the prosecutor to test the opinion's basis and inquire whether the witness knows particular items of derogatory information about the defendant.

This type of cross-examination is obviously highly prejudicial to the defense. However, the defendant has two safeguards. First, the defendant is entitled to a limiting instruction that the witness's answers are admissible only for the limited purpose of impeaching the witness. Second, the prosecutor must have a good faith belief that the report or fact he or she questions about is true. When the prosecutor asks a bad-faith question concerning prior convictions, arrests, or misconduct, the courts agree that the question may be a ground for reversal. Because of the dangers involved in this type of cross-examination, the trial judge in his or her discretion may inquire into the basis of the question the prosecution proposes. This inquiry may be made out of the jury's hearing so that it will have no impact on the fact finders. Any assurances by the prosecutor would have to be based on reliable evidence—either on the witness's firsthand knowledge or on documents or other proof of the prior conviction, arrest, or misconduct.

In addition to cross-examining the defense character witnesses, the prosecution may call its own character witnesses in rebuttal. If the defendant calls witnesses to testify that he or she possesses a certain character trait, the prosecutor may call wit-

15. Id.

16. Michelson v. United States, 335 U.S. 469, 69 S.Ct. 213, 93 L.Ed. 168 (1948).

17. 335 U.S. 469, 69 S.Ct. 213, 93 L.Ed. 168 (1948).

18. Fed.Evid.Rules 405, 608, 28 U.S.C.A.

19. Potts v. State, 502 P.2d 1287 (Okl.Cr.1972); Webber v. State, 472 S.W.2d 136 (Tex.Cr.App.1971).

nesses to testify that the defendant lacks the trait. Of course, the derogatory information the prosecution elicits must generally relate to the same character trait the defense witnesses testified to.[20] However, there is authority that if the defendant places in issue his or her general, law-abiding character, the prosecution may attack either the defendant's general character or a relevant character trait.

3. The Character of Third Parties

Just as the courts have permitted the defense to use the defendant's character evidence as circumstantial proof of his or her conduct, in some types of cases the courts have permitted the defense to use the alleged victim's character as circumstantial proof of that person's conduct.

The Alleged Victim of a Violent Crime. Suppose that the government charges the defendant with an assault and the defendant pleads self-defense, contending that the alleged victim was in truth the aggressor. In this circumstance, the alleged victim's character trait for violence is logically relevant: If the alleged victim had a violent, aggressive disposition, that disposition increases the probability that the alleged victim was the aggressor. Almost all courts permit the defendant to use the alleged victim's character trait for violence in this fashion.[21] The courts traditionally accepted reputation evidence of the alleged victim's character trait, and the modern trend is to admit opinion evidence and evidence of specific aggressive acts as well.[22]

After the defense places the alleged victim's character trait for violence in issue, the prosecution may present evidence of the alleged victim's character trait of peaceful-

ness. In most jurisdictions, the prosecution may present such evidence only after the defense has presented reputation evidence, opinion evidence, or evidence of other aggressive acts by the alleged victim.[23] A few jurisdictions permit the prosecutor to present evidence of the alleged victim's peacefulness whenever the defense makes the contention that the alleged victim was in reality the aggressor.[24]

Suggested Reading:

Freeman v. State, 204 So.2d 842 (Miss.1967).

The Alleged Victim of a Sex Offense. Assume that the government charges the defendant with a non-consensual sex offense and the defendant alleges that the alleged victim consented to the sexual intercourse. Here the alleged victim's sexual disposition is arguably logically relevant: The fact that the alleged victim previously engaged in consensual intercourse slightly increases the probability that he or she consented on the occasion in question. Many courts permit the defendant to use the alleged victim's sexual disposition as circumstantial evidence of consent. In rape prosecutions, these courts have admitted reputation evidence of promiscuity, opinion evidence of promiscuity, and evidence of specific instances of consensual intercourse.[25] As in the case of violent crime prosecutions, after the defendant attacks the alleged victim's character, the prosecution may defend the character.

Feminists and prosecutors have often criticized the admissibility of this type of

---

20. United States v. Wooden, 420 F.2d 251 (D.C.Cir. 1969).

21. Freeman v. State, 204 So.2d 842 (Miss.1967).

22. West's Ann.Cal.Evid.Code § 1103(1).

23. Id. at § 1103(1)(b).

24. Fed.Evid.Rule 404(a)(2), 28 U.S.C.A.

25. People v. Walker, 150 Cal.App.2d 594, 310 P.2d 110 (1957); People v. Battilana, 52 Cal.App.2d 685, 126 P.2d 923 (1942); People v. Pantages, 212 Cal. 237, 297 P. 890 (1931); People v. Biescar, 97 Cal.App. 205, 275 P. 851 (1929).

evidence.[26] First, they argue that given modern sexual mores, the evidence has minimal probative value. Second, they contend that the widespread knowledge of the liberal admissibility of the evidence deters victims from reporting rapes.[27] Several courts and legislatures have responded to this criticism by restricting or altogether excluding evidence of the alleged victim's previous sexual history. Some states completely ban the evidence,[28] others restrict the evidence to proof of the alleged victim's sexual conduct with the defendant,[29] and still others prescribe a special procedure for litigating the admissibility of the evidence.[30] The defense bar has already raised the argument that these limitations on evidence of the alleged victim's previous sexual history are unconstitutional.[31]

Suggested Reading:

Commonwealth v. Crider, 240 Pa.Super. 403, 361 A.2d 352 (1976).

People v. Walker, 150 Cal.App.2d 594, 310 P.2d 110 (1957).

---

26. See, e. g., Note, The Victim in a Forcible Rape Case: A Feminist View, 11 Am.Crim.L.Rev. 335 (1973); Comment, Rape and Rape Laws: Sexism in Society and Law, 61 Calif.L.Rev. 919 (1973).

27. Id. at 921–22.

28. Commonwealth v. Crider, 240 Pa.Super. 403, 361 A.2d 352 (1976).

29. West's Ann.Cal.Evid.Code § 1103(2). See People v. Blackburn, 56 Cal.App.3d 685, 128 Cal.Rptr. 864 (1976).

30. Nev.Rev.Stat. 48.045 & 50.085.

31. People v. Blackburn, 56 Cal.App.3d 685, 128 Cal. Rptr. 864 (1976).

CHAPTER 10
UNCHARGED MISCONDUCT

1. Introduction

Like the character evidence analyzed in Chapter 9, evidence of uncharged misconduct poses serious legal relevance problems. The defendant already stands accused of one crime. The prosecution now proposes to introduce evidence of an uncharged misdeed on the theory that that evidence will somehow tend to prove the charged crime. Although the evidence may be relevant in a criminal case when the defendant is charged with committing similar crimes, such evidence is excluded "not because it has no appreciable probative value, but because it has too much." [1] The evidence is logically relevant but is excluded because of the probative danger the jury may attach undue weight to it.[2] Other factors militating against the admissibility of such evidence are waste of time, unfair surprise, and distraction from the main point in issue.[3]

2. The Substantive Doctrine

Suggested Reading:

State v. Manrique, 271 Or. 201, 531 P.2d 239 (1975).

United States v. Woods, 484 F.2d 127 (4th Cir. 1973).

The uncharged misconduct doctrine is that *if evidence of an act of uncharged misconduct by the defendant is logically relevant to prove a fact in issue other than the defendant's character and the prosecution need for the evidence outweighs the evidence's prejudicial character, the evidence is admissible.* In the words of Federal Rule of Evidence 404(b), "(e)vidence of other crimes, wrongs, or acts is not admissible to prove the character of a person in order to show that he acted in conformity therewith. It may, however, be admissible for other purposes, such as proof of motive, opportunity, intent, preparation, plan, knowl-

---

1. 1 Wigmore, Evidence § 194 (3d ed. 1940).

2. Michelson v. United States, 335 U.S. 469, 69 S.Ct. 213, 93 L.Ed. 168 (1948).

3. Id.; Fed.Evid. Rule 404(b), 28 U.S.C.A.

edge, identity, or absence of mistake or accident." [4]

"If evidence of an act". When the proponent offers evidence on a character theory, the evidence usually takes the form of reputation or opinion testimony.[5] Under that theory, the proponent may not use evidence of a specific act to establish the character of the person in question.[6] In this respect a character theory of admissibility differs radically from an uncharged misconduct theory. Under the latter theory, the proponent may not introduce reputation or opinion evidence. Rather the proponent must prove the defendant's commission of a specific act. The proponent may use live testimony, competent hearsay, or a conviction to prove the act.[7] A witness may testify that he or she saw the defendant commit the act; the proponent may introduce an exceptionally admissible hearsay declaration that the defendant committed the act;[8] or the proponent may introduce a properly authenticated judgment convicting the defendant of the commission of the act.

"Of uncharged misconduct". The courts and commentators have used various labels to describe this theory of admissibility. They sometimes refer to "other crimes" or "similar crimes" evidence. The authors suggest that the title, "uncharged misconduct," is more accurate.

In the first place "other crimes" is imprecise: The act proven under this theory need not amount to a crime. The theory applies broadly to evidence of "a crime, civil wrong, or other act." [9] The evidence of the

act is not admissible *because* the act is a crime; rather the act, which coincidentally might be a crime, is logically relevant to prove some fact in issue and admissible *in spite of the fact* that the act might be a crime. For instance, in a homicide prosecution, the prosecution's theory might be that the defendant killed the alleged victim out of jealously over a woman. To prove the defendant's motive, the prosecution could introduce evidence of the defendant's acts of intercourse with the woman. If all three persons, the defendant, the alleged victim, and the woman were unmarried, the acts of intercourse could be perfectly lawful. The evidence of the acts would be admissible, for the acts are logically relevant to prove the defendant's motive. If the woman had been the alleged victim's wife and the acts had amounted to criminal adultery, the acts would still be logically relevant and might be admissible despite the fact that in introducing evidence of the acts of intercourse, the prosecution was coincidentally injecting evidence of uncharged crimes into the case.

In the second place, "similar crimes" is imprecise: The act need not be similar to the charged crime to be admissible under this theory. The litmus test is relevance rather than similarity, and the act can be relevant even if it is in no way similar to the charged crime. Suppose that the defendant is charged with a robbery. The robber dropped a pistol at the crime scene. To identify the defendant as the robber, the prosecution could introduce evidence that the defendant had stolen that pistol a month prior to the robbery. The uncharged larceny and the charged robbery are hardly similar crimes. Yet, proof that the defendant was the thief of the pistol is logically relevant to prove that the defendant was also the robber. There are numerous instances when the uncharged act is logically relevant even though the act is not at all similar to the charged crime.

"By the defendant". The act is logically relevant in the case only if the defendant

---

4. Fed.Evid. Rule 404(b), 28 U.S.C.A.

5. Chapter 9, § 2, supra.

6. Id.

7. United States v. Adderly, 529 F.2d 1178 (5th Cir. 1976).

8. For an analysis of the exceptions to the hearsay rule, see Chapter 13, infra.

9. West's Ann.Cal.Evid.Code § 1101(b).

committed the act. Thus, the prosecution must establish the defendant's connection with the act. Because uncharged misconduct evidence is highly prejudicial, many courts have imposed a strict standard of proof for the defendant's commission of the act. Some courts require "substantial evidence"; [10] other courts demand "clear and convincing evidence"; [11] and still other courts insist upon "plain, clear, and conclusive evidence." [12]

How can the prosecution meet this standard of proof? No jurisdiction requires that the evidence of the other crime be in the form of a prior conviction proven beyond a reasonable doubt.[13] However, a conviction for the act is obviously reliable evidence that the defendant committed the act, and a properly authenticated judgment of conviction satisfies the standard of proof. Likewise, live testimony by an eyewitness to the act is satisfactory if the eyewitness's identification of the defendant is relatively positive. The most difficult problems arise when the prosecution's only proof of the defendant's commission of the act is hearsay evidence. Even if the hearsay is admissible as falling within an exception to the hearsay rule, its reliability may be suspect.

"Is logically relevant". Like all other admissible evidence, proof of an act of uncharged misconduct must be logically relevant. Chapter 5 discusses the general test for logical relevance: Does the evidence make the desired inference more probable than it would be without the evidence? [14] The next subsection discusses the types of inferences

which the prosecutor may use uncharged misconduct evidence to prove.

It should be emphasized that mere logical relevance does not ensure the admissibility of uncharged misconduct evidence. Logical relevance is a necessary but not a sufficient condition for admissibility. Uncharged misconduct evidence is so prejudicial that as a practical matter, the courts usually demand that the evidence have substantial logical relevance to be admissible.[15]

"To prove a fact in issue other than the defendant's character". The courts often say that uncharged misconduct evidence must possess "independent" relevance. By that expression, they mean that the evidence must be logically relevant to prove a fact other than the defendant's character. Restating the common-law doctrine, California Evidence Code § 1101(b) declares that the act of misconduct must be logically relevant to prove a fact "other than (the defendant's) disposition to commit such acts." [16] Federal Rule of Evidence 401(b) similarly prohibits the prosecutor from using the evidence "to prove the character of a person in order to show that he acted in conformity therewith." [17] Negatively, the prosecutor must articulate a theory of admissibility other than character evidence.

Affirmatively, what may the prosecutor offer the evidence to prove? *Traditionally, the courts have formulated the uncharged misconduct doctrine in terms of a general rule excluding all evidence of uncharged misconduct unless it falls within a few stated exceptions.* The traditional courts have recognized some of the following exceptions:

(1) To show knowledge. Knowledge is an essential element of such crimes as receiving stolen property, uttering forged in-

---

10. People v. Donnell, 52 Cal.App.3d 762, 125 Cal. Rptr. 310 (1975).

11. United States v. Moody, 530 F.2d 809 (8th Cir. 1976).

12. United States v. Gocke, 507 F.2d 820 (8th Cir. 1974).

13. Cunha v. Brewer, 511 F.2d 894 (8th Cir. 1975); Manning v. Rose, 507 F.2d 889 (6th Cir. 1974).

14. Chapter 5, § 1, supra.

15. C. McCormick, Handbook of the Law of Evidence § 190 (2d ed. 1972).

16. West's Ann.Cal.Evid.Code § 1101(b).

17. Fed.Evid. Rule 401(b), 28 U.S.C.A.

struments, and wrongful possession of drugs.[18] Suppose that the defendant stands accused of knowing, wrongful possession of heroin. The prosecution must prove that the defendant knew that the substance in his or her possession was heroin. To prove that, the prosecution could introduce evidence that during an attempted sale of the substance, the defendant had described the substance as heroin. Although the defendant is not charged with sale or attempted sale, the evidence is logically relevant to prove knowledge, an essential element of the crime the defendant is charged with.

(2) To show consciousness of guilt. Certain misconduct by the defendant, such as flight from arrest or escape from confinement, may also be evidence of guilt.[19]

(3) To establish motive. Jealousies,[20] hostilities, the desire for property,[21] avoiding arrest, or escaping from custody may be motives for murder.[22] Motive may serve to show malice or intent or to identify the defendant as the perpetrator of another crime. It is a widely known fact that persons illegally using drugs often resort to other crimes to finance their drug purchases. Some courts are now permitting the prosecution to introduce evidence of uncharged drug abuse to prove the pecuniary motive for property crimes such as larceny or burglary.[23]

(4) To rebut defenses such as mistake, inadvertence, accident, or entrapment. When the defendant is charged with the wrongful possession of heroin, and he or she defends on grounds of entrapment, claiming that the sale was solicited by a government agent, evidence that on prior, recent occasions the defendant had sold heroin is admissible to show that he or she was a willing participant.[24] Evidence of similar conduct is also admissible when the accused is charged with poisoning someone. The accused may expressly or impliedly defend on the ground that he or she accidentally administered the poison to the victim. Evidence that the accused had poisoned other people is admissible if the other acts are so similar to the act charged that they tend to demonstrate that the poisoning was not the result of accident or mistake.

(5) To show plan or design. While intent refers to the state of mind at the time of the commission of the offense charged, plan or design points to a mental condition antecedent to the performance of a certain act.[25] A plan or design might be shown through the prior preparatory acts such as the purchase of suitable instrumentalities of crime. This exception often dovetails with the next exception, proof of identity. Suppose that the defendant is charged with a burglary. It would be logically relevant for the prosecution to connect the defendant to a series of uncharged, similarly perpetrated burglaries in the same neighborhood. The uncharged misconduct evidence here would directly establish a plan and inferentially identify the defendant as the perpetrator of the charged burglary.

(6) To show identity. Similarities between the crime charged and crimes previously committed by the defendant may es-

---

18. United States v. Brand, 79 F.2d 605 (2d Cir. 1935); State v. Renslow, 211 Iowa 642, 230 N.W. 316 (1930) (receiving stolen property).

19. People v. Gambino, 12 Ill.2d 29, 145 N.E.2d 42 (1957) (escape while awaiting trial); People v. Spaulding, 309 Ill. 292, 141 N.E. 196 (1923) (killing only eyewitness).

20. Commonwealth v. Heller, 369 Pa. 457, 87 A.2d 287 (1952).

21. State v. Browman, 182 N.W. 823 (Iowa 1921).

22. State v. Simborski, 120 Conn. 624, 182 A. 221 (1936) (murder of officer seeking to arrest defendant); State v. Griffin, 218 Iowa 1301, 254 N.W. 841 (1934) (prior offense providing motive for escape from and murder of sheriff).

23. United States v. Lee, 509 F.2d 400 (D.C.Cir. 1974).

24. United States v. Bailey, 505 F.2d 417 (D.C.Cir. 1974).

25. 2 Wigmore, Evidence §§ 300, 304 (3d ed. 1940).

tablish identity.[26] Numerous similarities may establish identity: place, time, tools used, clothing worn, character of victims, and modus operandi.[27] A modus operandi similarity is particularly probative. The charged crime might have been committed with a very unique, distinctive modus. Evidence that the defendant had committed uncharged crimes with the same distinctive modus would tend to identify the defendant as the perpetrator of the charged crime. To invoke this exception, the prosecution must demonstrate a very high degree of similarity between the charged crime and the uncharged acts.

(7) To show intent. This exception may come into play when the defendant is charged with larceny of property. Evidence that the defendant subsequently sold the property is admissible to show that the defendant had the intent to permanently deprive the victim of the property.[28] Likewise if the defendant is charged with knowingly receiving stolen property, evidence that the defendant had on another occasion received stolen goods under suspicious circumstances is admissible to prove that on the occasion charged he or she knew the goods in question had been stolen.[29] This exception is quite similar to the first exception.

The traditional formulation of the doctrine is a general rule of exclusion with a few exceptions. A second test for the admissibility of uncharged misconduct is a rule of inclusion employed in a minority of jurisdictions.[30] *Under this test, evidence of uncharged misconduct is admissible if it is relevant to any issue other than the defendant's propensity to commit a crime.* In United States v. Woods,[31] the Court of Appeals for the Fourth Circuit rejected the view that the prosecution must fit its evidence into a pigeon hole exception such as knowledge or motive. The court asserted that "evidence of other offenses may be received, if relevant, for any purpose other than to show a mere propensity or disposition on the part of the defendant to commit the crime."[32] Federal Rule of Evidence 404(b) codifies the *Woods* court's view.[33] Under this view, the prosecutor can satisfy this element of the foundation by articulating any theory of relevance other than character evidence.

"And the prosecution need for the evidence". As previously stated, the evidence's mere logical relevance does not ensure its admissibility. As in other legal relevance areas, the judge must balance the evidence's probative value against the attendant probative dangers. More specifically, the judge must balance the prosecution's need for the uncharged misconduct evidence against the evidence's prejudicial character. The extent of the prosecution need for the evidence is a function of four factors.

The first factor is how relevant the evidence is to the fact the prosecution offers the evidence to prove. The courts often say that the evidence must possess "substantial" relevance. In large part, the evidence's relevance depends on how recently the defendant committed the act. The second factor

---

26. See, e. g., Holt v. United States, 342 F.2d 163, 166 (5th Cir. 1965); State v. Bock, 229 Minn. 449, 39 N.W.2d 887 (1949).

27. State v. Calvert, 211 Kan. 174, 505 P.2d 1110 (1973) (plea of guilty to wrongful possession of same type of weapon used in two robberies); State v. Vince, 305 So.2d 916 (La.1974) (evidence of other rapes within short time of charged rape in same general area involving same modus operandi). But see State v. Manrique, 271 Or. 201, 531 P.2d 239 (1975) (three prior sales of heroin inadmissible on an identity issue because crime was not committed by the use of any "novel means" or in any "particular manner"); C. McCormick, Handbook of the Law of Evidence § 157 (1954). "The device used must be so unusual and distinctive as to be like a signature."

28. 2 Wigmore Evidence §§ 324–25 (3d ed. 1940).

29. Id.

30. Note, Development in Evidence of Other Crimes, 7 J.Law Reform 535 (1974).

31. See, e. g., United States v. Woods, 484 F.2d 127 (4th Cir. 1973).

32. Id. at 134.

33. Fed.Evid. Rule 404(b), 28 U.S.C.A.

is whether the fact the prosecution proposes to use the evidence to prove is itself an essential element of the crime or merely an intermediate fact in the case.[34] Exceptions (1), (6), and (7) usually coincide with essential elements of the charged crime. On the other hand, exception (3), motive, is merely an intermediate fact increasing the probability that the defendant committed the act. The third factor is whether the prosecution has available, alternative evidence to prove the fact. Some courts have held that the trial judge should not admit uncharged misconduct evidence if the offense can be proven by other, less prejudicial evidence.[35] Also courts have stated that when the prosecution has proven its case to the "hilt," [36] other evidence of misconduct is inadmissible.

The fourth factor is whether there is a genuine dispute over the fact the prosecution proposes to introduce the evidence to prove. If the defense offers to formally stipulate to the fact or the defendant admits the fact on the witness stand, the prosecution no longer needs the uncharged misconduct evidence to prove the fact. The most troublesome situation is the situation in which the defense simply fails to present any evidence to affirmatively controvert a fact. When the defense does not, the defense will argue solely that the prosecution evidence is insufficient to establish guilt beyond a reasonable doubt. Is there a sufficient prosecution need for the evidence in this variation of the record? Most courts have answered that

question in the affirmative.[37] A few courts have required that the prosecutor demonstrate there is a genuine dispute over the fact even though the defense has not presented any evidence on the fact.[38] Even in these jurisdictions, the evidence would be admissible if the defense cross-examination of the prosecution witnesses amounted to an attack on the existence of the fact the prosecution is offering its evidence to prove.

"Outweighs the evidence's prejudicial character". As in any other legal relevance problem area, the trial judge must make a discretionary determination whether the evidence's probative value outweighs its prejudicial character. The trial judge uses a balancing test to make the determination. The test gives the judge great latitude and discretion. However, if (1) there is a clear showing of the defendant's commission of the act, (2) the act is substantially relevant to a fact other than the defendant's character, and (3) that fact is genuinely disputed on the record, the judge will probably admit the evidence. However, the absence of any of these three elements often leads to the exclusion of the evidence.

"The evidence is admissible". If the prosecution satisfies all the foundational elements for uncharged misconduct evidence, the evidence is admissible. The prosecution may introduce the evidence during the defendant's cross-examination or through extrinsic evidence. In fact, although evidence impeaching the defendant's credibility would be admissible only if the defendant testified, uncharged misconduct evidence can be admitted even if the defendant does not testify at trial; uncharged misconduct is substantive evidence relating to the material, historical facts in issue rather than a witness's credibility.

---

34. United States v. Kasouris, 474 F.2d 689, 691 (5th Cir. 1973) (The "exception [to other crime evidence rule] contemplates that the prior acts would in fact be similar. Similarity, being a matter of relevancy, is judged by the degree in which the prior act approaches near identity with the elements of the offense charged. There is no necessity for synonymity but there must be *substantial* relevancy."), citing proposed Fed.Evid. Rules 403–04, 28 U.S.C.A.

35. C. McCormick, Handbook of the Law of Evidence 453 n. 56 (2d ed. 1972).

36. People v. Perez, 42 Cal.App.3d 760, 117 Cal. Rptr. 195 (1974); Banks v. State, 298 So.2d 543 (Fla. App.1974) (no need for "over-kill").

---

37. Chesnutt, The Admissibility of Other Crimes in Texas, 50 Tex.L.Rev. 1409 (1972).

38. United States v. Mahar, 519 F.2d 1272 (6th Cir. 1975); People v. Guzman, 47 Cal.App.3d 380, 121 Cal.Rptr. 69 (1975).

The prosecution may introduce its evidence during its case-in-chief or its rebuttal. When the prosecution offers the evidence during its case-in-chief, the prosecutor may have a difficult time persuading the trial judge that there is a genuine need for the evidence; at this point, the judge might not know which facts the defense intends to dispute. Hence the prosecution's chances of successfully introducing the evidence are much better during its rebuttal.[39] At the conclusion of the defense case-in-chief, the judge knows which elements of the crime the defense is actually controverting.

---

39. United States v. King, 505 F.2d 602 (5th Cir. 1974).

PART 4
RELIABILITY AND PRIVILEGE

CHAPTER 11
THE BEST EVIDENCE RULE

1. Introduction

We may assume at this point that the proffered evidence is both logically and legally relevant; the evidence has a tendency to prove some fact in issue, and the probative value of the evidence outweighs any attendant dangers of prejudice, confusion, time consumption, or unfair surprise. However, several evidentiary doctrines remain which may result in the evidence's exclusion. As the introduction noted, the generic term for these doctrines which have the effect of excluding relevant evidence is *competence rule*.

The Introduction also pointed out that there are two types of competence rules. Chapters 11–26 discuss these competence rules. Some are based on extrinsic social policy. The privileges discussed in Chapter 14 exclude relevant evidence in order to protect certain confidential relationships such as attorney-client and physician-patient. Chapters 15–26 discuss constitutional competence rules. These rules exclude evidence obtained in violation of the fourth, fifth, and sixth amendments; the rules render the evidence incompetent in order to discourage future violations of constitutional guarantees. Other competence rules are based on the supposed unreliability of the excluded evidence. The best evidence and hearsay rules are the most obvious examples of this type of competence rule.

The underlying assumption of the best evidence rule is that secondary evidence of a document's contents is not as reliable as the document itself. The best evidence rule is a preferential rule: Although the primary evidence, the original document, is preferred, in some circumstances secondary evidence of the document's contents is admitted. The doctrine is that *if a document's terms are in issue, the proponent must (1) produce an original or duplicate original or (2) prove an excuse for non-production and offer an admissible type of secondary evidence.* The doctrine necessitates analysis of five issues: (1) What is a document for purposes of the rule? (2) When are the document's terms in issue? (3) What are the definitions of original and duplicate original? (4) What is considered an adequate excuse for non-production? (5) What are the acceptable types of secondary evidence?

2. Definition of Document

Suggested Reading:

United States v. Gavic, 520 F.2d 1346 (8th Cir. 1975).

People v. Kirk, 43 Cal.App.3d 921, 117 Cal.Rptr. 345 (1974).

The term *best evidence rule* is misleadingly broad, for it suggests a general requirement that the proponent produce the best available evidence. The proponent's failure to offer the best available evidence may create an inference that that evidence is unfavorable;[1] however there is no general requirement that the proponent produce or account for the best available evidence. For example, a government expert testifying about a thin layer chromatography test to identify a drug may give oral testimony about the glass plates used in the experiment.[2] The prosecution need not produce the plates in the courtroom. Similarly, in a burglary prosecution, a police officer may give oral testimony about burglary tools found in the defendant's apartment. Although introducing the burglary implements would probably be sound trial strategy, the best evidence rule does not require that the prosecutor introduce the physical evidence. However, the courts apply the special preferential rule to documents because usually a greater need for precise detail exists in testimony about a document than it does in testimony about other physical evidence. Thus a more accurate label for the doctrine is *the original document rule*, for it applies only to articles in the nature of documents. When the court is hearing testimony about a document's contents, precision and detail are necessary; the outcome of a forgery prosecution may turn on whether the defendant used a certain word on a check, and the result in a threat prosecution could similarly depend on the exact language the defendant used in a letter.

The problem is definitional: How is *document* defined for purposes of the best evidence rule? Conventional writings certainly fall within the definition. Federal Evidence Rule 1001(1), which codifies the

---

1. See, e. g., United States v. Freeman, 514 F.2d 1314 (D.C.Cir. 1975): Comment, Drawing An Inference From the Failure to Produce a Knowledgeable Witness: Evidentiary and Constitutional Considerations, 61 Calif.L.Rev. 1422 (1973).

2. United States v. Gavic, 520 F.2d 1346 (8th Cir. 1975).

modern common-law view,[3] contains a broad definition of writing—"letters, words, or numbers, or their equivalent, set down by handwriting, typewriting, printing, photo-stating, photographing, magnetic impulse, mechanical or electronic recording, or other form of data compilation." The definition thus includes records prepared by handwriting, typewriting, printing, and by any other mechanical means of reproduction.

The courts have divided on the question of whether the best evidence rule applies to an inscribed piece of personal property or "chattel". For example, in order to connect the defendant with premises where drugs were found, the prosecutor may attempt to introduce testimony that a piece of luggage inscribed with the defendant's name was also found on the premises. If the court applies the best evidence rule here, the prosecutor must produce or account for the piece of luggage; the inscribed luggage would be the primary evidence while oral testimony about the inscription would be secondary evidence. However, while some jurisdictions extend the rule to inscribed chattels,[4] others narrowly limit the rule's scope to conventional writings.[5] Still other courts hold that the rule's application is within the trial judge's discretion.[6] In exercising this discretion, the judge should consider these factors: the difficulty of producing the chattel in the courtroom, the complexity of the inscription, and the importance of the inscription to the case.

The next question is whether the rule applies to sound recordings. Suppose that in a conspiracy prosecution, the government attempts to introduce the transcript of an intercepted, recorded conversation between two alleged conspirators. Does the original tape recording constitute a document? The prevailing view is that the best evidence rule applies and that the proponent must produce or account for the tape recording.[7] Like a conventional writing, a tape is simply a means of recording statements; thus the prevailing view is that a tape is indistinguishable from a writing in terms of the need for precise detail.[8]

The final issue is the application of the rule to photographs. Assume that the government is prosecuting the defendant for knowingly distributing pornographic photographs to minors. May the defense object if the police officer orally describes the photographs without actually producing them? Some courts continue to stubbornly exclude photographs from the definition of document. However, the emerging view is that a photograph constitutes a document,[9] and Federal Evidence Rule 1001(2) expressly extends the best evidence rule to photographs.[10]

3. When Terms Are In Issue

Suggested Reading:

United States v. Gonzales-Benitez, 537 F.2d 1051 (9th Cir. 1976).

Hill v. State, 201 Ga. 300, 39 S.E.2d 675 (1946).

3. C. McCormick, Handbook of the Law of Evidence § 232 (2d ed. 1972).

4. Uniform Rule of Evidence 1(13) (1953).

5. West's Ann.Cal.Evid.Code § 1500 applies the best evidence rule to any "writing." West's Ann.Cal. Evid.Code § 250 defines "writing" as including "any tangible thing." In B. Witkin, California Evidence § 689 (2d ed. 1966), the author argues that construed together, these statutes make the rule's application to inscribed chattels mandatory in California.

6. Quillen v. Commonwealth, 284 Ky. 792, 145 S.W. 2d 1048 (1940); State v. Lewark, 106 Kan. 184, 186 P. 1002 (1920).

7. People v. Kirk, 43 Cal.App.3d 921, 117 Cal.Rptr. 345 (1974); People v. King, 101 Cal.App.2d 500, 225 P.2d 950 (1950).

8. Id.

9. Comment, Contents of Writings, Recordings, and Photographs, 27 Ark.L.Rev. 357, 366–67 (1973).

10. Fed.Evid.Rule 1001(2), 28 U.S.C.A.

If the court concludes that the article involved is a document, the court proceeds to the next step in analysis—deciding whether the document's terms or contents are in issue. A witness may refer to a document's existence, execution, location, size, or length without triggering the best evidence rule. Like the first step in analysis, this decision poses a definitional problem. What does *in issue* mean? Generally speaking, the courts have defined the expression as including two fact situations.

In the first situation, the facts of consequence in the case automatically place the document's terms in issue. Here the content of the document is one of the material facts in issue. In the pornographic photograph prosecution, one of the historical facts in issue is the content of the photograph. Thus the substantive law and pleadings automatically trigger the best evidence rule.

This situation is distinguishable from one in which the document is convenient evidence of a fact which, however, exists independently of a document. For example, in a bigamy prosecution, one of the facts of consequence is that the defendant entered into a second marriage. An eyewitness to the marriage could orally testify about the marriage ceremony; although the marriage certificate would be convenient documentary evidence of the marriage, the facts of consequence do not automatically place the certificate's terms in issue.[11] A simple test which determines if the fact is independent is the inquiry whether an eyewitness could have observed the fact or event without examining the document.[12] If an eyewitness could have done so, the best evidence rule is not automatically triggered. Thus, if a police officer hears the defendant make an oral confession that is subsequently transcribed, the officer's testimony about the oral confession would not be subject to a best evidence objection.[13] The officer learned of the confession without ever inspecting the transcript.

In the second situation, the witness expressly or impliedly refers to a document's contents. Suppose that in the bigamy prosecution, the government cannot find any eyewitness to the second marriage. The prosecutor might then be forced to use the marriage certificate. If in the course of testifying, the county clerk expressly referred to the marriage certificate's contents, the reference would trigger the best evidence rule. Before eliciting the oral testimony, the prosecutor would have to produce or account for the certificate. An implied reference also invokes the best evidence rule. Suppose that on direct examination, the witness testifies to the marriage. On cross, the witness admits that the testimony on direct was based on an examination of the marriage certificate rather than on observation of the marriage ceremony. The direct testimony would be subject to a motion to strike on best evidence grounds.[14] In this situation, the facts of consequence do not automatically place the document's terms in issue, for the prosecution could prove the fact of the second marriage without resorting to the certificate. However, if the witness's testimony is expressly or impliedly based on the certificate, the certificate's terms come into issue.

Although the courts usually apply the best evidence rule in these two situations, the evidence may be removed from the purview of the best evidence rule by the collateral fact rule. This latter rule applies when

---

11. 2 Wharton, Criminal Evidence § 604 (12th ed. 1955).

12. Id. at § 607.

13. Hill v. State, 201 Ga. 300, 39 S.E.2d 675 (1946).

14. Since the question itself was proper, an objection would have been inappropriate. A motion to strike is the proper procedural device for attacking an improper answer.

the document's terms are technically in issue but the document relates to a collateral issue in the case. Federal Evidence Rule 1004(4) states that the collateral fact rule renders the best evidence rule inapplicable to a document if the document "is not closely related to a controlling issue." [15] For example, the prosecutor could use a copy of a prior inconsistent writing to impeach a witness; a prior inconsistent writing relates to credibility, a collateral fact, rather than to the ultimate facts on the merits. Or, to prove the defendant's standing to challenge the search of a house, the defense counsel could use a copy of the deed; the deed relates to the preliminary issue of standing rather than to the ultimate question of guilt or innocence.

Although some courts attempt to consistently apply an inflexible definition of collateral in such situations, most courts use the expression collateral fact rule as the shorthand label to describe a judgmental decision on the question of whether the document's terms are important enough to justify requiring the proponent to put forth the effort and expense of producing the document.[16] In making this judgmental decision, the courts balance three factors: the importance of the document to the pivotal issues in the case, the complexity of the document's contents, and the existence of a genuine dispute over the document's contents.[17] The less important the issue, the simpler the document, and the more frivolous the dispute, the more likely the judge is to permit the proponent to use secondary evidence. In the words of one state statute, the judge may admit secondary evidence if he or she concludes that "the writing is not closely related to the controlling issues and it would be inexpedient to require its production." [18]

---

15. Fed.Evid.Rule 1004(4), 28 U.S.C.A.

16. C. McCormick, Handbook of the Law of Evidence § 234 (2d ed. 1972).

17. Id.

18. West's Ann.Cal.Evid.Code § 1504.

4. Definition of "Original" and "Duplicate Original"

Suggested Reading:

United States v. Morgan, 555 F.2d 238 (9th Cir. 1977).

People v. Fujita, 43 Cal.App.3d 454, 117 Cal.Rptr. 757 (1974).

If the document's terms are in issue, the common law prefers that the proponent introduce an original or a duplicate original counterpart. In accordance with this preference, before resorting to secondary evidence, the proponent has to prove an adequate reason for the non-production of the original and any duplicates. Thus defining *original* and *duplicate original* becomes critically important.

The Definition of "Original". At common law, the original document is usually the first writing executed, the first tape made, or the negative of the photograph. However, it must be emphasized that the test is legal rather than chronological; the original is the document which has legal significance under the substantive law and pleadings. Suppose that the defendant is charged with sending an unlawful threat through the mails. In the hope of reducing the risk that the police laboratory will be able to trace the letter to him, the defendant makes a photostatic copy of the typed letter and mails the copy rather than the original. Although chronologically the typed letter is the original, the copy is the legally significant document: It is the document the defendant unlawfully sent through the mail. Using the legal test, the court would treat the photostatic copy as the original document.

The Definition of "Duplicate Original" or "Counterpart". *In General.* At first, the common law treated only contemporaneously prepared documents as duplicate originals. In order to qualify a document as a duplicate original, the proponent had to prove that: (1) The document was an exact copy of the original; (2) the parties executed the document with the same formalities as they used with the original; (3) the parties intended that the document would have the same legal effect as the original; and (4) the parties executed the document at the same time as the original, that is, simultaneously or at least in the same transaction.[19] In a commercial fraud prosecution, it might be relevant to prove the terms of a written contract between the defendant and the victim alleged in the indictment or information. Suppose that when the parties executed the contract, the original ribbon copy was on top of a carbon copy with carbon paper between. When the parties signed the ribbon copy in ink, the signatures were impressed on the carbon copy. The defendant retained the original typed copy, and the victim received the carbon copy. The carbon copy would qualify as a duplicate original, and the prosecutor could routinely introduce the victim's retained copy to prove the terms of the written contract.

Although contemporaneously prepared copies qualified at common law as duplicate originals, the general view was and still is that subsequently prepared copies do not.[20] Subsequently prepared copies are secondary evidence. The common-law courts treat subsequently prepared copies as secondary evidence even when a copy is reproduced by mechanical means and there is little likelihood of human error in duplication.[21]

At common law, the courts made some inroads into the general view treating subsequently prepared copies as secondary evidence. The first inroad related to photographs; courts treat all prints prepared from the original negative as duplicate originals.[22] In a few jurisdictions, the courts modified the general view to treat re-recordings [23] and even official transcripts of recordings [24] as duplicate originals.

Many legislatures have since intervened and relaxed the definition of *duplicate original* for business and public records. Most jurisdictions have now enacted some variation of the Uniform Photographic Copies of Business and Public Records as Evidence Act. One version of the Act reads: "A photostatic, microfilm, microcard, miniature photographic or other photographic copy or reproduction, or an enlargement thereof, of a writing is as admissible as the writing itself if such copy or reproduction was made and preserved as a part of the records of a business . . . in the regular course of such business." [25] Under the Act, a subsequently prepared copy qualifies as a duplicate original if the copy was prepared and preserved in the regular course of business.

The Federal Rules of Evidence represent a step beyond the Uniform Act. Rule 1001(3) contains very broad definitions of *original* and *duplicate*. The definition of *duplicate* is broad enough to include copies subsequently prepared by mechanical means of reproduction. With some exceptions, under the Federal Rules a duplicate is as admissible as an original.

19. C. McCormick, Handbook of the Law of Evidence § 235 (2d ed. 1972).

20. Id. at § 236.

21. Id.

22. Comment, Contents of Writings, Recordings, and Photographs, 27 Ark.L.Rev. 357, 366 (1973).

23. People v. Fujita, 43 Cal.App.3d 454, 117 Cal. Rptr. 757 (1974).

24. Id.; State v. McMullan, 223 La. 629, 66 So.2d 574 (1953).

25. West's Ann.Cal.Evid.Code § 1550.

5. Excuse for Non-Production

Suggested Reading:

Dean v. State, 240 Ala. 8, 197 So. 53 (1940).

McDonald v. United States, 89 F.2d 128 (8th Cir. 1937).

If the document's terms are in issue, the law prefers that the proponent introduce an original or duplicate original. However, this preference is not absolute; the proponent may offer secondary evidence if the proponent establishes an adequate excuse for the non-production of the originals and duplicates. The proponent must excuse the non-production of all the originals and duplicates.[26] The question then arises what the courts consider an adequate excuse for non-production. The following is a discussion of the most common excuses.

The Proponent Lost the Original or Duplicate. The proponent's loss of the original or duplicate is an adequate excuse for non-production.[27] The proponent ordinarily proves an unsuccessful search for the document as circumstantial evidence of its loss. In most jurisdictions the trial judge makes a discretionary determination whether the search was sufficiently diligent. In a few jurisdictions the courts have developed mechanical rules to determine whether the search was adequate; these jurisdictions always require that the proponent search the last known depository of the document or contact the last known custodian of the document.[28]

The Proponent Destroyed the Original or Duplicate Without Fraudulent Intent. The older cases indicated that the proponent could not introduce secondary evidence if the proponent had intentionally destroyed the original or duplicate. Modern courts realize that that standard is too harsh. Businesses often intentionally destroy their original records as part of their records retention and destruction policy; to conserve space, they destroy the originals and retain microcard, microfilm, or computerized records. The current test is whether the proponent destroyed the original or duplicate without fraudulent intent.[29] If the proponent did not destroy the documents for the specific purpose of making them unavailable at trial, the proponent may resort to secondary evidence.

The Original or Duplicate Is Bulky or Voluminous. Suppose that the government has charged a sole proprietor with willful tax evasion during a two-year period. The defendant does a large volume of business, and the relevant pages in the business' journal, ledgers, and account books number 2,000. A government accountant reviews the 2,000 pages and is prepared to testify that the records reflect $400,000 in taxable income while the defendant reported only $250,000. How may the prosecutor present the accountant's evidence to the jury in usable fashion? Obviously, it would be impractical to present the 2,000 pages of material to the jurors. In this situation, the law excuses the non-production of the original records and permits the auditor to give secondary oral testimony about the records' contents. The proponent of the secondary evidence must show that: (1) The originals or duplicates would be admissible; (2) the originals or duplicates are too numerous or too voluminous to conveniently introduce during trial; (3) the fact the proponent is

---

26. C. McCormick, Handbook of the Law of Evidence § 235 (2d ed. 1972).

27. Fed.Evid.Rule 1004(1), 28 U.S.C.A.; West's Ann.Cal.Evid.Code § 1501.

28. 2 Jones, Evidence § 7.13 (1972).

29. McDonald v. United States, 89 F.2d 128 (8th Cir. 1937).

attempting to prove is a summary of the records' contents, for example, the total taxable income reflected in the records; (4) the proponent granted the opponent access to the originals or duplicates for inspection; and (5) the witness personally reviewed all the records or was a member of a team of experts who reviewed the records.[30] In addition the judge has discretion to require that the originals or duplicates be produced at trial.[31]

The Original or Duplicate Is Physically Present in the Courtroom for Inspection. Suppose that the government has charged the defendant with the murder of a child. The prosecutor wants to introduce a photograph of the child. The parents have a beautiful photograph but are reluctant to part with it. The prosecutor is in a dilemma. On the one hand, the prosecutor does not want to upset the bereaved parents. On the other hand, the prosecutor fears a best evidence objection if he or she attempts to introduce a reprint from the parents' photograph. To resolve this dilemma, some jurisdictions permit the proponent to introduce secondary evidence so long as the original is in the courtroom and available for inspection.[32] The requirement of the original's presence in the courtroom serves to reduce the risk that the secondary evidence is unreliable; if a discrepancy exists between the original and the secondary evidence, the opponent can immediately point out the discrepancy to the jury.

After Notice to Produce, the Opponent Fails to Produce the Original or Duplicate in His or Her Possession. There are three conditions to invoking this excuse for nonproduction. First, the proponent must prove that the opponent has possession or control of the original or duplicate. The proponent may trace the document to the opponent by circumstantial evidence. Proving that the opponent has actual, physical possession of the document is unnecessary. It is sufficient to prove that the opponent has practical control over the document; for example, the proponent may trace the document to the opponent's employee or relative.

Second, the proponent must give the opponent notice to produce the original or duplicate at trial. As a precaution, the proponent should give the opponent express, written notice. This notice should include a reasonably specific description of the document and should request that the opponent bring the document to trial. The proponent should serve the notice on the opponent or the opponent's attorney sufficiently in advance of trial to give the opponent a fair opportunity to locate the document and bring it to trial.

The notice need not be express, and the courts sometimes find implied notice to the opponent. The court may draw the implication from the pleadings or the discovery proceedings in the case. For instance, the indictment might allege that a certain book the defendant held for sale is pornographic. This allegation impliedly gives the defendant notice that the book will be needed at trial. In a tax evasion prosecution, the government might send its accountants to the defendant's business premises to inspect the defendant's records. This inspection impliedly gives the defendant notice that the records will probably be needed at trial.

Third, the opponent fails to produce the original or duplicate at trial. If all conditions concur, the proponent may use secondary evidence. The opponent cannot complain because he or she has the original and has failed to produce it. In some criminal cases, the courts have eliminated the requirement that the prosecution give the defense notice to produce.[33] These courts argue that the

---

30. Fed.Evid.Rule 1006, 28 U.S.C.A.; West's Ann. Cal.Evid.Code § 1509.

31. Fed.Evid.Rule 1006, 28 U.S.C.A.

32. West's Ann.Cal.Evid.Code § 1510.

---

33. Lisansky v. United States, 31 F.2d 846 (4th Cir. 1929); Dean v. State, 240 Ala. 8, 197 So. 53 (1940).

notice would infringe upon the defendant's privilege against self-incrimination. This argument is tenable when the prosecutor demands production in the jury's presence, a demand which itself may be error.[34] However, the most expedient solution is (1) to require the prosecution to give the defense pretrial notice to produce but (2) to forbid the prosecution from demanding production in the jury's presence.[35]

The Opponent Admits the Contents of the Original or Duplicate. Some jurisdictions do not recognize this excuse. For example, the California statutes do not mention it, and California's statutory list of excuses seems to be exclusive.[36]

At the other extreme, some courts apply this excuse to any admission, written or oral, even if the opponent denies making the admission. So long as any credible evidence exists of an admission of the document's contents, the proponent may use the admission as secondary evidence of the document's contents. Other courts recognizing this excuse limit it to certain types of admissions. These courts believe that it is unfair to admit an oral admission the opponent denies making. They generally limit the excuse to the types of admissions listed in Federal Evidence Rule 1007: in-court admissions, admissions during deposition hearings, and written admissions.[37]

A Third Party Has the Original or Duplicate Beyond the Reach of the Court's Compulsory Process. The courts are in general agreement that if the third party possessing the document is within the reach of the court's compulsory process, the proponent must exhaust the court's process in an attempt to obtain the document. Thus, the proponent would have to try to depose the third party and to serve a subpoena duces tecum incident to the deposition.

However, the courts divide when the third party is beyond the territorial reach of the court's process. Federal Evidence Rule 1004(2) subscribes to the view that the mere presence of the document beyond the territorial reach of process is an excuse.[38] The proponent must exhaust all available compulsory process, including "subpoena duces tecum as an incident to the taking of a deposition in another jurisdiction," [39] but "no further showing is required." [40] Some state statutes require a further showing.[41] One such statute provides that the proponent must show that no "other available means" exist of obtaining the document.[42] Thus, the proponent would have (1) to attempt to contact the third party and induce the third party to voluntarily produce the document at trial or (2) to demonstrate that any attempt would be futile or prohibitively inconvenient.

The Original or Duplicate Is In Official Custody. There are several substantial reasons why official agencies are reluctant to release original official records in their possession. Even a temporary release may be inconvenient to other people who want to use the document, and the release creates a risk of losing the document. Finally, some statutes and regulations prohibit the official custodian from releasing the original document. For these reasons, the courts have been willing to treat a document's official custody as

---

34. McKnight v. United States, 115 F. 972 (6th Cir. 1902); Powell v. Commonwealth, 167 Va. 558, 189 S.E. 433 (1937).

35. West's Ann.Cal.Evid.Code § 1503(a); C. McCormick, Handbook of the Law of Evidence § 239 (2d ed. 1972).

36. West's Ann.Cal.Evid.Code § 1500 sets out the California best evidence rule. In pertinent part, the statute provides that secondary evidence is inadmissible "(e)xcept as otherwise provided by statute."

37. Fed.Evid.Rule 1007, 28 U.S.C.A.

38. Fed.Evid.Rule 1004(2), 28 U.S.C.A.

39. Id. at Advisory Committee Note.

40. Id.

41. West's Ann.Cal.Evid.Code § 1502.

42. Id.

an adequate excuse for its non-production. At first, the courts applied the excuse only to documents which could not legally be released from official custody. Although the case for reognizing an excuse is certainly clearest when such documents are concerned, the first two reasons apply to any document in official custody. Most courts now extend the excuse to any official document in official custody.[43] The trend is to extend the excuse to all documents in official custody—even private, original documents which have been deposited in a government office.[44]

6. Acceptable Secondary Evidence

Suggested Reading:

United States v. Gerhart, 538 F.2d 807 (8th Cir. 1976).

The Types of Secondary Evidence. If the proponent establishes an excuse for the non-production of all originals and duplicate originals, the proponent may introduce secondary evidence. However, there are limitations on the types of acceptabie secondary evidence.

The first type of secondary evidence is a written copy. Ordinarily the copy must be complete and verbatim. However, in the case of official records, the custodian sometimes prepares an extract. This extract is acceptable so long as it sets out part of the original verbatim rather than simply summarizing the original's legal effect. To establish the verbatim character of the copy, the proponent must comply with the authentication rules discussed in Chapter 6.

The second type of secondary evidence is oral recollection testimony. The witness testifies that he or she read the original and can recollect its substance. On the one hand, the witness need not recall the precise wording of the original. In an extortion prosecution, the witness could testify even if he or she could not quote the threatening letter they had previously read. On the other hand, the witness may not simply describe the legal effect of the document. If the witness had previously read the defendant's written confession, the witness may not say simply that the document was a full confession to all the essential elements of larceny. Rather the witness must be able to relate the substance of the document's contents.

Degrees of Secondary Evidence. The majority American rule is that there are degrees of secondary evidence.[45] For example, a written copy is preferred to oral recollection testimony. A court following the majority view would require the proponent to produce an existing copy or prove an excuse for its non-production. Some statutes modify the majority rule by limiting the preference for copies to copies in the proponent's possession. The wording of one statute illustrates this modification: "If the proponent does not have in his possession or under his control a copy of a writing . . ., other secondary evidence of the content of the writing is not made inadmissible by the best evidence rule." [46]

The minority English view is that there are no degrees of secondary evidence. Oral recollection testimony is as admissible as a written copy, and the proponent may present oral recollection testimony without proving an excuse for the non-production of any copies. The Advisory Committee's Note to Federal Evidence Rule 1004 states that "[t]he rule recognizes no 'degrees' of sec-

---

43. Fed.Evid.Rule 1005, 28 U.S.C.A.

44. West's Ann.Cal.Evid.Code § 1506.

45. C. McCormick, Handbook of the Law of Evidence § 241 (2d ed. 1972).

46. West's Ann.Cal.Evid.Code § 1505.

ondary evidence." [47] Although the minority jurisdictions generally do not recognize degrees of secondary evidence, these jurisdictions have carved out one exception to that general norm. Even these jurisdictions prefer a written, attested copy of an official record over oral recollection testimony of the official record's contents. Federal Evidence Rule 1005 states this preference: "The contents of an official record, or of a document authorized to be recorded or filed and actually recorded or filed, including data compilations in any form, if otherwise admissible, may be proved by copy, certified as correct in accordance with rule 902 or testified to be correct by a witness who has compared it with the original. If a copy which complies with the foregoing cannot be obtained by the exercise of reasonable diligence, then other evidence of the contents may be given." [48]

---

47. Advisory Committee Note, Fed.Evid.Rule 1004, 28 U.S.C.A.

48. Fed.Evid.Rule 1005, 28 U.S.C.A. See also West's Ann.Cal.Evid.Code § 1508.

CHAPTER 12
THE HEARSAY RULE

1. Reasons for the Hearsay Rule

Suggested Reading:

Barber v. Page, 390 U.S. 719, 88 S.Ct. 1318, 20 L.Ed.2d 255 (1968).

When Witness A swears to seeing B rob a bank, A's testimony is obviously logically relevant in B's trial on charges of robbery. If a proper foundation showing that A is competent has been laid, the court will admit A's testimony as proof of B's guilt. Assume, however, that A is unable or unwilling to testify at trial, but that A previously told C about the robbery. Should C be allowed to testify at trial as to what A said about B? This is the question posed by the hearsay doctrine. C's repetition of A's statement is an example of hearsay: an in-court report of an out-of-court statement which is offered to prove the truth of the statement. The answer to the question posed by C's testimony depends on an analysis of the definition of hearsay and the exceptions to the hearsay rule.

Like the best evidence rule, the hearsay doctrine is a competence rule. The doctrine operates to exclude logically relevant evidence by rendering the evidence incompetent. Again, like the best evidence rule, the doctrine is premised on the supposed unreliability of the excluded evidence. While competence rules such as the common-law privileges exclude relevant evidence in order to promote extrinsic social policies, both the best evidence and hearsay rules are based on the assumption that the excluded evidence is "untrustworthy." Of course, suggesting that all hearsay evidence is inherently or intrinsically weak would be unwarranted: The rule has been riddled with numerous exceptions precisely because there are many species of highly reliable hearsay. Hearsay evidence is untrustworthy only in the narrow sense that it has not been subjected to certain trial safeguards which test trustworthiness. The courts and commentators have named four safeguards missing in hearsay evidence.

The first three safeguards are secondary rationales for the hearsay rule. The first safeguard is the oath or affirmation. The administration of an oath or affirmation reminds the witness of the duty to testify truthfully. The scholarly consensus is that this safeguard is not the primary justification for the rule. Even if the out-of-court declarant reduces his or her statement to a sworn affidavit, the affidavit remains hearsay, and the conventional view is that a witness's testimony under oath at a prior trial is hearsay in the present hearing. The second rationale is the possibility of error in oral transmission of hearsay statements. When a witness relates what a declarant stated about an event the declarant observed, two human sources of possible error exist— the witness and the declarant. However, like the absence of oath, this rationale is merely an incidental justification for the rule. This justification does not account for the rule's well-settled application to writings. Moreover, courts routinely admit oral statements, such as prior inconsistent statements, for nonhearsay purposes even though the admission of the evidence presents the same danger of error in transmission. A third rationale is the lack of opportunity for the trier of fact to observe the declarant's demeanor. The admission of hearsay evidence denies the trier the opportunity to assess the declarant's demeanor. The Warren Court stressed the importance of demeanor evidence, pointing out that juror-witness confrontation is an aspect of sixth amendment confrontation.[1] Nevertheless, like the first two factors, this is a secondary reason for the rule. Even though the defendant's right to have the jurors observe the witnesses is of constitutional dimensions, courts dispense with this aspect of confrontation when they admit depositions.

The fourth and primary justification for the hearsay rule is that hearsay evidence denies the opponent the opportunity to conduct cross-examination.

These four safeguards provide both the justification for the hearsay rule and a basis for understanding the rule's exceptions which are presented in the next chapter. The hearsay rule crystallized during the Romantic age of trial advocacy when trial advocates greatly overestimated the importance of cross-examination. However, the contemporary view of cross-examination is more realistic. It is now conceded that the inexperienced trial attorney must learn several important facts: Most cases are won by painstakingly prepared direct examination rather than by divinely-inspired cross; because the eager attorney going for the opposing expert's jugular often succeeds only in cutting his or her own throat, overzealous cross can be counterproductive; and finally, the trial attorney must acquire the discipline to terminate a cross after eliciting a helpful admission or two and before the opposing witness has an opportunity to turn the tide of battle.

Nevertheless, cross-examination is an important test of reliability, for it can expose latent sources of error in direct examination. Cross gives the attorney an opportunity to explore the witness's testimonial ability (perception, memory, and narration) and willingness (sincerity)—the factors upon which the testimony's probative value depends. The admission of hearsay poses the danger that a latent error caused by a defect in one or more of these factors will go undetected. Moreover, the core of the confrontation clause is the guarantee that the adversary has the opportunity to cross-examine. Thus, most commentators concur that the hearsay rule's principal justification is the fact that hearsay evidence prevents the adversary from subjecting the evidence to the testing process of cross-examination.

2. Elements of the Rule

A common failure among trial attorneys is an inability to recognize inappropriate hearsay objections. Trial judges are usually irritated if counsel raise hearsay objections whenever a witness refers to an out-of-court statement. Equally disconcerting is the tendency of attorneys faced with hearsay objections to race to the argument that their evidence falls within an exception while they ignore the often available argument that the evidence is not hearsay to begin with. The basic cause of the problem is, of course, a misunderstanding of the scope of the hearsay rule. To understand the rule's scope, we

---

1. See, e. g., Barber v. Page, 390 U.S. 719, 88 S.Ct. 1318, 20 L.Ed.2d 255 (1968).

must turn to the definition of hearsay. As a tentative working guide, we will use the proposition that an *extra-judicial statement offered to prove the statement's truth is incompetent hearsay*. We can now analyze each of the definition's component elements.

"Extra-Judicial". The rule applies only to extra-judicial statements, that is, out-of-court declarations.

The Traditional View. The orthodox view is that the statement must be deemed extra-judicial so long as the declarant was not testifying during the present trial when he or she made the statement. Under this view, the statement remains hearsay even if the declarant subsequently becomes a witness at the trial. When a person makes a statement on Monday and testifies as a witness on Tuesday, Monday's statement is extra-judicial with respect to the trial.

It is important to remember that the hearsay rule applies also to writings: A person who authors a writing outside the courtroom is an out-of-court declarant. Thus, courts have held that the following documents are extra-judicial statements: newspaper stories;[2] grand jury reports;[3] invoices, bills, and receipts; markings on envelopes;[4] letters; affidavits for search warrants;[5] and even sketches and diagrams.[6]

The Opposite View. The polar view is that the declarant's out-of-court statements are not within the rule's purview if the declarant is present at the trial and available for cross-examination. If the declarant testifies on Tuesday, the declarant's statement on Monday would not be considered hearsay at the trial. Although to date, only one jurisdiction, Kansas, has adopted this approach,[7] it has received substantial scholarly support. In many, if not most cases, the prior declaration is more reliable than in-court testimony, for the prior declaration is both closer in time to the event and farther removed from the suggestive influences of the litigation.

This view gives the prosecution some protection against the so-called turncoat witness. Witness intimidation is an all too common occurrence in organized crime and family sex offense cases: Intimidated by threats, key prosecution witnesses feign lost memory at trial or radically change the tenor of their testimony. Under these circumstances, if the prosecution cannot use the witness's pretrial statements as substantive evidence, the prosecution may not be able to resist a motion for directed verdict or judgment of acquittal.

Compromise Views. Several jurisdictions generally apply the traditional view but except the witness's pretrial statements that are otherwise admissible for nonhearsay purposes. For example, in many jurisdictions if a statement is admissible as a prior inconsistent statement for impeachment, the statement may be used as substantive evidence. The compromise view necessitates a two-step analysis. First, the attorney must determine if the statement would be admissible for a nonhearsay purpose, e. g., as a prior consistent statement to bolster the witness's credibility. The threshold question here is whether the statement is admissible for any limited purpose. If it is, the attorney must then invoke the jurisdiction's rule permitting such statements to be used as substantive evidence.

---

2. State v. Aulds, 260 La. 869, 257 So.2d 642 (1972); Curtis v. State, 44 Ala.App. 335, 208 So.2d 245 (1967).

3. Oppenheimer v. Clunie, 142 Cal. 313, 75 P. 899 (1904).

4. United States v. Jackson, 469 F.2d 267 (9th Cir. 1972).

5. Hall v. State, 136 Tex.Cr.R. 320, 125 S.W.2d 293 (1939).

6. People v. Turner, 91 Ill.App.2d 436, 235 N.E.2d 317 (1968).

7. Kan.Stat.Ann. § 60–460(a).

The federal, California, and Wisconsin rules are illustrative. As originally enacted, Federal Rule 801(d)(1) contained a rather conservative provision. The Rule admitted: (1) statements otherwise admissible as prior consistent statements; and (2) statements otherwise admissible as prior inconsistent statements but only if the inconsistent statement "was given under oath subject to the penalty of perjury at a trial, hearing, or other proceeding, or in a deposition."[8] In late 1975, Congress amended the Rule to add statements of "identification of a person made after perceiving him" to the list of admissible statements.[9] Under this amendment, the pretrial identification is admissible even if the witness becomes frightened and is either unable or unwilling to repeat the identification in the courtroom.

The California view is more liberal. California statutes sanction the substantive use of statements otherwise admissible as prior inconsistent statements, prior consistent statements, and prior identifications.[10] Wisconsin limits the exception to the witness's prior written statements.[11]

Constitutional Issues Raised by Views (2) and (3). Defense counsel have argued that the second and third views represent too great an infringement on the right to cross-examine. Counsel point out that cross-examination at trial about the prior statement will sometimes be ineffective, for the witness can easily retreat behind testimony that he or she remembers making the statement but forgets the event that inspired the statement.[12] However, this argument did not persuade the Supreme Court. Re-

jecting an attack on one state's statutes, the Supreme Court held that trial cross-examination about the prior extra-judicial declaration generally satisfies the confrontation clause.[13] At minimum it is now settled that statutes implementing the compromise view are not facially invalid.

The remaining question is whether the statute is unconstitutional as applied to the facts of the case. In sustaining the state statutes, the Supreme Court emphasized the declarant's present availability for "full and effective cross-examination."[14] Obviously, the confrontation clause demands that the declarant be physically present in the courtroom. Query: Does the clause demand more? What if the declarant is physically present, but he or she precludes effective cross-examination by, for example, refusing to answer any questions about the statement? If the witness so refuses, the opportunity for cross is probably constitutionally inadequate.[15] If the witness denies making the statement and then testifies favorably to the defendant, no constitutional violation occurs.[16] When the witness limits cross by claiming to have forgotten, the courts are divided.[17]

Suggested Reading:

California v. Green, 399 U.S. 149, 90 S.Ct. 1930, 26 L.Ed.2d 489 (1970).

People v. Johnson, 68 Cal.2d 646, 68 Cal.Rptr. 599, 441 P.2d 111 (1968).

---

8. Fed.Evid.Rule 801(d)(1), 28 U.S.C.A.; United States v. Tavares, 512 F.2d 872 (9th Cir. 1975).

9. Fed.Evid.Rule 801(d)(1), 28 U.S.C.A.

10. West's Ann.Cal.Evid.Code §§ 1235–36 & 1238.

11. Gelhaar v. State, 41 Wis.2d 230, 163 N.W.2d 609 (1969), cert. denied 399 U.S. 929, 90 S.Ct. 2250, 26 L.Ed.2d 797 (1970).

12. People v. Johnson, 68 Cal.2d 646, 68 Cal.Rptr. 599, 441 P.2d 111 (1968).

13. California v. Green, 399 U.S. 149, 90 S.Ct. 1930, 26 L.Ed.2d 489 (1970).

14. Id. at 159.

15. Douglas v. Alabama, 380 U.S. 415, 85 S.Ct. 1074, 13 L.Ed.2d 934 (1965).

16. Nelson v. O'Neil, 402 U.S. 622, 91 S.Ct. 1723, 29 L.Ed.2d 222 (1971).

17. Compare People v. Woodberry, 10 Cal.App.3d 695, 89 Cal.Rptr. 330 (1970), with United States v. Payne, 492 F.2d 449 (4th Cir. 1974).

"Statement." All courts agree that the hearsay doctrine applies to assertive statements and conduct. The question in dispute is whether the doctrine should be extended to certain types of nonassertive conduct.

Assertive Statements. Because most assertive statements are declarative sentences, many trial judges use a rule of thumb that imperative, interrogative, and exclamatory sentences are not hearsay. However, the sentence's classification as assertive is a matter of interpretation. Suppose that the prosecutor offers the imperative sentence, "Place the baggie of marijuana in the trunk," as proof that the substance in the bag is marijuana. Here the prosecutor is relying upon the implied assertion that the substance is marijuana. For that purpose, the imperative sentence would be an assertive statement.

One often-neglected hearsay problem is police officers' use of assertive statements in explaining why they reported to the crime scene. The trial judge will usually permit the officer to make a statement along the lines that the officer proceeded to the scene after receiving a report that a burglary was in progress. The "report of a burglary in progress" is an out-of-court statement and is, thus, hearsay. The defense counsel should insist that the officer limit the detail of his or her testimony and, whenever there is a serious dispute over whether the crime was committed, should request a limiting instruction. Such statements are incompetent hearsay, and they should be admitted only for the limited purpose of explaining the officer's actions.

Assertive Conduct. Sometimes the actor intends his or her nonverbal conduct to be a true substitute for speech: The mute use sign language; a victim may point to a person in a lineup as a means of identifying the criminal; or people may nod or shake their heads to answer a question. Whenever the actor intends the conduct to be expressive or communicative, the hearsay rule applies to the conduct.

Nonassertive Conduct. Although the courts concur that the rule applies to assertive statements and conduct, they divide markedly on the question of whether the rule also encompasses nonassertive conduct. Suppose that the defendant's sanity is an issue. The prosecutor offers evidence that just prior to the crime, several of the defendant's acquaintances wrote him or her serious letters. The act of sending letters to the defendant is nonassertive conduct. Thus the prosecutor is relying upon the following chain of inferences: The authors would not have sent the letters to the defendant if they had thought that he or she was insane; the act therefore manifests their belief that he or she was sane; the fact that close acquaintances believed the defendant to be sane increases the probability that he or she was sane. In short, the prosecutor is using conduct actuated by a belief as proof of the belief's truth. Another common example of conduct actuated by a belief occurs in bookmaking cases. The police raid a bookie establishment. While the police are on the premises, they answer incoming phone calls. The callers, who attempt to place bets, would not have phoned unless they believed that they were calling a bookie establishment. The callers' act is also conduct actuated by a belief.

The traditional "Morgan hearsay" view is that the hearsay rule applies to such nonassertive conduct offered to prove the truth of a belief actuating the conduct. However, the emerging view, prevailing in the federal courts and many state courts, is that nonassertive conduct is simply relevant circumstantial evidence. The proponents of the emerging view point out that when the conduct is nonassertive, little risk of insincerity exists; actions speak louder than words, and the individual's willingness to act in reliance upon the belief obviates testing the individual's testimonial willingness. The counter-argument is that although the nature of nonassertive conduct eliminates the necessity to test for the hearsay danger of insincerity, the other hearsay dangers—errors in perception, memory, and narration—remain. Morgan argued that the opponent should be given an opportunity to probe the witness's testimonial ability. Morgan's argument is sound in principle, but the leading modern codifications of evidence law, including the Federal Rules and several state evidence codes, exclude nonassertive conduct.

Suggested Reading:

People v. Mendez, 193 Cal. 39, 223 P. 65 (1924).

"Offered to Prove the Statement's Truth." The hearsay rule applies only when the proponent offers the extra-judicial statement as evidence of the truth of the assertion or belief actuating the conduct. The declarant's credibility is critical usually only in this situation. When the courts say that the proponent is offering the evidence for "a hearsay purpose," they mean that the immediate inference the proponent seeks to draw from the evidence is the truth of the assertion or belief. The proponent can escape the rule by offering the evidence for any nonhearsay purpose, and the only limitations on the possible nonhearsay purposes are the doctrine of relevance and the attorney's imagination. When a court admits an extra-judicial statement for a nonhearsay purpose, it sometimes characterizes the evidence as "original."

There are three common, nonhearsay uses of out-of-court declarations. The first is to prove the declarations when they themselves are logically relevant. The courts invoking this theory often refer to the declarations as "operative facts," "verbal acts," or "res gestae." In a conspiracy prosecution, the prosecutor may introduce the conspirators' statements constituting the agreement. The agreement itself is a material fact, and the statements constituting the agreement are themselves legally significant.

A second nonhearsay purpose is to circumstantially prove the declarant's state of mind. If the defendant claims insanity, the defendant's apparently irrational or delusive statements are logically relevant to show insanity. The statements are circumstantial proof of the defendant's insanity.

A third nonhearsay purpose is to prove the effect of the declarations on the state of mind of the hearer or reader. If the defendant claims self-defense, the defendant may introduce proof of communicated threats by the alleged victim. The fact that the alleged victim communicated threats to the defendant increases the reasonableness of the defendant's apprehension.

The lowest common denominator of these cases is that the mere fact that the declaration was made is logically relevant, regardless of the statement's truth. At this point, re-emphasizing the limited nature of the hearsay definition is advisable. Evidence constitutes hearsay only if all the first three elements of the definition are present. If the statement is not deemed extra-judicial, or if the statement is not assertive, or if the proponent offers the evidence for a nonhearsay purpose, the rule is inapplicable. The proponent can defeat a hearsay objection by showing that any of the first three elements of the definition is missing.

Suggested Reading:

United States v. Pate, 543 F.2d 1148 (5th Cir. 1976).
United States v. Kutas, 542 F.2d 527 (9th Cir. 1976).
United States v. Grant, 519 F.2d 64 (5th Cir. 1975).

"Incompetent." The minority view is that hearsay evidence is absolutely incompetent; even if the opponent fails to object to the evidence's introduction, the evidence remains incompetent and cannot be relied upon to support any finding of fact necessary to sustain the judgment below. This minority view misconceives the nature of the hearsay rule. The rule is a competence rule excluding relevant evidence. The evidence excluded in fact has probative value. For this reason, the overwhelming majority of jurisdictions treat a failure to object as a waiver; the majority holds that if the evidence is admitted without objection, the trial court may give the evidence its natural probative value in disposing of motions for directed verdict, and the appellate court may do likewise if the defendant challenges the evidence's sufficiency on appeal.

CHAPTER 13
HEARSAY EXCEPTIONS

1. Introduction

Even if a statement falls within the definition of hearsay, the statement may be admissible under an exception to the hearsay rule. Ordinarily, two factors must concur before the court will recognize an exception to the rule: a circumstantial guarantee of trustworthiness and some necessity for resorting to the evidence. Although the two factors concur in most exceptions, they are not always present with equal force. In some exceptions, the first factor predominates; in others, the second is dominant; and in some exceptions, one factor will be virtually missing.

The first factor, the special guarantee of trustworthiness, serves as a substitute for the opportunity to cross-examine. This guarantee takes several forms. For example, the circumstances might be such that the declarant normally would be speaking sincerely, for a factor like fear of punishment might be present, counteracting any impetus to lie. Or the declarant might be speaking under conditions of publicity that would make him or her realize that any lie would immediately be detected and corrected.

The second factor, necessity, can be either absolute or relative. The necessity is absolute when the hearsay statement is the only evidence obtainable from that declarant; for instance, the declarant might be dead or otherwise unavailable.[1] Relative necessity occurs when the declarant is available to testify, but the hearsay evidence is more likely to be truthful than is the testimony the declarant would give on the witness stand. In this situation the hearsay might be an excited, evidently sincere statement while by the time of trial, the declarant has been subjected to numerous pressures and influences that can color testimony.

DISSERVING STATEMENTS

2. Admissions of a Party-Opponent

Suggested Reading:

Doyle v. Ohio, 426 U.S. 610, 96 S.Ct. 2240, 49 L.Ed. 2d 91 (1976).

One of the most important hearsay exceptions is the exception for admissions of a party-opponent. This exception permits prosecutors to introduce a defendant's confessions and admissions.[2] Scholars disagree on the related questions of whether admissions should be classified as hearsay and of the rationale for admissions' admissibility. While a defendant's extra-judicial admissions fall within the technical definition of hearsay, many commentators have argued

---

1. There are numerous hearsay exceptions which condition admissibility on the declarant's unavailability—e. g., former testimony and declarations against interest. Historically, the courts evolved different unavailability standards for each exception. The modern trend is toward statutory standards uniformly applied to all hearsay exceptions. See, e. g., Fed. Evid.Rule 804(a), 28 U.S.C.A.; West Ann.Cal.Evid. Code § 240.

2. Until recently, the courts distinguished confessions from admissions. A confession was a full acknowledgment of guilt of facts sufficient to authorize conviction. An admission was a concession of an incriminating fact or facts which was not sufficient to authorize conviction. Contemporary courts have virtually abolished the distinction and instead generally apply the same hearsay, corroboration, voluntariness, and *Miranda* rules to all the defendant's incriminating statements.

that the principal rationale for the hearsay rule is to give the adversary an opportunity to cross-examine and that it is nonsensical to talk about giving a party an opportunity to cross-examine himself or herself. Fortunately, the disputes are purely academic. Although the commentators disagree on the theoretical justification for admitting admissions, they agree on the necessary elements of the foundation.

The Elements of the Foundation. The proponent of an admission must lay the following foundation. First, the statement must be attributable to a party, here the defendant. The statement can be attributable on several bases. For example, the party might have personally spoken or written the statement; the party might have manifested assent to a statement spoken or written by a third person; or the party might be so related to a third person that it is just to impute the third person's statement to the defendant. Second, the statement must be offered by the declarant's opponent, here the prosecution. Third, the statement must be inconsistent with the position the declarant is defending at trial. However, the statement need not have been contrary to the declarant's interest at the time the declarant made the statement; at that point, the statement might have been positively self-serving. Thus the courts usually define the requirement negatively, saying that the statement must be contrary to or inconsistent with the position the defendant maintains at trial. Nevertheless restating the requirement affirmatively is more accurate: The statement must be helpful to the prosecution's case. So formulated, the requirement is simply an application of the relevance doctrine—the evidence must be logically relevant to prove an element of the prosecution's case.

These three requirements are the only elements of the foundation for this exception to the hearsay rule. Thus this exception is distinct from the prior inconsistent statement theory of impeachment. Under

that theory, before resorting to extrinsic proof of the statement, the proponent must ordinarily question the declarant and call the declarant's attention to the time, place, and tenor of the statement. In contrast the proponent does not have to follow this procedure to invoke the admission exception. However, peculiar criminal and constitutional law considerations may require a more extensive foundation. The prosecution may have to corroborate the confession, show the confession's voluntariness, and prove that the interrogators administered proper *Miranda* warnings. These other elements of the complete foundation are discussed in Chapters 21 and 23.

Traditionally the courts have been receptive to admissions, relaxing the application of many evidentiary rules. For example, most courts hold that an admission is competent even if it appears that the party did not have personal knowledge of the subject matter. Moreover, courts customarily accept conclusorily phrased admissions. Long before the courts began liberalizing the standards for admitting opinion evidence, they routinely accepted opinionated admissions couched as concessions of fault or guilt.

The Types of Admissions. There are three basic types of evidentiary admissions: personal, adoptive, and vicarious. The basis for classification is the reason for attributing the admission to the party. The evidence is a personal admission if the defendant himself or herself made or wrote the statement. The evidence is an adoptive admission if the defendant adopted or manifested assent to a statement made by a third person. The evidence is vicarious if some relationship, such as agency, existed between the defendant and the declarant at the time the statement was made.

Personal Admissions. Personal admissions take myriad forms. For example, a defendant might make a personal admission in an assertive statement. Of course, the defendant can personally make an oral or written confession. The admission can be a statement in a pleading or a motion the defendant signs or verifies. The defendant may make an admission while testifying as a deponent, and if the defendant does so, the admission is competent even though the prosecution cannot lay the normal foundation for a deposition's admission, e. g., the deponent's unavailability.

A defendant may also make a personal admission in the form of assertive conduct. During an interrogation, the suspect might nod a response rather than verbalize it. The nod is expressive, assertive conduct qualifying as an admission.

Finally, if the jurisdiction follows the Morgan hearsay theory, the court will have to resort to this exception in order to justify the admission of "consciousness of guilt" evidence: the defendant's flight after the crime's commission; the defendant's subornation of a witness's perjury; the defendant's refusal to take a physical or scientific test which might exonerate an innocent person; the defendant's threats against prosecution witnesses; the defendant's assumption of an alias; or his or her attempted suicide. In the jurisdictions subscribing to Professor Morgan's theory, these items of evidence constitute hearsay. The conduct is actuated by the defendant's belief in his or her own guilt, and the prosecution offers the evidence to prove the belief's truth.

The anomaly is that even in the jurisdictions following the emerging, narrow definition of hearsay, the courts often refer to these items of evidence as "admissions by conduct." This description is inaccurate and misleading, for the evidence is not hearsay, and the court need not resort to any hearsay exception to admit it.[3] The items are simply relevant circumstantial evidence of guilt.[4]

Adoptive Admissions. The second type of admission is an adoptive admission. In this situation, a third party makes the statement, and the defendant manifests assent to or acquiescence in the statement. He or she may demonstrate such assent either at the time the third party makes the statement or at a later point (ratification). The basic question here is inferential: May we infer assent from the defendant's words or acts? It is not enough that he or she simply describes or recites the third party's statement. Rather there must be a sufficient inference of approval of the statement's content.

Express adoption is quite common. Standard police operating procedure dictates that after eliciting an oral confession, the interrogator must reduce the confession to writing. The interrogator may either type the confession in a question-and-answer format or restate the interview in narrative form. After reducing the confession to writing, the interrogator tenders the document to the defendant for acknowledgment and signature. If the defendant reads the document and then signs, the signature is an express adoption of the document's contents. Alternatively, if the defendant reads the confession, acknowledges its correctness, but balks at signing the document, the document is nonetheless admissible as the defendant's adoptive admission. Although the lay defendant often attaches special significance

the defendant committed or authorized a third party to commit the act, e. g., suborn perjury. Second the defense counsel should attack the strength of the inference of consciousness of guilt of the crime charged. Some courts have already accepted the argument that evidence of the defendant's departure from the area is irrelevant unless the prosecution shows that the defendant knew the police were seeking him or her. Embree v. United States, 320 F.2d 666 (9th Cir. 1963); People v. Harris, 23 Ill.2d 270, 178 N.E.2d 291 (1961).

4. Embree v. United States, 320 F.2d 666 (9th Cir. 1963); People v. Harris, 23 Ill.2d 270, 178 N.E.2d 291 (1961).

3. Rather than focusing on the evidence's hearsay aspects, the defense counsel should attack its relevance. As in the case of uncharged misconduct evidence, the defense counsel should insist that the prosecution present clear and convincing evidence that

to the signature and refuses to sign after freely acknowledging the document's correctness, the acknowledgment is an express adoption, and it is immaterial that he or she refuses to sign.

The adoption can be either express or an *implied adoption by affirmative conduct.* Courts often find an implied adoption by an insured person when the insured includes a document in a proof of loss packet submitted to an insurer. Originally, some courts mechanically held that an adoption occurred whenever a person tendered someone else's writing to a third party. Modernly, the courts are assessing the strength of inference of adoption more realistically. In evaluating the inference's strength, the most important considerations are whether the insured had to submit that type of document and whether more than one possible source for the document existed. Suppose that the insurance policy requires that the insured submit both a doctor's certificate and any relevant police report. If the policy requires the insured to submit a specified doctor's certificate, the court certainly could not infer an adoption from the insured's submission of the certificate. However, if the policy does not require the insured to obtain the certificate from any particular physician, and if the insured submits his or her own doctor's certificate, the court may properly infer the insured's agreement with the certificate's contents. However, the insured has no choice with respect to the police report. If the insured includes the police report required by the policy, the court will probably refuse to infer assent. The strength of the inference depends upon whether the party can freely choose the document, and in turn the party's freedom often depends upon whether there are alternative sources for the document.

There can also be *implied adoption by silence.* This is known as the common-law doctrine of *tacit admission* or *assenting silence.* The following are the foundation elements of this doctrine: (1) Someone (a police officer, the victim, or even an accomplice) makes an accusatory statement in the

defendant's presence; (2) the defendant hears and understands the statement; (3) the defendant has an opportunity to deny the statement; (4) the defendant either remains silent or makes an evasive or equivocal answer; and (5) under similar circumstances, a reasonable innocent person would deny the statement. If the prosecutor can establish these foundational elements, a sufficient inference exists that the defendant's silence or evasion evidences acquiescence. The prosecutor may then present to the jury evidence of both the statement and the defendant's silence or evasion.

To attack prosecution evidence offered under this doctrine, the defense counsel should focus on the second and fifth elements of the foundation. For example, the counsel may be able to negative the second element by showing that the defendant had a mental disorder or was injured, shocked, or intoxicated. However, the fifth element is more troublesome. To establish it, the prosecutor must show that under the circumstances, the natural, normal reaction of an innocent person would have been to deny the statement. Thus, if the third party made the statement in a letter to the defendant, the defense counsel has a good chance of prevailing. Unless the defendant and the third party had engaged in mutual correspondence prior to the letter or unless they stood in a close relationship such as a business association, the court will be reluctant to find that the defendant was obliged to send a written denial. Even if the third party made an oral statement to the defendant, the defense counsel might nevertheless succeed. Courts have held that in the following circumstances the defendant did not manifest assent by silence: The defendant's attorney advised the defendant to remain silent; the defendant was surrounded by an angry mob, and his or her denial might have prompted violence; and the defendant overheard the statement in a conversation that he or she was not a party to. Significantly, some courts have held that the defendant's silence does not manifest assent if the defendant is already under arrest.[5] These courts recognize, partly because of the notoriety of *Miranda*, that many, if not most, laypeople now believe that the safest course for an arrestee is to invoke the fifth amendment and demand counsel. In effect, these courts judicially notice the existence of this widespread belief and recognize that in light of the belief, the arrestee's silence creates only a very weak inference of assent.

Constitutional Limitations on the Doctrine. In dictum in *Miranda*, the Supreme Court stated that "[t]he prosecution may not . . . use at trial the fact that he [the defendant] stood mute or claimed his privilege in the face of accusation."[6] The question thus arose whether the tacit admission doctrine could survive *Miranda*. The answer requires that we distinguish among several fact situations.

In the first situation, *Miranda* is simply inapplicable. The warning requirements apply only when law enforcement officers are interrogating a suspect in custody. A court will rule *Miranda* inapplicable if the prosecutor can demonstrate that: (1) police involvement in the confrontation between the defendant and the speaker was insufficient; *or* (2) at the time, the defendant was not in custody; *or* (3) at the time, the police were not interrogating the defendant. Suppose that the victim happens to walk past the defendant while the defendant is being detained at the police station. The victim then makes an accusatory remark to the defendant. If the meeting is truly by chance, *Miranda* would be inapplicable, for *Miranda* applies to only government officials, and the victim would be acting as a private individual. Moreover, suppose that a policeman makes a statement to the defendant before arresting the defendant or otherwise significantly restricting the defendant's free-

dom of movement. *Miranda* would be inapplicable because the defendant is not yet in custody. Finally, the prosecutor may be able to persuade the court that at the time, the police were not engaged in interrogation. In Miller v. Cox,[7] the defendant was present in the room while the police interrogated another suspect. The defendant remained silent when the other suspect confessed, implicating the defendant. The Fourth Circuit held that *Miranda* was inapplicable because the police were not interrogating the defendant. If the court accepts any of these arguments, *Miranda* is inapplicable, and the prosecutor may therefore use the adoptive admission as substantive evidence.

In a second situation, *Miranda* applies, but the police question the defendant without complying with *Miranda*, and the defendant makes an evasive or equivocal reply. Harris v. New York[8] and Oregon v. Hass[9] appear to be controlling here. In *Harris*, the Supreme Court held that the prosecution may use a voluntary but unwarned confession for impeachment. In *Hass*, the Court extended *Harris* to the situation in which the police elicit a statement from the defendant after the defendant has requested but before the police have furnished counsel. Thus in the second situation, although *Miranda* precludes the prosecutor from using the adoptive admission as substantive evidence, *Harris* and *Hass* seem to sanction its use for impeachment.

In the third situation, *Miranda* is applicable, the police give proper warnings, but the defendant waives. The defendant then makes an equivocal or evasive statement. Because the police complied with *Miranda*, the prosecutor is not barred from using the adoptive admission as substantive evidence.

---

5. United States v. Lo Biondo, 135 F.2d 130 (2d Cir. 1943).

6. Miranda v. Arizona, 384 U.S. 436, 468 n. 37, 86 S.Ct. 1602, 1624 n. 37, 16 L.Ed.2d 694 (1966).

7. 457 F.2d 700 (4th Cir. 1972), cert. denied 409 U.S. 1007, 93 S.Ct. 433, 34 L.Ed.2d 299. See Comment, 30 Wash. & Lee L.Rev. 311 (1973).

8. 401 U.S. 222, 91 S.Ct. 643, 28 L.Ed.2d 1 (1971).

9. 420 U.S. 714, 95 S.Ct. 1215, 43 L.Ed.2d 570 (1975).

The Supreme Court's recent decision in Michigan v. Mosley [10] will make it easier to find a waiver. The police arrested Mosley in connection with certain robberies. An officer advised Mosley of his *Miranda* rights, and he declined to discuss the robberies. The police immediately ceased interrogation. More than two hours later in another part of the building, another officer interrogated Mosley about an unrelated holdup murder. The officer gave Mosley a second set of warnings. Mosley waived, and the officer obtained an incriminating statement. The Court held that *Miranda* does not impose an absolute ban on reinterrogation after a suspect's claim of the privilege. The Court stated that the test was "whether his 'right to cut off questioning' was 'scrupulously honored.' " [11] In sustaining the waiver, the Court emphasized that "[t]he police here immediately ceased the interrogation, resumed questioning only after the passage of a significant period of time and the provision of a fresh set of warnings, and restricted the second interrogation to a crime that had not been a subject of the earlier interrogation." [12]

The fourth situation has generated substantial controversy. Here *Miranda* applies, the police give proper warnings, but the defendant remains silent or formally claims the privilege. There is general agreement that the defendant's invocation of the privilege precludes the prosecution from using the defendant's silence as substantive evidence. However, the courts divided on whether the prosecution may use the silence for impeachment as prior inconsistent conduct. If the defendant invoked the privilege during pretrial interrogation but at trial testifies to exculpatory facts, may the prosecutor impeach the defendant by showing that the defendant did not relate the facts to the police during the pretrial interview? Some courts held flatly that the defendant's silence is in-.

admissible even for the limited purpose of impeachment. [13] Two rationales were set forth for this position. One is that the admission of the evidence, even for the limited purpose of impeachment, would represent too great an infringement on the fifth amendment. This justification is questionable after *Harris* and *Hass*. The second rationale is that the belief that an arrestee's safest course is silence is now so widespread that the arrestee's silence is too ambiguous to support an inference of assent. This rationale is defensible.

Other courts permitted the prosecution to use the defendant's silence for impeachment at least when pretrial silence is "blatantly inconsistent" with the trial testimony —for example when the defendant testifies that he or she cooperated with the police. [14]

The issue first reached the Supreme Court in United States v. Hale. [15] In *Hale*, the defendant was charged with robbery. During pretrial interrogation, he offered no explanation for $158.00 found in his possession. At trial, however, he testified that the funds were the proceeds of his wife's welfare check. The prosecutor attempted to use the defendant's pretrial silence for impeachment. On appeal, the defendant presented alternative arguments. First, he argued that his silence was ambiguous and could not support a finding that it was inconsistent with his trial testimony. Second, he argued that *Miranda* barred the use of pretrial silence for impeachment. Writing for the majority, Mr. Justice Marshall ruled in Hale's favor on the first argument. Mr. Justices White and Douglas indicated that they also accepted Hale's second argument. However,

---

10. 423 U.S. 96, 96 S.Ct. 321, 46 L.Ed.2d 313 (1975).

11. Id. at 104.

12. Id. at 106.

13. United States v. Anderson, 498 F.2d 1038 (D.C. Cir. 1974); Johnson v. Patterson, 475 F.2d 1066 (10th Cir. 1973), cert. denied 414 U.S. 878, 94 S.Ct. 64, 38 L.Ed.2d 124. See Note, 13 Washb.L.J. 219 (1974).

14. United States v. Harp, 513 F.2d 786 (5th Cir. 1975); United States v. Fairchild, 505 F.2d 1378 (5th Cir. 1975); United States ex rel. Burt v. New Jersey, 475 F.2d 234 (3d Cir. 1973), cert. denied 414 U.S. 938, 94 S.Ct. 243, 38 L.Ed.2d 165.

15. 422 U.S. 171, 95 S.Ct. 2133, 45 L.Ed.2d 99 (1975).

the majority did not reach this second constitutional argument. Moreover, the Court did not state an absolute rule that pretrial silence always lacks sufficient probative value to be used as prior inconsistent conduct. The Court held only that on the specific facts of the case the inference of inconsistency was too weak. The Court cautioned that pretrial silence is too ambiguous "[i]n most instances," but it did not erect any absolute barriers to the use of pretrial silence for impeachment.

The Court finally reached the merits of the constitutional issue in Doyle v. Ohio.[16] Writing for the majority, Justice Powell stated that post-arrest silence is "insolubly ambiguous" and that the *Miranda* warnings contain an implicit assurance that "silence will carry no penalty." The justice announced a general rule that due process precludes the use of a suspect's pretrial silence to impeach "an explanation subsequently offered at trial." However, in a footnote, the Court noted an important exception to the general rule: "[I]t almost goes without saying that the fact of post-arrest silence could be used by the prosecution to contradict a defendant who testifies to an exculpatory version of events and claims to have told the police the same version upon arrest. In that situation the fact of earlier silence would not be used to impeach the exculpatory story, but rather to challenge the defendant's testimony as to his behavior following arrest."[17]

Vicarious Admissions. The third type of admission is a vicarious admission. In this situation, the defendant neither makes the statement nor manifests assent to it. Rather the statement is attributed to the defendant because of his or her close relationship to the declarant. For example, the relationship between co-conspirators is sufficiently close to permit the courts to attribute one conspirator's statements to another. Indeed, a general rule of criminal law is that one conspirator's acts and declarations in furtherance and during the pendency of a conspiracy can be attributed to all co-conspirators. The evidentiary application of the rule is the doctrine that *a statement by a co-conspirator in furtherance of a conspiracy then in progress is admissible against the defendant if the defendant was once a member of the conspiracy.* Because federal prosecutors use conspiracy counts quite liberally, the doctrine is one of the most important exceptions in federal courts.

"A Statement by a Co-conspirator." This element relates to the declarant's status. At the time the declarant makes the statement, he or she must be a member of the conspiracy. However, if the purported conspirator is actually an undercover agent, the statement is inadmissible.[18] Also if a conspirator effectively withdraws from the conspiracy before making the statement, the statement is inadmissible. A conspirator's arrest usually terminates his or her status as a conspirator. Nevertheless, when an imprisoned conspirator indicated he would resume active participation in the conspiracy as soon as he was released on bail, the Third Circuit held that a statement made while he was in jail was admissible.[19]

"In Furtherance." The conventional view is that as a separate element of the foundation, the prosecutor must show that the declarant made the statement in furtherance of the conspiracy's purposes. However, both the Uniform Rules and the Model Code completely dispense with this element, and the Kansas legislature followed their approach by enacting K.S.A. 60–460(i)(2). Under this statute, the prosecutor need not show that the declarant intended to further the conspiracy's purposes by making the

---

16. 426 U.S. 610, 96 S.Ct. 2240, 49 L.Ed.2d 91 (1976).

17. Id.

18. United States v. Williamson, 450 F.2d 585 (5th Cir. 1971), cert. denied 405 U.S. 1026, 92 S.Ct. 1297, 31 L.Ed.2d 486 (1972).

19. United States v. Armocida, 515 F.2d 29 (3d Cir. 1975).

statement. Instead he or she need show only that the statement's content relates to the conspiracy.

A second group of courts formally adheres to the conventional view but at times enforces it loosely. This looseness is particularly pronounced in anti-trust cases.[20] Although these courts occasionally refer to the furtherance requirement, they apply the requirement so laxly that it becomes almost inoperative.

Another group of courts enforces the conventional view rigorously. Federal Rule 801(d)(2)(E) preserves the furtherance requirement in federal practice. From the defense counsel's point of view, this requirement may be the most important element of the foundation, for counsel can often point to it as ground for excluding a conspirator's statement. If the counsel persuades the court to enforce the requirement rigorously, the court may exclude "mere conversations" between conspirators.[21] "Mere narratives" of past events may also be excludable.[22] Most importantly, a conspirator's post-arrest confession is excludable.[23]

"A Conspiracy." This element of the foundation, the conspiracy's existence, presents both pleading and proof questions. If the charging pleading does not contain a conspiracy count, may the prosecutor nevertheless invoke the exception? Although the answer is yes, there is authority that the conspiracy the prosecutor relies on must at least have been in furtherance of the charged

substantive offense.[24] Thus in a burglary case, the prosecutor may introduce a statement made during the course of a conspiracy to commit the burglary even though the indictment does not contain a conspiracy allegation. However, the prosecutor may not introduce the statement if the charged offense is rape.

There are three problems of proof. The first is that before introducing the statement, the prosecutor must establish the conspiracy's existence by "independent" evidence, that is, evidence *aliunde* the conspirator's hearsay assertions. The defense counsel should stress the requirement that the foundational evidence be independent; if the prosecutor attempts to use the proffered statement's contents to show the conspiracy's existence, the defense counsel should remind the judge that the prosecutor may not bootstrap. The prosecutor may use, inter alia, the following items of independent evidence: the parties' conduct indicating an illicit association, e. g., a clandestine meeting; the defendant's own admissions; the parties' statements constituting the illicit agreement;[25] and the conspirator's nonhearsay declarations offered as circumstantial evidence of the conspirator's subjective intention to effectuate the conspiracy's purposes.[26]

The second proof question is the quantum of proof of conspiracy. The majority view is that the necessary predicate is "a prima facie case" of conspiracy.[27] Sufficient evidence must be offered to support a

20. United States v. E. I. duPont de Nemours Co., 107 F.Supp. 324 (D.Del.1952); United States v. Imperial Chemicals, 100 F.Supp. 504 (S.D.N.Y.1952).

21. United States v. James, 510 F.2d 546 (5th Cir. 1975).

22. Levie, Hearsay and Conspiracy: A Reexamination of the Conspirators' Exception to the Hearsay Rule, 52 Mich.L.Rev. 1159, 1171 (1954).

23. People v. Morales, 263 Cal.App.2d 368, 69 Cal. Rptr. 402 (1968), cert. denied 393 U.S. 1104, 89 S.Ct. 907, 21 L.Ed.2d 798 (1969); People v. Roberts, 40 Cal. 2d 483, 254 P.2d 501 (1953).

24. United States v. Miller, 246 F.2d 486 (2d Cir. 1957), cert. denied 355 U.S. 905, 78 S.Ct. 332, 2 L.Ed. 2d 261; United States v. Olweiss, 138 F.2d 798 (2d Cir. 1944), cert. denied 321 U.S. 744, 64 S.Ct. 483, 88 L.Ed. 1047.

25. People v. Curtis, 106 Cal.App.2d 321, 235 P.2d 51 (1951).

26. C. McCormick, Handbook of the Law of Evidence § 267 n. 2 (2d ed. 1972).

27. United States v. Ragland, 375 F.2d 471 (2d Cir. 1967); State v. Seaman, 114 N.J.Super. 19, 274 A.2d 810 (1971).

finding of fact that a conspiracy existed. The minority view is that only "slight" evidence of a conspiracy is necessary.[28]

The final proof problem is the trial judge's treatment of the evidence of conspiracy. The prevailing view is that the judge decides only the question of law: Is there sufficient evidence to permit the jury to find that the conspiracy existed? The judge does not resolve the question of fact: Was there a conspiracy? If the jurisdiction follows this view, the defense counsel may both challenge the statement's admission and, if unsuccessful, request an instruction that the jurors must entirely disregard the statement if they find that there was no conspiracy. A counsel should always request this instruction in a multi-count prosecution in which the charging pleading contains both substantive and conspiracy counts.

The minority view is that the judge must resolve questions of credibility and decide as a matter of fact whether a conspiracy occurred. However, the judge should not inform the jury of his or her finding that there was a conspiracy. If the jurors somehow learn of the judge's finding, the defense counsel should insist that the judge instruct the jurors that his or her ruling is not binding upon them and that they must determine the conspiracy's existence by the stricter "beyond a reasonable doubt" standard. Some recent federal cases indicate that the new Federal Rules commit the federal courts to this minority view.

"Then in Progress." If the conspirator makes the statement before the conspiracy arises, the statement cannot qualify under the exception. Some courts have circumvented this rule by admitting the pre-conspiracy statement for a non-hearsay purpose such as circumstantially proving the declarant's motive for committing the crime.

After the prosecutor has presented evidence of the conspiracy's inception, he or she may invoke a permissive inference that the conspiracy continues to exist. The events the prosecutor relies upon as independent evidence of conspiracy need not coincide with the statement; the foundation is complete so long as the events antedate the statement. In effect, after the prosecutor presents evidence of the conspiracy's inception, the burden of going forward shifts to the defense to show either the declarant's withdrawal or the conspiracy's termination prior to the statement.

The question naturally arises: When does a conspiracy terminate? The conspiracy itself terminates when the conspirators have either achieved or abandoned their main objectives. In many cases, the conspiracy terminates when the conspirators actually commit the contemplated crime. For example, if the conspirators planned a battery, the court may hold that the conspiracy terminated as soon as the conspirators committed the battery. In contrast suppose that the conspirators plan to gain an illegal profit by a crime such as larceny. Here the conspiracy does not terminate at the crime's commission; rather the illegal agreement continues until the conspirators divide the fruits of the crime. Moreover, the conspiracy would certainly survive the crime's commission if the conspirators entered into a broad conspiracy to commit several crimes over a lengthy period of time.

The more difficult question is whether the conspiracy continues into the concealment phase when the conspirators attempt to avoid arrest and conviction. Occasionally, acts of concealment are part of the substantive offense. In kidnapping for ransom, the kidnappers must conceal both themselves and the victim before collecting the ransom. Here the conspiracy obviously continues while the conspirators commit the acts of concealment. However, most offenses do not contain concealment as an essential element, and the prevailing view is that the court will not infer a subsidiary agreement to continue to act in concert for concealment.

---

28. McColloch v. State, 45 Okla.Cr. 442, 283 P. 1026 (1930).

The prosecution must show an "express original agreement" to extend the conspiracy into the concealment phase.[29] Although this restrictive view commands widespread support among the courts, it is not constitutionally required. In Dutton v. Evans,[30] the Supreme Court sustained a Georgia statute which extends the conspiracy into the concealment phase even in the absence of an express agreement among the conspirators.

"If the Defendant Was Once a Member of the Conspiracy." If the statement occurred during the conspiracy's pendency but before the defendant joined the conspiracy, the statement is admissible against the defendant. The defendant is deemed to have ratified the prior statement. However, if the statement occurred after the defendant withdrew from the conspiracy, it is inadmissible against the defendant. To determine whether the defendant withdrew prior to the statement, counsel must consult the jurisdiction's substantive criminal law rules governing withdrawal.

Ordinarily, the judge will insist that the prosecutor prove these foundational elements before introducing the conspirator's statement. The judge has discretion to vary the order of proof and may admit the statement conditionally or provisionally, depending upon the prosecutor's subsequent presentation of "connecting-up" evidence. If the defense counsel believes that the prosecutor has not fulfilled the condition when the prosecution rests, the defense counsel should move to strike, and if the evidence is highly prejudicial, he or she should request a mistrial.

The Bruton Problem. Suppose that although the conspirator's statement does not fall within the exception, the conspirator and the defendant are being tried jointly. What is the evidentiary status of the statement? One fact is clear: The statement is not admissible as substantive evidence against the defendant. If the judge instructs the jury that they may consider the statement as evidence against the declarant conspirator only, may the prosecutor introduce the statement at the joint trial? Originally, the Supreme Court answered that question affirmatively. Later, reversing this position, the Court handed down its decision in Bruton v. United States.[31] There the Court held that if the statement does not fall within the exception and if the confessing conspirator does not subject himself or herself to cross-examination, it is a denial of confrontation to admit at the joint trial the statement implicating the other defendant. The Court assessed the jury's ability to follow the judge's limiting instruction and concluded that under these circumstances, the limiting instruction would be inadequate protection for the defendant.

The lower courts have not accepted *Bruton* enthusiastically. Rather they have uniformly refused to extend the doctrine and have strictly limited *Bruton* to its facts. A prosecutor can defeat a *Bruton* objection by showing that: the statement in question falls within the co-conspirator exception;[32] the confessing defendant's confession does not directly implicate the other defendant; the confessing defendant testifies and subjects himself or herself to cross-examination;[33] or the statement is substantially similar to the defendant's own admissible confession.[34] If the prosecutor convinces

---

29. Grunewald v. United States, 353 U.S. 391, 77 S.Ct. 963, 1 L.Ed.2d 931 (1957); Lutwak v. United States, 344 U.S. 604, 73 S.Ct. 481, 97 L.Ed. 593 (1953); Krulewitch v. United States, 336 U.S. 440, 69 S.Ct. 716, 93 L.Ed. 790 (1949).

30. 400 U.S. 74, 91 S.Ct. 210, 27 L.Ed.2d 213 (1970).

31. 391 U.S. 123, 88 S.Ct. 1620, 20 L.Ed.2d 476 (1968).

32. United States v. Adams, 446 F.2d 681 (9th Cir. 1971), cert. denied 404 U.S. 943, 92 S.Ct. 294, 30 L. Ed.2d 257.

33. Nelson v. O'Neil, 402 U.S. 622, 91 S.Ct. 1723, 29 L.Ed.2d 222 (1971).

34. United States ex rel. Duff v. Zelker, 452 F.2d 1009 (2d Cir. 1971).

the judge that the confessing defendant's statement falls within the exception, the statement is admissible as substantive evidence against the other defendant. If the judge relies upon any of the other limitations on the *Bruton* doctrine, the judge will receive the statement but give a limiting instruction.

What choices does the prosecution have if *Bruton* squarely applies? First, the prosecution may sever the trials. Second, the prosecution may proceed with a joint trial but forgo the use of the confession. Finally, the prosecution may attempt to redact the confession, that is, to strike all the statement's references to the other defendant. At the very least, the prosecution must delete all references to the other defendant's name. However, there is authority for the proposition that in some contexts, *Bruton* demands more than the deletion of the defendant's name. For example, if the prosecution substitutes a description such as "that white guy" and the defendant sitting before the jury fits the description, some courts find a *Bruton* violation.[35] If a court so finds the prosecution is placed in a difficult dilemma. On the one hand, if the prosecution insists on retaining the description, the court will find a *Bruton* violation of one defendant's confrontation right. On the other hand, if the prosecution agrees to redact all references to third parties in the confessing defendant's statement, that defendant's counsel can argue that the redaction violates due process, for by redacting all references to third parties, the prosecution is converting an admission of complicity in a conspiracy into an admission of sole responsibility for a crime.[36]

Statements of Agents. Although vicarious admissions of agents are encountered more frequently in civil cases, the doctrine is also important in criminal cases, especially when the named defendant is an entity such as a corporation. Generally, the courts have been less receptive to the admission of agents' statements than to the introduction of conspirators' statements; as we shall see, in one important respect the traditional requirements for agents' vicarious admissions are stricter than those for conspirator's statements. Essentially, the courts admit *agents' authorized admissions to proper addressees.*

"Agents'." The proponent must establish that the declarant was the party's agent. As in the case of conspirators' statements, the proponent may not bootstrap: The proponent must present independent evidence of the declarant's status as an agent. Surprisingly, the courts have not limited the doctrine to formal agents and employees. Instead they have sometimes admitted statements by attorneys and accountants who are technically independent contractors rather than agents.

"Authorized Admission." The courts are in sharp disagreement over the showing the proponent must make of the agent's authority. On the one hand, the traditional view is that the proponent must demonstrate that the agent had authority to speak for the principal. Courts subscribing to this view limit the doctrine to spokespersons. Thus the general doctrine governing agents is more restrictive than the specific doctrine governing conspirators. Suppose, for example, that the state is prosecuting a trucking firm for violating highway regulations. Under the traditional view, the prosecutor would have a difficult time introducing a vicarious admission by one of the firm's drivers. The judge is likely to rule that although the driver had authority to perform certain acts for the firm, the driver lacked authority to serve as the firm's spokesperson. Therefore the judge might dismiss the statement as "mere narration" and exclude the evidence.

---

35. Harrington v. California, 395 U.S. 250, 89 S.Ct. 1726, 23 L.Ed.2d 284 (1969); State v. Taylor, 104 Ariz. 264, 451 P.2d 312 (1969) ("another Negro male").

36. State v. Barnett, 53 N.J. 559, 252 A.2d 33 (1969).

On the other hand, there is growing support for a minority view that the proponent need show only that the statement relates to a matter within the scope of the agent's authority. Federal Rule 801(d)(2)(D) commits the federal courts to this approach. In the last hypothetical, a minority jurisdiction court might reach a different result, reasoning that the driver has authority to perform the act of driving the truck and that the statement is logically relevant to that act. ·

"To Proper Addressees." The traditional view is that the agent must make the statement to a third party outsider, someone outside the principal's business organization. The statement is inadmissible if the agent makes the statement to the principal or to another agent of the principal. Under this rationale, internal or intra-organizational reports are incompetent.

However just as the traditional view of the agent's authority is eroding, support is increasing for the abolition of the distinction among the various types of addressees. Rule 801(d)(2) follows this trend. Under the growing liberal view, the only questions are the declarant's status as an agent and the scope of the agent's authority. If the admission qualifies as an authorized admission by an agent, the addressee's identity is immaterial.

If the court refuses to accept the minority view, the proponent might nevertheless be able to introduce the statement. He or she would have to show that high-ranking organization officials, qualifying as spokespersons, approved the report. For example, the proponent might show that the officials took action based on the report. If the proponent can make this showing, the statement will qualify as an adoptive admission.

Suggested Reading:

Dutton v. Evans, 400 U.S. 74, 91 S.Ct. 210, 27 L. Ed.2d 213 (1970).

Bruton v. United States, 391 U.S. 123, 88 S.Ct. 1620, 20 L.Ed.2d 476 (1968).

3. Declarations Against Interest

Suggested Reading:

People v. Leach, 15 Cal.3d 419, 124 Cal.Rptr. 752, 541 P.2d 296 (1975).

Chambers v. Mississippi, 410 U.S. 284, 93 S.Ct. 1038, 35 L.Ed.2d 297 (1973).

Donnelly v. United States, 228 U.S. 243, 33 S.Ct. 449, 57 L.Ed. 820 (1913).

The Elements of the Foundation. The admission exception is often confused with another, distinct exception to the hearsay rule, the exception for declarations against interest. Under this exception, a hearsay statement is admissible if *at the time of the statement, the declarant realized that the statement was against his or her interest and at the time of trial, the declarant is unavailable.*

"At the Time of the Statement." At the time the declarant spoke or wrote, the declarant must have realized that the statement was contrary to his or her interest. Because the judge focuses on the declarant's state of mind at the time of the statement, this realization supplies the guarantee of the statement's trustworthiness.

"The Declarant Realized." In describing the exception, the courts sometimes state simply that the declaration must have been against the declarant's interest. This formulation of the rule is misleading. The pivotal fact is not that the statement is actually contrary to the declarant's interest but rather that the declarant believes that the statement is contrary to his or her interest. The declarant's willingness to make the statement despite that belief is the guaran-

tee of the statement's reliability.[37] If the statement was actually against the declarant's interest but the declarant did not realize the statement's disserving nature, the statement should be excluded. Conversely, if the proponent can prove that the declarant mistakenly thought that the statement was disserving, the statement should be admitted.

Although it is incorrect to formulate the rule as an objective test, many courts and a few statutes phrase the test in these terms: "Would a reasonable person in the declarant's position have realized that the declaration was against his or her interest?" However, again, the critical factor is the actual, subjective state of mind of the declarant. Nevertheless the reasonable person standard is helpful in ascertaining the declarant's state of mind, for the court will rarely have direct evidence of the declarant's state of mind. Instead the court will have to content itself with inferences from circumstantial evidence. The judge can speculate whether in similar circumstances, a reasonable person would have believed that the statement was against his or her interest. In the absence of evidence to the contrary, the judge may assume that the declarant entertained the same belief: "Perhaps a better statement would be that if a reasonable man would have had the belief, the declaration will be received unless there is a finding that the declarant did not believe the declaration to be against interest." [38]

"That the Statement Was Against His or Her Interest." The threshold question is: How does the judge determine whether the statement is contrary to the declarant's interest? May the judge consider both the statement's face and the extrinsic circumstances? While the English cases stress the

statement's prima facie aspect, the American cases permit the judge to range beyond the simple words of statement. Thus the proponent may resort to extrinsic factors to show the statement's disserving aspect, and the opponent may counter with evidence that the declarant had an ulterior motive to falsify.

Suppose that the evidence indicates that the declarant had both disserving and self-serving reasons for making the statement. The polar views are that: (1) The statement is admissible so long as the statement had a substantial, disserving aspect; and (2) the statement is inadmissible if the declarant had any motive to falsify. Most American jurisdictions have avoided either extreme. The prevailing practice is to "balance" the aspects and to admit the statement if the disserving aspect preponderates. Once again, it is important to remember that the pivotal fact is the declarant's state of mind; the issue is which aspect of the statement was actually uppermost in the declarant's thoughts. The courts fond of the objective formulation of the doctrine often seem to balance the aspects in the abstract. The problem becomes one of reconstructing the declarant's state of mind. In the absence of direct evidence, the judge must assume that the declarant entertained the same state of mind a reasonable person would have under the circumstances, but the objectively reasonable state of mind the hypothetical person would have entertained is relevant solely as circumstantial evidence of the declarant's actual, subjective belief.

"Interest." The courts have discussed two aspects of the interest: its magnitude and its type.

(1) The interest's magnitude. Courts often say that the interest must be both substantial and direct. If the interest is insubstantial or remote, the statement is inadmissible. However, like so many other statements about the doctrine, these are misleading. The interest's substantiality and re-

37. Morgan, Declarations Against Interest, 5 Vand. L.Rev. 451, 477 (1952); Jefferson, Declarations Against Interest: An Exception to the Hearsay Rule, 58 Harv.L.Rev. 1, 18, 23 (1944).

38. Id. at 22–23.

moteness are only relevant factors in determining the declarant's state of mind. The more substantial the interest, the more probable it is that the declarant had the interest in mind when he or she made the statement. The more immediate or direct the interest, the greater the probability that the declarant's mind naturally adverted to the interest. Thus elevating substantiality and directness to separate requirements of the foundation is a mistake. The judge should consider these items merely as factors affecting the strength of the inference that the declarant believed the statement to be contrary to interest.

(2) The type of interest. This exception first developed in English civil cases, and not surprisingly the early courts strictly limited it to declarations against proprietary and pecuniary interest. On the contrary American courts believed that the limitation was too restrictive; they reasoned that any substantial interest could furnish an adequate guarantee of trustworthiness.

The American courts first expanded the recognized types of interest by straining the meaning of "pecuniary." Using the classic example of a statement contrary to pecuniary interest as a declarant's statement admitting a debt, many American courts ruled that "pecuniary" interest included any statement which would help to subject the declarant to civil liability in tort or contract.

Until recently, even American courts were reluctant to recognize penal interest. However, in the past few years, the Supreme Court has on several occasions indicated its belief that declarations against penal interest are reliable, and on one occasion it ruled that the exclusion of a declaration against penal interest offered by a defendant (a third party's confession to the crime the defendant was charged with) violated due process.[39] The trend is now

toward the recognition of penal interest,[40] and Federal Rule 804(b)(3) has added impetus to the trend.

Nevertheless defense counsel should not leap to the conclusion that the recognition of penal interest will result in the automatic admission of any accomplice's statement helpful to the defense. In Commonwealth v. Colon,[41] the defendant was charged with murder. The prosecution theory was that the defendant and one Hernandez committed the murder. Using the theory that it qualified as a declaration against interest, the defense offered a statement by Hernandez that he had acted alone. The Pennsylvania Supreme Court upheld the statement's exclusion, saying in effect that the parts of Hernandez' statement exculpating alleged accomplices were not contrary to his penal interest.

Finally, some courts and legislatures have added social interest to the list of recognized interests. In their view, a declarant is unlikely to make a statement which would subject him or her to hatred, ridicule, or social disgrace unless the declarant is convinced that the statement is true. Although the original draft of Rule 804(b)(3) included social interest, the enacted Rule omits it.

"At the Time of Trial, the Declarant is Unavailable." The orthodox English view is that as a condition of admissibility the declarant must be dead. This view, which at one time had a large following in American jurisdictions, is now accepted by only a few courts.[42]

The prevailing modern view is that the statement is admissible so long as the de-

---

410 U.S. 284, 93 S.Ct. 1038, 35 L.Ed.2d 297 (1973); United States v. Harris, 403 U.S. 573, 91 S.Ct. 2075, 29 L.Ed.2d 723 (1971).

40. See Commonwealth v. Hackett, 225 Pa.Super. 22, 307 A.2d 334 (1973); Note, 79 Dickin.L.Rev. 189 (1974); Note, 10 Tulsa L.J. 313 (1974).

41. 461 Pa. 557, 337 A.2d 554 (1975).

42. McDonald v. Protestant Episcopal Church, 150 Mont. 332, 435 P.2d 369 (1967).

---

39. United States v. Matlock, 415 U.S. 164, 94 S.Ct. 988, 39 L.Ed.2d 242 (1974); Chambers v. Mississippi,

clarant is "unavailable." In this context, the courts ordinarily use the same tests for unavailability that they employ to determine former testimony's admissibility. In some jurisdictions, the courts tend toward an extraordinarily liberal test for the declarant's unavailability. There is even authority that proof of the declarant's mere hostility to the proponent is an adequate showing of unavailability.[43]

Heeding the commentators' pleas, Kansas and New Jersey have abolished the requirement of a showing of unavailability. California also did away with this requirement, but it has been reinstated in Evidence Code § 1230. The requirement's abolition is certainly defensible. If the court rigorously enforces the doctrine's other elements, there is a strong guarantee of the statement's trustworthiness; and comparative analysis suggests that like excited utterances, the declaration should be admissible irrespective of the declarant's availability. The drafters of Federal Rule 804(a) adopted a liberal definition of unavailability, but they balked at admitting the declarations of available declarants.

The Differences Between Declarations Against Interest and Admissions of a Party-Opponent. The reader should not think that these two exceptions are mutually exclusive, for they can overlap. For example, if the declarant is both related to the party and unavailable, the declaration might qualify as a vicarious admission and a declaration against interest. However, the counsel will ordinarily have to invoke either one exception or the other, and counsel should have a clear understanding of the major differences between the two exceptions.

First, an admission can be made only by a party or someone legally identified with the party. Anyone can make a declaration against interest.

Second, because the admission must be inconsistent with the position the party is defending at trial, the critical time for testing its disserving quality is the trial. In contrast the critical time for testing a declaration's disserving aspect is when the declarant makes the statement. If the declarant did not then realize the statement's disserving quality, the statement cannot qualify as a declaration against interest. However, this distinction is rarely critical, for the admission usually is contrary to the admitter's interest when he or she makes the statement.

Third, the declaration is admissible in most jurisdictions only if the declarant is unavailable at trial. The party defendant will almost always be available. Of course, because a defendant can sometimes be tried *in absentia*, a defendant's statement could qualify as both an admission and a declaration.

Finally, the courts have been reluctant to relax the application of the personal knowledge and opinion rules to declarations, and they only recently have become receptive to declarations couched as acknowledgements of "fault" or "responsibility." However, as we have seen, the courts often receive conclusory admissions and admissions not based on the admitter's personal knowledge.

Declarations as a Two-Edged Sword. The lowering of the unavailability standard and the recognition of penal interest will result in expanded use of declarations against interest in criminal prosecutions.

Defense Use. The defense can now argue more persuasively for the admission of two types of helpful evidence. First, the defense can argue for the admission of third party's confessions to the crime with which the defendant is charged. If the declarant is unavailable, such confessions will ordinarily qualify as declarations against penal interest. Counsel can argue alternatively that the court should recognize penal interest as a common-law exception and that in an appro-

---

43. State v. Sejuelas, 94 N.J.Super. 576, 229 A.2d 659 (1967).

priate case when the confession is demonstrably reliable, due process demands its admission.[44] Some jurisdictions recognizing penal interest impose limitations on introduction of third party confessions; they either limit admissibility to cases in which the prosecution relies solely on circumstantial evidence or they require corroboration that the declarant committed the offense. Federal Rule 804(b)(3) requires such corroboration. If the defense counsel is faced with one of these limitations and cannot comply, the counsel will have to rely upon the constitutional argument.

Second, the defense can urge the admission of victims' statements which do not qualify as dying declarations. Before dying, the victim might make statements helpful to the defense. In the past judges have excluded these statements if they did not satisfy the requirements for a dying declaration. Thus in a jurisdiction where suicide is still a crime, the victim's statement that he or she attempted suicide might be against penal interest; and in a jurisdiction where suicide is no longer an offense, the counsel could characterize the statement as against social interest.

Prosecution Use. Suppose that for some reason, a conspirator's statement implicating the defendant does not fall within the vicarious admission exception. May the prosecutor introduce the statement as substantive evidence against the defendant on the theory that the statement is a declaration against penal interest? In the past, the courts have refused to permit the prosecution to circumvent the conspirators' admission doctrine in this manner.[45] In People v. Leach,[46] a state

supreme court recently refused to permit the prosecution to use the declaration theory as an alternative "avenue of admissibility" for a co-conspirator's statement. However, one commentator predicted that if the courts ever recognized penal interest, they would ultimately permit the prosecution to use the declaration exception to introduce otherwise inadmissible conspirators' statements.[47] The comments to Federal Rule 804 suggest this possibility.[48]

The defense rejoinder will probably be that while the declarant's reference to his or her own acts is contrary to interest, the references to the defendant's acts are gratuitous and inadmissible. However, the courts applying the declaration exception developed a corollary doctrine that in addition to admitting the statements clearly contrary to interest, they would admit "collateral statements" in the declaration. In one case, the declarant stated that he and his wife were indebted to a third party.[49] The wife argued that while the husband's reference to his own indebtedness was against interest, his reference to hers was inadmissible. Rejecting this argument the court sustained the admission of the reference to her indebtedness as a collateral statement. One respected commentator makes an analogy between that case and the reference to the defendant in a conspirator's declaration.[50] Nevertheless the defense will probably prevail only if the court opts for the approach embodied in Rule 509 (2) of the Model Code of Evidence. Under that provision, collateral statements are admissible if the judge finds them "to be so closely connected with the declaration

44. Chambers v. Mississippi, 410 U.S. 284, 93 S.Ct. 1038, 35 L.Ed.2d 297 (1973); Commonwealth v. Hackett, 225 Pa.Super. 22, 307 A.2d 334 (1973); Imwinkelried, The Constitutional Right to Present Defense Evidence, 62 Mil.L.Rev. 225 (1973); Note, 79 Dickin. L.Rev. 189 (1974); Note, 10 Tulsa L.J. 313 (1974).

45. Commonwealth v. Antonini, 165 Pa.Super. 501, 69 A.2d 436 (1949).

46. 15 Cal.3d 419, 124 Cal.Rptr. 752, 541 P.2d 296 (1975).

47. Jefferson, Declarations Against Interest: An Exception to the Hearsay Rule, 58 Harv.L.Rev. 1, 62 (1944).

48. Advisory Committee Note, Fed.Evid.Rule 804, 28 U.S.C.A.

49. Turner v. Turner, 123 Ga. 5, 50 S.E. 969 (1905).

50. Jefferson, Declarations Against Interest: An Exception to the Hearsay Rule, 58 Harv.L.Rev. 1, 62 (1944).

against interest as to be equally trust-worthy."

DOCUMENTARY EXCEPTIONS

4. Business Entries

Suggested Reading:

United States v. Oates, 560 F.2d 45 (2d Cir. 1977).

State v. McGee, 131 N.J.Super. 292, 329 A.2d 581 (1974).

Johnson v. Lutz, 253 N.Y. 124, 170 N.E. 517 (1930).

The Elements of the Foundation. The business entry doctrine is the first in a series of documentary exceptions to the hearsay rule. The doctrine is that *a routine, original, factual, contemporaneous record, made in the regular course of a business and based upon personal knowledge, is exceptionally admissible.*

"Routine." In part, the truthworthiness of business entries is based on this element of the foundation. The proponent must demonstrate that the organization has a regular, systematic practice of preparing this sort of record and that the record is one in a series of similar entries rather than a casual or isolated entry. Congress amended draft Rule 803(6) to specifically add the foundational requirement that "it was the regular practice of that business activity to make the memorandum, report, record, or data compilation". In recent years, courts have applied this requirement rather laxly. There is now authority permitting the introduction of special reports about nonrecurring events if the report is prepared in the course of a business duty.[51]

"Original." At common law, the entry had to be in a book of original entry, the first permanent record of the data. In the business in question, as soon as a transaction is complete, employees might make up temporary slips and memoranda, which the bookkeeper uses as the basis for entries in a permanent journal or ledger. The journal or ledger would then be the book of original entry. The courts have not enforced this requirement strictly. In many cases, the facts suggest that the business used a double-entry system of accounting, transferring data from the temporary slips to a chronological journal and specialized ledgers. The courts have often permitted the proponent to use either the journal or a ledger.

The modern Uniform and Model acts do not expressly require that the entry be in a book of original entry. In jurisdictions which have enacted the acts the originality element becomes simply an application of the best evidence rule.[52] Of course, many of these jurisdictions have special statutes governing the best evidence rule's application to photographic and microfilm copies and to the situation in which the business has destroyed the original as part of its records retention and destruction policy.

"Factual." The traditional view is that the entry has to be a statement of observed fact about an act, transaction, condition, or event and that statements couched as opinions or conclusions are inadmissible. Some jurisdictions continue to insist that the entry be factual in nature.

Other jurisdictions have accepted an opposite approach, developing the rule that the declarant may make any statement in a business entry which he or she can make on the witness stand. Consider, for example, a hospital record purportedly prepared by the attending physician. The court might first state that because the hospital is repu-

---

51. Jones, Evidence § 12.5 (6th ed. 1972); B. Witkin, California Evidence § 577 (2d ed. 1966).

52. Laughlin, Business Entries and the Like, 46 Iowa L.Rev. 276, 292–93 (1961).

table, the court will assume that the physician is qualified. Then the court will admit any opinion in the entry which a qualified physician can testify to on the witness stand. Rule 803(6) now provides that "opinions or diagnoses" in business entries are admissible.

The modern trend is toward a compromise view. If the opinion's subject matter is relatively simple and non-controversial, the court will admit the opinion. For example, an entry in a hospital record listing physical symptoms such as blood pressure or heart beat would certainly be admissible. Most courts have also concluded that the forensic procedures for identifying suspected contraband drugs are so reliable that police laboratory reports analyzing substances seized from defendants are admissible. However, the court will exclude the opinion entry if the opponent has a substantial need to cross-examine the declarant. This need is a function of two criteria. The first is the opinion's complexity or subjectivity. If the opinion is conjectural or highly evaluative, the policy underlying the hearsay rule mandates that we afford the opponent an opportunity to cross-examine. Many courts are inclined to classify diagnoses of mental disorders in this category. The second factor is the importance of the issue in the context of the particular case. The more central the issue in the case, the more likely the court is to hold that the opponent is entitled to confront a witness rather than a document.

"Contemporaneous." This element is another key to the trustworthiness of business entries. If a substantial period of time elapses between the event and the entry's preparation, the entrant's memory might fail, and the entry therefore might be inaccurate. For this reason, courts demand that the entry be made at or near the time of the event recorded. They do not however require literal contemporaneity: The book need not be a daybook. In fact, courts have placed little emphasis on prompt recording. In some cases, despite the fact that months

elapsed between the event and the entry's preparation, courts have admitted the entry. If the entry is prepared in the regular course of business—that is, the normal course of accounting—the entry satisfies the contemporaneity requirement.

"Record." Although a few jurisdictions have admitted oral reports made in the course of business, the overwhelming majority view is that the exception applies only to documents. But courts have interpreted the term "document" expansively, treating writings, tape recordings, and computer printouts as documents.[53] The emerging principle is that any physical medium for recording and preserving information qualifies as a record.

"Made in the Regular Course of." This is one of the most troublesome elements of the foundation. Even though the type of record need not be essential or even customary in the line of business, the entry must nevertheless be incident to the business's operations; the entry's subject matter must somehow relate to the business' purposes. The language, "made in the regular course of a business," requires at least this minimal connection between the entry and the business. However, some courts have read much more into the language.

In Palmer v. Hoffman,[54] the Supreme Court seemed to infer the meaning not only that the entry must be affirmatively related to the business's purposes but also that the entry cannot have been prepared specifically for litigation. In *Palmer*, the proponent was a railroad, offering a statement contained in a litigation report. The Supreme Court held that the entry must relate to the operations of business *qua* business and that the report in question concerned litigating rather than railroading. The lower courts are divided in their interpretation of *Palmer*.

---

53. See, e. g., Transport Indemnity Co. v. Seib, 178 Neb. 253, 132 N.W.2d 871 (1965).

54. 318 U.S. 109, 63 S.Ct. 477, 87 L.Ed. 645 (1943).

A few courts have developed a rule of thumb that litigation reports such as accident reports are inadmissible. Most courts, however, read *Palmer* as granting the trial judge discretion to determine whether an ulterior motive existed for preparing the report, negativing the business entry's trustworthiness.

The courts have applied the *Palmer* limitation in a criminal context. In a case in which a prisoner alleged brutal treatment by guards,[55] the prison offered its records, containing versions of the incidents as described by the guards. Citing *Palmer*, the Seventh Circuit excluded the records, stating that they could not be presumed to be objective. On similar rationales, courts have excluded notations about the defendant's identity as the source of a drug on chain-of-custody receipts prepared by a narcotics officer.[56] Some courts have also excluded National Crime Information Center printouts.[57] The application of the *Palmer* doctrine to data stored in computers is rather subtle, for actually the record is contained in the computer's memory, lodged in its ferrite core. If no ulterior motive existed for falsifying the record when the business fed the data into the computer, it is immaterial that the business did not prepare the printout until prosecution was imminent.

Like *Palmer*, the New York case of Johnson v. Lutz [58] reads additional meaning into the language, "made in the regular course of a business." In *Johnson*, the proferred document was a police report. The pertinent part of the report was based on a bystander's statement to a policeman about an accident the bystander had witnessed. The court held that the record was not made in the regular course of business, for the by-stander was not a part of the business organization, the police department. *Johnson* requires that everyone contributing information to the report have a business duty to transmit the information; all the contributors must be engaged in and part of the business organization. Modernly, most courts and Federal Rule 803(6) follow *Johnson*. In a jurisdiction adopting this view, the defense counsel can usually exclude reports of investigation by government agencies because these reports are based on both the investigator's personal observation and hearsay statements by third parties outside the government. If the defense counsel invokes *Johnson*, the judge will probably admit only these portions of the report based on the government investigator's personal observation. If prosecution was foreseeable when the investigation began, counsel can succeed in excluding report by citing both *Palmer* and *Johnson*.

"*A.*" The record may be prepared by any business, even a business which is a complete stranger to the action. The source business need not be joined as a defendant. This exception is distinct from the admission exception.

"*Business.*" The courts have construed this term to include almost any regularly conducted activity. It encompasses, for example, private and public activities (a government agency's records can sometimes qualify as business entries as well as official records.), nonprofit activities such as hospitals and churches, and even unlawful activities (organized crime follows the corporate model). In the rare situation in which the prosecution locates an organized crime activity's records, they will be admissible as business entries. Moreover, in drug trafficking cases, courts have admitted the defendant's customer book on both business entry and admission theories.

"*And Based on Personal Knowledge.*" Traditionally, the courts required the proponent to show either that the entrant (the person making the entry) had personal

55. Bracey v. Herringa, 466 F.2d 702 (7th Cir. 1972).

56. United States v. Goodlow, 500 F.2d 954 (8th Cir. 1974); State v. Branch, 222 N.W.2d 423 (Iowa 1974).

57. State v. McGee, 131 N.J.Super. 292, 329 A.2d 581 (1974).

58. 253 N.Y. 124, 170 N.E. 517 (1930).

knowledge of the facts recorded or that the original informant in the business organization had such knowledge. Federal Rule 803(6) preserves this requirement, referring to "a person with knowledge."

A minority of jurisdictions have abolished this requirement. They have adopted the Model Act for Proof of Business Transactions, upon which 28 U.S.C.A. § 1732 was patterned. In pertinent part, this Act provides that "all other circumstances of the making of such writing or records, including the lack of personal knowledge by the entrant or maker," affect weight but not admissibility. In short, Congress's adoption of Rule 803(6) should have the important effect of reinstating this element in the foundation for business entries in federal courts.

The Method of Laying the Foundation. In the typical large business organization, identifying or locating the person who made an entry in business records will be difficult. Even if the entrant can be identified, producing him or her at trial will be inconvenient, and the likelihood is that an entrant who has made thousands of similar entries will be unable to recall the circumstances surrounding the entry in question. For these reasons, courts have liberalized the foundation for business entries. The witness first authenticates the record simply by testifying he or she removed it from the files where the business customarily stores its records. After authenticating the record, the witness lays the foundation for the business entry exception. The witness may be the document's custodian, the entrant's supervisor, or any other "qualified witness." In this context "qualified witness" means someone who has personal knowledge of the business' procedures for preparing records. The witness describes the business' method of preparation, including the sources of information normally used and the time the record is ordinarily prepared. The witness need not have any personal knowledge of the circumstances surrounding the preparation of

the particular record. So long as the witness can describe the business' record preparation procedures, the court can use that description as habit or practice evidence to support the inference that on the occasion in question, the business probably followed its habitual practice.

Examples of Competent Business Entries. Commercial records can be competent business entries in criminal prosecutions. The classic example is a book account showing debits and credits. The prosecution might introduce a motel record to show the defendant's proximity to the scene of the crime, or the defense might offer hotel registration or time cards to establish an alibi. If a pistol is found at the scene of the crime, the prosecution can offer the sales slip to connect the defendant with the pistol. In a theft prosecution, the government might introduce the victim firm's records or an invoice to show its ownership of the property subsequently found in the defendant's possession.

Moreover, business entries are useful in presenting scientific evidence. Some courts now permit the prosecution to offer police chain-of-custody receipts to establish the fact that the substance analyzed was the substance taken from the defendant or the crime scene. Additionally courts are receiving business entries reflecting maintenance on the instruments used to conduct scientific tests; they have admitted entries showing tuning fork tests for radar and breathalyzer inspection certificates. Finally, many courts are now routinely accepting laboratory reports of the tests themselves when the courts feel that the opinions expressed are not highly subjective or evaluative. For instance, courts have accepted laboratory reports of chemical analyses of suspected contraband drugs, blood alcohol concentration, and vaginal swab tests.

Palmer notwithstanding, for certain purposes courts have received police business records based on the officers' personal knowledge. It is often relevant in a criminal prosecution either to show that the police had notice of a fact or that they arrested the defendant at a certain time; such information can be critical in the litigation of voluntariness and *Miranda* challenges to confessions. Thus the judge might admit an arrest record, police blotter, police radio log, or arrest register at a hearing on a motion to suppress.

5. Official Records

Suggested Reading:

Commonwealth v. Perdok, 411 Pa. 301, 192 A.2d 221 (1963).

The Elements of the Foundation. Like business entries, official records constitute a documentary exception to the hearsay rule. Because modern government generates so many documents, prosecutors and defense counsel often invoke this exception to the rule. This basic doctrine is that *a factual, contemporaneous, public record, properly prepared by an official with a duty to record the fact and based on personal knowledge, is exceptionally admissible.*

"Factual." All courts will admit an entry in an official record which is a statement of observed fact. However, the courts split when the entry relates to such matters as medical causation or legal responsibility. Coroner reports, police reports, and death certificates frequently contain such statements. The traditional view is that these entries are inadmissible.[59] In recent years, however, major changes have taken place.

The first occurred in cases admitting entries relating to causation. If the court believes that the physical cause of death is readily diagnosable, it might admit the entry of causation. The traditional view has not, however, been completely supplanted, for some recent cases exclude entries attributing death or injury to battered child syndrome, trauma, and asphyxia. Although on its face, Rule 803(8) does not limit admissible entries to statements of observed fact, its legislative history is unclear.[60] Nevertheless in federal courts the Rule will probably liberalize admissibility of statements concerning medical causation.

Other inroads have been made in admission of entries relating to legal responsibility. It is a common practice for the death certificate or county pathologist's report to characterize a death as homicidal, accidental, or suicidal. Some courts will now admit such characterizations especially when the official who prepared the report is a qualified forensic pathologist. Probably a majority of courts still exclude such entries.

"Contemporaneous." A minority of courts have applied the contemporaneity requirement to official records as well as to business entries. For example, California Evidence Code § 1280(b) requires that the report be prepared "at or near the time of the act, condition, or event." Understandably the courts applying this requirement rarely enforce it strictly.

In contrast the majority does not impose any contemporaneity requirement. In these jurisdictions, the courts demand only that the document comply with the fifth

---

59. See, e. g., People v. Holder, 230 Cal.App.2d 50, 40 Cal.Rptr. 655 (1964).

60. The debate in the House suggests that that body intended to limit the provision's scope to statements of observed fact. Congressional Records, February 6, 1974, pp. H563–65, quoted in West's Federal Rules of Evidence for United States Courts and Magistrates 120–25 (1975). However, the Report of the Senate Committee on the Judiciary states: "The House Judiciary Committee report contained a statement of intent that the phrase 'factual findings' in subdivision (c) be strictly construed and that evaluations or opinions contained in public reports shall not be admissible under this rule. The committee takes strong exception to this limited understanding of the rule." Id. at 126.

foundational element; namely, that it be "properly prepared." If, following proper procedures, an official makes a corrected entry months or even years after the event, the record will be admissible in most jurisdictions.

"Public." The English courts and a minority of American courts limit the exception to records open to public inspection. However, the majority of American courts require at most that the document be in official custody, and when they admit certificates they dispense even with that requirement.

"Record." An official record can take virtually any form: a writing, a tape recording, or a computer printout. Federal Rule 803(8) specifically states that the record may be "in any form."

"Properly Prepared." The official preparing the record must comply with the prescribed procedures for doing so. The courts sensibly require substantial rather than strict compliance. If the only defect in the record is a minor irregularity such as a typographical error or misspelling, the court can admit the record. However, if there is an omission or misstatement of an important item of information, the court will exclude the document.[61]

"By an Official." The class of officials includes government employees. The employee can be assigned to the legislative, judicial, executive, or administrative branch, or to a local, state, national, or foreign government. Some courts have treated even employees of heavily regulated public utilities as officials.[62]

A person can qualify as an official even if he or she lacks general official status;

thus a person can be an ad hoc public official for the purpose of preparing a specific report. A statute or regulation can impose upon a private citizen the duty to prepare a report or to both prepare and file the report. For example, many statutes require physicians, undertakers, and ministers to prepare certificates to be given to other citizens or reports to be filed with the government. Courts have treated such vital statistic certificates and reports as official records.

"With a Duty to Record the Fact." The courts often say that the official must prepare the report "in the scope of duty." This phrase means simply that the official must have had a duty to make the specific entry offered. If the official did not have any duty to prepare the document, it cannot qualify as an official record. If the official had a duty to prepare a document but gratuitously included extraneous entries, these entries are inadmissible. The rules governing the existence of a duty to record the fact vary, depending upon the nature of the official record offered.

(1) Registers. The record can be a register—a record of the official transactions occurring on the official's business premises. An official ordinarily has an implied duty to maintain a register. For instance, the county clerk might maintain a registry of deeds which shows when deeds are recorded on the business premises.

(2) Returns. The record can take the form of a return. A return is a record of an act the official personally performs outside the business premises where the record will be maintained. While the official might maintain a single register for all homogeneous transactions, he or she usually prepares a separate return for each transaction. Police officers execute returns on search and arrest warrants and then file the returns with an official such as the clerk of the issuing court. A minister performs a marriage ceremony, executes the return on the marriage license, and then files the return

61. Mutual Life Ins. Co. v. Bell, 147 Fla. 734, 3 So. 2d 487 (1941); Portland Maine Pub. Co. v. Eastern Tractors Co., 289 Mass. 13, 193 N.E. 888 (1935).

62. Southern Express Co. v. Byers, 240 U.S. 612, 36 S.Ct. 410, 60 L.Ed. 825 (1916); Virginia v. West Virginia, 238 U.S. 202, 35 S.Ct. 795, 59 L.Ed. 1272 (1915).

with the marriage license bureau. The duty to prepare a return must be either expressly imposed or implied from the nature of the official's position. For example, a surveyor has an implied duty to file the maps he or she prepares in surveying land.

(3) Certificates. The record can also be a certificate. An official gives a certificate to a private citizen, and the citizen retains the certificate. If the document is truly a certificate, it need not be filed in any public office to qualify as an official record. At early common law, the courts demanded that the proponent show that the certifier had an express duty to prepare and issue the certificate. Modernly, the courts have found implied duties in two instances. First, notaries have authority to issue certificates about acts authorized to be performed in their presence, e. g., executions and acknowledgements. Second, custodians of official records have authority to execute attesting certificates that attached documents are true and accurate copies of original official records in the certifier's custody.

(4) Reports. Finally, the record can take the form of a report. A report of investigation is a record of an investigation the official conducts, usually off the business premises. Here the courts insist that the duty be expressly imposed or implied from the very nature of the official's position.

"And Based on Personal Knowledge." The traditional view is that the document must be based on the official's personal knowledge. This requirement does not pose any barrier to the admission of the first three types of records, for the deputy clerk making the entry in the deed registry will be the clerk who personally handled the registration; the officer executing the search warrant return will have participated in the search; and the notary executing the certificate will have observed the person signing. If the person preparing the record lacks personal knowledge, the record is probably improperly prepared and inadmissible for that reason.

The real problems arise with reports of investigation. During the course of the investigation, the investigator will usually consult hearsay sources. The report's recitals of facts or events the investigator personally observed are admissible. Additionally the report's findings, based on facts the investigator personally observed, are admissible unless excludable as improper opinion. If the findings rest in large part on hearsay information, the court will probably exclude them. Finally, the report might cite statements made by third parties. The citation is admissible to prove that the third party made the statement, but the statement itself is inadmissible as subtantive evidence unless it falls within a separate hearsay exception.

Under the traditional view, findings based on hearsay information can be admitted only if a statute abrogates the common law. Such a statute might require the official to include a certain entry and then provide that the record will be admissible as "prima facie" or "presumptive" evidence of the truth of all the required entries.[63] The courts have construed such statutes as authorizing the entry's use as substantive evidence. If the statute requires the finding to be entered but states only that the record will be admissible as evidence of "the facts recited" a difficult problem of statutory construction arises. Here the question is whether the factual finding is a "fact" within the statute's intendment and the courts have divided on the answer.

Professor McCormick forcefully advocated that the trial judge be granted discretion to admit entries in evaluative investigative reports.[64] Other modern commentators concurred in urging the courts to liberalize the traditional view without enabling

---

63. The Advisory Committee Note to Rule 803(8) contains a list of federal statutes authorizing the introduction of evaluative reports.

64. McCormick, Can The Courts Make Wider Use of Reports of Official Investigations? 42 Iowa L.Rev. 363 (1957).

legislation. The commentators have been successful in persuading some legislatures to make changes in the traditional view. For example, California Evidence Code § 1280 (c) does not require that the record be based on personal knowledge; rather the statute authorizes the presiding judge to weigh "the sources of information and method and time of preparation" to determine whether the record is trustworthy. Uniform Rule 63(15) would also have a liberalizing effect. Rule 803(8) effects a less sweeping change, admitting factual findings in investigative reports "in civil actions and proceedings and against the Government in criminal cases."

The Method of Laying the Foundation. The introduction of an official record is a disarmingly simple process. Sometimes the proponent simply marks the document for identification, hands it to the opposing counsel and judge for inspection, and the judge then admits the document. However, in reality, the foundation consists of two evidentiary doctrines. One is judicial notice in which the judge sub silentio judicially notices the statute or regulation imposing the duty to record the fact. The second is presumption or inference. If the document is fair on its face, a presumption or inference arises that the official properly prepared the document. If the document's face is regular, the opponent has the burden of coming forward with evidence that the document was not properly prepared.

Examples of Competent Official Records. Innumerable varieties of official records exist. For instance, courts have admitted department of motor vehicle records, weather reports, Selective Service records, and occasionally even letters. When a public official's letter, otherwise qualifying as an official record, is addressed to another public official, courts have sometimes treated the letter as an official record.[65] However, the

courts have been reluctant to treat letters addressed to private individuals as official records.

6. Past Recollection Recorded

Suggested Reading:

United States v. Marshall, 532 F.2d 1279 (9th Cir. 1976).

The Elements of the Foundation. The forgetful witness is a common phenomenon in criminal prosecutions. He or she may forget the relevant incident entirely, or as is usually the case, forget pertinent numbers, times, or quantities. When the witness's memory fails, counsel can sometimes resort to a document the witness prepared prior to trial. As previously stated, a few jurisdictions such as Kansas subscribe to the view that if an out-of-court declarant subsequently becomes a witness at trial, the declarant's prior, extra-judicial statements are no longer deemed hearsay. In these jurisdictions, the witness's prior written statements would certainly be admissible. However, in most jurisdictions, the document would constitute hearsay. Nevertheless counsel might be able to introduce the document as a record of the witness's past recollection. The past recollection recorded doctrine is that *when a witness has personal knowledge of a fact and prepares a record while the event is still fresh in the witness's memory, the record is admissible if at trial, the witness cannot recall the fact but can vouch for the record.*

"When a Witness Has Personal Knowledge of a Fact." The courts are in agreement that the record is inadmissible unless the witness had personal knowledge of the data recorded.

"And Prepares a Record." With respect to this element of the foundation, we must distinguish among three fact situations. In

---

65. United States v. Corwin, 129 U.S. 381, 9 S.Ct. 318, 32 L.Ed. 710 (1889); Dinsman v. Wilkes, 53 U.S. (12 How.) 390, 13 L.Ed. 1036 (1851).

the first situation, the witness on the stand personally prepared the record. Here all courts agree that the witness's personal preparation of the record satisfies the foundation. In the second situation, a third party prepared the record, but the witness examined the document and found it correct. The courts agree that the witness's verification of the record is satisfactory. The third situation is the most troublesome, for it involves the cooperative record: *A* orally reports facts to *B*, who transcribes the oral report, but *A* never verifies the record. The predominant modern view is that such a cooperative record is admissible. The proponent may call both *A* and *B* to have them describe their parts in the record's preparation. If they prepared the record in the course of a business, the court may accept habit evidence of the business' record preparation practices.

The third situation may present difficulties under the new Federal Rule 803(5), which requires that the record be "made or adopted by the witness." If the courts read this language literally, they will exclude cooperative records, for with a cooperative record, the original informant neither makes nor adopts the document by verification. If the courts find the language ambiguous, they may resort to the Rule's legislative history; and turning to the report of the Senate Committee on the Judiciary, they will find only a broad statement that the Rule applies to "situations involving multiple participants." [66] How the federal courts will resolve this constructional issue remains to be seen.

"While the Event Is Still Fresh in the Witness's Memory." The traditional view is that the witness had to prepare or verify the record contemporaneously with the event—that is, at or near the time of the event. Modern courts use a more liberal formulation of this element, requiring only that the witness prepare the record while the event is still fresh in his or her memory. However, even these courts demand that the witness prepare the record within a relatively short period of time. Although they will tolerate a lapse of several days between the event and the record's preparation, when the delay reaches weeks or months, the probability of the record's admission decreases sharply.

"The Record Is Admissible." If the proponent lays a proper foundation, the witness may read the record to the jury, and the jury may treat the record as substantive evidence. Moreover, in many jurisdictions, the proponent may formally introduce the document and submit it to the jurors for their inspection. Though a minority precludes the proponent from introducing the record, even these jurisdictions allow the opponent to introduce it. Rule 803(5) commits the federal courts to this approach.

"If at Trial, the Witness Cannot Recall the Fact." This foundational element creates the necessity for resorting to the evidence itself. The question here is how incomplete must the witness's memory be before the proponent may introduce the record. The early view was that the record is admissible only if the witness's memory fails completely—that is, the witness has no independent recollection of the event. However modern courts take a more realistic view. For example, Federal Evidence Rule 803(5) permits the proponent to introduce the record if the witness cannot recall "fully and accurately." Thus, if the witness testifies either that he or she cannot recall details of the event or that his or her present recollection is hazy, the court can permit the proponent to introduce the record to supplement the in-court testimony.

"But Can Vouch for the Record." The witness can vouch for the record in several ways. Ideally, the witness will testify that he or she distinctly recalls preparing or verifying the record. If, however, the witness is a police officer or business employee who has prepared hundreds or even thousands of similar records, it is doubtful that he or she

66. Quoted in West's Federal Rules of Evidence for United States Courts and Magistrates 112 (1975).

will recall the circumstances surrounding the preparation of any specific report. If the witness is unable to give the ideal foundational testimony, the proponent can resort to habit evidence. Thus, the proponent can elicit the witness's testimony that the witness is in the habit of carefully recording this sort of information. If even habit evidence is unavailable the proponent can, as a last resort, elicit the witness's testimony that the witness recognizes his or her own handwriting and is certain that he or she would not have signed the document unless convinced that it was correct. This sort of testimony is obviously weak; the witness is actually vouching for his or her own integrity rather than the document's accuracy.

The Method of Laying the Foundation. The fifth foundational element, the witness's present inability to remember, is the one new trial attorneys have the most difficulty properly laying. The proponent must demonstrate on the record that even after reading the document, the witness lacks present recollection. The proponent can effectively lay this element in the following fashion. As soon as the witness indicates that he or she cannot remember a specific fact, the proponent should lay the other foundational elements, e. g., the document's authorship and its time of preparation. Then the proponent should mark the document for identification, hand it to the witness, and ask the witness to read it silently. After the witness has done this, the proponent should ask the witness to return the document. The proponent should then hold the document away from the witness, asking that the record reflect this act. Finally, the proponent should directly ask whether after having read the document, the witness can presently recall the event. If the witness says "no," the foundation is complete, and the proponent in most jurisdictions can then formally introduce the record. If the witness says "yes," the witness can then testify under a present recollection revived theory.

The Distinction Between Past Recollection Recorded and Present Recollection Revived. The past recollection recorded doctrine is closely related to the present recollection revived theory. Unfortunately, precisely because of the close relationship, counsel often confuse the two doctrines. In truth, fundamental differences exist between them. If the document's tender to the witness actually revives the witness's memory, the witness can testify from refreshed, independent recollection. The evidence admitted is the witness's testimony rather than the document. Under the present recollection refreshed theory, which is not a hearsay exception, the document functions solely as a memory aid.

The Proponent. A proponent attempting to invoke the present recollection revived theory faces two questions.

First, what may the proponent use to refresh the witness's memory? Practitioners are not the only people guilty of confusing past recollection recorded and present recollection refreshed; appellate judges have sometimes committed the same error. For this reason, there is a minority view that the restrictions applicable to past recollection recorded apply with equal force to documents used to refresh recollection. In a court following the minority view, the judge would insist that the proponent show the document's authorship and time of preparation.

However, the majority of courts clearly distinguish the two theories. In a majority court, the proponent could use anything in the nature of a document to refresh the witness's recollection: a newspaper clipping, a deposition, a letter, a transcript of a former trial, a transcript of the witness's grand jury testimony, statements, an investigative police report, a tape recording, or a photograph. Some jurisdictions take an even broader view, suggesting that a proponent can use anything—an odor, a song or an exercise—to revive recollection.

Second, how should the proponent use the document to refresh the witness's memory? In a few jurisdictions, the customary practice is that when it becomes apparent the proponent will resort to present recollection revived, the witness temporarily retires from the stand to examine the document. However, in the overwhelming majority of jurisdictions, the witness remains on the stand. In some courts, the proponent or trial judge reads the document to the witness even when the jury is present. Nevertheless, the preferable practice is to tender the document to the witness, ask the witness to read the document silently, and then inquire whether the document refreshes recollection. If the memory aid is a tape recording, the witness should be provided with earphones, or the tape should be played to the witness in the jury's absence. Although under the theory of present recollection refreshed, the proponent cannot offer the record into evidence, some courts insist that the proponent at least mark the record for identification; and in any case the proponent should certainly physically insert the document into the record for the appellate court's benefit. If the witness says that he or she now recalls the event and the testimony's subject matter is fairly simple, the opponent should insist that the witness testify without holding the document. When the subject matter is fairly complex, such as a lengthy list of stolen articles, many judges permit the witness to intermittently consult the document even under the theory of present recollection refreshed.

The Opponent. Objecting to the Document's Use to Revive Recollection. The foundational requirements for present recollection refreshed are so minimal that the opponent rarely can object successfully. If the case arises in a minority jurisdiction applying the past recollection recorded restrictions to present recollection refreshed, the opponent may of course insist that the proponent lay the same foundation. The opponent may also object if the proponent re-

sorts to the document before the witness indicates that he or she has forgotten a specific fact; there must be some indication in the record that the witness's memory needs refreshment. Finally, while the courts generally liberally permit the proponent to use almost any document to refresh recollection, authority exists that the proponent may not use a document prepared specially for trial, for such specially prepared testimonial notes are too suspect.[67]

Procedures if the Judge Permits the Proponent to Use the Document. If the judge permits the proponent to use the document on the stand, the opponent has a right to inspect it. In some jurisdictions, the right is deferred until the conclusion of the direct examination; in other jurisdictions, the opponent may inspect the document before the proponent hands it to the witness. While the courts uniformly confer a right to inspect a document consulted in the courtroom, they divide on the right to inspect a document the witness consults prior to trial.[68] Though the traditional view is that the opponent does not have a right to inspect such documents, under Rule 612 the judge has discretion to grant the opponent the right. A few jurisdictions have statutes giving the opponent an absolute right to inspect documents consulted prior to trial. After inspection the opponent may use the document to cross-examine the witness.

Finally, the opponent may formally introduce those parts of the document relevant

---

67. N.L.R.B. v. Federal Dairy Co., 297 F.2d 487 (1st. Cir. 1962).

68. State v. Miller, 368 S.W.2d 353 (Mo.1963); Peters v. People, 151 Colo. 35, 376 P.2d 170 (1962); State v. Paschall, 182 Wash. 304, 47 P.2d 15 (1935); State v. Deslovers, 40 R.I. 89, 100 A. 64 (1917). These cases deal with a right under the evidence law of present recollection revived. The defense counsel often has an alternative discovery theory. For example, he or she might invoke a statutory discovery right such as the Jencks Act, 18 U.S.C.A. § 3500, or a common-law discovery right. People v. Estrada, 54 Cal.2d 713, 7 Cal.Rptr. 897, 355 P.2d 641 (1960).

to the witness's direct testimony. The document may reveal affirmative discrepancies between its contents and the direct examination. Also the opponent might want to introduce the document to cast doubt on the witness's testimony that reading the document refreshed his or her recollection; the document's content might seem so unrelated to the witness's testimony or so lacking in detail that the jury will doubt the witness's veracity.

7. Learned Treatises

Suggested Reading:

Allison v. State, 203 Md. 1, 98 A.2d 273 (1953).
Moore v. State, 184 Ark. 682, 43 S.W.2d 228 (1931).

The Elements of the Foundation. With forensic science playing a greater role in criminal trials, the learned treatise exception to the hearsay rule takes on more importance. The counsel does not have to produce a live witness to introduce scientific evidence, for the counsel may use a learned text or periodical as the means of introducing the evidence. At this point, we are not dealing with use of scholarly texts to cross-examine an expert. Rather we are dealing with use of the text's contents as substantive evidence. For example, this use might occur during the direct examination of a friendly expert who authenticates the text. Here the proponent is not only showing the basis of the expert's testimony, but he or she is also using statements in the text as evidence of the truth of the assertions. The learned treatise doctrine is that *statements in authoritative, learned publications, written by impartial persons, are competent as substantive evidence.*

"*Statements.*" Some jurisdictions follow the simple rule that any relevant statement in a qualified text is admissible. Although Federal Rule 803(18) uses the term "statement," most of the jurisdictions with statutes authorizing the admission of learned treatises contain more restrictive language. The statutes in Iowa and California, for example, permit the introduction only of statements concerning "facts of general notoriety and interest." Some courts in these states have seized upon that language as grounds for excluding specialized information in medical texts, reasoning that such specialized information is of neither general notoriety nor interest.

"*In Authoritative.*" The proponent must establish that the publication in question is a standard authority in the field, specifically showing that the publication is currently accepted and recognized as authority in the profession. Especially in the inexact, inductive sciences, the state of the art is constantly advancing, and texts written only a few years before might be outdated by the time of trial. The proponent must show that the publication is a contemporary standard authority.

"*Learned.*" The courts have gradually expanded the fields of learning in which texts can be competent evidence. At first, the courts conservatively limited the exception to rather static bodies of knowledge: the exact sciences, history, and geography. Because mathematic, historical, and geographic facts are "certain and constant," publications such as logarithm tables, history texts, and maps were admitted. Even in jurisdictions with statutes broadly authorizing the admission of "books of science," the courts were reluctant to admit medical, psychiatric, or surgical texts,[69] for they believed that these bodies of knowledge change so rapidly that a statement in a text written only a few years previously might be outdated at trial.

---

69. See, e. g., Allison v. State, 203 Md. 1, 98 A.2d 273 (1953); Moore v. State, 184 Ark. 682, 43 S.W.2d 228 (1931); Eggart v. State, 40 Fla. 527, 25 So. 144 (1898).

Modernly, courts and legislatures are more flexible, and are beginning to recognize as competent evidence texts in the fields of the inexact, inductive sciences, especially medicine. The scope of the most recent statutes is especially broad. Federal Rule 803 (18) sanctions the admission of texts "on a subject of history, medicine, or other science or art." California Evidence Code § 1341 has a similarly broad ambit: "historical works, books of science or art, and published maps or charts." Some courts are now admitting even driver braking distance and reaction time tables.[70]

"Publications." Most of the decided cases involve true treatises—that is, textbooks. However, the doctrine is not so limited; Rule 803(18), for example, refers to "published treatises, periodicals, or pamphlets." In Alabama, courts have admitted publications such as the *American Medical Association Journal, Clinics of North America, Journal of Industrial Medicine, New England Journal of Medicine,* and *Mayo Clinics.*[71] Although establishing the authoritative status of an article is usually more difficult than establishing that of a textbook, counsel should realize that the doctrine is not restricted to textbooks.

"Written by Impartial Persons." One of the primary guarantees of the trustworthiness of learned treatises is the fact that their authors are scholars. Though the Federal Rules do not make this foundational element explicit, many statutes expressly state that the treatise's author must be a "person indifferent between the parties." Affirmatively, because the scholar is writing for his or her colleagues, he or she knows that the publication will be subjected to rigorous peer scrutiny. Negatively, the scholar

is not connected with the litigation and thus has no motive to misrepresent.

"Are Competent as Substantive Evidence." The traditional view, which most jurisdictions continue to follow, is that statements in even authoritative, learned treatises are incompetent hearsay. The courts believe that in addition to presenting the normal hearsay dangers, a learned treatise poses the problem that the lay jurors might be unable to evaluate the treatise's technical statements. However, a small group of jurisdictions including Alabama, Wisconsin, and California [72] admit as substantive evidence statements from publications so long as the proponent can authenticate the works as learned treatises.

Recently, there has been some movement toward a compromise view illustrated by Rule 803(18), which will probably continue to gain new adherents. Rule 803(18) permits the treatise's use as substantive evidence if the publication is "called to the attention of an expert witness upon cross-examination or relied upon by him in direct examination." Thus Rule 803(18) conditions the treatise's admissibility on the presence in the courtroom of an expert who can explain, interpret, and apply the text for the jury. The proponents of this view fear that if the treatise is admitted in the absence of an expert, the jury either might not comprehend the technical terminology or might misapply the principle enunciated. However, even though proponents may now authenticate an especially well-known treatise by judicial notice, they usually rely upon authenticating witnesses. Therefore, the imposition of a formal requirement of an expert's presence would not impose any serious

---

70. West's Ann.Cal.Evid.Code § 1341.

71. Comment, Learned Treatises As Direct Evidence: The Alabama Experience, 1967 Duke L.J. 1169, 1182 n. 53.

72. Goldman, The Use of Learned Treatises in Canadian and United States Litigation, 24 U.Tor.L.J. 423 (1974); Comment, Admissibility of Medical Books in Evidence, 8 U.S.F.L.Rev. 364 (1973); Comment, Learned Treatises As Direct Evidence: The Alabama Experience, 1967 Duke L.J. 1169; 66 Mich.L.Rev. 183 (1967); Note, 46 Iowa L.Rev. 463 (1961); Note, 29 U.Cin.L.Rev. 255 (1960).

hardship on the proponent and would allay the most serious fear of the adherents of the traditional view.

The Method of Laying the Foundation. The first problem facing the proponent is the authentication of the text. To lay the foundation, he or she must establish that the publication is an authoritative, learned treatise. To lay an absolutely complete foundation, the proponent should show both the author's qualifications and the text's status as a standard authority. After establishing that the author is an expert, the proponent could show that the text is used extensively by practitioners as a sourcebook or that it is a recognized reference in professional schools. The proponent may use several methods of laying the foundation: stipulation; judicial notice of very well-known texts such as *Gray's Anatomy*; testimony of an opposing expert; testimony of one of the proponent's own experts; testimony of a professional librarian such as a medical librarian; and documents in those jurisdictions where the courts relax the competence rules for foundational matters. Even where this last method of proof is permissible, the proponent should not rely solely upon it, for the courts rarely sustain a finding of authoritativeness based only on written, biographical data about the author.[73]

In all jurisdictions if the judge rules that the foundation is sufficient, the attorney may then read the pertinent passage to the jury. It is apparently customary in most jurisdictions to formally admit the treatise into evidence and then permit the jury to take the text into the deliberation room. However, this practice creates the risk that the jury either will attach undue weight to the text or will consult other passages during deliberation. To eliminate this risk, Federal Rule 803(18) mandates that "the statements may be read into evidence but may not be received as exhibits." Even in jurisdictions formally admitting the text into evidence, some judges insist that the proponent submit a xeroxed or photographic copy of the pertinent passage to the jury rather than tender the entire textbook to the jury.

APPARENTLY SINCERE STATEMENTS

8. Excited Utterances

Suggested Reading:

United States v. Napier, 518 F.2d 316 (9th Cir. 1975).

The Elements of the Foundation. The frequently used excited utterance doctrine is one of the hearsay exceptions for apparently sincere statements.[74] The doctrine evolved from the *res gestae* exception, whose core concept, Wigmore believed, is *spontaneity*. Accordingly, the courts developed the doctrine that *a factual statement by any participant in or observer of a startling event about the event is exceptionally admissible if the declarant made the statement while still in a state of nervous excitement caused by the event.*

"A Factual." At early common law, the courts applied the opinion prohibition to excited utterances, but modernly they have relaxed the prohibition's application, realizing that the prohibition is merely a rule of preference and that it should apply loosely, if at all, to extra-judicial statements. The courts will now accept statements in the form of conclusory opinions such as acknowledgements of fault or responsibility.

---

73. Goldman, The Use of Learned Treatises in Canadian and United States Litigation, 24 U.Tor.L.J. 423, 447 (1974).

74. Fed.Evid.Rule 803(2), 28 U.S.C.A.

"Statement." The statement will almost always be oral. The fact that the declarant had the presence of mind to reduce the statement to writing tends to negative spontaneity. Nevertheless, on rare occasions courts have held that written statements qualified as excited utterances.[75]

"By Any." Courts have often stated that the declaration may be made by any person. Perhaps surprisingly, most courts take the statement literally, holding that the declarant need not be a party; that the declaration is admissible even if the declarant is available; that the declarant may be unidentified—for example, a member of a crowd who witnessed the event; and that it is immaterial that the declarant would have been an incompetent witness because of insanity, infancy, or spousal privilege. However, a few courts attach such weight to the policy underlying the spousal privilege that they will not admit even an excited utterance by a spouse. Other courts believe that a statement by an exceedingly young child or a severely mentally disordered person simply lacks probative value.[76]

"Participant in or Observer of." This element of the foundation restates the general requirement that the declarant have acquired personal knowledge of the fact stated by observing or participating in the event. The declarant can acquire the knowledge either as an actor in the event or as an eyewitness spectator.

The courts are wary when the declarant is unidentified. The declarant's personal knowledge may be shown inferentially, and some courts go to the length of admitting the statement so long as the facts are consistent with the inference that the declarant observed the event. However, other courts insist on some affirmative showing of personal knowledge on declarant's part. When the declarant is an unidentified member of a crowd which gathered near the crime scene, the opponent should emphasize the personal knowledge element of the foundation. In such circumstances, it might be virtually impossible for the proponent to make an affirmative showing of the declarant's personal knowledge, and if the opponent can persuade the trial judge to require at least a minimal showing, the opponent's objection will be successful.

"A Startling." This element focuses on the type of event: It must be startling enough to produce a spontaneous reaction of nervous excitement. This element is the objective element of spontaneity; the event must be startling, and as a further element the declarant must in fact have been subjectively startled. As we shall see, if the declarant has a particularly high excitement limen and remains calm in the face of an objectively startling event, his or her statement is not deemed spontaneous. However, in practice, the courts rarely question the former element of the foundation. They are more concerned with the showing of the declarant's actual, subjective excitement than with the event's objectively startling character.

"Event." It is well-settled that the startling event need not be the act charged in the indictment or information. Rather the event may be any relevant transaction. The question which has divided the courts is whether the proponent must present independent evidence of the event's occurrence: evidence apart from the proferred declaration.

A minority of courts demand such independent evidence. However, the trial judges in even these jurisdictions usually are content with only slight independent evidence. Generally, the judge will admit the statement if the declarant's physical appearance and demeanor suggested the event.

75. United States v. O'Brien, 51 F.2d 37 (4th Cir. 1931) (suicide note).

76. Ketcham v. State, 240 Ind. 107, 162 N.E.2d 247 (1959); State v. Rothi, 152 Minn. 73, 188 N.W. 50 (1922); Huntley v. State, 73 Fla. 800, 75 So. 611 (1917).

For example, if the declarant appeared dazed, disheveled, agitated, or bruised, the judge will usually accept these circumstances as sufficient evidence of an assault. Additionally courts are especially liberal in child molestation cases in which the infant is probably the only witness to the crime.

The majority of courts do not require any independent evidence. In short, they effectively eliminate this element of the foundation. So long as it purports to relate to a relevant event, the statement is admissible. The Advisory Committee's Note to Federal Rule 803(2) specifies that the Rule follows the prevailing practice making independent evidence unnecessary.

"About the Event." The opponent should carefully scrutinize the content of the proferred statement. Under the prevailing view, the statement's subject must be the event itself, and the statement's content must concern the facts and circumstances surrounding the event rather than those surrounding antecedent or subsequent events. Only one jurisdiction, the District of Columbia, has dispensed with this foundational requirement.[77]

"The Declarant Made the Statement While Still in a State of Nervous Excitement." Affirmatively, the statement must be spontaneous and impulsive. Negatively, it must not be the product of deliberation and design. The statement must be made under stress rather than being a calm narrative of a past event. At root, the question is the strength of the inference of nervous excitement. Like most inferential questions, the issue does not lend itself to any hard and fast rules. However, some of the relevant factors may be identified.

(1) The lapse of time between the event and the statement. In rare cases, the state-

ment may antedate the event, for the event might have been anticipated when the declarant made the statement. For example, perceiving that a collision is imminent, the declarant might make an exclamation about the anticipated crash. Nevertheless, in most of the decided cases, the event antedates the statement; and the courts consider the time interval between the event and the statement as a relevant factor. Indeed, they usually say that the time interval or element is the most important factor. Thus the greater the time lapse, the less the likelihood that the statement will qualify as an excited utterance. However, most courts are especially lax in sex offense cases and cases involving minors.[78] They reason that the offense's nature or the victim's identity ensures a relatively long period of trauma. The victim of a sex offense can hardly brush aside the event quickly, and children are more impressionable than adults. However, whenever the delay exceeds an hour, the likelihood of the statement's admission decreases markedly.[79]

A few jurisdictions are not content with mere spontaneity. Indiana, Mississippi, and Vermont insist also upon contemporaneity when the proferred statement is an accusatory statement by a homicide victim.[80] In these jurisdictions, the statement may not follow the event but instead must be contemporaneous with it, and the opponent should demand that the proponent show both contemporaneity and spontaneity. If the basic guarantee of trustworthiness is spontaneity, this strict view seems unreasonably

---

77. The cases are civil actions. Sawyer v. Miseli, 156 A.2d 141 (D.C.App.1959); Felder v. Pinckney, 244 A.2d 481 (D.C.App.1968); Murphy Auto Parts Co. v. Ball, 249 F.2d 508 (D.C.Cir. 1957), cert. denied 355 U.S. 932, 78 S.Ct. 413, 2 L.Ed.2d 415 (1958).

78. Beausoliel v. United States, 107 F.2d 292 (D.C. Cir. 1939); People v. Baker, 251 Mich. 322, 232 N.W. 381 (1930).

79. See, e. g., Sanders v. State, 127 Tex.Cr.R. 55, 75 S.W.2d 116 (1934). But see Guthrie v. United States, 207 F.2d 19 (D.C.Cir. 1953); People v. Noble, 23 Mich.App. 100, 178 N.W.2d 118 (1970).

80. State v. Peebles, 170 N.C. 763, 87 S.E. 328 (1915); Brown v. State, 78 Miss. 637, 29 So. 519 (1900); Parker v. State, 136 Ind. 284, 35 N.E. 1105 (1894).

severe; a statement can certainly be spontaneous and impulsive even if it follows the event.

(2) The declarant's location at the time of the statement. If the declarant either has moved or has been moved from the site of the event, the probability that the court will find spontaneity is reduced. But no hard and fast rule exists. If the declarant speaks about a startling event while he or she is in a hospital's emergency room, his or her absence from the crime scene will not preclude a finding of spontaneity.

(3) The declarant's conduct and the conduct of other involved persons. The opponent should inquire into the conduct of the declarant between the event and the statement. If in the interim the declarant performed tasks requiring reflective thought, this action tends to negative spontaneity. The opponent should also consider whether the declarant made the statement on his or her own motion or whether a bystander elicited the statement. A few jurisdictions have a strict rule that the statement is inadmissible if the declarant spoke in response to a question. However, most jurisdictions do not adhere to this rule of exclusion. Realistically, people who rush to a crime or accident scene usually ask, "What happened?" The fact that a bystander asked that question does not preclude an inference of spontaneity. Nevertheless even in a majority jurisdiction, the opponent should emphasize the length of the interrogation and the leading character of the question, for the trial judge may exclude the statement if it was a product of a long, leading interrogation.

(4) The declarant's condition at the time of the statement. If the declarant was experiencing severe pain caused by injuries suffered in the startling event, the statement can be spontaneous even when several hours have elapsed since the event. For example, a robbery victim who had been beaten and tied can make a spontaneous statement when

police untie him or her a substantial period of time after the crime.[81]

Even more dramatic are those situations in which the declarant became comatose during the event and made the statement as soon as he or she regained consciousness—sometimes hours or days after the crime. If the declarant makes the statement immediately upon regaining consciousness, the courts usually allow the statement's admission. Thus these cases highlight the ultimate issue: the declarant's state of mind when he or she makes the statement. The lapse of time, the distance traveled, the statement's character, the declarant's conduct, and his or her condition are all relevant factors; but the ultimate issue is whether a sufficiently strong inference exists that at the time of the statement, the declarant's mind remained under the event's influence. Whenever there is such an inference, the statement satisfies this element of the foundation.

The Fresh Complaint Doctrine. In addition to the excited utterance doctrine, courts often utilize the fresh complaint doctrine. The complaint in question is the complaint of a sex offense victim: the report that the offense occurred. Courts have taken three different approaches to this doctrine.

First, some courts simply do not recognize a separate fresh complaint doctrine. They hold that in order to be admissible, the complaint must qualify under one of the conventional evidence doctrines, usually prior consistent statement or excited utterance.[82] If the statement qualifies as a prior consistent statement, it might be admissible after the opponent has impeached the complaining witness. Under this theory, although the complaint's details are admissi-

---

81. United States v. Merrill, 484 F.2d 168 (8th Cir. 1973), cert. denied 414 U.S. 1077, 94 S.Ct. 594, 38 L. Ed.2d 484.

82. Jones, Evidence § 10:20 n. 65 (6th ed. 1972).

ble, the judge will give a limiting instruction that the jury may consider the statement only for the purpose of rehabilitating the complaining witness's credibility. If the statement qualifies as an excited utterance, the statement is admissible even if the victim does not testify. The details concerning the startling assault are admissible, and the statement can be used as substantive evidence.

A second group of courts treats fresh complaint as a separate bolstering doctrine. When the proponent lays a proper foundation, he or she may introduce evidence of the complaint to bolster the complaining witness's credibility even before impeachment. These courts have developed the view that *in sex offense cases in which lack of consent is an element or in which the victim testifies to lack of consent, evidence of the victim's fresh complaint to authorities about the fact of the offense and the offender's identity is admissible for the limited purpose of bolstering the victim's credibility.*

"In Sex Offense Cases." This doctrine is limited to sex offense prosecutions for crimes such as rape, assault with intent to rape, and sodomy.

"In Which Lack of Consent Is an Element or in Which the Victim Testifies to Lack of Consent." The fact of the complaint is logically relevant only if the crime was non-consensual; when such a crime is committed, the victim is outraged and will usually complain. The courts admit the evidence whether lack of consent is an essential element of the offense—e. g., rape—or the victim testifies to lack of consent—e. g., statutory rape.

"Evidence." Several types of evidence are admissible to prove the complaint. The victim may testify to his or her own complaint; the recipient of the complaint may testify; or someone who overheard the complaint may testify.

"Of the Victim's." The complainant, who may be male or female, must have been

the victim; bystanders' statements are inadmissible under this doctrine.

"Fresh." A few courts sometimes confuse the excited utterance and fresh complaint doctrines, holding that the latter must be made as promptly as the former. However, most courts can distinguish the doctrines and hence relax the time requirement for fresh complaint. They do not demand that the declarant still be in a state of nervous excitement; the complaint is "fresh" even though the declarant has had an opportunity to reflect.[83] Although the opinions' wording sometimes suggests that only the first complaint is admissible, there is authority that if the victim makes two reports within a short period of time, both may qualify as fresh complaints. Some courts have gone even further, virtually dispensing with any timeliness requirement. They state that the delay is "subject to explanation" and goes to the complaint's weight rather than to its admissibility.[84] Courts of this persuasion have admitted complaints made months after the offense's commission.[85]

"Complaint." The statement must be in the nature of a complaint or grievance. The statement is inadmissible if the declarant was gossiping or bragging when he or she made the statement. It is the sense of outrage which ensures trustworthiness, and if the declarant was not outraged, the statement cannot qualify under this theory.

"To the Authorities." The courts have admitted complaints made to police officers, family members, or simply to people whom the victim encountered after escaping.

"About the Fact of the Offense." The courts recognizing this doctrine permit the witness to testify to "the fact of the com-

83. People v. Damen, 28 Ill.2d 464, 193 N.E.2d 25 (1963).

84. State v. Grady, 183 N.W.2d 707 (Iowa 1971).

85. Coffman v. State, 3 Tenn.Cr.App. 634, 466 S.W. 2d 241 (1971), cert. denied 404 U.S. 1019, 92 S.Ct. 689, 30 L.Ed.2d 668 (1972); People v. Damen, 28 Ill. 2d 464, 193 N.E.2d 25 (1963).

plaint." They customarily permit the witness to relate that the victim complained, that the victim complained of a certain type of offense, and that the victim complained about an offense committed at a certain time and place. These details inform the jury of the complaint's relevance to the case. However, with one exception courts do not permit the witness to recite any other details of the complaint.

"And the Offender's Identity." This one exception is the fact some courts permit the witness to add that the victim identified a certain person as the offender. Even the courts recognizing the basic doctrine divide on the identity's admissibility.[86] The majority rule appears to be that the detail of identity is inadmissible.[87]

"Is Admissible for the Limited Purpose of Bolstering the Victim's Credibility." The separate fresh complaint doctrine is not a hearsay exception, and courts admit the statement for the limited purpose of bolstering credibility before impeachment. Thus the complaint is admissible only if the victim testifies at trial.

There is language in some cases suggesting a third approach to fresh complaint; the language suggests that fresh complaint is a separate exception to the hearsay rule. Some cases assert that the fresh complaint doctrine is an exception to the hearsay rule.[88] However, these statements are dicta. In no decided case has a court admitted the complaint's details as substantive evidence in the absence of circumstances establishing the excited utterance exception. In one respect, though, some courts have treated the fresh complaint doctrine as if it were a true hearsay exception. If the court applies fresh complaint as a strictly bolstering doctrine, the court should not admit the complaint unless the victim testifies at trial; a few courts have admitted fresh complaint evidence when the victim was unavailable.[89] However, no court has taken the ultimate step of elevating the fresh complaint doctrine to the status of a new exception to the hearsay rule and using the complaint's details as substantive evidence on that basis alone.

Suggested Reading:

People v. Crume, 61 Cal.App.3d 803, 132 Cal.Rptr. 577 (1976).

People v. Butler, 249 Cal.App.2d 799, 57 Cal.Rptr. 798 (1967).

9. Present Sense Impressions

Suggested Reading:

United States v. Kehoe, 562 F.2d 65 (1st Cir. 1977).

As we previously stated, Professor Wigmore thought that spontaneity is the underlying rationale of the *res gestae* cases. In contrast his predecessor, Professor Thayer identified contemporaneity as the basic rationale. Believing that the two theories of admissibility are mutually exclusive, most courts accepted Wigmore's and rejected Thayer's. Fortunately, Professor Morgan resurrected the contemporaneity theory and pointed out that either contemporaneity or spontaneity justifies a hearsay statement's admission. Professor Morgan's work accounts for the modern present sense impression exception: *A declarant's statement about an event is*

---

86. State v. Grady, 183 N.W.2d 707, 716 (Iowa 1971).

87. See, e. g., Aaron v. State, 273 Ala. 337, 139 So. 2d 309 (1961), cert. denied 371 U.S. 846, 83 S.Ct. 81, 9 L.Ed.2d 82 (1962).

88. State v. Tirone, 124 N.J.Super. 530, 308 A.2d 38 (1973); 65 Am.Jur.2d Rape § 76 (1972); People v. Stevens, 11 Ill.2d 21, 141 N.E.2d 33 (1957).

89. 65 Am.Jur.2d Rape § 76 (1972).

exceptionally admissible if the declarant made the statement while observing the event and if the witness who relates the declaration at trial observed the event.

"A Declarant's Statement." The courts have not demanded that the statement be a mere recitation of observed fact. Instead they have frequently admitted opinions such as statements that a car was traveling too fast.

"About." This element of the foundation defines the declaration's permissible subject matter—what it must describe or explain. In most jurisdictions, the subject matter may be any event, and the declarant may be participant or spectator. Federal Rule 803(1) has especially broad language, referring to "an event or condition." California Evidence Code § 1241 contains the peculiarly restrictive language that the declaration's subject matter must be the "conduct of the declarant." Under this statute, the declarant cannot be a mere bystander. Furthermore, even if the declarant was a participant, the statement must relate to the declarant actor's own conduct.

"An Event." The event need not be the act charged in the indictment or information; it may be any logically relevant occurrence. Moreover, in contrast to excited utterances, the event need not be startling, for in the instant case, the statement's guarantee of trustworthiness is its contemporaneity.

One unresolved question is whether independent evidence of the event's occurrence must be shown. Although there is authority that such evidence is necessary,[90] foundations rarely fail for this element alone. In jurisdictions requiring the last foundational element, the witness on the stand must be capable of supplying the needed corroboration; that witness must have observed the described event. If no independent evidence

exists, the foundation will fail on both elements. In the jurisdictions where the issue is unsettled the judge will probably refer to the jurisdiction's rules governing excited utterances which usually do not require independent evidence of the startling event's occurrence.

"The Declarant Made the Statement While." Because the exception is for *present* sense impressions, the statement must temporally accompany the event. Many jurisdictions insist upon strict contemporaneity. For example, California Evidence Code § 1241 requires that declarant make the statement "while the declarant was engaged in such conduct." Of course, exact contemporaneity is usually impossible, for the sense impression is a reaction to an external stimulus—an event—and the event will literally antedate the impression. Thus courts are usually content with substantial contemporaneity, admitting the statement if it is made a few seconds or sometimes minutes after the event transpires. Federal Rule 803(1) contains the especially liberal provision that the declarant may make the statement "while the declarant was perceiving the event or condition, or immediately thereafter." However, under even this provision, a court would undoubtedly enforce the timeliness requirement more strictly than in the case of excited utterances.

"Observing the Event." To be admissible, the statement must be a sense impression of the event. The declarant must have had personal knowledge of the facts asserted in the statement.

"The Witness Who Relates the Declaration at Trial Observed the Event." When Professor Thayer was developing his contemporaneity theory, he argued that one of the conditions of admissibility should be that the witness on the stand have observed the event.[91] If the court imposed this require-

90. Fitzpatrick v. Woodmen of the World Life Ins. Soc., 238 Mo.App. 385, 179 S.W.2d 753 (1944).

91. Thayer, Bedingfield's Case—Declarations as a Part of the Res Gestae, 15 Am.L.Rev. 6, 83, 107 (1881).

ment, the opponent could then cross-examine the witness about the statement's correctness. Many subsequent commentators concurred with Thayer's judgment that the court should require this additional element in the foundation.[92] Even the courts enforcing the requirement never insisted that the witness be a third-party observer. If the statement was otherwise admissible, the witness could be the declarant; the declarant-turned-witness had observed the event, and the opponent could cross-examine the declarant-witness about the accuracy of his or her prior statement.

The commentators have presented a strong argument for the inclusion of this element in the doctrine's foundation. However, the common-law courts occasionally disregarded the element.[93] In addition, this element does not appear to be a requirement under modern statutes. For example, on its face, Federal Rule 803(1) does not contain such a requirement. If the judge refuses to add the element by judicial gloss, the proponent could introduce evidence of a declarant's sense impression through a third party witness who had heard the statement but had not observed the event.

10. Dying Declarations

Suggested Reading:

People v. Bagwell, 38 Cal.App.3d 127, 113 Cal.Rptr. 122 (1974).

The introduction of a homicide victim's death-bed statements can have a dramatic impact on the outcome of a case. Such statements are admitted under the dying declaration exception to the hearsay rule. The exception's premise is that the approach of the awful event of death induces a sincere state of mind in the declarant. The exception is that *in certain types of cases, the decedent victim's complete, factual declaration about the cause and circumstances surrounding his or her death is exceptionally admissible if, at the time of the statement, the declarant had a hopeless expectation of imminent death.*

"In Certain Types of Cases." At early common law, dying declarations were admissible only in homicide prosecutions. Thus, courts admitted dying declarations in prosecutions for murder, manslaughter, and abortion when under the jurisdiction's substantive criminal law, the victim's death was an element of the charged offense. The courts excluded the declarations in rape and common abortion cases. The draft Federal Rule 804(b) would have increased the types of federal prosecutions in which declarations are admissible, but Congress decided to restrict Rule 804(b)(2) to the traditional scope.

Modernly, by decisional or statutory law, many states have broken away from the restrictive common-law view. Some courts admit dying declarations in any case in which the charged offense results in death; so long as the evidence shows that the charged crime was the cause of death, the decedent's statements are admissible. For example, suppose that the prosecution charges the defendant with assault and after the prosecution files its charge, the victim dies from the injuries inflicted in the assault. The victim's dying declarations would be admissible even if the prosecution does not amend the charge. Other jurisdictions such as Colorado and Kansas admit dying declarations in any case in which the statement is logically relevant.

"The Decedent." The overwhelming majority view is that when the proponent offers the declaration at trial, the declarant must be dead. Surprisingly, Federal Rule

---

92. Comment, Spontaneous Exclamations in the Absence of a Startling Event, 46 Colum.L.Rev. 430, 439 (1946).

93. Id. citing Simpson v. Miller, 97 Mont. 328, 34 P.2d 528 (1934) and Thompson v. State, 166 Ga. 512, 143 S.E. 896 (1928).

804(b)(2) has changed the standard in federal court. Under the Federal Rule, a statement may qualify as a dying declaration even if the declarant is not dead; it is sufficient if at the time the statement was made, the declarant believed he or she was dying and at the time of trial, the declarant is unavailable. Rule 804(a) defines "unavailability."

"Victim's." The traditional view is that the prosecution not only must be a homicide prosecution but it also must be for the declarant's homicide. The declarant must be the charged victim. Under this view a statement by any person other than the named victim is inadmissible. Thus, the prosecution could not offer an inculpatory statement by another victim whom the defendant killed at the same time, and the defense could not offer a third party's death-bed confession which exculpated the defendant. Most modern codifications of the dying declaration exception dispense with this element of the foundation, permitting either side to use any decedent's dying declarations.

"Complete." At one time, the courts subscribed to the view that the declaration was inadmissible unless it represented everything the declarant intended to say. The statement was admissible even if the declarant knew and could have said more about the incident. However, fragmentary declarations were inadmissible; if coma or some other factor interrupted the statement before the declarant could finish, the partial declaration was inadmissible.

Even at common law, courts began disregarding this element,[94] and modern statutes do not include it. At most, the judge has discretion to exclude a fragmentary declaration if he or she thinks that the declaration might mislead the jury. When the declaration's wording suggests that the declarant was about to add an important qualifi-

cation just before the declarant lapsed into a coma, the judge can exclude the statement. However, in most jurisdictions, there is no longer a strict rule excluding incomplete statements.

"Factual." This element of the foundation consists of two aspects. The first aspect is the application of the opinion prohibition to dying declarations. The opinion problem arises quite frequently, for the victim's declarations often characterize the defendant's conduct in a conclusory fashion.[95] At first, the courts rigidly enforced the opinion prohibition. For example, the courts excluded the decedent's statements to the effect that the defendant assaulted him or her in cold blood or intentionally. The courts even-handedly enforced the rule against the defense as well as the prosecution, excluding declarants' statements that the killing was accidental, that the defendant did not intend to harm the declarant, or that the defendant was insane at the time of the incident.

However, some courts were more lenient in their treatment of defendants' evidence, and eventually most courts generally liberalized the opinion prohibition's application to dying declarations. The courts now routinely admit conclusory declarations. For example, the court will admit the decedent's statement that the defendant acted without provocation or cause.

The second aspect is the application of the personal knowledge requirement to dying declarations. Both courts and commentators are in general agreement that the personal knowledge requirement applies to the declaration; it is admissible only if the declarant had personal knowledge of the fact stated. However, especially in poisoning cases, courts have sometimes overlooked the requirement, admitting a decedent's statement that the defendant poisoned him or her. Al-

---

94. Kliks, Impeachment of Dying Declarations, 19 Or.L.Rev. 265, 279 (1940).

95. See, e. g., People v. Bradfield, 300 Mich. 303, 1 N.W.2d 550 (1942); Mann v. Commonwealth, 215 Ky. 731, 286 S.W. 1044 (1926).

though the opinions usually contain insufficient information to clearly resolve the issue, it is doubtful whether the declarant had personal knowledge of the fact of poisoning. Uniform Rule 63(5) does not require the declarant to have personal knowledge.[96]

"Declaration." The declarations may be oral, written, partly oral and partly written, or even non-verbal. If a decedent assented to a document, the document is admissible as the declarant's statement in spite of the fact that the declarant did not sign the document. Sometimes the declarant will communicate by non-verbal conduct, making signs, blinking eyes in response to questions, or squeezing a bystander's hand in response.

"About the Cause and Circumstances Surrounding His or Her Death." This element regulates the scope of the admissible statement. The courts generally use the phrasing, "the cause or circumstances of his or her death," thus limiting the declaration's subject to the *res gestae* of the homicide. However, it would be more precise to say that the declaration must relate to the circumstances causing the declarant's dying condition. The statement may describe the assault or other incident causing the injury, but it may not relate to the defendant's previous threats or attempts against the declarant or to previous hostilities or quarrels between the two parties.

This is another element which courts have often relaxed. While some courts strictly confine the admissible statement to the cause of the dying condition, other courts have admitted evidence of the threats the defendant made the morning of the assault, remarks pertaining to a wife's adultery, and the identity of the person who furnished the instrumentalities for the abortion.[97] In a recent case, a court admitted a victim's statement about why he was murdered—the fact

that he "knew too much" about a bank robbery.[98]

Some jurisdictions have taken the next step and formally abolished the scope limitation on dying declarations. In Colorado and Kansas, for example, the practice follows Uniform Rule 63(5), admitting any logically relevant statement.

"If at the Time of the Statement, the Declarant Had a Hopeless Expectation of Imminent Death." The declarant may make the statement at any time between the infliction of the injury and his or her death. The test is whether at the time of the statement, the declarant had the requisite state of mind, ensuring the statement's sincerity. Although all courts essentially require a showing that the declarant believed immediate death was certain, they have used numerous expressions to describe this critical state of mind: the declarant must be *in extremis* or *in articulo mortis*; the declarant must have an unconditional belief that death is impending or imminent; the declarant must have despaired and abandoned all hope; the declarant must believe that doom will be swift, certain, and inevitable. It is insufficient that the declarant believed death to be certain or immediate death to be probable. If the declarant had even a faint or slight hope of recovery, the declaration is inadmissible.

Which factors should the proponent rely upon in laying the foundation? If the declarant expressly stated that he or she believed death is near, the statement is direct evidence of the requisite state of mind. Unfortunately, the proponent rarely has such direct evidence and ordinarily must rely upon circumstantial evidence. The proponent may show that a physician told the declarant that the wound was fatal; that the declarant probably overheard the physician tell a third party that the wound was mortal; that the

---

96. Quick, Some Reflections on Dying Declarations, 6 How.L.J. 109, 126 (1960).

97. See cases collected at 2 Wharton, Criminal Evidence § 317 n. 54 (13th ed. 1972).

98. United States v. Etheridge, 424 F.2d 951 (6th Cir. 1970).

declarant received the last rites; that the wound was so severe that the declarant must have known that death was near—e. g., the decedent had a large wound and intestines were visibly protruding. The courts have permitted physicians and even lay bystanders to express their opinions of the declarant's state of mind at the time of the declaration.

Which factors should the opponent rely upon in resisting the statement's admission? The declarant might have made a statement that he or she "will get" the defendant. Such statements indicate that the declarant had not abandoned all hope of surviving. The opponent can also use the injured person's requests for assistance as some evidence that the declarant hoped for recovery. However, numerous courts have upheld the admission of dying declarations even though the record clearly indicated that the declarant had requested aid.[99]

11. Statements of Bodily Condition

In this area, new counsel often make a fundamental mistake, overlooking the threshold question of whether the evidence offered is actually hearsay. First, the statement itself might not be assertive; the proponent of an involuntary, inarticulate exclamation such as a groan or scream does not have resort to a hearsay exception. Second, the proponent might be offering the statement for a non-hearsay purpose. Thus before rushing to this exception, the proponent should always carefully consider whether the statement falls within the definition of hearsay.

Statement of Present Bodily Condition. The statement is admissible if it relates to proper subject matter and if it was made to a proper addressee. The statement must purport to be a description of a then existing sensation or condition. An injured or diseased person might describe such sensa-

tions as pain, suffering, or as any other feeling he or she is then experiencing.[1] Except in Georgia, such a statement is admissible to prove the existence, nature, and location of the sensation. Most courts extend the exception to conditions as well as sensations, with some courts admitting a declarant's statement that she was pregnant. So long as the declarant purports to describe a then existing sensation or condition, it is immaterial that a substantial time interval passed between the event inflicting the injury and the statement. In addition to describing proper subject matter, the statement must have been made to a proper addressee.

A layperson is a proper addressee. A treating physician is also a proper addressee. If the declarant consulted a physician for treatment or diagnosis with a view toward treatment, the physician qualifies. However, treatment need not have been the declarant's sole motive in consulting the physician; if the trial judge can find any significant treatment motive, he or she will ordinarily admit the statement as substantive evidence.

While the courts are in agreement concerning laypersons and treating physicians, they divide when the physician addressee was a prospective witness at the time of consultation. A defendant declarant might have consulted a physician, such as a psychiatrist, solely to qualify him or her to testify at trial, or the court might have appointed the physician to examine the defendant, report to the court, and testify at trial. Under these circumstances do the declarant's statements to the physician fall within the exception? Although some courts have said that the statements are inadmissible for any purpose,[2] the majority view perhaps is now that even if the statement is inadmissible as substantive evidence, it is admissible to show the

---

99. See, e. g., People v. Tahl, 65 Cal.2d 719, 56 Cal. Rptr. 318, 423 P.2d 246 (1967).

1. But see Paulk v. Thomas, 115 Ga.App. 436, 154 S.E.2d 872 (1967).

2. United States v. Calvey, 110 F.2d 327 (3d Cir. 1940); United States v. Roberts, 62 F.2d 594 (10th Cir. 1932).

basis of the expert opinion the physician expresses at trial.

A growing number of courts have opted for a third view that the statements fall within the hearsay exception and that the fact the declarant consulted the physician witness solely to qualify the physician as an expert at trial affects only the testimony's weight. Several courts have adopted the third view as a matter of decisional law, and Federal Rule 803(4) commits the federal courts to this view. The Rule's text authorizes the admission of statements made "for purposes of medical diagnosis *or* treatment," and the Advisory Committee's Note indicates that a diagnosis which enables the physician to testify at trial meets this standard.

Statement of Past Bodily Condition. In the course of examining the patient, a physician will elicit his or her case history. This history will include the patient's statements about past as well as present symptoms. Once again, there are subject matter and addressee restrictions on the statements' admissibility.

The majority view might still be that a declarant's statements of past bodily condition are inadmissible for any purpose. However, substantial authority now exists that the statements are admissible for the limited purpose of showing the basis of an expert physician's opinion. Moreover, in recent years support has grown for the view that statements of past bodily condition are admissible as substantive evidence.[3] The courts adopting this view usually admit only statements made to treating physicians. They reason that the declarant probably realized that for treatment purposes his or her description of past symptoms is as important as the description of present symptoms. Some jurisdictions have governing statutes of which California's Evidence Code § 1251 is a particularly interesting example. The statute admits statements of past bodily condition as substantive evidence only when the declarant is unavailable and if his or her prior bodily condition is itself an issue in the case.

At common law, courts have rejected statements made to testifying physicians, admitting only statements addressed to physicians consulted for treatment. The modern statutes liberalize the rule. Some state statutes seem to authorize the admission of a statement made to any type of addressee. Federal Rule 803(4) effects a less sweeping change and admits only statements made "for purposes of medical diagnosis or treatment." The Advisory Committee's Note explains that given the Rule's limitation to those purposes, the admissible statements will probably be limited to statements addressed to physicians, "hospital attendants, ambulance drivers, or even members of the family."

Suggested Reading:

Meaney v. United States, 112 F.2d 538 (2d Cir. 1940).

Accompanying Statements of Causation. At the same time the declarant describes present and past symptoms, he or she might describe the events which in his or her mind resulted in the symptoms—the time, place, conditions, and circumstances of the objective cause. Should the court admit the statement of objective cause as well as the statement of subjective symptoms? At common law, almost all courts answered that question in the negative, justifying the evidence's exclusion not only on the possibility that the patient will color the description of external events but also on the theory that in most cases, the statements of external cause are not "pathologically germane."

---

3. Meaney v. United States, 112 F.2d 538 (2d Cir. 1940).

Federal Rule 803(4) departs from this conventional view, authorizing the admission of statements of "the inception or general character of the cause or external source thereof insofar as reasonably pertinent to diagnosis or treatment." As adopted, the Rule contains two significant limitations. First, the statement must be generalized. The Advisory Committee's Note specifies that "statements as to fault" will ordinarily be inadmissible. Second, even if the statement is generalized, it is competent only if the statement of causation was "reasonably pertinent to diagnosis or treatment." For example, a rape victim's generalized statement to a physician that she has been raped is pathologically germane, for it will affect the nature of the treatment the physician prescribes for the declarant. However, the victim's assertion of the rapist's identity would be inadmissible, perhaps for two reasons. The statement is dangerously specific, and in most cases, the rapist's identity is not pertinent to treatment.

12. Statements of Mental or Emotional Condition

From a practical perspective, the problems related to this exception are perhaps more important than the exception itself. The first related problem is a familiar one—the proponent's failure to recognize nonhearsay theories for the evidence's admissibility. In many cases in which the proponent invokes the "state of mind" exception, he or she should simply have asserted that the evidence is not hearsay. For example, the prosecution may offer a defendant's statements as circumstantial evidence of the defendant's malice toward or hatred of the victim. The defense may offer the defendant's statements reflecting delusions for the nonhearsay purpose of proving insanity. In an extortion case, the prosecution may offer the victim's statements as circumstantial evidence of the requisite fear. The defense may offer the alleged victim's statements indicating a suicidal intent.

A second, related problem is the opponent's failure to attack the effectiveness of limiting instructions on state-of-mind evidence offered for nonhearsay purposes. The classic case in point is Shepard v. United States.[4] In *Shepard*, the prosecution charged the defendant with murdering his wife, and the defense contended that the wife committed suicide. To rebut the defense contention, the prosecution offered evidence of the wife's statement, "Doctor Shepard has poisoned me." On appeal the prosecution argued the statement was admissible for a nonhearsay purpose—that is, for negativing a suicidal frame of mind. As a matter of hearsay law, this theory of admissibility is sound. The prosecution's use was nonhearsay, for the fact that the wife made that statement tends to negative suicidal intent. Ordinarily, then, the judge could simply admit the evidence and give a limiting instruction. Here, however, the Supreme Court held that the statement was so prejudicially accusatory that any limiting instruction would have been ineffective. *Shepard* thus counsels defense attorneys resisting state-of-mind evidence that even when the prosecution can articulate a nonhearsay purpose for an accusatory statement, the defense attorney has a second line of attack; citing *Shepard*, the counsel should argue that the statement is so directly accusatory that even a limiting instruction will probably not prevent jury misuse of the evidence for hearsay purposes.

The third related problem is that counsel tend to use "state of mind" as a magical expression. The proponent incants the phrase without explaining which of the various state-of-mind doctrines he or she is relying upon. As we shall see, there are several variations of this exception. To determine which is appropriate, the proponent must consider two factors. First, the proponent should consider the statement's purport. Does it purport to be an expression

---

4. 290 U.S. 96, 54 S.Ct. 22, 78 L.Ed. 196 (1933).

of present rather than past state of mind? In order to answer this question correctly, the proponent should subject his or her evidence to careful, facial analysis. Second, the proponent must consider the purpose for offering the evidence. Is the statement being offered to prove state of mind as an end in itself or as the basis for a further inference of some conduct? To ensure the admission of state-of-mind evidence, the proponent should articulate precisely the theory of admissibility.

Use of Statements of Present State of Mind or Emotion When That State Is in Issue. Sometimes the proponent will attempt to prove state of mind or emotion as an end in itself when the state itself is in issue. It is well-settled that even outright declarations of state of mind are admissible for this latter purpose. However, to understand the decided cases, we must distinguish between two fact situations.

In this first situation, the declarant makes the statement at the operative time. For example, under substantive criminal law, in an extortion case the operative state of mind is the victim's state when he or she surrenders the property to the defendant. If at time of surrender, the victim makes a declaration of a fearful state of mind, the declaration is admissible. The proponent is offering a declaration of then existing state of mind simply to prove that state of mind.

In the second situation, the declarant's statement of state of mind is not made at the operative time, but the court nevertheless permits the proponent to use the statement to prove the state at the operative time. For example, shortly after surrendering the property to the defendant, the extortion victim might make a declaration of his or her still subsisting fear. On its face, although the declaration expresses presently existing fear, it is not made at the operative time. However, the court might admit the statement on a "continuity of state of mind" or "stream of consciousness" theory. The court initially admits the statement for the

hearsay purpose of proving the victim's state of mind when the declaration was made; and if the interval between the operative time and the declaration is short enough, the court then permits the proponent to draw the permissive inference that the declarant's state of mind was the same at both times. The assumptions are that the state of mind continues and that a declaration of state of mind at one time supports an inference of state of mind at another time. This continuity concept can look forward or backward. The prosecution may use the extortion victim's declaration shortly before surrendering the property to prove the victim's state of mind at the subsequent surrender, or the prosecution may use the victim's declaration shortly after the surrender to prove the victim's state of mind at the prior surrender. The test is essentially inferential: Is the time lapse so short that we can permissibly infer that the declarant's state of mind was the same at the two points in time?

Some courts continue to labor under the misapprehension that a general rule excludes self-serving statements. For this reason some judges exhibit an unfortunate tendency to exclude the defendant's statements when the defense offers them to negative *mens rea*. However, the standard of admissibility is roughly the same for the defendant's exculpatory state-of-mind declarations as it is for those which inculpate the defendant. If the defendant made exculpatory statements under unsuspicious circumstances prior to the alleged crime, the judge should admit those statements.[5] One of the issues in the Chicago conspiracy trial was the intent with which each alleged conspirator traveled to Chicago, and the Seventh Circuit held that the defendants' declared plans and intents should have been admitted on the defense's behalf.[6]

---

5. White v. United States, 216 F.2d 1 (5th Cir. 1954).

6. United States v. Dellinger, 472 F.2d 340 (7th Cir. 1972).

Use of Present Plan Declarations to Prove Subsequent Conduct. This theory of admissibility is similar to the continuity-of-state-of-mind theory, for both involve two steps of analysis. A person declares a plan, intention, or design to commit a future overt act. In the first step of analysis, the court permits the proponent to draw the hearsay inference that at the time of the declaration, the declarant entertained that plan, intention, or design. In the second step, the court permits the proponent to use the evidence as proof that the declarant in fact committed the act. Although the declaration standing alone will rarely be sufficient to support a finding that the declarant subsequently committed the act, the declared intent slightly increases the probability of the commission of the act and, hence, is logically relevant, circumstantial evidence of commission. The courts have applied this theory to statements by the defendant, the victim, and third parties. If prior to the offense, the defendant threatened to commit the same type of offense, the prosecution may introduce the threat as evidence that the defendant subsequently carried out the threat. Some courts have relied on this theory even when the defendant made a general threat to commit some crime.

In homicide cases, if the alleged victim made a prior declaration of suicidal intent, the defense may use the declaration as the basis for an inference that the alleged victim actually committed suicide. In homicide and assault cases, when the victim threatened the defendant, the defense may introduce evidence of even uncommunicated threats to support a self-defense claim; the defense may imply that the alleged victim was in reality the aggressor. However, some courts have been reluctant to admit evidence of the victim's uncommunicated threats and have done so only in limited circumstances such as when there are no eyewitnesses or when there is some corroborating evidence, perhaps the defendant's own testimony, that the decedent initiated the fray.[7]

As in the case of the alleged victim's uncommunicated threats, courts have been reluctant to admit the threats of a third party to commit the offense the defendant is charged with, often saying that they will do so only if there is corroborating evidence of the third party's motive, opportunity, or act. Federal Rule 804(b)(3) conditions the admission of such third party confessions on the presence of "corroborating circumstances" which "clearly indicate the trustworthiness of the statement." Perhaps Chambers v. Mississippi[8] will make the trial courts more receptive to third-party confessions.

If the declarant announces an intention to travel to a certain place, the proponent may use the statement as evidence that the declarant went there. The leading opinion is a civil case, Mutual Life Insurance Co. v. Hillmon,[9] in which the beneficiaries under a life insurance policy alleged that the body found at a certain location was Hillmon's, the insured's. The insurer alleged that the body was that of one Walters and attempted to prove that he had journeyed to the location where the body was found by introducing Walters' letters, declaring such an intention. The Supreme Court held that the letters were admissible to prove that Walters traveled to his declared destination. In applying this theory, it is important to distinguish among three situations. In the first situation, the declarant announces an intent

7. See, e. g., State v. Johnson, 162 Iowa 597, 144 N.W. 303 (1913).

8. 410 U.S. 284, 93 S.Ct. 1038, 35 L.Ed.2d 297 (1973).

9. 145 U.S. 285, 12 S.Ct. 909, 36 L.Ed.2d 706 (1892).

to commit an act he or she can perform unaided. It is well-settled that such a statement is admissible to prove the declarant's subsequent act.

In the second situation, the declarant announces an intent to commit an act requiring a third party's cooperation, but the proponent offers the statement to prove only the declarant's subsequent act. In *Hillmon*, Walters announced his intention to go with Hillmon to the location. Even though the execution of the plan required Hillmon's cooperation, the Supreme Court admitted the statement to prove Walter's subsequent act. As a matter of relevance theory, the *Hillmon* result is sound; even if the commission of the act requires a third party's aid, the declarant's announced intention to cooperate in committing the act increases the probability that the act was committed. The trial judge, of course, should give a limiting instruction to the effect that while the jury may consider the declaration as evidence of the declarant's subsequent act, they may not consider the declaration as evidence of the third party's act.

In the third situation, the declarant announces an intent to commit an act requiring a third party's cooperation, and the proponent offers the statement to prove the third party's act. Surprisingly, *Hillmon* suggests that the proponent may do this.[10] However, most of the recent cases consider the evidence incompetent hearsay for this purpose.[11] Because one person's state of mind is not reliable evidence of another person's act, the courts insist that the trial judge admit the evidence only to prove the declarant's act under appropriate limiting instructions. In its report on the Federal

Rules, the House Judiciary Committee stated that Rule 803(3) permits the use of a declarant's statements of intention "only to prove his future conduct, not the future conduct of another person." [12]

The second and third situations are appropriate occasions for a defense argument that the limiting instruction will be ineffective. The prosecution often offers evidence of the victim's plan to commit an act with the defendant. For example, the declarant might assert an intention to meet the defendant at the place where the declarant's body is subsequently found. At most, such statements are admissible to prove that the victim carried out his or her intent. Thus the trial judge instructs the jury that they may not consider the victim's declared intent as evidence of the defendant's act. Query: Is such an instruction any more effective than the instruction the Supreme Court invalidated in *Shepard*? In a California case, Mr. Justice Traynor expressed his serious doubts about the limiting instruction's effectiveness.[13] Therefore, after arguing that the statement does not fall within the exception, an opponent defense counsel should cite *Shepard* and attack the limiting instruction's effectiveness.

Suggested Reading:

United States v. Pheaster, 544 F.2d 353 (9th Cir. 1976).

Use of Declarations of Past State of Mind or Emotion to Prove the Prior State. Suppose that the declarant refers to his or her state of mind on a prior occasion. May the proponent use the declaration as evidence

---

10. Mutual Life Ins. Co. v. Hillmon, 145 U.S. 285, 295–96, 12 S.Ct. 909, 912, 36 L.Ed. 706 (1892) (The letters were competent evidence "both that he did go and that he sent with Hillmon.").

11. People v. Reddock, 13 Ill.App.3d 296, 300 N.E.2d 31 (1973); State v. Perelli, 125 Conn. 321, 5 A.2d 705 (1939).

---

12. Quoted in West's Federal Rules of Evidence for United States Courts and Magistrates 110 (1975).

13. People v. Alcalde, 24 Cal.2d 177, 189, 148 P.2d 627, 633 (1944) (dissenting opinion).

of that state of mind? Although most courts have said that the declaration is incompetent to prove the prior mental or prior mental or emotional state, a few courts are contra. For example, one state statute permits the proponent to use the declaration for that purpose if: (1) The declarant is unavailable at the time of trial; (2) the declarant's state of mind or emotion at that prior time is a material issue in the case; and (3) the proponent is offering the evidence solely to prove the state at that time.[14]

Suggested Reading:

United States v. Mandel, 437 F.Supp. 262 (D.Md. 1977).

13. Former Testimony

Suggested Reading:

Mancusi v. Stubbs, 408 U.S. 204, 92 S.Ct. 2308, 33 L.Ed.2d 293 (1972).

People v. Enriquez, 19 Cal.3d 221, 137 Cal.Rptr. 171, 561 P.2d 261 (1977).

United States v. Lynch, 499 F.2d 1011 (D.C.Cir. 1974).

If a witness testifies at one trial but is unavailable at a subsequent trial, the witness's testimony might nevertheless be admissible at the second trial. The proponent may certainly use the prior testimony for nonhearsay purposes either as a prior inconsistent statement to impeach or as a prior consistent statement to rehabilitate. Also the proponent may use the testimony to refresh the witness's recollection. Finally, if the witness is now a defendant charged with perju-

ry, the prosecutor may prove the content of the allegedly perjurious testimony.

If the proponent wants to use the testimony as substantive evidence, several hearsay exceptions might apply: admission of party-opponent, declaration against interest, or even past recollection recorded.[15] If the proponent wants to use the testimony as substantive evidence, but none of the listed exceptions applies, the proponent must resort to the instant exception, former testimony.

The Elements of the Foundation. The former testimony doctrine is that *a witness's testimony at a prior adversary hearing is exceptionally admissible at a subsequent trial if the witness is now unavailable and there is an identity of parties and issues between the two hearings.*

"A Witness's Testimony at a Prior Adversary Hearing." Like the admission exception, the former testimony exception is a product of the adversary system of litigation. Testimony falls within the exception only if the witness gave the testimony at a procedurally fair adversary hearing. The hearing qualifies as such if it had the following incidents.

First, the witness testified under oath. If the hearing occurred in a court of record, the proponent can ordinarily persuade the trial judge at the second trial to presume that the witness testified under oath.

Second, the opposing party had the opportunity to cross-examine the witness. The opponent need not actually conduct cross-examinations; it is sufficient if he or she had an opportunity to do so. What if a fortuitous event such as the witness's death precludes the completion of cross-examination? Some courts automatically exclude the testimony at the second trial. Others, however, admit the testimony so long as neither the original nor the present opponent

---

14. West's Ann.Cal.Evid.Code § 1251.

15. Tatum v. United States, 249 F.2d 129 (D.C.Cir. 1957), cert. denied 356 U.S. 943, 78 S.Ct. 788, 2 L.Ed. 2d 818 (1958).

was responsible for the preclusion. If the opponent has completed part of the cross-examination, some courts will admit those portions of the direct that are relevant to the matters covered on cross.

Third, if the hearing was a critical stage in a prosecution, the defendant must have been afforded the right to counsel. The theory is that counsel's presence is necessary for an effective cross-examination.

Finally, some courts say and a few have even held that the tribunal conducting the prior hearing must have had jurisdiction over both the subject matter and the parties. However, the trend in the case law is to dispense with this additional requirement. The witness will have the requisite incentive to testify truthfully so long as it appears that the court has jurisdiction.

Given these requirements, the courts have treated many types of hearings as fair adversary hearings. Prior trials certainly qualify. Preliminary examinations and hearings on motions to suppress also qualify. Finally, nonjudicial proceedings might qualify. Administrative hearings, driver license revocation hearings, and even arbitration proceedings have been held to be fair adversary hearings.

"If the Witness Is Now Unavailable."

(1) General. At early common law, some courts admitted former testimony only if the witness was dead at the time of the second trial. Modernly, courts take a much more liberal view of the still requisite showing of unavailability. Some state statutes now provide that the proponent can establish unavailability by proving that the witness is dead; that a privilege exempts or precludes the witness from testifying;[16] that the witness is now incompetent to testify about the subject matter; that a mental or physical illness disables the witness from attending or testifying; that after exer-

cising due diligence, the proponent cannot locate the witness within the jurisdiction; or that the witness is beyond the reach of the jurisdiction's compulsory process and cannot be induced to come to the place of trial. Although some courts balk when the stated ground of unavailability is the witness's wrongful refusal to testify or his or her claimed loss of memory, many others accept even these grounds. Federal Rule 804 (a), which represents the laxest standard for unavailability, includes all the traditional grounds and also expressly recognizes wrongful refusal to testify and loss of memory.

(2) The proponent's inability to bring the witness to the place of trial. At early common law, many courts subscribed to the view that the witness was automatically deemed unavailable if he or she was beyond the territorial reach of the court's process. The courts did not require the prosecution to attempt to induce a nonresident witness to return voluntarily to the site of trial. However, in recent years, courts have demanded more impressive showings of unavailability.

The original impetus for this trend was Barber v. Page,[17] in which the Supreme Court held that the confrontation clause mandates that the prosecution make a good faith, diligent effort to bring the witness to the site of trial. The Court noted the options open to the prosecution. If the witness is in a state prison, the prosecution may seek a writ of habeas corpus *ad testificandum* in the courts of the custodian state. If the witness is in federal custody, a federal court may issue a similar writ under 28 U.S. C.A. § 2241(c), and the United States Bureau of Prisons has a general policy of permitting prisoners to testify in state criminal proceedings. Finally, if the witness is not in prison, the prosecution may resort to the Uniform Act to Secure the Attendance of Witnesses from Without the State in Criminal Cases. Soon after *Barber*, the Court

16. See, e. g., Exleton v. State, 30 Okl.Cr. 224, 235 P. 627 (1925).

17. 390 U.S. 719, 88 S.Ct. 1318, 20 L.Ed.2d 255 (1968).

strongly suggested in Berger v. California [18] that the prosecution can never establish good faith unless it exhausts all means of compulsory process or makes a persuasive showing that it would be futile to resort to the process.

Some commentators have suggested that the Burger Court's decision in Mancusi v. Stubbs [19] presaged a retreat from the strict *Barber* standard, but that prediction has not come to pass. In *Mancusi,* the witness was an American citizen who resided permanently in a foreign country, and at the time the federal statute did not authorize federal process to return a citizen to the United States for a state trial. The *Mancusi* case has not led to any noticeable relaxation of the *Barber* standard, and Congress has now amended 28 U.S.C.A. § 1783 to authorize worldwide process against American citizens.

The emerging consensus is that the prosecution must exhaust every available means of compulsory process. Although a few decisions are contra, substantial state authority now exists that the prosecution must utilize the Uniform Act.[20] Federal Rule 804(a)(5) embodies the developing principle that in addition to exhausting compulsory process, the prosecution must use any reasonable means of inducing the witness to voluntarily return to the site of trial. The Rule explicitly requires the proponent to show that he or she could not induce the witness to return by "process or other reasonable means." Thus the prosecution cannot prevail simply by showing that it would be very expensive to return the witness to the place of trial.[21]

(3) The proponent's inability to locate the witness.

While the problem of the witness's absence beyond the court's process has attracted more attention, the problem of the proponent's inability to locate the witness within the jurisdiction is probably more common and, hence, more important. The prosecution's general responsibilities are (1) to maintain contact with the witness after it becomes apparent that the witness's testimony will be needed at trial and (2) to arrange for the witness's presence after the trial date has been set. The prosecution must exercise reasonable diligence to discharge these responsibilities. Proof that a subpoena was issued but returned unserved is not a sufficient showing of diligence. In this situation police should consult such sources of information as the witness's place of employment, utility companies, the post office, welfare agencies, etc. If the witness was previously cooperative, the prosecution has little reason to suspect that the witness will go into hiding, and therefore the prosecution need not maintain close supervision over the witness's whereabouts.[22]

Although the courts usually purport to apply the same standard of unavailability to defense offers of former testimony, a few have explicitly adopted a laxer standard for the defense. The justification is two-fold: (1) The reason for imposing a strict standard on the prosecution is the sixth amendment confrontation clause, which the prosecutor does not have standing to raise; and (2) especially when the defendant is indigent, the prosecution, assisted by the police investigative machinery, has a much greater ability to locate witnesses.

"And There Is an Identity of Parties." Like the requirement for a hearing with the incident of cross-examination, this element of the foundation is designed to ensure that the opponent or a similarly situated person had an opportunity to test the witness's testimony.

---

18. 393 U.S. 314, 89 S.Ct. 540, 21 L.Ed.2d 508 (1969).

19. 408 U.S. 204, 92 S.Ct. 2308, 33 L.Ed.2d 293 (1972).

20. State v. Brookins, 478 S.W.2d 372 (Mo.1972); In re Terry, 4 Cal.3d 911, 95 Cal.Rptr. 31, 484 P.2d 1375 (1971).

21. United States v. Edwards, 469 F.2d 1362 (5th Cir. 1972).

22. People v. Benjamin, 3 Cal.App.3d 687, 83 Cal. Rptr. 764 (1970).

At early common law, the courts required complete identity of parties. However, it soon became apparent that the standard was unduly strict, so the courts then shifted to a requirement of substantial identity of parties. Even if there were additional parties in the prior or subsequent suit— e. g., co-defendants—the testimony was admissible.

Today almost all courts have progressed to the position that the testimony is admissible if the present opponent was a party to the prior suit. Thus courts focus on the party the testimony is now offered against. If that party was also a party to the first suit, the testimony is competent. It is immaterial whether the present opponent offered the testimony or the testimony was offered against that party, for the courts have concluded that the opportunity to test the testimony is adequate whether the means is direct or cross-examination.

Sentiment is now growing for a radical step beyond the prevailing view. In civil cases, many jurisdictions have eliminated the requirement that the present opponent have been a party to the prior suit, holding that the evidence is sufficiently reliable if *a* party to the prior suit had an interest and motive to develop the testimony similar to the interest and motive of the present opponent. In the view of these courts, the similarly situated third party's opportunity to develop the testimony renders the testimony sufficiently reliable to admit it against the present opponent. Although some commentators have urged that this view be extended to criminal cases,[23] the courts have disagreed. For example, they have uniformly held that testimony admitted against an accomplice at a prior trial is inadmissible against the present defendant. The courts' rationale is that the confrontation clause gives each defendant a personal right to cross-examine the witness. Unless the present defendant was a party to the prior hearing, the testimony cannot qualify as former testimony in the present prosecution. The drafters of the Federal Rules were willing to follow the commentators' urgings, for as originally worded, Rule 804(b)(1) would have authorized the admission of former testimony against a criminal defendant if a party to the prior hearing had a similar motive and interest to test the testimony. However, Congress was not persuaded that the proposed Rule comported with the confrontation clause and therefore amended the Rule to conform to the traditional view.

"And Issues Between the Two Hearings." This element of the foundation ensures that the opponent in the prior hearing had an adequate motive and incentive to exercise the opportunity to test the testimony. The closer the identity of issues between the two cases, the greater the likelihood that the first opponent conducted the same type of examination the present opponent would conduct.

As in the case of identity of parties, the common-law courts initially insisted upon strict, complete identity of issues. Of course, the proponent could satisfy this requirement only if the prior hearing was a preliminary examination or trial for the same crime. Modernly, courts insist only upon substantial identity of issues. The prosecution can satisfy this requirement if the second charge arises from the same transaction or act, and the court will overlook the fact that the second charge is for a different crime or a different degree of the same generic crime. The more astute courts point out that the customary formulation of the requirement, "substantial identity of issues," is misleading, for it suggests that the trial judge ruling on the former testimony's admissibility should compare all the issues in the first hearing with the issues in the second. However, the judge should focus on *the* issue on which the evidence was offered in the first hearing and *the* issue on which the former

---

23. Falknor, Former Testimony and the Uniform Rules: A Comment, 38 N.Y.U.L.Rev. 651, 659–60 (1963).

testimony is now offered. If those two issues are similar, the testimony is admissible.
If the evidence is offered to serve roughly
the same purposes in both hearings, adequate assurance exists that the prior examination is a satisfactory substitute for the
examination the present opponent would conduct.[24]

Methods of Laying the Foundation. The
witness's unavailability is the most difficult
problem of proof. Here the question is
whether the usual competence rules apply to
preliminary facts such as unavailability. The
majority opinion appears to be that even
when the judge is deciding preliminary facts,
he or she must observe these rules.[25] However, some jurisdictions have statutes expressly providing to the contrary. For instance, Federal Rule 104(a) states that "in
making its determination it [the court] is
not bound by rules of evidence except those
with respect to privileges." In such a jurisdiction, the proponent could use otherwise
incompetent hearsay reports to establish the
witness's unavailability. In fact, many jurisdictions have permitted the proponent to
disregard at least the hearsay rule in laying
the foundation for former testimony. Courts
have permitted the proponent to use doctors' certificates, witnesses's letters and post-
cards, and affidavits to establish unavailability. Some courts have even permitted
the proponent to use unauthenticated documents which simply purported to have been
signed by the witness. Counsel should check
the local rules on proof of preliminary facts
to determine whether he or she must comply
with competence rules in establishing the
witness's unavailability.

14. Miscellaneous Hearsay Exceptions

Suggested Reading:

United States v. Medico, 557 F.2d 309 (2d Cir.
1977).

United States v. Iaconetti, 406 F.Supp. 554 (E.D.
N.Y.1976).

The previous sections of this chapter discuss
the most frequently used hearsay exceptions.
The listing of hearsay exceptions in the present chapter is not exhaustive, for numerous
other exceptions exist. For example in a
theft case, the maximum sentence might depend upon the value of the property stolen,
and to prove that value, the prosecutor might
rely upon the exception for published market
reports and trade journals.[26] In a nonsupport case, the prosecutor might have to prove
parentage, resorting to the exception for
declarations of family history.[27] If the case
is a trespass prosecution, the prosecutor will
have to establish the ownership of the property invaded; here he or she could invoke
the exception for public matters, including
title to realty.[28] The case might involve a
defendant who does not speak English and
therefore uses an interpreter; there is an
exception for statements by interpreters.[29]
Finally, the prosecutor might have recourse
to the exception for statements in ancient
writings.[30] These examples are simply illustrative of the many hearsay exceptions upon which creative counsel can rely. With
the exception of dying declarations, the

24. United States v. Lynch, 499 F.2d 1011 (D.C.Cir.
1974); Government of Virgin Islands v. Aquino, 378
F.2d 540 (3d Cir. 1967).

25. E. Morgan, Basic Problems of Evidence 262
(1962); Maguire and Epstein, Preliminary Questions
of Fact, 36 Yale L.J. 1101, 1121 (1927).

26. See, e. g., Fed.Evid.Rule 803(17), 28 U.S.C.A.

27. See, e. g., Fed.Evid.Rule 803(19) and 804(b)(4),
28 U.S.C.A.

28. See, e. g., Fed.Evid.Rule 803(20), 28 U.S.C.A.

29. See, e. g., Kelly v. Ning Yung Benev. Assn., 2
Cal.App. 460, 84 P. 321 (1905).

30. See, e. g., Fed.Evid.Rule 803(16), 28 U.S.C.A.

courts have generally recognized the same exceptions in criminal and civil cases. Even though some of the exceptions almost always arise in civil cases, a counsel should not be reluctant to invoke any hearsay exception in a criminal case.

CHAPTER 14
PRIVILEGES

1. Introduction

The immediately preceding chapters discuss the best evidence and hearsay rules, competence rules excluding relevant evidence because of the evidence's supposed unreliability. Like the best evidence and hearsay rules, privileges are competence rules, excluding logically relevant evidence. However, privileges exclude relevant evidence for an entirely different reason: namely, to promote a social policy such as the protection of a confidential relationship.

Privileges must be distinguished from the competency rules discussed in Chapter 2. The competency rules might completely preclude a witness from testifying. The priv-

ilege rules have a narrower effect: They preclude the witness from testifying about certain types of information. The rules relating to spouses illustrate the distinction. Chapter 2 discussed the marital disqualification—the defendant spouse's ability to prevent the witness spouse from testifying at all.[1] This chapter discusses the privilege for confidential marital communications. Even if the witness spouse is a competent witness, he or she might not be able to testify about a conversation with the other spouse. The disqualifications discussed in Chapter 2 render the witness incompetent, while the priv-

---

1. See Chapter 2, § 4, supra.

ileges discussed in this chapter merely render certain testimony incompetent.

PRIVILEGES FOR CONFIDENTIAL RELATIONSHIPS

2. General

The common law recognizes the social practice of treating certain relationships as confidential. For example, society commonly views the client-attorney and patient-physician relationships as professional relationships of trust and confidence. Moreover, the professional cannot render effective service unless the layperson makes frank, full disclosure of all the relevant facts. Without these facts, the attorney cannot give sound advice, and the physician cannot form an accurate diagnosis. Therefore society has decided to encourage the layperson's candor by protecting what he or she confides from the risk of compelled disclosure in judicial proceedings; the layperson can divulge the information to the professional without fear that in subsequent litigation the judge will compel the professional to reveal the confidence.

There are numerous privileges for confidential relationships, including client-attorney, patient-physician, patient-psychotherapist, spouses, and client-accountant. Some privileges, such as the client-attorney privilege, are common-law creations. Others, notably the patient-physician privilege, are statutory creatures. Because reviewing the privileges one by one would be too time-consuming, this part of the chapter analyzes only the fundamental structure of a common-law privilege. In the final analysis, the law of privilege is that *in certain types of proceedings, the holder has certain privileges with respect to certain types of information unless (1) the holder has waived the privilege or (2) a special exception to privilege exists*. We shall now address the following questions in sequence: Which types of proceedings do the privileges apply to? Who is

the holder of the privilege? What is the nature of the privilege? What is the nature of privileged information? Which acts constitute waiver? What are the special exceptions to the privilege? The first four questions relate to the four basic elements of a common-law privilege, all of which the claimant must establish to make out the prima facie case. If the right type of claimant asserts the right type of privilege with respect to the right type of information in the right type of proceeding, there is prima facie case of privilege. Even then, the opponent can defeat the privilege by showing waiver or a special exception.

3. Proceedings Where the Privilege Applies

The norm is that the privileges apply to all types of legal proceedings, civil and criminal, judicial and non-judicial. The underlying justification for the privileges' existence is protecting the speaker from the risk of subsequently compelled disclosure of the statement. From the speaker's perspective, it is a matter of indifference whether the compelled disclosure occurs in a civil action, criminal prosecution, or administrative proceeding; whenever the compelled disclosure occurs, chilling effect on the confidential relationship can result. On the one hand, modern codifications of the privileges sometimes broadly state that the privileges apply in "any action, hearing, investigation, inquest, or inquiry (whether conducted by a court, administrative agency, hearing officer, arbitrator, legislative body, or any other person authorized by law) in which, pursuant to law, testimony can be compelled to be given."[2]

On the other hand, the courts and legislatures have occasionally excluded entire categories of proceedings from the scope of particular privileges. Illustrative are the state statutes rendering the marital privilege completely inapplicable in juvenile

---

2.   West's Ann.Cal.Evid.Code §§ 901 & 910.

court proceedings [3] and the patient-physician privilege completely inapplicable in criminal proceedings.[4] This latter privilege has produced the sharpest disagreement among the legislatures. Most statutes apply the privilege to both civil actions and criminal prosecutions. However, the California statute represents one extreme, applying the privilege to civil actions, but excluding criminal prosecutions.[5] Louisiana has gone to the other extreme, applying the privilege in only criminal prosecutions.[6]

4. Holders of the Privilege

Suggested Reading:

Fraser v. United States, 145 F.2d 139 (6th Cir. 1944).

People v. Holtz, 294 Ill. 143, 128 N.E. 341 (1920).

Identifying the holder of the privilege is critical, for in general only a holder has standing to invoke or claim the privilege. Thus most courts treat privileges as personal to the holder, and a third party cannot invoke the privilege even if he or she is a formal party to the suit. For this reason, a criminal defendant has no right to claim a witness's attorney-client privilege,[7] the victim's patient-physician privilege,[8] or a code-fendant's spousal privilege.[9] The procedural consequences of status as a holder become clearest on appeal. If the trial judge erroneously denies a claim of privilege, an appellant may assign the denial as error only if the appellant is also the holder.[10]

Who is the original holder of the privilege? The holder need not be a party to the suit, for the intended beneficiary of a privilege is the person whose disclosures the law hopes to encourage. Consequently, the original holder is usually the communicator, the layperson making the disclosures. The client is the original holder of the client-attorney privilege,[11] the patient the original holder of the patient-physician privilege,[12] and the patient or research subject the original holder of the patient-psychotherapist privilege.[13]

The spousal and penitent-clergyman privileges have received somewhat different treatment. Consistent with the above reasoning, the common-law view is that only the communicating spouse is a holder.[14] However, many statutes confer holder status on both spouses.[15] Also if the legislatures strictly limited the scope of the penitent-clergyman privilege for the communicator's protection, only the penitent would qualify for holder status. However, many legislatures have granted the clergyman a separate privilege in recognition that religious scruple will often prevent the clergyman

3. Id. at § 986.

4. Id. at § 998.

5. Id.

6. La.Stat.Ann. 15:476; Moosa v. Abdalla, 248 La. 344, 178 So.2d 273 (1965).

7. Commonwealth v. McKenna, 206 Pa.Super. 317, 213 A.2d 223 (1965); State v. Snook, 93 N.J.Law 29, 107 A. 62 (1919), aff'd 94 N.J.Law 271, 109 A. 289 (1920); State v. Leek, 152 Iowa 12, 130 N.W. 1062 (1911); People v. Patrick, 182 N.Y. 131, 74 N.E. 843, reh. denied 183 N.Y. 52, 75 N.E. 963 (1905).

8. State v. Boehme, 71 Wash.2d 621, 430 P.2d 527 (1967); Wimberley v. State, 217 Ark. 130, 228 S.W.2d 991 (1950); Vance v. State, 182 Miss. 840, 183 So. 280

(1938); Thrasher v. State, 92 Neb. 110, 138 N.W. 120 (1912); State v. Depoister, 21 Nev. 107, 25 P. 1000 (1891).

9. People v. Holtz, 294 Ill. 143, 128 N.E. 341 (1920).

10. West's Ann.Cal.Evid.Code § 918; State v. Knight, 204 Iowa 819, 216 N.W. 104 (1927).

11. West's Ann.Cal.Evid.Code § 953.

12. Id. at § 993.

13. Id. at § 1013.

14. Fraser v. United States, 145 F.2d 139 (6th Cir. 1944).

15. See, e. g., West's Ann.Cal.Evid.Code § 980.

from divulging the communication even though the penitent is willing to disclose.[16]

If the original holder is incompetent or deceased, who then qualifies as a successor holder who may claim the privilege in his or her own right? Most courts hold that the privilege survives the original holder's incompetency and permit the guardian or conservator to assert the privilege as a successor holder.[17] However, some courts have difficulty with the issue when the original holder dies. Even if the court decides that the privilege survives death, the question then becomes the selection of an appropriate successor holder. Among the jurisdictions ruling that the privilege survives the original holder's death, almost all grant the personal representative status as a successor holder.[18] Many of the courts go no further, taking the view that "the privilege ceases to exist when the client's estate is finally distributed and his personal representative (executor or administrator) is discharged."[19] Nevertheless, in civil cases, numerous authorities state that after the personal representative's discharge, the heirs become successor holders of the privilege.[20] On the basis of these civil authorities, some commentators have asserted that the same rule applies in criminal cases.[21]

Suppose that neither an original nor a successor holder is present to claim the privilege. May an agent claim the privilege for the holder? If the holder has granted the agent actual authority to assert the privilege, there is no reason to frustrate the holder's wishes. Suppose, however, that the attorney, the recipient of the communication, is present but the client has not given the attorney actual authority to claim the privilege. Does the attorney have implied-in-law authority to invoke the privilege? In several cases, courts have permitted attorneys to use the privilege as a defense to contempt citations for refusals to disclose confidential communications from clients.[22] These cases present a special fact situation, for two interests are at stake: the attorney's interest in liberty and the client's interest in confidentiality. However, the courts have often used forceful language to the effect that even in the absence of actual authority, the attorney has not only the right but also the duty to invoke the privilege for the client.[23] The trend in both the case law and the statutes appears to be to grant the professional recipient of the communication implied-in-law authority to invoke the privilege as the holder's agent.[24]

Finally, what happens if no original holder, successor holder, or agent is present when a party attempts to elicit a privileged communication? At common law, although anyone may call the privilege to the judge's attention, the judge has no duty to honor the privilege. Instead the judge has discretion (1) to permit the testimony, (2) to continue the case and have the holder notified, or (3) to sustain the claim. Some statutes now require that the judge sustain the privilege even in the absence of a holder or agent.[25]

16. Id. at § 1034.

17. West's Ann.Cal.Evid.Code §§ 953, 980, 993 & 1013.

18. West's Ann.Cal.Evid.Code §§ 953, 980, 993 & 1013.

19. Law Revision Commission Comment, West's Ann.Cal.Evid.Code § 954.

20. Walton v. Van Camp, 283 S.W.2d 493 (Mo.1955); Buuck v. Kruckenberg, 121 Ind.App. 262, 95 N.E.2d 304 (1950); Wilcox v. Coons, 359 Mo. 52, 220 S.W.2d 15 (1949).

21. 3 Wharton, Criminal Evidence § 566 (13th ed. 1973).

22. United States v. Kovel, 296 F.2d 918 (2d Cir. 1961); In re Selser, 15 N.J. 393, 105 A.2d 395 (1954).

23. See, e. g., Schwimmer v. United States, 232 F.2d 855 (8th Cir. 1956).

24. Fisher v. United States, 425 U.S. 391, 96 S.Ct. 1569, 48 L.Ed.2d 39 (1976); West's Ann.Cal.Evid. Code §§ 954–55.

25. West's Ann.Cal.Evid.Code § 916 provides:
"(a) The presiding officer, on his own motion or on the motion of any party, shall exclude in-

5. Nature of the Privilege

Suggested Reading:

United States v. Tapia-Lopez, 521 F.2d 582 (9th Cir. 1975).

The privileges are evidentiary privileges, for they operate to exclude evidence at the time of trial. If the relationship and other requisites such as confidentiality existed at the time of the communication, the privilege attaches, and it survives even if the relationship is terminated in the interim between the communication and trial.[26]

What are the privileges that the holder can assert at trial? The first is the right to personally refuse to disclose the confidential communication. The court cannot compel the holder to reveal the communication. Thus the privilege immunizes the holder from both contempt citations and discovery sanctions.[27] While some of the shield laws for reporters create true privileges, others afford only immunity from contempt cita-

tions.[28] A limited shield law of this nature "does not create a [true] privilege." [29]

The second privilege is to prevent third parties from disclosing the communication.[30] Which third parties are bound by the privilege? The holder can certainly prohibit the recipient from disclosing; for example, the client can preclude the attorney from making the disclosure. But what if the recipient connives with a party to enable the third party to eavesdrop on the communication? The courts have responded that the third party may not divulge the communication; if the recipient may not directly violate the privilege, the law will not permit the recipient to do so indirectly by conniving with the third party. The difficult question arises when, without the recipient's connivance, a third party learns of the communication by accident or design. Suppose that the third party either eavesdrops on a confidential oral conversation or intercepts a confidential letter. The prevailing common-law view has been that the eavesdropper or interceptor may testify to the communication. This view reflects hostility to the very existence of the privilege and its unavoidable tendency to suppress the truth. However, modernly, the courts and legislatures are attaching greater importance to privacy, and the trend is toward silencing the eavesdropper and interceptor.[31]

---

formation that is subject to a claim of privilege under this division if:

    (1) The person from whom the information is sought is not a person authorized to claim the privilege; and

    (2) There is no party to the proceeding who is a person authorized to claim the privilege.

(b) The presiding officer may not exclude information under this section if:

    (1) He is otherwise instructed by a person authorized to permit disclosure; or

    (2) The proponent of the evidence establishes that there is no person authorized to claim the privilege in existence."

26. People v. Dorsey, 46 Cal.App.3d 706, 120 Cal. Rptr. 508 (1975); Carter v. State, 167 Miss. 331, 145 So. 739 (1933); Mercer v. State, 40 Fla. 216, 24 So. 154 (1898); Lingo v. State, 29 Ga. 470 (1859); State v. Jolly, 20 N.C. 108 (1838).

27. Discovery statutes normally provide that privileged matter is not discoverable. See, e. g., Fed.Civ. Proc.Rule 37, 28 U.S.C.A.; West's Ann.Cal.Code Civ. Proc. § 2034.

28. West's Ann.Cal.Evid.Code § 1070.

29. Assembly Committee Comment, Parker's Cal. Evid.Code § 1070.

30. When a clergyman has a privilege separate from the penitent, the clergyman's privilege usually does not include this right. See, e. g., West's Ann.Cal. Evid.Code § 1034. The legislatures grant the separate privilege solely to permit the clergyman to observe personal religious scruple against disclosure. The penitent's privilege is adequate to protect the relationship's confidentiality.

31. West's Ann.Cal.Evid.Code § 954 grants the holder the privilege "to prevent another from disclosing, a confidential communication." The accompanying Law Revision Commission Comment states: "Under Section 954, the lawyer-client privilege can be asserted to prevent *anyone* from testifying to a confi-

In some jurisdictions, the holder has a third privilege to preclude the judge and counsel from making unfavorable comments about the privilege's invocation. At common law, a rather even division of authority exists on the propriety of comment. In some jurisdictions, the opposing counsel may comment in closing argument, and the judge may do so in instructions.[32] Thus the counsel and judge can invite the jury to draw the adverse inference that the witness's testimony would have been unfavorable. However, a growing number of courts prohibit such comment.[33] These courts reason that it is inconsistent to, on the one hand, confer the privilege and, on the other hand, make its assertion costly. In some jurisdictions, the holder has a right to an instruction that the jury may not draw an adverse inference from the privilege's invocation.[34]

6. Nature of the Privileged Information

Suggested Reading:

Branzburg v. Hayes, 408 U.S. 665, 92 S.Ct. 2646, 33 L.Ed.2d 626 (1972).

Blau v. United States, 340 U.S. 332, 71 S.Ct. 301, 95 L.Ed. 306 (1951).

In re Ryder, 263 F.Supp. 360 (E.D.Va.1967).

United States v. Kovel, 296 F.2d 918 (2d Cir. 1961).

Most privileges protect a very narrow type of information—confidential communica-

dential communication. Thus, clients are protected against the risk of disclosure by eavesdroppers and other wrongful interceptors of confidential communications between lawyer and client. Probably no such protection was provided prior."

32. Hampton v. State, 7 Okl.Cr. 291, 123 P. 571 (1912); O'Connor v. Detroit, 160 Mich. 193, 125 N.W. 277 (1910); People v. Hovey, 1 Cr.R. 283, 92 N.Y. 554 (1883).

33. United States v. Tapia-Lopez, 521 F.2d 582 (9th Cir. 1975).

34. West's Ann.Cal.Evid.Code § 913(b).

tions which occur between properly related parties and which are incident to the relationship. Thus, to be privileged, the information must satisfy four requirements. First, the information must have been a communication. Second, the communication must have been confidential. Third, the parties to the communication must have stood in a confidential relationship. Finally, the communication must have been incident to that relationship. The information is protected only if all four conditions are satisfied.

Communications. For most privileges, the courts use *the usual, narrow definition of communication*, limiting the privilege's protection to words and expressive acts. Therefore, both the client's oral, "Yes, that is correct," and nod in response to the question of whether a statement was correct qualify as a communication. The early common-law view is that the only privileged part of a verbal conversation is the statements made by the holder. However, with respect to the marital and professional privileges, the modern trend is to protect the statements by both parties to the conversation.[35] Indeed, some statutes now expressly protect both the communicated advice the professional gives and the uncommunicated opinion the professional forms.[36]

Like oral statements, written statements can qualify as communications. The test is whether the document came into existence as a communication between properly related parties. Thus, a letter from the client to the attorney will qualify. However, if the document did not come into existence as a communication, the document is unprotect-

35. United States v. Osborn, 409 F.Supp. 406 (D.Or. 1975); People v. Eckert, 2 N.Y.2d 126, 157 N.Y.S.2d 551, 138 N.E.2d 794 (1956); State v. Emmanuel, 42 Wash.2d 799, 259 P.2d 845 (1953); Keir v. State, 152 Fla. 389, 11 So.2d 886 (1943); Casey v. State, 37 Ark. 67 (1881).

36. See, e. g., West's Ann.Cal.Evid.Code §§ 952, 992 and 1012.

ed.[37] For example, suppose that the client has a pre-existing record, generated before the client-attorney relationship arose. The client cannot privilege that document by the simple expedient of delivering it to the attorney. Generally, if a document would be subject to production if it remained in the client's hands, the document is discoverable after the client transmits it to the attorney.

Although oral and written statements can qualify as communications, nonassertive, nonverbal conduct falls outside the definition's scope,[38] for such conduct is not communicative.[39] The act of taking money from somebody is an example of nonassertive conduct. Under the usual, narrow definition of communication, testimony about the act would not be privileged even if the witness is a wife testifying about her husband taking money from her.[40]

Like testimony about nonassertive conduct, testimony about tangible objects is generally unprivileged.[41] If the client turns over a knife[42] or stolen proceeds,[43] the prevailing view is that the transfer is unprotected; the attorney must surrender the object to the authorities.[44] Although a consensus exists on the attorney's duty to surrender the relevant physical evidence to the authorities, there is division on the question of whether the privilege allows the attorney to refuse to disclose the source of the evidence. Some relatively recent cases recognize this right.[45] These cases represent an expansion of the definition of communication, for the client's act of delivering the object to the attorney is not truly communicative. Unlike a person nodding in response to a question or pointing at a lineup, the client does not subjectively intend the act to serve as a true substitute for words. Nevertheless, the client would probably not perform the act but for his or her confidence in the attorney, and the cases have in effect broadened the definition of communication to include acts the client would not perform in the attorney's presence but for the professional confidence.

Finally, sometimes the very knowledge of the recipient of the communication will be privileged. However, knowledge will not be privileged simply because it is the professional's knowledge or even simply because the professional acquired the knowledge during the relationship. If the attorney observes the client in an intoxicated condition, the knowledge gained by that observation will not be privileged.[46] Similarly, during the course of the professional relationship, the attorney might form an opinion about the client's mental competence. That opinion would also be unprivileged. In both instances, the knowledge is independently acquired; the attorney gained the knowledge by means other than communications from the client. Thus independently acquired knowledge is unprivileged. Conversely, if knowledge is based solely on communications, the knowledge is privileged.[47] For example, the Supreme Court has held that

---

37. Fisher v. United States, 425 U.S. 391, 96 S.Ct. 1569, 48 L.Ed.2d 39 (1976); Falsone v. United States, 205 F.2d 734 (5th Cir. 1953), cert. denied 346 U.S. 864, 74 S.Ct. 103, 98 L.Ed. 375.

38. People v. Loper, 159 Cal. 6, 112 P. 720 (1911).

39. Pereira v. United States, 347 U.S. 1, 74 S.Ct. 358, 98 L.Ed. 435 (1954).

40. United States v. Mitchell, 137 F.2d 1006 (2d Cir. 1943).

41. People v. Lee, 3 Cal.App.3d 514, 83 Cal.Rptr. 715 (1970).

42. State ex rel. Sowers v. Olwell, 64 Wash.2d 828, 394 P.2d 681 (1964).

43. In re January 1976 Grand Jury, 534 F.2d 719 (7th Cir. 1976); In re Ryder, 263 F.Supp. 360 (E.D. Va.1967).

44. State ex rel. Sowers v. Olwell, 64 Wash.2d 828, 394 P.2d 681 (1964) held that the client-attorney privilege applied to the transfer of a knife to the attorney but that the attorney must surrender the weapon after a reasonable period of time.

45. See, e. g., State ex rel. Sowers v. Olwell, 64 Wash.2d 828, 394 P.2d 681 (1964).

46. State v. Fitzgerald, 68 Vt. 125, 34 A. 429 (1896).

47. United States v. Osborn, 409 F.Supp. 406 (D.Or. 1975).

a husband's knowledge of his wife's where-abouts is privileged if the husband gained the knowledge solely through the wife's confidential communications.[48]

Broader Definitions of Communication. We have already seen that some courts have broadened the definition of communication in applying the client-attorney privilege to the client's transfers of physical evidence to the attorney. Other courts and legislatures have expanded the definition in the context of either the spousal or the patient-physician privilege.

Some courts have radically expanded the definition of communication for purposes of the spousal privilege.[49] These courts have taken two approaches to the definition's expansion. One group expands the definition to include any information the spouse gained by virtue of the marital confidence. In these courts, an act will be privileged if one spouse would not have performed it in the other spouse's presence but for the marital confidence.[50] This view applies to such acts as secreting evidence in the spouse's presence. A second group of courts takes an even more expansive view, privileging any information the second spouse gains by virtue of the marital relation.[51] Under this view, the test is whether the witness spouse would have acquired the information but for the marital relation; if the witness probably would not have gained the information in the absence of marital cohabitation, the information is considered a communication.

Finally, many legislatures have expanded the definition of communication for pur-poses of the patient-physician and patient-psychotherapist privileges. The California statutes illustrate the statutory trend. California Evidence Code § 992 defines communication for purposes of the patient-physician privilege as "information, including information obtained by an examination of the patient."[52] The accompanying Assembly Committee note states that "[t]he definition here is sufficiently broad to include matters that are not ordinarily thought of as 'communications.'"[53] Evidence Code § 1012's definition for purposes of the patient-psychotherapist privilege parallels that of § 992.[54]

Confidential Communications. The courts and legislatures have developed privileges to protect the confidentiality of certain important social relationships. Given this policy, it is understandable that only confidential communications qualify for protection. In some jurisdictions, there are statutory or common-law presumptions that certain communications between properly related persons are confidential.[55] However, if there is no applicable presumption or if there is adequate evidence to rebut the presumption, the trial judge must decide as a matter of fact whether the communication was confidential. To establish confidentiality, the holder must prove that (1) the communication was physically private, and (2) at the time of the communication, the holder intended that the communication's secrecy would be maintained.

Physical Privacy. To the holder's knowledge, the communication must have been physically private. If the holder believes that the conversation is private but an eaves-dropper overhears the conversation, the priv-

---

48. Blau v. United States, 340 U.S. 332, 71 S.Ct. 301, 95 L.Ed. 306 (1951).

49. State v. Robbins, 35 Wash.2d 389, 213 P.2d 310 (1950); People v. Daghita, 299 N.Y. 194, 86 N.E.2d 172 (1949); Menefee v. Commonwealth, 189 Va. 900, 55 S.E.2d 9 (1949); Beyerline v. State, 147 Ind. 125, 45 N.E. 772 (1897).

50. State v. Robbins, 35 Wash.2d 389, 213 P.2d 310 (1950).

51. State v. Americk, 42 Wash.2d 504, 256 P.2d 278 (1953).

52. West's Ann.Cal.Evid.Code § 992.

53. Id.

54. Id. at § 1012.

55. Blau v. United States, 340 U.S. 332, 71 S.Ct. 301, 95 L.Ed. 306 (1951); United States v. Long, 468 F.2d 755 (8th Cir. 1972); West's Ann.Cal.Evid.Code § 917.

ilege can attach; however, in most jurisdictions the eavesdropper will not be bound by the privilege.[56] Although the eavesdropper could testify to the communication, the client could nevertheless prevent the attorney from divulging the communication. In contrast, if the holder knows that third parties are within hearing distance, this knowledge negatives privacy. The clear inference is that the holder did not intend the conversation to be private and confidential.

The starting point for analysis is that the known presence of a third party negatives physical privacy. However, there are numerous exceptions to this proposition. For example, the third party might be a child too young to understand the communication. If a very young child is present during a spousal conversation, the conversation might still qualify as a confidential communication.

Perhaps the third party is someone with whom the holder has a separate confidential relationship. Suppose the client husband and wife have a conference with the attorney. Again, the cases indicate that the privilege attaches.

Also the third party may be an agent of the professional. Thus the attorney might have a clerk or confidential secretary present, or a nurse might be present during an examination or treatment session between the patient and physician. In both these cases, because the agent's assistance and presence are customary professional practices, the way the profession does business, the agent's presence will not destroy confidentiality.

In addition, the third party's presence might be necessary for effective communication between the parties. The classic example is an interpreter.[57] If the client is not fluent in English and the attorney cannot understand the client's foreign language, an interpreter might be absolutely necessary,

and his or her presence will not destroy confidentiality. Moreover, the courts have extended this doctrine to cases of relative necessity. In United States v. Kovel,[58] the third party was an accountant. Analogizing to the interpreter cases, the court reasoned that the accountant's presence was necessary for effective communication on business matters between the client and attorney.

Suppose that the government forces the third person's presence upon the parties in the confidential relationship. For example, the local police practice may require that an officer accompany the prisoner whenever the prisoner consults a physician with whom the prisoner would otherwise have a confidential relationship. The traditional view is that the officer's presence negates confidentiality.[59] However, because the patient has no choice, there is a strong argument here for recognizing the privilege. For this reason, the trend in the case law is to apply the privilege at least to silence the professional,[60] and some courts have been courageous enough to prevent the officer's testimony as well.[61]

California has assumed the most liberal stance on the issue of confidentiality. California Evidence Code § 952 on the client-attorney privilege typifies this liberality,[62] providing that a third party's presence does not negate confidentiality if the third party is "present to further the interest of the client in the consultation." [63] The California Law Revision Commission explained the provision: "The words 'other than those who are present to further the interest of the client in the consultation' indicate that

---

56. See § 5, supra.

57. Hawes v. State, 88 Ala. 37, 7 So. 302 (1890).

58. 296 F.2d 918 (2d Cir. 1961).

59. State v. Thomas, 78 Ariz. 52, 275 P.2d 408 (1954).

60. People v. Decina, 2 N.Y.2d 133, 157 N.Y.S.2d 558, 138 N.E.2d 799 (1956).

61. State v. Gibson, 3 Wash.App. 596, 476 P.2d 727 (1970).

62. West's Ann.Cal.Evid.Code § 952.

63. Id.

a communication to a lawyer is nonetheless confidential even though it is made in the presence of another person—such as a spouse, parent, business associate, or joint client—who is present to further the interest of the client in the consultation. This may change existing law, for the presence of a third person sometimes has been held to destroy the confidential character of the consultation, even where the third person was present because of his concern for the welfare of the client." [64]

The Intent to Maintain Secrecy. Confidentiality requires more than proof that at the time of the communication, physical privacy existed. It also demands a showing that the holder intended that the communication remain secret. Thus at the time of the communication, the original holder must have intended that the recipient would not subsequently divulge the confidence.

Ideally, the holder will make his or her intention express. Unfortunately, the holder rarely does so. Therefore, the judge usually must decide whether the holder inferentially manifested an intention to maintain secrecy. For example, if the holder privately relates an embarrassing or humiliating experience to the professional, the court can find an implied intent to maintain secrecy. The more reasonable inference is that the holder would not want the experience publicized in the community. The contrary inference is the more reasonable if the client gives the attorney information to be included in a public pleading. The inference then is that the holder contemplated that the attorney would subsequently disclose the information to third parties outside the circle of confidence. Whenever the surrounding circumstances create an inference that the holder authorized subsequent disclosure, the court will probably find confidentiality lacking.

What is the result if subsequent disclosure is necessary to accomplish the purpose of the consultation? Suppose that the

client privately tells the attorney his or her symptoms and authorizes the attorney to disclose the information to a physician for medical evaluation. Authority exists that the holder's authorization of such a disclosure does not destroy confidentiality. [65] Because the attorney needs the physician's expert evaluation of the client's disclosures, the client should not forfeit the privilege by authorizing the recipient attorney to make subsequent disclosure to the physician.

Confidential Communications Between Properly Related Parties. The privilege attaches only if the proper relationship existed at the time of the communication. Although the relationship is two-sided, only one side poses serious definitional problems—that is, the side of the confidant, usually the professional. With the exception of corporate clients, the lay communicator can easily establish his or her side of the relationship, for few problems of proof arise when the communicator is a natural person. The other side of the professional relationship poses difficulties; the holder must demonstrate that the confidant qualifies as an attorney, a physician, or a clergyman.

Under the spousal privilege, the holder must show that the confidant was the communicator's spouse. For this purpose either a valid or a voidable marriage suffices. If under choice-of-law rules the appropriate jurisdiction recognizes common-law marriages, such a marriage will qualify as valid. However, because a bigamous marriage is void, no privilege exists. Moreover, some courts treat sham marriages as void; if the parties never intended to live together as husband and wife, there is no privilege.

Under the penitent-clergyman privilege, the confidant must be a religious functionary—a Protestant minister, a Catholic priest, a Jewish rabbi, or a similar representative in

---

64. Id.

65. West's Ann.Cal.Evid.Code § 952 ("or those to whom disclosure is reasonably necessary for . . . the accomplishment of the purpose for which the lawyer is consulted.").

the religious organization.[66] The clergyman's denomination is immaterial, and the clergyman need not be full-time. Many denominations have part-time ministers, and these ministers can qualify as confidants under the privilege.

Like the penitent-clergyman privilege, the patient-physician privilege has statutory origins; a statute must create the privilege.[67] Thus deciding whether the confidant qualifies is essentially a question of statutory construction. Most statutes mention only licensed physicians and surgeons, impliedly omitting nurses, dentists, druggists, and interns.

Two related questions in this area are: (1) Is it sufficient that the communicator reasonably believes that the confidant is a physician? And (2) must the physician be licensed in the jurisdiction in which the communication occurs? The modern statutes tend to resolve these questions in the communicator's favor, expanding the privilege's scope. Thus California Evidence Code § 990 states: "As used in this article, 'physician' means a person authorized, or reasonably believed by the patient to be authorized, to practice medicine in any state or nation." [68]

The patient-psychotherapist privilege is also statutory in origin. In some jurisdictions, the statute creating the patient-physician privilege is worded broadly enough to encompass psychiatrists. However, a growing number of jurisdictions have special statutes for psychotherapists.[69] Here again the California legislation is easily the most protective, for its statutory definition of "psychotherapist" includes physicians practicing psychiatry, licensed psychologists, licensed clinical social workers, credentialed school psychologists, and people licensed as marriage, family, and child counselors.[70]

Over half the states have enacted statutory shield laws allowing reporters to protect their sources.[71] The privilege's scope varies from state to state. Although most statutes limit the scope to the news source's identity, a few extend protection to news reports as well. A few statutes create absolute privileges, but many create only a conditional privilege that can be defeated by a showing of need for the evidence. Whatever their other parameters are, the privileges almost uniformly protect all types of reporters for all types of media.[72]

Finally, we turn to the client-attorney privilege. The trends in judicial and legislative treatment of this privilege are similar

---

66. West's Ann.Cal.Evid.Code § 990.

67. United States v. Meagher, 531 F.2d 752 (5th Cir. 1976).

68. West's Ann.Cal.Evid.Code § 990.

69. Id. at §§ 1010–28.

70. Id. at § 1010.

71. Council of State Governments, Shield Laws: A Report on Freedom of the Press, Protection of News Sources, and the Obligation to Testify (1973).

The media have attempted to construct a constitutional argument for a first amendment privilege. The Supreme Court has been generally unreceptive to the argument. See Note, 24 Syracuse L.Rev. 731 (1973). The leading precedents are Branzburg v. Hayes, 408 U.S. 665, 92 S.Ct. 2646, 33 L.Ed.2d 626 (1972) and Caldwell v. United States, 408 U.S. 665, 92 S.Ct. 2646, 33 L.Ed.2d 626 (1972). However, these cases rejected the radical contention that the first amendment gave reporters the privilege to dishonor a grand jury subpoena and simply refuse to appear. The cases left open the question whether a reporter has the limited privilege to refuse to answer specific questions in first amendment grounds. Note, 24 Syracuse L.Rev. 731, 755 (1973). Since Branzburg, several courts have recognized this limited, first amendment privilege. Brown v. Commonwealth, 214 Va. 755, 204 S.E.2d 429 (1974); State v. St. Peter, 132 Vt. 266, 315 A.2d 254 (1973); Bursey v. United States, 466 F.2d 1059 (9 Cir. 1972), petition for reh. denied Id. at 1091 (9th Cir. 1972). But see Farr v. Pitchess, 522 F.2d 464 (9th Cir. 1975); Rosato v. Superior Court of Fresno County, 51 Cal.App.3d 190, 124 Cal.Rptr. 427 (1975). Of course, the existence of broad shield statutes tends to moot out the constitutional question.

72. West's Ann.Cal.Evid.Code § 1070(a) protects "(a) publisher, editor, reporter, or other person connected with or employed upon a newspaper, magazine, or other periodical publication." § 1070(b) extends protection to "a radio or television news reporter or other person connected with or employed by a radio or television station."

to those in treating other privileges. One trend is to grant protection so long as the client reasonably believed the confidant was a licensed attorney.[73] The national, interstate character of commerce is creating another trend, undermining the view that the attorney must be licensed in the state where the communication occurs.[74]

These trends relate to the confidant side of the client-attorney relationship. The communicator side of the relationship poses problems if the client is a corporation. When should a communication emanating from a corporate employee be deemed a communication from the defendant corporation itself? Although the case law is almost entirely civil, the views should be transferable to criminal actions.

There are three different tests for determining whether the communication emanates from the corporation. The traditional view allows the corporation to claim the privilege for any employee's communication if the employee acted as an authorized agent in making the communication. If the employer orders or authorizes the communication with the intent of obtaining legal advice, the corporation will be deemed the communicator.[75]

The second view is the control-group test. Under this approach, the communication qualifies as a corporate communication only when the communicating employee is a member of the control group—the small group of executives (directors and officers) authorized to seek legal advice about a corporate matter and to act upon the matter. As one commentator stated: "To apply the test a judge divides documents according to the issues on which counsel's advice is sought, and determines who belongs to the control

group for each issue. . . . [A]n individual should be considered a member of the control group for a particular issue if action would not normally be taken without considering his opinion, and if he needs access to legal advice in order to carry out the duties of his office."[76]

The final view, which takes an intermediate position, is that the communication's status depends upon its subject matter. Under this approach, the statement of any corporate employee can qualify as the corporate client's communication if the statement's subject matter is the performance of the employee's own duties.[77] The leading case espousing the third view is D. I. Chadbourne, Inc. v. Superior Court.[78] In this case the court declared that: "When an employee has been a witness to matters which require communication to the corporate employer's attorney, and the employee has no connection with those matters other than as a witness, he is an independent witness; and the fact that the employer requires him to make a statement for transmittal to the latter's attorney does not alter his status or make his statement subject to the attorney-client privilege. Where the employee's connection with the matter grows out of his employment to the extent that his report or statement is required in the course of the corporation's business, the employee is no longer an independent witness, and his statement or report is that of the employer."[79] If the employee satisfies this test, the employee is a corporate representative, and his or her statement to or for the attorney will be considered a statement by the defendant corporation to its attorney.

Intermediaries Between the Parties Proper. Sometimes, rather than communi-

73. West's Ann.Cal.Evid.Code § 950; People v. Barker, 60 Mich. 277, 27 N.W. 539 (1886).

74. West's Ann.Cal.Evid.Code § 950.

75. Note, 84 Harv.L.Rev. 424, 433 n. 29 (1970); Simon, The Attorney-Client Privilege as Applied to Corporations, 65 Yale L.J. 953, 960–61 (1956).

76. Note, 84 Harv.L.Rev. 424, 430 (1970).

77. Harper & Row Publishers, Inc. v. Decker, 423 F.2d 487 (7th Cir. 1970).

78. 60 Cal.2d 723, 36 Cal.Rptr. 468, 388 P.2d 700 (1964).

79. Id. at 737, 36 Cal.Rptr. at 477, 388 P.2d at 709.

cating directly, the parties use intermediaries. The interposition of a third party between the communicator and confidant ordinarily prevents the privilege from attaching. In one leading case,[80] a husband dictated to his stenographer a letter to his wife. The Court held that the interposition of the stenographer destroyed the spousal privilege.

However, in two exceptional situations relating to professional privileges, the privilege attaches even though the parties communicate indirectly through an intermediary. The first situation relates to the use of business agents to make or receive communications. When a client makes a statement to an attorney's agent for transmission to the attorney, the statement is treated as a communication between client and attorney.[81] The same rule applies when a patient makes a statement to a nurse acting as the physician's assistant.[82] Moreover, if the jurisdiction protects communications flowing from the professional to the holder, statements the professional makes to his or her agent for transmission to the client or patient should also be protected.

The second exception concerns the client's consultation of an expert in the course of trial preparation. For example, the attorney might refer the client to an expert such as a physician so that the expert can study and evaluate the client's physical or mental condition. In a sense, the client and attorney are using the independent contractor expert as a means of communication. The client "possesses" private data about his or her physical or mental condition but lacks

the expertise to properly evaluate the condition, and the attorney needs the evaluation to prepare for trial. There is authority that the client-attorney privilege protects both the client's disclosures to the expert and the expert's subsequent report to the attorney. The authorities have applied this view to the client's consultation of physicians [83] and psychiatrists,[84] and some courts have gone so far as to extend the privilege to a client's consultation with an accountant.[85]

Confidential Communications Incidental to the Relationship Between Properly Related Parties. The final requirement for privileged information is that the communication occur incident to the relationship. The courts sometimes say that the communication must occur "in the course" of the relationship. This requirement necessitates analysis of the purpose of the statement. Why did the communicator make the statement to the confidant? Was that purpose specifically related to the nature of the relationship, or was it simply a casual statement between two people who happened to stand in another relationship?

For the client-attorney privilege to attach, the client must consult the attorney *qua* attorney—that is, in the attorney's professional legal capacity. Suppose that the attorney is also an accountant or business advisor. If the client consults the attorney in one of the latter capacities, the client-attorney privilege will not protect the communication.[86] However, if the client consults the attorney in his or her legal capacity, it is immaterial that the attorney

---

80. Wolfle v. United States, 291 U.S. 7, 54 S.Ct. 279, 78 L.Ed. 617 (1933).

81. State v. Krich, 123 N.J.Law 519, 9 A.2d 803 (1939); Hawes v. State, 88 Ala. 37, 7 So. 302 (1890) (dictum).

82. State v. Tornquist, 254 Iowa 1135, 120 N.W.2d 483 (1963); State v. Anderson, 247 Minn. 469, 78 N.W. 2d 320 (1956); Jasper v. State, 269 P.2d 375 (Okl.Cr. 1954); Clapp v. State, 73 Okl.Cr. 261, 120 P.2d 381 (1941), rev'd on other grounds 74 Okl.Cr. 144, 124 P.2d 267 (1942).

83. State v. Kociolek, 23 N.J. 400, 129 A.2d 417 (1957).

84. People v. Lines, 13 Cal.3d 500, 119 Cal.Rptr. 225, 531 P.2d 793 (1975); People v. Torres, 50 Cal. App.3d 778, 123 Cal.Rptr. 553 (1975).

85. United States v. Schmidt, 42 U.S.L.W. 2029 (M.D.Pa.1973); United States v. Kovel, 296 F.2d 918 (2d Cir. 1961).

86. Olender v. United States, 210 F.2d 795 (9th Cir. 1954); In re Fisher, 51 F.2d 424 (2d Cir. 1931).

renders the services gratuitously or that the attorney has not yet made a final commitment to represent the communicator. So long as the communicator consults the attorney with an ultimate goal of employment, the communication is incident to a client-attorney relationship.

Although there are no serious divisions among the courts or legislatures over the incidence requirement for the client-attorney privilege, a serious division does exist over the incidence requirement for the penitent-clergyman privilege. One view is that the communication must be a doctrinally required confession; the communicator must be a confessant. Arizona, for example, demands that the communication be "a confession . . . made . . . in the course of discipline enjoined by the church to which he [the confessant] belongs."[87] The contra view is that the incidence requirement demands only that the communicator consult the religious functionary in the latter's capacity as spiritual advisor. Thus the Florida statute is satisfied by a showing that the "person so communicating . . . is seeking spiritual counsel and advice."[88]

The patient-physician privilege also has an incidence requirement. The early view was that the communication had to have a significant treatment motive; the patient had to be immediately or ultimately seeking treatment, and it was insufficient if the patient sought diagnosis merely for trial purposes.[89] While most statutes retain the treatment requirement, inroads have been made into this traditional view. Some statutes now liberally protect any statement made to a physician "for the purpose of securing a diagnosis or preventive, palliative, or curative treatment."[90] These statutes protect statements made to physicians consulted with a view to trial, for confirmation of another diagnosis, or for treatment from another physician.[91] The incidence requirement here is quite important. In the course of treatment, the patient might make statements about the fight or accident in which the patient was injured. The courts generally hold that such statements are not incident to the relationship; because the statements are clinically irrelevant, they are unprivileged.[92]

The incidence requirement for the patient-psychotherapist privilege is expectably similar to the requirement for the patient-physician privilege. Again, most statutes preserve the treatment-diagnosis dichotomy, but a distinct minority privilege the communication even if the patient sought only diagnosis. A few states have gone even further, extending protection to research subjects as well as to patients.[93] For example, if the communicator makes the statement incident to a research project on mental disorder, the statement will be protected.

Perhaps the most difficult privilege to defeat on the basis of the incidence requirement is the spousal privilege. Because the spousal relationship affects so many aspects of the spouses' lives, convincing a judge that a statement is not at least marginally relevant to the spousal relationship is often difficult. Usually the best approach is demonstrating that the communication is affirmatively related to a second relationship between the spouses. For example, the spouses might be business partners; and if the statement relates to the partnership business rather than to family matters, the statement

---

87. Ariz.Rev.Stats. § 12–2233.

88. Fla.Stats.Ann. § 90.241.

89. People v. Sliney, 137 N.Y. 570, 33 N.E. 150 (1893).

90. West's Ann.Cal.Evid.Code § 991.

91. Senate Committee Comment, Parker's Cal.Evid. Code § 991.

92. Taylor v. United States, 222 F.2d 398 (D.C.Cir. 1955); State v. Riggle, 76 Wyo. 1, 298 P.2d 349 (1958), cert. denied 352 U.S. 981, 77 S.Ct. 384, 1 L.Ed. 366 (1959); People v. Barnes, 197 Misc. 477, 98 N.Y.S.2d 481 (Wayne County Ct.1950).

93. See, e. g., West's Ann.Cal.Evid.Code § 1011.

is unprivileged.[94]　Similarly, the spouses might be co-conspirators in an illegal venture, and if it relates to the illegal enterprise, the statement is not incident to the marriage.[95]

7.　Waiver of the Privilege

If the party claiming the privilege can establish the first four elements of the privilege, he or she has a prima facie case. The claimant has the burden of proving those elements.[96] However, even if the claimant can establish the prima facie case, the opponent can defeat the privilege by demonstrating a waiver or some special exception to the privilege. We shall first discuss the waiver problem. The general problem is reducible to three questions: (1) Who can waive the privilege? (2) How can the privilege be waived? And (3) what is the extent of the waiver?

The first question can be answered with relative ease. A privilege can be waived by an original holder, a successor holder, or someone the holder has authorized to waive. One of these people must either personally perform the act constituting the waiver or consent to the act.

The second question is more complex. A holder can waive by an act committed inside or outside the courtroom. Inside the courtroom, the holder can waive in three different capacities: as party to the action, as witness, and as proponent of evidence. In the capacity of a party to the action, the holder can waive expressly or by silence. For example, a criminal defendant can announce in the courtroom that he or she is waiving the privilege. This express

waiver is sometimes tactically advisable to impress the jury that the defendant is not attempting to hide the truth. The court will also find a waiver if the holder neglects to object to privileged evidence. "[F]ailure to claim the privilege in any proceeding in which he has the legal standing and opportunity to claim the privilege" effects a waiver.[97]

The holder can also waive in the capacity of a witness. However, the holder does not waive simply by becoming a witness. Moreover, under the majority view, the holder does not waive by simply testifying about the subject matter of the privileged communication. Thus, if the defendant disclosed to the attorney confidential information about an assault, the defendant could testify about the assault at trial without waiving the privilege. However, the holder commits a fatal slip if he or she expressly refers to a communication with the confidant. If the defendant testifies that he or she told the attorney a certain fact about the assault, that testimony constitutes a waiver. A minority view finds a waiver only if the holder makes the statement on direct examination. The theory is that cross-examination is necessarily compulsive and that any statement on cross is practically involuntary. The prevailing, more realistic view is that a reference to the privileged communication effects a waiver whether the reference occurs on direct or cross. Even on cross, the holder could claim the privilege, and characterizing the statement on cross as involuntary is unsound.

Finally, the holder can waive in the capacity of proponent of evidence. The holder generally does not waive simply by putting the confidant on the witness stand. The defendant thus does not waive the patient-physician privilege by calling the physician as a witness. Moreover, the dominant view is that the holder does not waive by eliciting

94. Dyer v. State, 88 Ala. 225, 7 So. 267 (1889).

95. United States v. Kahn, 471 F.2d 191 (7th Cir. 1972), cert. granted 411 U.S. 980, 93 S.Ct. 2275, 36 L.Ed.2d 956 (1973).

96. United States v. Tratner, 511 F.2d 248 (7th Cir. 1975); United States v. Stern, 511 F.2d 1364 (2d Cir. 1975); United States v. Osborn, 409 F.Supp. 406 (D. Or.1975).

97. West's Ann.Cal.Evid.Code, § 912(a).

testimony from the confidant about the subject matter of the privileged communication. Suppose that in the previous hypothetical the attorney had independently acquired knowledge of the assault. If the attorney is a competent witness in the jurisdiction, the defendant could elicit the independent knowledge without waiving the privilege. But, again, the holder would make a fatal slip by eliciting testimony expressly referring to the privileged communication. If the defendant asks the attorney to testify about a conversation between the defendant client and attorney, responsive testimony would waive whatever privilege otherwise cloaked the conversation.

There is some authority that extra-judicial waivers are ineffective and that the holder can waive only by an act performed inside the courtroom.[98] However, the overwhelming majority view is that the holder can make a waiver outside the courtroom. If the holder either voluntarily discloses a significant part of the communication to a third party outside the circle of confidence or consents to such a disclosure by the confidant, a waiver occurs. Two notable exceptions to this norm exist. First, there is no waiver if the person to whom the holder discloses stands in a separate confidential relationship with the holder.[99] For example, after consulting his attorney, the client husband confidentially relates the statements to his wife. Because the wife stands in a separate confidential relation with the client, the client's voluntary disclosure to the wife is not a waiver. Second, in some jurisdictions, if the confidant's subsequent disclosure to the third party is essential to accomplish the purpose of the original consultation, the holder can authorize the disclosure without forfeiting the privilege: "For example, where a confidential communication from a client is related by his attorney to a physician, . . . or other expert in order to obtain that person's assistance so that the attorney will better be able to advise his client, the disclosure is not a waiver of the privilege, even though the disclosure is made with the client's knowledge and consent."[1]

8. Special Exceptions to the Privileges

Suggested Reading:

Clark v. United States, 289 U.S. 1, 53 S.Ct. 314, 77 L.Ed. 519 (1933).

United States v. Gordon-Nikkar, 518 F.2d 972 (5th Cir. 1975).

Even in the absence of a waiver, the opposing attorney can defeat a claim of privilege by establishing a special exception to the privilege. Because they operate to suppress the truth, judicial and legislative hostility to privileges is widespread, and for this reason, the courts and legislatures have created exceptions too numerous to discuss in a text of this size. The courts create an exception when they believe either that applying it in a particular situation would not serve the privilege's purpose or that a conflicting social interest outweighs the interest in the relationship's confidentiality. The following discussion highlights some of the more important exceptions for criminal practice.

There are significant exceptions to the client-attorney privilege. The first arises if the client sought legal advice to facilitate the commission of a future crime or fraud.[2] The controlling intent is the client's subjective purpose at the time of the communication.[3] Unless the client realizes the attor-

---

98. State v. Powell, 217 S.W. 35 (Mo.1919); State v. Miller, 105 Wash. 475, 178 P. 459 (1919).

99. West's Ann.Cal.Evid.Code § 912(c).

1. Senate Committee Comment, Parker's Cal.Evid. Code § 912(d).

2. See, e. g., West's Ann.Cal.Evid.Code § 956.

3. United States v. Calvert, 523 F.2d 895 (8th Cir. 1975).

ney's state of mind, it is immaterial that the attorney knows that the course of conduct the client desires to pursue is illegal. Moreover, the client can safely seek advice concerning a past crime or fraud. The exception applies in the limited situation in which the client subjectively desires the advice to enable him or her to commit a future crime or fraud.[4]

The second exception comes into play when the defendant attacks the attorney's competence.[5] For example, in a habeas corpus proceeding collaterally attacking his or her conviction, the defendant might contend that the attorney rendered ineffective assistance, mandating reversal under the sixth amendment. The defendant has mounted an attack against the attorney, and the attorney may respond by disclosing confidential communications relevant to his or her competency as an attorney.[6]

The patient-psychotherapist and physician privileges also admit an important exception, the patient-litigant exception. If the patient tenders his or her condition as an issue in the case, the general belief is that permitting the patient to use the privilege to suppress highly relevant evidence is unfair.[7] Thus, if the defendant pleads insanity, the defendant injects the issue of his or her mental competence into the case. Any

psychiatrists the defendant had contacted would be critical witnesses on the issue. The case law and statutes take the position that in these circumstances, the defendant patient has lost the privilege with respect to the psychiatrists' testimony.[8]

There are several important exceptions to the spousal privilege. The first is the injured spouse exception. The defendant spouse loses the privilege if the offense alleged in the pleading is an offense against the marital relation. The list of offenses against the marital relation varies from jurisdiction to jurisdiction. However, one state's statute is illustrative: "There is no privilege under this article in a criminal proceeding in which one spouse is charged with:

"(a) A crime committed at any time against the person or property of the other spouse or of a child of either.

"(b) A crime committed at any time against the person or property of a third person committed in the course of committing a crime against the person or property of the other spouse.

"(c) Bigamy

"(d) A crime defined by Section 270 or 270a of the Penal Code [nonsupport offenses]."[9]

The most commonly named victims are the other spouse, children, and third parties injured in the course of an offense against the other spouse or the children. The listed offenses routinely encompass crimes against the person or property of one of the victims, and the list often includes bigamy, nonsupport, and other crimes tending to undermine the marital relation.

The second exception applies when the witness spouse attempts to invoke the privilege over the defendant spouse's objection.

---

4. Ordinarily, when the trial judge deals with competence rules, the judge finally decides as a matter of fact whether the preliminary facts exist. Fed.Evid. Rule 104(a); West's Ann.Cal.Evid.Code § 405. However, since it will be extraordinarily difficult for the prosecution to marshal evidence of the defendant's state of mind, the courts and legislatures have adopted a special procedure for applying this exception. The prosecution need present only a prima facie case that the defendant had the requisite guilty state of mind when he or she sought the legal advice. Clark v. United States, 289 U.S. 1, 53 S.Ct. 465, 77 L.Ed. 993 (1933); Unif.Rule 26(2)(a) (1953).

5. West's Ann.Cal.Evid.Code § 958.

6. Tasby v. United States, 504 F.2d 332 (8th Cir. 1974); Hunydee v. United States, 355 F.2d 183 (9th Cir. 1965); People v. Tucker, 61 Cal.2d 828, 40 Cal. Rptr. 609, 395 P.2d 449 (1964).

7. See, e. g., West's Ann.Cal.Evid.Code § 1023.

8. Id.

9. West's Ann.Cal.Evid.Code § 985.

Suppose the witness spouse is the holder and claims the privilege when the defendant spouse's attorney seeks to elicit favorable testimony. Some courts and legislatures have fashioned an exception allowing the defendant spouse to elicit the testimony.[10] For example, Texas overrides the privilege "where one or the other [spouse] is on trial for an offense and a declaration or communication made by the wife to the husband or by the husband to the wife goes to extenuate or justify the offense."[11] Although some courts have refused to recognize the exception,[12] it has a sound basis in the policy judgment that the defendant's interest in liberty outweighs the witness spouse's interest in confidentiality.

OTHER PRIVILEGES

9. General

There are myriad privileges in addition to those for confidential relations. This part of the chapter is admittedly incomplete, for it does not discuss the privileges peculiar to only one or a few jurisdictions. However, it does analyze some of the generally recognized privileges commonly encountered in criminal practice. Both the prosecution and defense utilize the work-product privilege to protect their trial preparation materials. The prosecution often resorts to the privileges for major and minor government secrets. Throughout this part of the chapter, we shall generally use the same analytic framework employed to dissect the privileges for confidential relations: To which types of proceedings does the privilege apply?

Who is the holder of the privilege? What is the nature of the privilege? What is the nature of the privileged information? Which acts constitute waiver? And finally, are there any special exceptions to the privilege's scope?

10. The Work-Product Privilege

Suggested Reading:

Goldberg v. United States, 425 U.S. 94, 96 S.Ct. 1338, 47 L.Ed.2d 603 (1976).

The United States has adopted an adversary model for its litigation system. Given that model, an attorney who expends time and effort preparing the case has a reasonable expectation that the adversary will not be permitted to profit from his or her efforts. The courts and legislatures have attempted to safeguard that expectation by creating a work-product privilege for trial preparation materials.

To which types of proceedings does the privilege apply? The seminal case, Hickman v. Taylor,[13] is a civil case, and the most of the decisional law is civil. However, there is substantial authority that the work-product privilege also applies in criminal prosecutions.[14]

Who is the holder? The courts have permitted both the attorney and the client

---

10. See, e. g., West's Ann.Cal.Evid.Code § 987.

11. Vernon's Ann.Tex.C.C.P. art. 38.11 (Code of Criminal Procedure).

12. Steeley v. State, 17 Okl.Cr. 252, 187 P. 821 (1920).

13. 329 U.S. 495, 67 S.Ct. 385, 91 L.Ed. 451 (1947).

14. Goldberg v. United States, 425 U.S. 94, 96 S.Ct. 1338, 47 L.Ed.2d 603 (1976) (application of the work product privilege to Jencks Act material); Duffy v. United States, 473 F.2d 840 (8th Cir. 1973); In re Grand Jury Investigation (Sturgis), 412 F.Supp. 943 (E.D.Pa.1976); United States v. Booth, 399 F.Supp. 975 (D.S.C.1975) (United States Attorney's interview notes); United States v. Marks, 364 F.Supp. 1022 (E.D.Ky.1973); People v. Moore, 50 Cal.App.3d 989, 123 Cal.Rptr. 837 (1975).

to invoke the privilege. At first glance, it might seem that the attorney is the sole holder. After all, the immediate object of the privilege is the protection of privacy of the attorney's case file. However, it is equally clear that the ultimate beneficiary is the client. Because we protect the attorney's privacy to enable the attorney to better serve the client, both attorney and client should have standing to claim the privilege.

What is the nature of the privilege? The decided cases are discovery cases in which one side seeks discovery of the other side's material. The only privilege the second side needs to assert is the first privilege to refuse to disclose the privileged material. Apparently no case law exists on the question of whether the holder may prevent an interceptor from divulging the material. However, conceivably that issue may arise. Suppose that a private party stole a defense attorney's material and handed it on the proverbial silver platter to the authorities. Because the thief is a private party, the seizure did not involve state action and thus is not violative of the fourth amendment. Could the defense suppress the material on a work-product theory? In a jurisdiction where the holder of a privilege for a confidential relation can silence an eavesdropper or interceptor, the court would probably extend the same protection to a holder of the work-product privilege.

The major work-product issue, however, is the fourth question: What is the nature of the privileged information? Some trial preparation materials are absolutely privileged, but others are only conditionally privileged.

Absolutely Privileged Material. Some statutes create absolute privileges for limited types of trial preparation material. The federal and California provisions are illustrative. Federal Rule 26(b)(3) [15] grants an absolute privilege against "the disclosure of

the mental impressions, conclusions, opinions, or legal theories of an attorney or other representative of a party concerning the litigation." California Code of Civil Procedure § 2016(b) [16] is analogous: "[A]ny writing that reflects an attorney's impressions, conclusions, opinions, or legal research or theories shall not be discoverable under any circumstances." Thus when the attorney writes either a memorandum to file, stating impressions of a witness or an opinion letter to a client, summarizing legal research, the memorandum and letter will be absolutely privileged.

In the absence of statute, the state courts have refused to create an absolute privilege. *Hickman* [17] did not purport to create an absolute work-product privilege, and the common-law courts have refused to go beyond *Hickman*. However, even the courts refusing to create an absolute privilege realize that some types of trial preparation material are more sensitive than are others and, hence, more deserving of protection. It is well-settled that both an attorney's memorandum outlining trial strategy [18] and a witness's statement [19] qualify as trial preparation materials. However, obviously the memorandum is much more sensitive than is the statement; the opposition can question the witness but has no method of divining the attorney's trial strategy. Even if the court is unwilling to grant the memorandum an absolute privilege, it will require a greater showing of need before ordering production of the memorandum. Because the opponent can rarely demonstrate a legitimate need for the materials qualifying for absolute privilege under the federal statute, discovery is rarely ordered

---

16. West's Ann.Cal.Code Civ.Proc. § 2016(b).

17. Hickman v. Taylor, 329 U.S. 495, 67 S.Ct. 385, 91 L.Ed. 451 (1947).

18. People v. Cathey, 186 Cal.App.2d 217, 8 Cal.Rptr. 694 (1960).

19. Edens v. State, 235 Ark. 178, 359 S.W.2d 432 (1962), cert. denied 371 U.S. 968, 83 S.Ct. 551, 9 L.Ed. 2d 538 (1963).

---

15. Fed.Civ.Proc.Rule 26(b)(3), 28 U.S.C.A.

even in jurisdictions without an absolute privilege.

Conditionally Privileged Material. In the absence of an absolute privilege, trial preparation material is conditionally privileged. The claimant establishes the privilege by demonstrating that the document qualifies as trial preparation material, but the opponent can defeat the privilege by demonstrating an overriding need or good cause for discovery.

What must the claimant prove to qualify the document as trial preparation material? Essentially, the claimant must show that the document is the derivative work product of an attorney, prepared in anticipation of litigation. The claimant must show that: (1) the document is derivative material rather than primary data; (2) the document is the work product of an attorney; and (3) the document was prepared in anticipation of litigation.

To be protected, the material must be derivative rather than primary.[20] A witness's knowledge of relevant facts is primary data as is physical evidence historically connected with the case. Even if an attorney had discovered and previously interviewed a witness, the attorney could not bar the opposition from interviewing or deposing the witness on a work-product theory. Similarly, the attorney could not resist a motion for the production of real, original physical evidence on work-product grounds. However, a statement from the witness[21] would be protected as would a model or mock-up the attorney prepared for trial. Likewise, a report the attorney acquires from an expert is derivative material.[22]

In addition to being derivative, the material must be the work product of an attorney. A few jurisdictions rigidly insist that the attorney personally prepare or obtain the material. Obviously, this requirement is highly inconvenient, for in the modern practice of law, the attorney often uses agents and the client as aides in trial preparation. Therefore, the prevailing view is that if the attorney is supervising the trial preparation, materials gathered by the client or the attorney's agents (such as investigators) can qualify.[23]

Finally, the material must be prepared in anticipation of litigation. If suit is pending (filed) and the material is relevant to the suit's subject matter, this requirement poses no problems. If suit has not as yet been filed, the material can nevertheless qualify if the attorney foresaw the possibility of litigation and prepared the material with a view to that possibility. It is relatively easy to make the required showing if the attorney in question is not on permanent retainer, for the mere fact that the client brings the problem to the attorney presages the possibility of litigation.

Even if the claimant establishes that the document is conditionally privileged, the opponent can then attempt to defeat the privilege by showing necessity for discovery. In the words of one state statute, the opponent must show that "denial of discovery will unfairly prejudice the party seeking discovery in preparing his claim or defense or will result in an injustice."[24] However, the language in the federal rule is much more informative; the opponent can defeat the conditional privilege "upon a showing that the party seeking discovery has substantial need of the materials in the preparation of his case and that he is unable without undue hardship to obtain the substantial equivalent of the materials by other means."[25] Thus under this rule the opponent must demon-

---

20. Mack v. Superior Court, 259 Cal.App.2d 7, 66 Cal.Rptr. 280 (1968).

21. State v. Aubuchon, 381 S.W.2d 807 (Mo.1964).

22. But see State v. Healey, 106 N.H. 308, 210 A.2d 486 (1965).

23. Alltmont v. United States, 177 F.2d 971 (3d Cir. 1949).

24. West's Ann.Cal.Code Civ.Proc. § 2016(b).

25. Fed.Civ.Proc.Rule 26(b)(3), 28 U.S.C.A.

strate that the material sought is substantially relevant to his or her own case and that no reasonable alternative means exists of obtaining equivalent material. For example, suppose that a key eyewitness to the crime dies before trial but after giving the prosecution a detailed witness statement. This statement might contain unique, valuable investigative leads, and a judge would probably overrule a claim of work-product privilege.

11. Government Privileges

Although both the prosecution and defense invoke the work-product privilege, it is the prosecution which resorts to government privilege. This section deals with the privilege for major and minor government secrets: major military and state secrets; confidential government information in general; and informer's identity in particular. Usually, the claimant government has the burden of proving that one of these privileges attaches.[26]

Major Government Secrets. The case law has created an absolute privilege for major government secrets, both military and state.[27] The privilege protects sensitive information relating to national defense and international relations. The privilege applies in criminal and civil actions. The government is the holder, and the chief officer of the interested government agency or department usually asserts the privilege on the government's behalf. The nature of the privilege enables the government to refuse to disclose the privileged information and to prevent third parties from making unauthorized disclosure. The only difficult element of the prima facie case is the fourth,

the nature of the privileged information. To date although no court has formulated a simple definition of the privilege's scope, one commentator has furnished helpful guidance: "The specific areas of sensitive information appear to be: (a) The plans and capabilities of specific combat operations; (b) the official estimates of the military plans and capabilities of potential enemy nations; (c) the existence, design, and production of new weapons or equipment or the existence and results of research programs specifically directed toward producing new weapons and equipment; (d) the existence and nature of special ways and means of organizing combat operations; (e) the identity and location of vulnerable areas such as production facilities, critical supply depots, or weapons installations; (f) the existence and nature of clandestine intelligence operations, special plans, or data; (g) the keys to communication codes; (h) the existence and nature of international agreements relative to military plans and capabilities and the exchange of intelligence." [28]

What is the procedural effect of the government's invocation of the privilege? The effect depends upon whether the government is a party to the suit. If the government is not a party and the court finds the information unprivileged, the court can order production; and the only remaining issue is the constitutional question of the government agent's immunity from compulsory process. If the government is not a party and the court sustains the privilege claim, the evidence is simply unavailable to the parties; this is the only consequence when the government is not a party to the action. Suppose that the federal government successfully invokes the privilege in a state criminal prosecution. Although the information is unavailable to the parties, the state may nevertheless proceed with the prosecution.[29]

---

26. State v. Lender, 266 Minn. 561, 124 N.W.2d 355 (1963).

27. United States v. Reynolds, 345 U.S. 1, 73 S.Ct. 528, 97 L.Ed. 727 (1953) (secret military equipment); Totten v. United States, 92 U.S. 105, 23 L.Ed. 605 (1875) (contracts for secret spying services).

28. Zagel, The State Secrets Privilege, 60 Minn.L. Rev. 875, 884–85 (1966).

29. People v. Parham, 60 Cal.2d 378, 33 Cal.Rptr. 497, 384 P.2d 1001 (1963).

However, the procedural consequences are radically different if the government claiming the privilege is a formal party to the action. Suppose, in a prosecution it initiated, the government claims the privilege in order to suppress information relevant to the defense. Although there is contrary authority,[30] the prevailing view is that even if the information qualifies as a major government secret, the government must either disclose the information or dismiss the charges to which the information relates.[31] As Judge Hand stated: "While we must accept it as lawful for a department of the government to suppress documents, even when they will help determine controversies between third persons, we cannot agree that this should include their suppression in a criminal prosecution, founded upon those very dealings to which the documents relate, and whose criminality they will, or may, tend to exculpate. So far as they directly touch the criminal dealings, the prosecution necessarily ends any confidential character the documents may possess; it must be conducted in the open, and will lay bare their subject matter. The government must choose; either it must leave the transactions in the obscurity from which a trial will draw them, or it must expose them fully."[32]

Suggested Reading:

United States v. Reynolds, 345 U.S. 1, 73 S.Ct. 528, 97 L.Ed. 727 (1953).

United States v. Andolschek, 142 F.2d 503 (2d Cir. 1944).

Minor Government Secrets—General. The privilege for major secrets does not ex-

haust the government's interest in confidentiality. Sensitive information relating to national defense and foreign policy presents the most compelling case for a privilege, but a persuasive case can also be made for a privilege to protect minor government secrets. However, the magnitude of the government interest in maintaining major secrets such as weapons developments is obviously much greater than the interest in maintaining minor secrets such as confidential letters to a state parole board.[33] For this reason although the privilege for major secrets is absolute, the privilege of minor secrets is conditional.

In applying the privilege for major secrets, the court resolves an essentially definitional problem: Does the information fall within the definition of a military or state secret? If the answer is affirmative, the privilege is absolute. However, when the court applies the privilege for minor secrets, the court must proceed through a two-step analysis. First, the court addresses the definitional problem: namely, whether the information falls within the definition of confidential government information used in the particular jurisdiction. If the answer is affirmative, the court must proceed to a second step in analysis. This is deciding whether "disclosure of the information is against public interest because there is a necessity for preserving the confidentiality of the information that outweighs the necessity for disclosure in the interest of justice."[34]

The courts and legislatures have developed two competing definitions of confidential government information. The federal courts have evolved a relatively narrow definition, focusing on the confidentiality of the decision-making process. They limit the privilege to internal working papers—documents which are integral parts of the decision-making process and which reflect advisory opin-

---

30. United States v. Haugen, 58 F.Supp. 436 (E.D. Wash.1944).

31. United States v. Andolschek, 142 F.2d 503 (2d Cir. 1944).

32. Id. at 506.

33. Runyon v. Board of Prison Terms and Paroles, 26 Cal.App.2d 183, 79 P.2d 101 (1936).

34. West's Ann.Cal.Evid.Code § 1040(b)(2).

ions, recommendations, and deliberations.[35] The draft of proposed Federal Rule of Evidence 509(a)(2)(A) would have codified the federal case law definition—"intragovernmental opinions or recommendations submitted for consideration in the performance of decisional or policy-making functions."[36] This definition's "policy basis . . . is . . . the desirability of encouraging candor in the exchange of views within the government."[37]

The narrow scope of the federal definition places the historical data in investigative reports outside the scope of the privilege. However, such data could fall within the broader definition used in many states. For example, one state's privilege broadly protects "information acquired in confidence by a public employee in the course of his duty."[38] Modern government regulates so many aspects of life that it needs a good deal of data to operate efficiently. The government cannot obtain certain types of information without assuring the source confidentiality. Thus a parole board will have difficulty obtaining frank evaluations of prisoners eligible for parole unless it can assure its sources confidentiality,[39] and likewise the health department may have difficulty gathering information on venereal disease unless it can use an assurance of confidentiality to encourage reporting. If the court uses this broad definition, it must ask whether the government agency has a legitimate need for the type of information contained in the report and whether the government needs an assurance of confidentiality to maintain the free flow of that type of information to the

government agency. Using this test, some courts have gone so far as to protect police reports from defense discovery.[40]

It is important to bear in mind that unlike the privilege for major government secrets, this privilege is merely conditional.[41] Even if the information falls within the jurisdiction's definition of confidential government information, the defense may nevertheless obtain discovery by demonstrating an overriding need for the information. The defense prevails on the first step in analysis if the information in question falls outside the jurisdiction's definition. Alternatively, the defense prevails if the judge decides that "the consequences to the litigant of nondisclosure" outweigh the government interest in secrecy.[42] The privilege is qualified;[43] and as in the case of work-product privilege, the defense resisting the claim of privilege can prevail by showing that the information is both highly relevant and practically unavailable through other sources.

Suggested Reading:

United States v. Berrigan, 482 F.2d 171 (3d Cir. 1973).

United States v. Germain, 411 F.Supp. 719 (S.D. Ohio 1975).

Minor Government Secrets—The Identity of an Informer. The previous subsection deals with the general privilege for confidential government secrets. This subsection deals with a particular type of minor government secret, the identity of an informer. Although the privilege applies in both civil and criminal proceedings, the issue arises

---

35. United States v. Berrigan, 482 F.2d 171 (3d Cir. 1973). See also Ackerly v. Ley, 420 F.2d 1336 (D.C. Cir. 1969); Machin v. Zuckert, 316 F.2d 336 (D.C.Cir. 1963).

36. Draft Fed.Evid.Rule 509(a)(2)(A).

37. Advisory Committee Note, id.

38. West's Ann.Cal.Evid.Code § 1040(a).

39. In re Muszalski, 52 Cal.App.3d 475, 125 Cal.Rptr. 281 (1975).

40. State v. Hill, 193 Kan. 512, 394 P.2d 106 (1964).

41. Assembly Committee Comment, Parker's Cal. Evid.Code § 1040.

42. Id.

43. Advisory Committee Note, Draft Fed.Evid.Rule 509.

more frequently in the latter context. Once again, the government is the holder, and in the typical criminal proceeding, the claimant is a government agent.[44] With one exception, the nature of the privilege is the same as that of a general government information privilege. As in the case of the general privilege, the government may refuse to disclose an informer's identity and usually can prevent third parties from making unauthorized disclosure.[45] However, the whole purpose of the privilege is to protect the informer from reprisal and embarrassment, and the exception is that the government cannot preclude the informers themselves from admitting their identity [46]—if an informer is brave or foolhardy enough to do so, the informer may acknowledge his or her status as an informant.

The privileged information is the identity of a person who has confidentially reported a law violation to a law enforcement agency, including legislative committees investigating law violations. The informer's identity is privileged, but the content of the report itself is ordinarily protected only to the extent necessary to prevent disclosure of the informer's identity.[47]

The primary problem in administering the general privilege for government information is the fourth element, the definition of the privileged information. Here the primary problem is the sixth element: namely, the special exceptions to the privilege. The Supreme Court has stated that "no fixed rule" exists to determine when the privilege must yield and the identity be disclosed.[48] Although there are no hard-and-fast rules,

tentative working guides are available to the courts.

The First Exception—The Percipient Witness. Roviaro v. United States [49] is the leading authority on the percipient witness exception to the privilege. In *Roviaro*, the informer was the only other participant in the crime, the only person who could furnish testimony to contradict the police officers who had observed and overheard the offense. The Supreme Court held that in these circumstances, the defendant was entitled to know the informer's identity. The lower courts have extended the same due process reasoning to situations in which the informer was not a participant in the offense but rather was a material witness to facts determining guilt or innocence.[50]

Although the courts use various labels such as "participant," "eyewitness," and "material witness" to rationalize the results, a common theme runs through the decided cases: The informer was in a position to have personal knowledge of the historical facts which will determine guilt or innocence. On the one hand, the defense does not have to shoulder the impossible burden of showing in advance that the informer's testimony would be favorable.[51] On the other hand, the defense must show a reasonable possibility that the informer has personal knowledge of the facts on the merits of the case.[52] Thus the defense must show that the

---

44. West's Ann.Cal.Evid.Code § 1041(a).

45. Id.

46. West's Ann.Cal.Evid.Code § 1041(c).

47. Roviaro v. United States, 353 U.S. 53, 60, 77 S.Ct. 623, 627, 1 L.Ed.2d 639 (1957); Bowman Dairy Co. v. United States, 341 U.S. 214, 71 S.Ct. 675, 95 L.Ed. 879 (1951).

48. Roviaro v. United States, 353 U.S. 53, 62, 77 S.Ct. 623, 628, 1 L.Ed.2d 639 (1957). See also United States v. Leo, 406 F.Supp. 1174 (E.D.Wis.1976).

49. 353 U.S. 53, 77 S.Ct. 623, 1 L.Ed.2d 639 (1957).

50. United States v. Fischer, 531 F.2d 783 (5th Cir. 1976); United States v. Barnes, 486 F.2d 776 (8th Cir. 1973); People v. Anderson, 43 Cal.App.3d 94, 117 Cal.Rptr. 507 (1974); Commonwealth v. Ennis, 1 Mass.App. 499, 301 N.E.2d 589 (1973); James v. State, 493 S.W.2d 201 (Tex.Cr.App.1973); People v. Garcia, 67 Cal.2d 830, 64 Cal.Rptr. 110, 434 P.2d 366 (1967); People v. McShann, 50 Cal.2d 802, 330 P.2d 33 (1958).

51. Price v. Superior Court of San Diego County, 1 Cal.3d 836, 83 Cal.Rptr. 369, 463 P.2d 721 (1970).

52. People v. Kelly, 49 Cal.App.3d 214, 122 Cal. Rptr. 393 (1975); People v. Alcala, 169 Cal.App.2d 468, 337 P.2d 558 (1959).

informer was more than "a mere tipster"[53] who pointed a finger of suspicion at the defendant.[54] As a practical matter, the defense must pay a price for the informer's identity. Before the court can decide whether the informer is a percipient witness to the relevant facts, the court must know the general nature of the defense the defendant intends to put on at trial.[55] In effect, the defendant must partially disclose trial strategy in order to demonstrate a genuine need for the informer's testimony.[56]

When the defense makes a prima facie showing of need, the rapidly spreading practice is to examine the informer in camera to determine whether his or her testimony would be helpful to the defense. Some courts exclude the defendant from the hearing, admit the defense attorney, and place him or her under protective orders.[57] Other courts have excluded both the defendant and the defense attorney.[58] If the court finds that the informer is a percipient witness but that his or her testimony would not benefit the defense, the judge denies discovery.[59] Although the Supreme Court has not yet passed upon the constitutionality of the procedure, several lower federal courts have upheld the procedure against confrontation and due process challenges.[60]

What is the procedural consequence if the court orders discovery but the prosecution refuses to comply with the order? If the court orders disclosure under this exception, the judge has necessarily found that disclosure is essential to a fair trial. If the prosecution refuses to comply, due process mandates dismissal of the charges.[61]

The Second Exception—An Informer Whose Report Was a Necessary Part of the Showing of Probable Cause. The first exception deals with an informer who can give testimony on the case's merits. The second exception relates to an informer whose testimony concerns the showing of probable cause for an arrest or search. The exception applies only when the informer's report is necessary to establish probable cause. Thus if the prosecution can establish probable cause apart from the informer's report, the exception is inapplicable.[62]

Assume that the prosecution must rely upon the informer's report to establish probable cause; the description of the report was an essential part of the affidavit supporting the warrant or of the information the officer relied upon in conducting a warrantless arrest or search. Even here a sharp disagreement exists among the courts over the propriety of recognizing an exception to the privilege.

One group of courts takes the view that there is no exception if the informer's testimony relates to a fourth amendment issue rather than to the merits.[63] The argument

---

53. United States v. Freund, 525 F.2d 873 (5th Cir. 1976); McLawhorn v. State of North Carolina, 484 F.2d 1 (1973).

54. People v. Martin, 2 Cal.App.3d 121, 82 Cal.Rptr. 414 (1969).

55. People v. Thomas, 12 Cal.App.3d 1102, 91 Cal. Rptr. 867 (1970).

56. Melendez v. Superintendent, 399 F.Supp. 430 (E.D.N.Y.1975). The defense attorney will understandably be reluctant to grant the prosecution informal discovery. Some trial judges permit defense counsel to make the disclosure in camera in the absence of the prosecutor.

57. United States v. Anderson, 509 F.2d 724 (9th Cir. 1975).

58. United States v. Howell, 514 F.2d 710 (5th Cir. 1975).

59. United States v. Doe, 525 F.2d 878 (5th Cir. 1976).

60. Id; United States v. Rawlinson, 487 F.2d 5 (9th Cir. 1973).

61. People v. McShann, 50 Cal.2d 802, 330 P.2d 33 (1958).

62. Lopez v. United States, 370 F.2d 8 (5th Cir. 1966); People v. Hunt, 216 Cal.App.2d 753, 31 Cal. Rptr. 221 (1963); Assembly Committee Comment, West's Ann.Cal.Evid.Code § 1042.

63. McInes v. United States, 62 F.2d 180 (9th Cir. 1932), cert. denied 288 U.S. 616, 53 S.Ct. 507, 77 L.

runs that *Roviaro* does not extend to fourth amendment issues, for in *Roviaro*, the prosecution was attempting to suppress information necessary to a fair trial on the merits. However, when the defense moves, under the fourth amendment, to suppress information, it is the defendant who is attempting to suppress the truth. With a few exceptions,[64] the cases following this view involve searches pursuant to warrants. Indeed, in some jurisdictions, the rule is limited to searches and arrests under warrants valid on their face.[65] In the warrant situation, a neutral and detached magistrate has already been interposed between the citizen and the police.

A second group of courts adheres to the view that disclosure is mandatory if the informer's report is an essential part of the showing of probable cause.[66] The argument in favor of mandatory disclosure is that the defendant is entitled to a procedurally fair hearing on the motion to suppress and that disclosure under this exception is just as essential to a fair hearing on the motion as disclosure under the first exception is to a fair trial on the merits. The cases adopting this view involve warrantless searches and arrests.[67]

A third group of courts has taken an intermediate position, holding that disclosure is at the judge's discretion. If the judge decides to believe the police officer's testimony about the informer's report and if that testimony is sufficient to establish probable cause,[68] the judge does not have to order disclosure. Numerous statutes apply this view to warrantless searches,[69] and the Supreme Court upheld such a statute in McCray v. Illinois.[70] Although it is now clear that the second view is not constitutionally required, it remains to be seen whether the Burger Court will sustain the first view, recognizing only the percipient witness exception to the privilege.

Suppose that the judge orders disclosure but that the prosecution refuses to comply. What is the procedural consequence? The consequence under the second exception is much more limited than under the first. Because the first exception relates to the merits of the charge, due process requires that the charge is dismissed. However, here the information relates only to probable cause, and the usual consequence is that the judge grants the motion to suppress. As a practical matter, granting the motion to suppress might result in the charge's dismissal, for granting the motion often deprives the prosecution of evidence necessary to sustain its burden of going forward and to withstand a motion for a directed verdict or judgment of acquittal.

Suggested Reading:

McCray v. Illinois, 386 U.S. 300, 87 S.Ct. 1056, 18 L.Ed.2d 62 (1967).

Roviaro v. United States, 353 U.S. 53, 77 S.Ct. 623, 1 L.Ed.2d 639 (1957).

Ed. 989 (1933); Segurola v. United States, 16 F.2d 563 (1st Cir. 1926); People v. Keener, 55 Cal.2d 714, 12 Cal.Rptr. 859, 361 P.2d 587 (1961).

64. See, e. g., Segurola v. United States, 16 F.2d 563 (1st Cir. 1926).

65. West's Ann.Cal.Evid.Code § 1042(b).

66. Priestly v. Superior Court of San Francisco, 50 Cal.2d 812, 330 P.2d 39 (1958).

67. See, e. g., United States v. Keown, 19 F.Supp. 639 (D.Ky.1937).

68. The testimony shows both that (1) the informer was reliable and that (2) the report's underlying basis made it more likely than not that the defendant had committed a crime (probable cause for arrest) or that an item subject to seizure was located at the place to be searched (probable cause for search).

69. See, e. g., West's Ann.Cal.Evid.Code § 1042(c).

70. 386 U.S. 300, 87 S.Ct. 1056, 18 L.Ed.2d 62 (1967).

PART 5

FOURTH AMENDMENT PROTECTIONS

CHAPTER 15

SEARCH OR SEIZURE

1. Overview

Suggested Reading:

Katz v. United States, 389 U.S. 347, 88 S.Ct. 507, 19 L.Ed.2d 576 (1967).

Olmstead v. United States, 277 U.S. 438, 48 S.Ct. 564, 72 L.Ed. 944 (1928).

United States v. Johnson, 561 F.2d 832 (D.C.Cir. 1977).

United States v. Pretzinger, 542 F.2d 517 (9th Cir. 1976).

Hernandez v. United States, 353 F.2d 624 (9th Cir. 1965).

The preceding four chapters dealt with common-law competence rules: best evidence, hearsay, and privileges. We now turn to an analysis of constitutional competence rules, doctrines which exclude relevant evidence to promote constitutional policies. Most of these policies are stated in the fourth, fifth, and sixth amendments to the United States Constitution. The following five chapters consider the fourth amendment exclusionary rule.

The fourth amendment provides: "The right of the people to be secure in their persons, houses, papers, and effects, against unreasonable searches and seizures, shall not be violated, and no warrants shall issue, but upon probable cause, supported by oath or affirmation, and particularly describing the place to be searched, and the persons or things to be seized." [1]

The modern understanding of the fourth amendment is that *if evidence is the product of an illegal, government search or seizure of a protected person, place, or thing, the evidence is inadmissible against a party with standing.* The next five chapters expand upon that proposition. This chapter discusses: the definitions of search and seizure; the requirement for government involvement in the search; and the list of protected persons, places, and things. Chapters 16 and

---

1. U.S.C.A.Const. Amend. IV.

17 analyze the rules determining the legality of searches and seizures. Chapter 18 deals with the standing doctrine. Chapter 19 discusses the fourth amendment exclusionary rule itelf, mandating the inadmissibility of illegally seized evidence.

"Search or Seizure". In considering the fourth amendment, the first issue to explore is whether a "search" or a "seizure" has occurred. Both a search without seizure and a seizure without a search are possible. The former occurs when law enforcement officials engage in visual surveillance rather than in seizure of physical objects. Of course, if the search is unlawful, any information the officers obtain is ordinarily inadmissible. The seizure without a search occurs when an item is seized solely because it is in plain sight, for example, on a sidewalk or in an open field. Here the individual seizing the object does not violate any right of privacy, for the seizure occurs in a public place.[2]

Whether there is a search or a seizure is one of the most puzzling questions that have plagued both courts and commentators. The answer might depend on an historical analysis, that is, on a consideration of the meaning of the fourth amendment at the time it was written. The advocates of this concept would argue that the fourth amendment prohibits only those searches or seizures which it was originally meant to prevent: searches or seizures made pursuant to a general warrant or writ of assistance.[3] Under this approach, the amendment would protect society against police action which is similar to the forcible rummagings of the English messengers or the Colonial customs officials.

In contrast to an historical interpretation, a philosophic analysis attempts to identify the social interests the fourth amendment was meant to protect and then to apply those interests and values in light of modern social conditions.

As the following chapters will document, the Supreme Court has tended to use a philosophic approach in answering the question whether a search or seizure has occurred. From time to time the Court has focused on different social values and interests in applying the philosophic approach. At one time the Court used a property law test: Did the police commit a technical trespass in obtaining the evidence?[4] Since its 1967 decision in Katz v. United States,[5] the Court has often used an expectation of privacy test: Did the police violate a reasonable expectation of privacy in obtaining the evidence? Finally the Court sometimes employs a motivational test: Were the police seeking evidence for a criminal prosecution or performing a non-prosecutorial function? The Court struggles with these philosophic issues whenever it addresses the initial question whether there has been a search or seizure. The Supreme Court has already resolved that intrusions such as the electronic surveillance in *Katz* amount to searches under the fourth amendment. However, the Court has not as yet had an occasion to decide such intriguing questions as whether the use of a detection dog or the attachment of an electronic beeper to an automobile constitutes a search. By freeing fourth amendment analysis from the old, mechanical property concepts, the Court may have made it more difficult than ever before to answer the threshold question whether there has been an intrusion under the fourth amendment.

"A Protected Person, Place, or Thing." What objects of search or seizure are pro-

2. Chapter 17, § 19, infra.

3. James Otis and Oxenbridge Thacker attacked the general writs of assistance. In John Adams' words, Otis' attacks on writs of assistance "breathed into this nation the breath of life." 10 C. Adams, Life and Works of John Adams 276 (1856).

4. Olmstead v. United States, 277 U.S. 438, 48 S.Ct. 564, 72 L.Ed.2d 944 (1928) illustrates this approach. In that case, the Supreme Court held that wiretapping did not constitute a search within the fourth amendment because the interception was effected "without trespass."

5. 389 U.S. 347, 88 S.Ct. 507, 19 L.Ed.2d 576 (1967).

tected under the fourth amendment? The amendment refers to *persons, houses, papers, and effects.* Thus a *person* is protected against forceful stops,[6] arrests,[7] and the taking of fingernail scrapings,[8] but not against being compelled by legal process to give handwriting[9] or voice exemplars.[10] The term *house* has been extended to include apartments,[11] hotel rooms,[12] and business offices.[13] Although it does not extend to open fields, it does protect the "curtilage" around the house. The phrase *papers and effects* includes letters,[14] cabinets,[15] automobiles,[16] and other items so long as they are not abandoned.[17]

"A Government Search or Seizure". The fourth amendment regulates only government searches and seizures. To invoke the fourth amendment, the defendant must demonstrate the government's involvement in the search or seizure. If private parties conducted the search or seizure, the fourth amendment exclusionary rule is inapplicable. To trigger the fourth amendment, the defendant must demonstrate that: (1) a

government employee conducted the search or seizure; or (2) the formally private party who conducted the search or seizure was cooperating with government employees and was acting as a de facto government agent. In the absence of such a demonstration, the defendant may have a tort or property cause of action against the private party who invaded his or her privacy, but the defendant will be unable to invoke the fourth amendment exclusionary rule at the criminal prosecution.

"An Illegal, Government Search or Seizure". Assume that there has been a government search or seizure of a protected person, place, or thing. The next major question is the legality of the search or seizure. The exclusionary rule comes into play only when the search or seizure is illegal; the rule excludes only illegally obtained evidence. To determine the legality of search or seizure, the court must resolve several subsidiary issues. The court first addresses the issue whether there is a basis for the search or seizure. The court must then apply the rules peculiar to warranted and warrantless intrusions.

The first issue is whether there is a basis for the search or seizure. The courts have recognized several legitimate bases, including consent, but by far the most common basis is probable cause. The fourth amendment provides that "no warrants shall issue, but upon probable cause," and the basis for a search or seizure may be probable cause or the diminished probable cause standard which has been applied to stops and frisks,[18] administrative inspections,[19] and airport searches.[20] Included in the issue of probable cause are the following: (1) What is the definition of probable cause? (2) Does the court judge probable cause by an objective standard or the officer's sub-

---

6. Terry v. Ohio, 392 U.S. 1, 88 S.Ct. 1868, 20 L.Ed. 2d 889 (1968).

7. Henry v. United States, 361 U.S. 98, 80 S.Ct. 168 4 L.Ed.2d 134 (1959).

8. Cupp v. Murphy, 412 U.S. 291, 93 S.Ct. 2000, 36 L.Ed.2d 900 (1973).

9. United States v. Dionisio, 410 U.S. 1, 93 S.Ct. 764, 35 L.Ed.2d 67 (1973).

10. United States v. Mara, 410 U.S. 19, 93 S.Ct. 774, 35 L.Ed.2d 99 (1973).

11. Clinton v. Virginia, 377 U.S. 158, 84 S.Ct. 1186, 12 L.Ed.2d 213 (1964) (per curiam).

12. Stoner v. California, 376 U.S. 483, 84 S.Ct. 889, 11 L.Ed.2d 856 (1964); United States v. Jeffers, 342 U.S. 48, 72 S.Ct. 93, 96 L.Ed.2d 59 (1951).

13. United States v. Lefkowitz, 285 U.S. 452, 52 S.Ct. 420, 76 L.Ed. 877 (1932).

14. Amos v. United States, 255 U.S. 313, 41 S.Ct. 266, 65 L.Ed. 654 (1921).

15. Holzhey v. United States, 223 F.2d 823 (5th Cir. 1955).

16. Chambers v. Maroney, 399 U.S. 42, 90 S.Ct. 1975, 26 L.Ed.2d 419 (1970).

17. Chapter 17, § 20, infra.

18. Chapter 17, §§ 2–4, infra.

19. Id. at § 17.

20. Id. at § 15.

jective belief? (3) Which facts may be used to establish probable cause?[21] (4) If a magistrate issued a warrant based upon an affidavit, may the showing of probable cause in the affidavit be bolstered by facts outside the affidavit?[22] (5) If the affidavit's showing of probable cause is facially sufficient, may the defendant attack[23] the showing by demonstrating mis-statements in the affidavit?[24] The Supreme Court recently made a definitive pronouncement on this last issue in Franks v. Delaware.[24a]

If there is a recognized basis for the search, the court then applies the rules for warranted and warrantless searches. Over the past twenty years the Supreme Court has emphasized that "the police must, whenever practicable, obtain advance judicial approval of searches and seizures through the warrant procedure."[25] The fourth amendment provides that the warrant shall specifically describe the place to be searched and the things to be seized. In addition there is a requirement that the warrant be issued by a neutral and detached magistrate. Chapter 16 discusses these requirements for warranted searches.

The Court has indicated that warrantless searches or seizures are unreasonable unless they fall within a few "jealously and carefully drawn" exceptions.[26] Among these exceptions are seizures of evidence in plain view of the police officer,[27] searches under certain exigent circumstances,[28] searches of automobiles,[29] searches incident to a lawful arrest,[30] and stops.[31] If the search or seizure was warrantless, the prosecution must establish that the intrusion falls within one of these recognized exceptions to the warrant requirement. There is an extensive body of case law setting out the elements of the various exceptions. Chapter 17 analyzes the exceptions in detail.

"The Evidence Is Inadmissible". The exclusionary rule operates as an evidentiary competence rule. If the prosecution offers relevant evidence which is the product of an illegal, government search or seizure, the fourth amendment mandates that the judge exclude the evidence. Simply stated, the fourth amendment exclusionary rule renders the evidence incompetent. As we shall see in Chapter 19, the exclusionary rule is not absolute. Sometimes the relationship between the initial illegal intrusion and the evidence is so attenuated that the court concludes that it would not be sensible to apply the exclusionary rule to the evidence. Chapter 19 discusses the exclusionary rule itself and the rule's application to derivative evidence.

---

21. Chapter 16, infra.

22. Generally the courts hold that the government may not resuscitate an affidavit by the use of oral evidence presented to the magistrate. Compare United States v. Anderson, 453 F.2d 174 (9th Cir. 1971), with Leeper v. United States, 446 F.2d 281 (10th Cir. 1971). See also Stone v. Powell, 429 U.S. 465, 96 S.Ct. 3037, 49 L.Ed.2d 1067 (1976). "[W]e have several times rejected [such resuscitation]."

23. The majority rule has been that such challenge is not permitted. People v. Bak, 45 Ill.2d 140, 258 N.E. 2d 341 (1970). The federal courts have required a hearing when the defense has made a "strong and substantial showing" of error. See, e. g., United States v. Bolton, 458 F.2d 377 (9th Cir. 1972).

24. The courts may exclude the evidence depending on the nature of the misconduct that led to the mis-statement or exclude the misstatement and reexamine the affidavit after such deletion to see if probable cause is established. See generally Kipperman, Inaccurate Search Warrant Affidavits as a Ground for Suppressing Evidence, 84 Harv.L.Rev. 825 (1971).

24a. —— U.S. ——, 57 L.Ed.2d 667, 98 S.Ct. 2674 (1978). The Court prescribed a procedure for the situation in which the alleged false statement is necessary to a finding of probable cause. The defendant must make a substantial preliminary showing that the affiant made the false statement knowingly or recklessly. If the defendant does so, he or she is entitled to a hearing on the allegedly false statements in the affidavit. If the defendant proves perjury or recklessness by a preponderance of evidence at the hearing, the exclusionary rule applies.

25. Terry v. Ohio, 392 U.S. 1, 88 S.Ct. 1868, 20 L.Ed. 2d 889 (1968).

26. Chapter 17, infra.

27. Id. at § 19.

28. Id. at §§ 7, 18.

29. Id. at § 9.

30. Id. at § 5.

31. Id. at §§ 2–4.

"Against a Party with Standing". In considering a fourth amendment issue, the last question that must be answered is: Does the party have standing to challenge the illegal search or seizure—that is, was he or she the person "whose rights were violated by the search itself?"[32] To show standing a person may prove that he or she has an interest in the property searched or seized, or that he or she had an expectation of privacy in the area searched, or that he or she was present legitimately on the premises at the time of the search. If the person proves any one of these conditions, he or she may object to the admission of the evidence.

The preceding subsections dissect the fourth amendment into six primary issues: the definition of search and seizure; the list of protected persons, places, and things; the requirement for government participation in the search or seizure; the legality of the search or seizure; the scope of the exclusionary rule; and the standing doctrine. The Supreme Court itself has treated these issues as discrete. The Court has treated the first issue as a threshold question.[33] The Court has decided that electronic surveillance,[34] stop and frisk procedures,[35] and administrative inspections[36] constitute searches and seizures within the meaning of the fourth amendment. When the Court held that handwriting and voice exemplars fall outside fourth amendment coverage, further inquiry became unnecessary: The focus shifts to the legality of the intrusion only after the Court decides that the government intrusion in question is a "search" or "seizure."

---

32. Alderman v. United States, 394 U.S. 165, 89 S.Ct. 961, 22 L.Ed.2d 176 (1969). Chapter 18, infra.

33. Katz v. United States, 389 U.S. 347, 88 S.Ct. 507, 19 L.Ed.2d 576 (1967).

34. Id.

35. Terry v. Ohio, 392 U.S. 1, 88 S.Ct. 1868, 20 L.Ed.2d 889 (1968).

36. Camara v. Municipal Court, 387 U.S. 523, 87 S.Ct. 1727, 18 L.Ed.2d 930 (1967).

CHAPTER 16

PROBABLE CAUSE AND WARRANTS

1. Introduction

If, in the first step of analysis, the court concludes that the activity amounts to a search or seizure, the court must then reach the other fourth amendment issues. Most importantly, the court must adjudicate the legality of the search or seizure. The most common basis for upholding an intrusion's legality is probable cause. §§ 1–5 of this chapter analyze the probability and reliability tests for probable cause. §§ 6–8 of this chapter discuss other rules governing the legality of warranted searches. The next chapter contains a similar discussion of the rules governing the legality of warrantless searches.

A search warrant may be issued only upon an affidavit or complaint setting forth probable cause. Because the requirement when a warrantless search is performed "surely cannot be less stringent"[1] than when a warrant is obtained, probable cause is required.[2] Thus probable cause is required for an arrest, a search authorized by a judge or magistrate, a search justified on the basis of hot pursuit, a warrantless search of an automobile under the *Carroll* doctrine,[3] and a warrantless search of premises under the exigent circumstances doctrine.

2. Probable Cause

Suggested Reading:

Beck v. Ohio, 379 U.S. 89, 85 S.Ct. 223, 13 L.Ed.2d 142 (1964).

Brinegar v. United States, 338 U.S. 160, 69 S.Ct. 1302, 93 L.Ed. 1879 (1949).

Ricehill v. Brewer, 459 F.2d 537 (8th Cir. 1972).

The Definition of Probable Cause. The Supreme Court has stated probable cause for an arrest exists when, at the time of arrest, the police have "reasonably trustworthy information" that a crime was or is being committed and that the arrestee committed or is committing the crime.[4] The Court has also defined probable cause to search: "In determining what is probable cause, we are not called upon to determine whether the offense charged has in fact been committed.

We are concerned only with the question whether the affiant had reasonable grounds at the time of his affidavit and the issuance of the warrant for the belief that the law was being violated on the premises to be searched".[5]

Although "probable cause" means more than mere suspicion,[6] it does not require proof sufficient to establish guilt beyond a reasonable doubt,[7] and it does not have to be competent evidence at trial.[8] Literally, probable cause to search means either that it is more likely than not that the items searched for will be in the place where the search is made, or that a greater than fifty percent probability exists of finding the items for which the search is made.[9] Probable cause is not a fixed test but rather a standard which varies with the seriousness of the offense. In Brinegar v. United States,[10] Mr. Justice Jackson described the standard's variability: "If we assume, for example, that a child is kidnapped and the officers throw a roadblock about the neigh-

---

1. Wong Sun v. United States, 371 U.S. 471, 83 S.Ct. 407, 9 L.Ed.2d 441 (1963).

2. Spinelli v. United States, 393 U.S. 410, 89 S.Ct. 584, 21 L.Ed.2d 637 (1969).

3. See Chapter 17, § 9, infra.

4. Beck v. Ohio, 379 U.S. 89, 91, 85 S.Ct. 223, 225, 13 L.Ed.2d 142 (1964); Henry v. United States, 361 U.S. 98, 102, 80 S.Ct. 168, 171, 4 L.Ed.2d 134 (1959); Brinegar v. United States, 338 U.S. 160, 175–176, 69 S.Ct. 1302, 1310, 1311, 93 L.Ed. 1879 (1949).

5. Dumbra v. United States, 268 U.S. 435, 441, 45 S. Ct. 546, 548, 69 L.Ed. 1032 (1925).

6. Henry v. United States, 361 U.S. 98, 80 S.Ct. 168, 4 L.Ed.2d 134 (1959).

7. Draper v. United States, 358 U.S. 307, 79 S.Ct. 329, 3 L.Ed.2d 327 (1959).

8. United States v. Matlock, 415 U.S. 164, 94 S.Ct. 988, 39 L.Ed.2d 242 (1974); Jones v. United States, 362 U.S. 257, 80 S.Ct. 725, 4 L.Ed.2d 697 (1960).

9. La Fave, "Street Encounters" and the Constitution: *Terry, Sibron, Peters,* and Beyond, 67 Mich.L. Rev. 29, 73–75 (1968). But see Model Code of Pre-Arraignment Procedure, § 120.1(2), Comment 134 (Official Draft No. 1, 1972). "An arrest standard more stringent than reasonable cause would, to be sure, provide increased assurance against interferences by the police with the liberty of innocent persons. It is the Reporters' belief, however, that society would and should be unwilling to pay the price in less efficient crime prevention and prosecution which this assurance would entail." See also Browne v. State, 24 Wis.2d 491, 129 N.W.2d 175 (1964). In determining the lawfulness of an arrest, it is not necessary to prove that guilt is more probable than innocence. It is necessary only that the information lead a reasonable officer to believe that guilt is more than a possibility.

10. 338 U.S. 160, 69 S.Ct. 1302, 93 L.Ed. 1879 (1949).

borhood and search every outgoing car, it would be a drastic and undiscriminating use of the search. The officers might be unable to show probable cause for searching any particular car. However, I should candidly strive hard to sustain such an action, executed fairly and in good faith, because it might be reasonable to subject travelers to that indignity if it was the only way to save a threatened life and detect a vicious crime. But I should not strain to sustain such a roadblock and universal search to salvage a few bottles of bourbon and catch a bootlegger." Some lower courts [11] and the Restatement of Torts have also recognized the seriousness of the offense as a relevant factor in determining probable cause.[12]

Objective Versus Subjective Standards. The civilian courts are split over whether the probable cause test is an objective [13] or objective-subjective test.[14] Under an objective test, the court reviewing the officer's decision to arrest or search (1) identifies the information the officer had in his or her possession and (2) determines whether objectively that information amounts to probable cause. Under an objective-subjective test, the court imposes an additional requirement. In addition to establishing objective probable cause, the prosecution must show that the officer subjectively believed that he or she had probable cause for the arrest or search. Thus, under this test, two questions arise. First, did the arresting officer have a subjective belief that the person he or she apprehended had committed an offense? Second, if the officer had the subjective belief, was the belief objectively reasonable?

There are at least three situations in which the subjective test should not be applied to determine whether there was probable cause for an apprehension. First, when an officer has to apprehend a respected friend, who the officer believes is incapable of committing a crime, an objective test for probable cause must be employed.[15] The subjective test is also inapplicable if there is a possibility that two or more individuals committed a specific offense. For example, A sees B and C bending over a dead man, D; B and C each accuse the other of murdering D. Although A is not sure that either B or C killed D, he has a reasonable ground that one of them is the killer. A is privileged to arrest either or both.[16] In the third situation, the perpetrator's identity is the key issue. The subjective test requires initially that the arresting officer determine if objective probable cause to arrest exists. In many cases, the officer is unsure whether there is probable cause. If a subjective test is applied here, the officer would be unable to make any arrest. In many situations, absent an arrest, the suspect's identity might be lost, and a failure to protect society would occur.

Some courts applying the subjective test have even gone to the extreme of holding that the legality of the arrest should be tested solely on the basis of the legal theory the officer had in mind at the time of mak-

---

11. United States v. Kancso, 252 F.2d 220 (2d Cir. 1958); United States v. Smeal, 23 U.S.C.M.A. 347, 49 C.M.R. 751 (1975); People v. Sirhan, 7 Cal.3d 710, 102 Cal.Rptr. 385, 497 P.2d 1121 (1972).

12. Restatement of Torts, 1934, § 119, Comment j.

13. United States v. Atkinson, 450 F.2d 835 (5th Cir. 1971); Klingler v. United States, 409 F.2d 299 (8th Cir.), cert. denied 396 U.S. 859, 90 S.Ct. 127, 24 L.Ed.2d 110 (1969); State v. Delmondo, 54 Haw. 552, 595, 512 P.2d 551 (1973); People v. Smith, 62 Misc. 2d 473, 308 N.Y.S.2d 909 (1970).

14. Moss v. Cox, 311 F.Supp. 1245, 1252 (E.D.Va. 1970); Winkle v. Kropp, 279 F.Supp. 532, 537 (E.D. Mich.1968), cert. denied 394 U.S. 1003, 89 S.Ct. 1600, 22 L.Ed.2d 781 (1969); People v. Superior Court, 7 Cal.3d 186, 101 Cal.Rptr. 837, 496 P.2d 1205 (1972); People v. Miller, 7 Cal.3d 219, 101 Cal.Rptr. 860, 496 P.2d 1228 (1972).

15. See W. LaFave, Arrest: The Decision to Take a Suspect into Custody 254–55 (1965); Williams, Arrest for Felony at Common Law, 1954 Crim.L.Rev. 408, 417.

16. Second Restatement of Torts, 1965, § 119, Illustration 2.

ing the arrest.[17] There are additional reasons why this extreme subjective test should not be applied. First, the arresting officer might not know the elements of every possible offense. Second, the offense which he or she used to justify the arrest might be declared unconstitutional between the arrest and a motion to suppress. A final reason for not requiring that the officer have a subjective belief about a specific offense is that at times an officer is unsure which crime has been committed: "If an officer, who has received a call to investigate a report of a serious disturbance, sees a disheveled man in bloodstained clothing flee from the area to which the officer has been called, there may be no way of knowing at the time whether the crime, if any, which has been committed, was a rape, a robbery, or a murder." [18] In this situation the officer should not be concerned with the legal subtleties surrounding probable cause.

However there is some justification for using the subjective-objective test; it does prevent the prosecution from gathering facts prior to trial to retroactively establish probable cause for the apprehension. As Judge Skolnick stated: "[T]he policeman perceives his job not simply as requiring that he arrest where he finds probable cause. In addition, he sees the need to be able to reconstruct a set of complex happenings in such a way that, subsequent to arrest, probable cause can be found according

to appellate court standards. In this way, as one district attorney expressed it, 'the policeman fabricates probable cause.' By saying this, he did not mean to assert that the policeman is a liar, but rather that he finds it necessary to construct a fact description of the preceding events so that these conform to legal arrest requirements, whether in fact the events actually did so or not at the time of arrest. Thus, the policeman respects a necessity for 'complying' with the arrest laws. His 'compliance' however, may take the form of *post hoc* manipulation of the facts rather than before-the-fact behavior." [19] When the court applies an objective test rather than a subjective-objective test, the probable cause standard can be met on the basis of information known to the police department as a whole rather than on the basis of facts known to the arresting officer.[20] Such an approach might encourage law enforcement officials to arrest even though they themselves do not have a valid reason, for they might be able to establish probable cause from information known to the police department.[21]

On the whole, the subjective-objective approach provides little fourth amendment protection. The prosecution can easily coach a witness prior to testifying, and once the police officer testifies that he or she thought there were grounds for the arrest, the defense could probably not rebut such testimony except in extreme cases. When the testimony cannot be rebutted, the after-the-fact review determines if the apprehension was based on objective probable cause. For

---

17. People v. Superior Court, 7 Cal.3d 186, 101 Cal.Rptr. 837, 496 P.2d 1205 (1972). But see South Dakota ex rel. Thunderhorse v. Ericson, 328 F.Supp. 1149 (D.S.D.1971); People v. Superior Court, 15 Cal. App.3d 146, 92 Cal.Rptr. 916 (1971) (defendant arrested for "investigation of burglary"; court held even though no basis for arrest on stated grounds there was probable cause to believe him guilty of disorderly conduct, burglary, and attempted burglary); Commonwealth v. Lawton, 348 Mass. 129, 202 N.E.2d 824 (1964) (court indicated it was not necessary to decide the constitutionality of the statute under which defendant was arrested because there was probable cause to arrest for second offense).

18. Model Code of Prearraignment Procedure § 120.0 Comment (Proposed Official Draft No. 1, 1972).

---

19. J. Skolnick, Justice Without Trial 214–15 (1966).

20. Ricehill v. Brewer, 459 F.2d 537 (8th Cir. 1972) (Although arrest for vagrancy was improper, the court expressly applied an objective test and rejected a subjective test, upholding arrest for murder. Police in good faith believed there were grounds for the vagrancy arrest.) See also United States v. Atkinson, 450 F.2d 835 (5th Cir. 1971); Klingler v. United States, 409 F.2d 299 (8th Cir.), cert. denied 396 U.S. 859, 90 S.Ct. 127, 24 L.Ed.2d 110 (1969).

21. Ricehill v. Brewer, 459 F.2d 537 (8th Cir. 1972).

all the above reasons, the trend in the case law is to apply the objective test.

The Distinction Between Probable Cause to Search and Probable Cause to Arrest. Establishing probable cause for apprehension does not establish probable cause for a search of a person or place. Establishing probable cause for a search does not establish probable cause for an apprehension. Each requires probabilities about different facts and circumstances. In order to obtain either authorization to search or a search warrant issued by a judge, an officer does not have to identify any particular person as the likely offender. Although the fact that the person controlling the place is connected with a crime is a frequent and primary justification presented to the judge, it is not decisive. When an individual has committed a crime involving fruits, instrumentalities, or other evidence with a nexus to criminal prosecution, opposing conclusions might be drawn about the search of a place. One might conclude that the probability that the individual has the property on his or her premises is no greater than the probability that he or she has it at some other place under his or her control. Or one might conclude that the probability that the accused has the items hidden in some place under his or her exclusive control justifies authorizing a search of any place he or she controls. Some courts support the latter proposition.[22]

3. The Probability Test

Suggested Reading:

United States v. Harris, 403 U.S. 573, 91 S.Ct. 2075, 29 L.Ed.2d 723 (1971).

Spinelli v. United States, 393 U.S. 410, 89 S.Ct. 584, 21 L.Ed.2d 637 (1969).

Draper v. United States, 358 U.S. 307, 79 S.Ct. 329, 3 L.Ed.2d 327 (1959).

There are various methods of obtaining evidence to establish probable cause to search or arrest. An officer who is planning an arrest or warrantless search may gain information in at least three ways. In many instances, he or she personally observes the criminal activity or its results. Second, he or she might receive information about the criminal activity from another police official. Finally, they might obtain information from an informant.

In a determination whether probable cause exists, two questions arise: (1) Is the evidence given either at the time of a motion to suppress or at the time of issuing the warrant worthy of belief? (the reliability test) and (2) If so, does the evidence lead to the reasonable belief that an offense has been committed by a particular person (probable cause for arrest) or that items connected with criminal activity are presently located in the place or on the person to be searched? (the probability test)

Whenever the officer making a warrantless arrest or search does not rely upon his or her personal observations, he or she is using hearsay to establish probable cause. Likewise, when the officer appearing before the magistrate is not relying upon his or her own personal observations to establish probable cause, he or she is using hearsay. In many instances, the officer will be willing to identify the hearsay source of information. However, in other cases, for example when the informant is still serving as an undercover investigator for the police, the officer will be reluctant to name the hearsay source.

---

22. See, e. g., U. S. v. Klapholz, 17 F.R.D. 18 (S.D. N.Y.1955), aff'd 230 F.2d 494 (2d Cir. 1956); Commonwealth v. De Masi, 362 Mass. 53, 283 N.E.2d 845 (1972). But see United States v. Flanagan, 423 F.2d 745 (5th Cir. 1970).

In Aguilar v. Texas,[23] the Supreme Court stated that if hearsay is relied upon, the magistrate must be informed of (1) some of the underlying circumstances which led the informant to conclude that the items are where he or she claims they are; and (2) some of the underlying circumstances which led the person seeking the warrant to believe his or her information is credible or his or her informant reliable. The first prong is *the "basis-of-knowledge" or probability test.* The second prong is *the "reliability test."* Although the Court spoke in terms of probable cause for a warrant, a similar test applies to an arrest.

Aguilar's two-prong test has been criticized as a prophylactic that is not constitutionally mandated.[24] Some courts are sympathetic to the criticism. To restrict the test, some courts have held that *Aguilar* and its progeny do not apply to information obtained from a known informant.[25] Others have held that the reliability test is to be relaxed when the information comes from a known informant.[26] However, the prevailing view is that regardless of whether the information relied upon to establish probable cause is hearsay or non-hearsay, the ba-

sis-of-knowledge or probability test must be satisfied.[27]

Personal Observation of the Informant. Under the basis-of-knowledge or probability test, the magistrate must be given facts from which he or she can judge the validity of the informant's conclusion. The test can be satisfied by a statement that the informant was relying on his or her personal observation.[28] The affidavit should set forth the conditions under which he or she made the observation, the opportunity he or she had to observe the items, and the expertise or background which led him or her to believe that the items were stolen or that they are a specific type of drug.[29] If the informant did not personally observe the items but rather drew a conclusion from circumstantial evidence, the judge must be informed of this fact.

Statement of the Defendant. Another means of passing the probability test is showing that the informant obtained his or her information directly from the defendant.[30] The purpose of the test is to ensure that the information establishing probable cause is not based on rumor, gossip, or solely on the defendant's reputation in the community. Although the basis-of-knowledge test is also satisfied by establishing that the

---

23. 378 U.S. 108, 114, 84 S.Ct. 1509, 1513, 12 L.Ed. 2d 723 (1964). Aguilar's conviction followed a search based on an affidavit which recited only that: "[a]ffiants have received reliable information from a credible person and so believe that heroin, marihuana, barbiturates and other narcotics and narcotic paraphernalia are being kept at the above described premises for the purpose of sale and use contrary to the provisions of the law." Id. at 109.

24. Spinelli v. United States, 393 U.S. 410, 417 n. 5, 89 S.Ct. 584, 589, 21 L.Ed.2d 637 (1969). See generally Rebell, The Undisclosed Informant and the Fourth Amendment: A Search for Meaningful Standards, 81 Yale L.J. 703 (1972); Note, The Informer's Tip as Probable Cause for Search or Arrest, 54 Cornell L.Q. 958 (1969).

25. United States v. Unger, 469 F.2d 1283, 1286 (7th Cir. 1972) (test needs to be applied when the complaint was based "solely on hearsay information from an unidentified informant"); United States v. Bell, 457 F.2d 1231, 1238 (5th Cir. 1972).

26. United States v. Brooks, 350 F.Supp. 1152 (D.C. Wis.1972).

27. Campbell v. Minnesota, 487 F.2d 1 (8th Cir. 1973) (statement of affiant detective must satisfy the basis-of-knowledge—probability test).

28. Spinelli v. United States, 393 U.S. 410, 423, 89 S.Ct. 584, 592, 21 L.Ed.2d 637 (1969) (White, J., concurring); People v. Arnold, 186 Colo. 372, 527 P.2d 806 (1974); State v. Adams, 109 Ariz. 556, 514 P.2d 477 (1973). But see Commonwealth v. Emerich, 225 Pa.Super. 163, 310 A.2d 390 (1973) (conclusory statement insufficient).

29. Hegdal v. State, Tex.Cr.App., 488 S.W.2d 782 (1972). The tip did not satisfy the basis-of-knowledge test because there was no information demonstrating the informant's expertise with drugs—that is, on the basis of past experience or because he is a user himself, the informant was qualified to recognize what he says he saw.

30. United States v. Hennig, 22 U.S.C.M.A. 377, 380, 47 C.M.R. 229, 232 (1973).

information was obtained from an accomplice,[31] the affidavit must set forth circumstances demonstrating that the informant is an accomplice.

Self-Verifying Detail. In Spinelli v. United States,[32] the Supreme Court stated: "In absence of a statement detailing the manner in which the information was gathered" the tip may be self-verifying when the defendant's "criminal activity is described in sufficient detail so that the magistrate may know that he is relying on something more substantial than a casual rumor." Although in *Spinelli* Mr. Justice Harlan offered little guidance for determining if a tip is detailed enough to be self-verifying, he did say that Draper v. United States [33] provided a "suitable benchmark" for indicating when a tip is sufficiently detailed.[34]

In *Draper* an informant who had been reliable in the past (1) informed the FBI on September 7 that Draper would arrive in Denver on a train from Chicago on September 8 or 9; (2) described Draper's appearance and how he would be dressed; (3) said that the defendant walked with a fast gait; (4) stated that he would be carrying a tan zipper bag; and (5) maintained that he would be carrying heroin. The court held that the apprehending officer had probable cause to arrest the defendant when the officer corroborated four of the five allegations prior to the defendant's arrest.

It is the nature of the facts rather than their number or detail that is determinative. The detail of the tip and the nature of the facts must be such that a reasonable person can draw the conclusion that the informant must have obtained the information by personal observation or by some other trustworthy manner. A detailed tip that contains easily predictable or ascertainable facts will not satisfy the test.

Corroboration. In *Spinelli*, Mr. Justice Harlan indicated that independent corroboration may satisfy both the basis-of-knowledge and the reliability tests.[35] Although this is the converse of what was actually stated,[36] it is supported by other language in the opinion.[37] In determining whether the tip has been sufficiently corroborated, Justice Harlan used *Draper*[38] as a standard of comparison.[39] In *Draper*, the apprehending officer had corroborated four of the five allegations prior to the defendant's arrest. However, in *Spinelli* only "one small detail" (the presence of two phones) had been corroborated by

---

31. Cf. United States v. Viggiano, 433 F.2d 716, 718 n. 3 (2d Cir. 1970); McCarthy v. State, 22 Md.App. 722, 325 A.2d 132 (1974). Remarking on the reliability test, the court stated there was "no reason for the accomplice to . . . state [that the drugs were kept at the defendant's house] if it were not so." But see Bridger v. State, 503 S.W.2d 801 (Tex. Cr.App.1974).

32. 393 U.S. 410, 416, 89 S.Ct. 584, 589, 21 L.Ed.2d 637 (1969).

33. 358 U.S. 307, 79 S.Ct. 329, 3 L.Ed.2d 327 (1959).

34. Id. See also United States ex rel. Saiken v. Bensinger, 489 F.2d 865 (7th Cir. 1973); United States v. Chavez, 482 F.2d 1268 (5th Cir. 1973); United States v. Marihart, 472 F.2d 809, 813 (8th Cir. 1972); Boyer v. Arizona, 455 F.2d 804 (9th Cir. 1972); Stanley v. State, 19 Md.App. 507, 313 A.2d 847 (1974).

35. This view seems to be accepted by the entire Court. See id. at 438 (Fortas, J., dissenting). See also United States v. Archuleta, 446 F.2d 518 (9th Cir. 1971) (corroboration of information in tip was sufficient to pass both prongs of test).

36. Spinelli v. United States, 393 U.S. 410, 415–16, 89 S.Ct. 584, 588, 589, 21 L.Ed.2d 637 (1969). "A magistrate cannot be said to have properly discharged his constitutional duty if he relies on an informer's tip which—even when partially corroborated—is not as reliable as one which passes Aguilar's requirements when standing alone."

37. Id. at 415. "If the tip is found inadequate under Aguilar, the other allegations which corroborate the information contained in the hearsay report should then be considered. Can it fairly be said that the tip, even when certain parts of it have been corroborated by independent sources, is as trustworthy as a tip which would pass Aguilar's test without independent corroboration?"

38. Draper v. United States, 358 U.S. 307, 79 S.Ct. 329, 3 L.Ed.2d 327 (1959).

39. Spinelli v. United States, 393 U.S. 410, 417, 89 S.Ct. 584, 589, 21 L.Ed.2d 637 (1969).

independent investigative efforts; [40] and that fact revealed "nothing unusual," [41] for "[m]any a householder indulges himself in this petty luxury." [42]

The Defendant's Reputation. In *Spinelli*, a search warrant for gambling paraphernalia was obtained on the basis of an affidavit indicating that (1) the defendant had been observed on several occasions going into a certain apartment; (2) a check with the telephone company disclosed that there were two telephones in this apartment listed in a name other than defendants; (3) the defendant was "known to this affiant and to federal law enforcement agents and local law enforcement agents as a bookmaker"; [43] and (4) the affiant had been "informed by a confidential reliable informant that the defendant [was] operating a handbook and accepting wagers and disseminating wagering information by the means of the telephones" [44] in the apartment. Mr. Justice Harlan, speaking for the majority of the Court, stated that "[t]he first two items reflect[ed] only innocent-seeming activity and data." [45] He continued by saying that the third allegation (defendant's reputation as a gambler) was "but a bald and unilluminating assertion of suspicion that is entitled to no weight in appraising the magistrate's decision." [46] The fourth allegation (the informant's tip) did not pass either prong of *Aguilar*.

In United States v. Harris, the affiant stated that the unidentified informer told the federal tax investigator that he had purchased bootlegged whiskey at the defendant's residence "for a period of more than

two years, and most recently within two weeks." [47] The informer also maintained that he had "personal knowledge that illicit whiskey was consumed by purchasers in the outbuilding known as and utilized as the 'dance hall,' and [had] seen Roosevelt Harris go to the other outbuilding, located about 50 yards from the residence, on numerous occasions, to obtain whiskey for this person and other persons." [48] Although no indication exists that the informer had given reliable information in the past, the tip was supported by the affiant's recitation of the facts in the warrant as follows: (1) The defendant had a reputation as a bootlegger. (2) "[A]ll types of persons" had supplied information about the defendant's "activities." (3) Another police officer had made a seizure of illicit whiskey from an "abandoned house under Harris' control" within the past four years. [49] The affiant also said that he had "interviewed this person [the informant], and found this person to be a prudent person." [50]

In a 5–4 decision written by Chief Justice Burger, the Court implied that the information in the tip was sufficiently corroborated for the magistrate to conclude that it was "reliable." Because of the detailed tip and the fact that the information was based on "personal and recent observations," [51] Chief Justice Burger concluded "that the affidavit in the present case contains an ample factual basis for believing the informant which, when coupled with affiant's own knowledge of the respondent's background, afforded a basis upon which the magistrate could reasonably issue the warrant." [52] The information within the

---

40. Id.

41. Id. at 414.

42. Id.

43. Spinelli v. United States, 393 U.S. 410, 89 S.Ct. 584, 21 L.Ed.2d 637 (1969).

44. Id.

45. Id.

46. Id.

47. United States v. Harris, 403 U.S. 573, 91 S.Ct. 2075, 29 L.Ed.2d 723 (1971).

48. Id. at 575–76.

49. Id. at 575.

50. Id.

51. Id. at 579.

52. Id. at 579–80. The opinion of the Court was divided in three parts. The entire opinion was

affiant's "own knowledge" deemed corroborative of the tip was the policemen's knowledge of the accused's reputation and of the seizure of illicit whiskey from the accused within the last four years. This reasoning is supported by the second portion of the opinion.[53] Here Chief Justice Burger wrote that the statement in *Spinelli* that the evidence of the defendant's reputation was "bald and unilluminating" was based on a misreading of Nathanson v. United States.[54] He limited *Nathanson* by holding that "reputation, *standing alone,* was insufficient; it surely did not hold it irrelevant when supported by other information."[55] Reputation evidence certainly must be considered, for it is a factual and practical consideration of everyday life upon which reasonable and prudent people act.[56]

An individual's reputation can establish a suspect's prior weaknesses which might lead him or her to engage in criminal activity.[57] It now seems fairly well-settled that the officer may consider a suspect's criminal reputation as increasing the probability of the suspect's guilt.

4. The Reliability Test

Suggested Reading:

United States v. Ventresca, 380 U.S. 102, 85 S.Ct. 741, 13 L.Ed.2d 684 (1965).

Jones v. United States, 362 U.S. 257, 80 S.Ct. 725, 4 L.Ed.2d 697 (1960).

United States v. Spach, 518 F.2d 866 (7th Cir. 1975).

In addition to satisfying the probability test, the prosecution must meet the reliability test. The reliability test, which guards against tips provided by untruthful or unreliable informers, speaks of two possibilities: (1) a "credible" informant, or (2) "reliable" information. This distinction suggests that an informant is credible if he or she provided truthful tips in the past and that the information is reliable if corroborated by independent investigation.

Past Reliability. In establishing reliability or credibility, a mere assertion that the information was obtained from "a confidential, reliable informant" is a "bald and unilluminating" statement which does not pass the reliability test.[58] Also it is insufficient to state simply that the informant is a "prudent person".[59] Citing Jones v. United States,[60] some courts hold that an assertion that the informer has given truthful tips on prior occasions is sufficient to establish credibility.[61] *Jones* upheld an affidavit stating

---

joined by Justices Black and Blackmun, who favored overruling *Spinelli* or *Aguilar*. Justice White agreed with the portion of the opinion dealing with the weight to be attached to declarations against interest and "concluded that the affidavit, considered as a whole, was sufficient to support issuance of the warrant." Id. at 585. Justice Stewart agreed with the part of the opinion dealing with the corroboration of the tip. Id. Justice Harlan wrote a lengthy dissent; he was joined by Justices Brennan, Douglas, and Marshall. Id. at 586.

53. Justices Black and Blackmun concurred in this position. Id. at 585.

54. 290 U.S. 41, 54 S.Ct. 11, 78 L.Ed. 159 (1931).

55. United States v. Harris, 403 U.S. 573, 582, 91 S.Ct. 2075, 2081, 29 L.Ed.2d 723 (1971).

56. Id. at 583–84.

57. Note, 1969 Wash.U.L.Q. 339.

58. Id.

59. United States v. Harris, 403 U.S. 573, 91 S.Ct. 2075, 29 L.Ed.2d 723 (1971).

60. 362 U.S. 257, 270, 80 S.Ct. 725, 735, 4 L.Ed.2d 697 (1960).

61. People v. McNeil, 52 Ill.2d 409, 288 N.E.2d 464 (1972); People v. Hendricks, 25 N.Y.2d 129, 133–34, 303 N.Y.S.2d 33, 36–37 (1967). See also United States v. Malo, 417 F.2d 1242 (2d Cir. 1969) (The tip was held sufficient to pass the reliability test when it was shown that the informant had given reliable

that the informant had previously given the affiant reliable information.[62] The affiant also related that Jones had "admitted to the use of narcotic drugs and display[ed] needle marks as evidence of same"[63] and that "[t]his same information"[64] regarding the accused had been given the narcotic squad by "other sources of information."[65] Other courts have held that merely stating that the informant has given reliable information in the past does not set forth enough of "the underlying circumstances" from which the officer concluded the informant is reliable.

In Hooper v. Commonwealth,[66] two affidavits were presented for the court's consideration. One recounted facts obtained from a participant in a burglary about where the stolen items were kept. This was held sufficient under *Aguilar*. The other affidavit, reporting where narcotics were hidden, was based on an account given by "a reliable source of information that has given information in the past, that has resulted in arrest being made for narcotics violation."[67] This was held insufficient information to enable the court to evaluate the tip.

The Colorado Supreme Court held insufficient an affidavit which stated that a reliable informer had given accurate information in the past, had purchased LSD from the subject and was to do so again on the day the warrant was sought.[68] The court said: "[A]n affidavit established the credibility

of informant by merely stating that the informant is known to be reliable based on past information supplied by the informer which has proven to be accurate. Although the words 'past information' might conjure up in the minds of the officer some knowledge of the underlying circumstances from which the officer might conclude that the informant was reliable, the judge has not been apprised of such facts, and consequently, he cannot make a disinterested determination based on such facts."[69]

The import of these decisions is that if the judge is to determine probable cause, he or she must know more than the fact that the informer has provided reliable information in the past.[70]

Declaration Against Interest. In the third part of the plurality opinion in United States v. Harris,[71] Chief Justice Burger stated that "there was an additional reason for crediting the informant's tip."[72] This reason was the informant's declaration against penal interest[73]—that is, his assertion that

69. Id. at 373.

70. United States v. Acosta, 501 F.2d 1330 (5th Cir. 1974) ("informant has on another occasion assisted Federal Agents in initiating cases" insufficient); People v. Arnold, 186 Colo. 372, 527 P.2d 806 (1974) (sufficient to say prior tips have resulted in two arrests); State v. Holloway, 187 Neb. 1, 187 N.W.2d 85 (1971); Horner v. State, 483 P.2d 744 (Okl.1971); Sturgeon v. State, 483 P.2d 335, 337 (Okl.1971) (The court expressed dissatisfaction with an affidavit which indicated only that the informant had proved reliable in the past; "[t]he affidavit must detail why the informant is deemed reliable . . . the affidavit in the instant case recites . . . no details as to why the informant is deemed reliable which would enable the magistrate to judicially determine whether the informant was in fact reliable."); Leonard v. State, 453 P.2d 257 (Okl.1969); Wiles v. Commonwealth, 209 Va. 282, 163 S.E.2d 595 (1968). Cf. Foxall v. State, 157 Ind.App. 19, 298 N.E.2d 470 (1973) (sufficient to state past information "proved to be valid").

71. 403 U.S. 573, 91 S.Ct. 2075, 29 L.Ed.2d 723 (1971). Justices Black, Blackmun and White concurred in this part of the opinion.

72. Id. at 583.

73. 26 U.S.C.A. § 5205(a)(2)

information in the past. Alternatively, there was corroboration of non-criminal behavior furnished the police by the informant.); United States v. Gazard Colon, 419 F.2d 120 (2d Cir. 1969) (Informant is deemed reliable if he has given arresting officer "at least six tips—three of which had led to arrest.").

62. Jones v. United States, 362 U.S. 257, 267–70, 80 S.Ct. 725, 734–735, 4 L.Ed.2d 697 (1960).

63. Id. at 267 n. 2.

64. Id.

65. Id.

66. 212 Va. 49, 181 S.E.2d 816 (1971).

67. Id. at 51, 181 S.E.2d at 817.

68. People v. Brethauer, 174 Colo. 29, 482 P.2d 369 (1971).

he had purchased illicit whiskey from the accused over a long period of time and in fact had bought whiskey within the last two weeks. The informant's statement by "itself and without more . . . furnished probable cause to search" the accused's premises.[74] Although this language in *Harris* did not have a majority of the Supreme Court's support, a number of lower courts have held that the declaration against interest by itself, or together with other factors, establishes the informant's reliability.[75]

Before a declaration against penal interest should be considered in determining probable cause, it must be examined to establish that it is truly against the informer's interest and that the informer has no motive to falsify the facts declared.[76] In support-

ing his statement in *Harris*, Chief Justice Burger relied upon the Proposed Rules of Evidence for the United States Courts and Magistrates, Rule 804, which became effective July 1, 1975. However, Rule 804 conditions the admissibility of declarations against penal interest upon proof of the declarant's unavailability.[77] The relevant factors in deciding admissibility of the declarant's statement, as set forth in Chambers v. Mississippi,[78] are first, whether the person is under charges at the time of the statement; second, whether the statement was made soon after the crime; third, whether the informer is aware that he or she is admitting a criminal offense; and fourth, whether any possible benefit to the declarant exists. When the declarant has been charged with an offense, especially in a narcotics case, he or she might be motivated to give additional information in order to receive an offer of immunity or a sentence reduction. If in a pretrial agreement the government gives the informant a grant of immunity or a reduction in sentence, the reliability of information received usually is suspect.[79] Moreover, especially in narcotic cases, the informant might be motivated by the promise of payments.[80]

---

74. United States v. Harris, 403 U.S. 573, 584, 91 S.Ct. 2075, 2082, 29 L.Ed.2d 723 (1971).

75. United States v. Neal, 500 F.2d 305 (10th Cir. 1974) (dictum); United States v. Golay, 502 F.2d 182 (8th Cir. 1974); United States v. Damitz, 495 F.2d 50, 55 (9th Cir. 1974) (The informant's "reliability is demonstrated by his admitted participation in the conspiracy to obtain marihuana as well as his voluntary surrender of two marihuana bricks to federal agents." The court held the admission and surrender to be sufficient proof of reliability. In addition, the informant had personally appeared before the magistrate.); Agnellino v. New Jersey, 493 F.2d 714 (3d Cir. 1974); Armour v. Salisbury, 492 F.2d 1032, 1035 (6th Cir. 1974) ("An admission against penal interest . . . is a significant, and sometimes conclusive, reason for crediting the statements of an informant."); Quigg v. Estelle, 492 F.2d 343, 345 (9th Cir. 1974) ("This declaration was against the informant's penal interest and as such could be used to credit his reliability and the information which he gave to the affiant"); United States v. Carmichael, 489 F.2d 983, 986 (7th Cir. 1973) (en banc) ("The statement by the second informer was an admission against his penal interest thus manifesting his reliability and constituting an exception to the hearsay rule."); United States ex rel. Griffin v. Vincent, 359 F.Supp. 1072, 1075 (D.C.N.Y.1973) ("An informant who accompanies the police to a confrontation with the defendant is unlikely to be a perpetrator of a deliberate fabrication . . . especially since civil or criminal liability may exist for inducing a false arrest."). But see Wilson v. State, 314 A.2d 905 (Del.Ch.1973) (Declaration against interest by itself was held insufficient.).

76. See C. McCormick, Handbook of the Law of Evidence § 256 (1954).

77. Fed.Evid.Rule 804(b)(3), 28 U.S.C.A. "A statement which . . . so far tended to subject [the informer] to civil or criminal liability . . . that a reasonable man in his position would not have made the statement unless he believed it to be true [will be admissible]." However, Rule 804 is not intended to apply to probable cause hearings. Fed.Evid. 1101(d) (3), 28 U.S.C.A.

78. 410 U.S. 284, 300–01, 93 S.Ct. 1038, 1048, 35 L.Ed.2d 297 (1973) (exclusion of exculpatory declarations against penal interest is a violation of due process). See also United States v. Matlock, 415 U.S. 164, 94 S.Ct. 988, 39 L.Ed.2d 242 (1974).

79. Siebert and Gitchoff, The Strategy of Narcotics Law Enforcement; Its Implication and Effects, 2 J. Drug Issues 29 (1972).

80. See S. Drodsky, Search Warrants, Hearsay Evidence in the Federal Constitution: A Critique Based on California Experience 35 (1969) (The California municipality studied by the author averaged $10. This amount was generally used to finance the informant's drug habit.); Jones v. United States, 266

The Citizen-Informant Doctrine. Another factor to consider in determining reliability is the relationship of the informant to criminal activity. In a recent case, Adams v. Williams,[81] the Supreme Court recognized this concept: "[W]hen the victim of a street crime seeks immediate police aid and gives a description of his assailant . . . the subtleties of the hearsay rule should not thwart an appropriate police response." [82]

When information is obtained from a person other than an unidentified informant, some courts have held that the *Aguilar* test does not apply.[83] In United States v. Bell,[84] a court of appeals stated: "It is now a well-settled and familiar concept, as enunciated by *Aguilar* and *Spinelli*, that supporting affidavits in an application for a search warrant must attest to the credibility of the informant and the reliability of his information. We have discovered no case that extends this reliability requirement to the identified bystander or the victim-eyewitness [85] to a crime, and we now hold that no such requirement need be met."

Those courts that have not eliminated the reliability test when the information is obtained from an individual who is not from a criminal environment have relaxed it in various ways. If information is obtained from the "ordinary citizen," some courts have held the reliability test is automatically satisfied.[86] Other courts have held that an eyewitness to or a victim of an offense is presumed reliable, and this presumption has been extended even to the anonymous victim. In Brown v. United States,[87] Judge Burger, now Chief Justice of the United States Supreme Court, stated: "That the information came from an unknown victim of the crime did not preclude the policeman's having probable cause to arrest Appellant on the basis of it. Although the police could not here judge the reliability of the information on the basis of the past experience with the informant, the victim's report has a virtue of being based on personal observation . . . and is less likely to be colored by self-interest than is that of an informant." [88] When a jurisdiction does not allow an attack on an affidavit sufficient on its face, no practical difference exists between a presumption of reliability and automatic reliability. In such a jurisdiction the reliability test should not be held satisfied merely because an informant is named. If this were done, there would be little to deter the police from naming any informant in the affidavit, particularly if they do not plan on using him or her in the future.

Finally, rather than automatic reliability or a presumption of reliability, some courts have stated that they will be less demanding in determining whether the reliability test of *Aguilar* has been met.[89]

Law Enforcement Officers. The Supreme Court has held that the agents of the Federal Bureau of Investigation are presumed reliable.[90] While some state courts have held that local law enforcement officials

---

F.2d 924, 928 (D.C.Cir. 1959). See also Note. The Outwardly Sufficient Search Warrant Affidavit, 19 U.C.L.A.L.Rev. 96 (1971).

81. 407 U.S. 143, 92 S.Ct. 1921, 32 L.Ed.2d 612 1972).

82. Id. at 147.

83. United States v. Sellers, 483 F.2d 37 (5th Cir. 1973); United States v. Bell, 457 F.2d 1231 (5th Cir. 1972).

84. 457 F.2d 1231 (5th Cir. 1972).

85. Id. at 1238.

86. Pendleton v. Nelson, 404 F.2d 1074 (9th Cir. 1968); State v. Paszek, 50 Wis.2d 619, 184 N.W.2d 836 (1971). But see United States v. Brooks, 350 F.Supp. 1152, 1154–55 (D.C.Wis.1972).

87. 365 F.2d 976 (D.C.Cir. 1966).

88. Id. at 979.

89. United States v. Brooks, 350 F.Supp. 1152 (D.C. Wis.1972).

90. United States v. Ventresca, 380 U.S. 102, 111, 85 S.Ct. 741, 747, 13 L.Ed.2d 684 (1965). "Observations of fellow officers of the Government engaged in a common investigation are plainly a reliable basis for a warrant applied for by one of their number."

are also presumed reliable,[91] the Maryland Court of Special Appeals has gone even further, stating that "the informant's status as an undercover agent employed by Pinkerton Detective Agency adequately established 'his credibility.' "[92]

Circumstantial Proof of Reliability. A number of courts have interpreted *Harris* as relaxing the credibility requirements enunciated in *Aguilar*.[93] These courts have indicated that other factors may be used to establish reliability circumstantially. For example, a court may infer reliability from the detail of the tip and a showing that the information is not obtained as the result of gossip in the underworld.[94] A second circumstance showing reliability is found in cases in which the informant is continuously employed by the government. The courts reason that the employee must be dependable, or he or she would be fired.

The Informant's Reputation. In Yantis v. State,[95] the court held that the informant's reliability "had been established by his excellent reputation in the neighborhood in which he resides, the lack of criminal record, and his continuous gainful employment."[96] The court treated the informant's reputation as one of the factors which together satisfied the reliability test.

Informant's Personal Appearance Before Magistrate. There are non-hearsay methods of establishing probable cause. In many instances the person who observed the criminal activity will testify before the issuing magistrate. The person gives the information under oath or affirmation and is subject to the personal scrutiny of the magistrate, who may question the witness.[97] If the magistrate issues the warrant, a presumption arises that he or she found the individual credible.

5. Probable Cause and Miscellaneous Matters

Imputed Knowledge. Many arrests by police officers are not based upon the personal observations of the arresting officer. Rather they are based solely upon a request from a superior officer, a request from a fellow officer, or information obtained by radio. Thus the officer acts upon the direction of a communication received through proper channels.[98] There is substantial au-

---

91. French v. State, 256 Ark. 298, 506 S.W.2d 820 (1974); Waugh v. State, 20 Md.App. 682, 318 A.2d 204 (1974).

92. Schmidt v. State, 17 Md.App. 492, 302 A.2d 714 (1973).

93. United States ex rel. Saiken v. Bensinger, 489 F.2d 865, 867 (7th Cir. 1973); United States v. McNally, 473 F.2d 934, 938–39 (3d Cir. 1973); United States v. Unger, 469 F.2d 1283, 1286 (7th Cir. 1972).

94. United States v. Principe, 499 F.2d 1135 (1st Cir. 1974) ("The informant was both named and was revealed as a participant in the crime. The informant's knowledge was obtained from recent personal observation. That the affidavit admitted details which could have strengthened it . . . is not fatal."); United States v. Smith, 499 F.2d 251 (7th Cir. 1974) (Detail was one factor as to reliability.); United States v. Carmichael, 489 F.2d 983 (7th Cir. 1973) (en banc) ("[T]he credibility of the informant was established by his personal observation" and his past reliability.); United States v. Unger, 469 F.2d 1283, 1287 (7th Cir. 1972) ("We are of the opinion that the reliability of the citizen's tip is further underwritten by his knowledge of the weapon viewed in the locker and the specificity with which he reported its contents to the police."); United States v. Bolton, 458 F.2d 377, 378 (9th Cir. 1972) ("The sharpness of the details concerning the instant crime underscored reliability," citing *Harris*.); Hughley v. State, 161 Ind.App. 583, 316 N.E.2d 586 (1974) ("The informant had proven to be reliable in the past. Furthermore, this informant gave accurate, detailed information about the plan.").

95. 476 S.W.2d 24 (Tex.Cr.App.1972).

96. Id. at 27.

97. People v. Coleman, 28 Cal.App.3d 36, 104 Cal. Rptr. 363 (1972) (The question of reliability is not involved when the informant himself personally signs the affidavit and appears before the magistrate. In such a case the magistrate determines reliability as would the trier of fact in court.); Dawson v. State, 11 Md.App. 694, 276 A.2d 680 (1971); People v. Wheatman, 29 N.Y.2d 337, 327 N.Y.S.2d 643 (1971).

98. Whitely v. Warden, 401 U.S. 560, 91 S.Ct. 1031, 28 L.Ed.2d 306 (1971) (dictum) (The Court was careful to point out that the person relaying the information must have had probable cause to execute the arrest himself.); Chambers v. Maroney, 399 U.S. 42, 90 S.Ct. 1975, 26 L.Ed.2d 419 (1970) (partial holding).

thority that under these circumstances the arresting ofifcer need not know personally the reliability of the informer in order to possess information sufficient to constitute probable cause. The court imputes the other officers' information to the arresting officer. The imputation is helpful in satisfying both the probability and reliability tests.

Suggested Reading:

United States ex rel. LaBelle v. LaVallee, 517 F.2d 750 (2d Cir. 1975).

Stale Information. Once it is shown that probable cause for arrest exists, the probable cause will remain for weeks, months or even years. However, this is not true when information is furnished to support probable cause for a search of a person or place. In such a situation the passage of time results in the likelihood that the goods will no longer be in the original location. For this reason information given in an affidavit or orally to a judge must state the time when the facts occurred.[99] Although this statement should be reasonably definite, declarations that the observations were made "recently" or "within" a named period have been approved.[1] Just how long a period may elapse from the time the facts are obtained until a search is authorized depends upon many things such as the location involved, the type of crime, the nature of the articles to be seized and whether the crime is a continuing operation. Although courts often refer to "the staleness doctrine" as if it were a separate fourth amendment doctrine, in reality staleness problems are simply an aspect of the probability test. The informa-

tion must make it probable that the item is *presently* located at the place to be searched.

Suggested Reading:

United States v. Brinklow, 560 F.2d 1003 (10th Cir. 1977).

6. General Warrant Requirements

Suggested Reading:

United States v. Chadwick, 429 U.S. 814, 97 S.Ct. 2476, 50 L.Ed.2d 74 (1977).

United States v. United States District Court, 407 U.S. 297, 92 S.Ct. 2125, 32 L.Ed.2d 752 (1972).

With varying degrees of emphasis the Supreme Court has stressed that "the definition of 'reasonableness' turns, at least, in part, on the more specific commands of the [fourth amendment's] warrant ·clause."[2] This reliance on the warrant clause has led the Court to apply a per se rule of illegality. Except in a few limited and carefully defined situations, a warrantless search is per se unreasonable.[3] The preferred search is made with a warrant, which must be based on probable cause and issued by a neutral, detached magistrate. It must also specifical-

---

99. Chin Kay v. United States, 311 F.2d 317 (9th Cir. 1962).

1. Rugendorf v. United States, 376 U.S. 528, 84 S.Ct. 825, 11 L.Ed.2d 887 (1964).

2. United States v. United States Dist. Court for the Eastern Dist. of Mich., 407 U.S. 297, 315, 92 S.Ct. 2125, 2135, 32 L.Ed.2d 752 (1972).

3. See, e. g., United States v. Robinson, 414 U.S. 218, 224, 94 S.Ct. 467, 471, 38 L.Ed.2d 427 (1973); Schneckloth v. Bustamonte, 412 U.S. 218, 219, 93 S. Ct. 2041, 2043, 36 L.Ed.2d 854 (1973) (dictum); Coolidge v. New Hampshire, 403 U.S. 443, 454–55, 478–82, 91 S.Ct. 2022, 2031–2032, 2044–2046, 29 L.Ed.2d 564 (1971); Vale v. Louisiana, 399 U.S. 30, 34–35, 90 S.Ct. 1969, 1971–1972, 26 L.Ed.2d 409 (1970); Chimel v. California, 395 U.S. 752, 762, 89 S.Ct. 2034, 2039, 23 L.Ed.2d 685 (1969); Katz v. United States, 389 U.S. 347, 356–57, 88 S.Ct. 507, 514, 19 L.Ed.2d 576 (1967).

ly describe the place to be searched and the things to be seized.

7. Technical Warrant Requirements

Neutral and Detached Magistrate. A search warrant must be issued by a "neutral and detached" magistrate. The information establishing probable cause must be given under oath or affirmation. The warrant must be signed by the magistrate, and it must direct the police officer to search a specified place and seize specific items. Also the warrant will usually specify when the warrant must be executed. The officer is normally required to inventory the items seized and return the inventory and warrant to the issuing magistrate.

In Coolidge v. New Hampshire,[4] the Supreme Court held that a state attorney general was disqualified from issuing the search warrant because he "was actively in charge of the investigation and later became the chief prosecutor at the trial."[5] On this point the Court quoted Johnson v. United States:[6] "Prosecutors and policemen simply cannot be asked to maintain the requisite neutrality with regard to their own investigations— the 'competitive enterprise [of ferreting out crime]' must rightly engage their single-minded attention."[7] Although the warrant must be issued by a neutral and detached magistrate, no requirement exists that the magistrate be a judge or a lawyer. In Shadwick v. City of Tampa,[8] the Supreme Court upheld a city charter provision authorizing municipal court clerks to issue arrest warrants for municipal violations. The Court concluded that "an issuing magistrate must meet two tests. He must be neutral and de-

tached, and he must be capable of determining whether probable cause exists for the requested arrest *or* search." [9] A compendium of state cases concerning the authority to issue a warrant is set forth in *Shadwick*.[10] If the magistrate helps prepare and type the original affidavit, he or she might be disqualified.[11] However, the magistrate is not required to divorce personal knowledge from his or her mind.[12]

Suggested Reading:

Coolidge v. New Hampshire, 403 U.S. 443, 91 S.Ct. 2022, 29 L.Ed.2d 564 (1971).

Specifying the Place to be Searched. The fourth amendment provides that the warrant specify the place to be searched. As a general rule, the warrant must describe the single dwelling unit to be searched. A warrant directed at a multiple dwelling unit is too broad if it does not describe a particular sub-unit to be searched.[13] The first exception to this rule has been made when the affiant did not realize the place was a multiple dwelling unit and the person executing

---

9. Id. at 350 (emphasis added).

10. Id. at 353 n. 12.

11. Compare United States v. Steed, 465 F.2d 1310 (9th Cir. 1972) (Preparing and typing affidavit were harmless error but should be avoided), with Albitez v. Beto, 465 F.2d 954 (5th Cir. 1972) (Help by magistrate in preparing affidavit was not error).

12. United States v. Marihart, 472 F.2d 809 (8th Cir. 1972) (Reliability established on the basis of the magistrate's knowledge of the informant); State v. Mandravelis, 114 N.H. 634, 325 A.2d 794 (1974) (Magistrate not disqualified because of his knowledge of defendant's drug problem).

13. United States v. Higgins, 428 F.2d 232 (7th Cir. 1970); United States v. Esters, 336 F.Supp. 214 (D.C. Mich.1972); Athens v. Wolf, 38 Ohio St.2d 237, 313 N.E.2d 405, 67 O.O.2d 317 (1974) (must specify college dormitory room). See generally Mascolo, Specificity Requirements for Warrants under the Fourth Amendment: Defining the Zone of Privacy, 73 Dickin.L.Rev. 1 (1968).

---

4. 403 U.S. 443, 91 S.Ct. 2022, 29 L.Ed.2d 564 (1971).

5. Id. at 450.

6. 333 U.S. 10, 13–14, 68 S.Ct. 367, 368–369, 92 L. Ed. 436 (1968).

7. Coolidge v. New Hampshire, 403 U.S. 443, 450, 91 S.Ct. 2022, 2029, 29 L.Ed.2d 564 (1971).

8. 407 U.S. 345, 92 S.Ct. 2119, 32 L.Ed.2d 783 (1972).

the warrant went directly to the specific apartment to be searched.[14] A second exception to the single-dwelling-unit rule comes into play when the warrant names the occupant of the particular sub-unit to be searched.[15] Of course the requirement of specifying the single dwelling unit does not apply when there is probable cause to search all the units.[16] Nor is a specific description of the sub-unit required when a multiple dwelling unit is occupied by several people in common or when the defendant has control over or access to the entire dwelling.[17] A final exception has been made when the multi-unit character of the premises was not known or reasonably apparent.[18]

Nevertheless, whenever possible it is advisable for the officer to identify the place to be searched, specifying the location as well as the name of the occupant. In any case if the court can conclude that only one place is obviously referred to and that the officer executing the warrant could not have been confused,[19] minor omissions or inac-

curacies respecting the particular subunit to be searched will not be fatal.

Suggested Reading:

United States v. Gusan, 549 F.2d 15 (7th Cir. 1977).

Specifying the Items to be Seized. The fourth amendment provides that the warrant must describe the "things to be seized."[20] Therefore a general warrant describing the place to be searched but not specifying the items to be seized is invalid even if it is based on probable cause. There is no restriction on what may be specified so long as these items will aid in a criminal prosecution. The courts apply a common-sense test in determining whether the warrant is specific. "Gaming apparatus" might be sufficient,[21] but "stolen tires" would be insufficient[22] because the tires obviously can be described by reference to a brand name or to a serial number. Generally if it is readily apparent that an item is contraband, the courts will accept a general description such as "narcotics paraphernalia"[23] and "narcotics consisting of dangerous drugs, heroin and marijuna, together with paraphernalia instrumental in the use of said contraband."[24] However, if it is not apparent that the items would aid in criminal prosecution, the use of generic terms such as "books", "records", "pamphlets", and "receipts" does not meet the fourth

---

14. Kenney v. United States, 157 F.2d 442 (D.C.Cir. 1946); United States v. Poppitt, 227 F.Supp. 73 (D.C. Del.1964); Butler v. State, 19 Md.App. 601, 313 A.2d 554 (1974).

15. United States v. Contee, 170 F.Supp. 26 (D.D.C. 1959); People v. Estrada, 234 Cal.App.2d 136, 44 Cal.Rptr. 165 (1965); Seymore v. State, 110 So.2d 460 (Fla.App.1959).

16. United States v. Olt, 492 F.2d 910 (6th Cir.1974); Hogrefe v. United States, 30 F.2d 640 (9th Cir.1929).

17. People v. Coulon, 273 C.A.2d 148, 78 Cal.Rptr. 95 (1969); People v. Gorg, 45 Cal.Rptr. 253 (1958); Plumlee v. State, 78 Okl.Cr. 201, 146 P.2d 139 (1944); Gill v. State, 71 Okl.Cr. 247, 110 P.2d 926 (1941); Renner v. State, 187 Tenn. 647, 216 S.W.2d 345 (1948).

18. Minovitz v. United States, 298 F.2d 682 (D.C. Cir. 1962); Hutto v. State, 50 Ala.App. 636, 282 So.2d 75 (1973); Jackson v. State, 129 Ga. 901, 201 S.E. 2d 816 (1973); People v. Frank, 54 Mich.App. 729, 221 N.W.2d 441 (1974); State v. Willcutt, 19 Or.App. 93, 526 P.2d 607 (1974); Commonwealth v. Johnson, 229 Pa.Super. 182, 323 A.2d 26 (1974).

19. United States v. Sklaroff, 323 F.Supp. 296 (D.C. Fla.1971); State v. Bisaccia, 58 N.J. 586, 279 A.2d 675 (1971); People v. Burrell, 8 Ill.App.3d 14, 288 N.E.2d 889 (1972).

20. U.S.C.A.Const. Amend. IV.

21. People v. Reid, 315 Ill. 597, 146 N.E. 504 (1925).

22. People v. Prall, 314 Ill. 518, 145 N.E. 610 (1924).

23. People v. Henry, 173 Colo. 523, 482 P.2d 357 (1971). But see State v. Stewart, 129 Vt. 175, 274 A.2d 500 (1971) (insufficient to state "contraband, to wit: regulated drugs").

24. People v. Walker, 257 Cal.App.2d 494, 58 Cal. Rptr. 495 (1967).

amendment specificity requirement.[25] One
of the bases for the fourth amendment was
the framers' fear of writs of assistance used
in seizing otherwise undefined "libelous"
matter.[26] If the warrant is so vague that it
vests the arresting officer with wide discretion, it should be held invalid.[27]

Suggested Reading:

United States v. Klein, 565 F.2d 183 (1st Cir. 1977).

In re Search Warrant, 436 F.Supp. 689 (D.C.Cir. 1977).

Incorporation of Affidavit into Warrant.
Although the warrant itself might not meet
the specificity requirement, the affidavit or
complaint for the warrant might contain a
complete description of the place to be
searched or things to be seized. When such
an affidavit is considered part of the warrant, the specificity requirement is satisfied.
Also the incorporation doctrine might remedy an unsigned, additional affidavit consisting of more than one page.[28] Some
courts have held that the incorporation of
documents supporting probable cause or satisfying the specificity requirement need not
be accomplished by any particular words or

attachment; rather these courts use a case-
by-case approach.[29]

Any test must guard against the use
of general warrants that are corrected after
the fact by attachment of an affidavit or
other document. Some courts apply the
stringent test that the affidavit must be
physically attached to the warrant and that
the warrant must incorporate the affidavit
by an express reference.[30] Other courts
consider the affidavit part of the warrant
when it is physically attached to and served
with the warrant.[31] Usually the affidavit is
attached to the copy of the warrant served.
When the affidavit is attached to but is not
served with the warrant, some courts have
held that the affidavit is nevertheless incorporated into the warrant.[32] Although this
view does not prevent altering the affidavit,
rules governing the fourth amendment
should not be based on a presumption of bad
faith by law enforcement officials. Another
approach is that the affidavit is deemed incorporated into the warrant if the issuing
magistrate testifies that he or she considered
the affidavit at the time the warrant was
issued.[33] Closely related to this approach
are those decisions interpreting the affidavit
as an integral part of the warrant.[34]

25. Stanford v. Texas, 379 U.S. 476, 85 S.Ct. 506, 13 L.Ed.2d 431 (1965).

26. United States v. McSurely, 473 F.2d 1178 (D.C. Cir. 1972) ("seditious materials" insufficient).

27. See Cook, Requisite Particularity in Search Warrant Authorization, 38 Tenn.L.Rev. 496, 505–07 (1971). See also People v. Holmes, 20 Ill.App.3d 167, 312 N.E.2d 748 (1974) (A description to seize "unde-termined amount of United States currency" and a "weapon" was held insufficient.). Cf. Taylor v. Minnesota, 466 F.2d 1119 (8th Cir. 1972) (Sufficient to list number of items of clothing, toiletries, photo-graphs, "and other material related to this crime of kidnapping, aggravated assault, sodomy, abduc-tion.").

28. People v. Johnson, 13 Ill.App.3d 1020, 304 N.E.2d 681 (1973).

29. State v. Stone, 322 A.2d 314 (Me.1974).

30. United States v. Meeks, 313 F.2d 464 (6th Cir. 1963). See also Booze v. State, 291 So.2d 262 (Fla. App.1974).

31. United States v. Rael, 467 F.2d 333 (10th Cir. 1972); Clay v. United States, 246 F.2d 298 (5th Cir. 1957).

32. Sherrick v. Eyman, 389 F.2d 648 (9th Cir. 1968); United States v. Averell, 296 F.Supp. 1004 (D.C.N.Y. 1969).

33. United States v. Horton, 503 F.2d 810, 812 (7th Cir. 1974) "We are reinforced in our conclu-sion because the defendant did not attempt to cross examine" the issuing magistrate or the police officer regarding the affidavits.

34. United States v. Lightfoot, 506 F.2d 238, 243 (D.C.Cir. 1974). See also Frey v. State, 3 Md.App. 38, 237 A.2d 774 (1968); People v. De Lago, 16 N.Y. 2d 289, 266 N.Y.S.2d 353, 213 N.E.2d 659 (1965).

Suggested Reading:

United States v. Meeks, 313 F.2d 464 (6th Cir. 1963).

Other Warrant Requirements. The officer seeking the warrant usually submits a signed and dated *affidavit or sworn complaint*. However, if the affiant's name appears in the affidavit, the failure to sign is not fatal.[35] Likewise the negligent misidentification of the affiant does not render the warrant invalid.[36]

If the affidavit is post-dated, the warrant is void.[37] In People v. Murgia,[38] the California Supreme Court stated: "The danger posed by the possible use of presigned warrants or the alteration of affidavits after issuance is too great for this Court to consider this matter an inconsequential irregularity."

If it appears on its face that the affidavit is sworn and signed by the officer, absent contrary testimony a presumption arises that it was signed in the presence of the issuing magistrate.[39] The oath requires no particular ceremony, and it is sufficient if the signing takes place before the magistrate.

Read Affidavit and Sign Warrant. The magistrate's function is to read the affidavit and issue the warrant only if he or she is satisfied that probable cause exists.[40] If the magistrate is satisfied, he or she will issue the warrant by affixing his or her name. If the affidavit is not sufficient on its face, the magistrate may hear additional sworn testimony. Under Rule 41 of the Federal Rules of Criminal Procedure [41] and some state statutes,[42] if the magistrate determines that the information is insufficient he or she may call the affiant or a third party as a witness. Such testimony must be given under oath and recorded as part of the affidavit. In some instances the judge may rely on his or her personal knowledge to establish probable cause.[43]

Generally, if the magistrate fails to sign the warrant after satisfying himself or herself that probable cause exists, the search is not rendered invalid. The court in Sternberg v. Superior Court [44] stated: "[A]ny insufficiency on the face of the warrant, because the magistrate inadvertently failed to sign it, was cured by his affixing his signature at the earliest opportunity after such omission was discovered and prior to any challenge to the warrant. The fact remains that here there was clear and convincing evidence that the magistrate had determined that there was probable cause and had authorized the search and seizure. No one's position was changed in reliance on the omission of the signature and the defect was promptly cured." [45]

---

35. Cf. Barnes v. State, 504 S.W.2d 450 (Tex.Cr. App.1974).

36. United States v. McCoy, 478 F.2d 176 (10th Cir. 1973). But see United States ex rel. Pugh v. Pate, 401 F.2d 6 (7th Cir. 1968).

37. Larkins v. State, 213 Tenn. 520, 376 S.W.2d 459 (1964); Harvey v. State, 166 Tenn. 227, 60 S.W. 2d 420 (1933) (Testimony that there was a clerical error was held inadmissible.).

38. 43 Cal.App.3d 85, 87, 117 Cal.Rptr. 564, 565 (1974).

39. Simon v. State, 515 P.2d 1161 (Okl.Cr.1973).

40. Rooker v. Commonwealth, 508 S.W.2d 570 (Ky. 1974) (the failure to read the warrant is fatal); State v. Dudick, 213 S.E.2d 458 (W.Va.1975).

41. Fed.Cr.Proc.Rule 41, 18 U.S.C.A.

42. Colo.Rev.Stat. § 16–3–303; Me.Cr.Proc. Rule 41.

43. Compare United States v. Marihart, 472 F.2d 809 (8th Cir. 1972) (reliability established by judge's prior knowledge of informer), with United States v. Acosta, 501 F.2d 1330 (5th Cir. 1974) (judge's knowledge of the informant's reliability cannot be used to save defective affidavit).

44. Sternberg v. Superior Court, 41 Cal.App.3d 281, 115 Cal.Rptr. 893 (1974) (officer acted in good faith without knowledge of defect); Commonwealth v. McAfee, 230 Pa.Super. 336, 326 A.2d 522 (1974).

45. Sternberg v. Superior Court, 41 Cal.App.3d 281, 115 Cal.Rptr. 893 (1974).

Directions to Officers. The warrant sets forth general instructions or directions for the executing officers. The warrant may also have special directions for a night search.[46]

Designation of the Executing Officer. Rule 41(c) of the Federal Rules of Criminal Procedure states: "The warrant shall be directed to a civil officer of the United States authorized to enforce or assist in enforcing any law thereof or to a person so authorized by the President of the United States."[47] The Fifth Circuit Court of Appeals has held that failure to name in the warrant the officer to conduct the search does not necessitate suppression of the evidence when the magistrate knows in advance who is to serve the warrant.[48]

When the Warrant Shall be Executed. The warrant shall be served in the daytime, unless the issuing authority, by appropriate provision in the warrant, and for reasonable cause shown, authorizes its execution at times other than daytime.[49] Rule 41(c) commits the federal courts to the prevailing view that the warrant must be executed within a specified period of time after issuance. Rule 41(c) specifies ten days as the time period in federal practice. The failure to execute the warrant within the specified period is fatal if the items authorized to be seized are easily movable.[50] However, if the items are not easily movable, the delay is not automatically fatal; the defendant must show that the delay prejudiced him or her.[51]

Execution of the Warrant. The executing officer will often have to enter premises to execute an arrest or search warrant. Many jurisdictions have statutes imposing knock-and-announce requirements: The statute may require that the officer knock, identify himself or herself, and state the purpose of the visit before demanding admission. The courts do not insist on strict, exact compliance with these statutory requirements; rather they demand only "substantial" compliance. Thus, the officers need not state their purpose with the specificity necessary in a pleading to be filed with the court. Moreover, the courts will excuse non-compliance in exigent circumstances. If the officer has reason to believe that the suspect has a hostage who may be harmed or that the suspect is in the process of destroying evidence, the courts often permit the officer to dispense with the knock-and-announce requirements.

The officer seizing property under the warrant is usually required to give a copy of the warrant to the person whose property is seized.[52] Additionally an inventory of the items must be made in the presence of the person from whose possession they are taken if he or she is present. The courts have held that the person whose house is being searched has no constitutional right to a lawyer's presence during the search.[53]

Return with Inventory. The inventory must be returned to the officer specified in the warrant.[54] Although failure to provide for the return has been held fatal,[55] some courts have held that failure to make the return for even a substantial period of time

---

46. Fed.Cr.Proc.Rule 41, 18 U.S.C.A.; State v. Marko, 36 Ohio App.2d 114, 65 O.O.2d 134, 303 N.E. 2d 94 (1973) (no specific direction as to time of day needed if property is movable).

47. Fed.Cr.Proc.Rule 41(c), 18 U.S.C.A.

48. United States v. Soriano, 482 F.2d 469 (5th Cir. 1973).

49. Fed.Cr.Proc. Rule 41(c), 18 U.S.C.A.

50. United States v. Wilson, 60 F.R.D. 55 (E.D. Mich.1973).

51. Commonwealth v. Cromer, 365 Mass. 519, 313 N.E.2d 557 (1974).

---

52. Fed.Cr.Proc.Rule 41(d), 18 U.S.C.A.

53. State v. Wheeler, 215 Kan. 94, 523 P.2d 722 (1974).

54. Id.

55. Laiser v. State, 299 So.2d 39 (Fla.App.1974); State v. Montoya, 86 N.M. 119, 520 P.2d 275 (1974). But see United States v. Hall, 505 F.2d 961 (3d Cir. 1974); United States v. Kennedy, 457 F.2d 63 (10th Cir. 1972); United States v. McKenzie, 446 F.2d 949 (6th Cir. 1971).

is not fatal.[56] To hold that both the execution and return may be delayed would make the warrant similar to the writs of assistance which British officials used during the Colonial period.

Suggested Reading:

Ker v. California, 374 U.S. 23, 83 S.Ct. 1623, 10 L.Ed.2d 726 (1963).

People v. Maddox, 46 Cal.2d 301, 294 P.2d 6 (1956).

Scope of the Search. When a warrant authorizes a search of a specific premises or part of a premises, the officer may search that portion and look anywhere professional experience leads him or her to believe the items might be found.[57] Thus a warrant authorizing the search of a house for a tape deck and television set does not permit the officer to search the dressers and desk drawers. When the designated items have been found and seized, the search must cease.[58] Even when the search does not exceed its specified bounds, it may be unreasonable if conducted in an unreasonable manner. For example, it would be unreasonable for police officers to tear out part of a ceiling in order to reach the area in the roof which might hold the sought for items.[59] When officers look for marijuana, searching a matchbox and wallet found on top of the defendant's dresser is proper.[60] A search for marijuana and paraphernalia might also justify seizing a notebook.[61]

A warrant authorizing a search of a single dwelling unit includes not only the principal building but also those areas of the curtilage where the specified items might be hidden.[62] The warrant also authorizes a search of vehicles on the premises, provided that they are owned or under the control of someone named in the warrant.[63] In State v. Reid,[64] the court upheld the search of an automobile not described in the warrant but located on the premises of a service station cited in the warrant.

Suggested Reading:

State v. Naharro, 55 Haw. 583, 525 P.2d 573 (1974).

Individuals Present on the Premises. A lawfully issued search warrant, while giving general authority to search reasonably for objects within the described place, does not *alone* give authority to search people on the premises.[65] When an individual is fortuitously on the premises at the time the search is made, the police should not have the authority to search his or her person. Nevertheless an examination of the circum-

---

56. Derrickson v. United States, 321 A.2d 497 (Del. 1974).

57. State v. Nabarro, 55 Hawaii 583, 525 P.2d 573 (1974); State v. Davenport, 55 Hawaii 90, 516 P.2d 65 (1973).

58. United States v. Highfill, 334 F.Supp. 700 (D.C. Ark.1971).

59. See, e. g., United States v. Markis, 352 F.2d 860 (2d Cir. 1965), vacated on other grounds, 387 U.S. 425, 87 S.Ct. 1709, 18 L.Ed.2d 864 (1967). The police officers seized 300,000 books on the specified premises. Only 60,000 of the books bore titles mentioned in the supporting affidavits. The court held the search had become general, thus rendering it void in its entirety.

60. State v. Davenport, 55 Hawaii 90, 516 P.2d 65 (1973).

61. United States v. Damitz, 495 F.2d 50, 56 (9th Cir. 1974).

62. United States v. Combs, 468 F.2d 1390 (6th Cir. 1972); State v. Ogden, 210 Kan. 510, 502 P.2d 654 (1973) (search of trash can at rear of yard upheld).

63. State v. Brochu, 237 A.2d 418, 422–24 (Me. 1967); Worden v. State, 197 Tenn. 340, 273 S.W.2d 139 (1954) (dictum).

64. 23 N.C.App. 194, 208 S.E.2d 699 (1974).

65. United States v. Di Re, 332 U.S. 581, 68 S.Ct. 222, 92 L.Ed. 210 (1948) (dictum); State v. Wise, 284 A.2d 292 (Del.Super.1971); State v. Bradbury, 109 N. H. 105, 243 A.2d 302 (1968). But see Guerra v. State, 496 S.W.2d 92 (Tex.Cr.App.1973).

stances might make reasonable a search of everyone present—for example, if the premises is used for the distribution of drugs which are openly displayed.[66] Likewise, a person who enters a house, known in the community as a center for criminal activity, assumes the risk of being searched. Here the strong probability exists that all those on the premises are participants in the criminal activity. Some jurisdictions permit both a protective search for weapons and an evidentiary search of persons on the premises even though neither is authorized by the warrant.[67]

In People v. Easterbrook,[68] the search warrant authorized the search of an apartment for narcotics and of "any other person who may be found to have such property in his possession or under his control or to whom such property may have been delivered." The court allowed a search of the defendant and of individuals in the hallway who had just left the apartment.

When a person arrives after the police officer has entered, it is difficult, if not impossible, to justify a full search of his or her person to find items named in the warrant, for those items were supposed to have been at the place before the officer arrived.[69] There is nevertheless authority to justify a frisk of the late comer for the police officer's safety.[70] The frisk might then justify

an arrest and full search of the individual frisked or of others on the premises.

Suggested Reading:

United States v. Di Re, 332 U.S. 581, 68 S.Ct. 222, 92 L.Ed. 210 (1948).

People v. Easterbrook, 43 A.D.2d 719, 350 N.Y.S. 2d 442 (1973).

Personal Property Present on the Premises. Does a warrant for a search of the premises authorize the search of movable personalty on the premises? The courts ordinarily sustain a search of the personality if the police know of some relationship between the object and premises.[71] The overwhelming majority of courts have held that the possessions of a resident of the named premises may be searched if they are "plausible repositories" of the items searched for.[72] Many jurisdictions have also permitted the search of the effects of non-residents.[73] Some courts have even authorized searches

---

66. United States v. Johnson, 475 F.2d 977 (D.C. Cir. 1973); United States v. Pentado, 463 F.2d 355, 363 (5th Cir. 1972); State v. DeSimone, 60 N.J. 319, 288 A.2d 849 (1972).

67. 23 U.S.C.A. § 524 (1970); Smith-Hurd Ill.Ann. Stat. ch. 38, § 108–9. Some jurisdictions permit a full search of a person on the premises if the search warrant names only the place and not the person. Ferguson v. State ex rel. Biggers, 250 So.2d 634 (Miss.1971); State v. McClelland, 215 Kan. 81, 523 P.2d 357 (1974) (authorized search of person standing in parking area of premises).

68. 43 A.D.2d 719, 350 N.Y.S.2d 442 (1973).

69. Smith v. State, 292 Ala. 120, 289 So.2d 816 (1974); State v. Wise, 284 A.2d 292 (Del.Super.1971).

70. United States v. Peep, 490 F.2d 903 (8th Cir. 1974); Smith v. State, 292 Ala. 120, 289 So.2d 816 (1974).

71. United States v. Micheli, 487 F.2d 429 (1st Cir. 1973) (permitted search of defendant's brief case on floor under desk because defendant was co-owner of printing plant being searched); United States v. Johnson, 475 F.2d 977 (D.C.Cir. 1973) (upheld search of visitor's purse lying on coffee table in house known as distribution point for drugs); State v. Naharro, 55 Haw. 583, 525 P.2d 573 (1974) (personal property which police know belongs to non-resident cannot be searched on basis of warrant); Commonwealth v. Platou, 455 Pa. 258, 312 A.2d 29 (1973) (upheld search of suitcase under authority of warrant because police were initially told suitcase was owned by the defendant); Commonwealth v. Snow, 363 Mass. 778, 298 N.E.2d 804 (1973) (upheld search of patron's coat under warrant for search of barbershop). Cf. McAllister v. State, 306 N.E.2d 395 (Ind. App.1974) (warrant to search inn does not justify search of patron's pocket).

72. Walker v. United States, 327 F.2d 597 (D.C. Cir. 1963); Clay v. United States, 246 F.2d 298 (5th Cir. 1957); State v. Davenport, 55 Hawaii 90, 516 P.2d 65 (1973).

73. United States v. Micheli, 487 F.2d 429 (1st Cir. 1973) (Campbell, J., concurring); United States v. Teller, 397 F.2d 494 (7th Cir. 1968); United States v. Riccitelli, 259 F.Supp. 665 (D.C.Conn.1968).

when the police did not know who owned the particular item of personal property.[74] Of course, while executing a search warrant, the police officer may seize any items in plain view which will aid in a criminal prosecution.[75]

Suggested Reading:

United States v. Micheli, 487 F.2d 429 (1st Cir. ed 442 (1973).

---

8. Arrest Warrants

Suggested Reading:

United States v. Santana, 427 U.S. 38, 96 S.Ct. 2406, 49 L.Ed.2d 300 (1976).

People v. Ramey, 16 Cal.3d 263, 127 Cal.Rptr. 629, 545 P.2d 1333 (1976).

When Warrant Required. On a number of occasions the Supreme Court expressed its preference for a search pursuant to a warrant. Except for a few "jealously and carefully drawn" exceptions, warrantless searches are per se unreasonable. This preference was emphasized by the holdings in Chimel v. California[76] and *Coolidge.* Yet, the Court had not voiced a similar preference for arrest warrants. The requirement of a search warrant without the parallel requirement of an arrest warrant probably is based on property law concepts which have been rejected by the Supreme Court on a number of occasions. The freedom of movement should be more sacred than the protection of property rights. However, the Supreme Court has refused to require arrest warrants.

In Trupiano v. United States,[77] the Court stated that the "absence of a warrant of arrest, even though there was sufficient time to obtain one, does not destroy the validity of an arrest under these circumstances."[78] Again in *Chimel,* the majority proceeded on the "hypothesis" that a warrantless arrest was legal even though the officers had almost thirty days to secure a warrant. The failure to require arrest warrants has been criticized by Professor Barrett: "The police decision to arrest an individual and initiate the process of criminal prosecution is in itself a signficant invasion of personal liberty even though the individual's innocence is ultimately established . . . [I]n terms of practical consequences the damage suffered is primarily to property interest and is not significantly different from the damage resulting from illegal entries by burglars or other criminals."[79] However, the consensus on the Court is so strong that even in his dissent in *Chimel* Mr. Justice White offered an explanation for not requiring a warrant for an arrest: "It must very often be the case that by the time probable cause to arrest a man is accumulated, the man is aware of police interest in him or for other good reasons is on the verge of flight. Moreover, it will likely be very difficult to determine the probability of his flight. Given this situation, it may be best in all cases simply to allow the arrest if there is probable cause, especially since that issue can be determined very shortly after the arrest."[80]

The Court first squarely faced the issue of the necessity for an arrest warrant

---

74. State v. Naharro, 55 Hawaii 583, 525 P.2d 573 (1974); Commonwealth v. Platou, 455 Pa. 258, 312 A. 2d 29 (1973).

75. Chapter 17, § 19, infra.

76. 395 U.S. 752, 89 S.Ct. 2034, 23 L.Ed.2d 685 (1969).

77. 334 U.S. 699, 68 S.Ct. 1229, 92 L.Ed. 1663 (1948).

78. Id. at 705.

79. Barrett, Personal Rights, Property Rights, and the Fourth Amendment, 1960 Sup.Ct.Rev. 46–47.

80. Chimel v. California, 395 U.S. 752, 779, 89 S.Ct. 2034, 2048, 23 L.Ed.2d 685 (1969).

in United States v. Watson.[81]   In *Watson*, seven days elapsed between the time when the police originally learned of the defendant's criminal activity and the subsequent arrest of the defendant in a restaurant. The Ninth Circuit found that the police had ample time to obtain a warrant and that there was no exigency excusing the failure to obtain a warrant.[82]   Given those findings, the Ninth Circuit invalidated the arrest.[83] The Supreme Court reversed.[84]   The Court held that at least when the police arrest the suspect outside his or her home, the police do not need a warrant.[85]   Writing for the Court, Justice White reviewed the historical practice and numerous statutes authorizing warrantless arrests based on probable cause.   The justice acknowledged that there is a policy preference for warrants, but added: "[W]e decline to transform this judicial preference into a constitutional rule when the judgment of the Nation and Congress has for so long been to authorize warrantless public arrests on probable cause rather than to encumber criminal prosecutions with endless litigation with respect to the existence of exigent circumstances, whether it was practicable to get a warrant, whether the suspect was about to flee, and the like." [86]

In United States v. Santana,[87] the Court amplified on *Watson*.   In *Santana*, the police went to the defendant's house. They first observed her standing in the doorway. As the police approached, the defendant retreated into the vestibule of her house. The police arrested her there. The defendant challenged her arrest, but the Court upheld the arrest.   Justice Rehnquist delivered the Court's opinion.   The justice first cited *Watson* as authority that "the warrantless arrest of an individual in a public place upon probable cause [does] not violate the Fourth Amendment." [88]   He pointed out that the defendant did not have any reasonable expectation of privacy where she was standing.   He held that the defendant was in a public place when the police first attempted to arrest her outside her house.   He finally invoked the hot pursuit doctrine to justify the actual arrest within the house.

The Court has yet to decide the question of whether a warrant is necessary for a non-exigent arrest in a home.   On their face, the *Watson* and *Santana* opinions deal only with arrests in public places.   An arrest within a home is a much greater invasion of privacy than a public arrest.   There is some state authority that if the police have sufficient time to obtain a warrant for an arrest within a home, they have a constitutional obligation to do so.   The leading authority for that proposition is the California Supreme Court's decision in People v. Ramey.[89]   Even the California court did not impose an absolute requirement for warrants for home arrests.   The court stated that the police could dispense with a warrant for a home arrest in "an emergency situation requiring swift action to prevent danger to life or . . . to property, or to forestall the . . . escape of a suspect or destruction of evidence." [90]

Scope of the Incidental Search.   The scope of the search incident to a warranted arrest is at least as broad as that of the search incident to a warrantless arrest. *Chimel* generally governs the arresting officer's authority to search beyond the immediate area of the arrestee.[91]

---

81. 423 U.S. 411, 96 S.Ct. 820, 46 L.Ed.2d 598 (1976).

82. Id.

83. Id.

84. United States v. Watson, 423 U.S. 411, 96 S.Ct. 820, 46 L.Ed.2d 598 (1976).

85. Id.

86. Id.

87. 427 U.S. 38, 96 S.Ct. 2406, 49 L.Ed.2d 300 (1976).

88. Id.

89. 16 Cal.3d 263, 127 Cal.Rptr. 629, 545 P.2d 1333 (1976).

90. Id. at 277, 12 Cal.Rptr. at 637, 545 P.2d at 1341.

91. Chapter 17, § 5, infra.

CHAPTER 17

WARRANTLESS SEARCHES

We now turn to the rules governing the legality of warrantless intrusions. In many cases an arrest or search results from a sequence of events or a chain reaction. A police officer's initial contact with an individual often concerns minor violations such as parking on the grass, in an unauthorized area, or in a loading zone. However, the initial contact can rapidly escalate. A police officer makes a contact, and the response or action of the individual whom he contacts might indicate a stop and frisk are called for. The frisk might furnish the basis for an arrest and an incidental search of both the individual and the immediate area. This search might give the officer a reason for a further search, warranted or unwarranted. This chapter is organized roughly along the lines of such a sequence of events.

1. Contacts

Suggested Reading:

Commonwealth v. Meadows, 222 Pa.Super. 202, 293 A.2d 365 (1972).

Not all communications between a citizen and the police amount to "seizure" of the person within the meaning of the fourth amendment. For example, many times these encounters occur without indication of any criminal activities. The police may assist a drunk by providing shelter, help a disabled person across the street, go to an individual's house to resolve a marital difficulty, and warn individuals of dangerous areas or dangerous conduct. The police officer, like any other citizen, has a right to stop and make inquiry concerning matters of interest.[1] These encounters do not amount to seizures under the fourth amendment.

Moreover, a police officer has a right to make a "contact," a face-to-face communication between an officer and an individual involving either criminal conduct or matters wholly unrelated to criminal conduct. The courts, particularly the Supreme Court, have recognized the right of the police officer to make a contact even though no reasonable suspicion exists that criminal activity is afoot and even though no probable cause exists for an arrest. In Terry v. Ohio,[2] the majority opinion of Chief Justice Warren stated that "not all personal intercourse between policemen and citizens involves 'seizures' of persons."[3] Mr. Justice Harlan stated that the right to stop must itself "be more than the liberty [possessed by every citizen] to address questions to another person, for ordinarily the person addressed has an equal right to ignore his interrogator and walk away."[4] In the concurring opinion in *Terry*, Mr. Justice White was even more explicit: "There is nothing in the Constitution which prevents a policeman from addressing

---

1. Cady v. Dombrowski, 413 U.S. 433, 441, 93 S.Ct. 2523, 2528, 37 L.Ed.2d 706 (1973) (recognized "police-citizen contacts" involving automobiles); Terry v. Ohio, 392 U.S. 1, 19 n. 16, 88 S.Ct. 1868, 1879 n. 16, 20 L.Ed.2d 889 (1968) ("not all personal intercourse between policemen and citizens involves 'seizures' of persons"); Batts v. Superior Court, 23 Cal.App.2d 435, 100 Cal.Rptr. 181 (1972); State v. Sheffield, 62 N.J. 441, 303 A.2d 68 (1973); State v. Evans, 16 Or. App. 189, 517 P.2d 1225 (1974).

2. 392 U.S. 1, 88 S.Ct. 1868, 20 L.Ed.2d 889 (1968).

3. Id. at 19 n. 16.

4. Id. at 32–33.

questions to anyone on the streets. Absent special circumstances, the person approached may not be detained or frisked but may refuse to cooperate and go on his way." In Cady v. Dombrowski [5] the Supreme Court noted the frequency of "police-citizen contacts" involving automobiles: "Some such contacts will occur because the officer may believe the operator has violated a criminal statute, but many more will not be of that nature. Local police officers . . . frequently investigate vehicle accidents in which there is no claim of criminal liability and engage in what, for want of a better term, may be described as community caretaking functions, totally divorced from the detection, investigation, or acquisition of evidence relating to the violation of a criminal statute." [6]

The basis for a contact has been defined differently in different jurisdictions. Some courts have sanctioned investigative questioning by police even when the officer has neither probable cause nor reasonable suspicion. In Commonwealth v. Meadows,[7] the court stated in dictum that although an officer may legally stop a person and question him or her, the officer may not restrain that person from walking away absent probable cause for an arrest or reasonable suspicion for a stop. In *Meadows*, the officer had neither probable cause nor reasonable suspicion. The defendant did not run when called, and his carrying a brown bag in the morning did not indicate criminal activities. However, the court stated that the circumstances justified "investigative questioning," [8] a type of questioning which can furnish the basis for a legitimate stop. In People v. Hines,[9] the court took the position that calling a defendant to the police car does not

amount to an arrest, nor does it amount to a seizure when there is no element of force or threat of force which could constitute a restraint on his or her freedom to walk away.

Other courts have indicated that the police may engage in investigative questioning only if either a "well founded" [10] or "reasonable suspicion" [11] exists. In Stone v. People,[12] the Colorado Supreme Court realistically recognized that when a police officer asks an individual to stop, he or she will usually obey the request, believing it is his or her duty to do so. "In order to lawfully detain an individual for questioning, (1) the officer must have a reasonable suspicion that the individual has committed, or is about to commit, a crime; (2) the purpose of the detention must be reasonable; and (3) the character of the detention must be reasonable when considered in light of the purpose." [13]

2.　Stops

Suggested Reading:

Adams v. Williams, 407 U.S. 143, 92 S.Ct. 1921, 32 L.Ed.2d 612 (1972).

Terry v. Ohio, 392 U.S. 1, 88 S.Ct. 1868, 20 L.Ed. 2d 889 (1968).

The officer's initial contact with a citizen can easily escalate into a stop. The pos-

---

5. 413 U.S. 433, 93 S.Ct. 2523, 37 L.Ed.2d 706 (1973).

6. Id. at 441.

7. 222 Pa.Super. 202, 293 A.2d 365 (1972).

8. Id. at 367.

9. 12 Ill.App.3d 582, 299 N.E.2d 581 (1973).

10. Gaines v. Craven, 448 F.2d 1236 (9th Cir. 1971); Wade v. United States, 457 F.2d 335 (9th Cir. 1972). The court stated the police may "detain" and make inquiry when there is a "founded suspicion . . . some basis from which the court can determine that the detention was not arbitrary or harassing." Id. at 336.

11. Stone v. People, 174 Colo. 504, 485 P.2d 495 (1971) (en banc).

12. 174 Colo. 504, 485 P.2d 495 (1971) (en banc).

13. Id. at 497.

sibility of such escalation raises two issues. First, what constitutes a stop for fourth amendment purposes? Second, what quantum of suspicion must the officer have before stopping a private citizen?

Stop and Question. A stop differs from an arrest in that the former lasts only briefly—that is, only as long as is necessary to identify the detainee and to receive an explanation of his or her activities. Generally, if the stop continues for more than a brief period, it becomes an arrest.[14]

Although after he or she is stopped, a person cannot be compelled to answer, the officer may question him or her in an attempt to obtain his or her name and address, and an explanation of activities. Schneckloth v. Bustamonte [15] indicates this type of stop does not constitute custody within the meaning of Miranda v. Arizona, [16] for in *Schneckloth* the Supreme Court suggested that questioning taking place on the street, in the house, or at a person's business is generally not custodial.[17] In *Miranda* itself, the Court stated: "Our decision is not intended to hamper the traditional function of police officers in investigating crime. General on-the-scene questioning as to facts surrounding a crime or other general questioning of citizens in the fact-finding process is not affected by our holding. It is an act of responsible citizenship for individuals to give whatever information they may have to aid law enforcement. In such situations the compelling atmosphere inherent in the process of in-custody interrogation is not necessarily present." [18] Again, in Adams v. Wil-

liams,[19] the Court noted that "a brief stop of a suspicious individual, in order to determine his identity or to maintain the status quo momentarily while obtaining more information, may be most reasonable in light of the facts known to the officer at the time."

The refusal to answer questions or produce identification does not establish probable cause to arrest, but evasive answers or other actions by the detainee can combine with other circumstances to support further seizures.[20]

Basis for a Stop. If an officer reasonably suspects that a person has committed, is committing, or is about to commit any crime, he or she has the right to stop that person.[21] This right may be exercised any place where the officer has a right to be, and both pedestrians and people in vehicles may be stopped.[22] The term *reasonable suspicion* cannot be precisely defined. However, there are a number of factors which taken alone or in combination with one another might be sufficient to establish reasonable suspicion for a stop.

The Person's Appearance. The appearance of the individual might indicate that he or she is under emotional strain—nervous, perspiring, or breathing heavily.[23] The individual might be under the influence of drugs, suffering from a recent injury, or

14. See People v. Gale, 9 Cal.3d 788, 108 Cal.Rptr. 852, 511 P.2d 1204 (1973).

15. 412 U.S. 218, 93 S.Ct. 2041, 36 L.Ed.2d 854 (1973).

16. 384 U.S. 436, 86 S.Ct. 1602, 16 L.Ed.2d 694 (1966).

17. Schneckloth v. Bustamonte, 412 U.S. 218, 93 S.Ct. 2041, 36 L.Ed.2d 854 (1973).

18. Miranda v. Arizona, 384 U.S. 436, 477–78, 86 S.Ct. 1602, 1629–30, 16 L.Ed.2d 694 (1966).

19. 407 U.S. 143, 146, 92 S.Ct. 1921, 1923, 32 L.Ed.2d 612 (1972).

20. The frisk in *Terry* followed "mumbled" responses to the officer's questions. In United States v. West, 460 F.2d 374 (5th Cir. 1972), the court held that when one defendant gave evasive answers to routine questions and another refused to identify himself and made furtive movements, the officer had a right and duty to investigate further. Mr. Justice White in *Terry* recognized that the refusal to answer questions must be given some weight. Terry v. Ohio, 392 U.S. 1, 34, 88 S.Ct. 1868, 1886, 20 L.Ed. 2d 889 (1968).

21. See Terry v. Ohio, 392 U.S. 1, 88 S.Ct. 1868, 20 L.Ed.2d 889 (1968).

22. See § 3, infra.

23. United States v. Lindsey, 451 F.2d 701 (3d Cir. 1971) (not nervousness alone); Moya v. Zelker, 329 F.Supp. 120 (S.D.N.Y.1971) (perspiring and breathing heavily as two factors).

have a bulge under his or her coat.[24] Also the person may look like a suspect wanted for a known offense.[25]

The Person's Actions. The actions of the individual may raise a reasonable suspicion—for example, attempting to conceal identity or to avoid the police. Depending on the area, flight itself might also raise reasonable suspicion.[26] Although the person does not flee, he or she might "concentrate his [or her] attention" on the police, or his or her action might be inconsistent with a response to police.[27] In many cases the person may have abandoned incriminating evidence.

Reputation. The reputation of the defendant or his or her companions is important,[28] for the defendant may have an arrest record or be known for committing a specific type of offense.

Factors Pertaining to the Person's Companion.[29] The action of the person's companions or their appearance may serve as a basis for a stop.

Demeanor of the Person During the Contact.[30] The person who is asked to respond to questions during a contact may give evasive, suspicious, or incriminating answers.

Area of the Stop.[31] The stop may be in a high-crime area near the scene of the offense. A reasonable suspicion may be based on the fact that the place of the stop is either a base of criminal activities or an unusual location.

The Time of Day.[32] It may be a time of day when no one should be in that area or when someone's being there is unusual.

Police Training and Experience.[33] The person's conduct may resemble the pattern or *modus operandi* followed in particular criminal offenses. The investigating officer's experience could lead him or her to believe that a certain criminal act is about to be committed.

Police Purpose.[34] The police may have been investigating a specific crime or specific type of criminal activity.

Source of Information.[35] If the officer makes the stop as a result of a tip, the tipster's reliability has a bearing on the reasonableness of the stop.

---

24. United States v. Miller, 452 F.2d 731 (10th Cir. 1971); Cox v. State, 254 Ark. 1, 491 S.W.2d 802 (1973).

25. United States v. Garr, 461 F.2d 487 (5th Cir. 1972); Murphy v. United States, 293 A.2d 849 (D.C. App.1972).

26. United States v. Hines, 455 F.2d 1317 (D.C.Cir. 1972); Dotson v. State, 260 So.2d 839 (Miss.1972).

27. United States v. Owens, 472 F.2d 780 (8th Cir. 1973) (action of defendant inconsistent with response to police); State v. Head, 13 Or.App. 317, 509 P.2d 52 (1973) (defendant "concentrate[d] his attention" on the police); State v. Ramey, 30 Ohio Misc. 89, 282 N.E.2d 65, 58 O.O.2d 442, 59 O.O.2d 405 (1971) (failure to flee as negative factor).

28. United States v. Owens, 472 F.2d 780 (8th Cir. 1973); United States v. Garr, 461 F.2d 487 (5th Cir. 1972); State v. Beaty, 57 Wis.2d 531, 205 N.W.2d 11 (1973).

29. Smith v. United States, 295 A.2d 64 (D.C.App. 1972).

30. Stephenson v. United States, 296 A.2d 606 (D.C. App.1972).

31. Adams v. Williams, 407 U.S. 143, 92 S.Ct. 1921, 32 L.Ed.2d 612 (1972) (high crime area); United States v. Hines, 455 F.2d 1317 (D.C.Cir. 1972) (near scene of crime); United States v. Rodriquez, 459 F.2d 983 (9th Cir. 1972) (seen leaving base of criminal activity); United States v. Mallides, 339 F.Supp. 1 (S.D.Cal.1972) (vehicle seen in isolated area).

32. Onofre v. State, 474 S.W.2d 699 (Tex.App.1972) (defendant observed behind lounge at 2:30 a. m., which was closed and unlighted).

33. Terry v. Ohio, 392 U.S. 1, 88 S.Ct. 1868, 20 L.Ed.2d 889 (1968); United States v. Catalano, 450 F.2d 985 (7th Cir. 1971).

34. Terry v. Ohio, 392 U.S. 1, 88 S.Ct. 1868, 20 L.Ed. 2d 889 (1968).

35. Adams v. Williams, 407 U.S. 143, 92 S.Ct. 1921, 32 L.Ed.2d 612 (1972).

3. Automobile Stops

Suggested Reading:

Pennsylvania v. Mimms, 434 U.S. 106, 98 S.Ct. 330, 54 L.Ed.2d 331 (1977).

United States v. Brignoni-Ponce, 422 U.S. 873, 95 S.Ct. 2574, 45 L.Ed.2d 607 (1975).

Inspection Stops of Automobiles. A police officer may make selective, non-arbitrary, nondiscriminatory, uniform inspection stops of automobiles.[36] The purpose of these stops, which are permitted under a number of state statutes,[37] is to check the operator's license, vehicle registration, and inspection stickers. In the recent case of United States v. Brignoni-Ponce,[38] the Supreme Court held that the random stopping of vehicles by border patrol agents to inquire about the occupants' citizenship was violative of the fourth amendment absent "specific articulable facts, together with rational inferences from those facts, that reasonably warrant suspicion that the vehicles contain aliens who may be illegally in the country."[39] However, in a footnote the Court recognized that border patrol agents have no part in enforcing laws that regulate highway use, declaring: "Our decision thus does not imply that state and local enforcement agencies are without power to conduct such limited stops as are necessary to enforce laws regarding driver's license, vehicle registration, truck weights, and similar matters."[40] After the officer has determined that the occupants' documents are in order and that no indication of criminal conduct exists the driver cannot lawfully be ordered to get out of the automobile.[41] Such selective inspections may be conducted randomly or at roadblocks or checkpoints established on the highway.

Investigative Stops of Automobiles. An investigative stop differs from an inspection stop, for the former is made on the "basis of suspicion of a law enforcement official that the occupants of the vehicle are involved in criminal activity."[42] Thus an officer may make an investigative stop when he or she reasonably suspects that the driver or passenger in an automobile has committed, is committing, or is about to commit a criminal act.[43] Vehicles not in proper operating condition or lacking license plates may be stopped. In some jurisdictions the basis of an investigative stop is similar to that of an individual stop.[44] Other jurisdictions use a general reasonableness standard that considers the totality of circumstances[45] while a third view uses the test of "founded suspicion."[46] Regardless of the test used, the courts have granted people in private passenger vehicles more protection than those in commercial vehicles.[47]

During a legitimate inspection or investigative stop, the police officer may examine the vehicle identification number.[48]

---

36. United States v. Cupps, 503 F.2d 277 (6th Cir. 1974) (dictum); United States v. Lepinski, 460 F.2d 234 (10th Cir. 1972); United States v. Turner, 442 F.2d 1146 (8th Cir. 1971); State v. Swift, 232 Ga. 535, 207 S.E.2d 459 (1974); State v. Ingle, 36 N.Y.2d 413, 369 N.Y.S.2d 67, 330 N.E.2d 39 (1975). But cf. State v. Ochoa, 23 Ariz.App. 510, 534 P.2d 441 (1975); Commonwealth v. Swanger, 453 Pa. 107, 307 A.2d 875 (1973).

37. Idaho Code § 49–319; Ky.Rev.Stats. 186.510; N.J.Rev.Stat. 39:3–29.

38. 422 U.S. 873, 95 S.Ct. 2574, 45 L.Ed.2d 607 (1975).

39. Id. at 884.

40. Id. at 883 n. 8.

41. United States v. Cupps, 503 F.2d 277 (6th Cir. 1974).

42. United States v. Harris, 404 F.Supp. 1116, 1123 n. 7 (E.D.Pa.1975) ("founded suspicion").

43. United States v. Larios-Montes, 500 F.2d 941 (9th Cir. 1974); State v. Maynard, 114 N.H. 525, 323 A.2d 580 (1974) (good faith belief based on driver's action that he is not fit to drive).

44. See § 2, supra.

45. United States v. Harris, 404 F.Supp. 1116 (E.D. Pa.1975) and cases cited therein.

46. United States v. Larios-Montes, 500 F.2d 941 (9th Cir. 1974).

47. United States v. Harris, 404 F.Supp. 1116 (E.D. Pa.1975).

48. Commonwealth v. Navarro, 2 Mass.App. 214, 310 N.E.2d 372 (1974) and cases cited therein.

Even absent an actual stop, if a car is parked in an area accessible to the police, they are permitted to ascertain the vehicle identification number by looking through the windshield.[49]

In addition, in Pennsylvania v. Mimms,[50] the Supreme Court held that if a police officer has pulled over a traffic offender, the officer may order the offender out of the car. Citing *Terry* and *Adams*, the Court balanced the competing interests. On the one hand, the Court stressed that an order to alight is a minimal intrusion. On the other hand, the Court emphasized that the factor of the officer's safety was overriding in its mind. The dissenters would have required an "individualized inquiry into the particular facts justifying every police intrusion,"[51] but the majority thought that police safety considerations were so weighty that they warranted generally sanctioning police orders that traffic offenders alight from their vehicles.

4. Frisk

The next step in escalation is a frisk of the person stopped.

Basis for a Frisk. An officer may frisk any person whom he or she has lawfully stopped when the officer reasonably suspects that the person is carrying a concealed weapon or a dangerous instrument and the frisk is necessary to protect the officer or others.[52] The frisk may be conducted immediately after making or at any time during the stop—that is, whenever a reasonable suspicion to frisk arises.[53] Although there

is no precise definition of reasonable suspicion to frisk, a number of factors exist which alone or in combination are sufficient to create this suspicion. Some of the factors relevant to determining whether there is a basis for a stop are relevant here as well.

The Person's Appearance.[54] An individual may have a bulge in his or her clothing, suggesting the presence of a weapon or other object capable of inflicting injury.

The Person's Actions.[55] The person may have attempted to flee, may have made a furtive movement as if to hide a weapon, or may appear nervous during the detention.

Prior Knowledge of the Person.[56] The person may have a reputation for being belligerent or a record for weapons offenses, assaults, or other violent crimes.

Location.[57] The stop may occur in a high-crime area near the scene of an offense or at a known base of criminal activity.

Time of Day.[58] Again depending on the location, a nighttime stop may contribute to the likelihood that the officer will be attacked.

Police Purpose.[59] The purpose of the stop may be suspicion that a serious or violent crime has been committed.

Companions.[60] A frisk of a companion may reveal a weapon. However, the arrest or stop of one individual by itself would not justify a frisk of the companion absent reasonable suspicion that the companion is carrying a concealed weapon or dangerous instrument.[61]

---

49. See, e. g., United States v. Wagner, 497 F.2d 249 (10th Cir. 1974).

50. 433 U.S. 1, 97 S.Ct. 2476, 53 L.Ed.2d 538 (1977).

51. Id.

52. Adams v. Williams, 407 U.S. 143, 92 S.Ct. 1921, 32 L.Ed.2d 612 (1972); Terry v. Ohio, 392 U.S. 1, 88 S.Ct. 1868, 20 L.Ed.2d 889 (1968); People v. Mack, 26 N.Y.2d 311, 310 N.Y.S.2d 292, 258 N.E.2d 703 (1970).

53. See Adams v. Williams, 407 U.S. 143, 92 S.Ct. 1921, 32 L.Ed.2d 612 (1972).

54. § 2 *The Person's Appearance, supra.*

55. § 2 *The Person's Actions, supra.*

56. § 2 *Reputation, supra.*

57. § 2 *Area of the Stop, supra.*

58. § 2 *The Time of Day, supra.*

59. § 2 *Police Purpose, supra.*

60. § 2 *Factors Pertaining to the Person's Companion, supra.*

61. United States v. Tharpe, 526 F.2d 326 (5th Cir. 1976).

Scope of a Frisk. In a frisk or pat down, the officer usually starts with the person's hat and hair, and then proceeds down the person, feeling for an object or dangerous weapon. If while conducting the frisk, the officer feels an object which he or she reasonably believes is a weapon, dangerous instrument, or other item that will aid in a criminal prosecution, the officer may remove this object. The pat down is generally limited to the outer clothing unless this clothing is too bulky to allow the officer to determine if a dangerous instrument is concealed underneath or unless the officer has a reasonable belief, based on reliable information or personal knowledge or observation, that a weapon is concealed in a particular place on the person—for example, in a pocket, waistband, or sleeve. In this situation, the officer may reach directly into the suspected area.

5. Search Incident to Arrest

Suggested Reading:

United States v. Edwards, 415 U.S. 800, 94 S.Ct. 1234, 39 L.Ed.2d 771 (1974).

Gustafson v. Florida, 414 U.S. 260, 94 S.Ct. 488, 38 L.Ed.2d 456 (1973).

United States v. Robinson, 414 U.S. 218, 94 S.Ct. 467, 38 L.Ed.2d 427 (1973).

Chimel v. California, 395 U.S. 752, 89 S.Ct. 2034, 23 L.Ed.2d 685 (1969).

Just as the initial contact can escalate to a stop, a stop can escalate to a full-fledged arrest.

General. An arrest occurs when four elements concur: real or assumed authority; actual or constructive seizure or detention of the person; expressed or implied communication of intent to take the person into custody; and an understanding by the arrestee that he or she is being taken into custody. If an arrest occurs, the prosecution must demonstrate probable cause for the arrest.[62]

Just as a frisk often accompanies a stop, the officer usually conducts a search incidental to the arrest.

Search Prior to Arrest. A number of courts have stated that an arrest must precede a search.[63] However, this is a misstatement of law, probably based either on (1) earlier decisions that a search cannot be justified as incident to an arrest if conducted without an actual arrest or on (2) statements that the fruits of a search cannot be used to justify an arrest. Most of these earlier cases found the search unreasonable on other grounds and the statement that the arrest must precede the search is dictum.[64]

In Warden v. Hayden,[65] the Supreme Court held that a search may under certain circumstances precede an arrest. This holding leaves open the possibility that seizures would be legal even if the defendant is not present on the premises and cannot be arrested immediately. Likewise, a search may be justified as incident to an arrest, although no arrest is made, if grounds exist to justify an arrest.[66] Courts have also held that a search may precede an arrest if the two events are substantially contemporaneous.[67]

When Is an Incidental Search of the Individual and the Immediate Area Permitted? In United States v. Robinson [68] and Gustafson v. Florida,[69] the Supreme Court held that

---

62. Chapter 16, supra.

63. See, e. g., United States v. Waller, 108 F.Supp. 450 (N.D.Ill.1952); United States v. Fleener, 21 U.S. C.M.A. 174, 44 C.M.R. 228 (1972).

64. M. Paulsen & S. Kadish, Criminal Law and Its Processes 740 n. i (1962).

65. 387 U.S. 294, 87 S.Ct. 1642, 18 L.Ed.2d 782 (1967).

66. See People v. Gavin, 21 Cal.App.3d 408, 98 Cal. Rptr. 518 (1971).

67. United States v. Jenkins, 496 F.2d 57, 75 (2d Cir. 1974); United States v. Riggs, 474 F.2d 699, 704 (2d Cir. 1973); United States v. Maynard, 439 F.2d 1086 (9th Cir. 1971); United States v. Collins, 439 F.2d 610 (D.C.Cir. 1971).

68. 414 U.S. 218, 94 S.Ct. 467, 38 L.Ed.2d 427 (1973).

69. 414 U.S. 260, 94 S.Ct. 488, 38 L.Ed.2d 456 (1973).

when a "lawful custodial arrest" occurs, a full search of the arrestee may be made even though no basis exists to believe that either evidence of a crime or a weapon is on the person. In these cases the defendants were arrested for traffic infractions and were transported to the police station—Robinson pursuant to police department regulations and Gustafson pursuant to the arresting officer's standard operating procedures. Perhaps because both defendants conceded that there had been a "custodial arrest," [70] the Supreme Court did not define this phrase.

However in the two opinions the Court did use several terms which, in conjunction with one another, might define *custodial arrest*. The Court spoke of "lawful custody," "custody," and "transportation to the police station" without indicating the relationship of these terms to "custodial arrest." Following *Robinson* and *Gustafson,* many state and federal courts are attempting to define *lawful custodial arrest.* The Florida Supreme Court has defined the phrase in a rule of the court. [71] The attempts to define the phrase have divided the courts into two schools of thought. The first school of thought is that all that is needed for a lawful custodial arrest is simply a lawful arrest, for, as mentioned above, custody is an element of any arrest. [72] The second school is that the Supreme Court used the phrase *lawful custodial arrest* to distinguish an arrest from the issuance of a traffic citation. Concurring in *Gustafson* Justice Stewart wrote: "[A] persuasive claim might have been made in this case that the custodial arrest of the petitioner for a minor traffic offense violated his rights under the Fourth and

Fourteenth Amendments." [73] A number of courts have stated that a stop to issue a traffic citation or other summons to appear in court does not constitute an arrest in the absence of a statute to the contrary. [74] In some states a person who is stopped for a misdemeanor or a traffic offense must be released unless the citation comes within certain exceptions. Usually these exceptions fall into one of two categories: (1) Because of the offense—for example, driving with a suspended driver's license or driving under the influence of alcohol—the individual must be taken before the magistrate. Or (2) at the police officer's option, the individual either may be released after the issuance of a traffic citation or may be taken before a magistrate. [75] A variation occurs in some states which require that the officer make a stationhouse arrest for certain offenses. Whether he or she makes such an arrest for the other offenses is at the officer's discretion. [76] In this light lawful custodial arrest probably means a lawful arrest for which the officer has at least discretion to transport the arrestee to the police station. This interpretation is consistent with the Court's remark in Terry v. Ohio: [77] "It is quite plain that the Fourth Amendment governs 'seizures' of the person which do not eventuate in a trip to the stationhouse and prosecution for crime—'arrest' in traditional terminology."

---

70. Gustafson v. Florida, 414 U.S. 260, 267, 94 S.Ct. 488, 492, 38 L.Ed.2d 456 (1973); Robinson v. United States, 414 U.S. 218, 221, 94 S.Ct. 467, 470, 38 L.Ed. 2d 427 (1973).

71. Fla.Traffic Ct. Rule 6.13. See also Me.Dist. Civ.Rule 80F(b).

72. People v. Briesendine, 13 Cal.3d 528, 119 Cal. Rptr. 315, 531 P.2d 1099 (1975); State v. Kaluna, 55 Haw. 361, 520 P.2d 51 (1974).

73. Gustafson v. Florida, 414 U.S. 260, 266–67, 94 S.Ct. 488, 492–93, 38 L.Ed.2d 456 (1973).

74. People v. Nunn, 264 Cal.App.2d 919, 923, 70 Cal.Rptr. 869, 872 (1968); Hart v. Herzig, 131 Colo. 458, 283 P.2d 177, 180–81 (1955); Conn v. Commonwealth, 387 S.W.2d 285, 286 (Ky.1965); Chrestman v. State, 148 Miss. 673, 678, 114 So. 748, 749 (1927); State v. Murray, 106 N.H. 71, 73, 205 A.2d 29, 30–31 (1964). But see United States v. Kinane, 24 U.S.C. M.A. 120, 51 C.M.R. 310 (1976); State v. Cook, 194 Kan. 495, 498, 399 P.2d 835, 838 (1965).

75. West's Ann.Cal.Vehicle Code §§ 40302–40303; Mich.Comp.Laws Ann. §§ 257, 727–28.

76. Vernon's Ann.Tex.Stat. art. 6701(b), §§ 147–53.

77. 392 U.S. 1, 16, 88 S.Ct. 1868, 1877, 20 L.Ed.2d 889 (1968).

In addition to dividing over the interpretation of *lawful custodial arrest*, the courts differ over the wisdom of permitting broad evidentiary searches incident to traffic arrests.

Some states have not followed *Robinson* and *Gustafson*, but rather have applied more stringent standards than constitutionally required.[78] These courts distinguish between evidentiary searches (those aimed at seizing contraband, fruits, instrumentalities of a crime, or other items that would aid in a criminal prosecution) and protective frisks for weapons. The officer will be allowed to make a limited protective frisk of the arrestee when he or she is required or has discretion to make a stationhouse arrest or when he or she reasonably suspects that the arrestee is armed. However, the officer may make an evidentiary search only when probable cause exists to believe that there is evidence on the person or in the immediate area. These rules are similar to those currently applied in Britain.[79]

On the other hand, some lower courts seem eager to liberalize the standards for evidentiary searches. In *Robinson* the Court stated that its decision dealt only with a *search of a person* and not with a search of the immediate area. This limitation was emphasized again in United States v. Stevens.[80] However, *Robinson's* rationale is that the right to make a search incident to an arrest rests not only on the need to disarm the arrestee but also on the need to preserve evidence.[81] This rationale is strikingly similar to the Supreme Court's language in Chimel v. California defining the immediate area as the one from which the individual can obtain a weapon or destroy evidence.

Logically, the security of the officer and the preservation-of-evidence rationale would also allow a search of the immediate area when a traffic arrest has been made. Recently some lower courts have extended the *Robinson* holding, but not yet to *Chimel's* "immediate area." Rather than allowing a full search of the immediate area, the Illinois Court of Appeal[82] held that when a person, stopped for a defective light, gets out of the car on demand, the officer has the right to make a "cursory search of the driver's seat."[83] In contrast to this approach, the Texas Court of Criminal Appeals has held that stopping a motorist for running a red light does not give the officer reason for searching between the front seats of the car.[84]

The basis of both *Robinson* and *Gustafson* is the Supreme Court's concern for the police officer's safety. At the outset of a street encounter, the person does not know what the officer intends to do. Therefore, a risk exists whether the officer approaches the individual to issue a traffic citation or to make a stationhouse arrest. Drawing distinctions between the right to search the person and the right to search the immediate area on the basis of the officer's subjective state of mind overlooks the Court's concern for his or her safety. What an officer may or may not do under a state statute or local ordinance is probably not known to the armed, dangerous criminal at the outset of a street encounter. The reasoning underlying *Robinson* and *Gustafson* suggests that a lawful custodial arrest justifies a full search of the immediate area.

---

78. Uniform and Model Traffic Ordinance § 16–203–204.

79. G. Wilson, Cases and Materials on the English Legal System 285–86 (1973).

80. 509 F.2d 683 (8th Cir. 1975).

81. Robinson v. United States, 414 U.S. 218, 235, 94 S.Ct. 467, 476, 38 L.Ed.2d 427 (1973).

82. 18 Ill.App.3d 781, 310 N.E.2d 673 (1974).

83. 310 N.E.2d at 676. See also State v. Venezia, 515 S.W.2d 492 (Mo.1974). An officer making a lawful, warrantless custodial arrest of the driver for a minor offense may, as an incident thereto, search any part of the interior of the automobile from which the driver might obtain a weapon, and this is true even though the arrestee has been required to get out of the car and is standing nearby.

84. Wilson v. State, 511 S.W.2d 531 (Tex.Cr.App. 1974).

Spatial Limitations on the Scope of the Incidental Search—How Is the "Immediate Area" Defined? Absent exigent circumstances the police officer may search only the arrestee's person and the area within his or her immediate control—that is, the area from which the arrestee might grab a weapon or destructible evidence.[85] However, even absent exigent circumstances that would permit a search beyond the spatial limitation of *Chimel*, the search of a home, business, automobile, or container carried by the individual may be justified as being within the area of the arrestee's "immediate control."

An ambiguity in *Chimel* is whether the standard is meant to define: (1) an area with specified radius; (2) an area that depends on the arresting officer's subjective evaluation of the arrestee's ability; (3) an area that depends on the officer's reasonable evaluation of the arrestee's ability; or (4) an area that the officer may reasonably search for self-protection.

Radius Test. Many courts have applied a linear test.[86] The radius test allows the police to search within a specified area of the arrest. Establishing a linear measurement as the standard for the proper area is unsatisfactory, for such a test could result in allowing a search much broader than necessary. Conversely, in other instances, this test would so severely limit the search that

the officer would not be adequately protected. Assume the defendant is arrested in his or her dining room which is connected to the kitchen by an open door. If the kitchen is beyond the mandated linear distance, a search of the area is impermissible, and thus the officer would not find any unseen weapons in the kitchen unless he or she searches beyond the limit set in the jurisdiction.[87] The advantages of a linear rule are that it is more understandable to the law enforcement official and tends to eliminate litigation.[88] The latter factor, although entitled to some weight, is not controlling, for the test is inconsistent with *Chimel*.[89] It is permissible to search the individual and the immediate area on the bases of the arresting officer's safety, the potential for the arrestee to escape, and possibility of destruction of evidence.[90]

Subjective Evaluation Test. Chimel's intent can be satisfied by applying a test which recognizes the arresting officer's evaluation of the arrestee's abilities. This test can be subjective or objective. However, a subjective test places a heavy burden on the defense and encourages perjury or educating police officers about the proper scope of the search.[91] Additionally, it means that the defendant's right against the governmental intrusion is dependent on the frailties and idiosyncrasies of the arresting officer. Therefore this test must also be rejected.

---

85. See Chimel v. California, 395 U.S. 752, 89 S.Ct. 2034, 23 L.Ed.2d 685 (1969).

86. United States v. Jenkins, 496 F.2d 57, 73 (2d Cir. 1974) (search of motorcycle saddlebag within immediate area); Strader v. Estelle, 491 F.2d 969, 970 (5th Cir. 1974) (search of glove compartment permissible); United States v. Frick, 490 F.2d 666 (5th Cir. 1973) (applying "yardstick test", the court upheld the search of attache case belonging to defendant who was handcuffed and surrounded by five FBI agents); People v. Perry, 47 Ill.2d 402, 408, 266 N.E.2d 330, 333 (1971) (a subsequent search of dresser and purse in room in which the defendant had been arrested but removed from sustained "since it was within the area from which defendant could have obtained a weapon or something that could have been used as evidence against him").

87. See United States v. Robinson, 471 F.2d 1082, 1101 n. 31 (D.C.Cir. 1972); Oaks, Studying the Exclusionary Rule in Search and Seizure, 37 U.Chi.L. Rev. 665, 727–29 (1970).

88. See Kirby v. Illinois, 406 U.S. 682, 92 S.Ct. 1877, 32 L.Ed.2d 411 (1972) (rule as to right to counsel can be easily followed). See also Packer, Two Models of the Criminal Process, 118 U.Pa.L.Rev. 1 (1964).

89. Chimel v. California, 392 U.S. 752, 89 S.Ct. 2034, 23 L.Ed.2d 685 (1969).

90. Id.

91. See Chevigny, Police Power (1969); Chevigny, Police Abuse in Connection with the Law of Search and Seizure, 5 Crim.L.Bull. 3 (1969); Younger, The Perjury Routine, May 8, 1967, The Nation, 596–97.

Objective-Subjective Evaluation Test. A test consistent with the rationale of *Chimel* is one based on both the objective and the subjective beliefs of the arresting officer.[92] This test requires that the officer entertain a subjective belief and measures the belief's reasonableness. Although no court has precisely articulated this test, some have implied its application in their holdings.[93]

Totality of Circumstances Test. Another test that has been used in evaluating other constitutional rights is an objective test which considers the totality of circumstances. In analyzing the area which is within the immediate reach of the arrestee, the courts examine all factors including the arrestee's cooperation, the linear distance, the number of police officers present, the age and agility of the arrestee, whether he or she was handcuffed, and the number of suspects present.[94]

Temporal Limitations on the Scope of the Incidental Search. In order for a search to be incident to an arrest, it must not only be within *Chimel's* spatial limitations but it must also be within the temporal limitations set forth by the courts. When the search is made contemporaneously with or shortly after the arrest, the evidence seized will usually be admissible as within the temporal limitation.[95] Under some circumstances, even a substantial delay might not invalidate a search. As the Supreme Court stated in United States v. Edwards:[96] "[O]nce the [defendant] is lawfully arrested and is in custody, the effects in his possession at the place of detention that were subject to search at the time and place of his arrest may lawfully be searched and seized without a warrant even though a substantial period of time has elapsed between the arrest and the subsequent administrative processing, on the one hand, and the taking of the property for use as evidence, on the other." The search incident to the arrest in *Edwards* took place approximately ten hours after the defendant had been incarcerated. However, this delay occurred during the evening hours when clothing was not available to replace that worn by the defendant, and his clothing was the subject of the seizure. The courts have also allowed a subsequent search when a search at the time of arrest would have been impractical.[97] Other courts permit a delayed search on the basis of the belief that after an individual is arrested, his or her right to privacy no longer exists.[98]

---

96. 415 U.S. 800, 807, 94 S.Ct. 1234, 1239, 39 L.Ed. 2d 771 (1974).

97. United States v. Gonzalez-Perez, 426 F.2d 1283, 1287 (5th Cir. 1970) ("The arresting officers are not required to stand in a public place examining papers or other evidence on the person of the defendant in order for such evidence to be admissible."); United States ex rel. Montgomery v. Wallack, 255 F.Supp. 566, 569 (S.D.N.Y.1966) ("We need no current reminder that arrests in a crowded, substandard neighborhood oft times trigger explosive action."). See also United States v. DeLeo, 422 F.2d 487, 493 (1st Cir. 1970); United States v. Davis, 43 C.M.R. 516, 520 (ACMR 1970); McCoy v. State, 491 P.2d 127 (Alaska 1971).

98. United States v. Jeffers, 524 F.2d 253 (7th Cir. 1975); United States v. Manar, 454 F.2d 342 (7th Cir. 1971). See also United States v. Robinson, 414 U.S. 218, 237, 94 S.Ct. 467, 477, 38 L.Ed.2d 427 (1973) (Powell, J., concurring).

---

92. United States v. Jones, 475 F.2d 723 (5th Cir. 1973). In determining if the search of a suitcase was proper, the court must determine the reasonableness of the officers' conclusion that the defendant could have "attempt[ed] to lay his hands on a weapon inside the suitcase."

93. See, e. g., People v. Floyd, 26 N.Y.2d 558, 563, 312 N.Y.S.2d 193, 195, 260 N.E.2d 815, 817 (1970) ("Nothing is within grabbing distance once the individual is handcuffed."). Contra, United States v. Ciotti, 469 F.2d 1204 (3d Cir. 1972); United States v. Mehciz, 437 F.2d 145 (9th Cir. 1971).

94. United States v. Gonzalez-Perez, 426 F.2d 1283 (5th Cir. 1970); United States v. Salatino, 22 U.S.C. M.A. 530, 48 C.M.R. 15 (1973).

95. Westover v. United States, 394 F.2d 164 (9th Cir. 1968).

6. Search of Premises

Suggested Reading:

Vale v. Louisiana, 399 U.S. 30, 90 S.Ct. 1969, 26 L.Ed.2d 409 (1970).

United States v. Briddle, 436 F.2d 4 (8th Cir. 1970).

General. After a seizure of the person, the police may escalate their investigation by a seizure of real or personal property. The courts have traditionally stated that when probable cause to search and exigent circumstances exist together, the police may make a warrantless search of the premises.[99] "Exigent circumstances" in this context mean reasonable grounds to believe that items on the premises are in danger of being removed, destroyed, or concealed before a warrant can be obtained. In determining whether there is a danger of evidence being destroyed, concealed, or removed, various factors are considered: the absence of probable cause to search the premises before the police arrived; the presence of confederates, accomplices, accessories, or relatives who might destroy evidence or assist in an escape; the feasibility of temporarily detaining the occupants of the premises; or a lack of concern about the evidence being destroyed.

These factors are merely illustrative, for many others can justify a warrantless search. However, if the officer has probable cause to believe that seizable items are on the premises but there are no exigent circumstances, the officer may instruct anyone who subsequently arrives at the premises that they have a right to enter but are subject to surveillance until a warrant can be obtained.[1] If the individuals are already on the premises, the officer may instruct them to stay in one portion of the premises until a warrant is obtained.[2]

Security of Arresting Officer. In many cases the police may search beyond the immediate area of an arrest on the premises. For example, the police officer may search for other individuals on the premises.[3] Such a search is entirely reasonable and necessary for the arresting officer's safety. Again, for security purposes, some courts have allowed the police to make a cursory view of the premises, looking for other individuals who might attempt to prevent the arrest of the defendant or to secure his or her escape.[4] Many courts require probable cause to believe that other individuals are on the premises.[5] Others rely upon the presence of unusual circumstances,[6] and some permit a cursory view at any time in order to prevent harm to the arresting officers.[7]

Obtaining Wearing Apparel. An individual who is arrested at his of her house or place of business might have to obtain wearing apparel or a change of clothing for a stay at the detention cell. If the arrestee requests permission to bring things to the cell, the officer may search the immediate

---

99. Vale v. Louisiana, 399 U.S. 30, 90 S.Ct. 1969, 26 L.Ed.2d 409 (1970); Chimel v. California, 392 U.S. 752, 89 S.Ct. 2034, 23 L.Ed.2d 685 (1969).

1. See United States v. Christophe, 470 F.2d 865, 868–869 (2d Cir. 1972). But see Shuey v. Superior Court, 30 Cal.App.3d 535, 106 Cal.Rptr. 452 (1973).

2. United States v. Christophe, 470 F.2d 865 (2d Cir. 1972). Cf. United States v. Agosto, 502 F.2d 612 (9th Cir. 1974). The court stated that it is not per se coercive for police officers to tell a defendant who is being requested to consent to a search of the premises that if consent is not given, the police will get a search warrant and will secure the premises while the warrant is obtained. See also United States v. Faruolo, 506 F.2d 490 (2d Cir. 1974).

3. Notes 4–7, infra.

4. United States v. Rich, 518 F.2d 980 (8th Cir. 1975). But see United States v. Carter, 522 F.2d 666 (D.C.Cir. 1975); United States v. Cooks, 493 F.2d 668 (7th Cir. 1974).

5. People v. Block, 6 Cal.3d 239, 103 Cal.Rptr. 281, 499 P.2d 961 (1971). Cf. United States v. Sellers, 520 F.2d 1281 (4th Cir. 1975).

6. See United States v. Carter, 522 F.2d 666 (D.C. Cir. 1975); United States v. Broomfield, 336 F.Supp. 179 (E.D.Mich.1972).

7. United States v. Briddle, 436 F.2d 4 (8th Cir. 1970).

area before these additional items are obtained, both to protect the arresting officer and to prevent the destruction of evidence.[8] However, the need for wearing apparel cannot be used as a pretext to make an additional search of the house.

7. Hot Pursuit

Suggested Reading:

United States v. Santana, 427 U.S. 38, 96 S.Ct. 2406, 49 L.Ed.2d 300 (1976).

Warden v. Hayden, 387 U.S. 294, 87 S.Ct. 1642, 18 L.Ed.2d 782 (1967).

Basis. The hot pursuit doctrine can also justify an intrusion onto realty. An officer who is pursuing an individual may make a warrantless entry into a building if he or she (1) has probable cause to believe a serious crime has been committed or is about to be committed; (2) has probable cause to believe the individual is in the building; (3) began the pursuit when the crime was committed, or shortly after the crime was committed; and (4) believes there is a need for immediate arrest and identification because of danger to the police or others. This doctrine commonly referred to as hot pursuit, is based on Warden v. Hayden.[9] There the Supreme Court held that when the police had been informed that an armed robbery had taken place and that the suspect had been seen entering a certain building five minutes before they reached it, the officers could make a warrantless search of the building because "exigent circumstances" existed. Some courts have held that to make hot pursuit, the police need both probable cause to believe a serious crime was committed and probable cause to believe the in-

dividual is in the particular building.[10] Some courts have indicated that a probable cause standard must be applied to the offense but that something less is required concerning the belief the individual is in the building.[11] In some cases no standard has been established.[12]

As to element (3), showing an uninterrupted investigation is not enough. Rather the pursuit must take place shortly after the commission of the crime.[13] Although the fact that the police momentarily lost sight of the suspect does not negate the exigent circumstances,[14] a two-hour delay will preclude a search on the basis of a hot pursuit.[15] If more than one family lives in an apartment complex, and probable cause exists to believe that the suspects are in the complex, courts have permitted hot pursuit into more than one dwelling unit.[16]

In its recent decision, United States v. Santana,[17] the Supreme Court seemed to conclude that element (4) is not a requirement of the hot pursuit doctrine. The majority stated that after the suspect who was carrying a package had retreated into the vestibule of her home, the hot pursuit doctrine permitted the officers to follow her to apprehend her and prevent the destruction of evidence. The Court acknowledged that although she was standing in her doorway when the police called to her, she could not

---

8. Giacalone v. Lucas, 445 F.2d 1238 (6th Cir. 1971); United States v. Kee Ming Hsu, 424 F.2d 1286 (2d Cir. 1970).

9. 387 U.S. 294, 87 S.Ct. 1642, 18 L.Ed.2d 782 (1967).

10. Frager v. United States, 258 A.2d 259, 260 (D.C.App.1969). Cf. Fellows v. State, 13 Md.App. 206, 283 A.2d 1 (1971); Nichols v. State, 501 S.W.2d 107 (Tex.Cr.App.1973).

11. Greer v. State, 253 Ind. 609, 255 N.E.2d 919 (1970).

12. See People v. Broyles, 28 Mich.App. 83, 184 N.W.2d 373 (1970).

13. United States v. Scott, 520 F.2d 697 (9th Cir. 1975).

14. Styles v. Commonwealth, 507 S.W.2d 487 (Ky. 1974).

15. People v. Hill, 12 Cal.3d 731, 117 Cal.Rptr. 393, 528 P.2d 1 (1975).

16. United States v. Scott, 520 F.2d 697 (9th Cir. 1975); People v. Bradford, 28 Cal.App.3d 695, 104 Cal.Rptr. 852 (1972).

17. 427 U.S. 38, 96 S.Ct. 2406, 49 L.Ed.2d 300 (1976).

avoid a lawful arrest by retreating into the privacy of her home. For fourth amendment purposes she was in a "public" place when she was standing in her doorway, and thus she lost all reasonable expectation of privacy despite her property interest in the premises. The holding here makes clear that the "reasonable expectation-of-privacy" doctrine which was set forth in *Katz* and which replaced property law concepts, can cut both ways. In a concurring opinion, Mr. Justice Stevens, joined by Mr. Justice Stewart, stated: "The decision was justified by the significant risk that the marked money [which was used to buy heroin] would no longer be in Santana's possession if the police waited until a warrant could be obtained." [18]

Scope of the Search. Before the suspects are found, the police may search any area where the individuals or weapons might be.[19] Additionally, evidence that is discovered contemporaneously with the arrest of individuals on the premises will be admissible.[20] However, if the police determine that no one is present, usually the search must stop.[21] Arguably even though no one is on the premises, the officers may search for evidence of the suspect's identity or whereabouts if the suspect is believed to be armed and dangerous and if his or her identity or the location to which he or she is fleeing is unknown.

8. Open Fields

Suggested Reading:

Air Pollution Variance Board v. Western Alfalfa Corp., 416 U.S. 861, 94 S.Ct. 2114, 40 L.Ed.2d 607 (1974).

---

18. Id.

19. Warden v. Hayden, 387 U.S. 294, 87 S.Ct. 1642, 18 L.Ed.2d 782 (1967).

20. Kirkpatrick v. Cox, 321 F.Supp. 284 (W.D.Va. 1971).

21. United States v. Goldstein, 456 F.2d 1006 (8th Cir. 1972); People v. Broyles, 28 Mich.App. 83, 184 N.W.2d 373 (1970).

Hester v. United States, 265 U.S. 57, 44 S.Ct. 445, 68 L.Ed. 898 (1924).

A third doctrine justifying intrusion onto realty is "open fields".

The protection of the fourth amendment extends to "persons, houses, papers, and effects." Relying on this language, Mr. Justice Holmes in Hester v. United States [22] stated that the fourth amendment does not protect property abandoned in an open field. In 1967, when the Supreme Court adopted its expectation of privacy approach, many courts thought that the open-fields doctrine would be abandoned.[23] However, a number of courts have indicated either than the concept is still viable [24] or that even if an expectation of privacy exists society will not recognize such an expectation in certain areas of an open field.[25] No matter which test is applied, an officer may enter open fields to the same extent as the public. In Air Pollution Variance Bd. v. Western Alfalfa Corp.,[26] the Supreme Court reaffirmed the open-fields doctrine by stating that it was "not advised" that the inspector conducting the environmental tests "was on premises from which the public was excluded.[27]

Regardless of whether the fourth amendment protects open fields, it does protect the curtilage of a house. Thus the concept of curtilage is important in deciding which areas are entitled to fourth amendment pro-

---

22. 265 U.S. 57, 44 S.Ct. 445, 68 L.Ed. 898 (1924).

23. Cf. Wattenburg v. United States, 388 F.2d 853 (9th Cir. 1960).

24. Conrad v. State, 63 Wis.2d 616, 218 N.W.2d 252 (1974).

25. Patler v. Slayton, 503 F.2d 472 (4th Cir. 1974).

26. 416 U.S. 861, 94 S.Ct. 2114, 40 L.Ed.2d 607 (1974).

27. Id. at 865.

tection and in determining the scope of a search incident to a warrant. The term *curtilage* has been defined as a "[y]ard, courtyard, or other piece of ground included within a fence surrounding a dwelling house." [28] "Generally speaking, curtilage has been held to include all buildings in close proximity to a dwelling, which are continually used for carrying on domestic employment; or such place as is necessary and convenient to a dwelling and is habitually used for family purposes." [29]

9. Automobile Search

Suggested Reading:

Coolidge v. New Hampshire, 403 U.S. 443, 91 S.Ct. 2022, 29 L.Ed.2d 564 (1971).

Chambers v. Maroney, 399 U.S. 42, 90 S.Ct. 1975, 26 L.Ed.2d 419 (1970).

We now shift our focus from real to personal property. Generally, if there is probable cause to believe that it contains seizable items, a warrantless search of an operational vehicle may be conducted, except when the vehicle is located on private property. In the past the Supreme Court has indicated that probable cause to search the vehicle and exigent circumstances must be present.[30] For example, the arrest in Chambers v. Maroney [31] took place late at night in a parking lot about two miles from a gas station that had been robbed. The defendant's vehicle was removed from the parking lot near the gas station and taken to the stationhouse where a search resulted in the seizure of two pistols found concealed in a compartment under the dashboard. The Court held that the exigent circumstance in this case was the fact that the opportunity to search is fleeting, for a car is "readily movable." [32] Removing the car to the stationhouse did not render the search illegal because it could have been temporarily detained until a warrant was obtained. The Court stated that once a basis for searching the car was established, the Court could not discern which was the greater intrusion—holding the car until a warrant was obtained or searching the car without a warrant. On this rationale they upheld the search.

Coolidge v. New Hampshire [33] seems to undermine the *Chambers* case. In *Coolidge*, the Supreme Court held that exigent circumstances did not exist when the following factors were present: (1) The police knew in advance that the defendant's car was associated with a crime. (2) The defendant had been "extremely cooperative throughout the investigation." (3) There was no indication the defendant might flee. (4) The vehicle was regularly parked in the driveway. (5) The vehicle was guarded prior to being moved to the police station. (6) No accomplices were known. (7) At the police's request the defendant's wife had spent the night at the home of a relative miles from her own residence. (8) No proof existed that anyone else had a motive to interfere with the vehicle.

The lower courts have found it difficult to reconcile *Chambers* and *Coolidge*. Some have opted for the view that if there is probable cause to search the vehicle at the location where it is found or stopped, the police may do so later at the stationhouse without first obtaining a warrant. Recently the Court has indicated that the fact that the vehicle is operational may be sufficient to satisfy the exigent circumstances test.[34]

---

28. Marullo v. United States, 328 F.2d 361, 363 (5th Cir. 1964).

29. United States v. Potts, 297 F.2d 68, 69 (6th Cir. 1961).

30. Chambers v. Maroney, 399 U.S. 42, 90 S.Ct. 1975, 26 L.Ed.2d 419 (1970).

31. Id.

32. Id. at 51.

33. 403 U.S. 443, 91 S.Ct. 2022, 29 L.Ed.2d 564 (1971).

34. Cardwell v. Lewis, 417 U.S. 583, 594, 94 S.Ct. 2464, 2471, 41 L.Ed.2d 325 (1974). The Supreme

Others have indicated that the decision of Texas v. White [35] has eliminated the exigent circumstances requirement.[36]

10. Movable Objects

Suggested Reading:

United States v. Chadwick, 433 U.S. 1, 97 S.Ct. 2476, 53 L.Ed.2d 538 (1977).

United States v. Van Leeuwen, 397 U.S. 249, 90 S.Ct. 1029, 25 L.Ed.2d 282 (1970).

Extending the "automobile exception," a number of courts have held that a suitcase, flight bag,[37] attache case,[38] and footlocker,[39] may be searched without a warrant when a showing of both probable cause to search the container and exigent circumstances is made. The courts upholding the search of closed containers under the *Chambers* rationale have said that the container is more analogous to an automobile than to a house.[40]

Court upheld the warrantless seizure of an unoccupied car parked in a public parking lot even though the accused was in custody at the police station. See also Texas v. White, 423 U.S. 67, 96 S.Ct. 304, 46 L.Ed.2d 209 (1975).

35. 423 U.S. 67, 96 S.Ct. 304, 46 L.Ed.2d 209 (1975). The courts are split on the effect of *White*.

36. Compare Haefeli v. Chernoff, 526 F.2d 1314, 1318 (1st Cir. 1975), with United States v. Robinson, 533 F.2d 578 (D.C.Cir. 1976). "We assume that if a Supreme Court majority intends to institute such a rule, and depart from its prior approach, it would do so by express pronouncement to all concerned."

37. United States v. Payseur, 501 F.2d 966 (9th Cir. 1974).

38. United States v. Frick, 490 F.2d 666 (5th Cir. 1973).

39. United States v. Evans, 481 F.2d 990 (9th Cir. 1973).

40. United States v. Soriano, 497 F.2d 147, 149 (5th Cir. 1974) (en banc); United States v. Valen, 479 F.2d 467, 471 (3d Cir. 1973); People v. McKinnon, 7 Cal.3d 899, 908–09, 103 Cal.Rptr. 897, 903–04, 500 P.2d 1097, 1103–04 (1972).

"Is a box or trunk consigned to a common carrier for shipment to a remote destination a 'thing readily moved' or a 'fixed piece of property'? The answer, self-evidently, is the former. To be sure, such a box has neither wheels nor motive power; but these features of an automobile are legally relevant only insofar as they make it movable despite its dimensions. A box, which is a fraction of the size and weight of an automobile, may serve the double purpose of both storing goods and packaging them for shipment. But whenever such a box is consigned to a common carrier, there can be no doubt that it is intended, in fact, to be moved. What is true of a box or trunk is true of all goods or chattels consigned to a common carrier for shipment. As they are no less movable than an automobile, the reasons for the rule permitting a warrantless search of a vehicle upon probable cause are equally applicable to the search of such a chattel." [41] The reason courts allow the search of the automobile is that it is "readily movable" [42] and has traditionally enjoyed a special status under the fourth amendment. Throughout *Chambers* refers to the "automobile and other conveyances," thus indicating a possible limitation of the holding.[43] Subsequently in *Coolidge* four justices stated they had "found no case that suggests . . . an extension . . . to containers that are equally movable, e. g., trunks, suitcases, boxes, briefcases and bags." [44]

---

41. People v. McKinnon, 7 Cal.3d 899, 900, 103 Cal. Rptr. 897, 904, 500 P.2d 1097, 1104 (1972). See also United States v. Valen, 479 F.2d 467 (3d Cir. 1973); United States v. Smeal, 23 U.S.C.M.A. 347, 49 C.M.R. 751 (1975).

42. Chambers v. Maroney, 399 U.S. 42, 51, 90 S.Ct. 1975, 1981, 26 L.Ed.2d 419 (1970).

43. Id. at 48.

44. Coolidge v. New Hampshire, 403 U.S. 443, 461 n. 18, 91 S.Ct. 2022, 2035 n. 18, 29 L.Ed.2d 564 (1971). See also Nugent v. United States, 409 U.S. 1065, 93 S.Ct. 564, 34 L.Ed.2d 518 (1972) (dissent of Justice White as to the denial of certiorari, joined by Douglas and Brennan). These justices candidly admitted that the mobility of these items is similar to that of automobiles. The language in Preston v. United

However, in United States v. Van Leeuwen,[45] the Supreme Court upheld the warrantless temporary detention of containers that postal officials had probable cause to believe contained contraband or some item that would aid in a criminal prosecution. A unanimous Court, although acknowledging that "detention of mail could at some point become an unreasonable seizure within the meaning of the Fourth Amendment,"[46] cited Terry[47] in validating the one-day "detention, without a warrant, while an investigation was made."[48]

As the previous section noted, Chambers approved some warrantless searches of automobiles. Chambers also indicated that an automobile can be held in status quo until a warrant is obtained. There seems to be even greater justification for warrantless detention of containers, for a substantial difference exists between maintaining the status quo over a container and over an automobile. The seizure of a car may deprive an individual of a primary means of transportation.[49] To acknowledge the distinction between a house and a car does not automatically validate every warrantless detention of a movable object. A preference for warranted detentions and searches remains.

The Supreme Court stressed that preference in United States v. Chadwick.[50] In Chadwick, the defendants loaded a 200 pound double-locked footlocker onto a train in San Diego. Railroad officials became suspicious because of several circumstances, including the facts that the locker leaked talcum powder (often used to mask marijuana odor) and that one defendant matched the profile of a drug trafficker. The footlocker was unloaded in Boston. There federal officers were waiting with a detection dog. The dog alerted, the suspects were arrested, and the footlocker was impounded. The officers opened the locker an hour and a half later at the federal building; they discovered that it contained a large quantity of marijuana.

The Supreme Court first held that the defendants had a reasonable expectation of privacy in the footlocker. The Court then declared that since the search was neither consensual nor incident to an arrest, a warrantless search would be legal only if there were exigent circumstances. Finding no exigent circumstances, the Court invalidated the search. The government analogized to automobile searches, but the majority emphasized that there are "significant differences between motor vehicles and other property which permit warrantless searches of automobiles in circumstances in which warrantless searches would not be reasonable in other contexts."[51] The Court reasoned that since luggage is "intended as a repository of personal effects,"[52] there is a greater expectation of privacy in luggage than in an automobile.

11. Inventories

Suggested Reading:

South Dakota v. Opperman, 428 U.S. 364, 96 S.Ct. 3092, 49 L.Ed.2d 1000 (1976).

We first discussed doctrines justifying intrusions upon the person. We then focused

States, 376 U.S. 364, 366, 84 S.Ct. 881, 882, 11 L.Ed. 2d 777 (1964) indicates that despite the tendency to label the Carroll doctrine the automobile exception, the doctrine may be applicable to other items: "Common sense dictates, of course, that questions involving searches of motorcars or other things readily moved cannot be treated as identical to questions arising out of searches of fixed structures like houses".

45. 397 U.S. 249, 90 S.Ct. 1029, 25 L.Ed.2d 282 (1970).

46. Id. at 252.

47. Terry v. Ohio, 392 U.S. 1, 88 S.Ct. 1868, 20 L. Ed.2d 889 (1968).

48. United States v. Van Leeuwen, 397 U.S. 249, 252, 90 S.Ct. 1029, 1032, 25 L.Ed.2d 282 (1970).

49. Cardwell v. Lewis, 417 U.S. 583, 94 S.Ct. 2464, 41 L.Ed.2d 325 (1974).

50. 433 U.S. 1, 97 S.Ct. 2476, 53 L.Ed.2d 538 (1977).

51. Id.

52. Id.

on doctrines supporting intrusions onto realty. Third, we turned to doctrines supporting intrusions into personal property. We shall now analyze several doctrines which can support intrusions relating to both persons and property. An inventory rationale can often be used to justify an intrusion upon a person or into property.

Inventory of the Person. Even though a search cannot be justified as incident to an arrest, the seizure of evidence may be sustained on the basis that the evidence was found during an inventory of the defendant's property prior to placing him or her in confinement. A key issue is when the inventory takes place. Some courts have implied that the inventory may take place when a possibility of detention exists.[53] Other courts have added that the inventory may take place at the time of booking [54] or after the decision to incarcerate has been made. However, even after the decision to incarcerate has been made, a number of courts limit the inventory. Some indicate that the inventory may not be made unless the individual has been offered the opportunity to make bail and cannot do so.[55] Others have said that the inventory may not be made absent confinement for an extended period of time.[56] One court has stated in dictum that the defendant must have been given "an opportunity like that accorded someone given a bathhouse locker for temporary use, to check his belongings in a sealed envelope, perhaps upon executing a waiver releasing the officer of any responsibility."[57]

Inventory of an Automobile. If the search of an automobile cannot be justified under the *Chambers* doctrine, it may be justified under the inventory exception but only if the inventory is not a subterfuge for a search. There are three reasons that legitimate an inventory of an automobile. First, it protects the police from fraudulent claims. Second, it protects the individual's property. And third, it protects the public from the possibility that a weapon in a car might fall into dangerous hands.[58]

Deciding whether the inventory is a subterfuge for a search is difficult. No hard and fast rule can be given, but in each instance a number of factors should be examined: the basis for impoundment; the procedure used in conducting the inventory; the time of inventory; the person who conducted the inventory; and the scope of the inventory. As to the first factor, the arrest of the driver does not itself justify removing the automobile from the highway.[59] Among the various legitimate reasons for impoundment are: The vehicle is unattended, illegally parked, or otherwise illegally obstructing traffic. After an accident the driver is physically or mentally incapable of deciding what to do with his or her property. The vehicle has been stolen or used in the commission of a crime. The vehicle is abandoned and creating a danger on a public highway. The impoundment is pursuant to an ordinance or statute which provides for forfeiture of the automobile.

The second factor is the procedure used to conduct the inventory. Because the rationale behind an inventory is protecting the police against fraudulent claims and guarding an individual's property, justifying a search on the basis of the inventory is diffi-

---

53. Charles v. United States, 278 F.2d 386 (9th Cir. 1960); United States v. Brashears, 21 U.S.C.M.A. 552, 45 C.M.R. 326 (1972).

54. Kaufman v. United States, 453 F.2d 798 (8th Cir. 1971).

55. People v. Overlee, 174 Colo. 202, 483 P.2d 222 (1971).

56. United States v. Mills, 472 F.2d 1231, 1239 n. 11 (D.C.Cir. 1972); People v. Superior Court, 7 Cal.3d 186, 101 Cal.Rptr. 837, 496 P.2d 1205 (1972).

57. United States v. Mills, 472 F.2d 1231, 1239 n. 11 (D.C.Cir. 1972).

58. Cady v. Dombrowski, 413 U.S. 433, 93 S.Ct. 2523, 37 L.Ed.2d 706 (1973).

59. Virgil v. Superior Court, 268 Cal.App.2d 127, 73 Cal.Rptr. 793 (1968).

cult if the trunk of a car must be opened by force.[60]

Both the time of the inventory and the person conducting it are also important factors. For example, if the car had been parked in an open parking lot and inventoried ten days after impoundment, the argument that the inventory is necessary to protect the police and the individual's property seems specious. Also the fact that the arrest is made by local officials, but the inventory is conducted at the local police department by federal officials is evidence that inventory is a subterfuge for a search.[61]

The factor causing the most controversy is the scope of the inventory. Some courts have held that regardless of where it is located, every item in the vehicle may be inventoried.[62] Some courts have stated that the inventory of hidden areas is justifiable only under unusual circumstances. Other courts have indicated that the police are not allowed to inventory items in locked or closed containers.[63] Some courts have strictly limited the inventory by deciding that once a basis for impoundment has been established, police officers may close and lock the vehicle, and if during the process, they observe evidence in plain view, the evidence may be seized and will be admissible. However, these courts have declared that opening or prying into compartments or containers

within the vehicle constitutes a search, which absent a warrant or special circumstances is illegal.[64] However, in South Dakota v. Opperman,[65] the Supreme Court held that evidence found in an unlocked glove compartment of a car that had been impounded for parking violations was admissible even though the police would have been protected from claims under state law if they had merely closed and locked the vehicle. In *Opperman* the Court recognized at least two other reasons for making an inventory: protecting the individual's property and protecting the police and the public from personal injury.

12. Consent

Suggested Reading:

United States v. Matlock, 415 U.S. 164, 94 S.Ct. 988, 39 L.Ed.2d 242 (1974).

Schneckloth v. Bustamonte, 412 U.S. 218, 93 S.Ct. 2041, 36 L.Ed.2d 854 (1973).

Frazier v. Cupp, 394 U.S. 731, 89 S.Ct. 1420, 22 L.Ed.2d 684 (1969).

Bumper v. North Carolina, 391 U.S. 543, 88 S.Ct. 1788, 20 L.Ed.2d 797 (1968).

Like the inventory rationale, a consent theory can justify an intrusion upon a person or into property. The consent theory is frequently used to validate a search or seizure. At trial proof of consent is less time consuming than proof of probable cause. The officer testifies briefly that consent was requested and granted. The consent theory is also useful because it is one of the few warrantless search doctrines which can validate a search even when probable cause is lacking.

---

60. People v. Garrison, 189 Cal.App.2d 549, 11 Cal. Rptr. 398 (1968). See also United States v. Lawson, 487 F.2d 468 (8th Cir. 1973); People v. Robinson, 36 A.D.2d 375, 320 N.Y.S.2d 665 (1971) (removing hubcaps, deflating tires, and examining interior of hubcaps and tires is not proper inventory).

61. Williams v. United States, 382 F.2d 48 (5th Cir. 1967).

62. State v. Wallen, 185 Neb. 44, 173 N.W.2d 372 (1970); People v. Sullivan, 29 N.Y.2d 69, 323 N.Y.S. 2d 945, 272 N.E.2d 464 (1971).

63. Mozzetti v. Superior Court, 4 Cal.3d 699, 94 Cal.Rptr. 412, 484 P.2d 84 (1971). See also United States v. Gravitt, 484 F.2d 375 (5th Cir. 1973); State v. Opperman, —— S.D. ——, 228 N.W.2d 152 (1975), cert. granted 423 U.S. 923, 96 S.Ct. 264, 46 L.Ed.2d 249; State v. McDougal, 68 Wis.2d 399, 228 N.W.2d 671 (1975).

64. United States v. Lawson, 487 F.2d 468, 477 (8th Cir. 1973); Commonwealth v. Dawson, 17 Crim.L. Rep. 2198 (Ky. May 9, 1975).

65. 428 U.S. 364, 96 S.Ct. 3092, 49 L.Ed.2d 1000 (1976).

Knowing Consent. Although the theoretical basis of the consent doctrine is the waiver concept,[66] the focus in the fourth amendment context is not the state of mind of the defendant but instead whether the defendant has voluntarily consented to the search.[67] In Schneckloth v. Bustamonte, the Supreme Court stated that in determining if consent is voluntary, one must examine the totality of the surrounding circumstances, including the conduct and statements of both the defendant and the police. The Court rejected the contention that voluntariness requires proof that the individual knows his or her fourth amendment rights. The Court stated that a fourth amendment waiver differs from a waiver of the right to counsel in that the fourth amendment does not affect the reliability or fairness of the truth-determining process. Also the burden of proof upon the prosecutor to establish that an individual subjectively knew he or she could withhold consent would be a "near impossibility."[68] Moreover, it would be thoroughly impractical to impose on the normal consent search the detailed requirements of an effective waiver."[69]

Voluntary Consent. Although the government must establish by "clear and positive" evidence that consent was "freely" given, the degree of proof may depend on the identity of the person consenting, the conduct of the police and the consenting party, and the nature of the property searched. If an officer says, "I am here to search your house," or "I have come to search your house," the statement will probably be deemed coercive.[70] Furthermore if there is a show of force or if the police officers falsely indicate that they have a search warrant,

any consent will be involuntary.[71] The Supreme Court has stated that under these circumstances there can be no consent, for "[w]hen a law enforcement officer claims authority to search a home under a warrant, he announces in effect that the occupant has no right to resist the search."[72] However, courts disagree on the effect of the officer stating that he or she intended to secure a warrant. Some courts view such statements as coercive, but most courts take a contra view if the officer has a good faith belief that there is probable cause that would justify the issuance of a warrant.[73]

Like the officer's conduct, the statement or actions of the defendant are relevant. For example, consent has been found when the defendant talked to a lawyer prior to the search, asked to speak to the investigators, was advised of the right to refuse to consent, and initialed the form reflecting he or she did not want a lawyer.[74] Moreover if the suspect assists in the search by providing a key, consent may be inferred.[75] In contrast a denial of guilt and the presence of incriminating objects on the premises militate against finding consent, for a rational individual who denies guilt would not willingly permit a search when incriminat-

---

66. Schneckloth v. Bustamonte, 412 U.S. 218, 93 S.Ct. 2041, 36 L.Ed.2d 854 (1973).

67. Id. at 224.

68. Id. at 230.

69. Id. at 231.

70. Amos v. United States, 255 U.S. 313, 41 S.Ct. 266, 65 L.Ed. 654 (1921).

71. Compare United States v. Dorman, 294 F.Supp. 1221 (D.D.C.1967), with Bumper v. North Carolina, 391 U.S. 543, 88 S.Ct. 1788, 20 L.Ed.2d 797 (1968).

72. Bumper v. North Carolina, 391 U.S. 543, 550, 88 S.Ct. 1788, 1792, 20 L.Ed.2d 797 (1968).

73. Compare United States v. Faruolo, 506 F.2d 490 (2d Cir. 1974) (not coercive where it was "well founded" warrant would be issued) and Hamilton v. North Carolina, 260 F.Supp. 632 (E.D.N.C.1966) (not coercive), with United States v. Boukater, 409 F.2d 537 (5th Cir. 1969) (coercive unless the officer actually had basis for warrant or said only that he would seek warrant). See also United States v. Agosto, 502 F.2d 612 (9th Cir. 1974) (must examine totality of circumstances).

74. United States v. Busby, 126 F.Supp. 845 (D.D.C.1954).

75. Higgins v. United States, 209 F.2d 819 (D.C.Cir. 1954); United States v. Kidd, 153 F.Supp. 605 (W.D. La.1957).

ing evidence will probably be found.[76] Also some courts have relied on the suspect's lack of cooperation in finding the consent "involuntary." [77]

Third Party Consent. Sometimes a person other than the suspect consents to the search. Various theories have been applied to find a valid third party consent. The common use theory is used when a third party who owns, uses, or possesses the property consents to a search.[78] Assumption of risk is applied when, as between the defendant and the third party, no reasonable expectation of privacy exists, and the defendant therefore assumes the risk of the third party's consent.[79] Finally, an apparent authority theory is employed if the police acted reasonably in believing the third party had authority to consent to a search of the property.[80]

Withdrawing Consent. The majority rule is that consent to search may be withdrawn before the search has commenced.[81] Withdrawal after the search is completed is

obviously ineffective.[82] Moreover, in some jurisdictions, an "attempted rescission . . . by the defendant does not render the original consent invalid for the reason that at a later time the defendant realized that his acquiescence might incriminate him." [83] Courts allowing such a withdrawal base their decision on the *Miranda* rule that a person subject to custodial interrogation may withdraw the waiver at any time. However, a substantial difference exists between the rights protected by the fourth and fifth amendments in their effect on a fair trial. There is not the possibility of admitting unreliable evidence with a fourth amendment case that occurs when the fifth amendment is involved. This distinction, which was recognized by the Supreme Court in Schneckloth v. Bustamonte,[84] should influence the approach of lower courts to withdrawal of a waiver of a fourth amendment right.[85]

Assuming that a withdrawal is legally possible, how does the suspect withdraw? Any positive action inconsistent with consent may amount to a valid withdrawal.[86]

Limiting the Scope of the Consent. A person may limit the scope of his or her consent.[87] Thus consent to search only a barn does not imply consent to search the cellar

76. Robinson v. United States, 325 F.2d 880 (5th Cir. 1964).

77. Higgins v. United States, 209 F.2d 819 (D.C.Cir. 1954). But see Leavitt v. Howard, 462 F.2d 992 (1st Cir. 1972).

78. United States v. Matlock, 415 U.S. 164, 94 S.Ct. 988, 39 L.Ed.2d 242 (1974). It is arguable that this standard should not be employed when consent is given by a person such as a wife consenting to search belongings of husband purely out of animosity. See, e. g., Cabey v. Mazurkiewicz, 431 F. 2d 839 (3d Cir. 1970) (dictum); Kelley v. State, 184 Tenn. 143, 197 S.W.2d 545, 546 (1946). Generally, the underlying motive has not been taken into consideration. See, e. g., McCravy v. Moore, 476 F.2d 281 (6th Cir. 1973); Commonwealth v. Martin, 358 Mass. 282, 264 N.E.2d 366 (1970).

79. Frazier v. Cupp, 394 U.S. 731, 89 S.Ct. 1420, 22 L.Ed.2d 684 (1969) (alternative basis for holding).

80. Cf. United States v. Matlock, 415 U.S. 164, 94 S.Ct. 988, 39 L.Ed.2d 242 (1974); Stoner v. California, 376 U.S. 483, 488, 84 S.Ct. 889, 11 L.Ed.2d 856 (1964).

81. People v. Botos, 27 Cal.App.3d 774, 104 Cal. Rptr. 193 (1972); People v. Martinez, 259 Cal.App. 2d 943, 65 Cal.Rptr. 920 (1968); People v. Shelton, 60 Cal.2d 740, 36 Cal.Rptr. 433, 388 P.2d 665 (1964).

82. People v. West, 3 Cal.3d 595, 91 Cal.Rptr. 385, 477 P.2d 409 (1970) ("defendant did not withdraw his consent until the officer discovered the marijuana").

83. United States v. Cady, 22 U.S.C.M.A. 408, 47 C.M.R. 345 (1973). But see United States v. Young, 471 F.2d 109 (7th Cir. 1972).

84. Smith v. Commonwealth, 197 Ky. 192, 246 S.W. 449 (1923).

85. 412 U.S. 218, 93 S.Ct. 2041, 36 L.Ed.2d 854 (1973).

86. Id.

87. People v. Shelton, 60 Cal.2d 740, 36 Cal.Rptr. 433, 388 P.2d 665 (1964) (refusal to assist officers in gaining access to the apartment); People v. Botos, 27 Cal.App.3d 774, 104 Cal.Rptr. 193 (1972) (after giving "consent" to search his car, the defendant threw the car keys in some bushes).

of another building.[88] Likewise, consent may be limited to an automobile and not include the person of the consenting party.[89] Also consent may be limited to the trunk of the car and not extend to its interior [90] or conversely, the consent may be limited to the interior, excluding the trunk.[91]

13. Routine Border Searches

Suggested Reading:

Holt v. United States, 218 U.S. 245, 31 S.Ct. 2, 54 L.Ed. 1021 (1910).

United States v. Guadalupe-Garza, 421 F.2d 876 (9th Cir. 1970).

Like the inventory rationale and the consent theory, the border search doctrine can also validate intrusions upon both persons and property. In 1789, the first customs statute was passed by the First Congress,[92] giving customs officials authority to search ships for smuggled goods on "suspicion of fraud." However, the statute prohibited the warrantless searches of homes and businesses. Because this statute was passed by the same Congress that proposed the fourth amendment, many commentators have argued that "border searches" are exempt from the fourth amendment or at least from the warrant requirement.[93] A second reason advanced for excluding border searches from the probable cause, specificity, oath, and warrant requirements of the fourth amendment is the language of the Supreme Court in Carroll v. United States: [94] "Travellers may be stopped in crossing an international boundary, because of national self-protection reasonably requiring one entering the country to identify himself as entitled to come in, and his belongings as effects which may be lawfully brought in." The reasonableness standard in the border search context is much laxer because of the national interests in protecting the integrity of our borders and in excluding, taxing, or limiting merchandise entering this country.

This section analyzes cases involving the boundaries of the United States with Mexico and Canada rather than in the airport context or international seaport standard.[95] The trigger for the border search doctrine is the individual's return to the United States across one of the boundaries.[96] Although each begins by stopping a person or vehicle, the searches at the border and its functional equivalent can be separated into several categories. The types of searches are an examination of the identification papers carried by the individual, an examination of the vehicle registration and license

amendment values are changing; second, the legislators may not have considered the fourth amendment; and third, the 1789 reasonableness standard is different from today's. This reasoning is based on a contemporary rather than an historical interpretation of the fourth amendment. See Chapter 15, supra.

94. 267 U.S. 132, 154, 45 S.Ct. 280, 285, 69 L.Ed. 543 (1925).

95. United States v. Ingham, 502 F.2d 1287 (5th Cir. 1974) (search of ship on docking); United States v. Skipwith, 482 F.2d 1272 (5th Cir. 1973) (applying border search rationale in airport context); United States v. Beck, 483 F.2d 203 (3d Cir. 1973) (border search rationale applied to justify search of two dock workers leaving pier at international port of entry).

96. Re-entry into the United States after being refused entry by both Mexico and Canada has been held to be a re-entry for border search purposes. People v. DeLoach, 58 Misc.2d 896, 297 N.Y.S.2d 220 (1969).

88. See United States v. Dichiarinte, 445 F.2d 126, 129 n. 3 (7th Cir. 1971).

89. Strong v. United States, 46 F.2d 257 (1st Cir. 1931).

90. Witt v. Commonwealth, 219 Ky. 519, 293 S.W. 1072 (1927).

91. State v. Johnson, 71 Wash.2d 239, 427 P.2d 705 (1967).

92. 1 Stat. 43 (1789).

93. For an argument that this history does not justify such a conclusion, see Note, Border Searches and the Fourth Amendment, 77 Yale L.J. 1007, 1011 (1968). The reasons are as follows: First, fourth

of the operator, a frisk of the person, a search of the individual's outer clothing, an examination of his or her arms, a strip search requiring a traveler to undress for visual examination and inspection of underclothing, and an examination of the body cavities such as the rectum and the vagina. Although none requires a warrant, the courts have set standards that must be met before the search may take place.

Examination of Identification Papers. The crossing of the border makes the examination of identification papers and citizenship reasonable.[97] Any invasion of privacy is minimal and outweighed by the national interest in preventing illegal entry.[98]

Examination of Vehicle Registration and Driver's License. Examination of vehicle registration and the driver's license is also reasonable, and occurs regularly even within this country during routine highway stops.[99]

Frisk, Search of Baggage, Clothing, and Vehicle. Although frisks of individuals and searches of outer clothing, baggage and vehicle are certainly searches within the meaning of the fourth amendment, they will not violate the amendment if conducted in a reasonable manner.[1] Most people crossing the border are on notice that they are subject to some type of examination. Moreover, because they are members of a neutral class and the search is conducted in the full view of other travellers it should not be considered

degrading, insulting, or peculiarly offensive. No alternative methods exist that could be used to perform this necessary function. Moreover, there is no reasonably articulable standard for probable cause that would be practical in light of the national interest.

Strip Search. The fact that the individual crosses an international border is justification for a frisk of his or her person and search of body clothing, baggage and vehicle. However, the courts have required additional justification for a "strip search." The following intrusions have been held too minor to constitute strip searches and thus do not require any additional justification:[2] orders to remove a coat;[3] roll up a sleeve,[4] remove a boot;[5] or expose the midriff.[6] These intrusions are much less than full disrobement. The exposure of the skin on the arm is common practice in today's society. The test that has been applied is whether the "suspect is forced to disrobe to a state which would be offensive to the average person."[7]

If there is justification for a strip search, which acts may the police require in addition to disrobing? The Ninth Circuit Court of Appeals has upheld the right of the agent to require a person to bend over at the waist and manually spread the buttocks.[8] This procedure allows the agent to examine

97. Witt v. United States, 287 F.2d 389, 391 (9th Cir. 1961). See also Ittig, The Rites of Passage: Border Searches and the Fourth Amendment, 40 Tenn.L.Rev. 329, 340 (1972); Note, From Bags to Body Cavities: The Law of Border Searches, 74 Colum.L.Rev. 53, 73 (1974).

98. Cf. California v. Byers, 402 U.S. 424, 91 S.Ct. 1535, 29 L.Ed.2d 9 (1971).

99. § 3, supra.

1. United States v. Flores, 477 F.2d 608, 609 (1st Cir. 1973) ("less objective and substantial than required for other searches"); United States v. Stornini, 443 F.2d 833, 835 (1st Cir. 1971) (search of baggage and clothing on subjective suspicion or random basis).

2. United States v. Chase, 503 F.2d 571, 574 (9th Cir. 1974).

3. Shorter v. United States, 469 F.2d 61 (9th Cir. 1972).

4. United States v. Murphree, 497 F.2d 395 (9th Cir. 1974).

5. United States v. Chase, 503 F.2d 571 (9th Cir. 1974).

6. United States v. Brown, 499 F.2d 829 (7th Cir. 1973).

7. Holt v. United States, 218 U.S. 245, 31 S.Ct. 2, 54 L.Ed. 1021 (1910); United States v. Chase, 503 F.2d 571, 574 (9th Cir. 1974).

8. United States v. Summerfield, 421 F.2d 684 (9th Cir. 1970) (per curiam); United States v. Castle, 409 F.2d 1347 (9th Cir. 1969). This does not include the vagina. United States v. Holtz, 479 F.2d 89 (9th Cir. 1973).

the thigh and crotch area. The examination of the rectal area includes wiping the area to determine if a lubricant has been applied.[9] (A lubricant, such as vaseline, facilitates placing items into the body orifice.)

The Ninth Circuit Court of Appeals has stated that a strip search must be based on real suspicion, that is, "subjective suspicion supported by objective, articulable facts." [10] In United States v. Guadalupe-Garza, the court indicated that these "facts must bear some reasonable relationship to suspicion that something is concealed on the body of the person to be searched." [11] Although it is unclear exactly which facts establish "real suspicion," the test seems to lie somewhere between mere suspicion and the indication required for a body cavity search. Some of the same facts used to justify a stop have been used to justify a strip search. Thus the search may be based on the actions of the defendant's companion.[12]

Although nervousness is insufficient by itself,[13] a corroborated tip [14] or information from a reliable informant [15] is sufficient. Also a strip search was held justified when an examination of defendant's pockets re-vealed several hundred undeclared emer-alds.[16]

The Fifth Circuit Court of Appeals has not adopted any specific test for when a strip search may be conducted. However, the Seventh Circuit Court of Appeals has applied a "real suspicion" test.[17]

Body Cavity Search. Many people have used their body cavities to smuggle contra-band into the country. Because of this fact at times searches are required which involve probing the vagina or rectum. Because of its intensity, a higher justification is re-quired for this type of search. "There must exist facts creating a clear indication, or plain suggestion, of smuggling. These facts (need not) reach the dignity of nor be the equivalent of "probable cause" necessary for an arrest and search at a place other than a border.[18]

Although some courts have held that even when time permits a warrant is not required for these searches,[19] these decisions may violate the fourth amendment or the due process clause of the fifth amendment.[20] The Ninth Circuit's view is that secreting con-traband in the rectum is more repulsive than invading the cavity to remove it.[21]

14. Extended Border Searches

Even after crossing the border, a person is not immune from searches by the Immigra-

---

9. See, e. g., United States v. Sosa, 469 F.2d 271 (9th Cir. 1972); United States v. Castle, 409 F.2d 1347 (9th Cir. 1969) (per curiam).

10. 421 F.2d 876, 879 (9th Cir. 1970).

11. Id.

12. United States v. Holtz, 479 F.2d 89, 91 (9th Cir. 1973).

13. United States v. Price, 472 F.2d 573 (9th Cir. 1973). Nervousness is not sufficient itself but when the defendant also has a bulge in his mid-section, it is sufficient. United States v. Mastberg, 503 F.2d 465 (9th Cir. 1974). When the defendant and two companions were nervous, all had needle marks on their arms, and an inspector found balloons in de-fendant's purse, a strip search of defendant was proper even though a strip search of her two male companions had yielded nothing.

14. United States v. Smith, 503 F.2d 1037 (9th Cir. 1974).

15. United States v. Castle, 409 F.2d 1347 (9th Cir. 1969) (per curiam).

16. United States v. Flores, 477 F.2d 608 (1st Cir. 1973).

17. United States v. Brown, 499 F.2d 829 (7th Cir. 1973).

18. Rivas v. United States, 368 F.2d 703, 710 (9th Cir. 1966).

19. United States v. Mason, 480 F.2d 563 (9th Cir. 1973). But see United States v. Holtz, 479 F.2d 89, 94 (9th Cir. 1973) (Ely, J., dissenting).

20. Cf. United States v. Carpenter, 496 F.2d 855 (9th Cir. 1974) (removal from rectum); United States ex rel. Guy v. McCauley, 385 F.Supp. 193 (E.D.Wis. 1974) (removal from pregnant woman's vagina).

21. Rivas v. United States, 368 F.2d 703 (9th Cir. 1966).

tion and Naturalization Service (INS) or by Border Patrol agents who have been authorized by the Attorney General to act as INS officers. These searches or seizures usually consist of stops for interrogation or searches of vehicles or persons conducted at either a permanent or temporary checkpoint or by a roving patrol.[22] Pursuant to statute an officer of the INS may "interrogate any alien or person believed to be an alien as to his right to be [in] or to remain in the United States."[23] Additionally, searching a car for aliens is permitted "within a reasonable distance of any external boundary" of this country.[24] This "reasonable distance" has been interpreted as one hundred air miles.[25] However, in Almeida-Sanchez v. United States,[26] the Supreme Court held that without probable cause or consent the roving border patrol may not stop and search a vehicle on an east-west California highway twenty miles north of the border. The Court refused to employ the border search doctrine to validate the search because the location of the search was neither the border itself nor the border's functional equivalent. The Court gave one example of a search at the functional equivalent of a border: "A search of the passengers and cargo of an airplane arriving at a St. Louis airport after a nonstop flight from Mexico City."[27] If the location is neither the border nor the border's functional equivalent, the authorities must establish consent to or probable cause for the search. In United States v. Ortiz,[28] the Court extended the same rule to searches at fixed checkpoints.

Then in United States v. Brignoni-Ponce,[29] the Court analyzed a less intrusive police practice, namely, a stop and inquiry into the detainee's citizenship by a roving patrol. The Court held that Border Patrol officers on roving patrol may stop vehicles and interrogate the occupants only if the officers have reasonable suspicion that the automobile contains illegal aliens. However, surprisingly, in United States v. Martinez-Fuente,[30] the Court declared that without either probable cause or reasonable suspicion, Border Patrol officers at permanent checkpoints may make warrantless stops and conduct limited interrogation concerning an automobile occupants' right to be in the United States. The Court sanctioned the traffic checking procedures at the San Clemente, California checkpoint.

15. Airport Searches

Suggested Reading:

United States v. Skipwith, 482 F.2d 1272 (5th Cir. 1973).

United States v. Epperson, 454 F.2d 769 (4th Cir. 1972).

A distinctive set of doctrines has evolved to justify searches of persons and property at airports. Various activities at the airport can amount to a search within the meaning of the fourth amendment. These include use of the profile and the magnetometer. The courts have uniformly indicated that the profile itself does not constitute a fourth amendment violation because it is reasonable under the circumstances.[31] Moreover, although

---

22. As to the categories, see United States v. Martinez-Fuerte, 428 U.S. 543, 96 S.Ct. 3074, 49 L.Ed.2d 1116 (1976).

23. 8 U.S.C.A. § 1357(a)(1).

24. 8 U.S.C.A. § 1357(a)(3).

25. 8 CFR 287.1.

26. 413 U.S. 266, 93 S.Ct. 2535, 37 L.Ed.2d 596 (1973).

27. Id. at 273.

28. 422 U.S. 891, 95 S.Ct. 2585, 45 L.Ed.2d 623 (1975).

29. 422 U.S. 873, 95 S.Ct. 2574, 45 L.Ed.2d 607 (1975).

30. 428 U.S. 543, 96 S.Ct. 3074, 49 L.Ed.2d 1116 (1976).

31. See, e. g., United States v. Skipwith, 482 F.2d 1272 (5th Cir. 1973); United States v. Lopez, 328 F. Supp. 1077 (E.D.N.Y.1971).

they have stated that the use of the magnetometer is a search under the fourth amendment,[32] it is reasonable in light of the minimal invasion of privacy, the security of travellers, and the necessity of preventing international incidents and providing for the orderly operation of commercial transportation.[33] While there can be disagreement whether the use of a profile or magnetometer constitutes a search, the frisk of a person is unquestionably a search requiring justification under the fourth amendment.[34] Some courts have held that if the profile is used with notice, fitting the profile alone is sufficient to justify a pat-down frisk.[35] Others have allowed a frisk if the person enters the boarding area.[36] Activating the magnetometer justifies a search of the person,[37] and some courts have held that the combination of fitting the profile and triggering the magnetometer is sufficient to justify a frisk.[38] However, one panel of the Second Circuit Court of Appeals has held that activating the magnetometer does not justify a frisk unless the individual is given an opportunity to withdraw or to remove items from his or her pockets and walk through the magnetometer a second time.[39]

Various theories are used to justify the airport search of the person including the stop and frisk theory,[40] the special area or boarding theory,[41] the administrative search theory,[42] the border search analogy,[43] and the implied consent theory.[44] Courts analyzing the frisk of a person have usually relied upon Terry v. Ohio.[45]

16. Detection Dogs

Suggested Reading:

United States v. Race, 529 F.2d 12 (1st Cir. 1976).

United States v. Solis, 393 F.Supp. 325 (C.D.Cal. 1975).

Is the Use of the Dog a Search? With the increased drug traffic in the United States, a new technique—the use of detection dogs—has developed. These dogs have been trained by federal and state agencies to detect the scent of marihuana, heroin, and some explosives. Because the dogs are now commonly used to examine people and parcels at customs points with the United States, the issue has arisen whether this constitutes a search. If the mere use of a detection dog is a search, the utility of the technique is severely limited. If the use of the dog is itself a search, the police must have an antecedent fourth amendment justification such

32. See, e. g., United States v. Bell, 464 F.2d 667 (2d Cir. 1972); United States v. Slocum, 464 F.2d 1180 (3d Cir. 1972); United States v. Epperson, 454 F.2d 769 (4th Cir. 1972); People v. Hyde, 12 Cal.3d 158, 115 Cal.Rptr. 358, 524 P.2d 830 (1974); People v. Kuhn, 33 N.Y.2d 203, 351 N.Y.S.2d 649, 306 N.E.2d 777 (1973).

33. People v. Hyde, 12 Cal.3d 158, 115 Cal.Rptr. 358, 524 P.2d 830 (1974).

34. United States v. Albarado, 495 F.2d 799 (2d Cir. 1974).

35. United States v. Dalpiaz, 494 F.2d 374 (6th Cir. 1974); United States v. Riggs, 474 F.2d 699 (2d Cir. 1973).

36. See, e. g., United States v. Fern, 484 F.2d 666 (7th Cir. 1973); United States v. Skipwith, 482 F.2d 1272 (5th Cir. 1973) (dictum).

37. United States v. Epperson, 454 F.2d 769 (4th Cir. 1972).

38. United States v. Bell, 464 F.2d 667 (2d Cir. 1972).

39. United States v. Albarado, 495 F.2d 799 (2d Cir. 1974).

40. United States v. Riggs, 474 F.2d 699 (2d Cir. 1973); United States v. Lopez, 328 F.Supp. 1077 (E.D.N.Y.1971).

41. United States v. Fern, 484 F.2d 666 (7th Cir. 1973); United States v. Mitchell, 352 F.Supp. 38 (E.D.N.Y.1972), aff'd 486 F.2d 1397 (2d Cir. 1973).

42. United States v. Davis, 482 F.2d 893 (9th Cir. 1973).

43. United States v. Skipwith, 482 F.2d 1272 (5th Cir. 1973); United States v. Moreno, 475 F.2d 44 (5th Cir. 1972).

44. United States v. Miner, 484 F.2d 1075 (9th Cir. 1973); United States v. Doran, 482 F.2d 929 (9th Cir. 1973).

45. 392 U.S. 1, 88 S.Ct. 1868, 20 L.Ed.2d 889 (1968).

as probable cause for employing the dog. If the use of the dog is not a search, the dog's alerts can be used to establish probable cause for an arrest or search. There are several theoretical approaches to the issue.

In deciding this issue, a determination could be made whether use of the dog is more analogous to the searches conducted by the King's messengers or to the use of a flashlight or an electronic bug. The answers to this question may depend on an analysis of the intent of the drafters of the fourth amendment.[46]

Another approach to the issue is a motivational concept, under which the test to determine the existence of a search is whether the law enforcement officials are seeking evidence of a crime. However, this simplistic approach has been rejected by the Supreme Court.[47]

Yet another approach is to analogize to the plain view doctrine. The Supreme Court has indicated that when a lawfully situated police officer detects evidence through his or her unaided senses, the evidence may be seized.[48] Therefore, the question becomes whether the use of the dog can be considered an extension of the natural senses. The Supreme Court has stated that the employment of sophisticated electronic eavesdropping devices used under certain circumstances constitutes a search.[49] If the function of a dog is closer to that of a policeman's flashlight rather than to that of an electronic bug, the use of the dog by itself is not a search.

Given the multitude of theoretical approaches to the issue, it is understandable that the courts have disagreed on whether the use of the dog constitutes a search. In United States v. Solis,[50] a federal district court equated the use of the dog with electronic recording equipment and held the use of the dog to be a search. The court asserted that "the use of the dogs constituted a search per se under the Fourth Amendment."[51] The court proceeded to hold that the use of the dog was an unreasonable search.

In United States v. Bronstein,[52] Judge Mansfield accepted the conclusion of the lower court in *Solis* that the use of a dog is a search. He rejected the "plain smell" analogy to the "plain view" doctrine. The judge argued that while a flashlight or binoculars merely enhance human senses, officers using a dog effectively replace their own senses "by the more sensitive nose of the dog in the same manner that a police officer's ears are replaced by a hidden microphone in areas where he could not otherwise hear because of the inaudibility of the sounds."[53] However, while the district court in *Solis* found the use of the dogs to be an illegal search, Judge Mansfield decided to uphold the search. He held that the use of detector dogs to search baggage consigned to a common carrier and placed in a common baggage area does not violate the fourth amendment when there are reasonable grounds to suspect the presence of contraband in the baggage.

To date, most of the courts that have passed on the issue have held that the use of the dog is not a search. In *Solis*, in reversing the lower court, the Ninth Circuit Court of Appeals accepted an analogy to the plain view doctrine. The court stated that the

---

46. Chapter 15, supra.

47. In Camara v. Municipal Court, 387 U.S. 523, 530, 87 S.Ct. 1727, 1731, 18 L.Ed.2d 930 (1967), the Court commented that it was "anomalous to say that an individual and his property would be fully protected by the Fourth Amendment only when he was suspected of criminal behavior."

48. § 19, infra.

49. Katz v. United States, 389 U.S. 347, 88 S.Ct. 507, 19 L.Ed.2d 576 (1967).

50. 393 F.Supp. 325 (C.D.Cal.1975).

51. Id. at 327.

52. 521 F.2d 459 (2d Cir. 1975). See also United States v. Race, 529 F.2d 12, 14 n. 2 (1st Cir. 1976). "We can discern no fourth amendment issue in the use of a dog for a routine check of commingled international and domestic freight in an airport warehouse." But see People v. Williams, 51 Cal.App.3d 346, 124 Cal.Rptr. 253 (1975).

53. United States v. Bronstein, 521 F.2d 459, 463 (2d Cir. 1975).

dogs "were not conducting an unconstitutional search, but rather monitoring the air in an area open to the public." [54] In *Bronstein*, the lead opinion analogized the dog to inanimate devices enhancing the natural senses. The court found that the dog is more analogous to a flashlight or binoculars than to a magnetometer: "The police dog sniffing procedure . . . is distinguishable in kind and degree. The magnetometer search is indiscriminate and the presence of sufficient metal willy-nilly leads to the body or baggage search." [55] The dog alerts only to contraband and does not indiscriminately disclose non-criminal conduct or conversations. Finally, the argument that the use of the dog is a search was rejected as "frivolous" in United States v. Fulero. [56]

Practical Aspects. If detector dogs are going to be used to establish probable cause, the police must meet certain standards. Unless probable cause already exists, the dog must be in an area where the police officer has a right to be—that is, where the police officer could use his own senses. When using the dog to establish probable cause, the police must prove the dog's reliability. At least one military court, however, has ruled that the mere certification of a detector dog by an appropriate canine training agency constitutes sufficient evidence of reliability for fourth amendment purposes. [57]

17. Inspections

Suggested Reading:

United States v. Biswell, 406 U.S. 311, 92 S.Ct. 1593, 32 L.Ed.2d 87 (1972).

Camara v. Municipal Court, 387 U.S. 523, 87 S.Ct. 1727, 18 L.Ed.2d 930 (1967).

Still another theory that can justify an intrusion upon either a person or property is the inspection rationale. The rationale is frequently used to justify searches of real property. Residential and commercial premises may be inspected for fire, health, and safety violations with the occupant's consent, with a search warrant, and in emergency circumstances. Although the courts require a less stringent standard for finding voluntary consent for administrative inspections,[58] coercion, intimidation, or misrepresentation will negate consent.[59] As with other consent searches, the search may not exceed the scope of the consent.[60]

In Camara v. Municipal Court,[61] the Supreme Court stated that the warrant requirement does not apply to emergency conditions,[62] citing the seizure of unwholesome food, compulsory smallpox vaccinations, health quarantine, and summary destruction of tubercular cattle. Other warrantless searches may relate to legitimate life-saving or emergency operations.[63] For example, during the course of fire fighting operations, firemen may seize evidence of arson or other

---

54. United States v. Solis, 536 F.2d 880 (9th Cir. 1976).

55. Id. at 882–83.

56. 498 F.2d 748 (D.C.Cir. 1974).

57. United States v. Thomas, 50 C.M.R. 114 (NCMR 1975); United States v. Black, 50 C.M.R. 15 (NCMR 1974).

58. United States v. Thriftimart, Inc., 429 F.2d 1006 (9th Cir. 1970).

59. United States v. Kramer Grocery Co., Inc., 418 F.2d 987 (8th Cir. 1969) (over objection, FDA inspector insisted on right to inspect); United States v. Anile, 352 F.Supp. 14 (N.D.W.Va.1973) (investigator told drug store owner he did not have choice about inspection).

60. Finn's Liquor Shop, Inc. v. State Liquor Authority, 31 A.D.2d 15, 294 N.Y.S.2d 592 (1968), aff'd 24 N.Y.2d 647, 301 N.Y.S.2d 584, 249 N.E.2d 440 (1969) (pocket of coat hanging in back room of liquor store).

61. 387 U.S. 523, 87 S.Ct. 1727, 18 L.Ed.2d 930 (1967).

62. Id. at 539.

63. See, e. g., United States v. Dunavan, 485 F.2d 201 (6th Cir. 1973); Perez v. State, 514 S.W.2d 748 (Tex.Cr.App.1974) (Search of unconscious defendant found in toilet stall was proper to learn identity and medical history).

crimes.[64] In Michigan v. Tyler,[64a] the Supreme Court upheld warrantless searches during fire fighting operations. The Court not only sanctioned such searches during the operations themselves; the Court also stated that once firefighters are in the building, they have a reasonable amount of time to investigate the cause of the fire and seize evidence of arson in plain view.

The search warrant required for an administrative inspection does not demand a showing of probable cause that a particular building or dwelling house violates a municipal ordinance. Rather a diminished probable cause standard governs. The inspector seeking a warrant can satisfy *Camara* by showing that it is likely that there are violations in the neighborhood or area where the particular building is situated. This diminished probable cause test was established by "balancing the need to search against the invasion which the search entails,"[65] that is by weighing the strong public interest in abating dangerous conditions against the limited invasion of privacy.[66] The Supreme Court recently reiterated the diminished probable cause warrant requirement in Marshall v. Barlow's Inc.,[66a] invalidating warrantless inspections under the Occupational Safety and Health Act of 1970. Even the diminished probable cause warrant requirement is inapplicable to the inspection of licensed premises, at least if a statute provides for unannounced inspections and if the conditions could be easily concealed.[67]

18. Emergency Searches

Suggested Reading:

People v. Neulist, 43 A.D.2d 150, 350 N.Y.S.2d 178 (1973).

A final doctrine capable of rationalizing a search of a person or property is the emergency doctrine. Pursuant to this doctrine, police officials may make a warrantless search to prevent either serious injury to people or substantial damage to property. The police must first have reasonable grounds to believe that an emergency exists that gives rise to a need for immediate action to protect life or property. The basis for this action must associate the emergency with the specific place to be searched. Examples of a connection between the objective signs and the place are screams coming from a building[68] or the odor of a decaying corpse emanating from the place.[69] Emergency action may not be primarily motivated by the intent to arrest or to seize evidence. Otherwise the action could serve as a subterfuge for a search.

After the police lawfully enter the premises, the issue arises of when the emergency ends. In Mincey v. Arizona,[69a] the Supreme Court rejected the argument that any search at the crime scene after a murder qualifies

---

64. Steigler v. Anderson, 496 F.2d 793 (3d Cir. 1974); State v. Felger, 19 Or.App. 39, 526 P.2d 611 (1974).

64a. 436 U.S. 499, 98 S.Ct. 1942, 56 L.Ed.2d 486 (1978).

65. Camara v. Municipal Court, 387 U.S. 523, 537, 87 S.Ct. 1727, 1735, 18 L.Ed.2d 930 (1967).

66. Id. at 532–40.

66a. 436 U.S. 307, 98 S.Ct. 1816, 56 L.Ed.2d 305 (1978).

67. United States v. Biswell, 406 U.S. 311, 92 S.Ct. 1593, 32 L.Ed.2d 87 (1972) (registered gun dealer); United States ex rel. Terraciano v. Montanye, 493 F.2d 682 (2d Cir. 1974) (pharmacist's records); Bren-

nan v. Buckeye Industries, Inc., 374 F.Supp. 1350 (S.D.Ga.1974) (warrantless inspection under the Occupational Safety and Health Act of 1970); Youghiogheny & Ohio Coal Co. v. Morton, 364 F.Supp. 45 (S.D.Ohio 1973) (warrantless inspection of coal mine under the Federal Coal Mine Health and Safety Act of 1969). But see Hogge v. Hedrick, 391 F.Supp. 91 (E.D.Va.1975) (inspection of massage parlor under local ordinance not permissible).

68. United States v. Barone, 330 F.2d 543 (2d Cir. 1964).

69. People v. Brooks, 7 Ill.App.3d 767, 289 N.E.2d 207 (1972).

69a. —— U.S. ——, 98 S.Ct. 2408, 57 L.Ed.2d 290 (1978).

as an emergency search. Most courts have indicated that once the police officers are properly on the scene, they are not constitutionally obligated to leave upon offering aid or removing the decedent's body.[70] When they have reason to believe that criminal activity is occurring or has taken place, the police may make an immediate search of the premises and maintain a status quo until evidence about the criminal activity can be gathered. In People v. Neulist,[71] the court stated that if after entering the police find evidence of a violent crime it is logical and necessary for the police to examine the crime scene, the entire premises. This is no more than "legitimate and restrained investigative conduct undertaken on the basis of ample factual justification." [72]

The emergency doctrine may justify a warrantless search of the person as well as the warrantless search of premises. Whenever an individual is found unconscious or incapacitated, the police may properly take necessary action to learn the identity of the person and to see if the person is carrying some indication of medical history.[73]

19. Plain View Seizures

Suggested Reading:

Coolidge v. New Hampshire, 403 U.S. 443, 91 S.Ct. 2022, 29 L.Ed.2d 564 (1971).

---

70. People v. Neulist, 43 A.D.2d 150, 350 N.Y.S.2d 178 (1973); United States v. Small, 23 U.S.C.M.A. 347, 47 C.M.R. 751 (1975). But see Root v. Gauper, 438 F.2d 361 (8th Cir. 1971).

71. 43 A.D.2d 150, 350 N.Y.S.2d 178 (1973).

72. Terry v. Ohio, 392 U.S. 1, 15, 88 S.Ct. 1868, 1876, 20 L.Ed.2d 889 (1968).

73. Vauss v. United States, 370 F.2d 250 (D.C.Cir. 1966); United States v. Yaraborough, 50 C.M.R. 159 (AFCMR 1975). "[C]onfronted with an unidentified airman in obvious distress . . . [the training instructor] had an unqualified right to detain the airman, have him searched and obtain medical assistance for him."

North v. Superior Court, 8 Cal.3d 301, 104 Cal. Rptr. 833, 502 P.2d 1305 (1972).

The last two warrantless search theories, plain view and abandonment, can be understood in two ways. One way is to consider the theories doctrines to support the conclusion that there is no fourth amendment intrusion in the case: There was no search because the item was in plain view, or there was no seizure because the item was abandoned property. The second way is to consider the doctrines theories for legalizing conceded fourth amendment intrusions. For sake of convenience, we have included the two doctrines in this chapter on warrantless searches.

A seizure may be justified under the plain-view doctrine if (1) the officer is lawfully situated at the time of the seizure [74] and if (2) a basis for the seizure exists.[75] A third requirement may be that the viewing or observation be inadvertent.[76]

There are three distinct factual variations of the first element of the doctrine. First, both a non-intrusive observation and the seizure take place in an area that is not constitutionally protected, such as a city street or open field.[77] This is the open-and-accessible concept. Second, a pre-intrusion observation is made of an area that is constitutionally protected, such as a house or automobile, from a vantage point outside the protected area.[78] This visual observation is not a search if the officer does not

---

74. This is the primary question and is probably the most difficult to answer. See Chapter 17, § 16. The various approaches are stated in this section dealing with dog searches.

75. Chapter 15, § 1, supra.

76. See generally Note, "Plain View"—Anything but Plain: Coolidge Divides the Lower Courts, 7 Loyola of Los Angeles L.Rev. 489 (1974).

77. See, e. g., Hester v. United States, 265 U.S. 57, 44 S.Ct. 445, 68 L.Ed. 898 (1924).

78. See, e. g., Brown v. State, 15 Md.App. 584, 292 A.2d 762 (1972).

violate an individual's right to privacy. The observation may furnish a basis for further action, such as immediate warrantless search of the premises, a warrant, hot pursuit, or immediate response by the police to protect life or to prevent serious damage to property. This is the open-view concept. Third, a post-intrusion observation occurs based on a prior valid intrusion into the constitutionally protected area.[79] This is the true plain-view concept. For example, an officer lawfully enters a house to serve an arrest warrant and observes contraband drugs in plain view in the living room.

Even if the object is in plain view, it may not be seized unless the second element of the doctrine is present: a basis for the seizure. The courts are divided over what standard is to be applied. The standard may depend on the nature of the object to be seized and where it is located at the time of the seizure. In Coolidge v. New Hampshire,[80] the Supreme Court stated that the seizure may take place when "it is immediately apparent to the police that they have evidence before them."[81] In rejecting the argument in Warden v. Hayden[82] that abolishing the "mere evidence" rule would lead to indiscriminate seizures, the Court stated that there "must, of course, be a nexus . . . between the item to be seized and the criminal behavior."[83] Recently, in a case upholding the seizure of documents not listed in a warrant, the Supreme Court stated, "[W]e conclude that the trained special investigators reasonably could have believed that the evidence specifically dealing with another lot in the Potomac Woods Subdivision could be used to show petitioner's intent

with respect to the Lot 13T transaction."[84] Because of the confusion concerning the correct standard, the lower courts have applied the immediately-apparent standard,[85] a probable-cause standard,[86] and a mere-suspicion standard.[87]

A third possible requirement of the plain-view doctrine is that the discovery of the evidence be inadvertent. The lead opinion in *Coolidge* indicates that the observation or viewing must be accidental. However, because only four justices joined in this portion of the *Coolidge* opinion, some state courts have indicated that inadvertence is not a requirement.[88] Even some adopting the requirement of inadvertence state that the requirement does not apply to contraband or stolen property.[89] Other courts adopting the requirement limit it to the third factual variation, the true plain-view context.[90]

---

79. See, e. g., Coolidge v. New Hampshire, 403 U.S. 443, 91 S.Ct. 2022, 29 L.Ed.2d 564 (1971).

80. 403 U.S. 443, 91 S.Ct. 2022, 29 L.Ed.2d 564 (1971).

81. Id. at 466.

82. 387 U.S. 294, 87 S.Ct. 1642, 18 L.Ed.2d 782 (1967).

83. Id. at 307.

84. Andresen v. Maryland, 427 U.S. 463, 96 S.Ct. 2737, 49 L.Ed.2d 627 (1976).

85. United States v. Gray, 484 F.2d 352 (6th Cir. 1973); United States v. Winston, 373 F.Supp. 1005 (E.D.Mich.1974).

86. People v. LaRocco, 178 Colo. 196, 496 P.2d 314 (1972); State v. Harwood, 94 Idaho 615, 495 P.2d 160 (1972); Shipman v. State, 291 Ala. 484, 282 So.2d 700 (1973); State v. Dimmer, 7 Wash.App. 31, 497 P.2d 613 (1973).

87. People v. Meneley, 29 Cal.App.3d 41, 55, 105 Cal.Rptr. 432, 436 (1972); North v. Superior Court, 8 Cal.3d 301, 104 Cal.Rptr. 833, 502 P.2d 1305 (1972).

88. Some courts have interpreted Mr. Justice Harlan's concurring opinion as an assent to this interpretation of the plain-view exception. Lewis v. Cardwell, 476 F.2d 467, 470 n. 4 (6th Cir. 1973). See also State v. Hills, 283 So.2d 220 (La.1973); State v. Bell, 62 Wis.2d 534, 215 N.W.2d 535 (1974) (dictum).

89. Coolidge v. New Hampshire, 403 U.S. 443, 471, 91 S.Ct. 2022, 2040, 29 L.Ed.2d 564 (1971). Compare United States v. Smollar, 357 F.Supp. 628 (S.D.N.Y. 1972), with Barnato v. State, 88 Nev. 508, 501 P.2d 643 (1972).

90. Brown v. State, 15 Md.App. 584, 292 A.2d 762 (1972).

20. Abandonment

Suggested Reading:

Abel v. United States, 362 U.S. 217, 80 S.Ct. 683, 4 L.Ed.2d 668 (1960).

United States v. Shelby, 431 F.Supp. 398 (E.D.Wis. 1977).

United States v. Maryland, 479 F.2d 566 (5th Cir. 1973).

People v. Krivda, 5 Cal.3d 357, 96 Cal.Rptr. 62, 486 P.2d 1262 (1971).

A police officer may lawfully seize without a warrant any item that has been discarded or thrown away and may examine the contents of the item, provided that he can lawfully proceed to the place where the item is located. If a person about to be arrested discards a piece of property, it may be lawfully seized by the police.[91] However, if the person was subjected to an illegal arrest or surveillance, any item discarded because of the arrest or surveillance will be held to have been illegally seized.[92]

Abandonment of Items in Trash Container. The earlier cases indicated that a warrantless seizure of items placed in a trash container did not violate the fourth amendment.[93] However, at least one recent California case has stated that a person has a reasonable expectation of privacy in garbage items with respect to all other people except garbage collectors until those items are so intermingled or comingled with other items as to be indistinguishable.[94] Other cases have indicated that whether trash will be considered abandoned depends on the location of the trash can.[95]

Abandonment of Vehicle. After a high speed chase, a driver of an automobile may abandon it and flee the scene. Such vehicle is considered abandoned, provided that the police officer's chase was lawful and that the driver has given up any reasonable expectation of privacy in the vehicle.[96]

Abandonment of Premises. When a suspect has demonstrated a lack of an intention to return to a premises, the police reasonably believe that the premises are abandoned, and the person entitled to possession allows the police to make a warrantless search, any items seized will be admissible. The key issue is whether there has, in fact, been an abandonment. In resolving this issue, the courts look at whether the rent was in arrears, whether a change of address card had been submitted to the post office, whether the renter had left the jurisdiction, leased another apartment, or changed his or her name, and whether the individual had checked out of the hotel or someone had seen the individual leave the hotel apparently with all his or her belongings.[97]

---

91. Capitoli v. Wainwright, 426 F.2d 868 (5th Cir. 1970); McClure v. United States, 332 F.2d 19 (9th Cir. 1964); Trujillo v. United States, 294 F.2d 583 (10th Cir. 1961).

92. Fletcher v. Wainwright, 399 F.2d 62 (5th Cir. 1968); United States v. Martin, 386 F.2d 213 (3d Cir. 1967). The court held that assuming the police action was illegal, if the defendant discards property because of a consciousness of guilt, the property will be admissible in evidence.

93. United States v. Dzialak, 441 F.2d 212 (2d Cir. 1971); United States v. Minker, 312 F.2d 632 (3d Cir. 1963).

94. People v. Krivda, 5 Cal.3d 357, 96 Cal.Rptr. 62, 486 P.2d 1262 (1971).

95. United States v. Jackson, 448 F.2d 963 (9th Cir. 1971) (trash placed in public receptables seizable); United States v. Harruf, 352 F.Supp. 224 (E.D.Mich. 1972) (seizure from containers used in common upheld); United States v. Kahan, 350 F.Supp. 784 (S.D. N.Y.1972) (defendant held to have right to privacy in waste basket in government office or basket located under the defendant's desk); People v. Superior Court, 23 Cal.App.3d 1004, 100 Cal.Rptr. 604 (1972) (loss of right to privacy where the defendant places the trash in his neighbor's trash can).

96. United States v. Edwards, 441 F.2d 749 (5th Cir. 1971).

97. United States v. Wilson, 472 F.2d 901 (9th Cir. 1973); Parman v. United States, 399 F.2d 559 (D.C. Cir. 1968).

CHAPTER 18

FOURTH AMENDMENT STANDING

1. Introduction

Assume that the government has conducted an illegal search or seizure and attempts to use evidence derived from the illegal intrusion at trial. The defendant will attempt to invoke the exclusionary rule to bar the admission of the evidence. In order to invoke the rule, the defendant must have a personal interest in the violation of fourth amendment rights. This requirement, called standing, is not unique to the fourth amendment, but rather is applicable generally to all constitutional challenges.[1] In Jones v. United States [2] the Supreme Court described the requisite relationship between an individual and the violation: "[O]ne must have been a victim of a search or seizure, one against whom the search was directed, as distinguished from one who claims prejudice only through the use of evidence gathered as a consequence of a search or seizure directed at someone else." [3]

The standing requirement is a corollary of the philosophic view that the primary purpose of the fourth amendment is to vindicate personal privacy rights. Given that premise, the Supreme Court has understandably required the defendant to show that the search or seizure violated the defendant's own fourth amendment rights. The standing requirement thus serves as a limitation on the exclusionary rule. If the philosophic purpose of the rule were to deter police misconduct, it should exclude all illegally seized evidence without inquiry into whose rights were violated. Beginning with the assumption that deterrence should be the rule's primary purpose, many commentators have urged the abolition of the standing requirement.[4]

---

1. See, e. g., Flast v. Cohen, 392 U.S. 83, 88 S.Ct. 1942, 20 L.Ed.2d 947 (1968) (As a constitutional minimum, standing requires that the party seeking relief have an adversary interest in the outcome of the controversy).

2. 362 U.S. 257, 80 S.Ct. 725, 4 L.Ed.2d 697 (1960).

3. Id. at 261.

4. Comment, Standing to Object to an Unreasonable Search and Seizure, 34 U.Chi.L.Rev. 342, 343 n. 8 (1967); Traynor, Mapp v. Ohio at Large in the Fifty States, 1962 Duke L.J. 319, 335; Allen, The *Wolf* Case: Search and Seizure, Federalism, and the Civil Liberties, 45 Ill.L.Rev. 1, 22 (1950).

2. "Vicarious" or "Third Party" Standing

Suggested Reading:

Alderman v. United States, 394 U.S. 165, 89 S.Ct. 961, 22 L.Ed.2d 176 (1969).

People v. Martin, 45 Cal.2d 755, 290 P.2d 855 (1955).

A number of states, including California, have heeded these urgings. In People v. Martin,[5] the California Supreme Court held that a defendant had standing to object at his trial to the admission of evidence illegally obtained from a third party. The court stressed the deterrent function of the exclusionary rule. The court reasoned that the traditional bar against 'third party" or "vicarious" standing "virtually invites law en-forcement officers to violate the rights of third parties and to trade the escape of a criminal whose rights are violated for the conviction of others by the use of the evidence illegally obtained against them." [6] The court concluded that judicial integrity dictated this result.[7]

However, in Wong Sun v. United States,[8] the Supreme Court rejected "third party" standing. The illegal arrest of Hom Way had led to the seizure of heroin from the home of Toy and the arrest of Wong Sun. The Court held that the heroin could be introduced against Wong Sun because he lacked standing to challenge the arrest of Hom Way or the search of Toy's home-laundry. In imposing the standing requirement, the Supreme Court attempted to reach a compromise between competing social values—control of police behavior and admissibility at trial of all material evidence. "The necessity for [the standing rule] was not eliminated by recognizing and acknowledging the deterrent aim of the rule. Neither those cases nor any others hold that anything which deters illegal searches is thereby commanded by the Fourth Amendment. The deterrent values of preventing the incrimination of those whose rights the police have violated have been considered sufficient to justify the suppression of probative evidence even though the case against the defendant is weakened or destroyed. We adhere to that judgment. But we are not convinced that the additional benefit of extending the exclusionary rule to other defendants would justify further encroachment upon the public interest in prosecuting those accused of crime and having them acquitted or convict-

---

5. People v. Martin, 45 Cal.2d 755, 290 P.2d 855 (1955). The court held that a defendant could properly invoke the exclusionary rule to bar the introduction of evidence obtained through the illegal search of a third party. See also People v. Sneed, 32 Cal.App.3d 535, 108 Cal.Rptr. 146 (1973); Yeargain v. State, 535 P.2d 693 (Okl.Cr.1973) (dictum). Oregon has proposed such a rule. Oregon Criminal Law Revision Commission, Part II, Pre-Arraignment Provisions, Art. 5, Search and Seizure § 40(1) (Prel.Draft No. 3, May 1972); ALI, § SS 290.1(5) (Proposed Official Draft 1975). But see Mabra v. Gray, 518 F.2d 512 (7th Cir. 1975) (defendant, who was with his wife in his automobile when both were arrested for armed robbery and murder, could not challenge a stationhouse search of his wife, for the search was not for the sole purpose of obtaining evidence against him); United States v. Jones, 518 F.2d 64 (9th Cir. 1975) (defendant has no standing to object to alleged unlawful vaginal search of female companion); United States v. Boston, 510 F.2d 35 (9th Cir. 1974) (defendant charged with illegal importation has no standing to object to vaginal search of female companion); United States v. Hunt, 505 F.2d 931, 942 (5th Cir. 1974) ("[A]lthough there may well be cases in which a principal may object to a search of his agent's papers or effects, this is not one."); United States v. Scheffer, 463 F.2d 567, 571–72 (5th Cir. 1972) (no standing to object to border search of co-defendant's automobile when defendants were not at scene of the first or second search); State v. Drake, 512 S.W.2d 166, 170 (Mo.App.1974) (no standing to object to illegal arrest of companion); Pilcher v. State, 503 S.W.2d 547 (Tex.Cr.App.1974) (no standing to object to search of companion).

6. People v. Martin, 45 Cal.2d 755, 760, 290 P.2d 855, 857 (1955).

7. Id. The defendant's right "to object to use the evidence must rest, not on a violation of his own constitutional rights, but on the ground that the government must not be allowed to profit by its own wrong and thus encouraged in the lawless enforcement of the law."

8. 371 U.S. 471, 83 S.Ct. 407, 9 L.Ed.2d 441 (1963).

ed on the basis of all the evidence which exposes the truth." [9] Since *Wong Sun*, the Supreme Court and most state courts have demanded that the defendant demonstrate personal standing.

3. Personal Standing

Suggested Reading:

Brown v. United States, 411 U.S. 223, 93 S.Ct. 1565, 36 L.Ed.2d 208 (1973).

Combs v. United States, 408 U.S. 224, 92 S.Ct. 2284, 33 L.Ed.2d 308 (1972).

Mancusi v. DeForte, 392 U.S. 364, 88 S.Ct. 2120, 20 L.Ed.2d 1154 (1968).

Jones v. United States, 362 U.S. 257, 80 S.Ct. 725, 4 L.Ed.2d 697 (1960).

United States v. Jeffers, 342 U.S. 48, 72 S.Ct. 93, 96 L.Ed. 59 (1951).

Because of the standing requirement, the defendant must demonstrate that the government intrusion violated his or her own privacy interests. What interests are sufficient to confer standing upon the defendant?

Interest in Premises Searched. The early law of standing derived from the common-law rules of trespass to real property.[10] Interpreting these rules, the courts held that standing applied only to a narrow class of people: the owners,[11] the lessee or licen-

see,[12] one with dominion,[13] an occupant of a boarding house,[14] or a guest in a hotel.[15] House guests[16] and employees[17] lacked standing. However, in the landmark case of Jones v. United States,[18] the Supreme Court declared: "[I]t is unnecessary and ill-advised to import into the law surrounding the constitutional right to be free from unreasonable searches and seizures subtle distinctions, developed and refined by the common law in evolving the body of private property law."[19] With this language the Court departed from conservative property law concepts in determining standing. The *Jones* Court announced new bases for establishing standing: (1) legitimate presence on the premises at the time of the search and (2) automatic standing when the defendant is charged with possessing the item seized.

Brown v. United States[20] emphasizes the restrictive nature of the interest in the property searched or seized. In order to confer standing, this interest must exist at the time of the alleged unlawful search or seizure. Defendants Brown and Smith were convicted of transporting stolen goods and conspiring with Knuckles to transport stolen goods in interstate commerce. Brown, together with Smith, was stealing goods from a warehouse. Both were arrested and placed in custody. After waiving their rights, they

---

9. Alderman v. United States, 394 U.S. 165, 174–75, 89 S.Ct. 961, 966–67, 22 L.Ed.2d 176 (1969).

10. See Edwards, Standing to Suppress Unreasonably Seized Evidence, 47 Nw.U.L.Rev. 471 (1952).

11. Id. United States v. Blok, 188 F.2d 1019 (D.C.Cir. 1951). "[Government employees] who merely work in a place no part of which is devoted to their exclusive use have been held to have no standing." Id. 1020–21. But the court of appeals stated that an employee does have standing with respect to lockers, desks, or other places in which he or she is "entitled to, and did, keep private property of a personal sort." Id. at 1021.

12. United States v. De Bousi, 32 F.2d 902 (D.Mass. 1929).

13. Steeber v. United States, 198 F.2d 615 (10th Cir. 1952).

14. McDonald v. United States, 335 U.S. 451, 69 S.Ct. 191, 93 L.Ed. 153 (1948).

15. Stoner v. California, 376 U.S. 483, 84 S.Ct. 889, 11 L.Ed.2d 856 (1964).

16. Gaskins v. United States, 218 F.2d 47 (D.C.Cir. 1955).

17. Kelley v. United States, 61 F.2d 843 (8th Cir. 1932).

18. 362 U.S. 257, 80 S.Ct. 725, 4 L.Ed.2d 697 (1960).

19. Id. at 266.

20. 411 U.S. 223, 93 S.Ct. 1565, 36 L.Ed.2d 208 (1973).

confessed that two months prior to their arrest, they had stolen goods from the warehouse and had sold the previously stolen goods after delivering them to Knuckles. A defective warrant to search Knuckles' store resulted in seizing some of the stolen property. Brown and Smith moved to suppress this evidence. However, they alleged no proprietary or possessory interest in Knuckles' premises or in the goods seized. The Supreme Court held that the defendants did not have standing, for at the time of the search they had an interest in neither Knuckles' store nor the property seized. The Court stated: "It is sufficient to hold that there is no standing to contest the search or seizure where, as here, the defendants: (a) were not on the premises at the time of the contested search or seizure; (b) had no proprietary or possessory interest in the premises; and (c) were not charged with an offense that includes as an essential element of the offense charged, possession of the seized evidence at the time of the contested search and seizure." [21]

Although *Brown* restricted this basis for standing by insisting that the interest exist at the time of the intrusion, since *Jones* the general trend has been to reduce the quantum of interest necessary in the property searched to establish standing. For example, a business person who regularly uses the suite of an associate might have a sufficient possessory interest to establish standing, [22] and a government employee has been held to have standing to object to a search of a wastebasket under his desk even though he had left his office for the day at the time of the search. [23] Also the defendant who intermittently lives in a house leased by a woman friend has standing. [24] However,

some courts have held that both a showing of a possessory interest and an expectation of privacy are necessary. [25] We shall analyze expectation of privacy as a basis for standing in a subsequent subsection.

Presence at the Site of the Search. *Jones* did not purport to discard the notion that standing could be established by showing a possessory or proprietary interest in either the premises searched or the property seized. The case merely added another interest to those protected by the fourth amendment—the interest of being "legitimately on [the] premises" at the time of the search. [26] Some courts have stressed *Jones'* language, holding that if a casual visitor is present at the time the police arrive, he or she has standing; [27] however, if the visitor leaves the premises before the police arrive or does not appear until after the police have made their search, he or she will not. [28] In a decision in late 1978, Rakas v. Illinois, [28a] the Supreme Court indicated that a mere casual visitor—in that case, a mere passenger in a car—would not have standing. The court stressed that in *Jones*, the defendant was an occupant of the apartment searched. In light of *Rakas*, mere presence at the site no longer seems to be an adequate basis for standing.

---

21. Id. at 229.

22. Baker v. United States, 401 F.2d 958 (D.C.Cir. 1968).

23. United States v. Kahan, 350 F.Supp. 784 (S.D. N.Y.1972).

24. Pierson v. State, 311 A.2d 854 (Del.1973).

25. United States v. Wilson, 472 F.2d 901 (9th Cir. 1972).

26. Jones v. United States, 362 U.S. 257, 267, 80 S.Ct. 725, 734, 4 L.Ed.2d 697 (1960). See also Mancusi v. DeForte, 392 U.S. 364, 368, 88 S.Ct. 2120, 2123, 20 L.Ed.2d 1154 (1968).

27. See, e. g., Brown v. United States, 411 U.S. 223, 93 S.Ct. 1565, 36 L.Ed.2d 208 (1973); Garza-Fuentes v. United States, 400 F.2d 219 (5th Cir. 1968); State v. Cadigan, 249 A.2d 750 (Me.1969).

28. But see Spinelli v. United States, 393 U.S. 410, 412 n. 2, 89 S.Ct. 584, 587 n. 2, 21 L.Ed.2d 637 (1969). "[I]t cannot matter . . . that the agents preferred to delay the arrest until petitioner stepped into the hallway."

28a. 24 Crim.L.Rep. 3,009 (U.S.S.C., December 5, 1978).

A person who is not legitimately on the premises [29] or in the vehicle certainly does not have standing.[30] One commentator has questioned the trespasser exception to the *Jones* rule: "The requirement of lawful presence would seem to run counter to the policy of Mapp. It is too late in the day to argue that a trespasser may be considered *caput lupinum* without constitutional rights." [31] This criticism is based on an erroneous view of the trespasser's position. The accused is not without rights—that is, even a trespasser may object to an illegal arrest. Moreover, the trespasser has standing to object to a search of his or her person.

Interest in the Property Seized. If the accused fails to show an interest in the place searched, the defendant can establish standing by demonstrating a possessory interest in the "property seized or examined" at the time of the contested search or seizure. This interest is sufficient to confer standing. This was the position taken by the Supreme Court in United States v. Jeffers.[32] In *Jeffers* narcotics had been seized in a hotel room occupied by the accused's two aunts, who had given him a key to the room and permitted him to come and go as he pleased. The government argued that the accused did not have standing because the search did not invade his privacy.[33] However, the Court held that the accused had standing to object, apparently on the basis of his interest in the drugs and not his interest in the room.[34]

Automatic Standing. The automatic standing rule is based on *Jones*. In that case, the accused was charged in a two-count indictment with having "purchased, sold, dispensed and distributed" narcotics not in or from the original stamped package and with having "facilitated the concealment and sale of" the narcotics knowing them to have been illegally imported. At trial, the accused's motion to suppress the evidence was denied on the ground that he lacked standing because he did not claim ownership of the narcotics found in the apartment where he was a guest. However, the Supreme Court held that the accused did have standing because of the nature of the government's case. "Since narcotics charges like those in the present indictment may be established through proof solely of possession of narcotics, a defendant seeking to comply with what has been the conventional standing requirement has been forced to allege facts the proof of which would tend, if indeed not be sufficient, to convict him." [35]

Thus the accused is in a dilemma and forced to elect between fourth and fifth amendment rights. To establish standing he or she is forced to claim either ownership of the premises searched or a possessory interest in the property seized. This testimony could then be used against him or her at trial.[36] The Court resolved the dilemma by holding that if possession at the time of

---

29. Cotton v. United States, 371 F.2d 385 (9th Cir. 1967).

30. Hodges v. State, 48 Ala.App. 217, 263 So.2d 518 (1972); Brisbane v. State, 233 Ga. 339, 211 S.E.2d 294 (1974) (no standing to object to search of stolen automobile); People v. Henenberg, 55 Ill.2d 5, 302 N.E.2d 27 (1973) (no standing to object to seizure of defendant's address book taken from automobile stolen by defendant); State v. Roberts, 210 Kan. 786, 504 P.2d 242 (1972); State v. Boutot, 325 A.2d 34 (Me.1974); Shope v. State, 18 Md.App. 472, 307 A.2d 730 (1973) (obtaining auto by false pretense); State v. Thompson, 490 S.W.2d 50 (Mo.1973) (passenger in stolen auto that was searched); Slyter v. State, 246 Miss. 402, 149 So.2d 489 (1963); Harper v. State, 84 Nev. 233, 440 P.2d 893 (1968); State v. Gaines, 40 Ohio App.2d 224, 318 N.E.2d 857, 69 O.O.2d 210 (1974) (no standing to object to search of stolen automobile); State v. Maloney, 111 R.I. 133, 300 A.2d 259 (1973); United States v. Simmons, 22 U.S.C.M.A. 288, 291, 46 C.M.R. 288, 291 (1973) ("[I]t is extremely difficult to believe that a trespasser in a motor vehicle can have standing."). But see United States v. McDonnell, 315 F.Supp. 152, 159 (D.Neb.1970).

31. Symposium, 59 Nw.U.L.Rev. 610, 630 (1964).

32. 342 U.S. 48, 72 S.Ct. 93, 96 L.Ed. 59 (1951).

33. Id. at 52.

34. Id.

35. Jones v. United States, 362 U.S. 257, 261–62, 80 S.Ct. 725, 731, 4 L.Ed.2d 697 (1960).

36. Fowler v. United States, 239 F.2d 93 (10th Cir. 1956); Heller v. United States, 57 F.2d 627 (7th Cir.

the contested search is an essential element of the offense charged, such possession confers standing without the accused's showing an interest in the premises searched or the property seized.[37] "The same element in this prosecution which has caused a dilemma, i. e., that possession both convicts and confers standing, eliminates any necessity for a preliminary showing of an interest in the premises searched or the property seized,

which ordinarily is required when standing is challenged." [38]

The dilemma that faced the accused in *Jones* no longer exists. In Simmons v. United States,[39] the Court held that testimony by an accused at a pretrial motion to suppress evidence cannot be used as part of the prosecution's case-in-chief against the accused. Because of *Simmons*, the accused can now establish the interest necessary for standing without fear that his or her words will be used against him or her at trial. However, no absolute prohibition exists against using this testimony for impeachment purposes. For example, in the federal courts if the accused's testimony during the case-in-chief is inconsistent with a pretrial statement, this statement may be used to impeach him or her.[40] Thus, if *Simmons* adequately protects the fifth amendment rights of an accused who wishes to establish standing, there is no basis for the continued application of the automatic standing rule.[41]

1932). See also Jones v. United States, 362 U.S. 257, 262, 80 S.Ct. 725, 731, 4 L.Ed.2d 697 (1960). "He has been faced . . . with the chance that the allegations made on the motion to suppress may be used against him at the trial, although that they may be is by no means an inevitable holding."

37. Simmons v. United States, 390 U.S. 377, 390, 88 S.Ct. 967, 974, 19 L.Ed.2d 1247 (1968) (emphasis added). The Court stated "that when . . . possession of the seized evidence is itself an *essential element of the offense* with which the defendant is charged," automatic standing should follow. Brown v. United States, 411 U.S. 223, 93 S.Ct. 1565, 36 L.Ed.2d 208 (1973). The defendants were convicted of transporting and conspiring to transport stolen goods in interstate commerce. The Court held that based on the nature of the prosecution case, the defendants did not have standing. "Here unlike *Jones*, the Government's case against petitioners does not depend on petitioners' possession of the seized evidence at the time of the contested search and seizure. The stolen goods seized had been transported and 'sold' by petitioners to Knuckles [a co-conspirator] approximately two months before the challenged search. The conspiracy and transportation alleged by the indictment were carefully limited to the period before the day of the search." Id. at 228–29. See also Jones v. United States, 362 U.S. 257, 263, 80 S.Ct. 725, 732, 4 L.Ed.2d 697 (1960); United States v. DeMarco, 488 F.2d 828, 829 n. 1 (2d Cir. 1973) ("[A]ll appellants have standing . . . because possession of the seized goods is an essential element of crime charged."); United States v. West, 453 F.2d 1351 (3d Cir. 1972) (if possession is essential element of offense, the defendant has standing to object to illegal search of third party.); United States v. Price, 447 F.2d 23 (2d Cir. 1971); State v. Matthews, 216 N.W.2d 90 (N.D.1974) (possession of goods is essential element of crime charged); Commonwealth v. Weeden, 457 Pa. 436, 322 A.2d 343 (1974). But when the defendants are charged with conspiracy to smuggle and transport heroin found in their car, they were held not to have standing; United States v. Sullivan, 488 F.2d 138 (5th Cir. 1973); United States v. Conrad, 448 F.2d 271 (9th Cir. 1973); United States v. Connor, 450 F.2d 334 (9th Cir. 1971). In none of these cases was the defendant present in the car at the time of the search; neither did they assert a possessory interest in the car.

38. Jones v. United States, 362 U.S. 257, 263, 80 S.Ct. 725, 732, 4 L.Ed.2d 697 (1960).

39. 390 U.S. 377, 88 S.Ct. 967, 19 L.Ed.2d 1247 (1968).

40. Harris v. New York, 401 U.S. 222, 91 S.Ct. 643, 28 L.Ed.2d 1 (1971); People v. Sturgis, 58 Ill.2d 211, 317 N.E.2d 545 (1974).

41. See Brown v. United States, 411 U.S. 223, 93 S.Ct. 1565, 36 L.Ed.2d 208 (1973). The Court stated that the "self incrimination dilemma, so central to the *Jones* decision, can no longer occur under the prevailing interpretation of the constitution." The Court "simply (saw) no reason to afford such 'automatic' standing where, as here, neither the risk of defendant's self-incrimination nor prosecutorial self-contradiction exists." United States v. Dye, 508 F.2d 1226, 1233 (6th Cir. 1974) ("The dilemma referred to in *Jones* . . . was removed by *Simmons*." The court held even though possession was an essential element, the defendant did not have automatic standing.); United States v. Smith, 495 F.2d 668, 670 (10th Cir. 1974) (dictum that automatic standing rule removed by *Simmons*). But see United States v. Hunt, 505 F.2d 931, 939 n. 9 (5th Cir. 1974); United States v. Mapp, 476 F.2d 67, 73 (2d Cir. 1973). In *Mapp*, the court refused to reject the automatic standing rule when possession is an essential element of the charged offense. United States v. Price, 447 F.2d 23, 29 (2d Cir. 1971).

Target of Search. An alternative method of establishing standing is showing that the individual was a "target" of the search in question. However, civilian jurisdictions have not dealt extensively with this issue. In *Jones*, Justice Frankfurter, writing for the Court, said: "In order to qualify as a 'person aggrieved by unlawful search and seizure' one must have been a victim of a search or seizure, one against whom the search was directed, as distinguished from one who claims prejudice only through the use of evidence gathered as a consequence of a search or seizure directed at someone else." [42] This passage was cited with approval in Alderman v. United States,[43] and apparently the concept continued to have some validity. In a concurring and dissenting opinion in *Alderman*, Mr. Justice Fortas stated that *Jones* "requires that we include within the category of those who may object to the introduction of illegal evidence 'one against whom the search was directed.' Such a person is surely the 'victim of an invasion of privacy' and a 'person aggrieved,' even though it is not his property that was searched or seized." [44] This language indicated that the target-of-the-search doctrine remained an open issue, and therefore it could be relied upon.[45] However, Illinois v. Rakas [45a] states that the target theory is not

an independent basis for standing. The court required that the defendant demonstrate that the search or seizure violated his or her personal expectation of privacy.

Expectation of Privacy. Mancusi v. DeForte [46] signals a further evolution in standing. The defendant, a teamster official, shared an office consisting of one large room with several other union officials. Although he was present and protesting, state law enforcement officials conducted a warrantless search of the office and seized certain union documents. The record does not indicate from which part of the office they were taken. However, the defendant spent a "considerable period of time" in the office and had "custody" of the documents "at the moment of their seizure." [47] The documents were admitted at the defendant's subsequent trial.

Despite the fact that the defendant was present on the premises at the time of the search, the Court used another rationale to justify its holding that standing existed. Citing Katz v. United States [48] for the proposition that the fourth amendment protection "depends not upon the property right in the invaded place but upon whether the area was one in which there was a reasonable expectation of freedom from governmental intrusion," [49] the Court posed the "crucial issue" as "whether . . . in light of all the circumstances, DeForte's office was such a place." [50]

The Court continued: "[I]t seems clear that if DeForte had occupied a 'private' office in the union headquarters, and union records had been seized from a desk or a filing cabinet in that office, he would have

42. Jones v. United States, 362 U.S. 257, 80 S.Ct. 725, 4 L.Ed.2d 697 (1960). See also United States ex rel. Coffey v. Fay, 344 F.2d 625 (2d Cir. 1965) (alternative holding); Wion v. United States, 325 F.2d 420 (10th Cir. 1963) (target test applied). Cf. Mabra v. Gray, 518 F.2d 512 (7th Cir. 1975) (target test rejected when search of wife was not "solely" directed at husband). But see United States v. Cangiano, 491 F.2d 906, 912 (2d Cir. 1974) (no standing to contest search of apartment in which defendant had no possessory interest, even though defendant was the target of investigation).

43. Alderman v. United States, 394 U.S. 165, 89 S.Ct. 961, 22 L.Ed.2d 176 (1969).

44. Id. at 173.

45. United States v. Mapp, 476 F.2d 67, 71 (2d Cir. 1973).

45a. 24 Crim.L.Rep. 3,009 (U.S.S.C., December 5, 1978).

46. 392 U.S. 364, 88 S.Ct. 2120, 20 L.Ed.2d 1154 (1968).

47. Id. at 368–69.

48. 389 U.S. 347, 88 S.Ct. 507, 19 L.Ed.2d 576 (1967).

49. Mancusi v. DeForte, 392 U.S. 364, 368, 88 S.Ct. 2120, 2123, 20 L.Ed.2d 1154 (1968).

50. Id.

had standing. In such a 'private' office, DeForte would have been entitled to expect that he would not be disturbed except by personal or business invitees, and that records would not be taken except with his permission or that of his union superiors." [51] The Court said that the defendant sharing an office did not "fundamentally" change his expectation of privacy.[52] Under these circumstances he could reasonably have expected that only the other union officials and their guests would enter the office and that the documents would not be examined without the permission of union officials.[53] The Court, referring to *Jones* to support their conclusion, then stated: "There was no indication that the area of the apartment near the bird's nest had been set off for Jones' personal use, so that he might have expected more privacy there than in the rest of the apartment." [54] The reference to *Jones* here raises the question of whether the standing concept was in fact expanded. As Mr. Justice Black pointed out in his dissent, if the majority was relying on the "legitimately on the premises" test,[55] there was no need for any analysis of "reasonable expectations."

Any argument that *DeForte* does not signal change is dispelled in Combs v. United States.[56] After a joint trial,[57] Combs

and his father were convicted of receiving, possessing, and concealing twenty-six cases of tax-paid whiskey.[58] The cases were seized from a shed on the father's farm pursuant to a warrant which the government conceded to be insufficient under *Aguilar's* [59] two-pronged test. The court of appeals did not rule on the sufficiency of the warrant, holding only that Combs lacked standing to challenge the legality of the search and seizure. However, the Supreme Court vacated the judgment and remanded the case because the record of trial was "virtually barren of the facts necessary to determine whether petitioner had an interest and connection with the searched premises that gave rise to a 'reasonable expectation [on his part] of freedom from governmental intrusion' upon those premises." [60]

Illinois v. Rakas [61] reinforced *Combs*. In *Rakas* the Court indicated that it is abandoning the traditional bases for standing; it will no longer be sufficient for the defendant to merely claim an interest in the premises or presence. Rather, to establish standing, the defendant will always have to show that the government conduct invaded his or her personal expectation of privacy.

---

51. Id. at 369.

52. Id.

53. Id.

54. Id. at 370.

55. Id. at 376.

56. 408 U.S. 224, 92 S.Ct. 2284, 33 L.Ed.2d 308 (1972). See also United States v. Burke, 506 F.2d 1165, 1170–71 (9th Cir. 1974) (repeated use of brother's van sufficient to grant defendant standing); United States v. Hunt, 505 F.2d 931, 941 (5th Cir. 1974) (Relying on expectation of privacy theory, the court denied standing even though defendant owned property seized illegally.); Commonwealth v. Hall, 366 Mass. 790, 323 N.E.2d 319 (1975) (Relying on expectation of privacy theory, the court held defendant had standing to object to search of hallway in apartment building subject to defendant's exclusive con-

trol.); Commonwealth v. White, 459 Pa. 84, 327 A.2d 40 (1974) (Defendant had reasonable expectation that items at mother's apartment would be free from governmental intrusion whether or not he was physically present when search was directed solely against him).

57. Combs v. United States, 408 U.S. 224, 225 n. 1, 92 S.Ct. 2284, 2285 n. 1, 33 L.Ed.2d 308 (1972). "Both men were convicted, but the accused's father did not appeal; another [co-accused] at the trial was the accused's brother, who was acquitted on a related charge."

58. 18 U.S.C.A. § 659.

59. Aguilar v. Texas, 378 U.S. 108, 84 S.Ct. 1509, 12 L.Ed.2d 723 (1964).

60. Combs v. United States, 408 U.S. 224, 227, 92 S.Ct. 2284, 2286, 33 L.Ed.2d 308 (1972).

61. 24 Crim.L.Rep. 3,009 (U.S.S.C., December 5, 1978).

CHAPTER 19

THE EXCLUSIONARY RULE AND DERIVATIVE EVIDENCE

1. Introduction

If the court concludes that there has been an illegal, government search or seizure and that the defendant has standing, the exclusionary rule applies. The exclusionary rule is a delicate balance of competing interests: the interests in aggressive law enforcement and protecting individual privacy rights. Despite the social cost, the Supreme Court has adopted the exclusionary rule, but it has recognized that when the cost to society of excluding reliable, relevant evidence outweighs the deterrent effect on police conduct, there is no reason to apply the rule.[1] In Alderman v. United States,[2] the Court pointed out that the denial of standing is a method of preventing the exclusionary rule from operating beyond the point of "diminishing returns."[3] The Court could grant a defendant standing to object to any illegally seized evidence, but instead it has decided that giving the exclusionary rule such broad applicability would be too costly. Similarly,

the Court could permit the rule to operate to exclude all evidence derived from an illegal intrusion. However, the Court has concluded that at times the relation between an illegal intrusion and derivative evidence is so attenuated that the balance of interests favors admitting the evidence. This chapter discusses the tests for determining when the exclusionary rule renders derivative evidence inadmissible.

2. The Norm of Inadmissibility

Suggested Reading:

Brown v. Illinois, 422 U.S. 590, 95 S.Ct. 2254, 45 L.Ed.2d 416 (1975).

Wong Sun v. United States, 371 U.S. 471, 83 S.Ct. 407, 9 L.Ed.2d 441 (1963).

The exclusionary rule applies not only to original evidence but may under some circumstances also apply to derivative evidence. The application of the rule to the latter has been commonly referred to as the "fruit of

---

1. Alderman v. United States, 394 U.S. 165, 89 S.Ct. 961, 22 L.Ed.2d 176 (1969).

2. Id.

3. Id. at 174.

the poisonous tree" doctrine.[4] In the absence of objection, the prosecution is not required to prove that its evidence has a lawful origin.[5] However, after the accused has raised the issue by objection or motion to suppress and has established a reasonable possibility that the evidence proffered by the government resulted from an unlawful intrusion, the evidence is inadmissible unless the prosecution can prove that it is not a product of illegal activity.[6] If the prosecution does not carry its burden, all the evidence which the record shows to be a result of the illegal activity is inadmissible. To shift the burden to the prosecution, the defense must prove more than that the police obtained the evidence after the illegal intrusion. The defense must show a reasonable possibility of a causal connection between the illegal intrusion and the evidence.[7]

The exclusionary rule was initially applied to derivative evidence by the Supreme Court in Silverthorne Lumber Co. v. United States.[8] Although the Court extended the rule to derivative evidence, the Court stressed the importance of a showing of substantial causal connection between the illegal intrusion and the evidence. The Court stated that if the knowledge of facts or evidence is "gained from an independent source they may be proved like any others." In Nardone v. United States,[9] the Court indicated that it is not enough to show a causal connection between the original evidence and the derivative evidence because as "a matter of good sense . . . such connection may have become so attenuated as to dissipate the taint." Another refinement occurred in Wong Sun v. United States,[10] where the Court stated: "We need not hold that all evidence is 'fruit of the poisonous tree' simply because it would not have come to light but for the illegal actions of the police. Rather, the more apt question in such a case is whether, granting establishment of the primary illegality, the evidence to which instant objection is made has been come at by exploitation of that illegality or instead by means sufficiently distinguishable to be purged of the primary taint."

At this point, the complexity of determining the admissibility of derivative evidence is apparent. On the one hand, *Silverthorne* and *Wong Sun* establish that evidence is inadmissible if a substantial causal connection exists between a prior illegal intrusion and the subsequent acquisition of the evidence by the police. On the other hand, *Wong Sun* precludes the lower courts from using a simple "but for" test in determining the existence of the substantial causal connection.[11] The *Wong Sun* Court rejected a "but for" test by declaring that evidence may be admissible even though "it would not have come to light but for the illegal actions of the police." To gain a better understanding of the meaning of "substantial causal

---

4. Nardone v. United States, 308 U.S. 338, 60 S.Ct. 266, 84 L.Ed. 307 (1939) (where the term was originally used).

5. Cf. Bivens v. Six Unknown Agents of the Federal Bureau of Narcotics, 403 U.S. 388, 91 S.Ct. 1999, 29 L.Ed.2d 619 (1971).

6. Oaks, Studying the Exclusionary Rule in Search and Seizure, 37 U.Chi.L.Rev. 665 (1970).

7. Harrison v. United States, 392 U.S. 219, 225, 88 S.Ct. 2008, 2011, 20 L.Ed.2d 1047 (1968); United States v. Decker, 16 U.S.C.M.A. 397, 402, 37 C.M.R. 17, 22 (1967) (Derivative evidence will not be held to be inadmissible when the "evidence . . . demonstrates that in the accused's 'own view . . . the confession was in no way a result of the search.'"); United States v. DeLeo, 5 U.S.C.M.A. 148, 162, 17 C.M.R. 148, 162 (1954) (Assuming the search was illegal, the court stated that the accused's confession could not have been the result of the search, for he testified that he did not know about the search and that the confession was drafted by the police officials.). Nardone v. United States, 308 U.S. 338, 341, 60 S.Ct. 266, 267, 84 L.Ed. 307 (1939).

8. 251 U.S. 385, 392, 40 S.Ct. 182, 183, 64 L.Ed. 319 (1920).

9. 308 U.S. 338, 341, 60 S.Ct. 266, 267, 84 L.Ed. 307 (1939).

10. 371 U.S. 471, 487–88, 83 S.Ct. 407, 417–18, 9 L.Ed.2d 441 (1963).

11. United States v. Bacall, 443 F.2d 1050 (9th Cir. 1971); United States v. Friedland, 441 F.2d 855 (2d Cir. 1971); People v. Pettis, 12 Ill.App.3d 123, 298 N.E.2d 372 (1973).

connection," we shall now consider two leading Supreme Court precedents on derivative evidence.

Wong Sun v. United States. In *Wong Sun*, federal narcotics agents arrested Hom Way for wrongful possession of heroin. He informed the agents that he bought the heroin from "Blackie Toy." On the morning of Hom Way's arrest, federal agents went to a laundry operated by the defendant, James Wah Toy, even though there was nothing indicating that James Toy was Blackie Toy. When Toy answered the door, an agent told him that they had come to pick up laundry. Toy informed him that the laundry was closed, and when the agent identified himself as a federal narcotics agent, Toy slammed the door and ran down the hallway through his laundry shop into the bedroom where his wife and child were sleeping. The agents knocked down the door and followed Toy into the living area, where he was apprehended in the bedroom.

Responding to an agent's question, he stated that he did not possess any narcotics but that he knew an individual, named "Johnny," who did have some. He then took the agents to Johnny's house. Entering the house pointed out by Toy, the agents found Johnny Yee in the bedroom where they seized some heroin.

Within an hour of these arrests, both individuals were taken to the stationhouse, where Yee said that he had bought the heroin four days earlier from a Chinese known only as "Sea Dog." Sea Dog was identified as the defendant, Wong Sun. Toy then led the narcotics agents to Wong Sun's house, and they were admitted by the defendant's wife, who told them that Wong Sun was sleeping in the bedroom. Seven agents went to the back bedroom, where they handcuffed Wong Sun and made a thorough search of the apartment.

On the same day as the arrest of Toy, Yee, and Wong Sun, Toy and Yee were arraigned before a magistrate and released on their own recognizance. The next day Wong Sun was also arraigned and released on his own recognizance. A few days after the arrest, all three were advised of their right to withhold information, that any information could be admitted in evidence, and that they were entitled to the advice of an attorney. After the agents questioned each one separately, the suspects made statements. Neither Toy nor Wong Sun would sign their statements.

The issues before the Supreme Court were the admissibility of Toy's oral statement in his bedroom at the time of his arrest, the admissibility of the heroin obtained from Yee, and the admissibility of Toy's and Wong Sun's unsigned pretrial statements. The Supreme Court held that no probable cause had existed to arrest Toy and that Toy's oral statement taken immediately after his unauthorized arrest was a fruit of the police officers' illegal activity. Because the heroin was also a fruit of Toy's illegal arrest, the majority held that the heroin taken from Yee was inadmissible against Toy. The Court rejected the government's argument that Toy's statement in his bedroom was a product of his own free will, for under the circumstances the statement could not be considered voluntary.[12] At least six officers had broken down his door and followed him into his bedroom, where he was immediately handcuffed and arrested in the presence of his wife and child.

However, the Court ruled that Wong Sun's unsigned oral statement was admissible because of the lack of connection between Toy's illegal arrest and the statement.[13] This statement was made after Wong Sun had been released on bail and had voluntarily returned to the police stationhouse. Wong Sun's statement was certainly derivative evidence; Toy's illegal arrest was the first link in a chain of events culminat-

---

12. Wong Sun v. United States, 371 U.S. 471, 482–83, 83 S.Ct. 407, 414–15, 9 L.Ed.2d 441 (1963).

13. Id. at 491.

ing in the statement. However, one of the events in the chain, Wong Sun's return to the stationhouse for further interrogation, was sufficiently voluntary to purge the statement from the taint of Toy's illegal arrest. *Wong Sun* was thus a significant pronouncement on the derivative evidence problem. The Court revisited the problem in Brown v. Illinois.[14]

Brown v. Illinois. In *Brown*, the Supreme Court identified various factors to be considered in determining whether a confession is the inadmissible fruit of an illegal arrest. At 7:45 p. m., police officials broke into Brown's apartment and searched it. Later when Brown was walking up the stairs leading to the rear entrance of his apartment, a man with a revolver approached him and said, "Don't move, you are under arrest." All this took place without probable cause or a warrant for either an arrest or a search. Two detectives then took Brown to the police station. During the twenty minute drive, one of the detectives asked Brown a number of questions, which he either evaded or answered falsely.

At the police station he was placed in a room containing only a table and chairs and left alone for some minutes while the police officers obtained the file on the murder he allegedly committed. Upon returning, the police officers advised the defendant of his *Miranda* rights. The defendant waived his rights, and the questioning produced a two-page statement. Several hours later Brown was again questioned by the prosecutor. At approximately 3:00 a. m., Brown gave a second statement, which he refused to sign.

The Illinois Supreme Court held that the defendant's confessions were admissible, for the *Miranda* warnings had automatically purged the taint of his illegal arrest. The Supreme Court unanimously rejected this view of the *Miranda* warnings' impact. A

majority also found that on the facts of the case, both statements were fruits of the illegal arrest. The Court stated that the *Miranda* warnings alone cannot sever the causal connection between the illegal arrest and the confession; to hold otherwise would dilute the effect of the exclusionary rule regardless of how wanton or purposeful the fourth amendment violation had been.[15] The Court indicated that no single fact is controlling on the issue of whether the confession is a fruit of the illegal arrest. Although *Miranda* warnings are important in determining if the confession is obtained by an exploitation of the arrest, they are not the only factor. "The temporal proximity of the arrest and the confession, the presence of intervening circumstances . . . and particularly, the purpose and flagrancy of the official misconduct are all relevant." [16] In analyzing these factors, the Court noted that Brown's first statement had been taken two hours after the illegal arrest and that the second statement was a result of the first. Additionally, the arrest here portrayed a "quality of purposefulness." [17] The "impropriety of the arrest was obvious," and the investigation was an "expedition for evidence." [18]

However, a person can confess as the result of "free will unaffected by the initial illegality. The question whether a confession is the product is a free will under *Wong Sun* must be answered on the facts of each case." [19] In this case the Court found Brown's statement to be more like Toy's than like Wong Sun's. *Brown* stands for the proposition that to purge the taint from derivative evidence, an intervening act must be truly voluntary. Wong Sun's confession after returning to the stationhouse was genuinely voluntary while the Court realisti-

14. 422 U.S. 590, 602, 95 S.Ct. 2254, 2261, 45 L.Ed. 2d 416 (1975).

15. Id.
16. Id. at 603–04.
17. Id. at 605.
18. Id.
19. Id. at 603.

cally concluded that at the time of his confessions, Brown was still acting under the duress of the illegal arrest.

3. Purging the Taint from Derivative Evidence

Suggested Reading:

United States v. Atkins, 22 U.S.C.M.A. 244, 46 C.M.R. 244 (1973).

Smith & Bowden v. United States, 324 F.2d 879 (D.C.Cir. 1963).

Wong Sun holds that acts intervening between an illegal intrusion and the subsequent acquisition of derivative evidence may purge the taint from the evidence. What factors should a court consider in deciding whether intervening events have sufficiently attenuated the connection between the initial illegality and the derivative evidence? In the light of *Wong Sun* and *Brown*, some factors to be considered are: the lapse of time between the illegal conduct and the obtaining of the derivative evidence; the nature of the relationship between the person engaged in the original illegality and the law enforcement agent obtaining the secondary evidence; the advice to the defendant of his or her rights under *Miranda* and of the fact that evidence obtained previously is inadmissible; the defendant's perception of the illegally seized evidence; the presence or absence of any aggravating circumstances; any voluntary act by the defendant severing the connection with the derivative evidence; and any voluntary act by a third party severing the connection between the primary evidence and the derivative evidence.

The Lapse of Time. A significant factor relied upon in *Wong Sun* was the lapse of time between the defendant's arrest and the obtaining of his oral statement. "On the evidence that Wong Sun had been released on his recognizance after a lawful arraignment, and had returned voluntarily several days later to make the statement, we hold that the connection between the arrest and the statement had 'become so attenuated as to dissipate the taint.' " [20]

The time factor was also important in *Brown*, where the defendant's first statement was made two hours after the illegal arrest and the second statement was "clearly the result and fruit of the first." [21] A comparison between *Brown* and *Wong Sun* demonstrates that time is a factor that can either support or negate an independent source. The Court found a "dramatic contrast" between the statement in *Wong Sun* and the statement in *Brown*. In *Wong Sun* the confession came several days after the illegality, and it was preceded by the defendant's lawful arraignment and release from custody.

However, as *Brown* implies, the time factor should not be controlling. If it were, the police could easily subvert the fruit of the poisonous tree rule.[22] The police could intentionally make an illegal raid, obtain evidence, postpone tasting the fruit for the required time span, and then use the primary evidence

---

20. Wong Sun v. United States, 371 U.S. 471, 491, 83 S.Ct. 407, 419, 9 L.Ed.2d 441 (1963). United States v. Beasley, 485 F.2d 60, 64 (10th Cir. 1973). One factor relied upon in concluding that the witness's testimony was not fruit was that her "decision to testify came some three days after the [illegal] arrest, and this time separation, together with the other circumstances, creates a high degree of probability that she exercised her own volition which leads to the conclusion that there was no exploitation of the illegal search."

21. Brown v. Illinois, 422 U.S. 590, 605, 95 S.Ct. 2254, 2262, 45 L.Ed.2d 416 (1975).

22. Collins v. Beto, 348 F.2d 823, 828 (5th Cir. 1965) ("To use time as a significant factor would postpone the tasting of the fruit but would not diminish its temptation."); Rogers v. United States, 330 F.2d 535, 541 (5th Cir. 1964); People v. Martin, 240 Cal. App.2d 653, 657, 49 Cal.Rptr. 888, 891 (1966) ("[W]e hasten to add that our interpretation of 'attenuated' does not rest on whether there is a time interval between the illegal arrest and the confession."). But see Commonwealth ex rel. Craig v. Maroney, 348 F.2d 22, 29 (3d Cir. 1965).

to obtain other evidence which would be admissible.

The States of Mind of the Police and the Defendant. The states of mind of the police and the defendant may help to establish or negate a causal connection between the original illegality and the derivative evidence. This principle was illustrated in United States v. Atkins.[23] The arresting officer in *Atkins* stated that he would not have arrested the defendant without knowing of the defendant's inadmissible statement. The court found that the arresting officer's testimony left no doubt that the apprehension was a direct exploitation of the defendant's unwarned statement. Because the officer did not regard the other circumstances as sufficient to amount to probable cause, the improperly obtained admission was a controlling factor in obtaining evidence of the defendant's guilt. The courts have also indicated that the defendant's view of the primary evidence may attenuate the causal connection. In United States v. Schafer,[24] the court held that even if the search had been illegal, the defendant's statement was not a result of the illegality, for when he made the statement, the defendant did not know about the incriminating evidence obtained in the search; moreover, the incriminating evidence was not used in questioning the defendant. Likewise, in United States v. DeLeo,[25] the court ruled that the defendant's confession would not be considered a fruit of the poisonous tree, for the defendant admitted that the confession was in no way the result of the search.

Aggravating Circumstances. The presence or absence of "oppressive," "coercive," or "aggravating" circumstances in obtaining subsequent statements "[has] more often than not been viewed as determinative in

subsequent decisions at lower court levels." [26] In *Brown* the Court said that the "purpose and flagrancy of the official misconduct" were relevant factors in deciding whether the confession was a fruit of the illegal arrest. The illegal arrest there had a "quality of purposefulness," [27] and as was noted, the officers "knew or should have known" that the arrest was without probable cause and unconstitutional.[28]

In his concurring opinion in *Brown*, Mr. Justice Powell wrote that he would "require the clearest indication of attenuation in cases in which official conduct was flagrantly abusive of Fourth Amendment rights." [29] An example of this flagrancy occurs when absence of probable cause is so obvious that it becomes clear that the arrest was used as a pretext for achieving collateral objectives. It is in these cases with intentional or aggravating circumstances that the "deterrent value of the exclusionary rule is most likely to be effective, and the corresponding mandate to preserve judicial integrity . . . most clearly demands that the fruits of official misconduct be denied." [30]

Miranda **Warnings.** In *Brown* the Court unanimously rejected the argument that a *Miranda* warning alone could sever a connection between an illegal arrest and subsequent confession. However, in his concurrence in *Brown*, Justice Powell stated: "[W]ith the exception of statements given in the immediate circumstances of the illegal arrest—a constraint I think is imposed by existing exclusionary rule of law—I would not require

---

26. Wong Sun v. United States, 371 U.S. 471, 486 n. 12, 83 S.Ct. 407, 417 n. 12, 9 L.Ed.2d 441 (1963); Pitler, "The Fruit of the Poisonous Tree" Revisited and Shepardized, 56 Calif.L.Rev. 579, 595 n. 80 (1968); Ruffin, Out on a Limb of the Poisonous Tree: The Tainted Witness, 15 U.C.L.A.L.Rev. 32, 65–66 & n. 120 (1967).

27. Brown v. Illinois, 422 U.S. 590, 605, 95 S.Ct. 2254, 2262, 45 L.Ed.2d 416 (1975).

28. Id. at 604.

29. Id. at 605.

30. Id. at 606.

---

23. 22 U.S.C.M.A. 244, 46 C.M.R. 244 (1973).

24. 13 U.S.C.M.A. 83, 87, 32 C.M.R. 83, 87 (1962).

25. 5 U.S.C.M.A. 148, 163, 17 C.M.R. 148, 163 (1954).

more than proof that effective *Miranda* warnings were given and that the ensuing statement was voluntary in the Fifth Amendment sense." [31]

Under *Miranda* the individual is warned of his or her rights to remain silent and to have counsel. However, he or she is not told that the illegally obtained evidence cannot be used. If the individual is warned that the evidence seized as a result of the arrest is inadmissible or that the evidence was illegally seized, the warning will sever any presumptive influence.[32]

Voluntary Act of the Defendant. One of the factors supporting the holding that Wong Sun's statement was not a fruit of the poisonous tree was the fact that several days after his arraignment he had voluntarily returned to the police station to make the statement.[33] The voluntariness of the defendant's act in producing the evidence was also emphasized in United States v. Bennett,[34] where the court stated that the presumptive influence would be severed if the government told the defendant that his prior statement was inadmissible in evidence. If after such a warning, he nevertheless makes a statement, the second statement would be admissible.

Voluntary Act of Third Party. Suppose that as a result of an illegal search, the police discover the identity of a potential prosecution witness. Can the witness's testimony be considered derivative evidence like the defendant's confession in *Brown?*

Until recently, the Supreme Court had not considered if the voluntary decision of a

witness to testify at trial severs the causal connection between the testimony and the illegality.[35] The Fifth Circuit Court of Appeals, however, had stated that the testimony of a witness is not to be treated the same as is physical evidence. "[B]eguiling as it is, we resist the temptations of the serpent of another tree, not only to eat, but swallow the fruit or the fruit of the fruit, or the theory of the fruit, poison, palatable or forbidden." [36]

A number of alternative positions should be considered in approaching the issue of a witness's testimony as "poisonous fruit": (1) The fruit of the poisonous tree doctrine does not apply to the testimony of a witness.[37] (2) When a witness has initially refused to testify but has then changed his or her mind, the testimony is deemed unpoisoned.[38] (3) The admissibility of the testimony depends upon the nature of the initial fourth amendment violation.[39] (4) The testimony of a witness should be treated no differently from other derivative evidence.[40] The following is an examination of these approaches to determining whether a witness's testimony is a fruit of the poisonous tree.

Volitional Act of the Witness. The language of Chief Justice Burger, then a member of the Court of Appeals, in Smith & Bowden v. United States,[41] has led some courts to believe that the simple volitional decision of the person to testify as a witness is enough to sever any connection with illegally obtained evidence. However, the facts in *Smith &*

31. Brown v. Illinois, 422 U.S. 590, 612, 95 S.Ct. 2254, 2266, 45 L.Ed.2d 416 (1975).

32. Cf. United States v. Bennett, 7 U.S.C.M.A. 97, 21 C.M.R. 223 (1956). But see Ruffin, Out on a Limb of the Poisonous Tree: The Tainted Witness, 15 U.C. L.A.L.Rev. 32, 68 (1967).

33. Wong Sun v. United States, 371 U.S. 471, 491, 83 S.Ct. 407, 419, 9 L.Ed.2d 441 (1963). See also People v. Walker, 203 Cal.App.2d 552, 556, 21 Cal. Rptr. 692, 695 (1962).

34. 7 U.S.C.M.A. 97, 21 C.M.R. 223 (1956).

35. Cf. Michigan v. Tucker, 417 U.S. 433, 94 S.Ct. 2357, 41 L.Ed.2d 182 (1974).

36. Gissendanner v. Wainwright, 482 F.2d 1293 (5th Cir. 1973).

37. Id. at 1296.

38. Smith and Bowden v. United States, 324 F.2d 879 (D.C.Cir. 1963).

39. Cf. Wong Sun v. United States, 371 U.S. 471, 486 n. 12, 83 S.Ct. 407, 417 n. 12, 9 L.Ed.2d 441 (1963).

40. Commonwealth v. Fogan, 449 Pa. 552, 296 A.2d 755 (1973); Commonwealth v. Cephas, 447 Pa. 500, 291 A.2d 106 (1973); People v. Albea, 2 Ill.2d 317, 118 N.E.2d 277 (1954).

41. 324 F.2d 879 (D.C.Cir. 1963).

Bowden square more with the second approach—that is, that the witness is not considered a fruit of the poisonous tree when the witness initially refuses to testify but then changes his or her mind. The identity of the witness in *Smith & Bowden* was discovered as a result of the defendant's confession during a period of illegal detention, which was violative of Federal Rule of Criminal Procedure 5(a). Although when the witness was first located, he gave no information adverse to the defendant, after reflecting on the matter, he agreed to testify at the defendant's trial. The court ruled that under these facts the witness's testimony could not be considered tainted. "The fact that the name of a potential witness is disclosed to police is of no evidentiary significance . . . since the living witness is an individual human personality whose attributes of will, perception, memory and volition interact to determine what testimony he will give. The uniqueness of this human process distinguishes the evidentiary character of a witness from the relative immutability of inanimate evidence." [42] Such reasoning is not foreclosed by *Wong Sun*, where the Court said: "Thus, verbal evidence which derives so immediately from an unlawful entry and an unauthorized arrest as the officer's action in the present case is no less the 'fruit of official illegality than the more common tangible fruits of the unwarranted intrusion.'" [43] This language refers to the defendant's statement made at the time of the illegal entry and arrest, not to a third-party utterance. The language in *Wong Sun* and *Smith & Bowden* has given some support to the position that the simple volitional decision to testify purges the taint.

Nevertheless, the argument that the volitional act is sufficient to purge a taint might be rejected, for such a rule encourages more widespread violation of constitutional rights, especially in the area of gambling, narcotics,

and illicit whiskey. In these areas a common investigative technique is to arrest the individuals at the bottom of a pyramid-type organization in order to obtain evidence against those controlling the operation. Admitting the testimony might encourage further fourth amendment violations. The principal purpose of the exclusionary rule is to deter police misconduct, not to encourage it. Using the volitional alternative or the alternative that the exclusionary rule does not apply to the testimony of a live witness would run counter to this primary purpose. Notwithstanding this policy argument, the Supreme Court seemed to adopt the volitional test in its 1978 decision in United States v. Ceccolini.[43a]

Initial Refusal to Testify. Some courts, relying on *Smith & Bowden*, have indicated that a witness's testimony is purged of any taint if he or she initially refuses to testify and then voluntarily changes his or her mind. However, it is doubtful whether the subsequent decision to testify is truly voluntary. The prosecution can resort to compulsory process and force the person to appear as a witness. If the person refuses to answer unobjectionable questions, the judge can hold him or her in contempt. The government can threaten a perjury prosecution to induce truthful testimony. In most cases, the potential witness's change of mind will not be as voluntary as the decision to return to the stationhouse in *Wong Sun*.

Outrageous or Substantial Violation Test. A third alternative is excluding the testimony of a witness when there has been an outrageous or substantial violation of the right to privacy, providing that the exclusion of the testimony would tend to deter similar violations in the future. This test, which has been proposed by the American Law Institute,[44] finds some support in *Wong Sun*.

42. Id. at 882.

43. Wong Sun v. United States, 371 U.S. 471, 485–86, 83 S.Ct. 407, 416, 9 L.Ed.2d 441 (1963).

43a. 435 U.S. 268, 55 L.Ed.2d 268, 98 S.Ct. 1054 (1978).

44. ALI Model Code of Pre-Arraignment Procedure § SS 290.2 (Official Draft 1975).

However, although the Court held that the bedroom statement by Toy was inadmissible because of the "oppressive" circumstances, the facts did not evince an outrageous violation.

An example of outrageous violation is the situation in Rochin v. California.[45] There three policemen broke into the defendant's house and arrested him in the bedroom. When the defendant swallowed what appeared to be drugs, the officers attempted to forcibly extract the drugs. Because that failed, the officers directed a doctor to induce vomiting by forcing an emetic through a tube into Rochin's stomach.

In determining whether a particular violation of the fourth amendment is "substantial," all relevant circumstances must be conjunctively considered; however, according to the ALI, the following factors are particularly important: the extent of the police deviation from sanctioned conduct; the willfulness of the violation; the extent to which privacy was invaded; and the prejudice to the defendant's ability to defend himself or herself. The first factor is the deviation from conduct permissible under the present norms governing the legality of searches and seizures—that is, probable cause for the search, valid authorization for the warrant, the execution of the warrant within the proper period, its return pursuant to the prevailing rules, a lawful entry, and proper

scope of the search. The second factor examines the flagrancy of the officer's conduct to determine whether there was a substantial violation. The third factor considers the extent of the violation. In applying this criterion the court will be able to distinguish among residences, businesses, cars, open fields, and curtilages. However, this criterion may be interpreted in various ways, for the "extent to which the privacy was invaded" can refer to property law concepts, to a subjective expectation of privacy, or to a reasonable expectation of privacy. The last criterion probably means that if the improper activity has impaired "the defendant's ability to defend himself or herself," for example, destruction of defense evidence, this activity by itself may show a substantial violation.

The outrageous and substantial violation test is objectionable in that it allows broad discretion in evaluating the criteria. One of the primary reasons the Supreme Court rejected the pre-*Miranda* voluntariness test was the Court's inability to supervise the lower courts'[46] administration of the vague voluntariness standard. The Court would encounter similar difficulty in supervising the lower courts' administration of the outrageous and substantial violation test.

---

45. 342 U.S. 165, 72 S.Ct. 205, 96 L.Ed. 183 (1952).

46. See Kamisar, A Dissent from the Miranda Dissents: Some Comments on the "New" Fifth Amendment and the Old "Voluntariness" Test, 65 Mich.L. Rev. 59 (1966).

PART 6
FIFTH AMENDMENT PROTECTIONS

CHAPTER 20
THE PRIVILEGE AGAINST SELF-INCRIMINATION

1. Overview of the Privilege

Despite its status as an element of the Bill of Rights, the fifth amendment privilege against self-incrimination remains one of the Constitution's most controversial provisions. Viewed by some as an essential ingredient of liberty,[1] the privilege has been characterized by others as an unnecessary infringement on the public's right to bring criminals to justice.[2] Both of these views have highly respected adherents and legitimate arguments behind them.

A brief caution is appropriate before proceeding. The privilege against self-incrimination in its most basic sense is the privilege of an accused or of a witness to refuse to testify in an incriminating fashion in a judicial proceeding. As such, the privilege, although related to, is distinct from the law of confessions dealing with the voluntariness and admissibility of pretrial statements. In the United States there has been a tendency, justified in part by the Supreme Court's decision in Miranda v. Arizona,[3] to combine the two areas. However, the privilege and the law of confessions[4] have somewhat different origins and justifications which merit separate treatment.

The privilege can be summarized in this fashion: *In an official proceeding, the holder may assert a privilege against compulsory, testimonial incrimination unless (1) the holder has waived the privilege or (2) the government has supplanted the privilege by granting immunity.* A study of the privilege resolves itself into an analysis of these issues: What types of proceedings does the privilege apply to? Who qualifies as a holder of the privilege? How does the holder assert the privilege? What is the nature of the privilege? What constitutes compulsion for purposes of the privilege? What kinds of acts are considered testimonial? What is in-

---

1. See, e. g., E. Griswold, The Fifth Amendment Today (1955); Boudin, The Constitutional Privilege in Operation, 12 Lawyer's Guild Rev. 128, 149 (1949).

2. See, e. g., Friendly, The Fifth Amendment Tomorrow: The Case for Constitutional Change, 37 U.Cin. L.Rev. 671 (1968).

3. 384 U.S. 436, 86 S.Ct. 1602, 16 L.Ed.2d 694 (1966).

4. See Chapter 21, infra.

crimination? What acts constitute waiver? And finally what sort of immunity must the government grant to supplant the privilege? We shall now briefly consider each of these issues.

The Types of Proceedings the Privilege Applies to. Before the privilege against self-incrimination can be asserted in an interrogation, the interrogation must have sufficient indicia of officiality.[5] The fifth amendment protects an individual from being compelled to be a witness against himself in any criminal case. The phrase "in any criminal case" has been construed broadly. The right against self-incrimination stems directly from *government* compulsion. Accordingly the privilege generally applies to government or quasi-government proceedings. Only government has the power to compel testimony on pain of contempt.

Suggested Reading:

Lefkowitz v. Turley, 414 U.S. 70, 94 S.Ct. 316, 38 L.Ed.2d 274 (1973).

McCarthy v. Arnstein, 266 U.S. 34, 45 S.Ct. 16, 69 L.Ed. 158 (1920).

Judicial Proceedings Including Discovery. It is well settled that the right against self-incrimination is applicable in all judicial proceedings,[6] including preliminary hearings and grand juries. Nevertheless a number of other questions about the privilege remain to be resolved. For example the privilege usually applies during judicial proceedings, but what of its application during discovery? This issue has tended to take two related forms: "alibi" statutes and prosecutorial discovery in general.

Under the alibi statutes, now in force in the federal courts and a number of states,[7] the accused must give advance notice of his or her intention to raise an alibi defense, his or her location at the time of the offense, and frequently the names of his or her witnesses. Failure to comply may result in preclusion of the alibi defense. The reason for the rule is clear; it prevents unnecessary surprise and avoids waste of judicial time. However, this attempt to remove part of the gamesmanship from criminal trials results in requiring the defendant to divulge information which may be incriminating. Traditionally the accused has had the right to refuse to present any evidence and to rely instead on the prosecution's inability to prove a case. Under the alibi statutes the defendant must decide his or her strategy in advance, chancing that he or she will supply vital information. Despite this, the alibi statutes have generally been upheld.

---

5. Lefkowitz v. Turley, 414 U.S. 70, 77, 94 S.Ct. 316, 322, 38 L.Ed.2d 274 (1973).

6. "The Amendment not only protects the individual against being involuntarily called as a witness against himself in a criminal prosecution but also privileges him not to answer official questions put to him in any other proceeding, civil or criminal, formal or informal, where the answers might incriminate him in future criminal proceedings." Lefkowitz v. Turley, 414 U.S. 70, 77, 94 S.Ct. 316, 322, 38 L.Ed.2d 274 (1973). The Court had previously found that the privilege extended to juvenile proceedings, In re Gault, 387 U.S. 1, 87 S.Ct. 1428, 18 L.Ed.2d 527 (1967), and also to civil proceedings, McCarthy v. Arnstein, 266 U.S. 34, 40, 45 S.Ct. 16, 17, 69 L.Ed.

158 (1920) (bankruptcy case), although its method of application may differ. Baxter v. Palmigiano, 425 U.S. 308, 96 S.Ct. 1551, 47 L.Ed.2d 810 (1976) (dicta stating that "the Fifth Amendment does not forbid adverse inferences against parties to civil actions when they refuse to testify in response to probative evidence offered against them").

7. In 1976 14 states had notice of alibi statutes that allowed preclusion of the defense in the event of non-compliance.

The federal government has adopted both a notice of alibi requirement, Fed.Cr.Proc.Rule 12.1, 18 U.S.C.A., and a general prosecution discovery right, Fed.Cr.Proc.Rule 16(b), 18 U.S.C.A. Florida's notice of alibi statute was sustained by the Supreme Court in Williams v. Florida, 399 U.S. 78, 90 S.Ct. 1893, 26 L.Ed.2d 446 (1970). However, the Court later indicated that to avoid due process pitfalls such statutes must be reciprocal in their operation. Wardius v. Oregon, 412 U.S. 470, 93 S.Ct. 2208, 37 L.Ed.2d 82 (1973).

Prosecutorial discovery raises much the same dilemma. While the defense now has rather wide-ranging discovery, any attempt by the prosecution to obtain material from the defense results in a possible violation of the defendant's privilege. In Jones v. Superior Court,[8] the defendant, charged with rape, gave notice of a defense of impotence and received a continuance to obtain necessary evidence. The prosecution replied with a request for the names and addresses of the doctors who were to be subpoenaed by the defense, the names and addresses of doctors who had treated Jones, and all medical records and X-rays. Jones raised his right against self-incrimination and lost. The issue reached the Supreme Court of California, where Chief Justice Traynor sustained the discovery order, holding in part that Jones was required to supply the names and addresses of witnesses he intended to call at trial and copies of the reports and X-rays he intended to offer. Justice Traynor's reasoning was simple: He was merely requiring an advance notice of material that would necessarily be revealed at trial. In dissent Justice Peters pointed out that the prosecution could now use the information in preparation of its case-in-chief. The dissent in *Jones* is probably correct. To hold otherwise is to coerce the accused into divulging critical information to be used against him or her on pain of its later inadmissibility.

The future of prosecutorial discovery is unclear.[9] Following *Jones*, Rule 16(b) of the

Federal Rules of Criminal Procedure allows prosecution discovery of defense papers, documents, or reports that the defense intends to offer at trial if the defense has first sought the same type of evidence from the prosecution. As McCormick suggests,[10] if such discovery is to be allowed, abandoning any effort to justify it under the privilege and conceding that this inroad is warranted by society's needs are more appropriate.

In all the discovery cases to date, the major element required of the defense (other than the accused's location at the time of offense and names of witnesses in the alibi cases) consists of documents, and in most of these cases the documents desired are not the defendant's private personal records. Since the Supreme Court's 1886 decision in Boyd v. United States,[11] it has been an article of faith that the fifth amendment extends to documents. Nevertheless recent Supreme Court decisions appear to be narrowing the scope of the privilege to private papers akin to diaries.[12] Should this trend

---

8. 58 Cal.2d 56, 22 Cal.Rptr. 879, 372 P.2d 919 (1962) (hereinafter cited as *Jones*). *Jones* has since been virtually limited to its facts. See Reynolds v. Superior Court, 12 Cal.3d 834, 117 Cal.Rptr. 437, 528 P.2d 45 (1974); Prudhomme v. Superior Court, 2 Cal. 3d 320, 85 Cal.Rptr. 129, 466 P.2d 673 (1970). See Louisell, Criminal Discovery and Self-Incrimination: Roger Traynor Confronts the Dilemma, 53 Calif.L. Rev. 89 (1965).

9. The ultimate future of alibi statutes is unclear despite Williams v. Florida, 399 U.S. 78, 90 S.Ct. 1893, 26 L.Ed.2d 446 (1970). Compare Brecheen v. Dycus, 547 P.2d 980 (Okl.Cr.App.1976) [Judge could not require defense to disclose all evidence intended

for use at trial during a preliminary hearing.]; Scott v. State, 519 P.2d 774 (Alaska 1974) [Mere notice of alibi is acceptable but other requirements such as names and addresses of witnesses violate the self-incrimination clauses of the federal and Alaska Constitutions.], with State ex rel. Keller v. Criminal Ct., 262 Ind.App. 420, 317 N.E.2d 433 (1974); People v. Sanders, 110 Ill.App.2d 85, 249 N.E.2d 124 (1969) [Discovery order requiring the defense to yield documents for impeachment sustained.]; People v. Damon, 24 N.Y.2d 256, 299 N.Y.S.2d 830, 247 N.E.2d 651 (1969); State v. Grove, 65 Wash.2d 525, 398 P.2d 170 (1967); State v. Malzac, 19 Crim.L.Rep. 2413 (Minn. July 9, 1976) (Defense required to disclose defense ballistics report and video tape deposition of defense expert); People ex rel. Bowman v. Woodard, 63 Ill.2d 382, 349 N.E.2d 57 (1976) (Defense required to disclose reports of experts which it intended to use at trial but not materials which would not be used or relating to experts not to be called). See also United States v. Wright, 489 F.2d 1181 (D.C. Cir. 1973), holding that the prosecution could not demand access to defense investigator's notes of witness interviews in the absence of defense discovery or use of the notes by witnesses.

10. C. McCormick, Handbook of the Law of Evidence 284 (2d ed. 1972).

11. 116 U.S. 355, 6 S.Ct. 524, 29 L.Ed. 746 (1886).

12. See, e. g., Fisher v. United States, 425 U.S. 391, 96 S.Ct. 1569, 48 L.Ed.2d 39 (1976). In *Fisher*, the

continue many of discovery cases will simply no longer come within the scope of the privilege.

Legislative Inquiries. Legislative bodies must conduct investigations to determine the necessity for new legislation.[13] Such official inquiries supply, via the power to hold witnesses in contempt, the coercion necessary to render the fifth amendment applicable. A number of Supreme Court cases [14] have clearly held that the privilege applies to legislative investigations.

Despite this fact a number of problems remain. One difficulty, applicable also to witnesses before courts, concerns the waiver doctrine, under which a witness who has answered one or more questions may be held to have lost his or her entire privilege.[15] More important is the fact that at times Congress and other legislatures have utilized their proceedings to harass witnesses.[16] While witnesses may be immunized against any prosecutorial use of their statements, such immunity does not protect against widespread press coverage of misdeeds or aberrant ac-

tions or views. For example, the charge "Fifth-Amendment Communist" made by the late Senator Joe McCarthy had serious effects on the reputations of many witnesses who exercised their privilege. While in judicial proceedings reason might exist to abandon self-infamy as an aspect of the right against self-incrimination, a limited form granting legislative witnesses the right to testify in secret might be appropriate. The difficulty with such a position is of course, that for every case of unfortunate exposure of private acts and beliefs to the public, there may be more instances when the public has a critical need to be exposed to the testimony (e. g. Watergate). The conflict between the positions seems irreconcilable and perhaps must be left in the hands of the legislators themselves.

Police Interrogations. Traditionally the right against self-incrimination did not apply to police interrogations, for police lack formal legal power to coerce answers in the same fashion as can courts and legislatures.[17] However, in Miranda v. Arizona,[18] the Supreme Court determined that the fifth amendment privilege does apply to police questioning because of the informal coercion during police interrogations. The expectation that suspects should talk to police is inherent in American society, and the police use psychologically coercive tactics to gain admissions. The police thus exercise the type of social coercion against which the original privilege against self-incrimination was designed to protect.

Psychiatric Inquiries. A problem not yet fully resolved is the application of the right against self-incrimination to compelled psychiatric examinations. In the usual criminal case a defendant who intends to offer an insanity defense is examined by a defense psychiatrist. To rebut expected testimony

---

Court acknowledged that surrender of documents "tacitly concedes the existence of the papers demanded and their possession or control" but held that the possible testimonial aspects of such a situation would depend on the individual facts of each case or class of cases. This in itself represents an inroad into the privilege (somewhat similar to the effects of prosecutorial discovery).

13. While not explicitly authorized by the Constitution, Congress has been found to have had inherent authority to conduct legislative investigations. Anderson v. Dunn, 19 U.S. (6 Wheat.) 204, 5 L.Ed. 242 (1821).

14. Hutcheson v. United States, 369 U.S. 599, 610, 82 S.Ct. 1005, 1011, 8 L.Ed.2d 137 (1962); Quinn v. United States, 349 U.S. 155, 75 S.Ct. 668, 99 L.Ed. 964 (1955); Emspak v. United States, 349 U.S. 190, 75 S.Ct. 687, 99 L.Ed. 997 (1955). Most of the cases have had to determine whether the witness had adequately invoked the fifth amendment. It behooves such a witness to do so in an unmistakeable fashion if unnecessary litigation is to be avoided.

15. See, e. g., Rogers v. United States, 340 U.S. 367, 71 S.Ct. 438, 95 L.Ed. 344 (1951).

16. See Meltzer, The Right to Remain Silent 98–118 (1972).

17. See generally 8 Wigmore, Evidence, § 2252 n. 27 (McNaughton rev. 1961).

18. 384 U.S. 436, 86 S.Ct. 1602, 16 L.Ed.2d 694 (1966).

the prosecution prefers that the accused submit also to an examination by its expert.

Under these circumstances may an accused be required to submit to a prosecution expert? At first glance the answer appears to be no, for the accused is being asked to involuntarily supply a testimonial utterance likely to have negative consequences at trial. Upon reflection, however, the problem becomes more complicated because the type of incriminating evidence that may result is twofold. It may bear simply on the accused's mental state and thus be incriminating only in the sense that it might lessen the defense chances of showing incompetency during the offense or at trial.[19] But it may also take the shape of specific incriminating facts regarding the offense. Although competency, despite its substantial effects on the defendant's future, does not constitute incrimination, specific admissions concerning the offense certainly do. Nevertheless, once the defendant has made a showing of insanity at the time of the offense, the government has an unusually heavy burden to overcome in order to establish the sanity of the accused. If the government is forced to rely only on cross-examination of the defense experts and other extrinsic evidence, its presentation is severely hampered.

Compelled psychiatric examinations of this kind, on pain of preventing the defense from presenting all or part of its evidence on insanity, generally involve the types of coercion that allow the privilege to be invoked. However, the overwhelming majority rule in the United States [20] is that when a defendant raises an insanity defense, he or she has impliedly waived in part the privilege against self-incrimination. Under the decisions, the defendant must submit to a government psychiatrist who need not give *Miranda* warnings but who will not be allowed to testify at trial to any specific incriminating remarks made during the interview. Moreover the psychiatrist must limit himself or herself to conclusions on the issue of sanity.[21] Refusal by the defendant to submit might result in an adverse inference, preclusion of the use of defense expert witnesses,[22] preclusion of the entire insanity defense, or perhaps even contempt.

---

19. Competency to stand trial must be distinguished from sanity at the time of the offense. The first has no direct bearing on the guilt or innocence of the accused, while by definition the second usually does. The federal courts have adopted a specific procedure to deal with determining the competency of the accused to stand trial. 18 U.S.C.A. § 4244 expressly allows an accused to be required to submit to a psychiatric examination to determine his or her competence to stand trial but states that no statement made by the accused during the examination will be admissible against the accused on the issue of guilt.

20. See for example United States v. Cohen, 530 F.2d 43 (5th Cir. 1976); Karstetter v. Cardwell, 526 F.2d 1144 (9th Cir. 1976); United States v. Barrera, 486 F.2d 333, 338–39 (2d Cir. 1973), cert. denied 416 U.S. 940, 94 S.Ct. 1944, 40 L.Ed.2d 291 (1974); United States v. Mattson, 469 F.2d 1234, 1236 (9th Cir. 1972), cert. denied 410 U.S. 986, 93 S.Ct. 1513, 36 L.Ed.2d 183 (1973); United States v. Julian, 469 F.2d 371, 375–76 (10th Cir. 1972); United States v. Bohle, 445 F.2d 54 (7th Cir. 1971); United States v. Albright, 388 F.2d 719 (4th Cir. 1968); United States v. Babbidge, 18 U.S.C.M.A. 327, 40 C.M.R. 39 (1969); Lewis v. Thulemeyer, 538 P.2d 441 (Colo.1975); Noyes v. State, 516 P.2d 1368 (Okl.Cr.1973); but see U. S. v. Alvarez, 519 F.2d 1036 (3d Cir. 1975). See generally Aronson, Should the Privilege Against Self-Incrimination Apply to Compelled Psychiatric Examinations? 26 Stan.L.Rev. 55 (1973); Danforth, Death Knell for Pre-Trial Mental Examination? Privilege Against Self-Incrimination, 19 Rut.L.Rev. 489 (1965); Lederer, Rights Warnings in the Military, 72 Mil.L. Rev. 1 (1976); Note, Requiring a Criminal Defendant to Submit to a Government Psychiatric Examination: An Invasion of the Privilege Against Self-Incrimination, 83 Harv.L.Rev. 648 (1970); Note, Protecting the Confidentiality of Pretrial Psychiatric Disclosures: A Survey of Standards, 51 N.Y.U.L.Rev. 409 (1976). An interesting case is State v. Smallwood, 25 Or.App. 251, 548 P.2d 1346 (1976), holding that the jury was entitled to know that the defendant's exercise of his fifth amendment rights limited the scope of the rebuttal testimony of the government's psychiatrist.

21. See, e. g., United States v. Bohle, 445 F.2d 54, 66–67 (7th Cir. 1971). Note that Virginia allows a coerced examination as long as the defendant is not forced to answer questions regarding the offense with which he or she is charged. Gibson v. Commonwealth, 216 Va. 412, 219 S.E.2d 845 (1975).

22. See Manual for Courts-Martial, United States, 1969 (rev. ed.), paras. 122(b)(2), 140(a)(2), 150(b), as amended by 40 Fed.Reg. 4247 (1975).

The cases in this area have attempted to reconcile competing societal interests. So long as insanity is viewed as a defense rather than as a post-conviction issue,[23] society must try to redress the imbalance that is possible when the accused can control access to his or her mind, the chief source of relevant evidence.[24] However, current methods resolve the imbalance by sacrificing the interests protected by the privilege.[25]

The Holder of the Privilege. The fifth amendment states that "no person . . . shall be compelled in any criminal case to be a witness against himself." From this phrasing is born the standing requirement of the fifth amendment. Loosely phrased, only an *individual* with a personal interest, exercising the privilege of his or her own behalf, may assert the right against self-incrimination.

The right against self-incrimination is personal. The Supreme Court has declared that its decisions "reflect the Court's consistent view that the privilege against self-incrimination should be 'limited to its historical function of protecting only the natural individual from compulsory incrimination through his own testimony or personal records.' "[26] The Court has consistently held that corporations,[27] partnerships,[28] and as-

sociations[29] may not assert the privilege. Nor may human agents of such organizations raise the right on behalf of their firms and organizations.[30]

The courts have also held that only the specific individual concerned may assert the right against self-incrimination. Thus accountants[31] and lawyers[32] may not raise the privilege on behalf of their clients if they are trying to prevent disclosure of client records in the attorney's or accountant's possession. Although some defendants have attempted to raise a violation of another per-

---

23. Michigan has now revised its law to make sanity an issue of post trial disposition only (e. g. the nature of the sentence to be imposed).

24. This is the primary justification for the balancing tests that most courts have used in this area. United States v. Cohen, 530 F.2d 43, 47 (5th Cir. 1976).

25. In addition to the interests protected by the privilege, the majority rule would appear to injure later patient-psychiatrist relationships—particularly in those cases in which the role of the pretrial examining psychiatrist is inadequately explained.

26. Bellis v. United States, 417 U.S. 85, 89–90, 94 S.Ct. 2179, 2183–84, 40 L.Ed.2d 678 (1974), citing United States v. White, 322 U.S. 694, 701, 64 S.Ct. 1248, 1252, 88 L.Ed. 1542 (1944). See generally 8 Wigmore, Evidence § 2259 (McNaughton rev. 1961).

27. See, e. g., Grant v. United States, 227 U.S. 74, 33 S.Ct. 190, 57 L.Ed. 423 (1913); Wheeler v. United States, 226 U.S. 478, 33 S.Ct. 158, 57 L.Ed. 309 (1913);

Drier v. United States, 221 U.S. 394, 31 S.Ct. 550, 55 L.Ed. 784 (1911); Wilson v. United States, 221 U.S. 361, 31 S.Ct. 538, 55 L.Ed. 771 (1911); Hale v. Henkel, 201 U.S. 43, 26 S.Ct. 370, 50 L.Ed. 652 (1906).

28. See, e. g., Fisher v. United States, 425 U.S. 391, 96 S.Ct. 1569, 48 L.Ed.2d 39 (1976); Bellis v. United States, 417 U.S. 85, 94 S.Ct. 2179, 40 L.Ed.2d 678 (1974).

29. See, e. g., Rogers v. United States, 340 U.S. 367, 71 S.Ct. 438, 95 L.Ed. 344 (1951) (Communist Party of Denver); United States v. White, 322 U.S. 694, 64 S.Ct. 1248, 88 L.Ed. 1542 (1944) (labor union). See also Note, The Constitutional Rights of Associations to Assert the Privilege Against Self-Incrimination, 112 U.Pa.L.Rev. 394 (1964).

30. See, e. g., Drier v. United States, 221 U.S. 394, 31 S.Ct. 550, 55 L.Ed. 784 (1911). As the officers and agents have no interest in the firm's records, they have no personal standing when the records are to be used against them.

31. Couch v. United States, 409 U.S. 322, 93 S.Ct. 611, 34 L.Ed.2d 548 (1973).

32. Fisher v. United States, 425 U.S. 391, 96 S.Ct. 1569, 48 L.Ed.2d 39 (1976). As in Couch v. United States, 409 U.S. 322, 93 S.Ct. 611, 34 L.Ed.2d 548 (1973), the primary rationale behind the Court's decision in *Fisher* was that the privilege is personal and "protects a person only against being incriminated by his own compelled testimonial communications." Thus so long as records are not in the possession of the accused, the accused may not assert the privilege to prevent their disclosure or surrender. Because the accountant or attorney will usually not be incriminated by a client's records, he or she may also not assert the privilege. The Court in *Fisher* did acknowledge that the attorney-client privilege might apply if the defendant would be privileged under the fifth amendment. As *Fisher* appears to have narrowly limited the application of the fifth amendment right to documents, such a situation might not occur in the future. Before one can criticize *Couch* and *Fisher*, a decision as to the scope of the privilege is required.

son's right, frequently in an effort to prevent receipt of a harmful admission or confession at trial, the courts have rejected such attacks. This practice does appear in accord with the primary purposes served by the privilege.[33]

Historically the right against self-incrimination has been a "fighting right," requiring a positive assertion. It has only incidentally been involved in the effort to protect the courts from unreliable evidence. Interestingly a few cases dealing with coerced confessions have allowed someone other than the maker of the statement to move to suppress.[34] In such cases, however, the court is usually concerned only with reliability.

Virtually every state has its own privilege against self-incrimination, whether constitutional or statutory.[35] In a number of cases the privilege in a specific state is broader than the federal privilege. One example will suffice. In Ohio a statutory right to refuse to answer interrogatories of the Ohio Civil Rights Commission on grounds of self-incrimination has been construed to include corporations.[36] Accordingly research into state law may be crucial when a case arises in a non-federal forum.

Suggested Reading:

Bellis v. United States, 417 U.S. 85, 94 S.Ct. 2179, 40 L.Ed.2d 678 (1974).

United States v. White, 322 U.S. 694, 64 S.Ct. 1248, 88 L.Ed. 1542 (1944).

Asserting the Privilege. As we shall see, the defendant's privilege is broader than a witness's privilege. The defendant can assert the privilege by failing to testify; the prosecution may not call the defendant to the stand. In contrast, the witness's privilege is limited to a right to refuse to answer specific, incriminating questions. The witness may assert the privilege on direct or cross-examination. Although asserting the right against self-incrimination on cross-examination is possible,[37] an argument that waiver has taken place is frequently made. Regardless of whether the witness has a proper claim or wrongfully refuses to testify, the judge must decide how to handle the testimony on direct. If the matters the witness has refused to testify to on cross are merely collateral, the judge need not strike the direct.[38] But if the witness's refusal makes testing the trustworthiness of his or her direct testimony impossible, part or all

---

33. See, e. g., Couch v. United States, 409 U.S. 322, 328, 93 S.Ct. 611, 615–16, 34 L.Ed.2d 548 (1973), stating: "The Constitution explicitly prohibits compelling an accused to bear witness 'against himself'; it necessarily does not proscribe incriminating statements elicited from another. It is extortion of information from the accused himself that offends our sense of justice."

34. See, e. g., LaFrance v. Bohlinger, 499 F.2d 29 (1st Cir. 1974) (use for impeachment of a statement allegedly obtained by threats required a prior voluntariness hearing by the trial judge).

35. See 8 Wigmore, Evidence § 2252 nn. 1 and 3 (McNaughton rev. 1961, Supp. 1975), setting forth the relevant constitutional and statutory provisions of every state.

36. Ohio Civil Rights Comm. v. Parklawn Manor, Inc., 41 Ohio St.2d 47, 322 N.E.2d 642, 702 O.O.2d 148 (1975).

37. See United States v. Gould, 536 F.2d 216 (8th Cir. 1976), sustaining the trial judge's actions in preventing the cross-examination of a witness (who had indicated his intention to exercise his privilege) respecting a prior criminal act with which the defense intended to impeach him. The witness had been completely cross-examined with respect to the offense for which the defendant was on trial. The Michigan Court of Appeal has sustained the assertion of the privilege by a witness during a cross-examination designed to lay the foundation for impeachment by prior inconsistent statement even though the assertion blocked the attempted impeachment. People v. Gunne, 65 Mich.App. 216, 237 N.W.2d 256 (1976).

38. See, e. g., United States v. Brierly, 501 F.2d 1024, 1027 (8th Cir. 1974), cert. denied 419 U.S. 1052, 95 S.Ct. 631, 42 L.Ed.2d 648; United States v. Cardillo, 316 F.2d 606, 610–13, 618 (2d Cir. 1963), cert. denied 375 U.S. 822, 84 S.Ct. 60, 11 L.Ed.2d 55.

of the direct may have to be struck.[39] The refusal of a witness to answer questions on cross-examination may not be used to suggest to the jury possible answers. Thus a prosecutor may not ask a witness a series of questions hoping that the jury will draw a favorable inference from the witness's refusal to answer.[40]

The Nature of the Privilege. In reality, the defendant, the formal accused in the trial, has two privileges. First, the defendant has a privilege not to testify at all. Second, the defendant has a privilege to prevent comment on his or her invocation of the privilege.

In a criminal trial neither the prosecution nor the trial judge may comment on a defendant's proper exercise of the right against self-incrimination nor may the jury draw an adverse inference from it.[41] Indeed the defense is entitled to have the jury instructed not to consider the accused's silence. The Supreme Court has also held that a defendant may not be impeached by the fact that he or she did not answer questions after having been told by the police of the right to remain silent.[42]

The witness's privilege is much narrower. The witness must comply with compulsory process and ascend the witness stand. The only privilege is to refuse to answer specific questions which tend to incriminate the witness.

Suggested Reading:

Griffin v. California, 380 U.S. 609, 85 S.Ct. 1229, 14 L.Ed.2d 106 (1965).

Testimonial Incrimination. The fifth amendment phrasing "shall be compelled to be a witness against himself" is too vague to be of great use in determining the scope of the privilege. The traditional expression of the scope of the right is that it includes evidence of a testimonial or communicative nature.

Suggested Reading:

United States v. Dionisio, 410 U.S. 1, 93 S.Ct. 764, 35 L.Ed.2d 67 (1973).

California v. Byers, 402 U.S. 424, 91 S.Ct. 1535, 29 L.Ed.2d 9 (1971).

United States v. Wade, 388 U.S. 218, 87 S.Ct. 1926, 18 L.Ed.2d 1149 (1967).

Schmerber v. California, 384 U.S. 757, 86 S.Ct. 1826, 16 L.Ed.2d 908 (1967).

Boyd v. United States, 116 U.S. 616, 6 S.Ct. 524, 29 L.Ed. 746 (1886).

Testimonial Utterances and Their Equivalents. Defining "testimonial or communicative" acts has proved surprisingly difficult. Speech intended to convey information, in contrast to speech intended as a voice sample,[43] is clearly covered. It is the extent to which speech analogs are protected that is unclear. Of course one cannot escape the fifth amendment by telling a witness to nod his or her head rather than to reply in words. But exactly where is the dividing line between speech equivalents and unprotected acts?

---

39. See, e. g., United States v. Newman, 490 F.2d 139, 144–46 (3d Cir. 1974); United States v. Colon-Atienza, 22 U.S.C.M.A. 399, 47 C.M.R. 336 (1973). Whether impeachment constitutes a collateral matter evidently depends on the facts of each specific case.

40. See, e. g., Douglas v. Alabama, 380 U.S. 415, 85 S.Ct. 1074, 13 L.Ed.2d 934 (1965).

41. Griffin v. California, 380 U.S. 609, 85 S.Ct. 1229, 14 L.Ed.2d 106 (1965). See generally Comment, Exercise of the Privilege Against Self-Incrimination by Witnesses and Codefendants: The Effect Upon the Accused, 33 U.Chi.L.Rev. 151 (1965). Improper comment upon the failure of the accused to take the stand remains a problem and causes the reversal of a number of cases every year.

42. Doyle v. Ohio, 426 U.S. 610, 96 S.Ct. 2240, 49 L.Ed.2d 91 (1976); United States v. Hale, 422 U.S. 171, 95 S.Ct. 2133, 45 L.Ed.2d 99 (1975).

---

43. United States v. Wade, 388 U.S. 218, 222–23, 87 S.Ct. 1926, 1929–30, 18 L.Ed.2d 1149 (1967).

To date, the Supreme Court has decided that extracting bodily fluids,[44] compelling production of handwriting [45] and voice exemplars,[46] and requiring a suspect to don or remove clothes [47] or to supply fingerprints [48] are unprotected. Apparently the Court believes that an act which is the functional equivalent of a verbal utterance carrying information is protected. Although exemplars of various kinds may require affirmative acts and mental action, they do not convey the type of information that could reveal the innermost thoughts of an individual. In addition, some acts discussed above occur so frequently in ordinary life (e. g. speaking) that the Court has found no expectation of privacy. However, an examination of the cases in other jurisdictions reveals that the court's finding was avoidable.[49]

A gray area remains in situations in which physical acts can convey information. Occasionally termed the "verbal act" problem, this area is subject to differing approaches throughout the various jurisdic-

tions. When a police officer says, "You know what I want, take it out of your pocket," [50] and the suspect complies, the prosecution can use the act to establish the element of knowing possession. The Supreme Court has recently suggested that the mere inference of knowing possession is a de minimis infringement of the privilege.[51] In one case a court held that requiring the accused to demonstrate his method of opening a pack of cigarettes was testimonial when the act linked him with an unusually opened pack found at the scene of the crime.[52] Such holdings are common in jurisdictions which have a constitutional or statutory right broadly framed in terms of preventing self-incrimination. In such cases the privilege's scope can be substantially broader than that of the fifth amendment, extending to affirmative nonverbal acts that supply incriminating evidence against the defendant.

Another problem area is that of identification. May an individual refuse to identify himself or herself? Although the cases are conflicting, the majority answer is in the negative.[53] The probable rationale is that

44. Schmerber v. California, 384 U.S. 757, 86 S.Ct. 1826, 16 L.Ed.2d 908 (1967).

45. United States v. Mara, 410 U.S. 19, 93 S.Ct. 774, 35 L.Ed.2d 99 (1973); Gilbert v. California, 388 U.S. 263, 266, 87 S.Ct. 1951, 1953, 18 L.Ed.2d 1178 (1967).

46. United States v. Dionisio, 410 U.S. 1, 93 S.Ct. 764, 35 L.Ed.2d 67 (1973); United States v. Wade, 388 U.S. 218, 222–23, 87 S.Ct. 1926, 1929–30, 18 L.Ed. 2d 1149 (1967).

47. See United States v. Wade, 388 U.S. 218, 222, 87 S.Ct. 1926, 1929, 18 L.Ed.2d 1149 (1967); Holt v. United States, 218 U.S. 245, 31 S.Ct. 2, 54 L.Ed. 1021 (1910).

48. Schmerber v. California, 384 U.S. 757, 764, 86 S.Ct. 1826, 1832, 16 L.Ed.2d 908 (1967).

49. A number of other jurisdictions have reached differing conclusions, usually because of the peculiar phrasing of their constitutional or statutory right. See, e. g., Note, Criminal Law: Nontestimonial Aspect of Oklahoma's Right Against Self-Incrimination, 28 Okl.L.Rev. 122 (1975); Lederer, Rights Warnings in The Military, 72 Mil.L.Rev. 1 (1976). See also City of St. Joseph v. Johnson, 539 S.W.2d 784, 787 (Mo. App.1976), holding that a motorist who refused to take a blood alcohol test and who has thus suffered revocation of license should not be compelled to explain at trial his refusal to take the test.

50. See, e. g., United States v. Kinane, 24 U.S.C. M.A. 120, 122 n. 1, 51 C.M.R. 310, 312 n. 1.

51. Fisher v. United States, 425 U.S. 391, 96 S.Ct. 1569, 48 L.Ed.2d 39 (1976) (holding that the effect of surrender of papers pursuant to subpoena presents difficult questions involving the definition of "testimonial" and incrimination, and resolution may depend on the facts and circumstances of particular cases; however, in *Fisher,* the act of surrender did not involve testimonial incrimination).

52. State v. O'Conner, 320 So.2d 188 (La.1975).

53. See United States ex rel. Hines v. LaVallee, 521 F.2d 1109 (2d Cir. 1975); United States v. Camacho, 506 F.2d 594 (9th Cir. 1974); United States v. Leyba, 504 F.2d 441, 444 (10th Cir. 1974); United States v. Menichino, 497 F.2d 935, 939–42 (5th Cir. 1974); United States v. La Monica, 472 F.2d 580 (9th Cir. 1972); cf. State v. Levy, 292 So.2d 220 (La.1974); but see Proctor v. United States, 404 F.2d 819 (D.C. Cir. 1968). As only a body with subpoena and contempt power can compel an answer, the identification issue usually arises only in terms of whether rights warnings were needed before identification could be requested.

identity is not usually incriminating.[54] However, identity may be privileged when, as in a forgery case, it might play a role in the offense itself.[55]

Documents. In England the privilege against self-incrimination was early presumed to extend to personal papers. In the 1765 case of Entick v. Carrington,[56] Lord Camden held that searching the plaintiff's home and subsequently examining his personal papers violated the plaintiff's right against self-incrimination. *Entick* was cited with approval by the United States Supreme Court in Boyd v. United States.[57] There the Court stated that "we have been unable to perceive that the seizure of a man's private books and papers to be used in evidence against him is substantially different from compelling him to be a witness against himself."[58] The Court likened the seizure of personal papers to the general writs of assistance which were so instrumental in fomenting the Revolution.[59]

After *Boyd* the fifth amendment was presumed to bar seizure of personal papers, but the limits of the rule were unclear. Corporate records and records of business associations obviously were not within the scope of the rule. Were personal business records, tax records, and personal papers? The ultimate result was perhaps foreshadowed in

Warden v. Hayden,[60] in which the Supreme Court held that "mere evidence" as well as contraband and proceeds of crime could be seized pursuant to the fourth amendment, thus negating *Boyd's* assumption that under no circumstances could papers be lawfully seized.[61] In a series of cases culminating in 1976 with Andresen v. Maryland,[62] the Court consistently either allowed seizure or compelled surrender of personal business and tax documents to such an extent that the vitality of *Boyd* is in severe doubt. In Fisher v. United States,[63] Justice Brennan stated that "it is but another step in the denigration of privacy principles settled nearly 100 years ago in Boyd v. United States."[64]

The rationale behind *Fisher* and *Andresen* is primarily that the forced production of papers[65] does not require the individual to create evidence but rather to disclose evi-

---

54. See California v. Byers, 402 U.S. 424, 433–34, 91 S.Ct. 1535, 1540–41, 29 L.Ed.2d 9 (1971).

55. Cf. American Law Institute, A Model Code of Pre-Arraignment Procedure § 140.8(5) (1975). As *Miranda* requires rights warnings only when a suspect is in custody and the questions are designed to elicit an incriminating response, the courts can usually avoid coming to grips with this issue by determining that the request for identification took place in a non-custodial setting.

56. 19 Howell St.Tr. 1029 (1765).

57. 116 U.S. 616, 6 S.Ct. 524, 29 L.Ed. 746 (1886).

58. Id. at 633.

59. It is an historical curiosity that Entick v. Carrington played a significant role in the expansion of the English privilege while in the United States the privilege was ultimately viewed as a fourth amendment precedent.

60. 387 U.S. 294, 87 S.Ct. 1642, 18 L.Ed.2d 782 (1967).

61. Warden v. Hayden was cited by the Supreme Court in Fisher v. United States, 425 U.S. 391, 96 S.Ct. 1569, 48 L.Ed.2d 39 (1976), for the proposition that "several of Boyd's express or implicit declarations have not stood the test of time." The Supreme Court then found that *Warden* had "washed away" the foundations of the document rule.

62. 427 U.S. 463, 96 S.Ct. 2737, 49 L.Ed.2d 627 (1976).

63. 425 U.S. 391, 96 S.Ct. 1569, 48 L.Ed.2d 39 (1976), holding that papers used to prepare tax returns and retained by the defendant's attorney were not privileged.

64. Id.

65. The cases discussed above involve private business papers. Insofar as Boyd v. United States dealt with a partnership's papers, it has been overruled. See, e. g., Bellis v. United States, 417 U.S. 85, 94 S.Ct. 2179, 40 L.Ed.2d 678 (1974). An individual in possession as custodian of papers belonging to a firm or to a governmental unit lacks standing to assert the privilege and must surrender the papers on demand. See, e. g., United States v. Sellers, 12 U.S.C. M.A. 262, 30 C.M.R. 262 (1961). Justifications for the rule include waiver and no expectation of privacy. 8 Wigmore, Evidence § 2259(c) (McNaughton rev. 1961). But see In re Bernstein, 20 Crim.L.Rep. 2429 (S.D.Fla. Jan. 3, 1977) (grand jury cannot subpoena tapes of incriminatory statements which are in the witness's possession; ownership, possession, and self-incrimination concur to protect the tapes).

dence already in existence. Furthermore the Court seems to imply that the "business" nature of the papers renders the fifth amendment protection unnecessary. It appears that the Court is utilizing a balancing test insofar as privacy interests are concerned. Perhaps an individual may assert the right against self-incrimination if compelled to disclose personal non-business papers—such as a diary. However, in view of the Supreme Court's increasing limitation of the privilege's scope, even this coverage may be abolished. Should this be the case, defense counsel may be expected to increasingly argue state constitutional provisions and statutes if they are broader than the fifth amendment.

Governmentally Required Records and Reports. For minimum efficiency, contemporary government demands a substantial amount of information from its citizens. Whether that information is designed to promote governmental efficiency, as in a census, or to control certain materials or substances, as in gun registration or drug control programs, the government has a critical need that certain records be kept and submitted to it.

The courts have consistently acknowledged the right of the government to require records and reports when the records are not inherently incriminating and are used for a proper government purpose. The first significant case is United States v. Sullivan,[66] in which the Supreme Court held that income tax returns could be required although the filing of the return might create a possibility of incrimination.[67] The leading case in

the area is Shapiro v. United States,[68] in which the Court sustained the legality of the Emergency Price Control Act of 1942. The Act required certain people to retain records of operation subject to inspection by the Office of Price Administration. Shapiro, a wholesale fruit dealer, had to surrender his records and was prosecuted for violation of the Act. He claimed that the coerced surrender violated his right against self-incrimination and thus tainted the prosecution. The Court sustained the record-keeping requirement on the grounds that the government had a right to regulate the activity and that a sufficient relationship existed between the activity and the records required.[69] The government had unquestioned power to regulate commodity prices, and the record keeping requirement was a proper exercise of that power. Again, as in the tax cases, the mere act of keeping records, to be produced in the future, was not necessarily incriminating.[70]

In subsequent cases [71] in which the reporting requirement appeared certain to yield incriminating material and the sole purpose of the requirement seemed to be to obtain information for prosecution, the Court struck down the reporting requirement. Thus the Court reversed convictions for fail-

---

66. 274 U.S. 259, 47 S.Ct. 607, 71 L.Ed. 1037 (1927).

67. The Court did indicate that the privilege might allow a refusal to answer specific questions on the return. In Garner v. United States, 424 U.S. 648, 96 S.Ct. 1178, 47 L.Ed.2d 370 (1976), the Court held that while a taxpayer may claim the privilege in respect to parts of the return, he or she must actually assert the privilege and may not later claim that because his or her answers were incriminating they cannot be used against him or her. The privilege must be asserted even though a prosecution may re-

sult because the claim of the privilege (perhaps only a valid claim) is a defense to a prosecution for a failure to make a return.

68. 335 U.S. 1, 68 S.Ct. 1375, 92 L.Ed. 1787 (1948).

69. Id. at 32.

70. See generally 8 Wigmore, Evidence § 2259(c) (McNaughton rev. 1961) for an outstanding analysis of the reporting requirements. Note that while prospective record keeping designed only for government use provides one set of justifications, reports historically kept and important to the business of an individual may require another.

71. Leary v. United States, 395 U.S. 6, 89 S.Ct. 1532, 23 L.Ed.2d 57 (1969); Haynes v. United States, 390 U.S. 85, 88 S.Ct. 722, 19 L.Ed.2d 923 (1968); Grosso v. United States, 390 U.S. 62, 88 S.Ct. 709, 19 L.Ed.2d 906 (1968); Marchetti v. United States, 390 U.S. 39, 88 S.Ct. 697, 19 L.Ed.2d 889 (1968). But see California v. Byers, 402 U.S. 424, 91 S.Ct. 1535, 29 L.Ed.2d 9 (1971); United States v. Freed, 401 U.S. 601, 91 S.Ct. 1112, 28 L.Ed.2d 356 (1971).

ure to register firearms or to pay gambling taxes when the act of registration or payment would undoubtedly lead to prosecution.

The reporting requirement is far from dead, however. Plans that escape the prosecutorial deadfall remain legitimate.[72] In California v. Byers,[73] the Court came to grips with California's hit-and-run statute requiring the driver of a vehicle involved in an accident to stop at the scene and to leave his or her name and address. Byers claimed that his conviction for failure to do so after an accident violated his privilege against self-incrimination. Reversing the Supreme Court of California, the Court upheld the statute, finding that it did not involve "a highly selective group inherently suspect of criminal activities" and did not apply only in an area "permeated with criminal statutes."[74] Leaving name and address was found to be an essentially neutral act even though it might supply a link in the evidentiary chain.[75] While the majority [76] opinion found that the privilege was inapplicable, the dissent stated that contrary to the Court's holding, the driver of a vehicle involved in an accident was so likely to have violated a criminal statute that Byers could not be distinguished from previous cases. However, the act of reporting in Byers was not necessarily incriminating. The prior reporting requirements that were overturned were almost equivalent to conviction.

The Court actually attempts to balance the rights of the individual against the rights of society.[77] With reporting requirements, the individual's rights have been limited; so long as a proper purpose is involved and the result of the report is not inherently incriminating, the requirement will be upheld.[78] The alternative is to find that the privilege is applicable but that to sustain the reporting requirements neither the information divulged nor derivative information may be used at a prosecution. The Court in Byers rejected this alternative, finding that it would place an insurmountable burden on prosecution.

Incrimination. The fifth amendment privilege has been interpreted by the Supreme Court as protecting the individual from self-incrimination.[79] In the technical

---

77. "Tension between the State's demands for disclosures and the protection of the right against self-incrimination is likely to give rise to serious questions. Inevitably these must be resolved in terms of balancing the public need on the one hand, and the individual claim to constitutional protections on the other." Note also the Court's approach in Fourth Amendment cases. E. g. California Bankers Ass'n v. Shultz, 416 U.S. 21, 94 S.Ct. 1494, 39 L.Ed.2d 812 (1974).

78. As Byers indicates, the probability of incrimination is relevant. The Government may not avoid the problem by using forfeiture proceedings rather than a criminal prosecution, United States v. United States Coin and Currency, 401 U.S. 715, 718, 91 S.Ct. 1041, 1043, 28 L.Ed.2d 434 (1971), although civil tax proceedings are possible. But compare Widdis v. United States, 395 F.Supp. 1015 (D.Alaska 1974), with Jensen v. United States, 29 AFTR.2d 72–1166, 72–1169 – 72–1171 (D.Colo.1972) (Civil C–2938 filed March 27, 1972). Note that the Virginia Supreme Court has accepted the social purpose test rather than considering the probability of self-incrimination. Banks v. Commonwealth, 20 Crim.L.Rep. 2263 (Va. Nov. 24, 1976) (state automobile accident disclosure statute sustained despite high probability of self-incrimination in case of licenseless defendant previously adjudged an "habitual traffic offender").

79. Some state constitutions and statutes have extended the privilege beyond the federal scope. See, e. g., Ga.Code § 38–1205; Iowa Code Ann. § 622.14; Neb.Rev.Stat.Supp. 1971, § 25–1210 (1956), extending the privilege to self-infamy, or the Uniform Code of Military Justice, Art. 31(a), 10 U.S.C.A. § 831(a), which appears to have been construed to include a less than honorable discharge as equivalent to in-

---

72. In United States v. Freed, 401 U.S. 601, 91 S.Ct. 1112, 28 L.Ed.2d 356 (1971), the Court sustained a firearms (hand grenades) registration requirement because no possibility of prosecution other than for failure to register existed; use immunity had been attached to the act of registration. Although the transferee had to supply fingerprints and a photograph to lawfully receive the weapons, the Court found any possibility of incrimination to be "trifling." The transferee could not claim that the possibility of future crimes allowed him to assert the privilege.

73. 402 U.S. 424, 91 S.Ct. 1535, 29 L.Ed.2d 9 (1971).

74. Id. at 430.

75. Id. at 434.

76. Consisting of a plurality and a concurrence in the judgment by Mr. Justice Harlan.

sense "an incriminating act" is an ambiguous expression, for *incrimination* may mean a *consequence* (such as a criminal conviction) or an *act* (such as a testimonial utterance) leading to a consequence. All acts leading to the consequence of a criminal conviction are not incriminating within the sense of the fifth amendment. This section addresses incrimination in terms of consequences.

The clearest form of incrimination is a judicially imposed criminal conviction. Even so, a number of minor problems surround a conviction. At which point does a conviction relieve a defendant of further incrimination? If an accused has been convicted but not sentenced or sentenced but is making an appeal that could result in reversal, he or she may usually invoke the privilege.[80] If a defendant has been tried but remains subject to trial in another jurisdiction[81] or for related offenses, he or she may also remain silent absent a grant of immunity. When there is no danger of criminal conviction, as in the case of a grant of immunity, an acquittal, a pardon, or the running of the statute of limitations, no justification exists to invoke the privilege. The risk of incrimination must of course be real before the right against self-incrimination may be asserted.[82]

The extent to which consequences other than a criminal conviction may constitute incrimination is unclear. In the past the Supreme Court has tended to look at the actual consequence of a proceeding rather than at its label in order to define incrimination. Thus juvenile proceedings were generally

found to be criminal.[83] However, the Court may be retreating from this position. In Baxter v. Palmigiano,[84] the Court allowed prison officials to draw an inference of guilt from Palmigiano's silence during a prison discipline proceeding. Because the Court found that the State of Rhode Island had not attempted to use his silence at a criminal proceeding distinct from the disciplinary proceeding, it found the adverse inference justifiable. Palmigiano was "sentenced" to thirty days in punitive segregation and a downgrading in classification; therefore, the Court obviously found that the consequence of restricted liberty is not incrimination. Here the Court appeared to look at the social purpose served by the proceeding rather than at its label or consequence. Thus this form of increased deprivation of liberty was noncriminal.[85]

Although civil liability per se does not constitute incrimination, a civil penalty having a punitive intent may.[86] Deportation is not equivalent to incrimination.[87] Loss of livelihood generally does not appear to be a

---

crimination. United States v. Ruiz, 23 U.S.C.M.A. 181, 48 C.M.R. 797 (1974).

80. See, e. g., Mills v. United States, 281 F.2d 736 (4th Cir. 1960); C. McCormick, Handbook of the Law of Evidence 257 n. 84 (2d ed. 1972).

81. Cf. Murphy v. Waterfront Comm., 378 U.S. 52, 84 S.Ct. 1594, 12 L.Ed.2d 678 (1964).

82. See, e. g., Rogers v. United States, 340 U.S. 367, 374–75, 71 S.Ct. 438, 442–43, 95 L.Ed. 344 (1951).

83. In re Gault, 387 U.S. 1, 87 S.Ct. 1428, 18 L.Ed.2d 527 (1967).

84. 425 U.S. 308, 96 S.Ct. 1551, 47 L.Ed.2d 810 (1976). The case is more than a little surprising because at the time of his hearing, Palmigiano had not been granted immunity and could have been prosecuted.

85. In a case even more disturbing than Baxter v. Palmigiano, the Supreme Court found military summary courts-martial, which can impose a sentence of thirty days' confinement at hard labor, to be similar to parole revocation hearings and not criminal convictions requiring counsel for the accused. Middendorf v. Henry, 425 U.S. 25, 96 S.Ct. 1281, 47 L.Ed.2d 556 (1976).

86. See generally 8 Wigmore, Evidence §§ 2256–57 (McNaughton rev. 1961). There is a historic precedent for equating some civil actions with criminal sanctions. See, e. g., Boyd v. United States, 116 U.S. 616, 634–35, 6 S.Ct. 524, 534–35, 29 L.Ed. 746 (1885).

87. See, e. g., Woodby v. Immigration & Naturalization Service, 385 U.S. 276, 87 S.Ct. 483, 17 L.Ed.2d 362 (1966); Abel v. United States, 362 U.S. 217, 80 S.Ct. 683, 4 L.Ed.2d 668 (1960); Chavez-Raya v. Immigration & Naturalization Service, 519 F.2d 397 (7th Cir. 1975).

relevant consequence [88] although disbarment may be.[89] Far more difficult to resolve than even the complex issues mentioned above is the concept of treatment. Prior to In re Gault, juveniles were unable to assert the right against self-incrimination because their proceedings were designed for beneficial corrective reasons rather than for punishment. Thus they were noncriminal. While *Gault* has bestowed the privilege on juvenile proceedings, the rationale of beneficial treatment remains. For example in one case, a student suspected of smoking in violation of school rules was held not entitled to *Miranda* warnings because "the purpose of most school-house rules is to find facts . . . relating to special maladjustments of the child with a view toward correcting it [*sic*]." [90] The same theory is used to justify denying the privilege to those who will be committed to mental institutions rather than to prisons.[91] The dividing line between a punitive consequence and legitimate treatment is rather fine. Although the Supreme Court will probably not expand the definition of *incrimination* in the future, it and the state courts will have to draw a clearer line between those consequences which are incriminating and those which are not.

Suggested Reading:

In re Gault, 387 U.S. 1, 87 S.Ct. 1428, 18 L.Ed.2d 527 (1967).

Hoffman v. United States, 341 U.S. 479, 71 S.Ct. 814, 95 L.Ed. 1118 (1951).

Rogers v. United States, 340 U.S. 367, 71 S.Ct. 438, 95 L.Ed. 344 (1951).

Incrimination in Foreign Jurisdictions. Despite the phrasing of the fifth amendment, the Supreme Court has, since 1892, construed the privilege against self-incrimination as allowing a jurisdiction to compel a witness to testify in a self-incriminating fashion if the witness is adequately immunized against the risk of subsequent prosecution.[92] However, even though a federal grant of immunity could prevent subsequent trial or use of immunized testimony by a state, states cannot guarantee freedom from prosecution by either the federal government or another state. All American jurisdictions are powerless to prevent possible prosecution by a

---

88. Cf. Gardner v. Broderick, 392 U.S. 273, 88 S. Ct. 1913, 20 L.Ed.2d 1082 (1968) (policeman may be dismissed if he fails to answer specific questions narrowly directed towards his duties despite failure to grant immunity). But see State ex rel. Vining v. Florida REC, 281 So.2d 487 (Fla.1973), finding that deprivation of livelihood may be penal in nature and compelling testimony when license revocation or suspension is the possible result is a violation of the self-incrimination clauses of the United States and Florida constitutions.

89. Disbarment has proven vexatious. In Spevack v. Klein, 385 U.S. 511, 87 S.Ct. 625, 17 L.Ed.2d 574 (1967), the Supreme Court reversed Spevack's disbarment for invoking the privilege when he was subpoenaed to produce financial records. While there is authority for believing that disbarment is quasi-criminal in nature despite its public service function (see In re Ruffalo, 390 U.S. 544, 550, 88 S.Ct. 1222, 1225–26, 20 L.Ed.2d 117 (1968)), most states have continued to treat it as civil in nature. See, e. g., Segretti v. State Bar of California, 15 Cal.3d 878, 126 Cal.Rptr. 793, 544 P.2d 929 (1967) ("the purpose of disciplinary proceedings against attorneys is not to punish but rather to protect the court and public from the official ministrations of persons unfit to practice."); Maryland State Bar Ass'n v. Sugarman, 273 Md. 306, 329 A.2d 1 (1974). See generally Note, Self-Incrimination: Privilege, Immunity, and Comment in Bar Disciplinary Proceedings, 72 Mich. L.Rev. 84 (1973); Chilingirian, State Disbarment Proceedings and the Privilege Against Self-Incrimination, 18 Buff.L.Rev. 489 (1969).

90. Doe v. New Mexico, 88 N.M. 347, 540 P.2d 827 (1975); the dissent is at 88 N.M. 489, 542 P.2d 834 (1975). Because the student was interrogated for forty minutes and ultimately confessed to smoking marijuana, the case seems far from a simple violation of school rules.

91. See, e. g., Williams v. Director, Patuxent Institution, 276 Md. 272, 347 A.2d 179 (1975) (defective delinquent treatment is not criminal in nature); Aronson, Should the Privilege Against Self-Incrimination Apply to Compelled Psychiatric Examinations? 26 Stan.L.Rev. 55 (1973).

92. Counselman v. Hitchcock, 142 U.S. 547, 12 S.Ct. 195, 35 L.Ed. 1110 (1891).

foreign government. Until 1964, the rule was simple—so long as a witness was immunized against prosecution in the jurisdiction compelling the testimony, the witness was unable to assert a fifth amendment privilege against testifying.

This "separate sovereignties" doctrine was overruled in 1964 by Murphy v. Waterfront Commission.[93] In *Murphy*, Mr. Justice Goldberg found that the policy behind the right against self-incrimination required that in our federal system a witness granted immunity by a state also be safe from the subsequent use or derivative use of that testimony in federal court. Seven members of the Court held that the Constitution mandated this result and that the prosecution in a federal trial of a witness granted immunity by a state would have to show that neither the testimony given at the state proceeding nor any information derived from it had been used to prepare the federal prosecution. In concurring, Justices Harlan and Clark objected to that part of the holding making the result a matter of constitutional law, preferring to use the Court's supervisory power over the federal courts.[94]

The federal government's grant of immunity to a witness must, to comply with *Murphy*, at least protect the witness against use of his or her testimony by a state.[95] A close reading of *Murphy* supports the conclusion that a witness immunized by one state is protected from use or derivative use of his or her testimony by another state. Remaining unresolved, however, is the possibility of incrimination outside the United States.

In view of the interrelationship among the states, the right to interstate travel, and the American federal system, *Murphy's* result was long overdue. However, the question of foreign prosecution is substantially different. Unless a treaty can be negotiated, the United States is without power to dictate foreign municipal law. Furthermore, although an American citizen may indeed have a right to travel beyond the national borders, neither the need nor the right to do so is equivalent to the need to travel freely throughout the United States. Counterbalancing these factors is the ever increasing interdependence of nations and the exchange of information among national police forces.

The English cases appear to allow a witness to refuse to incriminate himself or herself when a definite possibility of foreign prosecution exists.[96] The American cases, while increasing in number, are conflicting, and the Supreme Court has to date refused to decide the issue.[97] Most of these cases

---

93. 378 U.S. 52, 84 S.Ct. 1594, 12 L.Ed.2d 678 (1964).

94. 378 U.S. at 80.

95. Until 1970, most federal immunity statutes granted transactional immunity, which protected a witness against any prosecution for any offense (other than perjury) included in the immunized testimony. In 1972, the Supreme Court in Kastigar v. United States, 406 U.S. 441, 92 S.Ct. 1653, 32 L.Ed.2d 212 (1972), held that testimonial immunity (sometimes called *use immunity*) is sufficient. Testimonial immunity protects the witness from any use of his or her immunized testimony including any derivative use to obtain other evidence.

96. See, e. g., United States of America v. McRae, L.R., 3 Ch.App. 79 (1867), in which the United States sued for an accounting of money received by the witness as a Confederate agent during the Civil War. Because McRae could have had American property forfeited as a result of his testimony, his answers would have had a substantial risk of incrimination. A few earlier cases also existed in which the witness could have been prosecuted in other parts of the British empire. East India Co. v. Campbell, 27 Eng.Rep. 1010 (Ex.1749) (possible prosecution in India). *McRae* may have confined the previously principal English case, King of the Two Sicilies v. Willcox, 61 Eng.Rep. 116 (Ch.1851) to its facts. The Court of Chancellery had held that before prosecution in Sicily could take place, the witnesses would have to abandon their residence in England and that it was unclear that Sicilian law would make the information demanded incriminating. See generally Grant, Federalism and Self-Incrimination, Part II., Common Law and British Empire Comparisons, 5 U.C.L.A.L.Rev. 1 (1958).

97. Zicarelli v. Investigation Comm., 406 U.S. 472, 478–81, 92 S.Ct. 1670, 1674–76, 32 L.Ed.2d 234 (1972). The Court found in *Zicarelli* that the witness had not really been asked any questions that would have created a risk of incrimination abroad.

concern witnesses who asserted a right to refuse to testify before grand juries.[98] In general the witnesses have been compelled to testify so long as they were immunized under *Murphy* against American prosecution. The rationale used has been that grand juries are secret proceedings and that the likelihood of foreign discovery of the information is too minimal to invoke the privilege. Arguably this places too much trust in the prosecution (who can reveal information) and ignores the possibility of extradition.

Utilizing *Murphy's* rationale, if a witness at trial can show a real possibility of foreign prosecution, he or she should be allowed to assert the privilege despite a grant of immunity effective in the United States. This would of course deny the prosecution the witness's testimony unless a grant of immunity could be obtained from the foreign jurisdiction. However, before a real possibility of foreign incrimination can arise, the witness must show a likelihood of return to the foreign jurisdiction—either by possible extradition or for home or business interest.[99]

The Procedure for Determining Whether a Question Is Incriminating. A witness may successfully assert the privilege only if his or her answers might be incriminating. How does the judge determine whether the question is incriminating? The leading case in this area is Hoffman v. United States,[1] holding that so long as the witness's claim of privilege seems valid, the claim should be honored. For the court to overrule the claim, it must be *"perfectly clear"* that a witness's answers *"cannot possibly"* incriminate the witness.[2] The issue is one for the trial judge. Although most judges routinely excuse a witness who asserts the privilege, a number of cases exist[3] in which the court has either denied the claim or limited the questioning of the witness to avoid the self-incrimination problem. In such a case the judge may ask the witness to indicate where the potential for incrimination exists. Obviously this is a measure of last resort, for it may defeat the entire purpose of exercising the privilege. In view of the *Hoffman* decision, the trial judge should not place this burden of coming forward on the witness unless the judge would otherwise be compelled to deny the privilege.

Waiver. The privilege against self-incrimination is waived if not affirmatively exercised. The courts tend to be hostile to the fifth amendment privilege and have utilized waiver as a partial means of limiting it. The general rule is that if a witness has

98. See In re Quinn, 525 F.2d 222 (1st Cir. 1975) (alleged purchase of firearms later found in Ireland; insufficient risk of British prosecution shown); In re Weir, 495 F.2d 879 (9th Cir. 1974), affirming 377 F.Supp. 919 (S.D.Cal.1974); In re Cahalane, 361 F. Supp. 226 (E.D.Pa.), aff'd without opinion 485 F.2d 682 (3d Cir. 1973), cert. denied 415 U.S. 989, 94 S.Ct. 1587, 39 L.Ed.2d 886 (1974); In re Tierney, 465 F.2d 806, 811–12 (5th Cir. 1972); In re Parker, 411 F.2d 1067, 1069–70 (10th Cir. 1969), vacated 397 U.S. 96, 90 S.Ct. 819, 25 L.Ed.2d 81 (1970). The only case allowing a witness to assert the privilege is In re Cardassi, 351 F.Supp. 1080 (D.Conn.1972), which so held in an unusually well-written and persuasive opinion. See generally Comment, Fear of Foreign Prosecution and the Fifth Amendment, 58 Iowa L. Rev. 1304 (1973); Comment, The Fifth Amendment Protects a Witness Who Refuses to Testify for Fear of Self-Incrimination Under the Laws of a Foreign Jurisdiction, In re Cardassi, 351 F.Supp. 1080 (D. Conn.1972), 5 Rutgers-Camden L.J. 146 (1973).

99. This problem can be substantial for American military personnel stationed abroad. Service members are protected both by the fifth amendment and Article 31 of the Uniform Code of Military Justice, 10 U.S.C.A. § 831, which is broader in scope in many areas than is the fifth amendment. The only military case on point, United States v. Murphy, 7 U.S.C. M.A. 32, 21 C.M.R. 158 (1956), held that Article 31 protects military members only against possible incrimination in an American jurisdiction. Although the case is suspect in light of Murphy v. Waterfront, it has not yet been overruled.

1. 341 U.S. 479, 71 S.Ct. 814, 95 L.Ed. 1118 (1951).
2. Id. at 488, citing Temple v. Commonwealth, 75 Va. 892, 898 (1881).
3. See, e. g., United States v. Anglada, 524 F.2d 296 (2d Cir. 1975) ("carefully phrased, limited questions" may be permissible even if the witness may assert the privilege generally); State v. Hasney, 115 R.I. 210, 341 A.2d 729 (1975) (no possibility of further incrimination).

answered even one incriminating question, the witness has irretrievably waived the privilege unless "further" incrimination could result.

In the leading case of Rogers v. United States,[4] Ms. Rogers testified before a grand jury that she was the treasurer of the Denver Communist Party. She asserted her privilege when questioned about the identity of the individual to whom she had transferred the party's accounts. The Supreme Court held that she had waived her right to remain silent by revealing her party membership and possession. Her testimony had not conceded any criminal activity on her part, for the Smith Act proscribed only membership with knowledge of the goals of the Communist Party. However, the Court found that no reasonable danger of *further* incrimination existed [5] although the question was itself incriminating.[6] If further testimony would have opened up a new area or substantially increased the risk of self-incrimination, the privilege could have been asserted.

The court's use of the waiver doctrine usually prevents a witness from testifying to some questions while refusing to answer other questions on the same subject. While this approach is often salutary in that it prevents an abridged version of events from being presented,[7] it also has the curious result of forcing people to assert the privilege when asked any question, regardless of how trivial, for fear that they will waive their right to remain silent.[8]

The Supreme Court has recognized that a defendant may choose to testify on the issue of the voluntariness of a confession or of the legality of a search and seizure without waiving the privilege. In this situation the witness may not be cross-examined on the merits.[9] Similarly the Federal Rules of Evidence limit the waiver concept by stating [10] that the giving of testimony by an accused or a witness "does not operate as a waiver of his privilege against self-incrimination when examined with respect to matters which relate only to credibility."

A waiver problem not yet resolved centers on prior proceedings. Generally the rule is that a statement made at one proceeding does not waive the witness's rights at a subsequent independent proceeding. However recent cases [11] suggest that testimony given at a grand jury proceeding might operate as a waiver at trial.

Suggested Reading:

Rogers v. United States, 340 U.S. 367, 71 S.Ct. 438, 95 L.Ed. 344 (1951).

4. 340 U.S. 367, 71 S.Ct. 438, 95 L.Ed. 344 (1951). See generally Comment, Waiver of the Privilege Against Self-Incrimination, 14 Stan.L.Rev. 811 (1962).

5. 340 U.S. at 374. Chief Justice Vinson stated: "As to each question to which a claim of privilege is directed, the court must determine whether the answer to that particular question would subject the witness to a 'real danger' of further crimination."

6. Under the Court's decision in Rogers, the question is not whether a response would be incriminating but whether the response would yield a "real danger" of further incrimination or, in other words, would significantly increase the danger by opening up a new area or so expand the scope of reply as to increase the danger of prosecution. See, e. g., Brown v. United States, 356 U.S. 148, 78 S.Ct. 622, 2 L.Ed. 2d 589 (1958) (deportation case); In re Master Key Litigation (Illinois v. McCulloch), 507 F.2d 292 (9th Cir. 1974) (civil anti-trust suit).

7. Rogers v. United States, 340 U.S. 367, 371, 71 S.Ct. 438, 440–41, 95 L.Ed. 344 (1951).

8. In theory a witness must weigh each question and refuse to answer it individually. However, the circumstances of a specific case may justify blanket refusals. Cf. United States v. Harper, 397 F.Supp. 983 (E.D.Pa.1975).

9. Simmons v. United States, 390 U.S. 377, 88 S.Ct. 967, 19 L.Ed.2d 1247 (1968).

10. Fed.Evid.Rule 608, 28 U.S.C.A.

11. See, e. g., United States v. Seewald, 450 F.2d 1159, 1164 (2d Cir. 1971), cert. denied 405 U.S. 978, 92 S.Ct. 1206, 31 L.Ed.2d 253 (1972); Ellis v. United States, 416 F.2d 791, 800–05 (1969). This does not as yet appear to be a majority rule.

Immunity. As interpreted by the courts, the fifth amendment privilege is a right not to incriminate oneself. The distinction between this phrasing and the actual wording of the amendment ("nor shall [any person] be compelled in any criminal case to be a witness against himself") is critical, for the amendment taken literally appears absolute. Nevertheless when the narrower interpretation is accepted, immunity becomes possible. If the intent of the privilege is to safeguard an individual from criminal consequence, a statutory guarantee (immunity) that such an incrimination cannot take place should remove the privilege. Clearly, however, acceptance of immunity as a viable concept negates the possibility of the privilege expanding to include self-infamy (e. g. damage to reputation). Although self-infamy has been occasionally urged as a ground for refusal to testify,[12] the courts have uniformly, absent a state statute or constitutional provision, rejected the claim, fearing that any expansion of the privilege would unreasonably hinder law enforcement efforts. Accordingly, grants of immunity have become significant tools in the hands of prosecutors.

Supreme Court in 1892. Counselman, a grain dealer, was called before a grand jury to testify about certain improper railway rates. Counselman refused to respond to a number of incriminating questions despite the existence of a federal immunity statute stating that neither testimony nor other evidence gained during such proceedings could be used against its maker at a later trial. The Supreme Court found that Counselman's refusal to testify was justified because the statute did not bar derivative use—that is, using the testimony given before the grand jury to obtain other evidence for trial.

At the time *Counselman* was widely interpreted as requiring, before the privilege could be overcome, that a witness be granted immunity from subsequent prosecution for any transaction or offense testified to at the first proceeding. This interpretation became known as transactional immunity. The lesser form of immunity, seemingly justified in *Counselman* but rejected in federal and most state statutes, became known as testimonial or use immunity.[14] This immunity excludes any evidence gained at the first proceeding *and* any derivative evidence but allows subsequent prosecution of the witness if sufficient independent evidence exists.

Transactional immunity was approved by the Supreme Court in 1895.[15] However the minimum form of immunity necessary to remove the fifth amendment was undeter-

Suggested Reading:

Kastigar v. United States, 406 U.S. 441, 92 S.Ct. 1653, 32 L.Ed.2d 212 (1972).

What Type of Immunity Is Required? Although a number of decisions had dealt with the general issue of immunity, the first truly significant case in the United States is Counselman v. Hitchcock,[13] decided by the

12. See, e. g., Ullman v. United States, 350 U.S. 422, 445–55, 76 S.Ct. 497, 510–515, 100 L.Ed. 511 (1956) (Douglas, J., dissenting); Brown v. Walker, 161 U.S. 591, 631–32, 16 S.Ct. 644, 653, 40 L.Ed. 819 (1896) (Field, J., dissenting). Note that Mr. Justice Douglas rejected the notice of immunity because of self-infamy. 350 U.S. at 445.

13. 142 U.S. 547, 12 S.Ct. 195, 35 L.Ed. 1110 (1892).

14. Actually a number of terms are used for this type of immunity. The Court in *Counselman* interpreted the statute as barring use but not derivative use of the immunized evidence (arguably an improper interpretation of the statute). Accordingly that form of defective immunity is sometimes known as "use" immunity. Use and derivative use are known variously by that description, "use plus fruits," or testimonial immunity as well as by other terms. The key difference between transactional and testimonial immunity (also today occasionally called use immunity) is that testimonial immunity theoretically allows subsequent prosecution for the offense testified about while transactional immunity prevents prosecution about the offense or transaction.

15. Brown v. Walker, 161 U.S. 591, 16 S.Ct. 644, 40 L.Ed. 819 (1896).

mined until 1972, when the Supreme Court decided Kastigar v. United States.[16] In *Kastigar* the Court explicitly accepted testimonial immunity, stating that it was sufficiently broad to supplant the privilege. This decision had been foreshadowed by two earlier opinions. In Malloy v. Hogan [17] the Court held that the fifth amendment right against self-incrimination applies to the states as well as to the federal government, and in *Murphy*,[18] decided the same day, the Court held that a witness who testified pursuant to a state grant of immunity is protected from use or derivative use of his testimony by the federal courts. *Murphy* suggested that something less than transactional immunity would be acceptable by stating that the government, when prosecuting a previously immunized individual, could show that the evidence used was independent of the immunized testimony.

The power to grant immunity for the federal government was centralized in the Department of Justice by the Organized Crime Control Act of 1970,[19] providing for testimonial immunity. *Kastigar* sustained the legality of the Act, holding, however, that the government, when prosecuting a previously immunized witness, must show that its evidence is totally independent of the immunized evidence. Apparently the prosecution must affirmatively show independence by a preponderance of the evidence.[20] Although *Kastigar* settled the question of the minimum form of immunity, it did not preclude transactional immunity. Therefore, a number of jurisdictions continue to grant transactional immunity either by intent or by inaction,[21] and occasional efforts are made to statutorily require transactional immunity.[22]

The Derivative Evidence Problem. Under *Kastigar* the government must affirmatively show, in prosecuting an individual previously the recipient of a grant of immunity, that its case is untainted by any use or derivative use of the testimony given under the grant of immunity.[23] Although other prob-

---

16. 406 U.S. 441, 92 S.Ct. 1653, 32 L.Ed.2d 212 (1972). See also the companion cases of Zicarelli v. Investigation Comm., 406 U.S. 472, 92 S.Ct. 1670, 32 L.Ed.2d 234 (1972), and Sarno v. Investigating Comm., 406 U.S. 482, 92 S.Ct. 1677, 32 L.Ed.2d 243 (1972). See generally Comment, Constitutional Considerations of Federal and State Testimonial Immunity Legislation, 36 La.L.Rev. 214 (1975); Rubenstein, Immunity and the Self-Incrimination Clause, 2 Am.J.Crim.L. 29 (1973); Comment, Immunity from Prosecution: Transactional Versus Testimonial or Use, 17 S.D.L.Rev. 166 (1972); Note, Immunity Statutes and the Constitution, 68 Colum.L.Rev. 959 (1968). Comment, Standards for Exclusion in Immunity Cases After *Kastigar* and *Zicarelli*, 82 Yale L.J. 171 (1972).

17. 378 U.S. 1, 84 S.Ct. 1489, 12 L.Ed.2d 653 (1964).

18. 378 U.S. 52, 84 S.Ct. 1594, 12 L.Ed.2d 678 (1964). See also In re Birdsong, 216 Kan. 297, 532 P.2d 1301 (1975).

19. 18 U.S.C.A. § 6001 et seq. The Act provides for grants of immunity before grand juries, courts, and federal agencies (§ 6003) and Congressional proceedings (§ 6004).

20. The Court in *Kastigar* likened testimonial immunity to the result of a coerced confession. The Court has held in Lego v. Twomey, 404 U.S. 477, 92 S.Ct. 619, 30 L.Ed.2d 618 (1972), that the government must show a challenged confession to be admissible using a preponderance of the evidence standard.

21. In 1976, research indicated that of fifteen states selected at random, nine (Florida, Colorado, New Hampshire, New York, Washington, California, Nebraska, Hawaii, and Illinois) granted transactional immunity while only one (New Jersey) granted testimonial. Five other states (Virginia, Tennessee, Wisconsin, Mississippi, and Michigan) had limited or specialized immunity statutes. Military courts-martial serve as an excellent example of the situation in that both testimonial and transactional grants of immunity are in use depending upon the local command, although general policy seems to suggest that testimonial immunity be used. See Grants of Immunity, The Army Lawyer, December, 1973, at 22–25, as amended by the Army Lawyer, February, 1974, at 14.

22. See, e. g., H.R. 844, 95th Cong., 1st Sess. (1977), which would amend 18 U.S.C.A. §§ 6001–6005 to grant transactional rather than testimonial immunity.

23. 406 U.S. 441, 460–61, 92 S.Ct. 1653, 1664–65, 32 L.Ed.2d 212 (1972). See, e. g., United States v. First Western State Bank, 491 F.2d 780 (8th Cir. 1974) (en banc).

lems exist in the immunity area,[24] one of the primary difficulties posed by the Court's decisions is determining what constitutes improper derivative use. In *Kastigar* the Court found that the "sweeping proscription of any use, direct or indirect, of the compelled testimony and any information derived therefrom"[25] mandated by the Organized Crime Control Act of 1970 answered fears that testimonial immunity would be unable to cope with possible effects of the incriminating testimony, including obtaining prosecutorial leads, names of witnesses, and other information not otherwise available.[26] Unfortunately the Court failed to indicate how broad testimonial immunity might be in the absence of the statute.

At least one court has considered the derivative evidence problem carefully and has reached the conclusion that the smallest possible use constitutes taint. In United States v. Rivera,[27] the United States Court of Military Appeals indicated that the prosecution may not use the immunized testimony

"in any way to improve . . . a case against the accused" and that "the mere reading of the accused's immunized statement constitutes a prima facie use of the testimony which is prohibited." The court stated that in most cases a grant of testimonial immunity would effectively bar further prosecution of the immunized individual. Thus at least in the military, there is now little difference between testimonial and transactional immunity. This policy, currently a minority view, may bar subsequent prosecution unless the government can successfully demonstrate to the court's satisfaction that its case was complete prior to the testimony of the immunized witness. Furthermore the prosecution team in the second trial probably would have to consist of lawyers who had no contact with the first trial. Although extreme, this position seems defensible in view of the justifications behind the privilege against self-incrimination.

Procedures for Granting Immunity. The procedure for granting immunity depends upon the jurisdiction involved. Most grants of immunity are issued by the states simply because of the sheer number of state prosecutions. Of course, the source of and method of granting immunity depend on the particular state concerned and therefore vary considerably. In some states a grant is issued by a court upon motion of the District or County Attorney.[28] In others the state's Attorney General must first approve the grant before the court may issue a grant,[29] and in others the statutory language suggests that a court order is unnecessary, thus leaving the decision in the hands of the prosecution.[30] Thus in some jurisdictions the court controls the system and in others the prosecution does.[31]

---

24. The courts have yet to finally resolve the problem of possible incrimination in non-American jurisdictions, for example. Additionally it is unclear to what extent immunized evidence can be used against the immunized individual in non-criminal proceedings. See, e. g., Segretti v. State Bar of California, 15 Cal. 3d 878, 126 Cal.Rptr. 793, 544 P.2d 929 (1976), holding that a grant of immunity does not prevent use of the immunized testimony in bar disciplinary proceedings because of their non-criminal nature. In view of the Supreme Court's decision in Lefkowitz v. Turley, 414 U.S. 70, 94 S.Ct. 316, 38 L.Ed.2d 274 (1973), and Spevack v. Klien, 385 U.S. 511, 87 S.Ct. 625, 17 L.Ed.2d 574 (1967), the *Segretti* decision seems suspect.

25. 406 U.S. at 460.

26. Id. at 459. Note United States v. McDaniel, 482 F.2d 305 (8th Cir. 1973), holding that reading of immunized testimony was an "improper use." Determination of the possibility of derivative use can occasionally become a legal nightmare. See, e. g., United States v. Kurzer, 534 F.2d 511 (2d Cir. 1976) holding that when the result of witness A's immunized testimony was the incrimination of witness B, whose testimony led to the indictment of witness A, the District Court was obliged to determine the motivation that led witness B to testify in order to determine taint.

27. 23 U.S.C.M.A. 430, 50 C.M.R. 389 (1975).

28. E. g., Washington, New York, Colorado, California, and Nebraska (approval of states' attorneys-general is unclear).

29. E. g., New Hampshire and New Jersey.

30. E. g., Florida (but order seems likely).

31. In Florida a judge may not offer immunity; the relevant statute, Fla.Stat.Ann. § 914.04, has been

The primary source of federal immunity is the Organized Crime Control Act of 1970.[32] The Act centralizes control of federal immunity in the Attorney General of the United States. Usually the decision to immunize rests with the prosecution and not with the courts, for a federal district court must grant immunity when the prosecution has complied with the Act's requirements.[33] Eighteen U.S.C.A. § 6003 states that a U. S. Attorney "may, with the approval of the Attorney General, the Deputy Attorney General, or any designated Assistant Attorney General, request an order to testify when the testimony desired is in the public interest" and the "individual has refused or is likely to refuse to testify or provide other information on the basis of his privilege against self-incrimination." Under § 6004 an agency of the United States may issue an order to testify before an administrative proceeding if prior approval has been obtained from the Attorney General.

Other forms of immunity exist. Although there are no generally accepted designations for them, they may be termed informal [34] (or equitable) immunity and de facto immunity. Informal immunity is granted by the prosecution relying upon inherent prosecutorial discretion rather than upon statutory authority. Because the prosecution may always decide not to prosecute, it may promise to refrain from doing so. Unlike the usual grant of immunity, proof of such an arrangement may be difficult if the government reneges.

In some jurisdictions the government might not be bound by its promise, although

a confession resulting from such an arrangement might be considered involuntary. Informal immunity or clemency may frequently be promised in return for a plea of guilty and the term *equitable immunity* has been used in at least one case in which the accused claimed a breach of agreement.[35] De facto immunity is in effect a fifth amendment exclusionary rule. If a witness correctly asserts his or her privilege but then is improperly ordered to testify on pain of contempt, any testimony would be suppressed at a subsequent proceeding just as would any involuntary confession.[36] For this result to occur, however, the witness must have initially refused to answer rather than having simply bowed to what seemed to be inevitable.[37] Of course in such a circumstance, the witness may continue to refuse to answer and litigate the likely contempt citation.

This same doctrine provides a framework for dealing with improper or illegal offers of immunity. For example, in most jurisdictions police are totally unable to offer immunity. If a policeman or other state official obtains testimony by invalidly promising immunity, the jurisdiction may not be bound by the promise,[38] but the testimony

---

held to leave this issue to the prosecuting attorney. Fla.Att'y Gen. 073–150 (May 8, 1973).

32. 18 U.S.C.A. § 6001–05.

33. 18 U.S.C.A. § 6003(a) provides that "the United States district court . . . shall issue . . . upon the request of the United States attorney for such district, an order requiring such individual to give testimony."

34. United States v. Librach, 536 F.2d 1228 (8th Cir. 1976).

35. United States v. Donahey, 529 F.2d 831 (5th Cir. 1976) (the court found that the accused had not honored her part of the bargain and had thus freed the government from its promise to prosecute only a misdemeanor.).

36. Maness v. Meyers, 419 U.S. 449, 474, 95 S.Ct. 584, 599, 42 L.Ed.2d 574 (1975) (Stewart, J., concurring); cf. United States v. Pepe, 367 F.Supp. 1365 (D.Conn.1973).

37. See, e. g., State v. Wallace, 321 So.2d 349 (La. 1975); State v. Hall, 65 Wis.2d 18, 221 N.W.2d 806 (1974) (witness answered three or four questions after his first refusal to testify; he was not coerced into his answers and his testimony would not be suppressed.).

38. See, e. g., United States v. Long, 511 F.2d 878 (7th Cir. 1975). The actual phrasing of the promise becomes extremely important. See for example United States v. Nussen, 531 F.2d 15 (2d Cir. 1976), in which the FBI stated that information gained from Nussen would not be used to "further develop a more encompassing case involving any drug dealings, and other transactions he had engaged in pre-

will probably constitute an illegal admission which will be suppressed.

Results of a Grant of Immunity. A grant of immunity compels the recipient to testify to the topics covered by the grant. The individual generally cannot challenge the order to testify unless it is either too limited or procedurally improper. Some difficulties have arisen concerning the exclusion of perjury or false swearing from the crimes protected by immunity grants. Eighteen U.S.C.A. § 6002 provides that when an order to testify is given, "no testimony or other information compelled under the order (or any information directly or indirectly derived from such testimony or other information) may be used against the witness in any criminal case,[39] except a prosecution for perjury, giving a false statement, or otherwise failing to comply with the order." Although the exception appears to allow trial for perjury which is given as part of the immunized testimony, occasionally claims have been made that it allows prosecution with the immunized testimony for prior perjury.[40] Generally this letter argument seems incorrect.[41]

A witness refusing to testify after being granted immunity lacks any privilege and may be subject to a contempt citation [42] or in some jurisdictions to prosecution for the offense of refusal to testify.[43] The court may hold the witness in civil contempt and imprison him or her for the life of the grand jury or until he or she decides to testify. Criminal contempt is also possible. If a lawyer advises a client not to testify despite an order to do so, the lawyer may not be held in contempt,[44] but the client generally may not claim reliance on the attorney's advice as a defense. In addition a witness may not refuse to testify because of fear of retaliation against himself or herself or his or her family.[45]

Note, Statutory Immunity and the Perjury Exception, 10 Case W.Res.L.Rev. 428 (1974). See also In re Bonk, 527 F.2d 120 (7th Cir. 1975), stay denied, 423 U.S. 942, 96 S.Ct. 350, 46 L.Ed.2d 274.

42. See, e. g., In re Special September 1972 Grand Jury (Lufman), 500 F.2d 1283 (7th Cir. 1974) (criminal contempt citation may follow civil contempt); In re Manna, 124 N.J.Super. 428, 307 A.2d 619 (1973). In the event of criminal contempt, summary contempt is viewed as inappropriate in view of the complex legal issues generally involved.

43. See, e. g., Uniform Code of Military Justice, Art. 134, 10 U.S.C.A. § 934 punishing among other offenses "refusal to testify" which according to Manual for Courts-Martial, 1969 (rev. ed.), para. 127(c) carries a maximum punishment of a dishonorable discharge, confinement at hard labor for five years, total forfeitures and reduction to the lowest enlisted grade.

44. Maness v. Meyers, 419 U.S. 449, 95 S.Ct. 584, 42 L.Ed.2d 574 (1975).

45. See, e. g., Dupuy v. United States, 518 F.2d 1295 (9th Cir. 1975).

---

vious or subsequent to July 16, 1974." The court found that the further information gained was voluntary and was not in violation of the terms of the promise.

39. This does appear to leave open use of immunized testimony in "non-criminal" civil or administrative proceedings. See, e. g., Segretti v. State Bar of California, 15 Cal.3d 878, 126 Cal.Rptr. 793, 544 P.2d 929 (1976); Maryland State Bar Ass'n v. Sugarman, 273 Md. 306, 329 A.2d 1 (1974) (bar disciplinary proceedings).

40. See In re Baldinger, 356 F.Supp. 153 (C.D.Cal. 1973). A related problem is use of immunized testimony to obtain a perjury conviction when the perjured statements are made *after* the proceedings at which the immunized statements were given. See United States v. Tramunti, 500 F.2d 1334 (2d Cir. 1974), cert. denied 419 U.S. 1079, 95 S.Ct. 667, 42 L.Ed.2d 673.

41. See generally Comment, Constitutional Considerations of Federal and State Testimonial Immunity Legislation, 36 La.L.Rev. 214, 221–23 (1975);

CHAPTER 21

THE VOLUNTARINESS DOCTRINE

1. Introduction

A confession is a statement by an individual admitting all the elements of a crime. Historically, a confession took place before the court and was the equivalent of a conviction.[1] Distinct from a confession, an admission is a statement admitting some facts relevant to proof of a crime but not the crime itself. The difference can be seen in the following example. The police suspect Smith of a homicide. During the first police interview, Smith admits that he visited the deceased the afternoon of the offense. During a followup interview, Smith confesses that he shot the deceased during his visit. The first statement is an admission, and the second constitutes a confession. In terms of admissibility, there is generally[2] no difference between an admission and confession.[3]

A judicial confession is simply a confession made in court, usually by an accused who has taken the stand. A judicial confession normally takes place when a defendant admits commission of one offense while denying responsibility for another, more serious offense. All other confessions, which are technically extrajudicial, are usually referred to merely as confessions.

To successfully offer a confession or admission into evidence, a counsel must comply with the hearsay rule, the voluntariness doctrine, the *Miranda* warning requirements, and in the case of confessions, the corroboration requirement. Admissions and confessions made by a party to the trial are of course exceptions to the hearsay rule.[4]

---

1. See, e. g., 3 Wigmore, Evidence § 818 (Chadbourn rev. 1970); Blackstone, Commentaries on the Laws of England; of Public Wrongs 421 (Beacon Press ed. 1962).

2. In the past some jurisdictions distinguished between admissions and confessions for such matters as the effect of error in their admission at trial (admissions being more easily excused than confessions). Although some differences may continue to exist in the states (see, e. g., State v. Shaw, 284 N.C. 366, 200 S.E.2d 585 (1973); People v. Koch, 15 Ill.App.3d 386, 304 N.E.2d 482 (1973)), there appears to be no difference in their treatment under the Constitution. See Miranda v. Arizona, 384 U.S. 436, 476–77,

86 S.Ct. 1602, 1628–29, 16 L.Ed.2d 694 (1966). Within this chapter, reference to either admissions or confessions will include both possibilities unless otherwise indicated.

3. Exculpatory statements are those that deny wrongdoing. They were treated differently from admissions or confessions at common law. However, because of their use for impeachment, constitutional doctrine treats them as admissions. Miranda v. Arizona, 384 U.S. 436, 476–77, 86 S.Ct. 1602, 1628–29, 16 L.Ed.2d 694 (1966).

4. The underlying rationale for the recognition of the admission and confession exception to the hearsay

The voluntariness doctrine requires that admissions and confessions be shown to have been made voluntarily. The doctrine is designed to ensure reliable evidence and to protect against unfairness. The *Miranda* warning requirements reinforce the voluntariness doctrine. The corroboration requirement demands that before a confession can be admitted, enough other evidence must be shown to substantiate the commission of the offense or to establish the reliability of the confession.[5] This chapter focuses on the voluntariness doctrine and the corroboration requirement.

2. Background

Suggested Reading:

Brown v. Mississippi, 297 U.S. 278, 56 S.Ct. 461, 80 L.Ed. 682 (1936).

Professor Wigmore found four stages in the development of the English law of confessions:[6] total acceptance of confession evidence until approximately 1750; limited exclusion of involuntary confessions during approximately 1750 to 1800; hypersensitivity to confessions resulting in almost complete exclusion;[7] and the current rule characterized in the United States by constitutional underpinnings. Differing slightly from Wigmore, Professor Levy finds that the voluntariness rule was at least partially recognized by 1726[8] and suggests that its primary justification was preventing receipt of unreliable evidence.

Although separate and distinct from the right against self-incrimination, the voluntariness doctrine plainly had its origins in the same complex of values and social conflicts that gave rise to the right. Certainly much of the objection to self-incrimination was based on objection to torture-derived confessions. The English voluntariness rule appears to have been based primarily on reliability grounds. However, questions of fairness no doubt were also relevant.

The right against self-incrimination per se had no remedy, for it allowed an individual only to remain silent, and once testimony was given the right was waived. However, the voluntariness doctrine created a remedy in that if an individual was compelled to confess, his or her statement could be ex-

---

rule is unclear. However, it would seem to be based in part on the need for the evidence, for the declarant will be uncompellable under the privilege against self-incrimination, and in part on the same reasoning that underlies the declaration against interest exception. There are a number of types of admissions, including exculpatory ones, which prove difficult to explain on either rationale, and it may be that the rule should be considered as not falling within any one theory. See State v. Kennedy, 135 N.J.Super. 513, 343 A.2d 783 (1975). The requirement that the statement come from a party to the trial can be highly troublesome both in theory and in practice. For those jurisdictions lacking the declaration against penal interest exception to the hearsay rule, it can result in the exclusion of a confession made by an individual not on trial.

5. The majority rule requires independent evidence to establish the commission of an offense (the corpus delicti rule), and the minority rule requires only that other evidence be admitted to show the reliability of the confession.

6. 3 Wigmore, Evidence § 817 (Chadbourn rev. 1970).

7. Id. at §§ 820 & 820a. Wigmore postulates the following explanation for the English approach during the early 1800's: the character of the suspect— i. e., lower social class with a subordination to authority—the absence of a right to appeal and the resulting difficulty of obtaining a rule of general application; the inability of the accused to take the stand in his or her own behalf. Probably the large number of offenses which carried the death penalty during the first quarter-century also motivated exclusion.

8. L. Levy, Origins of the Fifth Amendment 327 (1968): "Lord Chief Baron Geoffrey Gilbert, in his *Law of Evidence*, written before 1726 though not published until thirty years later, stated that though the best evidence of guilt was a confession, this Confession must be voluntary and without Compulsion; for our Law . . . will not force any Man to accuse himself; and in this we do certainly follow the Law of Nature, which commands every Man to endeavor his own Preservation; and therefore Pain and Force compel Men to confess what is not the truth of Facts, and consequently such extorted confessions are not to be depended on."

cluded, thus attaching an exclusionary sanction to violations of the right against self-incrimination. This development should not be misconstrued; all coerced confessions were not inadmissible. Particularly during the 1700's in England, the question was one of apparent truthfulness rather than breach of a privilege.

As in the case of the right against self-incrimination, the voluntariness doctrine was transplanted to the American Colonies. For example, formal recognition took place in Pennsylvania by 1792[9] at latest. The common-law voluntariness doctrine was the rule in the United States during most of the 19th century, although presumably without the anti-confession bias common in England during the early 1800's.

Despite the existence of the fifth amendment and later of the fourteenth amendment (enacted in 1868), the Supreme Court failed to make use of constitutional rationales[10] until 1897 when the Court decided Bram v. United States.[11] In *Bram*, a murder case, the Court found the fifth amendment right against self-incrimination required reversal because of the receipt in evidence of an involuntary confession. *Bram* was the high point in applying the privilege against self-incrimination to confessions, and the Court subsequently retreated from the holding.[12]

Professor Otis Stephens[13] states that in its review of federal confession cases, the Supreme Court, while at first emphasizing the reliability test for coerced statements, began to swing toward concern about fair trial generally.[14] In 1936, the Court in Brown v. Mississippi[15] held that admission of a coerced confession into evidence violated fourteenth amendment due process. The facts in *Brown* demanded reversal. A white Mississippi farmer had been murdered. In order to coerce a confession from one Black "suspect," a deputy sheriff accompanied by a mob hanged him twice from a tree. Having refused to confess, the suspect was released, rearrested a day or so later, and beaten. He then signed the desired confession. The two other Black suspects, including Brown, were jailed and beaten until they too confessed as their captors desired.

Clearly, in reversing the conviction, the Supreme Court was motivated by the specific facts of the case and the obvious injustice. However, the Court's extension of due process standards to confessions was probably also motivated by the Wickersham Report,[16]

---

9. Commonwealth v. Dillon, 4 U.S. (4 Dall.) 116, 1 L.Ed. 765, cited in O. Stephens, The Supreme Court and Confessions of Guilt 23 (1973).

10. The Court did apply the common-law voluntariness test to federal cases. See Wilson v. United States, 162 U.S. 613, 621–25, 16 S.Ct. 895, 899–900, 40 L.Ed. 1090 (1896); Sparf v. United States, 156 U.S. 51, 53–56, 15 S.Ct. 273, 274–75, 39 L.Ed. 343 (1895); Hopt v. Utah, 110 U.S. 574, 584–87, 4 S.Ct. 202, 207–09, 28 L.Ed. 262 (1884).

11. 168 U.S. 532, 18 S.Ct. 183, 42 L.Ed. 568 (1897). Interestingly, the Court in Bram considered and rejected the argument that police interrogation was per se coercive. Id. at 556–58.

12. This may have been because of the Court's holding in Twining v. New Jersey, 211 U.S. 78, 29 S.Ct. 14, 53 L.Ed. 97 (1908), overruled by Malloy v.

Hogan, 378 U.S. 1, 84 S.Ct. 1489, 12 L.Ed.2d 653 (1964), that the fifth amendment right against self-incrimination was inapplicable to the states. But see the Court's admission that the voluntariness doctrine is grounded in the same policies giving rise to the privilege against self-incrimination. Davis v. North Carolina, 384 U.S. 737, 740, 86 S.Ct. 1761, 1763, 16 L.Ed.2d 895 (1966).

13. S. Otis, The Supreme Court and Confessions of Guilt 26 (1973).

14. See, e. g., Ziang Sung Wan v. United States, 266 U.S. 1, 45 S.Ct. 1, 69 L.Ed. 131 (1924) (one week's incommunicado detention and constant questioning without arrest while the suspect was ill; held that compulsion automatically required reversal).

15. 297 U.S. 278, 56 S.Ct. 461, 80 L.Ed. 682 (1936). *Brown* held that a state conviction resting solely on a coerced confession required reversal. Later cases indicated that reversal was merited in almost all cases involving coerced confessions—the automatic reversal rule. See Chapman v. California, 386 U.S. 18, 87 S.Ct. 824, 17 L.Ed.2d 705 (1967); Payne v. Arkansas, 356 U.S. 560, 78 S.Ct. 844, 2 L.Ed.2d 975 (1958).

16. Report on Lawlessness in Law Enforcement, National Commission on Law Observance and Enforcement (1931) (the Wickersham Report).

which had confirmed the use of the "third degree"—e. g., physical violence and psychological coercion—to obtain confessions across the country, particularly from the poor and disadvantaged. The Court's subsequent cases [17] tended to confirm a strong element of redress for racial discrimination of the worst sort, for many poor Blacks were the targets of brutal beatings designed to coerce confessions.

While the Court has consistently reaffirmed the voluntariness requirement of Brown v. Mississippi,[18] its application of the voluntariness doctrine has varied greatly. After *Brown* the Court made use of its supervisory powers to require that federal defendants be promptly brought before magistrates, thereby limiting the time available for police interrogation.[19] In the state arena, the Court took an active role in preventing coerced confessions [20] and then turned temporarily to considering primarily the trustworthiness [21] of the coerced confession—a standard that emphasized reliability. Beginning in the mid 1950's the Court returned to its earlier role and scrutinized confessions not so much from the perspective of reliability but more from the standpoint of the fairness of the procedure involved.[22] Ultimately the Court decided Miranda v. Arizona,[23] holding that the innate coercion of custodial interrogation required rights warnings, including the right to counsel, to dispel the coercive atmosphere. At present the test used throughout the United States emphasizes fairness rather than reliability and asks if the statement was the product of a free and unrestrained choice.[24]

3. Substantive Doctrine

Suggested Reading:

LaFrance v. Bohlinger, 499 F.2d 29 (1st Cir. 1974).

Rogers v. Richmond, 365 U.S. 534, 81 S.Ct. 735, 5 L.Ed.2d 761 (1961).

Ashcraft v. Tennessee, 322 U.S. 143, 64 S.Ct. 921, 88 L.Ed. 1192 (1944).

Although the voluntariness doctrine has been greatly affected by the Supreme Court's decision in Miranda v. Arizona,[25] it retains vitality as an independent doctrine in deter-

---

17. See, e. g., Ward v. Texas, 316 U.S. 547, 62 S.Ct. 1139, 86 L.Ed. 1663 (1942); Vernon v. Alabama, 313 U.S. 547, 61 S.Ct. 1092, 85 L.Ed. 1513 (1941); Lomax v. Texas, 313 U.S. 544, 61 S.Ct. 956, 85 L.Ed. 1511 (1941); White v. Texas, 310 U.S. 530, 60 S.Ct. 1032, 84 L.Ed. 1342 (1940); Canty v. Alabama, 309 U.S. 629, 60 S.Ct. 612, 84 L.Ed. 988 (1940); Chambers v. Florida, 309 U.S. 227, 60 S.Ct. 472, 84 L.Ed. 716 (1940) (lead case).

18. 297 U.S. 278, 56 S.Ct. 461, 80 L.Ed. 682 (1936).

19. 318 U.S. 332, 63 S.Ct. 608, 87 L.Ed. 819 (1942). See Chapter 22, infra.

20. In Lisenba v. California, 314 U.S. 219, 62 S.Ct. 280, 86 L.Ed. 166 (1941), an exceptional and unusually gruesome murder case, the Court upheld a coerced confession on the ground that the defendant's will had not been overcome. The Court did state, however, that the aim of the due process requirement was "to prevent fundamental unfairness in the use of evidence, whether true or false." 314 U.S. at 236. The cynical reader might infer that had it not been for the nature of the crime involved, the case would have been reversed. In Ashcraft v. Tennessee, 322 U.S. 143, 64 S.Ct. 921, 88 L.Ed. 1192 (1944), the Supreme Court recognized that both psychological coercion and physical brutality can make a statement involuntary. *Ashcraft* also introduced the short-lived test of "inherent coercion," a test which looked to the nature of the police misconduct. The test, superseded by the fair-trial test, eventually became a part of the contemporary voluntariness doctrine under a new name.

21. Stein v. New York, 346 U.S. 156, 73 S.Ct. 1077, 97 L.Ed. 1522 (1953), overruled Jackson v. Denno, 378 U.S. 368, 84 S.Ct. 1774, 12 L.Ed.2d 908 (1964).

22. See, e. g., Payne v. Arkansas, 356 U.S. 560, 78 S.Ct. 844, 2 L.Ed.2d 975 (1958); Fikes v. Alabama, 352 U.S. 191, 77 S.Ct. 281, 1 L.Ed.2d 246 (1957); Leyra v. Denno, 347 U.S. 556, 74 S.Ct. 716, 98 L.Ed. 948 (1954).

23. 384 U.S. 436, 86 S.Ct. 1602, 16 L.Ed.2d 694 (1966).

24. See, e. g., Culombe v. Connecticut, 367 U.S. 568, 602, 81 S.Ct. 1860, 1879, 6 L.Ed.2d 1037 (1961); Rogers v. Richmond, 365 U.S. 534, 540–41, 81 S.Ct. 735, 739–40, 5 L.Ed.2d 760 (1961).

25. 384 U.S. 436, 86 S.Ct. 1602, 16 L.Ed.2d 694 (1966).

mining the admissibility of confessions.[26] Nevertheless determining the exact nature of the doctrine is difficult in view of the ambiguity inherent in the term *voluntary*.[27] Each individual jurisdiction in the United States has its own statutorily [28] or judicially derived definition of voluntariness. Generally the states suppress confessions that are the product of coercion, threats, or improper inducements, just as they would be suppressed under the common law. However, the states may differ in respect to what constitutes improper inducements, what effect is to be given to the suspect's age, mentality, etc.

Regardless of the individual state test, the federal constitutional test is paramount.[29]

Under the due process clause, a court must determine whether a confession was "the product of an essentially free and unrestrained choice" by its maker.[30] If the individual's will was "overborne" by the interrogation, the resulting [31] confession is involuntary and inadmissible. In determining the voluntariness of a statement, the trial court must look to "the totality of the circumstances" surrounding it. The primary purpose of the due process test is to ensure fairness; the truth or falsity of the resulting confession is irrelevant.[32]

While the due process test suggests a case-by-case approach to determining the causal connection between police [33] misconduct and a confession, analysis of the cases suggests that in truth two separate rules are being applied.[34] In those cases in which the misconduct is extreme—e. g., in cases of physical brutality—the courts frequently

---

26. While the term *voluntariness* is still used, the voluntariness of a confession generally means that the rights warnings required by *Miranda* were properly given to the accused and that visible coercion was lacking. However, the rights warnings are merely one component of voluntariness. See, e. g., United States v. Chadwick, 393 F.Supp. 763 (D.Mass. 1975). The British continue to use a strict common-law standard. See C. Hampton, Criminal Procedure and Evidence 436–38 (London: Sweet & Maxwell 1973).

27. See Schneckloth v. Bustamonte, 412 U.S. 218, 223–27, 93 S.Ct. 2041, 2045–47, 36 L.Ed.2d 854 (1973).

28. See, e. g., Georgia: "To make a confession admissible, it must have been voluntarily, without being induced by another, by the slightest hope of benefit or remotest fear of injury." Ga.Code § 38–411; "The fact that a confession shall have been made under a spiritual exhortation, or a promise of secrecy, or a promise of collateral benefit, shall not exclude it." Ga.Code § 38–412; New York: "A confession, admission or other statement is 'involuntarily made' by a defendant when it is obtained from him: (a) By any person by the use or threatened use of physical force upon the defendant or other person, or by means of any other improper conduct or undue pressure which impaired the defendant's physical or mental condition to the extent of undermining his ability to make a choice whether or not to make a statement; or (b) By a public servant engaged in law enforcement activity or by a person then acting under his direction or in cooperation with him: (i) by means of any promise or statement of fact, which promise or statement creates a substantial risk that the defendant might falsely incriminate himself; or (ii) in violation of such rights as the defendant may derive from the constitution of this state or of the United States." McKinney Consol.Laws of N.Y.Code Cr.Proc. § 60.45.2.

29. Obviously the state's test may be more beneficial to the accused, in which case it is binding.

30. See, e. g., Schneckloth v. Bustamonte, 412 U.S. 218, 224–26, 93 S.Ct. 2041, 2046–47, 36 L.Ed.2d 854 (1973); Culombe v. Connecticut, 367 U.S. 568, 602, 81 S.Ct. 1860, 1879, 6 L.Ed.2d 1037 (1961); Rogers v. Richmond, 365 U.S. 534, 544, 81 S.Ct. 735, 741, 5 L.Ed.2d 760 (1961). *Voluntary* clearly does not mean that the decision to confess must be made without any pressure or with full awareness of the actual situation. The pressures inherent in arrest or questioning, for example, are not per se enough to render a statement involuntary.

31. An individual may confess to clear his or her conscience even after improper pressure. The test in such a case is whether the statement was the product of true remorse and intent or was in fact the product of the improper pressure and thus involuntary.

32. Rogers v. Richmond, 365 U.S. 534, 543–44, 81 S.Ct. 735, 740–41, 5 L.Ed.2d 760 (1961). Of course, if a statement was obtained correctly but is likely to be false, the trial judge should exclude it.

33. The voluntariness doctrine applies to confessions coerced by anyone. However, problems relating to improper threats and inducements are likely to pertain only to public officials. See McKinney Consol. Laws of N.Y.Code Cr.Proc. § 60.45.2, supra note 28. See generally 3 Wigmore, Evidence §§ 827–30 (Chadbourn rev. 1970).

34. See Gangi, A Critical View of the Modern Confession Rule: Some Observations on Key Confession Cases, 28 Ark.L.Rev. 1, 30–31 (1974); McCormick, Handbook of the Law of Evidence 317–21 (2d ed. 1972).

find that the misconduct has rendered the statement per se involuntary.[35] In all other cases the courts test the facts to determine if the misconduct actually overcame the will of the accused.[36] It is virtually impossible to set forth criteria, other than torture, which will result in automatic exclusion. The situation is very much like the famous *Rochin*[37] "shock the conscience" test used in search and seizure.

When applying the contemporary voluntariness doctrine, a court must look to numerous factors. According to Wigmore[38] among these factors are:

> the condition of the accused (health, age, education, intelligence, mental condition, physical condition); the character of detention, if any (delay in arraignment, warning of rights, holding incommunicado, conditions of confinement, access to lawyer, relatives, and friends); the manner of interrogation (length of session(s), relays, number of interrogators, conditions, manner of interrogators); the use of force, threats, promises, or deceptions.

The court weighs these factors to determine whether coercive interrogation factors overcame the suspect's ability to resist. *If coercive interrogation techniques overcame the suspect's ability to resist and the defendant has standing to challenge the resulting statement, the statement must be excluded on the defendant's objection.* This doctrine requires the court evaluate both the interrogation techniques used by the police and the suspect's subjective ability to resist coercive techniques.

Coercive Interrogation Techniques. Of all the possible forms of misconduct, the one most likely to result in automatic exclusion of a statement is *physical coercion*. Physical brutality, usually termed the "third degree," was of course at the heart of the Supreme Court's turn to due process standards[39] and is assumed not only to violate minimum standards of fairness but also to yield unreliable statements. When physical coercion is involved, it is generally irrelevant that the party responsible was not a police officer or a public official.[40] Because of the extreme concern that accompanies charges of police brutality, a number of states require in such cases that the government call all material witnesses who were connected with the alleged confession.[41]

In a discussion of coercion, any attempt to create separate and distinct categories is doomed to failure. While beatings, hangings, flogging, etc. are clearly forms of illegal coercion, other forms of mistreatment can also be identical in effect. In Stidham v. Swenson,[42] the United States Court of Appeals for

---

35. See, e. g., Brooks v. Florida, 389 U.S. 413, 88 S.Ct. 541, 19 L.Ed.2d 643 (1967) (15 days' solitary confinement, naked and on a restricted diet); Ashcraft v. Tennessee, 322 U.S. 143, 64 S.Ct. 921, 88 L.Ed. 1192 (1944) (36 hours of constant questioning by relays of interrogators).

36. See, e. g., United States v. Carmichael, 21 U.S. C.M.A. 530, 45 C.M.R. 304 (1972) (statement made after accused was led to believe that his failure to speak would result in trial by Nationalist Chinese court rather than by an Air Force court-martial held voluntary because of trial court's determination that it was not induced by the threat of foreign trial).

37. Rochin v. California, 342 U.S. 165, 72 S.Ct. 205, 96 L.Ed. 183 (1952).

38. 3 Wigmore, Evidence 352 n. 11 (Chadbourn rev. 1970).

39. See § 1, The Holder of the Privilege, Chapter 20, supra.

40. See, e. g., McKinney Consol.Laws of N.Y.Code Cr.Proc. § 60.45.2(1); Commonwealth v. Mahnke, 368 Mass. 662, 335 N.E.2d 660 (1975) (vigilante group); People v. Haydel, 12 Cal.3d 190, 115 Cal.Rptr. 394, 524 P.2d 866 (1974); 3 Wigmore, Evidence § 833 (Chadbourn rev. 1970).

41. See, e. g., Nabors v. State, 293 So.2d 336 (Miss. 1974); Smith v. State, 256 Ark. 67, 505 S.W.2d 504 (1974).

42. 506 F.2d 478 (8th Cir. 1974). Stidham, imprisoned for robbery, was convicted of murdering a fellow inmate during a prison riot. Although the facts as portrayed by the majority are shocking, the dissent suggests an entirely different view. *Stidham* is a sample of the difficulties sometimes caused by federal habeas corpus, for the actual case had been affirmed by the Missouri Supreme Court 13 years before the first federal attack was filed, making re-

the Eighth Circuit found a confession per se involuntary when it was preceded by 18 months of solitary confinement in subhuman conditions prior to the offense. After the offense the defendant was returned to those conditions and subjected to 25 interrogation sessions without any food or water during four days before he confessed. Courts have condemned as improper coercion denial of medical treatment,[43] prolonged detention,[44] sustained interrogation,[45] handcuffing for lengthy periods,[46] and brutal detention.[47] Of course this list is not exhaustive.[48] Other forms of coercion such as loss of employment[49] may also render a statement involuntary. Whether specific conditions other than physical punishment render a statement involuntary must depend on the facts of each case.

Threats. Coercion can of course also be supplied by threats, for coercion includes both the psychological and the physical.[50] Threats of violence,[51] refusal to supply medi-

cation,[52] removal of wife or children,[53] arrest or prosecution of friends or relatives,[54] and harsher consequences if a confession is not given[55] may all constitute sufficient coercion to render a statement involuntary.[56]

Promises and Inducements. Like threats, promises and inducements may cause involuntary confessions. Clearly a possibility of benefit may well result in an overborne will, rendering a statement violative of due process. Under the common-law test for voluntariness, which was mostly concerned with the reliability of the statement, some forms of inducement, such as religious appeals, did not result in a false confession.[57] This may no longer be the case after Miranda v. Arizona.[58]

In theory any promise or inducement should be analyzed under the usual due process test. However, perhaps because of the common-law heritage, many states almost automatically suppress a confession occurring after an improper promise or inducement. Most improper promises involve representations that the police will not arrest

---

buttal of Stidham's charges difficult. Stidham had also charged he was beaten, but the court discounted the allegation.

43. Cf. Commonwealth v. Purvis, 458 Pa. 359, 326 A.2d 369 (1974).

44. Cf. Stidham v. Swenson, supra note 42. While the issue may not yet be fully resolved, it would appear that the fact of an illegal arrest or detention will render a statement inadmissible. Wong Sun v. United States, 371 U.S. 471, 83 S.Ct. 407, 9 L.Ed.2d 441 (1963).

45. Commonwealth v. Irvin, 462 Pa. 383, 341 A.2d 132 (1975).

46. See, e. g., People v. Holder, 45 A.D.2d 1029, 358 N.Y.S.2d 54 (1974).

47. See, e. g., Stidham v. Swenson, supra note 42; United States v. O'Such, 16 U.S.C.M.A. 537, 37 C.M.R. 157 (1957).

48. See generally 3 Wigmore, Evidence § 833 (Chadbourn rev. 1970).

49. Garrity v. New Jersey, 385 U.S. 493, 496–500, 87 S.Ct. 616, 618–620, 17 L.Ed.2d 562 (1967).

50. Id. at 496–97.

51. See, e. g., ALI, Model Code of Pre-Arraignment Procedure §§ 140.3, 150.2(6) (1975).

52. See, e. g., Northern v. State, 257 Ark. 549, 518 S.W.2d 482 (1975).

53. See, e. g., Lynumn v. Illinois, 372 U.S. 528, 83 S.Ct. 917, 9 L.Ed.2d 922 (1963); People v. Richter, 54 Mich.App. 598, 221 N.W.2d 429 (1974).

54. See, e. g., People v. Helstrom, 50 A.D.2d 685, 375 N.Y.S.2d 189 (1975); People v. Haydel, 12 Cal. 3d 190, 115 Cal.Rptr. 394, 524 P.2d 866 (1974).

55. See, e. g., Sherman v. State, 532 S.W.2d 634 (Tex.Cr.App.1976) (threat by chief of police that accused would receive the death penalty if he did not confess).

56. See generally 3 Wigmore, Evidence § 833 (Chadbourn rev. 1970).

57. 3 Wigmore, Evidence § 840 (Chadbourn rev. 1970).

58. 384 U.S. 436, 86 S.Ct. 1602, 16 L.Ed.2d 694 (1966). *Miranda* requires not only that rights warnings be given but also that the suspect's decision to speak or remain silent not be affected in any way. Thus an exhortation to confess sin or to simply tell the truth is likely to be viewed as nullifying the right to remain silent and thus rendering a statement involuntary.

or prosecute,[59] that a lenient sentence will result,[60] or that friends or relatives will not be harassed, arrested, or prosecuted.[61] Exhortations to tell the truth are not in violation of the traditional voluntariness test [62] although they may interfere with the *Miranda* rights warnings and invalidate a statement. Statements resulting from immunity or plea bargains are inadmissible against the maker.[63]

According to Wigmore, for a promise to result in suppression, it should be possible of fulfillment and thus its maker must have some influence.[64] An accused who initiates a bargaining session with authorities, offering a statement in return for some concession, will not normally be heard to complain that his or her statement is involuntary.[65]

Psychological Coercion. It is well recognized that coercion need not be physical to be effective.[66] Indeed most successful interrogation techniques are almost purely psychological,[67] a fact which proved a major cause for the Supreme Court's decision in Miranda v. Arizona. Psychological techniques employed by interrogators may have coercive effect whether they are holding a suspect incommunicado, helping him or her to excuse the offense, supplying sympathy, or using a "Mutt and Jeff" routine.[68] The courts have recognized that such coercion may render a confession involuntary just as physical coercion may. However, in this area determination of what actually took place and its effect is particularly difficult, and a final judgment is likely to depend upon the character and background of the suspect.[69]

In State v. Edwards,[70] the police used sympathy, stressed a sisterhood between the

59. See, e. g., M.D.B. v. State, 311 So.2d 399 (Fla. App.1975); State v. Raymond, 305 Minn. 160, 232 N.W.2d 879 (1975); St. Jules v. Beto, 371 F.Supp. 470 (S.D.Tex.1974).

60. See, e. g., Freeman v. State, 258 Ark. 617, 527 S.W.2d 909 (1975) (implied promise of leniency found when prosecutor said that he could not promise anything but that defendant probably would not get more than 21 years in jail if he confessed); People v. Ruegger, 32 Ill.App.3d 765, 336 N.E.2d 50 (1975) (police conveyed the impression that they would "go to bat" for the accused in getting him probation).

61. See, e. g., Witt v. Commonwealth, 215 Va. 670, 212 S.E.2d 293 (1975) (Defendant claimed that he confessed because of his belief that his pregnant wife would be arrested if he did not; court found that even if the defendant drew the inference, it was unreasonable and that the confession was voluntary.); Jarriel v. State, 317 So.2d 141 (Fla.App.1975) (police threat to arrest wife unless defendant confessed made resulting statement involuntary). Note that a defendant's belief that confession will assist a friend or relative, when formed without any official representation to that effect, will usually not invalidate a statement. See, e. g., People v. Steger, 16 Cal.3d 539, 128 Cal.Rptr. 161, 546 P.2d 665 (1976); Witt v. Commonwealth, supra.

62. See, e. g., State v. Rollwage, 21 Or.App. 48, 533 P.2d 831 (1975) ("If you confess you'll feel better" held simply an admonition to tell the truth and therefore proper); 3 Wigmore, Evidence § 832 (Chadbourn rev. 1970).

63. See, e. g., Mobley ex rel. Ross v. Meek, 531 F.2d 924 (8th Cir. 1976) (Ross had confessed after making a plea bargain but then withdrew the agreement; held the confession was involuntary); State v. Hoopes, 543 S.W.2d 26 (Mo.1976); 3 Wigmore, Evidence § 834 (Chadbourn rev. 1970).

64. 3 Wigmore, Evidence §§ 827–30 (Chadbourn rev. 1970). The rule suggested is examining each case individually to determine the relationship between the suspect and the promisor. Note State v.

Hess, 9 Ariz.App. 29, 449 P.2d 46 (1969), holding a promise not to file a complaint an improper inducement.

65. See, e. g., United States v. Faulk, 48 C.M.R. 185 (ACMR 1973).

66. See, e. g., Ashcraft v. Tennessee, 322 U.S. 143, 64 S.Ct. 921, 88 L.Ed. 1192 (1944); ALI, Model Code of Pre-Arraignment Procedure § 140.4 (1975).

67. See, e. g., Inbau & Reid, Criminal Interrogations and Confessions (2d ed. 1967); Kamisar, What Is an "Involuntary" Confession? Some Comments on Inbau and Reid's Criminal Interrogation and Confessions, 17 Rut.L.Rev. 728 (1963).

68. This is an interrogation routine usually using two interrogators, one who is hostile and aggressive and the other who is sympathetic and somewhat passive. The intent is to build a sympathetic relationship between the suspect and the second interrogator. The same routine can be used with only one interrogator who will simply change his or her approach as necessary.

69. See *The Suspect's Ability to Resist the Coercive Interrogation Techniques,* infra.

70. 111 Ariz. 357, 529 P.2d 1174 (1974).

female suspect and a female officer, and minimized the moral seriousness of the charge. The Arizona Supreme Court held that these actions, in conjunction with other violations,[71] were more than enough to result in an overborne will, rendering the resulting confession involuntary.

Similarly, in State v. Pruitt [72] the North Carolina Supreme Court found that the interrogation of Pruitt by three police officers took place in a police dominated atmosphere characterized by repeated comments that the suspect's story had too many holes, that he was lying, and that they did not want to fool around. The court found that fear, augmented by a threat that things would be rougher if he did not cooperate, necessitated exclusion of the resulting statement.

A court's decision of course depends on the specific facts of each case. In State v. Iverson,[73] the Supreme Court of North Dakota sustained the admissibility of a statement given after an interrogation session which was attended by a bloodhound and which included a suggestion that Iverson take a lie detector test. Testing the circumstances of the interrogation, the suspect's past experience with the law, and his rational participation in the session, the court found that the statements were voluntary.

Deceit. The police have frequently used deceit to obtain confessions. Examples include misrepresenting that an accomplice has confessed,[74] misrepresenting the seriousness of the offense or condition of the victim,[75] misrepresenting that evidence has been found,[76] and disguising police officers.[77] While numerous courts and commentators have joined in condemning deceit,[78] most courts continue to sustain the admissibility of confessions obtained through its use. So long as the deceit does not nullify the *Miranda* warnings,[79] overcome another policy such as the right to counsel,[80] overbear the person's will, or make a false statement likely,[81] a resulting statement is usually deemed voluntary and admissible. Perhaps the general acceptance of deceit will diminish in the future, but at present most cases of deceit are not reversed on that ground.

The Polygraph. Although the results of the polygraph or lie detector are not yet generally admissible in evidence,[82] the polygraph

---

71. Other factors included continuous interrogation, a request that the suspect take a polygraph (and stating that a refusal indicated guilt) and most importantly, due to *Miranda*, ignoring the suspect's request for counsel. The last factor alone would have required suppression.

72. 286 N.C. 442, 212 S.E.2d 92 (1975).

73. 225 N.W.2d 48 (N.D.1974).

74. See, e. g., Frazier v. Cupp, 394 U.S. 731, 739, 89 S.Ct. 1420, 1424–25, 22 L.Ed.2d 684 (1969); People v. Houston, 36 Ill.App.3d 695, 344 N.E.2d 641 (1976); Commonwealth v. Jones, 457 Pa. 423, 322 A.2d 119 (1974).

75. See, e. g., In re Walker, 10 Cal.3d 764, 112 Cal. Rptr. 177, 518 P.2d 1129 (1974); State v. Cooper, 217 N.W.2d 589 (Iowa 1974).

76. Cf. State v. Oakes, 19 Or.App. 284, 527 P.2d 418 (1974) (defendant told that guns found on him were on the "hot sheet").

77. See, e. g., Milton v. Wainwright, 407 U.S. 371, 92 S.Ct. 2174, 33 L.Ed.2d 1 (1972) (police officer disguised as a cellmate). Cf. State v. McCorgary, 218 Kan. 358, 543 P.2d 952 (1975).

78. See, e. g., Miranda v. Arizona, 384 U.S. 436, 476, 86 S.Ct. 1602, 1628, 16 L.Ed.2d 694 (1966) ("any evidence that the accused was threatened, tricked, or cajoled into a waiver will, of course, show that the defendant did not voluntarily waive his privilege"); Hileman v. State, 259 Ark. 567, 535 S.W.2d 56 (1976); ALI Model Code of Pre-Arraignment Procedure §§ 140.2, 140.4(5) (1975).

79. The decision to speak must be voluntary; once the decision is made, deception appears acceptable. A number of cases hold that subterfuge does not necessarily preclude a knowing waiver of rights. See, e. g., Commonwealth v. Jones, 457 Pa. 423, 322 A.2d 119 (1974) (being deceived that codefendant had implicated him did not preclude a knowing waiver); State v. Cooper, 217 N.W.2d 589 (Iowa 1974).

80. See, e. g., Massiah v. United States, 377 U.S. 201, 84 S.Ct. 1199, 12 L.Ed.2d 246 (1964). But see Milton v. Wainwright, 407 U.S. 371, 92 S.Ct. 2174, 33 L.Ed.2d 1 (1972).

81. See, e. g., In re Walker, 10 Cal.3d 764, 777, 112 Cal.Rptr. 177, 184–85, 518 P.2d 1129, 1136–37 (1974). The due process test remains paramount. However, reliability is frequently discussed in deceit cases and occasionally appears to be the primary test exercised.

82. See generally Chapter 8, supra.

itself plays a major role in law enforcement. Invited to clear themselves via the machine, numerous suspects submit to polygraph examination only to be trapped by their own fears of the machines, occasionally augmented by police commentary.[83] Both the pretest and the examination itself tend to create fear and apprehension that result in the suspect confessing and throwing himself or herself on the interrogator's mercy.

The test itself is voluntary and cannot be compelled; indeed if a custodial situation exists, *Miranda* rights warnings are required. Nevertheless confessions continue. While at least one court has stated that "the situation a lie detector test presents can best be described as a psychological rubber hose," [84] courts across the country have ruled that the mere use of a polygraph does not render a confession involuntary.[85] What creates an involuntary statement is either coercion to take the test [86] or police misconduct.[87]

The Suspect's Ability to Resist the Coercive Interrogation Techniques. Under the federal due process test, a confession is involuntary if the person being questioned is denied the ability to make a free choice; in short, if his or her will is overborne. A court dealing with a challenged confession must not only explore the nature of the alleged coercion or inducement, but also, if the case does not involve inherent coercion, weigh the character and background of the person interrogated. Thus the totality of the circumstances includes the suspect. The subjective factors of age, intelligence, and mental or physical condition must be considered in determining voluntariness.

The fact that a minor makes the confession does not as such make a confession inadmissible.[88] Age and understanding are, however, substantial factors to be considered by judge and jury.[89] Nevertheless a major caveat exists in this area. A number of states have chosen to treat juvenile confessions differently from adult statements. Therefore, in some states a minor may not make a statement unless he or she has consulted a parent.[90] In others minors must be released to their parents or taken immediately to a juvenile court or detention home; failure to do so results in inadmissibility.[91] At least one case has declared inadmissible a statement given at the urging of a minor's mother because she was not informed of the child's right to remain silent.[92] Absent these special rules, no exceptional consideration exists for children.

---

83. See, e. g., Johnson v. State, 19 Crim.L.Rep. 2159 (Md.Ct.Spec.App. April 15, 1976).

84. State v. Faller, 227 N.W.2d 433, 435 (S.D.1976).

85. See, e. g., Sotelo v. State, 264 Ind. 298, 342 N. E.2d 844 (1976); State v. Bowden, 342 A.2d 281, 285 (Me.1975); People v. Wilson, 78 Misc.2d 468, 477–78, 354 N.Y.S.2d 296, 307–08 (Nassau County Ct. 1974); Jones v. Commonwealth, 214 Va. 723, 204 S.E.2d 247 (1974).

86. See, e. g., State v. Cullison, 215 N.W.2d 309 (Iowa 1974) (woman told that she should submit either to a medical examination or to a polygraph or the police would "leave no stone unturned" in their investigation).

87. Interestingly enough the courts, despite hostility to polygraphs, have not used accusations of lying or coaxing by police to invalidate confessions but rather have tried to determine whether the suspect's will had been overborne. See, e. g., State v. Bowden, 342 A.2d 281, 285 (Me.1975).

88. See, e. g., In re M.D.J., 346 A.2d 733 (1975); In re Mellott, 27 N.C.App. 81, 217 S.E.2d 745 (1975); Commonwealth v. Wilson, 463 Pa. 1, 329 A.2d 881 (1974).

89. Age may be a determining factor. See, e. g., Commonwealth v. Eden, 456 Pa. 1, 317 A.2d 255 (1974) (14 year old who had been sniffing glue with drug experience found to lack sufficient understanding of *Miranda* warnings for his confession to be voluntary).

90. See, e. g., Weatherspoon v. State, 328 So.2d 875, 876 (Fla.App.1976) (In Florida, juveniles are afforded rights and considerations not available to adult offenders); Crook v. State, 546 P.2d 648 (Okl.Cr. 1976) (10 Okl.Stat.Ann. § 1109 requires that questioning be done in the presence of guardian or legal custodian). See, e. g., Commonwealth v. Stanton, 466 Pa. 143, 351 A.2d 663 (1976).

91. See, e. g., State v. Wade, 531 S.W.2d 726 (Mo. 1976); State v. Strickland, 532 S.W.2d 912 (Tenn. 1975).

92. Commonwealth v. Starkes, 461 Pa. 178, 335 A. 2d 698 (1975).

Mentally retarded are in the same legal position as are any other group of people. If a retarded individual is an adult, or a minor in a state without special provision, the retardation is considered simply another factor in the voluntariness equation.[93] Similarly, the mentally ill are considered able to make a knowing, intelligent decision to confess in the absence of a specific disorder that would interfere with their ability to cope with reality to a significant extent.[94]

Physical illness as such is treated like any other factor and each case is determined on its specific facts.[95] However, difficulties exist in the areas of intoxication and drug abuse. The traditional rule for intoxication is that "proof of [voluntary] intoxication amounting to mania or such an impairment of the will and mind as to make the person confessing unconscious of the meaning of his words renders a confession so made by him inadmissible, but a lesser state of intoxication will not render the confession inadmissible."[96]

Although drug addiction per se does not make a confession involuntary,[97] withdrawal symptoms, threats, or promises connected with withdrawal may make a statement inadmissible.[98] There appears to be a strong trend in the alcohol and drug cases towards emphasizing reliability of a statement—perhaps to a greater extent than free choice. The law has never favored intoxication, and apparently in this area as well, an intoxicated individual is considered in effect to have waived his or her right to make a truly free and intelligent choice. However, if the alcohol or drug has rendered an individual peculiarly susceptible to some form of pressure, that factor will be taken into account.

Standing to Challenge the Statement. Because an involuntary statement must usually be excluded from evidence, the rule has evolved that before a party may challenge the admissibility of a statement on voluntariness grounds, he or she must have an adequate personal interest. This requirement, known as standing, has been held in the area of confessions to mean that a defendant may object only to his or her own statement. Hence the general rule is that an accused is unable to challenge a statement or derivative evidence made by another person although it is offered to prove the guilt of the accused.[99] This rule can be particularly important in cases involving accomplices.

Presumably the limitation is designed to balance the rights of the individual on trial against the societal interest in allowing as much probative evidence as possible

---

93. State v. Pyle, 216 Kan. 423, 532 P.2d 1309 (1975); State v. Ross, 320 So.2d 177 (La.1975) (low mentality and illiteracy); People v. Langston, 57 Mich.App. 666, 226 N.W.2d 686 (1975) (mentally deficient did not understand the situation rendering his confession involuntary); Commonwealth v. Tucker, 461 Pa. 191, 335 A.2d 704 (1975) (19 year old with second grade education, IQ 75–79 and constitutional psychopath).

94. Schade v. State, 512 P.2d 907, 916 (Alaska 1973); People v. Brown, 86 Misc.2d 339, 380 N.Y.S.2d 476 (Nassau County Ct. 1976) (internal pressures did not make confession involuntary).

95. See, e. g., Barnett v. State, 51 Ala.App. 470, 286 So.2d 876, cert. denied 291 Ala. 773, 286 So.2d 890 (1973).

96. Patterson v. State, 56 Ala.App. 359, 321 So.2d 698 (1975), citing Carter v. State, 53 Ala.App. 43, 297 So.2d 175 (1975). See also State v. Arredondo, 111 Ariz. 141, 526 P.2d 163 (1974); People v. Durante, 48 A.D.2d 962, 963, 369 N.Y.S.2d 560, 561 (1975); State v. Saxon, 261 S.C. 523, 201 S.E.2d 114 (1973). But see State v. Lloyd, 22 Or.App. 254, 538 P.2d 1278 (1975) (defendant in jail for detoxification could not understand *Miranda* warnings; statement must be suppressed).

97. See, e. g., Hayward v. Johnson, 508 F.2d 322 (3d Cir. 1975); United States v. Arcediano, 371 F. Supp. 457 (S.D.N.J.1974); People v. Delgado, 30 Ill. App.3d 890, 333 N.E.2d 633, 635–36 (1975); Fred v. State, 531 P.2d 1038 (Okl.Cr.1975) cert. denied 421 U.S. 966, 95 S.Ct. 1955, 44 L.Ed.2d 453.

98. See, e. g., United States v. Monroe, 397 F.Supp. 726 (D.D.C.1975).

99. Cf. Alderman v. United States, 394 U.S. 165, 174, 89 S.Ct. 961, 966–67, 22 L.Ed.2d 176 (1969) (fourth amendment electronic eavesdropping case).

to be brought before the jury.[1] However, one exception to the rule may exist. In LaFrance v. Bohlinger,[2] the United States Court of Appeals for the First Circuit determined that when the prosecution had attempted to impeach its own witness with an allegedly coerced confession, the trial court should have determined the voluntariness of the confession even though it had not been made by the defendant. The court's reasoning was primarily that "[t]he due process requirements of a fair trial clearly extend to matters dealing with a witness' credibility."[3] While the court limited its expansion of the traditional standing rule, the case does suggest that due process considerations may allow an accused to occasionally challenge statements made by other parties.

The Exclusionary Rule. An involuntary confession is usually inadmissible in evidence. Further, in most cases any evidence gained through the involuntary statement is also inadmissible.[4] The exclusion of derivative evidence under the "fruit of the poisonous tree" doctrine is necessitated by the desire to prevent any incentive for improper police conduct as well as by doubts about the propriety of courts using illegally obtained evidence. Although exclusion of coerced or induced statements may additionally be justified on the assumption that the evidence itself is unreliable, the same conclusion does

not necessarily flow from use of derivative evidence.[5] Accordingly, the ban on derivative evidence must be presumed to flow from policy considerations rather than from reliability grounds. The numerous problems associated with the exclusionary rule in the confessions context are discussed at length in Chapter 24.

4. The Corroboration Requirement

Suggested Reading:

Opper v. United States, 348 U.S. 84, 75 S.Ct. 158, 99 L.Ed. 101 (1954).

The same reluctance to convict defendants on the basis of confession evidence that helped give rise to the voluntariness doctrine gave rise also to the corroboration requirement. Originally dealing primarily with crimes of violence, the rule now generally requires that before a confession or an admission [6] be admitted, the statement must be corroborated by independent evidence.[7] Thus the courts have imposed an additional reliability check on confession evidence.

Two primary corroboration rules exist in the United States. Under the majority

1. Standing to challenge illegal searches and seizures appears to be broader, perhaps because the right involved is primarily one of privacy.

2. 499 F.2d 29 (1st Cir. 1974).

3. Id. at 34. In *LaFrance*, a Massachusetts habeas corpus case, the statement involved was alleged to be a police fabrication signed by a jailed accomplice while he was "strung out on drugs." It is questionable whether the court's decision would have been the same if a case of unlawful inducement had been claimed. Interestingly, the circuit court noted that despite the state rule requiring jury determination when the trial judge rules adversely to the defense on the voluntariness issue, only a decision by the trial judge was needed for this type of voluntariness issue.

4. See generally 3 Wigmore, Evidence § 859 (Chadbourn rev. 1970).

5. Derivative evidence (which could include proceeds of crime, weapons, or equipment used to accomplish the crime, or other witness, etc.) should usually be perfectly reliable and not susceptible to the doubts that accompany possible inaccurate or false statements. Note that the key theoretical difference between the fourth amendment exclusionary rule and the "fifth amendment" rule is that questions of reliability are completely absent from illegal searches and seizures which generally supply "hard" evidence such as crime proceeds.

6. There is no difference in treatment in the federal courts (Opper v. United States, 348 U.S. 84, 90–92, 75 S.Ct. 158, 162–64, 99 L.Ed. 101 (1954)), although some jurisdictions may apply the rule only to confessions.

7. See generally 7 Wigmore, Evidence § 2070–75 (3d ed. 1940); C. McCormick, Handbook of the Law of Evidence § 158 (2d ed. 1972).

rule, independent evidence must substantiate the corpus delicti, or in other words show that a criminal act has in fact occurred.[8] However, independent evidence is not needed to show the identity of the perpetrator.[9] Under the laxer minority rule, used by the federal courts,[10] independent evidence must be received to show that the confession is trustworthy.

As McCormick[11] suggests, the federal courts have tended to confuse the standards and thus frequently require that the corpus delicti be shown.[12] Since that standard almost always also establishes the truthworthi-

ness of the confession, the difference between the two standards tends to be purely academic.

Corroboration need not be shown beyond a reasonable doubt.[13] In some jurisdictions, the prosecution may rely on otherwise inadmissible evidence to corroborate the confession.[14] The presence of evidence sufficient to corroborate a confession is a question for the trial judge in some jurisdictions,[15] for the jury in others.[16] The minimum constitutional requirement thus remains unsettled, although in the light of Jackson v. Denno,[17] presumably a judicial determination is adequate. Traditionally the corroboration requirement has applied only to extra-judicial confessions. Accordingly the rule does not apply to confessions or admissions made during trial.[18]

---

8. See, e. g., Tanner v. State, 57 Ala.App. 254, 327 So.2d 749 (1976) (testimony showing that 988 tires with a value of $33,000 were missing from inventory corroborated the defendant's confession); People v. Ruckdeschel, 51 A.D.2d 861, 380 N.Y.S.2d 163 (1976) (failure of independent evidence to show a larcenous taking from the victim resulted in insufficient corroboration and compelled reversal of first degree robbery); Davis v. State, 542 P.2d 532 (Okl. Cr.1975) (independent evidence established that a dead body was found and the death was shown to have resulted from multiple stab wounds; the confession was corroborated).

9. See, e. g., People v. Reeves, 39 Cal.App.3d 944, 114 Cal.Rptr. 574 (1974). Usually this is the element of proof supplied by the confession.

10. See, e. g., Opper v. United States, 348 U.S. 84, 75 S.Ct. 158, 99 L.Ed. 101 (1954); Smith v. United States, 348 U.S. 147, 75 S.Ct. 194, 99 L.Ed. 192 (1954); United States v. Wilson, 529 F.2d 913, 915 (10th Cir. 1976).

11. C. McCormick, Handbook of the Law of Evidence § 159 (2d ed. 1972).

12. See, e. g., United States v. Daniels, 528 F.2d 705, 707–08 (6th Cir. 1976); United States v. Fleming, 504 F.2d 1045, 1048–49 (7th Cir. 1974).

13. See, e. g., Green v. State, 159 Ind.App. 68, 304 N.E.2d 845 (1973).

14. See, e. g., United States v. Stricklin, 20 U.S. C.M.A. 609, 44 C.M.R. 39 (1971) (hearsay evidence).

15. See, e. g., State v. Kelley, 308 A.2d 877, 885 (Me.1973); Felton v. United States, 344 F.2d 111 (10th Cir. 1965).

16. See, e. g., Burkhalter v. State, 302 So.2d 503 (Miss.1974). The Court of Military Appeals has been unable to resolve this problem definitively and has held in United States v. Seigle, 22 U.S.C.M.A. 403, 47 C.M.R. 340 (1973), that the issue is for the trial judge alone unless the evidence is "substantially conflicting, self-contradictory, uncertain, or improbable," in which case the court must, on defense request, instruct the jury on the issue.

17. 378 U.S. 368, 84 S.Ct. 1774, 12 L.Ed.2d 908 (1964).

18. See, e. g., Manning v. United States, 215 F.2d 945, 950 (10th Cir. 1954).

CHAPTER 22

THE McNABB-MALLORY RULE

1. Introduction

Suggested Reading:

McNabb v. United States, 318 U.S. 332, 63 S.Ct. 608, 87 L.Ed. 819 (1943).

Having incorporated the common-law voluntariness test for confessions into due process,[1] the Supreme Court in the 20th century found itself faced with a number of involuntary confession cases. A common thread that ran through these cases was incommunicado police detention of suspects for interrogation. Such interrogation, conducted in police stations on police terms, and with the suspect lacking all psychological support, was recognized as more likely to produce a statement than is questioning conducted under more neutral circumstances. One obvious method of minimizing the apparent "coercive"[2] effect of such an interrogation is to require that suspects be rapidly brought before a local magistrate who informs the

suspect of his or her rights.[3] This appearance was presumed to interrupt any psychological coercion flowing from partisan police questioning. Indeed, in 1932 a noted law review article[4] suggested that ideally the magistrate, not the police, should conduct interrogations.[5] While such an expansive role for the magistrate remained an interesting academic theory, the basic idea of using an appearance before a magistrate to deter involuntary confessions was accepted by the Supreme Court in McNabb v. United States.[6]

---

1. See generally Chapter 21, supra.

2. This is not to suggest that the mere existence of incommunicado interrogation was enough to render a confession involuntary. However, it has always been an important factor.

3. The requirement that arrested people be brought before a magistrate or judge for an initial appearance existed in statutory form as early as 1879. Act of March 1, 1879, ch. 125, 20 Stat. 327, 341 (limited to the offense of operating an illegal distillery). Under Rule 5 of the Federal Rules of Criminal Procedure, the current initial appearance rule, the federal magistrate shall, when the offense is not a minor one triable by magistrate, "inform the defendant of the complaint against him and of any affidavit filed therewith, of his right to retain counsel, of his right to request the assignment of counsel if he is unable to obtain counsel, and of the general circumstances under which he may secure pretrial release. He shall inform the defendant that he is not required to make a statement and that any statement made by him may be used against him." Rule 5(c).

4. Kauper, Judicial Examination of the Accused—A Remedy for the Third Degree, 30 Mich.L.Rev. 1224 (1932), reprinted, 73 Mich.L.Rev. 39 (1974).

5. Id.

6. 318 U.S. 332, 63 S.Ct. 608, 87 L.Ed. 819 (1943) (hereinafter cited as *McNabb*).

2. *McNabb-Mallory* in the Federal Courts

Suggested Reading:

Mallory v. United States, 354 U.S. 449, 77 S.Ct. 1356, 1 L.Ed.2d 1479 (1957).

McNabb v. United States. On July 31, 1940, officers from the Chattanooga office of the Alcohol Tax Unit of the Bureau of Internal Revenue arrested members of the McNabb family for selling illegal liquor. During the raid one federal officer was killed. Some members of the family[7] were arrested between one and two a. m. Thursday and were taken immediately to the local federal building where they were left in a detention room for fourteen hours; they were then transferred to the county jail and subsequently returned to the federal building. Questioning began at approximately nine p. m. Thursday and continued until one a. m. when the suspects were sent back to the county jail. They were taken to the federal building for further questioning on Friday morning. Another member of the family surrendered on Friday and confessed after five or six hours of questioning. On Friday night the other McNabbs were confronted with the confession, and a statement considered adequate was obtained from them three hours later at two a. m. Saturday.

At trial the McNabbs claimed that their confessions were involuntary. On appeal the Supreme Court failed to reach the constitutional issue, preferring to rely on its supervisory authority over subordinate federal courts.[8] The Court stated that Congress had statutorily required that federal officials arresting individuals take them before the nearest United States Commissioner (the forerunner of today's federal magistrate) for hearing, commitment, or bail.[9] The Court found that the legislation restricted "third-degree interrogations," protected defendants, and guaranteed methods commending "themselves to a progressive and self-confident society."[10] Because Congress had failed to include an exclusionary rule in the statute, the Court invoked its supervisory authority to suppress the confessions. However, the Supreme Court stated: "[W]here . . . it appears that evidence has been obtained in such violation of legal rights . . . it is the duty of the trial court to entertain a motion for the exclusion of such evidence."[11]

In theory, *McNabb* simply invoked a federal statute requiring that defendants be brought before a U. S. Commissioner after arrest. In actuality, by creating an exclusionary rule to enforce the statute, the Court was making a valiant and far from novel[12] attempt to prevent lengthy police interrogations. Congressional reaction to the experiment was loud and furious.[13]

From McNabb to Mallory. A number of attempts were made to statutorily overrule the judicially created exclusionary rule.[14] Al-

7. The McNabbs were in fact almost a perfect stereotype. Those arrested were in their mid- to late twenties; none had gone beyond the fourth grade, and none had ever traveled beyond the limits of the clan—an area known as the McNabb Settlement. 318 U.S. at 334–35. In view of the defendants' background, as well as the nature of the interrogation, the Court could certainly have found a violation of fifth amendment due process and held the resulting confessions involuntary.

8. 318 U.S. at 340.

9. Id. at 342, citing 18 U.S.C.A. § 595. The Court noted that virtually all the states had similar legislation. See 318 U.S. 342 n. 7.

10. 318 U.S. at 344.

11. Id. at 346.

12. See, e. g., Kauper, Judicial Examination of the Accused—A Remedy for the Third Degree, 30 Mich.L. Rev. 1224, 1226–31 (1932), reprinted, 73 Mich.L.Rev. 39, 41–46 (1974).

13. See generally O. Stephens, Jr., The Supreme Court and Confessions of Guilt 68–77 (1973).

14. For an excellent review of the historical development of the *McNabb-Mallory* rule, including efforts made to nullify it, see O. Stephens, Jr., The Supreme Court and Confessions of Guilt 63–89 (1973) (hereinafter cited as Stephens).

though the attempts were unsuccessful, sufficient anti-*McNabb* feeling existed to prevent positive enactment of the *McNabb* rule when the general initial appearance requirement was codified as Rule 5(a) of the Federal Rules of Criminal Procedure.[15]

The Supreme Court, in United States v. Mitchell,[16] sustained the admissibility of a statement given by a defendant soon after his arrest (and immediately upon his arrival at the police station) despite a subsequent eight-day delay in bringing him before a Commissioner for his initial appearance. The Court reasoned that the delay had not caused the confession in any way.

Although *Mitchell* appears to be a partial retreat from *McNabb*, the Supreme Court reaffirmed the *McNabb* rule in a 1948 case[17] in which the accused confessed after thirty hours of illegal detention which lacked any coercive features. Apparently crucial to the reversal was the fact that the accused had been detained on mere suspicion.

The Supreme Court's next significant decision in this area is Mallory v. United States.[18] Mallory, a rape suspect, was arrested in the early afternoon and taken with two other suspects to police headquarters. Mallory spent the afternoon in custody and, after having denied guilt during earlier questioning, consented to a polygraph examination. Mallory confessed during this examination. Only after the initial statement did the police attempt to reach a United States Commissioner in order to arraign Mallory. This attempt was unsuccessful. Following an examination by a deputy coroner, Mallory was confronted by the victim and a number of police. He then dictated his confession, finishing at approximately midnight and was arraigned the next morning.

To reach its decision the Supreme Court interpreted the language in Rule 5(a) of the Federal Rules of Criminal Procedure requiring that arrested people be taken "without unnecessary delay" before the nearest Commissioner for arraignment. In a unanimous opinion written by Mr. Justice Frankfurter, the Court held that the relevant provisions of Rule 5(a) "contemplate a procedure that allows arresting officers little more leeway than the interval between arrest and the ordinary administrative steps required to bring a suspect before the nearest available magistrate."[19] The Court conceded that "the command does not call for mechanical or automatic obedience. Circumstances may justify a brief delay between arrest and arraignment, as for instance, where the story volunteered by the accused is susceptible of quick verification through third parties. But the delay must not be of a nature to give opportunity for the extraction of a confession."[20] In *Mallory*, the Court found that unnecessary delay had in fact occurred and therefore reversed the conviction.

McNabb-Mallory in the Federal Courts Today. The *McNabb-Mallory* rule mandates exclusion of a statement whenever it is given during a period of "unnecessary delay" in

15. Stephens at 73, citing Note, 36 Am.J.Police Sci., Sept.-Oct. 1945, at 225. The proposed draft section 5(b), which would have excluded evidence obtained after an unnecessary delay in taking an accused before a commissioner, was deleted from the final draft after opposition from the American Bar Association. As currently phrased (unchanged in relevant detail since its enactment in 1946, 327 U.S. 821 (1946)), § 5(a) reads: "An officer making an arrest . . . or any person making an arrest . . . shall take the arrested person *without unnecessary delay* before the nearest available federal magistrate or, in the event that a federal magistrate is not reasonably available, before a state or local judicial officer authorized by 18 U.S.C. § 3041." (emphasis added). Because Rule 5 deals primarily with initial appearances before magistrates, a new Rule, 5.1, was promulgated in 1972 to deal specifically with preliminary examination.

16. 322 U.S. 65, 64 S.Ct. 896, 88 L.Ed. 1140 (1944).

17. Upshaw v. United States, 335 U.S. 410, 69 S.Ct. 170, 93 L.Ed. 100 (1948).

18. 354 U.S. 449, 77 S.Ct. 1356, 1 L.Ed.2d 1479 (1957). *Mallory* took place in Washington, D.C., thus making what would usually be a state offense a federal one.

19. 354 U.S. at 453.

20. Id. at 455.

bringing a defendant before a magistrate for an initial appearance. In interpreting Rule 5(a) of the Criminal Rules of Procedure,[21] the Supreme Court has refused to define unnecessary delay in terms of a specific time period [22] and has expressly held a post-arrest statement admissible despite a subsequent lengthy delay in araignment.[23] Because of such vague precedents, *McNabb-Mallory* has failed to ripen into a concise and easy-to-apply procedural rule. Lower federal courts appear to follow *McNabb-Mallory* with a notable lack of enthusiasm. Certainly cases finding exceptions to the rule predominate. Of course some exceptions are inherent in the rule's formulation. For example, following *Mitchell*,[24] a number of courts have found interrogation in the first minutes (or hours) of arrest appropriate and necessary. Others have determined that delays due entirely or in part to the unavailability of a magistrate [25] or to inadequate transportation to a hearing officer [26] are not "unnecessary." The hostility of some courts is evidenced by what appears to be a general presumption that magistrates are unavailable during evenings, holidays, and weekends

—a presumption that must be rebutted by the defense before the delay involved can be found unnecessary.[27]

While the motive for any delay as well as the actual use made by the police of the time involved have been considered factors,[28] only a few decisions have held that the police motive in delaying an appearance is conclusive.[29] Because *McNabb* and *Mallory* dealt only with post-arrest statements, non-arrest situations are not covered by the rule. Following the same reasoning—that in such a case an initial appearance is not critical to continued detention—most courts have held *McNabb-Mallory* irrelevant to defendants already in custody for other offenses.[30]

However, a truly significant exception has been developed from the *Miranda* warnings requirement. Despite the Supreme Court's obvious belief that *McNabb* is a procedural protection not affected by the voluntariness of a statement, a number of decisions have found that an otherwise valid *Miranda* rights waiver is also a waiver of the *McNabb-Mallory* right to a speedy appearance before a magistrate.[31]

---

21. *McNabb* actually addressed itself to Rule 5(a)'s predecessor, 18 U.S.C.A. § 595, which was similar in relevant part.

22. Mallory v. United States, 354 U.S. 449, 455, 77 S.Ct. 1356, 1359–60, 1 L.Ed.2d 1479 (1957). However, the time frame was to be extremely short.

23. United States v. Mitchell, 322 U.S. 65, 64 S.Ct. 896, 88 L.Ed. 1140 (1944).

24. Id. Note that a case-by-case approach has been adopted by most courts. See, e. g., United States v. Kershner, 432 F.2d 1066 (5th Cir. 1970); Gray v. United States, 394 F.2d 96 (9th Cir. 1967), cert. denied 393 U.S. 985, 89 S.Ct. 459, 21 L.Ed.2d 446 (1968).

25. See, e. g., United States v. Brown, 459 F.2d 319 (5th Cir. 1971); United States v. Sterling, 321 F.Supp. 1301 (D.La.1971). But see United States v. Feguer, 192 F.Supp. 377 (N.D.Iowa 1961).

26. See, e. g., United States v. Odom, 526 F.2d 339 (5th Cir. 1976); United States v. Hensley, 374 F.2d 341 (6th Cir. 1967), cert. denied 388 U.S. 923, 87 S. Ct. 2139, 18 L.Ed.2d 1373, rehearing denied 389 U.S. 891, 88 S.Ct. 25, 19 L.Ed.2d 210; Nez v. United States, 365 F.2d 286 (10th Cir. 1966).

27. See, e. g., United States v. Frazier, 385 F.2d 901 (6th Cir. 1967).

28. See, e. g., United States v. Chadwick, 415 F.2d 167 (10th Cir. 1969) (delay for verification of alibi proper); Wise v. United States, 383 F.2d 206 (D.C. Cir. 1967), cert. denied 390 U.S. 964, 88 S.Ct. 1069, 19 L.Ed.2d 1164 (1968) (delay for identification permitted when time was reasonable; United States v. Price, 345 F.2d 256 (2d Cir. 1965), cert. denied 382 U.S. 949, 86 S.Ct. 404, 15 L.Ed.2d 357 (unintentional 12-hour delay upheld); United States v. Middleton, 344 F.2d 78 (2d Cir. 1965) (delay to obtain evidence rendered statement inadmissible).

29. Naples v. United States, 382 F.2d 465 (D.C. Cir. 1967); United States v. Middleton, 344 F.2d 78 (2d Cir. 1965); Virgin Islands v. Berry, 385 F.Supp. 134 (D.V.I.1974).

30. See, e. g., United States v. Smith, 464 F.2d 194 (10th Cir. 1972), cert. denied 409 U.S. 1066, 93 S.Ct. 566, 34 L.Ed.2d 519; United States v. Ireland, 456 F. 2d 74 (10th Cir. 1972); United States v. Reid, 437 F.2d 1166 (7th Cir. 1971). But see United States v. Nygard, 324 F.Supp. 863 (D.Mo.1971).

31. See, e. g., United States v. Woods, 468 F.2d 1024 (9th Cir. 1972); Pettyjohn v. United States, 419

McNabb and *Mallory* are perhaps obsolete. In an effort to statutorily overrule *Miranda* and *McNabb-Mallory*, Congress passed the Omnibus Crime Control and Safe Streets Act of 1968.[32] Subsection (c)[33] of the Act states: "In any criminal prosecution by the United States or the District of Columbia, a confession made or given by a person who is a defendant therein, while such person was under arrest or other detention in the custody of any law-enforcement officer or law-enforcement agency, shall not be inadmissible solely because of delay in bringing such person before a magistrate . . . if such confession is found by the trial judge to have been made voluntarily and if the weight to be given the confession is left to the jury and if such confession was made or given by such person within six hours immediately following his arrest or other detention: *Provided*, That the time limitation contained in this subsection shall not apply in any case in which the delay . . . beyond such six hour period is found by the trial judge to be reasonable considering the means of transportation and the distance to be traveled to the nearest available such magistrate or other officer."

Clearly the intent of the Act, often called the Anti-*Miranda* Act, was to overrule *McNabb* and *Mallory*.[34] However, the Act's language has created a substantial problem of statutory interpretation. In subsections (a) and (b),[35] Congress attempted to adopt a traditional voluntariness standard for confession evidence and expressly stated that the presence or absence of any of the enumerated factors,[36] including "the time elapsing between arrest and arraignment of the defendant making the confession, if it was made after arrest and before arraignment . . . need not be conclusive on the issue of voluntariness of the confession." In view of this policy, the reason for the inclusion of the six-hour rule in subsection (c) is unclear. If the only test is voluntariness, (c)'s statement that a confession shall not be inadmissible solely because of delay if the confession was made within six hours after arrest or other detention appears to be surplusage *unless* Congress ineloquently intended to allow exclusion of an otherwise voluntary statement given during an unnecessary delay longer than six hours. The vast majority of court decisions that have considered this issue have construed the Act as overruling *McNabb* and *Mallory* completely and substituting voluntariness in their place.[37] However, while this tortured construction may in fact comply with the general intent behind the statute, it runs afoul of the logical interpretation of the wording of the statute itself.[38] If, as it appears to be, the Act is

F.2d 651 (D.C.Cir. 1969), cert. denied 397 U.S. 1058, 90 S.Ct. 1383, 25 L.Ed.2d 676 (1970); Virgin Islands v. Kirnon, 377 F.Supp. 601 (D.V.I.1974). Cf. United States v. Collins, 462 F.2d 792 (2d Cir.), cert. denied 409 U.S. 988, 93 S.Ct. 343, 34 L.Ed.2d 254 (1972).

32. 18 U.S.C.A. § 3501.

33. 18 U.S.C.A. § 3501(c).

34. See, e. g., II U.S.Code Cong. & Admin. News 2124–27 (1968).

35. 18 U.S.C.A. § 3501(a) & (b).

36. Other factors include the defendant's knowledge or lack thereof of the offense he or she is suspected of committing, his or her knowledge of the right to remain silent, whether the defendant had been advised of the right to counsel, and whether counsel was present when the defendant confessed.

37. See, e. g., United States v. Bear Killer, 534 F.2d 1253 (8th Cir. 1976); United States v. Crocker, 510 F.2d 1129, 1133, 1138 (10th Cir. 1975); Virgin Islands v. Gereau, 502 F.2d 914, 923–24 (3d Cir. 1974); United States v. Mandley, 502 F.2d 1103 (9th Cir. 1974); United States v. McCormick, 468 F.2d 68 (10th Cir. 1972). But see United States v. Erving, 388 F. Supp. 1011 (W.D.Wis.1975).

38. See, e. g., the excellent discussion of the problem in United States v. Erving, 388 F.Supp. 1011 (W. D.Wis.1975). The Act also attempts to statutorily overrule *Miranda*. However, the *McNabb-Mallory* portion of the statute will probably be held severable if the *Miranda* portion is declared unconstitutional. While there has been some suggestion that the *McNabb-Mallory* portion might be unconstitutional (see C. McCormick, Handbook of the Law of Evidence § 155(a) (2d ed. 1972)), this seems unlikely. The Court's exercise of its supervisory power, coupled with what was claimed to be interpretation and implementation of a Congressional statute, is probably constitutional, *McNabb-Mallory* has either been modified to exempt statements obtained during the first six hours after arrest or has been obliterated completely. As of 1979, however, this issue remained unanswered and in need of resolution by the Supreme Court.

3. *McNabb-Mallory* in the State Courts

Suggested Reading:

Commonwealth v. Boone, 467 Pa. 168, 354 A.2d 898 (1975).

By their very nature the *McNabb* and *Mallory* cases are limited to the civilian [39] federal courts.[40] However, analogs of Rule 5 (a)[41] are easily found in the states. As of 1975, twenty-eight states required that a defendant be brought before a magistrate for an initial hearing " 'without unnecessary delay,' 'with reasonable promptness,' 'without undue delay,' 'forthwith,' 'immediately' " or equivalents thereof.[42] Nine states [43] have statutes requiring production of the accused before a magistrate within a specific time period—usually either 24 or 48 hours.

Because Rule 5(a)'s predecessor existed for some time before the Supreme Court created the *McNabb* exclusionary rule, the remedy for a violation of a state appearance requirement is not necessarily suppression of any statement that took place during the delay. State rules range from *McNabb* equivalents [44] to rules stating that unnecessary delay is simply one factor to consider in determining the voluntariness of a statement.[45]

---

susceptible of Congressional modification. A.L.I. Model Code of Pre-Arraignment Procedure 323 (1975) states that "the general view is that Congress may permissibly alter (the *McNabb-Mallory* rule) in that the rule was merely one of federal judicial administration, and not of constitutional status."

39. *McNabb-Mallory* does not apply to military courts-martial which are not affected by the Federal Rules of Criminal Procedure. Boeckenhaupt v. United States, 392 F.2d 24 (4th Cir. 1968), cert. denied 393 U.S. 896, 89 S.Ct. 162, 21 L.Ed.2d 177; Burns v. Harris, 340 F.2d 383 (8th Cir. 1965), cert. denied 382 U.S. 960, 86 S.Ct. 439, 15 L.Ed.2d 363.

40. Both *McNabb* and *Mallory* were interpreting federal procedural statutes that applied only to the federal courts.

41. Fed.Cr.Proc. Rule 5(a), 18 U.S.C.A.

42. A.L.I. Model Code of Pre-Arraignment Procedure 626 (1975).

43. Id. at 627.

44. Pennsylvania, for example, seems to parallel federal practice, including the numerous exceptions. See, e. g., Commonwealth v. Boone, 467 Pa. 168, 354 A.2d 898 (1975) (statements made in first 2½ hours after arrest were unrelated to subsequent unnecessary delay); Commonwealth v. Abu-Ibn Hanifah Bey, 462 Pa. 533, 341 A.2d 907 (1975) (five-hour unnecessary delay after arrest for interrogation purposes renders confession inadmissible); Commonwealth v. Whitson, 461 Pa. 101, 334 A.2d 653 (1975); Commonwealth v. Futch, 447 Pa. 389, 290 A.2d 417 (1972) (*McNabb* "equivalent").

45. See, e. g., State v. Wyman, 97 Idaho 486, 547 P.2d 531 (1976); Austin v. State, 56 Ala.App. 307, 321 So.2d 272 (1975); Williams v. State, 542 P.2d 554 (Okl.Cr.1975); Apple v. State, 158 Ind.App. 663, 304 N.E.2d 321 (1973).

CHAPTER 23
THE MIRANDA DOCTRINE

1. Historical Background

Suggested Reading:

Escobedo v. Illinois, 378 U.S. 478, 84 S.Ct. 1758, 12 L.Ed.2d 977 (1964).

You have the right to remain silent;

anything you say may be used against you at trial;

you have a right to consult with a lawyer and have a lawyer present during this interrogation and if you cannot afford a lawyer one will be appointed for you.

Thus spoke the Supreme Court in Miranda v. Arizona,[1] surely one of its most controversial Criminal Law decisions and one almost certain to be modified by the Court in the near future. The decision is complex and will be discussed subsequently at length. However, it is important to note at this point that *Miranda* imposed an affirmative duty on police desiring to conduct custodial interrogations to warn an accused of his or her right to remain silent and to have counsel present at interrogations—a far broader

---

1. 384 U.S. 436, 86 S.Ct. 1602, 16 L.Ed.2d 694 (1966) [hereinafter cited as *Miranda*]. The warnings listed represent only one variation of those in general use and do not include the required waiver questions.

right than had existed before the decision. Yet, contrary to some commentators' impressions, the basic nature of *Miranda* was far from unpredictable.

The history of the Supreme Court's treatment of the confession problem is one of partially futile attempts to find a tool with which to control improper police conduct. Past chapters [2] have chronicled the various steps in the development of the contemporary law of confessions. The tool the Court ultimately seized was, of course, the right to counsel—not a perfect tool but at least far better than its nearest competitors. The first decision of nationwide relevance was Massiah v. United States,[3] finding a sixth amendment right to counsel at post-indictment interrogations when the defendant had retained counsel. *Massiah* was followed in a few months by Escobedo v. Illinois.[4]

However, *Miranda* is easily the most significant decision. In *Miranda* the Supreme Court announced a prospective rule [5] that required police to warn a suspect of the right to remain silent and to consult with a lawyer at an interrogation. In the oft-quoted, critical passage of the majority opinion, Chief Justice Warren declared: "Our holding will be spelled out with some specificity in the pages which follow but briefly stated it is this: the prosecution may not use statements, whether exculpatory or inculpatory, stemming from custodial interrogation of the defendant unless it demonstrates the use of procedural safeguards effective to secure the privilege against self-incrimination. By custodial interrogation, we mean questioning initiated by law enforcement officers after a person has been taken into custody or otherwise deprived of his freedom of action in any significant way. As for the procedural safeguards to be employed, unless other fully effective means are devised to inform accused persons of their right to silence and to assure a continuous opportunity to exercise it, the following measures are required. Prior to any questioning, the person must be warned that he has a right to remain silent, that any statement he does make may be used as evidence against him, and that he has a right to the presence of an attorney, either retained or appointed. The defendant may waive effectuation of these rights, provided the waiver is made voluntarily, knowingly, and intelligently. If, however, he indicates in any manner and at any stage of the process that he wishes to consult with an attorney before speaking there can be no questioning. Likewise, if the individual is alone and indicates in any manner that he does not wish to be interrogated, the police may not question him. The mere fact that he may have answered some questions or volunteered some statements on his own does not deprive him of the right to refrain from answering any further inquiries until he has consulted with an attorney and thereafter consents to be questioned." [6]

A definitive analysis of *Miranda* is beyond the scope of this work. However, if one presumes that incommunicado police interrogation is inherently coercive,[7] the Court's

---

2. See Chapters 20–22, supra.

3. 377 U.S. 201, 84 S.Ct. 1199, 12 L.Ed.2d 246 (1964). The Court had previously been disturbed by police interference with a suspect's desire to contact counsel. See, e. g., Haynes v. Washington, 373 U.S. 503, 83 S.Ct. 1336, 10 L.Ed.2d 513 (1963) (police refused to allow accused to call wife or attorney). See generally Chapter 21, supra.

4. 378 U.S. 478, 184 S.Ct. 1758, 12 L.Ed.2d 977 (1964) (hereinafter cited as *Escobedo*).

5. The Court subsequently announced that *Miranda* applied only to cases that came to trial after June 13, 1966, the date of the *Miranda* decision. Johnson y. New Jersey, 384 U.S. 719, 86 S.Ct. 1772, 16 L.Ed. 2d 882 (1966). But see Michigan v. Tucker, 417 U.S. 433, 94 S.Ct. 2357, 41 L.Ed.2d 182 (1974), allowing use of derivative evidence obtained in a pre-*Miranda* interrogation. Note that state rules may differ and may be more beneficial to an accused. See, e. g., Commonwealth v. Romberger, 454 Pa. 279, 312 A.2d 353 (1975).

6. 384 U.S. at 444–45 (footnotes omitted).

7. The Supreme Court had consistently held that police custody and questioning are not "inherently

decision is seen as flowing smoothly from its earlier voluntariness decisions. Accordingly, this coerciveness must be compensated for by explaining the suspect's rights and by extending the right to a lawyer to the interrogation. The Court drew this conclusion, relying on the fact that modern custodial interrogation is psychologically rather than physically coercive. The right to counsel was the "protective device to dispel the compelling atmosphere of the interrogation." [8] The Court also noted that without protections during pretrial interrogation, all the safeguards supplied at trial would become empty formalities.[9] The *Miranda* holding can hence be viewed as an extension of the voluntariness doctrine. The critical parts of the decision extend the right to counsel to custodial interrogations,[10] require that the suspect in such a setting be informed of his or her rights, and require an affirmative waiver before questioning may take place.

The Court chose to grant the right to counsel to all regardless of wealth. Thus the core of the *Miranda* decision is its affirmative extension of the right to counsel to all suspects subjected to custodial interrogation. The rights warnings required by the opinion not only directly implement the right against self-incrimination by informing suspects of its existence but also support the right through the mandatory statement that, the suspect may have counsel present regardless of the suspect's financial situation.

2. General Elements of the Doctrine

Suggested Reading:

Miranda v. Arizona, 384 U.S. 436, 86 S.Ct. 1602, 16 L.Ed.2d 694 (1966).

Despite the Supreme Court's attempt to be extremely specific in the *Miranda* decision, the Court left open a substantial number of questions about the decision's application. To best analyze the contemporary interpretation of *Miranda*, the following questions will be addressed in turn: (1) Who must give warnings? (2) When must warnings be given? (3) Who must receive warnings? (4) What warnings must be given? (5) What is the effect of asserting one's *Miranda* rights? (6) How is a *Miranda* waiver effected? and (7) What is the consequence if the police do not comply with *Miranda*?

At the risk of over-simplification, the answer to these questions is: *When a law enforcement officer interrogates a suspect in custody, the officer must give the suspect certain rights warnings. Unless the suspect makes an effective waiver, any statement by the suspect is inadmissible.*

3. "A Law Enforcement Officer"

Suggested Reading:

Tarnef v. State, 512 P.2d 923 (Alaska 1973).

coercive" so as to automatically render a statement involuntary. See, e. g., Bram v. United States, 168 U.S. 532, 556–58, 18 S.Ct. 183, 192–193, 42 L.Ed. 568 (1897). However, *Miranda* leaves the unmistakable impression that the Court finally held otherwise. Certainly custody is not the type of "inherent coercion" that makes all statements involuntary, for spontaneous statements are admissible without either warnings or counsel, and the *Miranda* rights may be waived despite custodial circumstances. Accordingly, the term "inherently coercive" is used here in an attempt to accurately describe the Court's reasoning despite clear restrictions on the ultimate utility of the expression.

8. 384 U.S. at 465.

9. 384 U.S. at 466, citing Mapp v. Ohio, 367 U.S. 643, 685, 81 S.Ct. 1684, 1707, 6 L.Ed.2d 881 (1964) (Justice Harlan dissenting).

10. If, after being warned, the suspect requests counsel and counsel is unavailable, the police may not question him or her. The police always have the option either of making counsel available or of not interrogating.

The *Miranda* warnings were designed to offset the psychological coercion presumed to be inherent in custodial questioning by law enforcement agents.[11] Generally the cases have required police officers, prosecutors, and law enforcement agents with official status to give warnings[12] and exempted private citizens from the warnings requirements.[13] Part-time police and private security guards pose some difficulty. The primary question appears to be their status as local, state, or federal officers.[14] Thus cases involving private guards frequently require a determination of the guard's arrest powers under local law. As one commentator has stated,[15] the private citizen exception to *Miranda* generally does not apply to citizens acting as police agents.[16] Although police officers must give warnings before conducting custodial interrogation, undercover agents are ordinarily exempt from the warning requirement simply because undercover work normally does not involve custodial interrogation.[17]

Of course a number of people who are not themselves law enforcement agents are likely to question a suspect as part of the law enforcement process. Cases involving clerical personnel should be analyzed in terms of the clerk's status, the purpose of the questioning, and the general policies served by *Miranda*. Government psychiatrists performing competency examinations, particularly examinations in response to sanity defenses, should theoretically present a problem, for the information gained from the suspect probably will be used against him or her. However, since the courts have nearly unanimously held that a suspect raising a sanity defense waives the privilege against self-incrimination and must consent to a government examination,[18] giving warnings in this situation seems unnecessary.[19]

---

11. 384 U.S. 436, 444, 86 S.Ct. 1602, 1612, 16 L.Ed. 2d 694 (1966).

12. See generally J. Zagel, Confessions and Interrogations After Miranda: A Comprehensive Guideline of the Law 46–47 (Nat'l Dist. Attorneys Ass'n 1972).

13. See, e. g., Reno v. State, 337 So.2d 122 (Ala. Crim.App.1976) (company officer); Commonwealth v. Mahnke, 368 Mass. 662, 335 N.E.2d 660 (1975) (vigilante group of private citizens was not required to give warnings to suspect subjected to custodial interrogation); Brown v. State, 293 So.2d 425 (Miss. 1974) (jail cell questioning by victim's mother did not require *Miranda* warnings when the conversation was not instigated by the police).

14. Official status or a significant police connection will require warnings. Compare Tarnef v. State, 512 P.2d 923 (Alaska 1973) (private arson investigator who was a former police officer and who worked closely with the police and considered himself part of the "team" was required to give warnings) and Allen v. State, 53 Ala.App. 66, 297 So.2d 391 (1974), cert. denied 292 Ala. 707, 297 So.2d 399 (interrogator who had occasionally acted as a part-time deputy sheriff in the past had sufficient connections with the sheriff that warnings should have been given), with United States v. Delay, 500 F.2d 1360 (8th Cir. 1974) (although interrogating newsman had acted as a part-time unpaid deputy sheriff, his past activities had been restricted to acting as a photographer or press secretary or helping to search for drowning victims; accordingly, he was not a law enforcement agent for *Miranda* purposes.).

15. Zagel, note 12, supra.

16. Citizens acting as police agents may have to give warnings. Compare People v. Baugh, 19 Ill.

App.3d 448, 311 N.E.2d 607 (1974) (victim's attorney who questioned suspect in police custody was acting as a police agent, and he should have given *Miranda* warnings), with State v. Jensen, 111 Ariz. 408, 531 P.2d 531 (1975) (prisoners who obtained a statement from cellmate were not "plants" and could testify to statements made by the accused). Note that a person who is investigating misconduct and who is not a law enforcement agent, may not have to give warnings despite the fact that he or she holds an official position. See, e. g., In re Brendan H., 82 Misc.2d 1077, 372 N.Y.S.2d 473 (Schenectady Fam.Ct.1975) (school principal investigating school misconduct not required to give warnings to students in the absence of police connection).

17. If one is concerned only with the issue of fairness, one should ask why undercover agents should be allowed to question suspects without warnings when uniformed officers would be prevented from doing so. However, this concern avoids the rationale for *Miranda*. Undercover agents questioning suspects in a noncustodial setting by definition do not create the type of coercive atmosphere found in a police station.

18. See Chapter 20, supra.

19. When no right to remain silent exists, there is no reason for warning of its existence. However,

Foreign police have not been required to give *Miranda* warnings [20] when interrogating an American suspect. The United States cannot compel foreign jurisdictions to comply with American law. Clearly the prophylactic function served by *Miranda* domestically is irrelevant in foreign jurisdictions. *Miranda* should apply to foreign investigations which are conducted in conjunction with American authorities and are simply part of an American investigation.[21] American efforts to circumvent the *Miranda* requirements should be discouraged. However, this approach creates a substantial risk of deterring American prosecution and leaving the American accused in the hands of foreign authorities. The balance is yet to be struck.

4. "Interrogates"

Suggested Reading:

Trail v. State, 552 S.W.2d 757 (Tenn.Cr.App.1977).
Norman v. State, 302 So.2d 254 (Miss.1974).

In General. The *Miranda* warnings are designed to protect against coercive interrogation. *Interrogation* has become a term of art and defies easy definition. In its usual sense, interrogation for *Miranda* purposes refers to police questioning designed to elicit

an incriminating response from a suspect. More than simple questioning is included, however. Any statement or action designed to elicit an incriminating response will be considered interrogation.[22]

Whether a statement or physical act will be considered interrogation is determined by the facts of each case.[23] Clearly exempt from *Miranda's* definition of interrogation, however, are volunteered or spontaneous statements.[24] If a suspect initiates a statement or responds to entirely neutral or innocuous questioning or statements with an incriminating comment, the comment is admissible,[25] and the police need not interrupt the statement with *Miranda* warnings.[26] Although the issue has not yet been resolved, once a spontaneous statement begins the police probably may seek to have it continue or to flesh it out with neutral questioning.[27]

the right to counsel at psychiatric examinations is not totally foreclosed, and in those few jurisdictions recognizing a limited right to counsel some form of rights warning is appropriate.

20. See, e. g., United States v. Mundt, 508 F.2d 904, 907 (10th Cir. 1974) (*Miranda* warnings were not required in a Peruvian investigation despite American participation when American officers did not play a "substantial role in events leading to the arrest.").

21. See, e. g., Cranford v. Rodriguez, 512 F.2d 860 (10th Cir. 1975) (Mexican police acting on behalf of New Mexico police should have given *Miranda* warnings).

22. See, e. g., Blackmon v. Blackledge, 396 F.Supp. 296, 299 (W.D.N.C.1975) (confronting defendant suddenly after four hours of police interrogation with witness who accused him of murder was a form of interrogation requiring warnings). Some courts have held confrontations not to be interrogations.

23. Police *statements* or actions are likely to be found non-interrogative. See, e. g., United States v. Raines, 536 F.2d 796 (8th Cir. 1976) (police remark to suspect that a search warrant would be applied for after arrest was not an interrogation, and suspect's subsequent admission and surrender of evidence were not in violation of *Miranda*).

24. 384 U.S. 436, 478, 86 S.Ct. 1602, 1629–30, 16 L.Ed.2d 694 (1966). See, e. g., Garcia v. State, 159 Ind.App. 64, 304 N.E.2d 812 (1973) (statement by rape suspect, "It wasn't rape, it was assault with a friendly weapon," was admissible without warnings); State v. Hobson, 309 Minn. 411, 244 N.W.2d 654 (1976) (defendant refused to leave the police station without "his" gun; volunteer statement held admissible to establish possession of stolen weapon).

25. See, e. g., People v. Potter, 20 Ill.App.3d 1049, 1054–55, 314 N.E.2d 201, 205 (1974) (deputy sheriff attempted to quiet a prisoner and had a neutral conversation with him; prisoner's volunteered statement that "he was going to con them like a snake and charm his way out" was not obtained in violation of *Miranda*).

26. Miranda v. Arizona, 384 U.S. 436, 478, 86 S.Ct. 1602, 1629–30, 16 L.Ed.2d 694 (1966).

27. See, e. g., United States v. Pauldino, 487 F.2d 127 (10th Cir. 1973) (police request for bill of sale

The spontaneous-statement exception to *Miranda* is difficult theoretically. If *Miranda* presumes that the psychological coercion of custody requires an offsetting warning, the same coercive atmosphere would seem to compel a suspect to make volunteered statements to seek police approval. Removing volunteered statements from *Miranda's* coverage is thus inconsistent with its basic rationale.[28] However, the exception appears to be too well accepted to be modified at this stage.

Administrative Questioning. *Miranda* was intended to deal with criminal interrogations; its purpose is to give meaning to the fifth amendment right against self-incrimination. By definition an administrative consequence is not criminal. Accordingly, interrogations which cannot result in criminal prosecutions are not interrogations within the scope of *Miranda*. The dividing line between criminal and administrative consequences is of course at times rather thin,[29] and absent judicial precedent, predicting *Miranda's* applicability can be difficult.

This has been particularly true with Internal Revenue Service investigations, for the transition between administrative tax investigation and criminal tax evasion investigation is elusive despite the I.R.S. use of Intelligence Division agents for tax evasion cases. The Supreme Court has refused to apply *Miranda* to noncustodial tax investigations,[30] regardless of the fact that most tax evasion prosecutions begin with "administrative" noncustodial investigations.

Although most tax investigations are noncustodial, deportation proceedings are often custodial. However, because deportation is viewed as a non-criminal consequence, *Miranda* does not apply to deportation interrogations.[31] Investigations which are primarily administrative may not require warnings despite the possibility of later criminal prosecution.[32] Since prison discipline proceedings have been determined to be administrative in nature,[33] *Miranda* warnings appears to be unnecessary within the prison discipline area.[34]

Thus, the courts have limited *Miranda* by characterizing civil tax investigations and deportation and prison discipline proceedings as administrative. The courts have even characterized some parts of the criminal justice process as administrative. Any arrest requires that a defendant be formally processed or "booked." Whether through formal booking or other administrative questioning, data is occasionally obtained which is incriminating and which proves at trial harmful to the defendant.[35] Four of

---

for vehicle was proper after arrested suspect volunteered the statement that he had a bill of sale for the vehicle); United States v. Vogel, 18 U.S.C.M.A. 160, 39 C.M.R. 160 (1968); State v. Taylor, 343 A.2d 11 (Me.1975) (policeman's question, "What do you mean?" held to be a neutral question following defendant's initiated statement, and reply was not in violation of *Miranda*); Commonwealth v. Yount, 455 Pa. 303, 314 A.2d 242 (1974) (defendant entered police station and announced that the police were looking for him; police questioning to determine why he had come and subsequently who was his homicide victim was proper). The issue of whether questions are sufficiently neutral or have become improper interrogation must be resolved from the individual facts of each case.

28. *Miranda* resolves the conflict by defining volunteered statements as those made "voluntarily without any compelling influences." 384 U.S. at 478. Query the application of this statement to a volunteered admission made after stationhouse detention?

29. See Chapter 20, supra.

30. Beckwith v. United States, 425 U.S. 341, 96 S.Ct. 1612, 48 L.Ed.2d 1 (1976).

31. See, e. g., Chen v. Immigration Naturalization Serv., 537 F.2d 566 (1st Cir. 1976).

32. Cf. United States v. Harris, 381 F.Supp. 1095 (E.D.Pa.1974) (officer at airport checkpoint did not have to warn suspect of his rights after being told that the suspect had a gun inside his bag).

33. Baxter v. Palmigiano, 425 U.S. 308, 96 S.Ct. 1551, 47 L.Ed.2d 810 (1976).

34. Id. at 315.

35. See, e. g., United States ex rel. Hines v. LaValle, 521 F.2d 1109 (2d Cir. 1975) (information gained through informal police administrative questioning while defendant was being transported to the station-

five federal circuit courts of appeals that had considered the issue by the end of 1978 held *Miranda* inapplicable to preliminary or administrative questions.[36] The rationale seems to be that the data is normally non-incriminating, is essential to an efficient criminal justice system, and constitutes non-investigative questioning.

As suggested by one commentator,[37] limited Supreme Court authority supports this rationale. In California v. Byers,[38] the Court upheld a state reporting system which required drivers involved in accidents to stop and leave names and addresses. Clearly the Court upheld a limited infringement on the driver's privilege against self-incrimination.[39] The same reasoning may be applicable to administrative questioning.

Emergency Questioning. There is general agreement that law enforcement officers may ask questions of suspects without *Miranda* warnings when the questions are motivated by safety considerations.[40] "While life hangs in the balance, there is no room to require admonitions concerning the right to counsel and to remain silent. It is inconceivable that the *Miranda* Court or the framers of the Constitution envisioned such admonishments first be given under the urgent circumstances involved."[41] While the suspects in these cases presumably retain their right to remain silent, the opinions suggest that safety considerations overcome the *Miranda* rationale and eliminate the need for warnings.

5. "A Suspect"

Although custodial interrogation of a person who is not a suspect is possible,[42] the nature of American law makes custodial interrogations of non-suspects extremely rare. If a person is not a suspect, the authorities will rarely have a justification for holding him or her in custody. Thus usually and in contrast to some statutory warning requirements,[43] the threshold issue is whether the person questioned was in custody and not whether he or she was a suspect. In this regard the cases frequently exhibit an ambiguous use of the word, *focus*. While courts often attempt to determine if an investigation focused on an individual to decide whether he or she was in custody at the time of questioning, the same issue is also raised to determine whether the person questioned was a suspect. Because the two

---

house proved important in identifying suspect as rapist).

36. The Courts of Appeals for the Second, Fifth, Eighth, and Ninth Circuits have held such questioning to be proper without warnings while the District of Columbia Circuit has allowed questioning but rejected its results from use in evidence at trial. Note, The Applicability of *Miranda* to the Police Booking Process, 1976 Duke L.J. 574, 576, and cases cited therein.

37. Id. at 585–86.

38. 402 U.S. 424, 91 S.Ct. 1535, 29 L.Ed.2d 9 (1971).

39. For a more complete examination of *Byers*, see Chapter 20, supra.

40. See, e. g., United States v. Castellana, 500 F.2d 325 (5th Cir. 1974) (en banc) (FBI agent participating in a gambling raid asked the defendant whether he had any weapons; the resulting seizure of illegal weapons was not in violation of *Miranda*); Norman v. State, 302 So.2d 254, 258 (Miss.1974) (questions to group which had fired at the police were motivated by safety and were not inquisitorial interrogation).

41. People v. Dean, 39 Cal.App.3d 875, 882, 114 Cal. Rptr. 555, 559 (1974).

42. A person in custody for one offense might be questioned merely as a witness to a second. Assuming that the questions relating to the second offense could not in any way touch on the first—a rather abstract and unlikely situation in view of possible derivative evidence and use of any information gained for impeachment and related purposes—by implication *Miranda* would not appear to apply, for its goal was to protect suspects from coercive questioning. Note that the *fact* of custody is the determining feature for a suspect. It is unimportant that he or she is in custody for another offense so long as he or she is a suspect. See, e. g., Mathis v. United States, 391 U.S. 1, 88 S.Ct. 1503, 20 L.Ed.2d 381 (1968).

43. The statutory military rights warnings, 10 U.S. C.A. § 31(b) (1970), apply, for example, whenever a suspect or accused is to be questioned. There is no requirement that the individual be in custody. In the military, determination of whether a person was actually a suspect is a question of fact.

separate criteria for *Miranda's* application are frequently merged, careful analysis may be needed to discern the court's true holding. One of the few situations in which a court could easily separate the issues would be the questioning of a material witness held in custody. There the court could hold that although the subject was in custody, the subject was not a suspect and hence not entitled to *Miranda* warnings.

6. "In Custody"

Suggested Reading:

Oregon v. Mathiason, 429 U.S. 492, 97 S.Ct. 711, 50 L.Ed.2d 714 (1977).

United States v. Mandujano, 425 U.S. 564, 96 S.Ct. 1768, 48 L.Ed.2d 212 (1976).

Beckwith v. United States, 425 U.S. 341, 96 S.Ct. 1612, 48 L.Ed.2d 1 (1976).

Orozco v. Texas, 394 U.S. 324, 89 S.Ct. 1095, 22 L.Ed.2d 311 (1969).

In General. *Miranda's* use of the expression, *custodial interrogation,* is deceptively simplistic. The case defines the term as "questioning initiated by law enforcement officers after a person has been taken into custody or otherwise deprived of his freedom of action in any significant way." [44] The problems engendered by this formulation can be grouped into two areas—the formulation of a test to define *custody* and the determination of the presence of custody in a particular case once a test has been formulated.

The difficulty in formulating a test is caused by *Miranda's* basic premise. If the warnings are to cope with psychological co-ercion felt by the suspect, should the test not be a subjective one that seeks to determine whether the suspect believed himself or herself to be in custody? Although that approach may most fully implement *Miranda's* intent, it may also unreasonably open the door to perjury by the defendant. Moreover, the test makes determinative the suspect's perhaps unreasonable view of the situation. While there is much to be said for requiring warnings whenever a doubtful situation exists, clearly the *Miranda* Court did not intend to foreclose all police questioning without warnings, and this foreclosure could easily result under a purely subjective test.

An alternative test chosen by some jurisdictions after *Miranda* was based on the police officer's view of the situation. [45] Although this subjective test eliminated the suspect's unreasonable perceptions, it substituted the perhaps unreasonable view of the police officer.

If the purely subjective tests are discarded, one is left with variations of an objective test. Two major variants are possible. A purely objective test—was the defendant in fact in custody? [46] And in light of the defendant's age, intellect, experience, physical condition, etc., could the defendant have reasonably believed that he or she was in fact in custody? [47] This latter version has the advantage of taking into account the factors that *Miranda* and its predecessors considered important.

The extent to which a jurisdiction utilizes any specific test is difficult to determine because of the courts' tendency to use a case-by-case approach and the ambiguous

---

44. 384 U.S. 436, 444, 86 S.Ct. 1602, 1612, 16 L.Ed. 2d 694 (1966). In the footnote which follows the quotation, the Court stated that "This is what we meant in *Escobedo* when we spoke of an investigation which had focused on an accused."

45. This test led to the question of the interrogating officer: "Would you have let the defendant leave?" Today no jurisdiction uses only this test.

46. See J.M.A. v. State, 542 P.2d 170 (Alaska 1975); State v. Thomas, 22 N.C.App. 206, 206 S.E.2d 390 (1974).

47. Or as often expressed—reasonably believe that he or she was free to leave. United States v. Luther, 521 F.2d 408 (9th Cir. 1975). See, e. g., State v. Mayes, 110 Ariz. 318, 518 P.2d 568 (1974).

language in some decisions. The plurality of American jurisdictions which seem to use a single test applies an objective standard to determine the presence of custody. Other jurisdictions choose to use instead what they characterize as a "focus test." [48] Deriving its origins from Escobedo v. Illinois,[49] this test in its purest sense (one seldom applied) attempts to determine whether the individual questioned was in fact the focus or central point of the investigation. As a definitional test for custody, the focus test has apparently been disavowed by the Supreme Court.[50] However, cleansed of its confusion with custody, focus is determinative of whether the person questioned was a suspect.[51] This use of the term may explain the frequent references to focus in many opinions.

Following focus in popularity is the variety-of-factors approach.[52] Perhaps best characterized by the Fifth Circuit's formulation, this test seeks to determine custody by a four-part approach: Did the police have probable cause to arrest the suspect? Did the officer intend to hold the suspect in custody? Did the suspect believe that he or she was not free to leave? Had the investigation focused on the suspect? [53] This approach allows the court to handle on an individual basis each case in which a formal arrest is lacking. While variously phrased, many opinions in this area appear to follow a multifactor approach. Thus the distinct possibility exists that no majority rule is now in use that provides a specific definition of custody.

Regardless of the test adopted, the court in any specific case must determine whether the interrogated suspect was in custody. This matter without question depends on the facts of the case. Factors which have been considered important in this determination include the place of interrogation,[54] the time of questioning,[55] the length of the interrogation, the use of weapons or other physical restraint, whether the interview was initiated by the suspect or the police,[56] whether the suspect voluntarily attended the interview,[57] and whether the suspect was or felt

---

48. See, e. g., Moore v. State, 54 Ala.App. 22, 304 So.2d 263 (1974); Reeves v. State, 258 Ark. 788, 528 S.W.2d 924 (1975).

49. The Supreme Court was perhaps attempting through *Miranda's* footnote 4 to bring *Escobedo* into line with *Miranda*. While this attempt may be successful, it is at best difficult and *Miranda* is better viewed as having created a new test for when warnings are required.

50. Beckwith v. United States, 425 U.S. 341, 96 S.Ct. 1612, 48 L.Ed.2d 1 (1976). In *Beckwith*, a case involving the failure of IRS special agents to give warnings to the suspect whom they interviewed in a private home, the Court did concede the possibility "that noncustodial interrogation might possibly in some situations, by virtue of some special circumstances, be characterized as one where the 'behavior of . . . law enforcement officials was such as to overbear petitioner's will to resist and bring about confessions not freely self-determined.'" Id. at 342–45 (citation omitted). While the failure to give warnings in such a case would be relevant, it would not be fatal. See also United States v. Gardner, 516 F.2d 334, 339–40 (7th Cir. 1975).

51. See, e. g., Steigler v. Anderson, 360 F.Supp. 1286 (D.Del.1973) (questioning of family member whose relatives had died in an arson-related fire was not a result of an investigation which had focused on him).

52. See, e. g., Smith v. State, 236 Ga. 12, 222 S.E. 2d 308 (1976); State v. Kalai, 56 Hawaii 366, 537 P.

2d 8 (1975); State v. Williams, 522 S.W.2d 641 (Mo.App.1975).

53. See United States v. Carollo, 507 F.2d 50, 52 (5th Cir. 1975); Brown v. Beto, 468 F.2d 1284 (5th Cir. 1972).

54. While a custodial interrogation may take place in the suspect's home (see, e. g., Orozco v. Texas, 394 U.S. 324, 89 S.Ct. 1095, 22 L.Ed.2d 311 (1969); Commonwealth v. Borodine, 353 N.E.2d 649 (Mass. 1976)), such a location is very likely to weigh heavily in a finding of no custody.

55. See, e. g., Commonwealth v. O'Shea, 456 Pa. 288, 318 A.2d 713 (1974).

56. See, e. g., United States v. Victor Standing Soldier, 538 F.2d 196 (8th Cir. 1976).

57. See, e. g., People v. Wipfler, 37 Ill.App.3d 400, 346 N.E.2d 41 (1976); Commonwealth v. Simpson, 345 N.E.2d 899, 904 (Mass.1976). This factor is by no means conclusive. See, e. g., State v. Mathiason, 375 Or. 1, 549 P.2d 673 (1976) (voluntary attendance overcome by coercive environment and circumstances).

free to leave the interrogation. The mere fact that a person has been questioned by the police does not create a custodial interrogation.[58] Accordingly, all the factors listed above may be relevant in determining whether custody existed for *Miranda* purposes. The reference in *Miranda* to any "significant" interference with the suspect's freedom of action is the key to the determination of custody. When the suspect has been formally arrested and brought to the police station house, the determination is usually simple. Only when the defendant has been questioned without an arrest and usually outside the station house do the numerous factors discussed above become critical.[59]

Stops for Traffic and Other Minor Offenses. A large number of courts have held that traffic offenses constitute an exception to *Miranda*.[60] Although generally such stops are noncustodial, the rationale for excluding them seems to be that they are common events expected by most citizens, that the usual traffic violation is not the sort of crime *Miranda* dealt with, and that traffic questioning fits the general investigatory exception to *Miranda*.[61] This rationale may be appropriate for simple driving violations; however the same rule has occasionally been applied to drunken driving and more serious offenses.[62] These latter cases tend to blend into those which hold that *Miranda* is inapplicable to misdemeanors.[63]

Street Encounters by Police. *Miranda* and its related cases [64] dealt primarily with station house interrogations or their equivalent. Thus the extent to which its broad holding involving custodial interrogations covered non-station house questioning was unclear. It is now apparent that questioning a suspect in police custody will generally trigger the warning requirements regardless of the location of the questioning.[65] However, some forms of street encounters are not covered by *Miranda*.

Miranda expressly recognized the need for police investigation: "General on-the-scene questioning as to facts surrounding a crime or other general questioning of citizens in the fact finding process is not affected by our holding." [66] The authors of the opinion seem to have envisioned a general investigation which lacked an identifiable suspect. The numerous cases in this area break down into three major groups: (1) those in which a known suspect did not exist at the time of questioning—e. g., the investigation had not yet focused on the individual questioned or a violation of law was

---

58. For example, a recognized "exception" to *Miranda* exists for "general investigative questioning," a police officer's general questions at the scene of the offense. Despite use of the term *exception* these cases frequently are ones in which a suspect does not yet exist (the investigation has not yet "focused" on someone) or the individuals questioned are not in custody. See, e. g., State v. Kalai, 56 Hawaii 366, 537 P.2d 8 (1975); People v. Langley, 63 Mich.App. 339, 234 N.W.2d 513 (1975); Jordan v. Commonwealth, 216 Va. 768, 222 S.E.2d 573 (1976).

59. See J. Zagel, Confessions and Interrogations After Miranda 12–36 (Nat'l Dist. Attorneys Ass'n 1972) for a complete list of factors with accompanying citation.

60. See, e. g., Clay v. Riddle, 541 F.2d 456 (4th Cir. 1976) (defendant questioned after arrest for drunken driving and after threatening police officers with a gun; *Miranda* held inapplicable); State v. Bowen, 336 A.2d 228 (Del.Super.1975) (*Miranda* held inapplicable to motor vehicle cases); State v. Cupp, 36 Ohio App.2d 224, 304 N.E.2d 598, 65 O.O. 2d 346 (1973) (*Miranda* inapplicable to questions accompanying arrest for drunken driving). But see State v. Lawson, 285 N.C.3d 320, 204 S.E.2d 843 (1974) (*Miranda* held applicable to traffic violations).

61. Cf. J. Zagel, Confessions and Interrogations After Miranda 34–35 (Nat'l Dist. Attorneys Ass'n 1972).

62. See note 60, supra.

63. See, e. g., State v. Glanton, 231 N.W.2d 31 (Iowa 1975); State v. Gabrielson, 192 N.W.2d 792 (Iowa 1971); State v. Pyle, 19 Ohio St.2d 64, 249 N.E. 2d 826, 48 O.O.2d 82 (1969).

64. Some courts have held *Miranda* inapplicable to stop and frisks under much the same reasoning. See, e. g., Crum v. State, 281 So.2d 368 (Fla.App. 1973); People v. Myles, 50 Cal.App.3d 423, 123 Cal. Rptr. 348 (1975).

65. See § 1, supra.

66. 384 U.S. at 477–78.

not yet clear; [67] (2) those in which a suspect may have existed but custody was lacking; [68] and (3) those in which there was a suspect in custody but police questioning was held to have been general investigation and not within the *Miranda* definition of interrogation.[69]

While some reason exists to doubt the propriety of this last group of cases, the Supreme Court in the years since *Miranda* has evinced a hostility both to the case itself and to its application outside the station house.[70] Accordingly, this limit on *Miranda's* scope may now be appropriate despite some uncertainty about *Miranda's* original meaning.

Similar to this last group of cases are those in which police surprise a person seemingly during the commission of an offense and they question the person—usually after he or she is taken into custody. A number of courts have approved questioning without warnings in these circumstances, reasoning that *Miranda* was never meant to ap-

ply to on-the-scene questioning. Presumably the courts involved believe that the coercive atmosphere of the station house is lacking here.[71] Additionally, a number of decisions have mentioned the possibility that the suspect is in fact innocent and simply found in an incriminating situation which can be explained quickly through limited police questioning.

Witnesses Appearing Before Grand Juries and Trial Courts. In United States v. Mandujano,[72] the Supreme Court expressly held *Miranda* inapplicable to grand jury proceedings. The Court stated that *Miranda's* concern was with custodial interrogation and "simply did not perceive judicial inquiries and custodial interrogation as equivalent." [73] The Court also stated that the right against self-incrimination at a grand jury was somewhat more limited for a witness than was the privilege available to a suspect being questioned by the police, that no right to counsel exists at grand juries, and that accordingly the *Miranda* warnings would be inappropriate.[74]

By implication and general custom, a trial judge need not warn a witness at trial who may be incriminating himself or herself of the right to remain silent.[75] However, although no legal duty mandates warning a witness of the right against self-incrimina-

67. See State v. Egger, 24 Or.App. 927, 547 P.2d 643 (1976) (vehicle stop for erratic driving); District of Columbia v. M. E. H., 312 A.2d 561 (D.C.App. 1973) (question about who owned the gun was addressed to the group, not to a given person). But see People v. Norwood, 68 Mich.App. 730, 243 N.W. 2d 719 (1976) (holding that sheriff's question, "What happened," to defendant who had summoned him to her home because she had shot the deceased was a violation of *Miranda*).

68. See, e. g., State v. Shepardson, 194 Neb. 673, 235 N.W.2d 218, 223 (1975) (vehicle registration check led to officer noting marijuana seeds; questioning prior to formal arrest did not require warnings); cf. Gedicks v. State, 62 Wis.2d 74, 214 N.W. 2d 569 (1974) (defendant's I.D. checked by policeman to determine his reason to be on university grounds).

69. See, e. g., Owens v. United States, 340 A.2d 821 (D.C.App.1975) (burglar was caught at the scene and handcuffed; his incriminating reply made one or two seconds after his apprehension to policeman's question about what he was doing on the roof was admissible, for warnings were not required); State v. Henson, 23 Or.App. 234, 541 P.2d 1085 (1975) (vehicle stop resulted in questioning about a hit and run; *Miranda* warnings held not to have been required despite fact that officer removed defendant's car keys and directed him to remain in the vehicle.).

70. See, e. g., Schneckloth v. Bustamonte, 412 U.S. 218, 247, 93 S.Ct. 2041, 2058, 36 L.Ed.2d 854 (1973).

71. See, e. g., United States v. Vigo, 487 F.2d 295 (2d Cir. 1973). The Supreme Court has found that the lack of a formal arrest to be of great—perhaps determinative—significance in a case involving the "voluntary" interrogation of a parolee. Oregon v. Mathiason, 429 U.S. 492, 97 S.Ct. 711, 50 L.Ed.2d 714 (1977). The Court's opinion suggests that the future may see *Miranda* limited to formal arrest situations that involve stationhouse interrogations.

72. 425 U.S. 564, 96 S.Ct. 1968, 48 L.Ed.2d 212 (1976). See also Commonwealth v. Columbia Investment Corp., 457 Pa. 353, 325 A.2d 289 (1974).

73. 425 U.S. at 547.

74. Id. at 577–80.

75. See, e. g., Manual for Courts-Martial, United States, 1969 (rev. ed.) para. 140a(2), stating that although a judge need not warn a witness at trial of the right to remain silent, he or she may do so.

tion at a grand jury proceeding or trial, warnings may be given.[76]

7. "Certain Rights Warnings"

Suggested Reading:

United States v. Cullinan, 396 F.Supp. 516 (N.D.Ill. 1975).

Commonwealth v. Spriggs, 463 Pa. 375, 344 A.2d 880 (1975).

At first impression, the *Miranda* Court seems to have been more than adequately specific in its rendition of the required warnings. The Court stated: "The person must be warned that he has a right to remain silent, that any statement he does make may be used as evidence against him, and that he has a right to the presence of an attorney, either retained or appointed." [77] Later in the opinion, the Court clearly indicated that the latter warning means not only that the suspect has a right to consult with an attorney but also that "if he is indigent a lawyer will be appointed to represent him." [78] Despite the seeming clarity of the *Miranda* opinion, numerous courts have been compelled to interpret the validity of variations on the *Miranda* commandments. Most of these cases concerned the right to counsel warning, although a respectable number consider the other warnings and suggestions that further warnings may be necessary.

The Right to Remain Silent. Perhaps the most important *Miranda* warning is the first warning that the suspect "has the right to remain silent, and that any statement he does make may be used as evidence against him." [79] The basic warning itself is simple and difficult to abuse. However, a number of formulations have been used by various jurisdictions to explain the right to remain silent. No specific phrasing seems required so long as the right to remain silent is sufficiently communicated to the suspect.[80] Occasionally police suggest that suspects may refrain from incriminating themselves but may not remain silent or that suspects may be charged with misprision of felony if they are not involved but nevertheless remain silent; these suggestions are improper and will cause suppression of any resulting statement.[81]

---

76. See, e. g., United States v. Jacobs, 547 F.2d 772 (2d Cir. 1976), suppressing the grand jury testimony of a perjury defendant for failure to warn her during the preceedings that she was a "target" of the investigation. In reaching its decision, the court exercised its supervisory powers while concurring in the Supreme Court's decision in *Mandujano*, 425 U.S. 564, 96 S.Ct. 1768, 48 L.Ed.2d 212 (1976). The court noted that within its circuit United States Attorneys had for 20 years been warning putative defendants of their status; the failure of a strike force prosecutor to do so resulted, in the court's opinion, in unequal protection of the law and required suppression in order to enforce conformity within the circuit. Arguably, *Mandujano* did not definitively deal with the applicability of *Miranda* to a grand jury witness who is also a putative defendant. That issue was partially answered by the Supreme Court in United States v. Wong, 431 U.S. 174, 97 S.Ct. 1823, 52 L.Ed.2d 231 (1977). The decision in *Wong* may ultimately prove of little consequence, for support is increasing for legislation that would grant witnesses the right to counsel when appearing before a grand jury. See, e. g., ABA Section on Criminal Justice, Criminal Justice, winter 1977, at 5. In *Wong*, the Supreme Court has held that as a matter of constitutional law, even putative defendants need not be warned of their right to remain silent. United States v. Wong, 431 U.S. 174, 97 S.Ct. 1823, 52 L.Ed.2d 231 (1977).

77. 384 U.S. 436, 444, 86 S.Ct. 1602, 1612, 16 L.Ed. 2d 694 (1966).

78. Id. at 473.

79. 384 U.S. 436, 444, 86 S.Ct. 1602, 1612, 16 L.Ed. 2d 694 (1966).

80. See, e. g., Commonwealth v. Spriggs, 463 Pa. 375, 344 A.2d 880 (1975) (warning that "you have the right to refuse to answer questions asked of you while you are in custody" was sufficient to convey the right to remain silent despite the failure to use the word *statement*.).

81. See, e. g., United States v. Allen, 48 C.M.R. 474 (A.C.M.R.1974); United States v. Williams, 2 C.M.A. 430, 9 C.M.R. 60 (1953) (*Williams* deals with the military's statutory analogue to *Miranda*).

The Consequences of Making a Statement. Under the *Miranda* formulation, an interrogator must secondly advise the suspect that any statement made "may be used as evidence against him." [82] Variations of the warning have used "will," "could," or "might" in place of the word "may" in the warning.[83] A statement that any comments "will be used against you" certainly provides the suspect with the strongest warning. However, it fails to take into account the possibility that the evidence might be used for the defendant. Paralleling the *Miranda* formulation, the English Judges' Rules provide that an interrogating constable must tell a suspect that anything he or she says "may be put into writing and given in evidence." [84] Telling the American suspect that a statement might be used for him or her may, however, be considered an improper inducement which will render a statement involuntary.[85]

The Right to Counsel. *Miranda* requires that a suspect next be warned that he or she has a right to have an attorney present during the interrogation and that if he or she cannot afford an attorney, one will be appointed.[86] Failure to advise the suspect of the right to free counsel is usually considered noncompliance with *Miranda* [87] and fatal

to the admissibility of any resulting statement.[88] While the use of the word *attorney* rather than *lawyer* has been challenged, there appears little general objection to the use of the former term.

Far more important has been the question of exactly when the right to counsel attaches in terms of the warning given the suspect by the police. The suspect has a right to consult with counsel before interrogation and to have counsel present during the interrogation. Until counsel is supplied, no interrogation may take place if the suspect wants a lawyer. A number of courts have held that the failure to advise suspects of their right to consult with counsel prior to interrogation does not constitute error when the right to have counsel present during interrogation is made clear.[89]

Cases in which the police warning has suggested that the right to counsel might attach at some substantially later time have been far more troublesome. In the usual case the suspect is either advised that a "court" will appoint counsel if needed or that "we have no way of giving you a lawyer if you cannot afford one, but one may be appointed for you, if you wish, if and when you go to court." [90] The typical warning that refers to a future right to counsel is confusing at best and creates a substantial risk of leading a suspect to believe that no effective right to appointed counsel exists at the interrogation. The courts are divided on the propriety of admitting statements obtained after

---

82. 384 U.S. 436, 444, 86 S.Ct. 1602, 1612, 16 L.Ed. 2d 694 (1966).

83. See generally Y. Kamisar, W. LaFave, & J. Israel, Modern Criminal Procedure 570–71 (4th ed. 1974).

84. Judges' Rules and Administrative Directions to the Police, Rules II, III, § IV (London 1964).

85. See Y. Kamisar, W. LaFave, & J. Israel, Modern Criminal Procedure 570–71 (4th ed. 1974) for a discussion of this issue.

86. Id.

87. See, e. g., United States v. Cullinan, 396 F.Supp. 516 (N.D.Ill.1975); People v. Hermance, 35 N.Y.2d 915, 364 N.Y.S.2d 900, 324 N.E.2d 367 (1974). Note Batteaste v. State, 331 So.2d 832 (Ala.Crim.App. 1976), holding that the warning that if the suspect cannot afford a lawyer, one will be appointed for him need not include the specific statement that such a lawyer will be "free of charge."

88. See, e. g., Commonwealth v. Romberger, 464 Pa. 488, 347 A.2d 460 (1975). For an interesting decision, see United States v. Cullinan, 396 F.Supp. 516, 518 (N.D.Ill.1975), holding that failure to warn a suspect of his right to free counsel in the event of indigency would be harmless if the prosecution could present adequate proof of the suspect's ability to afford to retain counsel.

89. See, e. g., United States v. Floyd, 496 F.2d 982 (2d Cir. 1974); Sands v. State, 542 P.2d 209 (Okl. Cr.1975); State v. Ralls, 167 Conn. 408, 356 A.2d 147 (1974).

90. Grennier v. State, 70 Wis.2d 204, 214, 234 N.W. 2d 316, 321 (1975).

warnings which indicate that counsel is not immediately available.[91] Although final resolution of the issue awaits future decisions, a trend toward acceptance of statements given after warnings of this kind seems to be developing.[92] Although the American Law Institute's Model Code of Pre-Arraignment Procedure expressly recognizes a warning that counsel will be appointed at a later time, it does so in an unusually clear and forthright manner that should cure most of the defects surrounding the present formulations.[93]

Other Warnings. Although *Miranda* explicitly sets forth a number of required rights warnings, defense counsel have often argued that the case demands additional warnings not specifically enumerated in the decision. Perhaps the most common additional warning said to be required is that the suspect who has chosen to make a statement may choose to change his or her mind at any time and subsequently remain silent. Although no doubt exists that the suspect may indeed

invoke the right to remain silent at any time during interrogation,[94] *Miranda* does not require that suspects be advised of that right to terminate an interview so long as their decision to stop talking is respected.[95] Accordingly, courts have almost unanimously denied the defense claim that such a warning is required.[96]

Perhaps more important is the occasional defense claim that the suspect should be notified of sufficient facts to allow him or her to make an intelligent decision whether to waive. At a minimum, some counsel have argued, the suspect should be told the nature of the offense of which he or she is suspected.[97] Others have argued that surrounding circumstances should be disclosed. For example, is the crime a felony or misdemeanor? Has the victim died or been seriously injured? Has the suspect been able to make a knowing and intelligent waiver? However, most courts have held that information about the nature either of the offense or of the surrounding circumstances is not required.[98] Re-

91. See, e. g., Wright v. North Carolina, 415 U.S. 936, 94 S.Ct. 1452, 39 L.Ed.2d 494 (1974) (Mr. Justice Douglas dissenting from denial of a petiiton for grant of a writ of certiorari), and cases cited therein. Note that both federal and state courts are divided on this issue. See also Note, Criminal Procedure: Miranda Warning and the Right to "Instant Counsel"—A Growing Schism, 29 Okla.L.Rev. 957 (1976).

92. See, e. g., Arnold v. State, 548 P.2d 659 (Okl.Cr. 1976); Grennier v. State, 70 Wis.2d 204, 234 N.W. 2d 316 (1975); State v. Maluia, 56 Hawaii 428, 539 P.2d 1200 (1975); United States v. Rawls, 322 A.2d 903 (D.C.App.1974); Schade v. State, 512 P.2d 907 (Alaska 1973) (police officer was only telling the truth).

93. "No law enforcement officer shall question an arrested person after he has been brought to the police station or otherwise attempt to induce him to make a statement unless he has been advised by the station officer in plain understandable language . . . that if he wishes to consult a lawyer or to have a lawyer present during questioning, but is unable to obtain one, he will not be questioned until a lawyer has been provided for him; such advice shall also include information on how he may arrange to have a lawyer so provided." ALI Model Code of Pre-Arraignment Procedure § 140.8(1)(c) (1975).

94. 384 U.S. 436, 473–74, 86 S.Ct. 1602, 1627–28, 16 L.Ed.2d 694 (1966).

95. Id. at 444–45, 467–70, 473–74.

96. See, e. g., Crowe v. State, 54 Ala.App. 121, 305 So.2d 396 (1974); State v. Cobbs, 164 Conn. 402, 418–17, 324 A.2d 234, 244, cert. denied 414 U.S. 861, 94 S.Ct. 77, 38 L.Ed.2d 112 (1973); State v. Sherwood, 139 N.J.Super. 201, 204–05, 353 A.2d 137, 139 (1976); Commonwealth v. Alston, 456 Pa. 128, 317 A.2d 241 (1974); State v. Harbaugh, 132 Vt. 569, 577–78, 326 A.2d 821, 826 (1974).

97. See, e. g., Uniform Code of Military Justice, art. 31(b), 10 U.S.C.A. § 831(b) (1970), requiring that a suspect be advised of the nature of the offense of which he or she is suspected. The warning need not be overly specific or technical. (E. g., "you are suspected of killing Smith" is enough). Miller v. State, 263 Ind. 595, 335 N.E.2d 206 (1975).

98. See, e. g., State v. Owen, 13 Wash.App. 146, 149, 534 P.2d 123, 125 (1975) (general nature of charges against defendant is required); State v. Kenner, 290 So.2d 299 (La.1974) (defendant was not entitled to be warned that he was confessing to a felony); People v. Lewis, 43 A.D.2d 989, 352 N.Y.S.2d 248 (1974) (defendant was not entitled to be warned that the rape victim had died). But see People v. Prude, 32 Ill.App.3d 410, 415–17, 336 N.E.2d 348, 352–54 (1975) (juvenile suspects should have been warned of

quiring the police to give a suspect a complete briefing prior to requesting a statement seems unreasonable. Nevertheless, no apparent reason exists not to require the police to warn the suspect of the basic nature of the offense of which he or she is suspected. This approach has been in use in the military since 1951 [99] and has not proven detrimental to investigation.

An additional warning that has been discussed by a number of noted commentators [1] is the statement that the silence of a defendant will not be used against him or her. In the light of recent Supreme Court decisions,[2] that warning would now be legally true insofar as admission of a warned witness's pretrial silence is concerned. However, as Professors Kamisar, LaFave, and Israel point out,[3] the suspect's silence may well have detrimental effects on police decision-making. Despite this and because most suspects feel a psychological necessity to speak (the underlying presumption of *Miranda*), a warning that the suspect's silence will not be used against him or her at trial is desirable. It would at least minimize the inherent compulsion with which *Miranda* deals. However, such a warning does not appear to be required at this time, and the present Supreme Court would probably not extend *Miranda*.

The Necessity for Repeating Warnings. The degree to which proper *Miranda* warnings and waiver may persist and excuse the absence of new warnings and waiver (or perhaps more importantly an incomplete or improper waiver) at a subsequent interrogation is unclear and is usually addressed by the courts on a case-by-case basis. If the time period between interrogations is short and the multiple interrogations can be characterized as continuous or a single transaction, the lack of warnings at the later interrogation is harmless.[4] However, the definition of a continuous transaction excusing warnings at a subsequent interrogation depends solely on the facts of each case and the approach of the particular court. Because a delay between waiver and interrogation or between successive interrogations may easily taint a statement,[5] warnings should be given and a new waiver obtained at each interrogation to moot possible error and exclusion.

---

4. See, e. g., United States v. Delay, 500 F.2d 1360, 1365 (8th Cir. 1974) (The ultimate question is only: Did the defendant with full knowledge of his or her rights, knowingly and intentionally relinquish them?); United States v. Schultz, 19 U.S.C.M.A. 311, 41 C.M.R. 311 (1970) (7-hour delay did not affect "single continuous interrogation"); Gregg v. State, 233 Ga. 117, 210 S.E.2d 659 (1974) (14 hours between waiver and final statement did not taint statement); State v. Myers, 345 A.2d 500, 503 (Me.1975) (17-hour period between warnings and statement did not vitiate warnings when defendant was reminded at the interrogation of the warnings previously given, and he acknowledged them); State v. Rhea, 86 N.M. 291, 523 P.2d 26 (1974), cert. denied 86 N.M. 281, 523 P.2d 16 (two sets of warnings were sufficient; third set was unnecessary in view of the short delay); State v. McZorn, 288 N.C. 417, 434–35, 219 S.E.2d 201, 212 (1975).

5. See, e. g., United States v. Weston, 51 C.M.R. 868 (A.F.C.M.R.1976) (20-day delay and different offenses required new waiver); United States v. Boster, 38 C.M.R. 681 (A.B.R.1968) (two interrogation sessions found separate and distinct); State v. White, 288 N.C. 44, 52, 215 S.E.2d 557, 562 (1975) (a number of hours' delay between statements required a new warning and waiver when the second interrogation took place at a new location and under different circumstances); Commonwealth v. Wideman, 460 Pa. 699, 334 A.2d 594 (1975) (12-hour delay between initial waiver and confession required a new set of warnings when the interrogation was broken a number of times and the suspect was allowed to sleep for a period.).

---

the possibility of trial for murder in adult courts); People v. Santos, 85 Misc.2d 602, 381 N.Y.S.2d 205 (Bronx Cy.Sup.Ct.1976) (suspect should have been told that she had been indicted).

99. See generally Lederer, Rights Warnings in the Armed Services, 72 Mil.L.Rev. 1 (1976).

1. See note 85, supra.

2. Doyle v. Ohio, 426 U.S. 610, 96 S.Ct. 2240, 49 L.Ed.2d 91 (1976); United States v. Hale, 422 U.S. 171, 95 S.Ct. 2133, 45 L.Ed.2d 99 (1975). See generally Comment, Impeaching a Defendant's testimony by Proof of Post-Arrest Silence: Doyle v. Ohio, 25 Clev. St.L.Rev. 261 (1976).

3. See note 85, supra.

8. "Unless the Suspect Makes an Effective Waiver"

Suggested Reading:

Brewer v. Williams, 430 U.S. 387, 97 S.Ct. 1232, 51 L.Ed.2d 423 (1977).

Michigan v. Mosley, 423 U.S. 96, 96 S.Ct. 321, 46 L.Ed.2d 313 (1975).

Asserting *Miranda* **Rights.** On the one hand, after rights warnings, the suspect may assert his or her rights. As has been previously discussed,[6] the Supreme Court in *Miranda* created a framework which prevents a statement from being obtained during a custodial interrogation unless a valid waiver has been obtained from the suspect. Although *Miranda* makes clear that a non-waiver is to be considered an assertion or affirmative exercise of the *Miranda* rights, the theoretical rule can be difficult to apply to the facts of an individual case, particularly when most courts recognize implied waivers.

The clearest invocation of *Miranda* is a suspect's affirmative refusal to speak accompanied by a request for a lawyer. In such a case the police must cease interrogation[7] and obtain counsel.[8] Either a refusal to speak or a request for counsel, unless qualified in some manner, will stop questioning. However, a qualified exercise of rights can be made. A suspect may refuse to discuss a specific topic but remain willing to talk about other matters; the suspect may wish counsel but only at a later time; discussion

at the moment may be rejected in favor of a later statement. Accordingly, each case must be examined closely to determine to what extent the suspect asserted the *Miranda* rights. To the extent to which they have been invoked, the police must comply and/or cease interrogation.

Waiving *Miranda* **Rights.** A suspect may not be subject to custodial interrogation unless he or she waives the right to remain silent and the right to counsel. To be effective, the waiver must be "made voluntarily, knowingly, and intelligently."[9] Thus in the absence of a "spontaneous" statement volunteered by the suspect, the police must obtain a valid *Miranda* waiver before interrogation may take place.[10] In the words of *Miranda:* "If the interrogation continues without the presence of an attorney and a statement is taken, a *heavy burden* rests on the government to demonstrate that the defendant knowingly and intelligently waived his privilege against self-incrimination and his right to retained or appointed counsel. An express statement that the individual is willing to make a statement and does not want an attorney followed closely by a statement could constitute a waiver. But a valid waiver will not be presumed simply from the silence of the accused after warnings are given or simply from the fact that a confession was in fact eventually obtained."[11]

It is apparent that no need exists for a suspect to affirmatively assert the right to remain silent;[12] rather he or she must

---

6. § 1, supra.

7. The extent to which interrogation may be resumed after the suspect has refused to make a statement is unclear and is discussed, infra.

8. However, the police may opt simply to discontinue the interrogation. Although the police may arbitrarily refuse to supply counsel, if counsel is in fact unavailable, the police may choose to notify counsel and to discontinue questioning.

9. Miranda v. Arizona, 384 U.S. 436, 444, 86 S.Ct. 1602, 1612, 16 L.Ed.2d 694 (1966).

10. If *Miranda* is violated, the resulting statement will be excluded from evidence.

11. Miranda v. Arizona, 384 U.S. 436, 475, 86 S.Ct. 1602, 1628, 16 L.Ed.2d 694 (1966) (emphasis added and citations omitted).

12. Because the suspect need not affirmatively exercise the right to remain silent, numerous cases have attempted to determine whether a suspect has in fact exercised, in whole or in part, this privilege. See, e. g., United States v. Marchildon, 519 F.2d 337, 343 (8th Cir. 1975) (defendant's response to police request to inform meant only that suspect would not talk

waive the privilege to make a statement. However, the right to counsel must be affirmatively exercised.[13] But when asserted, unless limited to future consultation [14] or some specifically defined use,[15] a request for a lawyer will stop interrogation completely.[16]

The ideal form of waiver consists of a proper rights warning followed by three questions: "Do you understand your rights? Do you want a lawyer? Do you wish to make a statement?" [17] A "yes" to the first and third questions and a "no" to the second create a proper waiver. However, such an express waiver is rare. Most cases dealt with in the courts [18] involve alleged waivers in which the suspect either stated he or she understood the rights and then proceeded to answer police questions [19] or went immediately from the warnings to the interrogation.[20] Faced with this situation, the courts have generally accepted implied waivers [21] whenever convinced of their existence. Of course, in doing so, the courts need to weigh all the surrounding circumstances, for the waiver must be voluntary.

It is important to distinguish between cases in which the suspect spontaneously began making a statement after receiving warnings [22] and those in which he or she began answering questions after receiving warnings. In the first situation, the statement is voluntary and spontaneous, and waiver is virtually automatic. In the second, waiver must be found from the circumstances. Presence of the suspect's attorney at the interrogation is persuasive, if not absolute, evidence of waiver and will usually obviate the need for waiver and/or warnings.[23]

A recurring problem is that of the suspect who refuses to sign a written waiver. The courts have consistently held that such refusal does not render a subsequent statement involuntary.[24] However, it may be

---

about his sources of supply, not that he wished to remain silent).

13. While a suspect who does not waive the right to counsel must be given a lawyer before an interrogation may take place (Miranda v. Arizona, 384 U.S. 436, 470–71, 86 S.Ct. 1602, 1625–26, 16 L.Ed.2d 694 (1966)), in the absence of interrogation, counsel need not automatically be supplied, and the suspect desiring counsel is well advised to affirmatively request one.

14. See, e. g., People v. Turnage, 45 Cal.App.3d 201, 119 Cal.Rptr. 237 (1975).

15. See, e. g., People v. Madison, 56 Ill.2d 476, 309 N.E.2d 11 (1974) (defendant's saying that he would give a statement, but not sign it until a public defender was present held not to prevent interrogation, for the suspect had not requested counsel).

16. Miranda v. Arizona, 384 U.S. 436, 444–45, 86 S.Ct. 1602, 1612, 16 L.Ed.2d 694 (1966). See, e. g., State v. Nicholson, 19 Or.App. 226, 232, 527 P.2d 140, 142 (1974) (contra People v. Madison, supra, the court held that a defendant's refusal to sign his statement until he had a lawyer present was a general request for counsel which should have stopped the interrogation immediately).

17. This form of express waiver is in use in the Army, for example. See Department of the Army Form 3881, Rights Warning/Waiver Certificate. Note that a defective warning will usually render any waiver a nullity.

18. Perfect waivers are seldom litigated. However the cases involving implied waiver will probably be challenged.

19. See, e. g., People v. Johnson, 13 Ill.App.3d 1020, 1025, 304 N.E.2d 681, 685 (1973).

20. See, e. g., State v. Pineda, 110 Ariz. 342, 519 P.2d 41 (1974).

21. See, e. g., United States v. Moreno-Lopez, 466 F.2d 1205 (9th Cir. 1972); United States v. Gochenour, 47 C.M.R. 979 (A.F.C.M.R.1973); Commonwealth v. Valliere, 366 Mass. 479, 321 N.E.2d 625, 631 (1974); Braziel v. State, 529 S.W.2d 501 (Tenn.Cr.App.1975); Moreno v. State, 511 S.W.2d 273, 276–77 (Tex.Cr. App.1974); State v. Breznick, 134 Vt. 261, 356 A.2d 540, 542 (1976).

22. Errors in warnings can frequently be cured by spontaneous statements from the suspect, for only rarely is such a statement found to have been an improper product of coercive circumstances.

23. See, e. g., White v. State, 294 Ala. 265, 314 So.2d 857 (1975). See generally J. Zagel, Confessions and Interrogations After *Miranda* (Nat'l District Attorney's Ass'n, 1972) at 58–59. While warnings in such a case *may* be unnecessary, as Mr. Zagel suggests, they should nevertheless be given in order to moot future claims of error.

24. See, e. g., United States v. Sawyer, 504 F.2d 878 (5th Cir. 1974); United States v. Cooper, 499 F.2d 1060, 1063 (D.C.Cir. 1974); United States v. Reynolds, 496 F.2d 158 (6th Cir. 1974); United States v. Crisp, 435 F.2d 354, 358 (7th Cir. 1970); Hewitt v.

strong evidence of the suspect's desire not to waive his or her rights and consequently may result in a finding of non-waiver.[25] A related problem is the suspect who makes an oral statement but refuses to make a written one. While such a refusal may mean only that the suspect has become frightened, it may also indicate a mistaken belief that *Miranda* bars oral but not written statements from use in court. In this situation, the oral statement will be inadmissible [26] because of a basic misunderstanding of the *Miranda* rights.

Knowing and Voluntary Waiver. A valid *Miranda* waiver presupposes that the suspect is aware of and understands his or her *Miranda* rights. A defect in the warnings may thus make waiver impossible.[27] The warnings must be properly communicated,[28] and the suspect must comprehend both them and the effects of waiver. If the suspect lacks the ability to understand the rights or to make an intelligent [29] waiver de-

cision, a waiver is void. Thus in any given case, questions relating to the suspect's intelligence, physical and mental condition,[30] and the circumstances surrounding the waiver are highly relevant.[31] To a large extent the determination of the waiver's voluntariness subsumes the traditional common-law determination of a confession's voluntariness. *Miranda* explicitly bars the use of threats, trickery, and cajolery to obtain waivers,[32] although trickery that does not overbear the suspect's will may be acceptable after a valid waiver.

Waiver After Initial Assertion of Miranda Rights. A difficult question is whether a suspect's assertion of the *Miranda* rights prevents questioning at a later time. Clearly, competing considerations are involved. *Miranda* expressly requires that questioning stop as soon as a suspect invokes his or her rights,[33] and allowing repetitive attempts at interrogation can be regarded only as a wearing away of the *Miranda* armor even if *Miranda* warnings are given during each attempt. However, a suspect may wish to change his or her mind and to make a statement—particularly if the suspect is aware of newly discovered evidence. If confession evidence is desirable, and society persists in viewing it as such, society has an interest in balancing the seemingly absolute privilege against self-incrimination

---

State, 261 Ind. 71, 300 N.E.2d 94 (1973); State v. Jones, 35 Ohio App.2d 92, 300 N.E.2d 230, 64 O.O.2d 208 (1973); Commonwealth v. Cost, 238 Pa.Super. 591, 362 A.2d 1027 (1976).

25. See, e. g., Millican v. State, 157 Ind.App. 363, 300 N.E.2d 359 (1973).

26. See, e. g., State v. Jones, 34 Ohio St.2d 21, 306 N.E.2d 409, 66 O.O.2d 79 (1974) (suspect made an oral statement but refused to continue when police began to take notes).

27. *Miranda* expressly rejects the possibility that warnings may be omitted because the suspect may have prior knowledge of his or her rights; "whatever the background of the person interrogated, a warning at the time of interrogation is indispensable to overcome its pressures and to insure that the individual knows he is free to exercise his privileges at that point in time." 384 U.S. 436, 468–69, 86 S.Ct. 1602, 1624–25, 16 L.Ed.2d 694 (1966).

28. The warnings must, for example, be given in a language that the suspect understands. Cf. People v. Gonzales, 22 Ill.App.3d 83, 316 N.E.2d 800 (1974). Another difficulty may be the rapid "ritualistic" fashion that the police sometimes use to give warnings. See, e. g., People v. Andino, 80 Misc.2d 155, 362 N.Y.S.2d 766, 770–71 (1974).

29. See, e. g., Greenwell v. State, 32 Md.App. 579, 363 A.2d 555, 561 (1976) (minimum ability to understand must be found).

30. See, e. g., Commonwealth v. Hosey, 368 Mass. 571, 334 N.E.2d 44, 48 (1975) (emotional upset complicated by gratuitous police information that getting a lawyer would be difficult voided the waiver). Poor physical or mental condition does not necessarily make waiver impossible. United States v. Choice, 392 F.Supp. 460, 469 (E.D.Pa.1975).

31. Any form of threat or inducement may make the waiver a nullity just as the same conduct may make a confession involuntary.

32. 384 U.S. at 476.

33. "[I]f the individual is alone and indicates in any manner that he does not wish to be interrogated, the police may not question him." 384 U.S. 436, 446, 86 S.Ct. 1602, 1613, 16 L.Ed.2d 694 (1966). See also id. at 473–74.

with a police right to ask a suspect to reconsider.

The law is unsettled in this area. During 1975, in deciding Michigan v. Mosley,[34] the Supreme Court attempted to resolve the problem. Richard Mosley was arrested in Detroit in connection with a series of robberies. He was brought to the police department, where he was advised of his rights, and he then affirmatively refused to answer any questions about the robberies. A few hours later a different detective approached Mosley in his cell, gave proper warnings, and questioned him about a homicide. Mosley admitted participation in the homicide. The majority of the Supreme Court held that Mosley's *Miranda* rights had not been violated, for the first interrogation had stopped immediately when he refused to answer questions and the second session pertained to an entirely different offense.[35] The majority apparently emphasized the fact that although Mosley asserted his privilege against self-incrimination, he did not request counsel.[36]

Justices Brennan and Marshall[37], dissenting, pointed out that the homicide was in fact connected with the robberies because Mosley had been arrested only after a tip that concerned both offenses. In addition, the interrogations were connected, for Mosley's refusal to discuss the robberies should have been construed to have included the homicide. More importantly, the dissenters properly criticized the majority's holding[38] that so long as a refusal to talk was "scrupulously honored," interrogation could resume

at some later time. Such an approach both further erodes *Miranda*[39] and creates a test without meaning, for the opinion does not indicate the proper time limit between interrogations. Justices Brennan and Marshall suggested that subsequent interrogation should be prohibited until counsel is appointed and present or until the suspect is arraigned.[40]

Thus, at present the police may attempt to question a suspect who has previously asserted the right against self-incrimination so long as they honor the original refusal to talk and so long as some unknown time period elapses between the two interrogations. Moreover, the Court has arguably ruled only on a subsequent interrogation for an offense unrelated to the first interrogation, although the Court's ultimate direction appears obvious.

The *Mosley* majority highlighted the fact that Mosley had not affirmatively requested counsel, suggesting strongly that a request for counsel might block subsequent interrogation until counsel is obtained.[41] Such a rule has some precedent in the decisions of a number of lower courts.[42]

At present the state of the law may be summarized as follows. Clearly it is constitutional to request a statement, after proper warnings and waiver, of a suspect who has previously refused to make a statement about a different offense if an "appreciable" delay has occurred between the interrogations and if the circumstances are not coercive. It is probably proper to attempt a later interrogation involving the same offense that the suspect originally refused to discuss so long as his or her original refusal

---

34. 423 U.S. 96, 96 S.Ct. 321, 46 L.Ed.2d 313 (1975), hereinafter cited as *Mosley*.

35. Mr. Justice White, concurring, stated: "I suspect that in the final analysis the majority will adopt voluntariness as the standard by which to judge the waiver of the right to silence by a properly informed defendant. I think the Court should say so now." 423 U.S. at 108.

36. Id. at 104 n. 10.

37. Id. at 111.

38. Id. at 114–15. For further discussion, see Note, 21 Vill.L.Rev. 761 (1975–76).

39. Compare *Mosley* with *Miranda*, 384 U.S. at 473–474.

40. 423 U.S. at 116.

41. Id. at 104 n. 10 "[*Miranda*] directed that 'the interrogation must cease until an attorney is present' only '[i]f the individual states that he wants an attorney.'"

42. See, e. g., United States v. Clark, 499 F.2d 802 (4th Cir. 1974).

to talk was "scrupulously honored." [43]　It is clear that the Court has rejected the notion that *Miranda* forbids renewal of interrogation.[44]　All other questions, particularly in those cases in which the suspect requests counsel,[45] are left open for later decision.

9. "Any Statement by the Suspect Is Inadmissible"

Suggested Reading:

Oregon v. Haas, 420 U.S. 714, 95 S.Ct. 1215, 43 L.Ed.2d 570 (1975).

Harris v. New York, 401 U.S. 222, 91 S.Ct. 643, 28 L.Ed.2d 1 (1971).

The Initial Statement. The price of noncompliance with *Miranda* is simple but critical—exclusion from trial of the resulting evidence.　Subject to the effects of statutory attempts to overrule *Miranda*,[46] the case requires that the product of a *Miranda* violation and its derivative evidence be excluded at trial.[47]　One significant exception to this exclusionary rule exists.　The Supreme Court has expressly approved the use of evidence obtained in violation of *Miranda* for impeachment purposes.[48]　This limited inroad to the exclusionary rule results from the Supreme Court's increasing dissatisfaction with exclusionary rules generally and *Miranda* specifically.　By allowing such evidence to be used for impeachment, the Court has expressly countenanced police violation of *Miranda* (and perhaps more importantly has encouraged it), for now the interrogator who has been frustrated by a suspect's refusal to talk has a reason to attempt to overcome the suspect's assertion of the right to remain silent.[49]　Perhaps for this reason,

---

43. See, e. g., State v. Travis, 26 Ariz.App. 24, 545 P.2d 986 (1976); People v. Almond, 67 Mich.App. 713, 717–19, 242 N.W.2d 498, 501 (1976); Commonwealth v. Reiland, 241 Pa.Super. 109, 359 A.2d 811 (1976); State v. Robbins, 15 Wash.App. 108, 547 P.2d 288 (1976).

44. Michigan v. Mosley, 423 U.S. 96, 101–04, 96 S.Ct. 321, 325–26, 46 L.Ed.2d 313 (1975).

45. While some courts have held that a request for counsel prevents later interrogation until counsel has been obtained and present (e. g., United States v. Flores, 540 F.2d 432 (9th Cir. 1976); People v. Parnell, 31 Ill.App.3d 627, 630, 334 N.E.2d 403, 406 (1975)), numerous courts have found a request for counsel to be of no particular significance in deterring a later interrogation.　E. g., United States v. Pheaster, 544 F.2d 353 (9th Cir. 1976); People v. Morgan, 39 Ill.App.3d 588, 350 N.E.2d 27 (1976); Commonwealth v. Orton, 355 N.E.2d 925, 927 (Mass.App. 1976); Buckingham v. State, 540 S.W.2d 660, (Tenn. Cr.App.1976), cert. denied 429 U.S. 1049, 97 S. Ct. 759, 50 L.Ed.2d 764 (1977).　See also Brown v. United States, 359 A.2d 600 (D.C.App.1976) (interrogating detective was unaware of suspect's prior request for counsel: statement was admissible).　In Brewer v. Williams, 430 U.S. 387, 97 S.Ct. 1232, 51 L.Ed.2d 424 (1977), the Supreme Court appears to accept the proposition that a defendant may always waive his or her right to counsel although it is "incumbent upon the State to prove 'an intentional relinquishment or abandonment of a known right or privilege.'"　Thus it seems that a defendant may be questioned a second time even though at the first session he or she requested counsel.　For the second session to yield an admissible statement, however, in the absence of counsel, the suspect must intentionally and knowingly give up the right to counsel—arguably under a higher standard than that normally used in *Miranda* cases.

46. 18 U.S.C.A. § 3501 (1970).

47. 384 U.S. 436, 479, 86 S.Ct. 1602, 1630, 16 L.Ed. 2d 694 (1966): "[N]o evidence obtained as a result of interrogation (in violation of *Miranda*) can be used."　Despite some early state decisions to the contrary, *Miranda* probably intended to ban derivative evidence (the fruit of the poisonous tree) as well as evidence obtained in direct violation of its tenets. But see Michigan v. Tucker, 417 U.S. 433, 460–61, 94 S.Ct. 2357, 2372, 41 L.Ed.2d 182 (1974) (Mr. Justice White concurring).　*Miranda's* ultimate effect on derivative evidence is now unclear in view of the Supreme Court's increasingly hostile treatment of the decision.　See Comment, The Effects of Tucker on the "Fruits" of Illegally Obtained Statements, 24 Clev.St.L.Rev. 689 (1975), discussing Michigan v. Tucker, 417 U.S. 433, 94 S.Ct. 2357, 41 L.Ed.2d 182 (1974).

48. Oregon v. Haas, 420 U.S. 714, 95 S.Ct. 1215, 43 L.Ed.2d 570 (1975); Harris v. New York, 401 U.S. 222, 91 S.Ct. 643, 28 L.Ed.2d 1 (1971). Note that although statements obtained in violation of *Miranda* may be used for impeachment, the statements must be voluntary in the non-*Miranda* sense.　See e. g., Kidd v. State, 20 Crim.L.Rep. 2238 (Md. Nov. 3, 1976); Booker v. State, 326 So.2d 791, 793 (Miss. 1976).

49. Oregon v. Haas, 420 U.S. 714, 725, 95 S.Ct. 1215, 1222, 43 L.Ed.2d 570 (1975) (Mr. Justice Brennan dissenting).

a number of jurisdictions have declined to follow the Supreme Court's lead and have expressly rejected the impeachment exception to the *Miranda* exclusionary rule.[50] The fifth amendment exclusionary rule is discussed at greater length in Chapter 24.

Subsequent Statements. The extent to which an improperly obtained statement may taint further interrogations despite an otherwise proper *Miranda* waiver is difficult to determine without reference to the specific facts of a given case. The law recognizes that any of the many factors[51] that could render a statement involuntary may well have a continued effect—enough effect to render a later statement involuntary. On the one hand, the mere knowledge that a statement has already been given can be considered a major factor in a suspect's decision to make a subsequent statement.[52] On the other hand, many of the errors that can cause a statement to be inadmissible either may be exceedingly minor in scope and have little continued effect or may be adequately counterbalanced by rights warnings and circumstances. The courts have generally treated these cases on a case-by-case basis, looking carefully at the unique facts of each to determine the probability that the impropriety of the first interrogation was overcome by the later interrogation.[53] The bur-

den to show voluntariness remains of course with the prosecution, which must demonstrate that the later statement was obtained in full compliance with *Miranda* and the voluntariness doctrine. The burden may be difficult to meet under these conditions.

The courts have apparently treated cases involving only *Miranda* violations at the earlier interrogation somewhat more leniently than cases involving violations of the pre-*Miranda* voluntariness doctrine.[54] In all cases involving a later custodial interrogation,[55] proper warnings must be given and a proper waiver obtained. If this procedure is complied with and the prosecution can show that any prior taint has been dissipated[56] by time, special warnings, or circumstances, the statement is probably admissible.[57] Statements involving physical coercion, threats, or unlawful inducement are more difficult to overcome.[58] Interrogators attempting to repair an improperly obtained statement not only should give the usual warnings but also should notify the

---

50. United States v. Girard, 23 C.M.A. 263, 49 C.M.R. 438 (1975); People v. Disbrow, 16 Cal.3d 101, 113–15, 127 Cal.Rptr. 360, 366–67, 545 P.2d 272, 280 (1976) (California Constitution construed); State v. Santiago, 53 Hawaii 254, 492 P.2d 657 (1971) (Hawaiian Constitution construed); Commonwealth v. Triplett, 462 Pa. 244, 341 A.2d 62 (1975).

51. Incomplete warnings, erroneous warnings, failure to comply with an attempted exercise of the right against self-incrimination or the right to counsel, physical coercion, threats, inducements, and psychological coercion are the usual violations.

52. The suspect may believe that the statement is a confession and that he or she has therefore nothing to lose by confessing further.

53. The courts have generally rejected the theory that the "cat-is-out-of-the-bag" rationale requires suppression of all subsequent statements perhaps unless the suspect is told that his or her prior statement is

inadmissible. See, e. g., Tanner v. Vincent, 19 Crim. L.Rep. 2509 (2d Cir. Aug. 27, 1976) and cases cited therein. However, the inadmissibility of the first statement is a factor that *must* be considered when weighing the admissibility of the later statement. See, e. g., State v. Silver, 286 N.C. 709, 213 S.E.2d 247 (1975).

54. See, e. g., United States v. Toral, 536 F.2d 893 (9th Cir. 1976) (When first interrogation had little that that was inherently coercive and was defective almost exclusively because of the police failure to give warnings, the later statement was untainted).

55. While *Miranda* warnings apply only to custodial interrogation, logically an inadmissible statement could taint a subsequent statement obtained during noncustodial interrogation.

56. An exploitation of the first statement will likely render the second inadmissible. Similarly, a statement by the accused to the effect that "I wouldn't tell you this if I hadn't talked to you yesterday" will probably doom the statement if the prior statement had been inadmissible.

57. See, e. g., Tanner v. Vincent, 541 F.2d 932 (2d Cir. 1976).

58. Violations of the traditional voluntariness doctrine are deemed more likely to have a substantial long-term effect than does the failure to give the prophylactic *Miranda* warnings.

suspect that the earlier statement will be considered inadmissible in court. Although this notification is not required,[59] it ought to be accomplished in order to moot later litigation.[60]

10. Future of *Miranda*

Suggested Reading:

Michigan v. Tucker, 417 U.S. 433, 94 S.Ct. 2357, 41 L.Ed.2d 182 (1974).

Believing that the objections to *Miranda* are well-founded, police, prosecutors, and much of the nation's citizenry greeted the decision with rage that has cooled only slightly with time. The national displeasure resulted in a Congressional attempt to overrule *Miranda* by statute, which President Johnson signed into law as part of the Omnibus Crime Control and Safe Streets Act of 1968.[61] The statute attempted to replace the *Miranda* exclusionary rule requiring suppression of a statement obtained without proper *Miranda* warnings and waiver with a pre-*Miranda* voluntariness test.[62] At the time of its en-

actment, the "Post-Miranda Act" was considered unlikely to affect *Miranda* directly, for *Miranda* was considered a decision resulting from constitutional interpretation and thus beyond statutory control.[63] Accordingly, while other sections of the statute had effect,[64] the *Miranda* portion tended to be ignored.[65] However, the Supreme Court's clear dislike for *Miranda* has resulted in a significant shift in the potential importance

take into consideration all the circumstances surrounding the giving of the confession, including (1) the time elapsing between arrest and arraignment of the defendant making the confession, if it was made after arrest and before arraignment, (2) whether such defendant knew the nature of the offense with which he was charged or of which he was suspected at the time of making the confession, (3) whether or not such defendant was advised or knew that he was not required to make any statement and that any such statement could be used against him, (4) whether or not such defendant had been advised prior to questioning of his right to the assistance of counsel; and (5) whether or not such defendant was without the assistance of counsel when questioned and when giving such confession.

The presence or absence of any of the above-mentioned factors to be taken into consideration by the judge need not be conclusive on the issue of voluntariness of the confession."

63. Despite some argument that Congress could have acted to limit the federal courts' jurisdiction to review on appeal a finding that a confession was voluntary in the § 3501 sense (see 1968 U.S.Code Cong. & Admin.News 2139–2150), Congress seems to have abandoned its attempt to expressly limit federal jurisdiction. Significant doubt remains that the statute could actually affect *Miranda*. Professor Stephens suggests at page 145 that the statutory effort to limit *Miranda* may have been intended to signal the Supreme Court that it had gone too far and that it should reconsider *Miranda* and its general approach in criminal matters. See Gandara supra note 61 at 311–13; O. Stephens, supra note 61 at 142–45.

64. The sections attempting to overrule the Court's decisions in McNabb v. United States, 318 U.S. 332, 63 S.Ct. 608, 87 L.Ed. 819 (1943), and Mallory v. United States, 354 U.S. 449, 77 S.Ct. 1356, 1 L.Ed. 2d 1479 (1957), were apparently successful.

65. See Gandara, supra note 61 at 311–13, indicating that federal law enforcement agents have adhered to *Miranda* and that many of the United States Attorneys did not urge § 3501 on federal District Courts to save confessions, although the Southern District of New York "had invoked section 3501 in several cases." Id. at 312.

59. See, e. g., Tanner v. Vincent, 541 F.2d 932 (2d Cir. 1976); State v. Dakota, 300 Minn. 12, 16, 217 N.W.2d 748, 751 (1974).

60. See, e. g., United States v. Seay, 24 C.M.A. 10, 51 C.M.R. 60 (1975) ("In addition to rewarning the accused, the preferable course in seeking an additional statement would include advice that prior illegal admissions or other improperly obtained evidence which incriminated the accused cannot be used against him.")

61. Pub.L.No. 90–351, 82 Stat. 197. The relevant portion of the Act, usually termed either the "Post-Miranda Act" or the "Anti-Miranda Act," is 18 U.S. C.A. § 3501 (1970). See generally O. Stephens, Jr., The Supreme Court and Confessions of Guilt 139–45, 163–64 (1973); Gandara, Admissibility of Confessions in Federal Prosecutions: Implementation of Section 3501 by Law Enforcement Officials and the Courts, 63 Geo.L.J. 305 (1974) (hereinafter cited as Gandara). For 18 U.S.C.A. § 3501's legislative history, see 1968 U.S.Code Cong. & Admin.News 2124–2150.

62. 18 U.S.C.A. § 3501(b) (1970): "(b) The trial judge in determining the issue of voluntariness shall

of the statute. In Michigan v. Tucker,[66] the Court apparently found that *Miranda* lacked constitutional dimension and served only as "prophylactic rules." [67]

Despite the fact that every reason exists to believe that the Warren Court had not intended to set *Miranda* in concrete for all time,[68] *Miranda* is clearly of constitutional dimension. With the Court's present view, however, the Post-Miranda Act could be held by the Court to have pre-empted the Court's "non-constitutionally required" *Miranda* doctrine. Although by early 1979 the Supreme Court had not had occasion to construe the effect and legality of the Post-Miranda Act, some courts had begun to apply it to prevent exclusion of statements that would have been suppressed under *Miranda*.[69] At present *Miranda* governs, but the long-term effect of the statutory attempt to overrule it is unknown and cannot be dismissed as wholly ineffective.

---

66. 417 U.S. 433, 94 S.Ct. 2357, 41 L.Ed.2d 182 (1974).

67. Id. at 466.

68. *Miranda* expressly recognized that other effective techniques might be developed which could replace the warnings. 384 U.S. 436, 467, 86 S.Ct. 1602, 1624, 16 L.Ed.2d 694 (1966).

69. See, e. g., United States v. Crocker, 510 F.2d 1129, 1136–38 (10th Cir. 1975).

CHAPTER 24

THE EXCLUSIONARY RULE AND DERIVATIVE EVIDENCE

1. Primary Taint

Suggested Reading:

People v. Disbrow, 16 Cal.3d 101, 127 Cal.Rptr. 360, 545 P.2d 272 (1976).

Any statement obtained in violation of the voluntariness rule [1] or *Miranda* [2] may not be used against its maker [3] at trial on the merits. However, the Supreme Court has held [4] that statements obtained in violation of *Miranda* but otherwise voluntary [5] may be used to impeach [6] the maker's testimony at trial.[7] In so holding, the Court has indicated both its displeasure with the exclusionary rule generally and its concern that to hold otherwise would allow some defendants to commit perjury with impunity.[8]

As a number of commentators have suggested, however, the Court's decisions in this area work to nullify the deterrent effect of the exclusionary rule and thereby the right against self-incrimination, for the police now have a logical reason for improperly interrogating a suspect.[9] Because of this concern and relying on state constitutions or local statutes, a number of courts have refused

---

1. See generally Chapter 21, supra.

2. Miranda v. Arizona, 384 U.S. 436, 86 S.Ct. 1602, 16 L.Ed.2d 694 (1966). See generally Chapter 24, supra.

3. Generally, only the maker of a statement, obtained in violation of either *Miranda* or the voluntariness doctrine, has standing to object at trial to its admission. Thus the exclusionary rule does not reach statements introduced against a person other than their maker. However, a defendant may have standing to contest the admissibility of an involuntary statement that may be untrustworthy. LaFrance v. Bohlinger, 499 F.2d 29 (1st Cir. 1974).

4. Oregon v. Haas, 420 U.S. 714, 95 S.Ct. 1215, 43 L.Ed.2d 570 (1975); Harris v. New York, 401 U.S. 222, 91 S.Ct. 643, 28 L.Ed.2d 1 (1971).

5. The Supreme Court has clearly distinguished between statements which are obtained in violation of *Miranda* and those which are otherwise involuntary and possibly untrustworthy. E. g., Oregon v. Haas, 420 U.S. 714, 722–23, 95 S.Ct. 1215, 1220–21, 43 L.Ed. 2d 570 (1975). Thus involuntary or unreliable statements may not be used even for impeachment. See,

e. g., State v. Denny, 19 Crim.L.Rep. 2540 (Ariz.App. Aug. 17, 1976).

6. A few courts have used the impeachment exception of *Harris* and *Haas* as grounds for expanding the use of evidence that would normally be suppressed. Compare Greenfield v. State, 20 Crim.L.Rep. 2119 (Fla.Dist.Ct.App. Sept. 24, 1976) (allowing admission of police testimony about defendant's exercise of his *Miranda* rights when defendant raised a defense of insanity even though the defendant did not take the stand), with Pyburn v. State, 539 S.W.2d 835 (Tenn.Crim.App.1976) (use of confession tainted by *Miranda* violation for evidence of defendant's sanity was improper, for the statement should have been limited to the defendant's credibility).

7. It is unclear whether statements obtained in violation of other limitations, such as United States v. Massiah, may also be used for impeachment. There is some reason to believe that such evidence may be so used. Cf. United States v. Frank, 520 F.2d 1287 (2d Cir. 1975).

8. See, e. g., Oregon v. Haas, 420 U.S. 714, 721–23, 95 S.Ct. 1215, 1220–21, 43 L.Ed.2d 570 (1975).

9. See, e. g., Id. at 725 (Mr. Justice Brennan dissenting).

to follow the Supreme Court's lead and have expressly rejected the impeachment exception.[10]   Despite the inroad the impeachment exception represents, the exclusionary rule at present appears relatively stable insofar as its effect on primary evidence is concerned.[11] Nevertheless, significant questions exist about the future of the derivative evidence rule.

2. The Fruit of the Poisonous Tree

Suggested Reading:

Brewer v. Williams, 430 U.S. 387, 97 S.Ct. 1232, 51 L.Ed.2d 423 (1977).

Michigan v. Tucker, 417 U.S. 433, 94 S.Ct. 2357, 41 L.Ed.2d 182 (1974).

United States v. Harris, 528 F.2d 914 (4th Cir. 1975).

The Derivative Evidence Rule Itself. The public's apparent disapproval of *Miranda* centers on the *Miranda*-imposed exclusionary rule, which is viewed as an improper interference with society's right to be protected from criminals.[12]   The exclusionary rule in this area, like the fourth amendment exclusionary rule, has two phases—direct and derivative.   Evidence, such as a confession, obtained directly from a violation of *Miranda* or the voluntariness doctrine is inadmissible but so too is any evidence derived from the primary evidence which was improperly obtained in the first instance.   In standard terminology, the first violation is considered a "poisonous tree" and the derivative evidence obtained with it is considered its "fruit."

At present, testimonial evidence derived through exploitation of a *Miranda* violation will be suppressed.   Statements obtained in violation of *Miranda* which are improperly admitted at trial may cause the defendant to take the stand to refute the statement.   Such "impelled" testimony is deemed coerced, and convictions resting on such testimony are often reversed.[13]   However, beyond this conclusion the state of the law of derivative evidence is not as clear as one would like.

Although the primary exclusionary rule itself is highly controversial, the derivative evidence rule is even more debatable.   Prior to *Miranda* and until comparatively recently in the history of the voluntariness doctrine in the United States, derivative evidence was

---

10. See, e. g., United States v. Girard, 23 U.S.C.M.A. 263, 49 C.M.R. 438 (1975); People v. Disbrow, 16 Cal. 3d 101, 113–15, 127 Cal.Rptr. 360, 363–67, 545 P.2d 272, 280 (1976); Commonwealth v. Triplett, 462 Pa. 244, 341 A.2d 62 (1975); State v. Santiago, 53 Hawaii 254, 492 P.2d 657 (1971).   Most states have, however, adopted the impeachment exception.   See also Wilson v. State, 56 Ala.App. 13, 318 So.2d 753 (1975); Zachry v. State, 260 Ark. 97, 538 S.W.2d 25 (1976); Stevens v. State, 265 Ind. 396, 354 N.E.2d 727 (1976). For an analysis of the Pennsylvania situation, see Note, 21 Vill.L.Rev. 769 (1976).

11. Of course, 18 U.S.C.A. § 3501 (1970), and the A.L.I. Model Code of Pre-Arraignment Procedure § 150.3 (1975) may yet have substantial effects on the basic fifth amendment exclusionary rule.   See, e. g., United States v. Crocker, 510 F.2d 1129, 1136–38 (10th Cir. 1975), holding that voluntariness is the only test for admissibility after 18 U.S.C.A. § 3501 (1970).

12. While the public should of course be deeply concerned about crime and its causes, it frequently appears that lack of comprehension is the root cause of much of the opposition to *Miranda*.   Increased familiarity with the decision's actual holding and its policy justifications is helpful in correcting years of myth and erroneous information.

13. See, e. g., Harrison v. United States, 392 U.S. 219, 88 S.Ct. 2008, 20 L.Ed.2d 1047 (1968); Smith v. Estelle, 527 F.2d 430 (5th Cir. 1976); United States v. Hundley, 21 U.S.C.M.A. 320, 45 C.M.R. 94 (1972); People v. Wilson, 60 Ill.2d 235, 326 N.E.2d 378 (1975). It should be noted that the mere wrongful admission of a statement at trial does not compel the conclusion that the defendant's testimony was impelled.   See, e. g., Commonwealth v. Saunders, 459 Pa. 677, 331 A. 2d 193 (1975) (defendant's in-court statement was virtually identical to the allegedly wrongfully admitted statement, and the court found that taking the stand was defendant's "most promising course" in view of the overwhelming evidence against her); People v. Wilson, 16 Ill.App.3d 473, 306 N.E.2d 626 (1973) (in-court testimony was motivated by testimony of other witnesses, not by admission of illegally seized evidence).

admissible.[14] This was perfectly reasonable, for the voluntariness doctrine was originally concerned with the reliability of the statement, and derivative evidence is generally not only completely trustworthy but may demonstrate the reliability of the original statement.[15] Indeed, in England today, derivative evidence is always admissible even when the primary evidence is suppressed.

In the United States the rationale for admission of derivative evidence was largely nullified when the Supreme Court held that due process considerations rather than considerations of reliability required suppression of evidence. Although *Miranda* does not expressly require suppression of derivative evidence, apparently the Court intended to exclude derivative evidence as well as the primary evidence.[16] However, the future of the *Miranda* branch of the derivative evidence rule is unclear. Although evidence derived from a *Miranda* violation is generally suppressed at present, the Supreme Court has laid the groundwork for limiting or abolishing the *Miranda* derivative evidence rule.

The Court did so in Michigan v. Tucker.[17] In *Tucker*, the Court dealt with a fact situation in which the interrogation occurred before *Miranda* but the trial occurred

after *Miranda*. The Court held that in that situation, *Miranda* did not require the suppression of the testimony of a witness discovered through Tucker's interrogation which had not been preceded by a warning of the right to appointed counsel. *Tucker* could be narrowly limited to the fact situation where the interrogation predates *Miranda*, but the Court's rationale seems broader. The Court declared that the *Miranda* warning requirements are merely "prophylactic standards" which safeguard the fifth amendment but which themselves are not of "constitutional dimension." [18] Thus precedent now exists for distinguishing evidence derived from a *Miranda* violation from evidence obtained in violation of the voluntariness doctrine and other constitutional rights.[19]

The Court's recent decision in Brewer v. Williams [20] underscores the possibility that a dual standard is developing. In *Brewer*, the Court was forced to come to grips with a textbook application of the derivative evidence rule. The defendant Williams was suspected of killing a ten year old girl. He voluntarily turned himself in. After arraignment, he was transported from Davenport, Iowa, to Des Moines, the scene of the

---

14. A.L.I., Model Code of Pre-Arraignment Procedure 410 (1975), citing 2 Wharton, Criminal Evidence § 357 (2d ed. 1955); 3 Wigmore, Evidence § 856 (3d ed. 1940); Scott, Federal Control Over Use of Coerced Confessions in State Criminal Cases—Some Unsettled Problems, 29 Ind.L.J. 151, 156 (1954).

15. Id.

16. For cases holding that *Miranda* does not require exclusion of derivative evidence, see J. Zagel, Confessions and Interrogations After Miranda 83 (Nat'l Dist. Attorneys Ass'n 1972). Following *Miranda*, the Supreme Court reversed a case in which a suspect, confronted at trial by statements obtained in violation of *McNabb-Mallory* (see Chapter 22, supra) took the stand to refute them. Harrison v. United States, 392 U.S. 219, 88 S.Ct. 2008, 20 L.Ed.2d 1047 (1968). While a *McNabb-Mallory* violation is not the equivalent of a *Miranda* violation, one would normally infer that the same result would follow from *Miranda* which is to some extent constitutionally based.

17. 417 U.S. 433, 94 S.Ct. 2357, 41 L.Ed.2d 182 (1974).

18. Id. at 443–44, 446. The Court's decision in *Tucker* is puzzling. The Court holds that the *Miranda* warnings and waiver requirements are merely "prophylactic standards" laid down by the Court to safeguard the right against self-incrimination. Yet those standards have sufficient constitutional status to bind the states. Perhaps the Court has created a new form of constitutional rule, one which changes depending upon the issue involved.

19. Compare United States ex rel. Hudson v. Cannon, 529 F.2d 890 (7th Cir. 1976) (holding that a statement obtained in violation of a suspect's right to counsel at an interrogation under Escobedo v. Illinois, 378 U.S. 478, 84 S.Ct. 1758, 12 L.Ed.2d 977 (1964) would taint the discovery of a third party's testimony), with Rhodes v. State, 91 Nev. 111, 530 P.2d 1199 (1975) (holding that third party testimony gained through a *Miranda* violation is admissible). The primary authority for suppressing derivative evidence is Wong Sun v. United States, 371 U.S. 471, 83 S.Ct. 407, 9 L. Ed.2d 441 (1963).

20. 430 U.S. 387, 97 S.Ct. 1232, 51 L.Ed.2d 423 (1977).

crime. Despite Williams' desire to remain silent and his lawyer's insistence that the police not question Williams, two police officers interrogated him during the trip.[21] Williams' disclosures led the police to the victim's body.

Speaking for the Court, Mr. Justice Stewart found that the interrogation violated Williams' sixth amendment right to counsel[22] and that the primary evidence, Williams' statements, should have been suppressed. The Court technically did not decide whether the derivative evidence, the body itself, should have been suppressed. However, its inadmissibility seems clear from the opinion itself, Mr. Justice Stewart's suggestion that perhaps the body would have been inevitably discovered,[23] and the dissents. Thus, barring a new decision by the Court, it seems clear that evidence derived from a non-*Miranda*, constitutional violation must be suppressed.

Exceptions to the Derivative Evidence Rule. Evidence obtained through exploitation of a violation of the *Miranda* or the fourth, fifth, or sixth amendments must be excluded from trial. However, the mere fact that evidence is connected with such a violation does not necessarily lead to exclusion. As the Supreme Court stated years ago in Wong Sun v. United States,[24] the test is not a "but for" one but is rather a question of "exploitation." Thus, if the prosecution can show an independent source for the evidence, the evidence will be admissible despite the

violation.[25] Similarly, if the violation and its primary taint have been sufficiently "attenuated" so that sufficient intervening events have rendered the causal effects of the violation minimal, the evidence will be admissible.[26]

More difficult to employ is the doctrine of inevitable discovery. Under this approach, the prosecution must demonstrate that the otherwise tainted evidence would inevitably and legally have come to the government's attention and the violation in question is in effect harmless. The Supreme Court has recently accepted this escape from

---

21. Knowing that the defendant was deeply religious, the officer engaged in a conversation emphasizing how unfortunate it was that the little girl would not receive a Christian burial and that in view of snow, how unlikely it was that the body would be found. Dissenting, Chief Justice Burger objected to the implicit finding of the majority that the police conversation constituted interrogation.

22. Thereby breathing new life into Massiah v. United States, 377 U.S. 201, 84 S.Ct. 1199, 12 L.Ed.2d 246 (1964). See generally Chapter 25, supra.

23. 430 U.S. 387, 406 n. 12, 97 S.Ct. 1232, 1243 n. 12, 51 L.Ed.2d 423 (1977).

24. 371 U.S. 471, 83 S.Ct. 407, 9 L.Ed.2d 441 (1963).

25. See, e. g., United States v. Harris, 528 F.2d 914 (4th Cir. 1975), cert. denied 423 U.S. 1075, 96 S.Ct. 860, 47 L.Ed.2d 86 (1976) [when Alcohol, Firearms, and Tobacco agents arrived at the location specified by the informant, they saw the defendant with part of a pistol protruding from his pocket. Erroneously failing to warn him of his rights, the agents asked if Harris had a gun. He replied by drawing the pistol. On appeal, the Court held that the weapons seizure was not the product of the *Miranda* violation—in effect an independent source existed.]; United States v. Martinez, 512 F.2d 830 (5th Cir. 1975) [assuming *Miranda* warnings were required of Immigration agents who asked the accused his country of origin, inspection of accused's file was not a tainted product because the file was already in existence and the accused's name and origin were also previously known]; Godwin v. State, 133 Ga.App. 397, 211 S.E.2d 7 (1974) [unwarned request of defendant to remove shoplifted merchandise from her product did not taint the merchandise when accused had previously been seen placing the merchandise in her pocketbook].

26. Attenuation requires that sufficient time and/or events intervene between the violation and the seizure of the evidence. See, e. g., United States v. Mullens, 536 F.2d 997 (2d Cir. 1976) [admission of guilt and fact that accused led police to evidence broke the causal chain between the evidence and an illegal search]; United States v. Trevino, 62 F.R.D. 74 (D.Tex. 1974) [defendant's acknowledgement that he would have made admissions in any event despite illegal search found to attenuate illegal search]; United States v. Harris, 381 F.Supp. 1095 (E.D.Pa.1974) [sufficient time between inadmissible state interrogation and properly warned federal questioning to attenuate taint]; State v. Wright, 515 S.W.2d 421 (Mo.1974) [day's delay between unwarned interrogation and confession was enough to attenuate taint when confession of juvenile was made at juvenile building and both a juvenile court officer and the accused's mother were present]. The classic attenuation case is Wong Sun v. United States, 371 U.S. 471, 83 S.Ct. 407, 9 L.Ed.2d 441 (1963).

the exclusionary rule.[27]   However a number of jurisdictions view it with disfavor, preferring to ask "what actually happened," rather than "what might have happened," [28] finding perhaps that the real probability of inevitable discovery is never high enough to render the doctrine applicable.   In any event, it should be clear that mere causation alone is insufficient to taint evidence seized through a voluntariness/*Miranda* violation.[29]

---

27.   Brewer v. Williams, 430 U.S. 387, 406 n. 12, 97 S.Ct. 1232, 1243 n. 12, 51 L.Ed.2d 423 (1976).   United States v. Falley, 489 F.2d 33 (2d Cir. 1973).   See also Mills v. State, 278 Md. 262, 363 A.2d 491 (1976) [defendant's address, which was obtained in violation of *Miranda*, could have been obtained from independent sources; in effect the address would have been inevitably discovered];   State v. Garrison, 21 Or.App. 155, 534 P.2d 210 (1975) [accomplice had told four other persons about the crime; consequently discovery of the evidence was inevitable].   See generally LaCount & Girese, The "Inevitable Discovery" Rule, An Evolv- ing Exception to the Constitutional Exclusionary Rule, 40 Alb.L.Rev. 483 (1976).

28.   Cf. United States v. Puerifoy, 22 U.S.C.M.A. 549, 552, 48 C.M.R. 34, 37 (1974).

29.   For a more detailed exposition of these various principles, see Chapter 19, supra.

PART 7
FURTHER CONSTITUTIONAL PROTECTIONS

CHAPTER 25
THE RIGHT TO COUNSEL

1. Introduction

In retrospect it is evident that the Supreme Court's attempts to resolve the question of coerced confessions changed several times over the years.[1] With its decisions in the federal cases of *McNabb* and *Mallory*,[2] the Court emphasized prompt arraignment, a requirement which not only stopped incommunicado interrogation, but also informed an accused of the right to counsel. However, *McNabb* and *Mallory* were merely resting places for the Court in its continued search for effective tools to prevent involuntary confessions at the state as well as at the federal level.

The next phase in the Court's search was the application of the sixth amendment right to counsel at interrogations. Exercising this right provides certain advantages akin to those given by the requirement of prompt arraignment: Consultation with counsel may interrupt the psychological and physical effects of interrogation, and counsel's advice may educate an uninformed defendant of the right to remain silent. The first significant decision[3] in this area is Massiah v. United States.[4]

2. The *Massiah* Case

Suggested Reading:

Massiah v. United States, 377 U.S. 201, 84 S.Ct. 1199, 12 L.Ed.2d 246 (1964).

In April 1958, Winston Massiah was arrested aboard a United States ship for possession of cocaine. Subsequently indicted for the same offense and "conspiracy to import, conceal, and facilitate the sale of nar-

---

1. See, e. g., Chapter 21, supra.

2. See Chapter 22, supra.

3. Earlier decisions involving the right to counsel had generally been resolved adversely to the defense. See, e. g., Crooker v. California, 357 U.S. 433, 78 S.Ct. 1287, 2 L.Ed.2d 1448 (1958) (5 to 4 decision that failure to allow the defendant to see his attorney was only one of the factors to be considered in determining whether a confession is involuntary). However, an undercurrent of dissatisfaction with denying the right to counsel appeared in a number of cases prior to Massiah v. United States.

4. 377 U.S. 201, 84 S.Ct. 1199, 12 L.Ed.2d 246 (1964) (hereinafter cited as *Massiah*).

cotics," Massiah, who had retained counsel and pleaded not guilty, was released on bail.[5] Unknown to Massiah, an indicted co-conspirator had decided to cooperate with the authorities and therefore had allowed agents to install a radio transmitter in his car. On November 19, 1959, Massiah, a guest in the vehicle, made incriminating remarks which were transmitted to and recorded by government agents and which were later admitted in evidence against him at trial.

Relying on the sixth amendment right to counsel, the Supreme Court reversed the conviction. The Court reasoned that the period between arraignment and trial was a "critical" one during which an accused had a constitutional right to counsel.[6] In holding that the bugging of Massiah's conversation had been improper, the Court emphasized that the federal agents had intentionally elicited incriminating evidence from Massiah after his indictment and in the absence of counsel. While the Court indicated that the authorities could continue to investigate the offense for which a defendant had been indicted, it stressed that they could not use incriminating statements obtained from the defendant, in the absence of his attorney, against him[7] at trial. The Court failed to address directly the question of a defendant under investigation for offenses other than those for which he had previously been indicted. In deciding the case, the Court explicitly followed the New York rule, which was said to have outlawed "secret interrogation of a defendant after indictment."[8]

The Supreme Court's decision in *Massiah* left undecided a number of major questions. Although it dealt with a post-indictment "interrogation," it was unclear if the Court meant to attach the right to counsel only at indictment or also at other critical stages such as arraignment.[9] The possibility of waiver of *Massiah* rights was unaddressed[10] as was the question of interrogation directed to offenses other than those for which the accused was indicted.[11] Perhaps most importantly the decision itself discussed expressly "secret" interrogation via bugging and left open the issue of application to more customary direct interrogation.

However, this latter question was apparently settled when the Court reversed,[12] without opinion, but citing *Massiah*, the Ohio Supreme Court's decision in State v. McLeod.[13] In *McLeod*, the indicted defendant had given incriminating information to a policeman and a prosecutor during a car ride in the absence of counsel. While *McLeod* appeared to delineate the scope of *Massiah*, incidentally making the case applicable to the states, its application was soon further

---

persons charged with crime." 377 U.S. at 205, citing People v. Waterman, 9 N.Y.2d 561, 565, 216 N.Y.S. 2d 70, 75, 175 N.E.2d 445, 448 (1961).

9. *Massiah* of course assumed that indictment was a critical stage.

10. See § 3, infra.

11. Although the Supreme Court's opinion in *Massiah* recognized the legitimacy of continuing a criminal investigation into the same offense or transaction involved in the indictment, it limited the use of any incriminating statements. 377 U.S. at 207. Investigations involving completely unrelated offenses were not discussed. See Grieco v. Meachum, 533 F.2d 713 (1st Cir. 1976) (finding admissible statements by an indicted defendant directly related to "another substantive offense" and "only incidentally admissible" at the trial of the offense for which the defendant was indicted); United States v. Merritts, 527 F.2d 713 (7th Cir. 1975).

12. 381 U.S. 356, 85 S.Ct. 1556, 14 L.Ed.2d 682 (1965) (per curiam).

13. 1 Ohio St. 60, 203 N.E.2d 349, 30 O.O.2d 34 (1964) (hereinafter cited as *McLeod*).

---

5. 377 U.S. at 202.

6. Id. at 205, citing Spano v. New York, 360 U.S. 315, 79 S.Ct. 1202, 3 L.Ed.2d 1265 (1959) (concurring opinions of Justices Douglas and Stewart) and Powell v. Alabama, 287 U.S. 45, 53 S.Ct. 55, 77 L.Ed. 158 (1932).

7. 377 U.S. 201, 207, 84 S.Ct. 1199, 1203, 12 L.Ed.2d 246 (1964).

8. "Any secret interrogation of the defendant, from and after the finding of an indictment, without the protection afforded by the presence of counsel, contravenes the basic dictates of fairness in the conduct of criminal causes and the fundamental rights of

complicated by the Court's decisions in Escobedo v. Illinois [14] and Miranda v. Arizona.[15]

3. *Massiah* and *Miranda*

Suggested Reading:

Brewer v. Williams, 430 U.S. 387, 97 S.Ct. 1232, 51
L.Ed.2d 423 (1977).

∴

The Supreme Court's 1966 decision in Miranda v. Arizona [16] held that a suspect could not
be subjected to custodial interrogation by
government agents without being informed
of right to counsel—a right which could be
waived, but only voluntarily, intelligently,
and knowingly.[17] *Miranda*'s effect on *Massiah* was and continues to be unclear. Although custodial interrogation generally
precedes either arraignment or indictment,
it need not do so. Similarly post-arraignment or indictment interrogation need not
be custodial in nature. Thus while the relevant time frame in both cases can overlap,
they also can be independent of each other.
In the absence of further decision by the Supreme Court, treating the two decisions as
generally complementary seems appropriate.

Such an approach allows resolution of
at least one problem—that of waiver. Under *Miranda*, the right to counsel may be
waived. However, waiver was not addressed
in either *Massiah* or *McLeod* because neither case contained relevant rights warnings. In light of *Miranda*, the majority of
courts have held [18] that the *Massiah* right to
counsel may be waived, using the rationale
of the *Miranda* rights warning and its waiver procedure.

Because *Massiah* deals with the right to
counsel at a critical stage of pretrial proceedings, a small but important minority of
judges [19] have urged that although waiver
may be possible, the warnings used at trial
to a pro se accused, desiring to represent
himself or herself, are more appropriate and
must be used instead of the *Miranda* procedure. While there is question in some juris-

---

14. 378 U.S. 478, 84 S.Ct. 1758, 12 L.Ed.2d 977
(1964).

15. 384 U.S. 436, 86 S.Ct. 1602, 16 L.Ed.2d 694
(1966). United States v. Frank, 520 F.2d 1287 (2d
Cir. 1975) (This decision contains dicta to the effect
that the trial court could have used evidence obtained
in possible violation of *Massiah* in trial of new offenses for which the defendant had not been indicted
at the time of the indirect interrogation. The court
rejected the defendant's claim that despite the suppression of the evidence at trial, he had been prejudiced by being unable to take the stand in his own
behalf because of the fear that he would be impeached
with the suppressed evidence); State v. Hill, 26 Ariz.
App. 37, 545 P.2d 999, 1002 (1976) (Interrogation of
robbery defendant involving unrelated offenses was
proper despite absence of counsel when evidence was
not introduced at the robbery trial but rather at trial
for unrelated offenses); Deskins v. Commonwealth,
512 S.W.2d 520 (Ky.1974) (Voluntary statements
made to friend who was acting as a government
agent were admissible when remarks were made in
course of attempt to steal prosecutorial files subsequent to a murder indictment).

16. 384 U.S. 436, 86 S.Ct. 1602, 16 L.Ed.2d 694
(1966).

17. See generally Chapter 23, infra.

18. See, e. g., United States v. Crook, 502 F.2d 1378
(3d Cir. 1974); United States v. Mandley, 502 F.2d
1103, 1104 (9th Cir. 1974) (defendant waived counsel
although he had a state-appointed counsel to represent him at a state proceeding); Moore v. Wolff, 495
F.2d 35, 37 (8th Cir. 1974); United States v. Barone,
467 F.2d 247, 249 (2d Cir. 1972); United States v.
Dority, 487 F.2d 846, 848 (6th Cir. 1973) (federal
defendant had had a state-appointed counsel designated to deal with state charges); United States v.
Cobbs, 481 F.2d 196 (3d Cir.), cert. denied 414 U.S.
980, 94 S.Ct. 298, 38 L.Ed.2d 224 (1973); United
States v. Crisp, 435 F.2d 354, 358–59 (7th Cir. 1970),
cert. denied 402 U.S. 947, 91 S.Ct. 1640, 29 L.Ed.2d
116 (1972); United States ex rel. Wooden v. Vincent,
391 F.Supp. 1260, 1263–64 (S.D.N.Y.), aff'd 508 F.2d
837 (2d Cir. 1974); People v. McCrary, 549 P.2d 1320
(Colo.1976).

19. See, e. g., United States v. Massimo, 432 F.2d
324, 327 (2d Cir. 1970) (Friendly, J., dissenting);
United States v. Satterfield, 19 Crim.L.Rep. 2381 (S.
D.N.Y. July 8, 1976); United States ex rel. Lopez,
344 F.Supp. 1050, 1054 (S.D.N.Y.1972).

dictions [20] about whether the right to counsel under *Massiah* may be waived at all, such waiver is probably constitutionally acceptable.

The Supreme Court dealt with this issue in 1977 in Brewer v. Williams.[21] In *Brewer,* the Court dealt with an arraigned defendant who was being transported by police from his point of surrender to the city in which the murder had taken place. Despite agreement between the police and defendant's lawyers not to question the defendant during the trip (and an affirmative statement by defendant that he would talk after speaking with counsel), the police began a conversation with each other [22] which resulted in the defendant leading the police to the victim's body. While holding the verbal admissions of the defendant [23] inadmissible on *Massiah* grounds, the Court stated that although the defendant could have waived his right to counsel, the state was required to show "an intentional relinquishment or abandonment of a known right or privilege." [24] The exact procedure for obtaining such a waiver and the difference, if any, between it and a *Miranda* waiver thus are still unclear.

4. *Massiah* Today

The *Massiah* case, as interpreted in the light of State v. McLeod,[25] is a fundamental sixth amendment decision applicable to the state as well as to federal proceedings. While it has for most purposes been overshadowed by the Supreme Court's subsequent decision in Miranda v. Arizona,[26] *Massiah* appears independent of *Miranda*—a highly significant conclusion in light of the likely future modification of the *Miranda* decision.

At minimum, *Massiah* provides a right to counsel at post-indictment [27] interrogations, direct or indirect, when the accused has already retained counsel. Arguably this right is essential to give meaning to the right to counsel at trial and is severable from concerns relating to police interrogation conduct, despite the case's clear effects on interrogations.[28] At present *Massiah* is of consequence primarily in cases involving undercover police activity in situations not governed by *Miranda*.[29] At the same time the case may be valuable to the defense when *Miranda* waivers have been made by post-

---

20. See note 18, supra. Of all American jurisdictions, New York has the most extreme rule in this area, holding that an accused represented by counsel may not waive his or her rights without the presence of counsel during the waiver. See, e. g., People v. Arthur, 22 N.Y.2d 325, 292 N.Y.S.2d 663, 239 N.E.2d 537 (1968). The same result can be reached by statutory interpretation. See, e. g., United States v. McOmber, 24 U.S.C.M.A. 207, 51 C.M.R. 452 (1976).

21. 430 U.S. 387, 97 S.Ct. 1232, 51 L.Ed.2d 423 (1977).

22. The conversation was implicitly found to constitute interrogation. But see Chief Justice Burger's vehement dissent. The conversation emphasized that the victim, a 10 year old girl, might never be found and that she would thus never have a Christian burial. The police knew that the defendant was highly religious, and it was snowing heavily.

23. The Court declined to deal directly with the discovery of the body.

24. 430 U.S. 387, 97 S.Ct. 1232, 51 L.Ed.2d 423 (1977), citing Johnson v. Zerbst, 304 U.S. 458, 464, 58 S.Ct. 1019, 1023, 82 L.Ed. 1461 (1938).

25. 381 U.S. 356, 85 S.Ct. 1556, 14 L.Ed.2d 682 (1965) (per curiam).

26. 384 U.S. 436, 86 S.Ct. 1602, 16 L.Ed.2d 694 (1966).

27. This minimum might apply at earlier stages following the formal initiation of the criminal case. See § 2, note 9, supra.

28. This conclusion is bolstered by the somewhat surprising rationale of the Supreme Court in Kirby v. Illinois, 406 U.S. 682, 688–89, 92 S.Ct. 1877, 1881–82, 32 L.Ed.2d 411 (1972). *Kirby* held that *Miranda* is a fifth and fourteenth amendment decision, independent of the sixth amendment.

29. See, e. g., United States v. Anderson, 523 F.2d 1192 (5th Cir. 1975) (paid informer obtained illegal drug prescription from doctor previously indicted for improper possession of amphetamines with intent to distribute); Dismukes v. State, 324 So.2d 201 (Fla. App.1975); State v. McCorgary, 218 Kan. 358, 543 P.2d 952, 957–58 (1975) (Mere placement of informer in jail cell of murder defendant after commencement of prosecution and appointment of counsel was error even if the informer did not elicit information directly).

indictment defendants.[30] A frequent argument is that *Massiah* applies to situations in which defendants are interrogated without notice to counsel but with the consent of the accused. However, in the vast majority of such cases,[31] the courts have refused to disturb even post-indictment defendants' waivers. Although it seems unlikely that the Supreme Court will overrule *Miranda* in toto, the *Massiah* decision represents the probable minimum application of the right to counsel at interrogations.

---

30. See § 3, note 21 and accompanying text.

31. See § 3, note 18. The question here is primarily one of notice to counsel of police interrogations. At the post-arraignment (indictment) stage, clear ethical prohibitions exist against prosecution counsel attempting to interview represented defendants without giving notice to their counsel. See Disciplinary Rule 7–104, A.B.A. Code of Professional Responsibility; Moore v. Wolff, 495 F.2d 35, 37 (8th Cir. 1974). The propriety of police doing what the prosecutor may not is at best questionable. However, few jurisdictions require such notice of police intent.

CHAPTER 26

EYEWITNESS IDENTIFICATION

1. Introduction

Prior to the landmark trilogy of *Wade-Gilbert-Stovall*,[1] eyewitness identification had been a neglected area of criminal law, even though it is probably the least reliable type of evidence.[2] English[3] and American[4] annals are replete with instances of mistaken eyewitness identification, whose unreliability has been scientifically demonstrated.[5] Despite this fact, juries attach a great deal of weight to this kind of evidence.[6]

---

1. United States v. Wade, 388 U.S. 218, 87 S.Ct. 1926, 18 L.Ed.2d 1149 (1967); Gilbert v. California, 388 U.S. 263, 87 S.Ct. 1951, 18 L.Ed.2d 1178 (1967); Stovall v. Denno, 388 U.S. 293, 87 S.Ct. 1967, 18 L.Ed.2d 1199 (1967).

2. Williams & Hammelmann, Identification Parades, Part I, 1963 Crim.L.Rev. 479, 480 [hereafter cited as Williams & Hammelman].

3. See G. Williams, The Proof of Guilt 106–24 (3d ed. 1963); Williams & Hammelmann, Parts I and II 479, 545.

4. See generally E. Borchard, Convicting the Innocent (1932); F. Block, The Vindicators (1963); J.

Frank & B. Frank, Not Guilty (1957); E. Gardner, The Court of Last Resort (1952).

5. See generally A. Anastasi, Fields of Applied Psychology 548–50 (1964); F. Berren, Practical Psychology 416–44 (rev. ed. 1952); H. Burtt, Applied Psychology 232–65 (2d ed. 1957); F. Ruch, Psychology and Life 291 (5th ed. 1958); Buckhout, Eyewitness Testimony, Scientific American 23 (Dec. 1974); Levine & Tapp, The Psychology of Criminal Identification: The Gap from *Wade* to *Kirby*, 121 U.Pa.L.Rev. 1079 (1973).

6. See E. Borchard, Convicting the Innocent XII (1932); P. Wall, Eye-Witness Identification in Criminal Cases 41 (1965); Williams & Hammelmann, Parts I and II at 480 and 545, 550.

In his study of eyewitness identifications, Professor Borchard concluded that the major source of error is the identification of the suspect by the victim of a violent crime.[7] This is especially true when the victim is a child or young person.[8] In such cases the emotional state of the witness or victim may render unreliable all recollections of the crime. Moreover, the victim or witness may desire to seek vengeance on the person believed guilty or merely to support the identification which he or she assumes, consciously or unconsciously, has already been made by another.[9] Even so, "juries seem disposed more readily to credit the veracity and reliability of the victims of an outrage than any amount of contrary evidence by or on behalf of the accused, whether by way of alibi, character witnesses, or other testimony." [10]

Once a witness has identified someone, he or she tends to maintain the decision "by a process of auto-suggestion which evidences itself in continually seeking means of justifying his opinion and reinforcing his belief. Questioned once more regarding the matter, the chances are that he would repeat, with even greater emphasis, his previous declaration." [11]

In addition a lineup only adds to unreliability of eyewitness identification, for certain suggestions are inherent in this proce-

dure. Foremost, it suggests that the guilty person is in the lineup. "Knowing that the man suspected by the police is present, and trusting the police not to have put up the wrong man, the witness may make every effort to pick out his man, on the mistaken assumption that if he can do so, this would provide the kind of corroboration of their suspicion that the police expect and require. His immediate reaction if he is not certain may be to strain his memory to the utmost to find some resemblance between one of the men before him and the offender as he remembers him. The witness may therefore be inclined to pick out someone, and that someone will be the one member of the parade who comes closest to his own recollection of the criminal. Discrepancies may be easily overlooked or explained away." [12]

Suggestions other than obvious differences in height, weight, age, race, etc., may be made by the participants in the lineup through nonverbal communication. Using police officers might be suggestive because altering their bearing and demeanor is difficult.[13] Furthermore, by their attitude the police participants might inadvertently suggest who is the suspect. This is true also of nonpolice participants who know the accused's identity.[14] The suspect too might

---

7. See E. Borchard, Convicting the Innocent XIII (1932); see also M. Houts, From Evidence to Proof 19–20 (1956).

8. Williams & Hammelmann, Part II at 545, 546.

9. E. Borchard, Convicting the Innocent XIII (1932).

10. Id.

11. Gorphe, Showing Prisoners to Witnesses for Identification, 1 Am.J.Police Sci. 79, 82 (1930). Moreover, "[i]t is a matter of common experience that, once a witness has picked out the accused at a lineup, he is not likely to go back on his word later on, so that in practice the issue of identity may (in the absence of other relevant evidence) for all practical purposes be determined there and then, before the trial." United States v. Wade, 388 U.S. 218, 229, 87 S.Ct. 1926, 1933, 18 L.Ed.2d 1149 (1967), quoting Williams & Hammelmann, Part I at 482.

12. Williams & Hammelmann, Part I at 486–87; see also C. Polph, Law and the Common Man 192 (1968); P. Wall, Eye-Witness Identification in Criminal Cases 47 (1965).

13. Williams & Hammelmann, Part I at 486–87. "[P]olice officers should never be used in a parade unless, indeed, it is a case in which a policeman is suspect." Williams, Identification Parades, 1955 Crim.L.Rev. 525, 534. Another reason for not using police officers is that police techniques have been developed to make sure that any particular person can, if necessary, be "forced" on a witness, the way a magician forces a card. One of the most popular means is to line the suspect up between a group of detectives who then cast their eyes slightly in the direction of the suspect, instead of straight ahead. Result: the witness's gaze is directed as though by arrows to the right place. M. Machline & W. Woodfield, Ninth Life 61 n. 2 (1961).

14. Williams & Hammelmann, Part I at 489.

communicate nonverbally if his or her shame or anxiety [15] is affecting facial expression, posture, or gait. The possibility of intentional suggestion is also present in a pretrial confrontation.[16] Some law enforcement officials are not impartial. "[W]ithout making any claim to generalization, it is common knowledge that the prosecuting technique in the United States is to regard a conviction as a personal victory calculated to enhance the prestige of the prosecutor."[17]

This chapter discusses defense attacks on eyewitness identification testimony. The defense can mount an attack on fourth, fifth, or sixth amendment grounds. The fourth amendment attack is that the testimony is inadmissible derivative evidence. The fifth amendment attack is that the lineup procedures were unfairly suggestive. The sixth amendment attack is that the police wrongfully denied the suspect counsel at the lineup.

2. Sixth Amendment Attack on the Pretrial Identification

Suggested Reading:

Gilbert v. California, 388 U.S. 263, 87 S.Ct. 1951, 18 L.Ed.2d 1178 (1967).

United States v. Wade, 388 U.S. 218, 87 S.Ct. 1926, 18 L.Ed.2d 1149 (1967).

15. See United States v. Wade, 388 U.S. 218, 230–31, 87 S.Ct. 1926, 1934, 18 L.Ed.2d 1149 (1967); P. Wall, Eye-Witness Identification in Criminal Cases 44–45 (1965); Napley, Problems of Effecting the Presentation of the Case for a Defendant, 66 Colum. L.Rev. 94, 99 (1966). See also R. Allen, E. Ferster, & J. Rubin, Readings in Law and Psychiatry 36 (1968).

16. See United States v. Wade, 388 U.S. 218, 230–35, 87 S.Ct. 1926, 1934–37, 18 L.Ed.2d 1149 (1967). See also Foster v. California, 394 U.S. 440, 89 S.Ct. 1127, 22 L.Ed.2d 402 (1969).

17. E. Borchard, Convicting the Innocent XV (1932). See also P. Wall, Eye-Witness Identification in Criminal Cases 46 (1965). Speaking for the majority in McDonald v. United States, 335 U.S. 451, 456, 69

In United States v. Wade,[18] the Supreme Court attempted to avert prejudice in a lineup situation and to ensure adequate cross-examination for a fair trial. In that case a witness had identified the accused in the absence of counsel at a post-indictment lineup [19] conducted approximately eight months after the crime.[20] The Court held that this witness's in-court identification must be excluded unless the prosecution could establish that such evidence was not tainted by the pretrial identification. In Gilbert v. California,[21] the Court held that the pretrial identification was conducted in derogation of the accused's right to counsel and that the in-court identification was inadmissible if it was "the direct result of the illegal lineup."[22] These rules apply to both state and federal prosecutions but affect only confrontations [23] which occurred after June 12, 1967.[24]

S.Ct. 191, 193, 93 L.Ed. 153 (1948), Mr. Justice Douglas said, "[H]istory shows that the police acting on their own cannot be trusted."

18. 388 U.S. 218, 87 S.Ct. 1926, 18 L.Ed.2d 1149 (1967).

19. A "lineup" for the purpose of this chapter describes an event in which the suspect is placed in a group of people and a witness viewing the group is asked to pick out the guilty party. A "showup" describes an event in which only the suspect is presented to the witness, who is then asked whether or not this was the person who committed the offense. See P. Wall, Eye-Witness Identification in Criminal Cases 27–28, 40–41 (1967).

20. United States v. Wade, 388 U.S. 218, 220, 87 S.Ct. 1926, 1928–29, 18 L.Ed.2d 1149 (1967).

21. 388 U.S. 263, 87 S.Ct. 1951, 18 L.Ed.2d 1178 (1967).

22. Id. at 272–73.

23. The term *confrontation* as used in this chapter describes a situation arranged by the police subsequent to the crime in which the witness or the victim observes the suspect or the accused for the purposes of identification. The victim or witness may or may not identify the suspect or accused.

24. Stovall v. Denno, 388 U.S. 293, 87 S.Ct. 1967, 18 L.Ed.2d 1199 (1967).

3. Accrual of the Right to Counsel at Lineup

Suggested Reading:

Moore v. Illinois, 434 U.S. 220, 98 S.Ct. 458, 54 L.Ed.2d 424 (1977).

United States v. Ash, 413 U.S. 300, 93 S.Ct. 2568, 37 L.Ed.2d 619 (1973).

Kirby v. Illinois, 406 U.S. 682, 92 S.Ct. 1877, 32 L.Ed.2d 411 (1972).

The impact of *Wade* has been severely limited by the Supreme Court's decision in Kirby v. Illinois.[25] There the Court indicated that an individual is not entitled to a lawyer at a lineup until the "initiation of adversary judicial criminal proceedings." [26] Initiation takes place when "the government has committed itself to prosecute" [27] and "the adverse positions of Government and defendant have solidified." [28] At this point the accused "finds himself faced with the prosecutorial forces of organized society, and immersed in the intricacies of substantive and procedural criminal law." [29]

Kirby's language is unclear as to exactly when the accused is entitled to counsel at a confrontation for identification. The opinion states only that the answer depends on when the "initiation of adversary judicial criminal proceedings" takes place. Although Chief Justice Burger seemed to indicate that this initiation occurs when formal charges have been made against the accused,[30] the plurality opinion suggests that this right accrues at the time of formal charge, preliminary hearing, indictment, information, or arraignment. While not naming a specific time when the accused is entitled to counsel, the Court did set forth a rule that can be easily followed by law enforcement officials: The accused is not entitled to counsel at any confrontation for identification prior to formal charge, preliminary hearing, indictment, information, or arraignment, provided that these stages of the prosecution are not purposefully delayed to deny the accused the right to counsel.[31]

The purpose of right to counsel announced in *Wade-Gilbert* was primarily to ensure the rights of cross-examination, confrontation, and fair trial. The *Kirby* Court's rejection of reliance on these rights was probably the reason for Mr. Justice White's dissent.[32] It is unrealistic to think that the risk of misidentification because of intentional or innocent suggestion is less when the suspect is in custody but no "initiation of the adversary criminal proceedings" has occurred.

This illogical position might be a primary reason that some lower courts have indicated that an arrest with or without a warrant,[33] an arrest pursuant to a warrant,[34] or an arrest plus confinement [35] triggers the right to counsel at a lineup. However, other courts have ruled that an arrest is not a "formal charge" [36] or "initiation of

---

25. 406 U.S. 682, 92 S.Ct. 1877, 32 L.Ed.2d 411 (1972).

26. Id. at 689.

27. Id.

28. Id.

29. Id.

30. Id. at 691. In a terse dissent Mr. Justice White stated that "Wade . . . and Gilbert . . . govern this case and compel reversal of the judgment below." Id. at 705.

31. Id. at 689. Compare Adams v. United States, 399 F.2d 574 (D.C.Cir. 1968), with United States v. Broadhead, 413 F.2d 1351 (7th Cir. 1969).

32. Kirby v. Illinois, 406 U.S. 682, 705, 92 S.Ct. 1877, 1890, 32 L.Ed.2d 411 (1972).

33. Commonwealth v. Richman, 458 Pa. 167, 320 A.2d 351 (1974).

34. Robinson v. Zelker, 468 F.2d 159 (2d Cir. 1972); State v. Morris, 484 S.W.2d 288 (Mo.1972).

35. Patler v. Slayton, 503 F.2d 472, 476 (4th Cir. 1974) (counsel present at police station).

36. Lane v. State, 506 S.W.2d 212 (Tex.Cr.App. 1974); West v. State, 229 Ga. 427, 192 S.E.2d 163 (1972).

adversary proceedings." A third line of cases declares that no right to counsel exists prior to information or indictment.[37] In the wake of *Kirby*, the Wisconsin Supreme Court stated: "While the presence of counsel at a lineup prior to the institution of formal charges is not mandatory henceforth, we nevertheless believe it is good police practice and in the interest of justice to afford such counsel where practicable. We also emphasize that the formal commencement of a criminal prosecution cannot be constitutionally delayed, while a suspect is in custody, merely for the purpose of holding a lineup without the benefit of counsel." [38]

The most recent Supreme Court pronouncement on this issue is its 1977 decision in Moore v. Illinois. The defendant was charged with rape. The alleged victim was in the courtroom when the defendant appeared for his preliminary hearing. After the judge informed the defendant of the charges and the State's attorney summarized the evidence, the alleged victim made an in-court identification of the defendant. At trial, the alleged victim testified to the pretrial identification. Writing for the Court, Justice Powell held that the defendant's right to counsel attached at the preliminary hearing. Justice Powell argued that at that point, the government had committed itself to prosecute and the defendant was faced with society's prosecutorial forces. Since the government had not afforded the defendant counsel at the preliminary hearing, the evidence of the pretrial identification was inadmissible.

Photographic Identification. In United States v. Ash,[39] the Supreme Court held there was no right to counsel at a photographic lineup even though the lineup occurred shortly before trial. However, in *Ash* the testimony had been introduced by the prosecution in rebuttal to defense evidence. The majority of courts have held no right to counsel exists at a photographic identification procedure even though the defendant is in custody.[40] When the defendant is not in custody, photographic identification procedures have been used "widely and effectively in criminal law enforcement from the standpoint both of apprehending offenders and of sparing innocent suspects the ignominy of arrest by allowing eyewitnesses to exonerate them through scrutiny of photographs." [41] The ruling of the *Ash* Court has resulted in increased reliance on photographic indentification procedures rather than corporeal lineups. The former saves time and labor, but it has led to requests to have a witness identification tested at a subsequent corporeal lineup.[42]

Although whenever photographic identification procedures are used, no duty to segregate all the photographs arises, a record should be kept so that the photographic display can be reconstructed.[43]

Accidental Viewing. The reason for fashioning the exclusionary rule in *Wade* and *Gilbert* was to "deter law enforcement authorities from exhibiting an accused to

37. Dearinger v. United States, 468 F.2d 1032 (9th Cir. 1972); Ashford v. State, 274 So.2d 517 (Fla. 1973); State v. St. Andre, 263 La. 48, 267 So.2d 190 (1972); State v. Carey, 486 S.W.2d 443 (Mo.1972); Chandler v. State, 501 P.2d 512 (Okl.Cr.1972) (better procedure is to afford defendant opportunity to obtain counsel).

38. State v. Taylor, 60 Wis.2d 506, 210 N.W.2d 873 (1973).

39. 413 U.S. 300, 93 S.Ct. 2568, 37 L.Ed.2d 619 (1973).

40. United States v. Ash, 413 U.S. 300, 301 n. 2, 93 S.Ct. 2568, 2569 n. 2, 37 L.Ed.2d 619 (1973).

41. Simmons v. United States, 390 U.S. 377, 88 S.Ct. 967, 19 L.Ed.2d 1247 (1968).

42. See § 10, Right to a Lineup, infra.

43. United States v. Clemons, 445 F.2d 711 (D.C. Cir. 1971); United States v. Hamilton, 420 F.2d 1292, 1295 (D.C.Cir. 1969); People v. Lawrence, 4 Cal.3d 273, 93 Cal.Rptr. 204, 481 P.2d 212 (1971); Commonwealth v. Gibson, 357 Mass. 45, 255 N.E.2d 742 (1970).

witnesses before trial for identification purposes without notice to and in the absence of counsel." [44] Thus applying the right to counsel rule to identification proceedings would be illogical when the suspect is inadvertently and unintentionally exposed to witnesses. Most jurisdictions follow the logical approach.[45] In addition to holding no right to counsel at accidental confrontations, the courts have uniformly indicated that such identifications do not violate due process of law if there is no deliberate misconduct by the police and if the confrontation is truly accidental.[46]

Many "accidental" indentifications, though seemingly spontaneous, may be the result of maneuvering by the police. The fact that a witness fortuitously "bumped into" the suspect should itself arouse suspicion, for the meeting could have been the result of a police ploy known as the "Oklahoma showup." [47]

Waiver of the Right to Counsel. A number of courts follow the *Wade* language that "counsel's presence should have been a requisite to conduct . . . the lineup, absent an 'intelligent waiver.' " [48] These courts have held that the defendant, following a description of his or her rights, may waive the presence of counsel.[49] A general *Miranda* warning is insufficient; the police must inform the defendant that he or she has a right to counsel at the lineup. The police must give the counsel a reasonable period of time to travel to the stationhouse where the lineup will be conducted.[50] The Model Rules for Law Enforcement, Eye Witness Identification, state that the suspect must be informed that he or she will be provided with a lawyer free of charge and that the lineup will be delayed for a reasonable time after his or her lawyer has been notified in order to allow the lawyer to appear.[51] In many cases unless he or she is notified that the proceedings will be delayed, a suspect feels that his or her lawyer may be busy at the time and unwilling to attend.

4. Content of the Right to Counsel at Lineup

Suggested Reading:

People v. Williams, 3 Cal.3d 853, 92 Cal.Rptr. 6, 478 P.2d 942 (1971).

State v. Jensen, 106 Ariz. 421, 477 P.2d 252 (1970).

Assume that the right to counsel attaches at the suspect's lineup. Do the police have to appoint an attorney who will continue to represent the suspect throughout all subsequent stages of the case? May the attorney testify about the lineup at a subsequent trial? What role does the attorney play during the lineup? These are the major problems which arise if the right to counsel attaches at the lineup.

Substitute Counsel. In *Wade* the Supreme Court stated that "[a]lthough the right to counsel usually means a right to the suspect's own counsel, provision for a sub-

---

44. Stovall v. Denno, 388 U.S. 293, 297, 87 S.Ct. 1967, 1970, 18 L.Ed.2d 1199 (1967).

45. See, e. g., People v. Covington, 47 Ill.2d 198, 265 N.E.2d 112 (1970); Robertson v. State, 464 S.W. 2d 15 (Mo.1971) (encounter at police station); State v. Turner, 81 N.Mex. 571, 469 P.2d 720 (1970)(no right to counsel where confrontation inadvertent); United States v. Young, 44 C.M.R. 670 (AFCMR 1971).

46. See United States v. Brown, 461 F.2d 134 (D.C. Cir. 1972).

47. See, e. g., United States ex rel. Ragazzini v. Brierley, 321 F.Supp. 440 (W.D.Pa.1970); People v. Winfrey, 11 Ill.App.3d 164, 298 N.E.2d 413 (1973).

48. United States v. Wade, 388 U.S. 218, 237, 87 S.Ct. 1926, 1937, 18 L.Ed.2d 1149 (1967).

49. United States v. Ayers, 426 F.2d 524 (2d Cir. 1970).

50. People v. Keim, 8 Cal.App.3d 776, 87 Cal.Rptr. 597 (1970) (half hour wait for counsel insufficient to constitute waiver).

51. Model Rules for Law Enforcement, Eye Witness Identification, Rule 404 (1974).

stitute counsel may be justified on the ground that the substitute counsel's presence may eliminate the hazards which render the lineup a critical stage for the presence of the suspect's *own* counsel." [52] Relying on this language, some courts have held that the requirement of the "presence of counsel" [53] is met when an attorney is present to ensure the fairness of the proceedings, even though he or she does not establish a confidential relationship with the accused.[54] This ad hoc counsel will meet the requirements of *Wade*, for his or her presence can serve to eliminate the hazards that make a pretrial identification potentially unfair to the accused.

Aside from the Court's comment that the police may not have adequate records to aid the suspect, they may also be determined to get a conviction, for they may have already concluded that the suspect they apprehended is guilty. Language in *Wade* indicates that the Court wishes to subject the police to the impartial scrutiny of an observer not connected with the prosecution. Therefore the use of a substitute counsel identified with the police will not satisfy the requirements of *Wade-Gilbert*.[55] However, the *Wade* Court did leave "open the question whether the presence of substitute counsel might not suffice." [56]

This issue is crucial when the suspect's own counsel either refuses to appear or is not able to come immediately. Furthermore counsel may appear and then walk away from the lineup in an effort to stop the procedure. However, the courts have stated that this action does not preclude continuing the lineup.[57] In many cases counsel refuse to attend or walk away from the lineup so they can object to the lineup at the time of trial, and the prosecution will not be able to point to defense counsel's presence in supporting the fairness of the lineup procedure. Prosecutors sometimes argue that the procedure must have been fair because the defendant's lawyer was present and had made no objection. This argument is certainly irrelevant and subject to objection, but it is questionable whether this sort of remark can be cured by an instruction of the judge.

Concerning the role of substitute counsel, one court has stated "it may well be incumbent upon the prosecution to insure that the observations and opinions of the substitute counsel are transmitted to the accused's subsequently appointed trial counsel." [58] However, when no request is made for these records until after trial, counsel has probably waived any objection that substitute counsel failed to turn over the records.

The Propriety of the Counsel's Testimony at Trial. Disciplinary Rules 5.101 and 5.102 of the A.B.A. Code of Professional Responsibility require that except when essential to the ends of justice, lawyers should not testify in court on behalf of clients.[59] Use of substitute counsel avoids placing the defendant's counsel in this difficult predicament. If eyewitness identification is material to the trial, obviously the testimony of the lawyer-witness would not be confined to merely formal matters, for example, to au-

52. United States v. Wade, 388 U.S. 218, 237 n. 27, 87 S.Ct. 1926, 1938 n. 27, 18 L.Ed.2d 1149 (1967) (emphasis in original).
53. Id. at 228, 236, 237.
54. Zamora v. Guam, 394 F.2d 815, 816 (9th Cir. 1968); State v. Griffin, 205 Kan. 370, 469 P.2d 417 (1970); Wright v. State, 46 Wis.2d 75, 175 N.W.2d 646 (1970). But see People v. Thorne, 21 Mich.App. 478, 175 N.W.2d 527 (1970) (suspect was not effectively represented when the attorney who was present at the lineup did not know he was representing the suspect).
55. But see State v. Lacoste, 256 La. 697, 237 So.2d 871 (1970). The court approved of the use of an assistant district attorney as a lineup counsel when no objection to his competency was raised until the end of trial. The court also noted that the accused did not show that the assistant district attorney did not "properly . . . represent him at the lineup."
56. United States v. Wade, 388 U.S. 218, 237, 87 S.Ct. 1926, 1937, 18 L.Ed.2d 1149 (1967).

57. Vernon v. State, 12 Md.App. 430, 278 A.2d 609 (1971). See also Redding v. State, 10 Md.App. 601, 272 A.2d 70 (1971) (counsel refused to attend).
58. Marshall v. United States, 436 F.2d 155, 160 n. 18 (D.C.Cir. 1970).
59. A.B.A. Disciplinary Rules 5.101–02.

thentication of documents or to ensuring attestation of the custodial instruments. If the lawyer believes he or she must testify either before the judge or jury and then argue in support of his or her own credibility, the lawyer must withdraw from the case. In order to avoid this situation the lawyer-witness should take a third party with him or her to view any lineup, thus eliminating the issue of withdrawal from the case.

The Role of Counsel at the Lineup. In United States v. Cole,[60] the defendant, the only Black present at the preliminary hearing, was seated with his counsel and was identified as one of the robbers. In determining whether the showup at the preliminary hearing was unduly suggestive, the court indicated that consideration may be given to "counsel's opportunity to inquire into circumstances of the challenged identification which existed at the time of the preliminary hearing."[61] In United States v. Allen,[62] the court indicated that the presence of counsel at a lineup allows counsel to reconstruct what happened and also "to minimize the likelihood of an unduly suggestive confrontation."[63] When counsel is allowed to "have a role in setting up a lineup and proposing changes to avoid suggestive features," "absent plain error or circumstances unknown to counsel at the time of the lineup, no challenges to the physical staging of the lineup could successfully be raised beyond objections raised at the time of the lineup."

In United States ex rel. Riffert v. Rundle,[64] the court held that no violation of due process occurred when the defendant was led into the courtroom for his preliminary hearing, handcuffed to two police officers and accompanied by his attorney and then identified by the witnesses. The court relied upon the fact that defense counsel did not cross-examine the witnesses at the preliminary hearing or at trial about the basis for their identification. Additionally, no suggestion was made that the police "aided" the two witnesses in their identification prior to the trial.[65]

Another approach taken by some courts is that if counsel remains passive at a lineup, he or she waives any claim of violation of due process of law.[66] The reluctance of the courts to find a violation of due process is underscored by the fact that only one case has been discovered in which a court found such a violation when counsel was present and passive.[67]

In their commentary the Reporters to the ALI Model Code of Pre-Arraignment Procedure have indicated that the defendant's lawyer, who was present at a lineup, should not be deemed to have waived objections if he or she does not immediately object upon noting some unfairness. Likewise, police officials are not required to follow the suggestions of counsel.[68] However the Model Code states that the absence of any objection by defense counsel is some indication of the fairness of the proceeding. This fact may provide some degree of incentive for defense counsel to make reasonable objection which

---

60.   449 F.2d 194 (8th Cir. 1971).

61.   Id. at 200.

62.   408 F.2d 1287 (D.C.Cir. 1969).

63.   Id. at 1289. Clemons v. United States, 408 F.2d 1230 (D.C.Cir. 1968) (en banc). See also United States v. Wade, 388 U.S. 218, 238, 87 S.Ct. 1926, 1938, 18 L.Ed.2d 1149 (1967).

64.   464 F.2d 1348 (3d Cir. 1972).

65.   Other cases that have considered the presence of counsel in the totality of circumstances to find no violation of due process of law are: Sutton v. United States, 434 F.2d 462 (D.C.Cir. 1970); People v. Thomas, 3 Cal.App.3d 859, 83 Cal.Rptr. 879 (1970); State v. Carpenter, 257 S.C. 162, 184 S.E.2d 715 (1971).

66.   See People v. Stearns, 14 Cal.App.3d 178, 92 Cal.Rptr. 69 (1971).

67.   Jones v. State, 47 Wis.2d 642, 178 N.W.2d 42 (1970).

68.   ALI Model Code of Pre-Arraignment Procedure, Comment 211 (Ten.Draft No. 6, 1974). See also id. at §§ 160.2(7)c and 160.4(5).

the police might heed, rather than to sit back and hope to attack the lineup procedures later.

5. Propriety of the In-Court Identification

Suggested Reading:

State v. Callahan, 526 S.W.2d 59 (Mo.App.1975).

United States ex rel. Woodward v. New Jersey, 474 F.2d 694 (3d Cir. 1972).

If the right to counsel accrued at a lineup and the police did not satisfy the right, the witness may not testify to an identification at the lineup. Rather than eliciting testimony about the pretrial lineup, the prosecution may then attempt to have the witness identify the defendant in the courtroom. The trial judge usually has discretion to permit an in-court identification or lineup.[69] What effect does the violation at the pretrial lineup have on the propriety of an in-court identification? In *Wade*, Mr. Justice Brennan wrote that violation bars an in-court identification unless the prosecution can "establish by clear and convincing evidence that the in-court identifications [are] based upon observations of the suspect other than the lineup identification."[70] The Court rejected "a per se rule of exclusion of courtroom identification"[71] and allowed the prosecution to establish an independent basis for the in-court identification.

6. Fifth Amendment Attack on Pretrial Identification

Suggested Reading:

Stovall v. Denno, 388 U.S. 293, 87 S.Ct. 1967, 18 L.Ed.2d 1199 (1967).

The primary concern of defense counsel and the prosecutor should not be when the individual is entitled to counsel, but whether a violation of fifth amendment due process of law has occurred. Even if there has been a violation of right to counsel, all testimony from the witness is not automatically precluded. The witness may make an in-court identification of the defendant provided an independent basis for the in-court identification exists. As indicated in Gilbert v. California, the per se exclusionary rule that comes into play when a violation of right to counsel has occurred is applicable only to testimony concerning an out-of-court identification. However, a violation of due process of law may be so gross that the prosecution will be forbidden from introducing any of the witness's testimony.

7. Proper Procedures for Conducting a Lineup

Before discussing improprieties in lineup procedures, we must outline the proper procedures for conducting a lineup.

Fillers. There should be at least four fillers in the lineup. The fillers in the lineup should resemble the suspect. If the police cannot find proper fillers, photographic identification should be used. Additionally, the fillers in a lineup should not be informed of who the suspect is; otherwise their nonverbal communication may affect the witnesses. If the suspect is required to try on clothing or perform other acts, all should have to do so.

---

69. United States v. Hamilton, 469 F.2d 880 (9th Cir. 1972); United States v. Williams, 436 F.2d 1166 (9th Cir. 1970); Commonwealth v. Jones, 362 Mass. 497, 287 N.E.2d 599 (1972); People ex rel. Blassick v. Callahan, 50 Ill.2d 330, 279 N.E.2d 1 (1972); People v. Maire, 42 Mich.App. 32, 201 N.W.2d 318 (1972) (No abuse of discretion was found in trial judge ordering an in-court identification lineup to be conducted at preliminary hearing).

70. United States v. Wade, 388 U.S. 218, 240, 87 S.Ct. 1926, 1939, 18 L.Ed.2d 1149 (1967).

71. Id.

Police Officers. In United States v. Rodriguez,[72] the court held that the use of police fillers is not impermissibly suggestive by itself, but it is a practice to be avoided.

Witnesses. The witnesses must be separated before and and after any identification. Allowing the witnesses to mingle together is not good practice, but it may not of itself amount to undue suggestiveness. The witnesses to the lineup should not be allowed to make an identification in the presence of one another; otherwise tailoring by the witnesses might occur.[73]

People Who Conduct the Lineup. The individual conducting the lineup should be a police official who is not involved with the specific investigation. Suggestions by the police may adversely affect the integrity of the lineup.

The Suspect. The prosecution may require the defendant to wear distinctive clothing at the lineup.[74] The prosecution may also require the defendant to shave, trim hair, or even grow a beard prior to participating in a lineup.[75] The suspect or his or her counsel should be allowed to determine the suspect's position in the lineup. In addition, the suspect or counsel should be permitted to change position after each viewing. Changes prevent tailoring by the witnesses.

8. Procedures Violating Due Process

Suggested Reading:

Manson v. Brathwaite, 432 U.S. 98, 97 S.Ct. 2243, 53 L.Ed.2d 140 (1977).

Neil v. Biggers, 409 U.S. 188, 93 S.Ct. 375, 34 L.Ed. 2d 401 (1972).

Simmons v. United States, 390 U.S. 377, 88 S.Ct. 967, 19 L.Ed.2d 1247 (1968).

Gilbert v. California, 388 U.S. 263, 87 S.Ct. 1951, 18 L.Ed.2d 1178 (1967).

The test determining if a violation of due process has occurred is whether, considering the totality of circumstances, the pretrial identification was so unnecessarily suggestive that it created a substantial likelihood of mistaken identification. The remaining issue is how the trial court applies this test. In the United States [76] the prevailing rule encompasses a two-step procedure. The trial court must examine the totality of circumstances first to decide if the pretrial identification was unnecessarily suggestive even if counsel was present. The second step is to determine if the pretrial identification was so suggestive that it created a substantial likelihood of mistaken identification. If the pretrial identification was suggestive and would lead to a mistaken identification, the prosecution is forbidden from proving the pretrial identification by that particular witness.

The two-step procedure was apparently applied in Neil v. Biggers.[77] The majority

---

72. 363 F.Supp. 499 (D.P.R.1973).

73. Rudd v. Florida, 477 F.2d 805 (5th Cir. 1973). The court indicated that an identification of the defendant by two or more witnesses in the presence of each other does not per se amount to a denial of due process. See also United States v. Henderson, 489 F.2d 802 (5th Cir. 1973); United States v. Rodriguez, 363 F.Supp. 499 (D.P.R.1973); Commonwealth v. Cofield, 1 Mass.App. 660, 305 N.E.2d 858 (1974).

74. United States v. King, 433 F.2d 937 (9th Cir. 1970).

75. United States v. O'Neal, 349 F.Supp. 572 (N.D. Ohio 1972); United States v. Barnaby, 17 C.M.R. 63, 65 (1954) (C. J. Quinn, dissenting).

76. Haberstroh v. Montanye, 493 F.2d 483 (2d Cir. 1974); United States v. Henderson, 489 F.2d 802 (5th Cir. 1973); Souza v. Howard, 488 F.2d 462 (1st Cir. 1973); United States v. Hurt, 476 F.2d 1164 (D.C.Cir. 1973); United States v. New Jersey, 472 F.2d 735 (3d Cir. 1973); United States v. Gambrill, 449 F.2d 1148 (D.C.Cir. 1971); United States ex rel. Phipps v. Follette, 428 F.2d 912 (2d Cir. 1970).

77. 409 U.S. 188, 93 S.Ct. 375, 34 L.Ed.2d 401 (1972).

opinion, written by Mr. Justice Rehnquist, stated that it is "less clear from our cases . . . whether, as intimated by the District Court, unnecessary suggestiveness alone requires the exclusion of evidence." [78] Without answering directly the question raised, he indicated that the per se exclusionary rule is meant to deter the police from using a less reliable procedure whenever a more reliable one is available. Justice Rehnquist stated that the police did not exhaust all possibilities in trying to find an individual who fit the physical description of the defendant. Even so, he thought the district court focused too much on the question of suggestiveness at the showup rather than on the question of the reliability of the identification. He said that in applying the totality of circumstances test, the "central question" is whether the pretrial identification is reliable. [79] The factors he examined in answering this question are the same factors that the Court uses to determine if an independent basis for an in-court identification exists when the right to counsel has been violated. In both situations these factors include: [80] the witness's opportunity to view the actual perpetrator of the offense; [81] the witness's degree of attention; the accuracy of the witness's prior description of the criminal; [82] the level of certainty demon-

strated by the witness at the confrontation; [83] and the length of time between the crime and the confrontation. [84]

The First Step: Unnecessary Suggestivity. The question of whether the pretrial identification is unnecessarily suggestive must be divided into its two component parts: Under the circumstances was the pretrial identification suggestive? If so, were the suggestive aspects of the identification unnecessary? These questions were central to Stovall v. Denno. [85]

In *Stovall*, the accused, a Black man handcuffed to a police officer, was presented to the victim one day after major surgery to save the victim's life. The confrontation took place in a hospital room containing, with the exception of the accused, only white people, five police officers and two hospital attendants. The victim was asked whether the accused "was the man." The Supreme Court stated that in determining whether there had been a denial of due process, the applicable test was whether, judged by the totality of the circumstances, the identification procedures were unnecessarily suggestive and conducive to irreparably mistaken identification. The Court stated that in this instance no denial of due process occurred, for the necessity of the sole surviving wit-

---

78. Id. at 198–99.

79. Id. at 199.

80. Id. at 199–200. See also United States ex rel. Lucas v. Regan, 503 F.2d 1 (2d Cir. 1974) (same five factors were decisive—prior misidentification did not render in-court identification unreliable); Souza v. Howard, 488 F.2d 462 (1st Cir. 1973); United States v. Clifton, 48 C.M.R. 852 (ACMR 1974).

81. Neil v. Biggers, 409 U.S. 188, 93 S.Ct. 375, 34 L.Ed.2d 401 (1972). See also United States ex rel. Lucas v. Regan, 503 F.2d 1 (2d Cir. 1974); Haberstroh v. Montanye, 493 F.2d 483 (2d Cir. 1973); United States v. Evans, 484 F.2d 1178 (2d Cir. 1973); United States v. Smith, 473 F.2d 1148 (D.C.Cir. 1972); People v. Owens, 54 Ill.2d 286, 296 N.E.2d 728 (1973); People v. Jackson, 54 Ill.2d 143, 295 N.E.2d 462 (1973); State v. McCollum, 211 Kan. 631, 507 P.2d 196 (1973); Rozga v. State, 58 Wis.2d 434, 206 N.W. 2d 606 (1973).

82. United States ex rel. Gonzalez v. Zelker, 477 F.2d 797 (2d Cir. 1973) (prior descriptions reason-

ably accurate); United States ex rel. Rivera v. McKendrick, 474 F.2d 259 (2d Cir. 1973) (no discrepancy as negating suggestive identification as impermissibly suggestive); United States ex rel. Miller v. La Valle, 320 F.Supp. 452 (E.D.N.Y.1970) (inaccurate description as negating independent basis); State v. Sadler, 95 Idaho 524, 511 P.2d 806 (1973); Rozga v. State, 58 Wis.2d 434, 206 N.W.2d 606 (1973) (prior correct identification).

83. Haberstroh v. Montanye, 493 F.2d 483 (2d Cir. 1974); United States ex rel. Lucas v. Regan, 503 F. 2d 1 (2d Cir. 1974); United States ex rel. Rivera v. McKendrick, 474 F.2d 259 (2d Cir. 1973); Goff v. State, 506 P.2d 585 (Okl.Cr.1973).

84. United States ex rel. Lucas v. Regan, 503 F.2d 1 (2d Cir. 1974); United States v. Evans, 484 F.2d 1178 (2d Cir. 1973); Souza v. Howard, 488 F.2d 462 (1st Cir. 1973) (one year as negative factor but outweighed by others).

85. 388 U.S. 263, 87 S.Ct. 1951, 18 L.Ed.2d 1178 (1967).

ness identifying the suspect outweighed the highly suggestive circumstances.

The only case in which the Supreme Court has found a violation of due process is Foster v. California.[86] There the Court held that the lineup procedures employed were unnecessarily suggestive and remanded the case for further proceedings. The facts in *Foster* were that the police first placed the defendant in a lineup with two shorter, heavier men; only the defendant was wearing clothes similar to those worn by the perpetrator of the offense. When these tactics failed to produce an identification, the police arranged a face-to-face confrontation between the victim and the accused. However, when the victim still could not make a positive identification, the police showed him the defendant in a five-man lineup in which the accused was the only person who had also appeared in the first lineup. Because of the unnecessarily suggestive face-to-face confrontation, the case was remanded to the trial court.

A review of the cases dealing with due process of the law indicates that the courts will find a denial of due process only if an outrageous violation of the individual's rights has occurred—that is, where a flagrantly suggestive pretrial identification took place.

The Second Step: Conducivity to Mistaken Identification. The prevailing view is that evidence of a pretrial lineup is not inadmissible simply because the lineup procedure was unnecessarily suggestive. In addition, the procedure must be conducive to mistaken identification. More specifically, in the totality of the circumstances, the procedure must create a very substantial likelihood of misidentification. The following is a list of the factors the trial judge should consider in deciding the likelihood of misidentification.

Supports or Negates a Finding of A Reliable Identification at the Time of Trial	Factors to be Considered
Negates finding a reliable identification	Existence of a discrepancy between any pre-lineup description and the actual appearance of the defendant [87]
Negates finding a reliable identification	Any identification of another person prior to the lineup [88]
Negates finding a reliable identification	Failure to identify the defendant on a prior occasion [89]
Ambiguous factor	Lapse of time between the criminal act and the lineup identification [90]
Ambiguous factor	Prior photographic identification from a large group of photographs [91]
Supports finding a reliable identification	The exercise of unusual care to make observation [92]
Supports finding a reliable identification	Prompt identification at first confrontation [93]
Supports finding a reliable identification	Fairness of lineup [94]
Supports finding a reliable identification	The presence of a perpetrator with distinctive physical characteristics [95]
Supports finding a reliable identification	Prior acquaintance of witness with suspect [96]

86. 394 U.S. 440, 89 S.Ct. 1127, 22 L.Ed.2d 402 (1969).

87. United States ex rel. Lucas v. Regan, 503 F.2d 1 (2d Cir. 1974) (discrepancy not controlling in light of other factors). See also note 80, supra.

88. Perryman v. State, 470 S.W.2d 703 (Tex.1971).

89. United States v. Wade, 388 U.S. 218, 241, 87 S.Ct. 1926, 1939, 18 L.Ed.2d 1149 (1967).

90. Id.

91. Id. See also United States ex rel. Woods v. Rundle, 326 F.Supp. 592 (E.D.Pa.1971); State v. Walters, 457 S.W.2d 817 (Mo.1970).

92. United States v. Sera-Leyva, 433 F.2d 534 (D.C. Cir. 1970); People v. Jackson, 54 Ill.2d 143, 295 N.E. 2d 462 (1973).

93. People v. Covington, 47 Ill.2d 198, 265 N.E.2d 112 (1970).

94. United States v. Evans, 484 F.2d 1178 (2d Cir. 1973).

95. State v. DeLuna, 107 Ariz. 536, 490 P.2d 8 (1971); People v. Bey, 42 Ill.2d 139, 246 N.E.2d 287 (1969) (distinctive bump on the head).

96. Stanley v. Cox, 486 F.2d 48 (4th Cir. 1973) (observed twice as robber of same premises); State v.

Ambiguous factor	Ability and training in identification procedures [97]

These same factors may be used to establish an independent basis for in-court identification.

In Neil v. Biggers,[98] the Supreme Court declared that the trial judge must balance these factors to determine whether there is a very substantial likelihood of misidentification. Even evidence of an unnecessarily suggestive lineup is admissible so long as, after considering all these factors, the judge decides that the pretrial identification was reliable. In Manson v. Brathwaite,[99] the Court announced that the *Neil* test applies whether the lineup occurs before or after the date of the decision in *Stovall*.

As in the case of the sixth amendment attack, the defense counsel may also attack the in-court identification. An in-court identification may be permissible even if the evidence of the out-of-court identification is inadmissible. Once again, the judge looks to the factors listed above. The in-court identification is permissible so long as the pretrial procedure did not create a very substantial likelihood of *irreparable* misidentification.[1]

Taylor, 109 Ariz. 518, 514 P.2d 439 (1973) (defendant seen on two prior occasions); People v. Mueller, 54 Ill.2d 189, 295 N.E.2d 705 (1973); People v. Covington, 47 Ill.2d 198, 265 N.E.2d 112 (1970); State v. Johnson, 457 S.W.2d 762 (Mo.1970); State v. Kandzerski, 106 R.I. 1, 255 A.2d 154 (1969); State v. McLeod, 260 S.C. 445, 196 S.E.2d 645 (1973).

97. United States ex rel. Geralds v. Deegan, 292 F. Supp. 968 (S.D.N.Y.1968). But see E. Gardner, The Court of Last Resort 81–82 (1952) (reports inability of trained, experienced officers to estimate accurately height, weight, and age).

98. 409 U.S. 188, 93 S.Ct. 375, 34 L.Ed.2d 401 (1972).

99. 432 U.S. 98, 97 S.Ct. 2243, 53 L.Ed.2d 140 (1977).

1. Neil v. Biggers, 409 U.S. 188, 93 S.Ct. 375, 34 L.Ed.2d 401 (1972); Simmons v. United States, 390 U.S. 377, 88 S.Ct. 967, 19 L.Ed.2d 1247 (1968).

9. Fourth Amendment Attacks on Pretrial Identification

Suggested Reading:

Davis v. Mississippi, 394 U.S. 721, 89 S.Ct. 1394, 22 L.Ed.2d 676 (1969).

Adams v. United States, 399 F.2d 574 (D.C.Cir. 1968).

Although most of the cases dealing with eyewitness testimony focus on fifth and sixth amendment issues, this type of testimony can also raise significant fourth amendment issues.

Ordering a Suspect to Appear for a Lineup. Until recently, if the suspect was not in custody and did not consent, the police could not force the suspect to appear at a stationhouse to appear in a lineup. In the past few years, several jurisdictions have adopted procedures for ordering a suspect to appear to permit observation and analysis of physical characteristics. There are state statutes, proposed federal statutes, amendments to the Federal Rules of Criminal Procedures, and American Bar Association Standards[2] specifically dealing with the issue. Three state statutes specifically permit compelling an individual to appear in a lineup.[3]

In addition to the statutes and rules, there is case law which lends support to the proposition that a court may issue an order, based on diminished probable cause, to compel a suspect to appear for a lineup. In Adams v. United States,[4] the court held inadmissible the testimony of the witness who had viewed the defendant at a lineup con-

---

2. A.B.A. Standards Relating to Discovery and Procedure Before Trial § 3.1 (1970).

3. Ariz.Rev.Stat. § 13–1424; Idaho Code § 19–625; Utah Code Ann. § 77–13–37.

4. 399 F.2d 574 (D.C.Cir. 1968).

ducted during a period of unnecessary delay violating Rule 5(a) of the Federal Rules of Criminal Procedure. However, the court suggested the police could have invoked "the aid of [the court] to make the [defendant who was then in custody] reasonably available" for lineup identification in respect of other crimes for which there is less than probable cause to arrest.[5] "But, had the police heeded Rule 5(a) and taken appellants after booking before a magistrate, it is by no means certain that the police could not have arranged for other victims to view appellants in lineups."[6] Relying upon this language, the Court of Appeals for the District of Columbia upheld a magistrate's order compelling an arrestee to participate in a lineup by witnesses to other crimes with similar modus operandi.[7] There are four Supreme Court cases that might justify compelling a person to appear in a lineup in the absence of probable cause to arrest: Davis v. Mississippi,[8] Terry v. Ohio,[9] United States v. Dionisio,[10] and Camara v. Municipal Court.[11]

Pretrial Identification After Illegal Arrest. While special orders for lineup appearances are becoming increasingly common, the police usually place persons in lineups while they are in post-arrest custody. Suppose that the arrest was illegal. How does the arrest's illegality affect the admissibil-ity of testimony about an identification at the lineup? When an intentional illegal arrest has occurred that is designed to produce an identification by a particular witness, any identification by that witness will be inadmissible regardless of the existence of an independent basis for the identification.[12] This type of illegal action can be deterred. However, if an identification takes place after a good faith arrest, which is later determined to be illegal, testimony about the pretrial identification is inadmissible, but the witness making the identification after the arrest may make an in-court identification if the prosecution can establish an independent basis for such identification.[13] Similarly, when a photograph of the defendant was illegally obtained and used in a "photographic lineup," this illegality will not affect an in-court identification if an independent basis exists.[14]

A few courts have held that an illegal arrest does not affect admissibility of testimony concerning pretrial or in-court identification if the illegal arrest did not suggest or influence the pretrial identification.[15]

---

5. Id. at 579.

6. Id. at 578.

7. United States v. Allen, 408 F.2d 1287 (D.C.Cir. 1969). Thus although *Adams* seems to indicate in dictum that a person who is in custody may be made to appear before a lineup in order to identify him or her as a participant in the crime for which he or she was arrested, the *Allen* court indicated that a person who is arrested for one offense may be placed in a lineup to determine if he or she committed other offenses for which there is no legal basis for arrest.

8. 394 U.S. 721, 89 S.Ct. 1394, 22 L.Ed.2d 676 (1969).

9. 392 U.S. 1, 88 S.Ct. 1868, 20 L.Ed.2d 889 (1968).

10. 410 U.S. 1, 93 S.Ct. 764, 35 L.Ed.2d 67 (1973).

11. 387 U.S. 523, 87 S.Ct. 1727, 18 L.Ed.2d 930 (1967).

12. United States v. Edmons, 432 F.2d 577, 584 (2d Cir. 1970). See also Commonwealth v. Jones, 362 Mass. 497, 287 N.E.2d 599, 603 (1972) (Deliberately holding the defendant incommunicado taints accidental confrontation unless the prosecution can "show beyond a reasonable doubt that the identification is untainted by the deprivation of the defendant's rights.").

13. Id. at 584. See also People v. Bean, 121 Ill. App.2d 332, 257 N.E.2d 562 (1970) (In-court identification inadmissible because "traceable" to pretrial identification after illegal arrest); State v. Accor, 277 N.C. 65, 175 S.E.2d 583 (1970) (Illegal arrest entitles defendant to suppress pretrial identification but in-court identification admissible if independent basis).

14. State v. Brown, 50 Wis.2d 565, 185 N.W.2d 323 (1971). See also Metallo v. State, 10 Md.App. 76, 267 A.2d 804 (1970).

15. People v. Owens, 54 Ill.2d 286, 296 N.E.2d 728 (1973) (illegally obtained from defendant's house); Rozga v. State, 58 Wis.2d 434, 206 N.W.2d 606 (1973) (photograph obtained during illegal detention).

10. Miscellaneous Identification Testimony Problems

Suggested Reading:

United States v. Amaral, 488 F.2d 1148 (9th Cir. 1973).

United States v. Telfaire, 469 F.2d 552 (D.C.Cir. 1972).

Evans v. Superior Court, 11 Cal.3d 617, 114 Cal. Rptr. 121, 522 P.2d 681 (1974).

Right to Counsel's Presence During the Interview of the Witness by the Police. Two bases for the *Wade-Gilbert* decisions are to allow counsel to reconstruct what happened at lineups and to detect any suggestive practices utilized at lineups. The periods before and after the lineup are also crucial because suggestions during these periods often influence the identification. These suggestions might be unintentional ones made when witnesses talk to one another or make an identification in the presence of one another, or they might be intentional ones by law enforcement officials. Nevertheless, many courts have indicated that the defendant does not have a right to have counsel present at the interviews when the witness is asked who committed the crime.[16] However, the Fifth Circuit Court of Appeals in United States v. Banks [17] stated: "We emphasize that similar procedures [requests for response of witness without the presence of counsel] might require a different result if counsel is denied the opportunity to reconstruct all elements of the lineup and related agent-witness interviews, or if any witness indicates suggestive statements or actions by prosecution agents while counsel for the accused is excluded.

Clandestine conferences may not be used for the purpose of evading the clear constitutional mandate of *Wade* and *Gilbert*." [18]

Right to a Lineup to Test the Witness's Identification of the Defendant. With the increased use of photographic identifications rather than corporeal identifications, many defense counsel are now requesting to have the witnesses's identification of the defendant in a photographic display tested at a corporeal lineup. Most courts have held that the defendant has no right to such a test.[19]

However, there is some authority supporting the defendant's right to a corporeal lineup.[20] One state supreme court has held that the defendant has a right to have a witness's testimony tested at a lineup when the identification is a material issue and mistaken identification a likelihood.[21]

Right to Have the Defendant Sit Among the Spectators at Trial. Because of the increasing use of pretrial photographic identifications, the witness may not have personally confronted and identified the defendant prior to trial. The prosecution will probably attempt to have the witness identify the defendant in court. As a tactical maneuver defense counsel may want the defendant to sit with the spectators at trial. However, the defense counsel should not direct the defendant to sit with the spectators without the permission of the trial court judge, whose decision on the matter is discretionary.[22]

16. See, e. g., United States v. Wilcox, 507 F.2d 364 (4th Cir. 1974); Nance v. State, 7 Md.App. 433, 256 A.2d 377 (1969). But see People v. Williams, 3 Cal. 3d 853, 92 Cal.Rptr. 6, 478 P.2d 942 (1971).

17. 485 F.2d 545 (5th Cir. 1973).

18. Id. at 548–49.

19. United States v. Zane, 495 F.2d 683 (2d Cir. 1974); United States v. McGhee, 488 F.2d 781 (5th Cir. 1974); United States v. White, 482 F.2d 485 (4th Cir. 1973); United States v. Furtney, 454 F.2d 1 (3d Cir. 1972); United States v. Kennedy, 450 F.2d 1089 (9th Cir. 1971).

20. United States v. Caldwell, 481 F.2d 487 (D.C. Cir. 1973).

21. Evans v. Superior Court, 11 Cal.3d 617, 114 Cal. Rptr. 121, 522 P.2d 681 (1974).

22. See § 5, note 69, supra.

Right to Present Psychological and Psychiatric Testimony. Because of the variables involved in eyewitness identification, the testimony of a psychologist or psychiatrist familiar with the area is helpful.[23] However, the courts have indicated that their testimony should be about only matter "within the common experience of men."[24] The trial judge has discretion to admit witness psychology testimony, but most judges exercise their discretion to exclude the testimony. Thus counsel must resort to the use of examples in his or her argument about the unreliability of eyewitness identification: for instance, the suggestiveness of a lineup;[25] the impact of intelligence on recollection; the impact of stress and perceptual readiness;[26]

perceptual selectivity;[27] and the time factor and its impact on memory.[28]

Cautionary Instructions About Eyewitness Identification Testimony. Most courts subscribe to the view that the trial judge is not required to instruct on the uncertainty and unreliability of eyewitness identification, nor is he or she required to instruct that identification testimony should be scrutinized with extreme care. Also a requested instruction that no class of testimony is more unreliable than that of eyewitness identification may be granted or denied at the judge's discretion.[29] It is sufficient for the trial judge to instruct the jury simply on the credibility of witnesses and the government's burden of proof.[30]

---

23. Levine & Tapp, The Psychology of Criminal Identification: The Gap from *Wade* to *Kirby*, 121 U. Pa.L.Rev. 1079 (1973).

24. Commonwealth v. Jones, 362 Mass. 497, 287 N.E.2d 599, 602 (1972). See also United States v. Amaral, 488 F.2d 1148 (9th Cir. 1973).

25. See § 6, supra.

26. Levine & Tapp, The Psychology of Criminal Identification: The Gap from *Wade* to *Kirby*, 121 U. Pa.L.Rev. 1079, 1097–99 (1973).

27. Id. at 1096–97.

28. Id. at 1099–1100.

29. United States v. Barber, 442 F.2d 517, 526 (3d Cir. 1971) and cases cited therein.

30. Id. at 528. For a set of model instructions, see United States v. Telfaire, 469 F.2d 552, 558 (D.C.Cir. 1972).

PART 8
SUFFICIENCY OF THE EVIDENCE
CHAPTER 27
BURDENS OF PRODUCTION AND PROOF

1. Introduction

The previous chapters deal with one topic, the admissibility of individual items of evidence. The trial attorney's first objective is to persuade the trial judge to admit his or her individual items of evidence. However, even if the attorney's individual items of evidence are admissible, the attorney's case might never reach the jury. The judge might rule that although admissible, the individual items do not have sufficient cumulative probative value to warrant submitting the case to the jury. In addition, even if the judge submits the case to the jury, the jurors might find the attorney's evidence insufficient; they might be unpersuaded that the fact in dispute exists. In short, after the judge passes on the individual items' admissibility, the judge and jurors must evaluate the evidence's sufficiency. The presumptions and inferences doctrine governs these evaluations. The doctrine employs two procedural devices, the burdens of going forward and of proof.

BURDEN OF PRODUCTION

2. The Initial Burden of Going Forward

The judge makes the initial assessment of the evidence's sufficiency, deciding whether the evidence is sufficient to sustain the proponent's initial burden of going forward with or producing evidence.[1] The burdened party has the duty to persuade the judge that there is sufficient evidence to submit the issue to the trier of fact. The burdened party must convince the judge that the evidence has sufficient cumulative probative value to permit the trier of fact to rationally conclude that the fact exists. The penalty for failing to fulfill the duty is that the judge will make an absolute peremptory ruling against the burdened party,[2] withdrawing the issue from the jury's consideration and resolving it against the burdened party.

In a criminal case, the prosecution is allocated the initial burden of going forward on all essential elements of the charged offense or crime. For its part, the defense has the burden on the essential elements of affirmative defenses. If the defendant wants the jury to consider a certain defense, he or she must come forward with evidence raising that defense.

3. Attempting to Sustain the Burden

Suggested Reading:

People v. Blakeslee, 2 Cal.App.3d 831, 82 Cal.Rptr. 839 (1969).

Isaac v. United States, 284 F.2d 168 (D.C.Cir. 1960).

Curley v. United States, 160 F.2d 229 (D.C.Cir. 1947).

Many evidence students have complained that this area of law is abstract to the point of being metaphysical. At the outset, diagraming the steps the proponent and opponent progress through is helpful. The following is a discussion of the most important steps depicted on the diagram.

PROPONENT

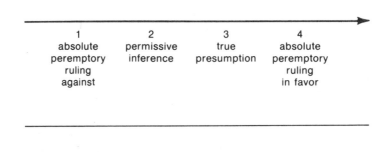

1	2	3	4
absolute peremptory ruling against	permissive inference	true presumption	absolute peremptory ruling in favor

OPPONENT

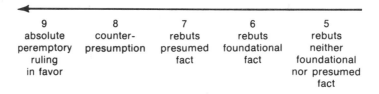

9	8	7	6	5
absolute peremptory ruling in favor	counter-presumption	rebuts presumed fact	rebuts foundational fact	rebuts neither foundational nor presumed fact

---

1. West's Ann.Cal.Evid.Code § 110.   **2.** Id.

The Proponent Fails to Sustain the Burden. In the first step, the proponent's evidence is insufficient to sustain the burden. The older view is that a mere scintilla of evidence is sufficient to sustain the burden.[3] Modernly, the prevailing view is that the evidence must have sufficient probative value to permit the jurors to rationally infer that the disputed fact exists.[4] A substantial minority finds that a stricter standard applies in criminal cases. This view is that the test in criminal cases is whether the evidence is so weak that the jurors must have a remaining lingering doubt; even if there is a permissive inference of the fact's existence, the evidence is insufficient if it would necessarily leave the jurors with a lingering doubt about the defendant's guilt.[5]

Suppose that the defendant attempts to raise the defense of insanity. The judge allocates the defendant the initial burden of going forward on that issue. Suppose further that the defendant's only evidence of insanity is the testimony of a lay witness to the crime. That witness gives conclusory testimony that, several hours before the crime, the defendant was acting "a bit peculiar." At the instructions conference, the defense attorney requests an instruction on insanity. The judge will undoubtedly deny the request, for logically, the evidence lacks sufficient probative value to support an inference of insanity. Thus to control the rationality of the jury's findings, the judge will withdraw the issue from the jury. This ruling can be restated symbolically. The proponent, the defense, has presented credible evidence of fact A, the defendant's slightly peculiar behavior shortly before the offense. The ultimate material fact in dispute is E, the defendant's sanity. In effect, the judge has ruled that *even if the jurors believe the evidence of A, they may not infer E*. A is the foundational or basic fact. E is the presumed fact. In this case, the foundational or basic fact does not have sufficient probative worth to permit an inference that E exists.

What is the procedural consequence if the proponent reaches only this step? As a matter of law, the judge will make an absolute peremptory ruling against the proponent.[6] If the prosecution has the burden on an issue and prosecution reaches only step #1, the judge will grant a motion for directed verdict, judgment of acquittal, or finding of not guilty. If the defense has the burden on a defense and reaches only step #1, the judge will not instruct the jury on the defense. The proponent suffers an absolute defeat on the issue.

The Proponent Barely Sustains the Burden. In the second step, the proponent barely sustains the burden of going forward. The proponent ordinarily reaches this step by presenting sufficient evidence to support a permissive inference of the existence of the fact in dispute. The judge assesses the probative value of the proponent's evidence and concludes that the value is sufficient to sustain the burden. Alternatively, for policy reasons the legislature can declare that if the proponent proves specified foundational facts, the jury may infer the fact in dispute. As we shall see, the creation of an inference by legislative fiat poses serious constitutional questions in criminal cases.[7]

Returning to the original hypothetical, suppose that the defense attorney now presents more extensive lay testimony. The lay witness states that he or she has known the defendant intimately for several years; at the time of the offense, the defendant was absolutely incoherent, lacked muscular control, and had a dazed appearance; and in the

---

3. 9 Wigmore, Evidence § 2494 (3d ed. 1940).

4. People v. Blakeslee, 2 Cal.App.3d 831, 82 Cal. Rptr. 839 (1969).

5. The seminal case in this line of authority is Curley v. United States, 160 F.2d 229 (D.C.Cir. 1947). For a recent case following the view, see United States v. Wiley, 519 F.2d 1348 (2d Cir. 1975).

6. West's Ann.Cal.Evid.Code § 550(a).

7. See § 8, *Limitations on the Creation of Inferences and Presumptions*, infra.

witness's opinion, the defendant was insane. Once again, the defense attorney requests an instruction on insanity. Now the judge will probably grant the request. The proponent defense has presented evidence of fact *B*, detailed testimony about bizarre behavior on the part of the defendant whom the witness knew well. The judge rules that *if the jurors believe the evidence of B, they may infer E.*

At this stage, the proponent has created a permissive inference or presumption of fact. The procedural consequence is that the judge will submit the issue to the jury. If the proponent reaches only step #2, neither party will be subject to a peremptory ruling by the judge.

The Proponent Creates a True Presumption. In the third step, the proponent goes beyond barely sustaining the burden, presenting sufficient evidence to create a true presumption or mandatory inference. In the second step, the proponent creates a mere permissive inference; the jury may infer the existence of the fact in dispute from the foundational evidence. The third step is qualitatively different. There is such a necessary or highly probable connection between the foundational fact and the fact in dispute that the inference is mandatory; if the jurors believe the foundational evidence, they must infer the existence of the fact in dispute. The California statutes clearly draw the distinction. California Evidence Code § 600(b) defines an inference as "a deduction of fact that may logically and reasonably be drawn from another fact or group of facts." [8] In contrast, Evidence Code § 600(a) declares that a presumption is "an assumption of fact that the law requires to be made from another or group of facts." [9] Ordinarily the proponent must rely upon the evidence's sheer probative value to carry the proponent to the third step. Of course,

as in the second step, a legislature may create a presumption by fiat, declaring that if the jury finds that specified foundational facts exist, they must infer the fact in dispute. Here again, in criminal cases, such legislative declarations pose constitutional issues. [10]

Revisiting the hypothetical, suppose that the defense attorney presents a properly authenticated copy of a judgment showing that shortly before the alleged offense, a court of competent jurisdiction adjudged the defendant permanently insane. [11] If the defendant suffered from a relatively permanent mental disorder such a short time before the offense, he or she was probably insane at the time of the alleged *actus reus*. The foundational evidence is so powerful that it creates a mandatory inference or true presumption of insanity. [12] The foundational evidence, fact *C*, gives rise to a mandatory inference of the existence of the fact in dispute. The judge would rule that *if the jurors believe the evidence of C, they must infer E.*

The proponent has now created a mandatory inference or presumption of law or prima facie case. [13] A true presumption has one and sometimes two procedural consequences. The first is that if the presumption does not disappear from the case, it will entitle the proponent to a conditional peremptory ruling which takes the form of a favorable instruction to the jury. Because the presumption does not entitle the proponent to an absolute peremptory ruling, the judge will not instruct the jury that *E*, the fact in dispute, exists. Rather, the ruling is conditional, and the condition is the jury's belief of the foundational evidence. Thus the judge instructs the jury that they must infer *E* *if* they believe the evidence of *C*.

---

8. West's Ann.Cal.Evid.Code § 600(b).

9. West's Ann.Cal.Evid.Code § 600(a).

---

10. See, § 8, infra.

11. See, e. g., Hurt v. United States, 327 F.2d 978 (8th Cir. 1964).

12. Id.

13. West's Ann.Cal.Evid.Code § 602. The same expression is sometimes used loosely in the sense of a permissive inference.

The conditional ruling is peremptory because the judge has withdrawn from the jury the issue of the connection between *C* and *E*, telling the jury that a necessary connection exists between the two facts. However, the jury must nevertheless decide whether to believe the evidence of *C*.

In some jurisdictions, a second procedural consequence flowing from the creation of a presumption is a shift of the ultimate burden of proof.[14] This consequence could conceivably operate against a criminal defendant. In a homicide case, the prosecution must prove the death of the alleged victim. Some jurisdictions recognize a burden-shifting presumption that a person is dead if he or she has not been heard from in seven years.[15] In a bigamy case, the prosecution must establish the validity of the first marriage. Several jurisdictions recognize a burden-shifting presumption that a ceremonial marriage is valid.[16] Some statutes creating burden-shifting presumptions expressly provide that the presumption may not operate against a criminal defendant.[17]

The Proponent Obtains an Absolute Peremptory Ruling. In the first step, the judge makes an absolute peremptory ruling against the proponent; the judge withdraws the issue from the jury and announces the proponent's loss. In the fourth step, the judge makes an absolute peremptory ruling in the proponent's favor; the judge withdraws the issue from the jury and announces the proponent's victory. In this situation the proponent presents such overwhelming evidence and the opponent presents such meager evidence that the jury's finding against the proponent would be irrational.

Understandably, a proponent rarely reaches the fourth step. The fifth and

fourteenth amendments probably preclude absolute peremptory rulings against the defendant on essential elements of the charged offense.[18] However occasionally, some defendants have won absolute peremptory ruling. In the original hypothetical, suppose that the defense presented extensive expert psychiatric testimony of schizophrenia, and the prosecution did not present even lay rebuttal testimony. Under these circumstances, some defendants have won absolute peremptory rulings which dismiss the charges against them.[19] There is also authority that if the defendant presents uncontradicted evidence of entrapment, the defendant is entitled to dismissal.[20] Such cases share several common elements. First, the proponent presents extensive, credible evidence of the foundational facts. Second, the opponent presents no or very meager rebuttal evidence. Third, the opponent usually has the ultimate burden of proof on the issue. In the insanity cases, although the defense has the initial burden of going forward on the insanity issue, in most jurisdictions the prosecution has the ultimate burden of proof. If all three elements are present, an absolute peremptory ruling in the proponent's favor is appropriate.

Here the foundational evidence is *D*. The judge rules that *(1) the jury must be-*

---

14. West's Ann.Cal.Evid.Code §§ 601 and 605.

15. Id. at § 667.

16. Id. at § 663.

17. See, e. g., West's Ann.Cal.Evid.Code §§ 665 and 668.

18. If the substantive Criminal Law prescribes a fact as an essential element of the crime and the defendant does not judicially admit the fact, the prosecution must prove the fact, and the jury must have an opportunity to decide whether the prosecution has proven the fact. United States v. Goings, 517 F. 2d 891 (8th Cir. 1975); United States v. Bosch, 505 F.2d 78 (5th Cir. 1974); United States v. Lee, 483 F. 2d 959 (5th Cir. 1973). Even if the defense does not dispute the prosecution evidence, the issue must be submitted to the jury. Bryan v. United States, 373 F.2d 403 (5th Cir. 1967); United States v. England, 347 F.2d 425 (7th Cir. 1965).

19. See, e. g., Isaac v. United States, 284 F.2d 168 (D.C.Cir. 1960); McKenzie v. United States, 266 F.2d 524 (10th Cir. 1959).

20. United States v. Bueno, 447 F.2d 903 (5th Cir. 1971).

lieve the evidence of D and (2) the jury must infer E from D. In the third step, the judge makes only the second ruling—the conditional peremptory ruling that a necessary connection exists between *C* and *E*. However, the judge does not direct the jury to believe the evidence of *C*. In the fourth step, the judge concludes that the jury's disbelieving the evidence of *D* would be irrational. Therefore, the judge removes the condition and makes an absolute ruling. For example, if several reputable psychiatrists testify that the defendant was suffering from a psychosis and the prosecution presents no rebuttal, the defense is entitled to an absolute peremptory ruling. The ruling for the defense takes the form of a directed verdict, judgment of acquittal, or finding of not guilty.

4. Attempting to Rebut the Evidence

Suggested Reading:

United States v. Hendrix, 542 F.2d 879 (2d Cir. 1976).

Assume that the proponent reaches either step #2 or #3. If the proponent reaches step #2, the proponent has barely sustained the burden; if the proponent reaches step #3, the proponent creates a true presumption. In both cases, the proponent has satisfied the burden of going forward. However, so long as the proponent does not reach step #4, the opponent escapes an absolute peremptory ruling. Moreover, the opponent usually has the opportunity to present rebuttal evidence to demonstrate that the presumed fact does not exist, for most presumptions are rebuttable.[21] Although the proponent gains the benefit of a permissive

or mandatory inference that *E* exists, the opponent may introduce evidence that *E* does not exist.[22]

The Opponent Does Not Present Sufficient Evidence to Rebut Either the Foundational or the Presumed Fact. In the fifth step, the opponent fails to present sufficient evidence to rebut either the foundational fact or the presumed fact. The form of the instruction the jury hears depends upon whether the proponent attained the second or the third step. If the proponent reached the second step, the instruction is that *if the jurors believe the evidence of B, they may infer E.* If the proponent attained the third step, the instruction is that *if the jurors believe the evidence of C, they must infer E.*

The Opponent Presents Sufficient Evidence to Rebut the Foundational Fact. In the sixth step, the opponent still fails to present sufficient evidence to rebut the ultimate fact in dispute, *E*. However, the op-

---

21. West's Ann.Cal.Evid.Code § 601.

22. There are conclusive or irrebuttable presumptions. Such presumptions are in this form: If the jurors believe the evidence of C, they must infer E. That statement is elliptical; to state the matter more starkly, if the jurors believe the evidence of C, they must infer E even if the opponent has credible evidence that E does not exist. The truth of the matter is that a conclusive presumption is a substantive rule of law rather than an evidentiary rule. 9 Wigmore, Evidence § 2492 (3d ed. 1940). The legal consequence flows from the foundational facts, and the existence or non-existence of the presumed fact is immaterial.

Consider this statutory presumption for criminal nonsupport actions. A child born while a husband and wife are cohabiting is conclusively presumed to be the husband's natural offspring. In a nonsupport action, the defendant husband could attack the foundational facts. The husband could introduce evidence that the woman was not his lawful wife or that they were not cohabiting when the child was born. However, the husband could not attack the presumed fact, the child's legitimacy. The husband could not introduce another man's admission that he considered himself the father. In reality, the child's legitimacy is immaterial in the nonsupport action. By enacting the statutory evidentiary presumption, the legislature has effectively promulgated a substantive rule of law that a husband has a legal duty to support a child born of his wife while they are cohabiting.

ponent does succeed in presenting sufficient evidence to rebut the foundational fact. With one exception, the jury instructions are the same as they are in the fifth step. This exception is that judge must call the jury's attention to the fact that the parties have presented conflicting evidence on the foundational fact. There is now a disputed question of fact over whether the foundational fact exists. The judge instructs that *the jurors must resolve the conflict in the evidence over whether the foundational fact, B or C, exists.* The judge then delivers the instructions previously outlined.

The Opponent Presents Sufficient Evidence to Rebut the Presumed Fact. In the seventh step, the opponent mounts a sufficient rebuttal against *E* itself, the ultimate fact in dispute. Two questions arise. The first is the standard for determining when the opponent has presented sufficient rebuttal evidence. The second is the procedural effect of the opponent's presentation of sufficient rebuttal evidence.

The Sufficiency of the Rebuttal Evidence. The courts have unfortunately articulated numerous conflicting standards for testing the sufficiency of the opponent's rebuttal evidence, including "substantial evidence to the contrary, any contradictory evidence, some evidence to the contrary, competent evidence, by evidence of equal weight, evidence legally sufficient to overcome the presumption, and testimony that outweighs the presumption." [23] Nevertheless, the wealth of verbal formulae is reducible to five primary standards: the Model Code standard of "any evidence contrary thereto, regardless of whether it is credible or substantial"; [24] substantial evidence to the contrary; evidence sufficient, standing alone, to support a finding that the material fact in dispute does not exist; [25] evidence sufficient

to leave the issue in equipoise; and finally, evidence which makes the fact's non-existence more likely than its existence.

The Effect of the Presentation of Sufficient Rebuttal Evidence. Suppose that under the prevailing standard in the jurisdiction, the judge decides that the opponent has presented sufficient rebuttal evidence. What is the procedural consequence? There are two schools of thought on this question. The first is the majority view, the "bursting bubble" theory, advocated by Thayer, Wigmore, and the drafters of the Model Code. [26] Their view is that the presumption disappears or self-destructs as soon as the opponent presents sufficient rebuttal evidence. If the opponent presents such evidence, the judge will not mention a mandatory inference or even the word *presumption* in the final jury charge. This school theorizes that presumptions are merely procedural devices for allocating the burden of going forward during the trial. If the judge has decided that the case should be submitted to the jury, the presumption has already spent its force and fulfilled its function.

Only the presumption has disappeared; the proponent is no longer at step #3. Usually a permissive inference remains, for the evidence of the foundational facts is still in the record, and that evidence ordinarily has sufficient probative value to keep the proponent at step #2, thus preventing an absolute peremptory ruling against the proponent. Conceivably, when the presumption disappears, the proponent could revert back to step #1. This possibility arises because, as previously stated, a legislature may create a presumption by fiat. If the foundational facts specified in the statute do not have sufficient probative value to support a permissive inference of the existence of the ultimate fact, *E*, the presentation of suf-

23. 2 Conrad, Modern Trial Evidence § 955 (1956).

24. Model Code of Evidence Rule 605.

25. West's Ann.Cal.Evid.Code § 604.

26. Model Code of Evidence Rule 704(2); 9 Wigmore, Evidence §§ 2485–91 (3d ed. 1940); Thayer, A Preliminary Treatise on Evidence at Common Law 313–52 (1898).

ficient rebuttal evidence is fatal to the proponent's case. The immediate effect is the disappearance of the presumption; the proponent is no longer at step #3. More importantly, because the foundational facts do not support a permissive inference of E, the proponent reverts to step #1 and suffers an unfavorable absolute peremptory ruling.

The second school of thought asserts that the presumption remains in the case even after the opponent presents sufficient rebuttal evidence. The adherents of this view include Morgan, McCormick, Bohlen, and the drafters of the Uniform Rules.[27] This view has significant procedural consequences. First, even after the opponent reaches step #7, the proponent remains at step #3. Hence, it is impossible for the proponent to revert to step #1 and suffer an unfavorable absolute peremptory ruling. Second, regardless of the rebuttal evidence, the proponent obtains a favorable jury instruction. However, even the courts subscribing to the second school of thought disagree over the instruction's wording.

Some courts prefer merely to inform the jury that the presumption exists and do not even attempt to explain the presumption's operation to the jury. Other courts inform the jury of the presumption's existence and then describe the presumption itself as evidence. Still other courts use the term, *presumption*, but describe the presumption as a permissive inference. The final group of courts urge that the presumption not only remains in the case but also shifts the ultimate burden of proof to the opponent. They instruct the jury if *the jurors believe the evidence of C, they must infer E unless the opponent proves by a certain measure of proof that E does not exist* —for example, by a preponderance of the

evidence. Morgan and McCormick would apply this view to all true presumptions.

BURDEN OF PROOF

5. The Ultimate Burden of Proof

The jurors make their own assessment of the evidence's sufficiency. While the judge decides whether the proponent's evidence is sufficient to sustain the initial burden of going forward, the jurors decide whether the evidence is sufficient to fulfill the ultimate burden of proof or risk of nonpersuasion.[28] The judge decides a question of law: Standing alone, does the proponent's evidence have sufficient probative value to support an inference that E exists? The jurors decide a question of fact: Does E exist? To decide this question, they consider the evidence presented by both the proponent and the opponent. The burden of going forward is a duty owed to the judge, and if the proponent does not satisfy the initial burden, the penalty is a peremptory ruling by the judge against the proponent.[29] The burden of proof is a duty owed to the triers of fact, and if the proponent does not satisfy this ultimate burden, the penalty is an adverse finding of fact by the jurors.[30]

6. Allocation of the Burden

With respect to each material fact in issue, the trial judge must allocate the ultimate burden to one of the parties.[31] No single test helps the judge to determine the allocation. He or she must consider factors of policy, probability, and fairness. A victory for one side may be preferable in terms of social policy; and if so, the judge will allocate the burden to the other side. One side

27. Morgan, Some Problems of Proof 81 (1956); C. McCormick, Handbook of the Law of Evidence § 317 (1954); F. Bohlen, The Effect of Rebuttable Presumptions of Law Upon the Burden of Proof, 68 U.Pa.L. Rev. 307 (1920); Uniform Rule of Evidence 14 (1953).

28. West's Ann.Cal.Evid.Code § 115.

29. Id. at § 110.

30. Id. at § 115.

31. Id. at § 502.

may be defending a markedly more improbable proposition, and if so, that side should bear the burden. Finally, one side may have superior access to the evidence relevant to the fact's existence, and fairness counsels assigning that side the burden. In the absence of a controlling common-law precedent or statute, the judge must consider all three factors in determining to whom to allocate the burden. Fortunately, the judge can usually rely on precedent or statute for guidance.

At common law, the norm is that the prosecution has the burden both on the crime's essential elements and on affirmative defenses. While the defendant has the initial burden to raise the defense, once it is raised the prosecution has the ultimate burden of proving that the defense does not exist in the present case. For its part defense need only raise a reasonable doubt that the defense exists.[32] There are exceptions to the common-law norm. For example, in some jurisdictions, the defendant has both the initial and ultimate burdens on insanity.[33] Also substantial authority mandates that the defendant has the ultimate burden on self-defense.[34] Still other courts assign the defendant the ultimate burden on entrapment.[35]

If the crime is statutory, the statute may dictate the allocation of the ultimate burden.[36] Suppose that the statute contains two physically separate clauses. The first, an enacting clause, sets forth the general prohibition. The second clause contains exceptive language. Some courts have inferred from the use of two clauses a legislative intention to make the exceptive language an affirmative defense and to assign the defendant the ultimate burden on the defense.[37] For example, in the enacting clause a statute might generally prohibit possession of narcotic paraphernalia and then, in a separate clause, except possession in the course of medical practice. A court could plausibly conclude that the defendant has the ultimate burden of proving that he or she is a physician who uses the paraphernalia in the course of medical practice.

The above discussion relates to the initial allocation of the ultimate burden. In fact, the ultimate burden does not come into play until the judge is ready to submit the case to the jury. Nevertheless, at the outset of the case, the judge can usually predict the ultimate allocation. Problems arise, however, in jurisdictions following the view that a presumption shifts the ultimate burden.[38] In these jurisdictions, the judge must first decide what the normal allocation of the burden is. Then the judge must review the record to determine whether the burdened party created any presumption which would shift the ultimate burden to the opponent.

7. The Measure of the Burden

Suggested Reading:

In re Winship, 397 U.S. 358, 90 S.Ct. 1068, 25 L.Ed. 2d 368 (1970).

In addition to allocating the ultimate burden, the trial judge must determine the measure—that is, the degree of belief the proponent must produce in the jury's mind in order to prevail.[39] There are three common measures of this burden.

---

32. Law Revision Commission Comment, West's Ann.Cal.Evid.Code § 501.

33. See, e. g., West's Ann.Cal.Evid.Code § 522.

34. Straughter v. State, 247 A.2d 202 (Del.1968); State v. Farley, 112 Ohio App. 448, 176 N.E.2d 232, 16 O.O.2d 343 (1960); State v. Zannino, 129 W.Va. 775, 41 S.E.2d 641 (1947).

35. United States v. Pugliese, 346 F.2d 861 (2d Cir. 1965).

36. McKelvey v. United States, 260 U.S. 353, 357, 43 S.Ct. 132, 134, 67 L.Ed. 301 (1922).

37. 1 Wharton, Criminal Evidence § 20 (1955).

38. See § 4, supra.

39. West's Ann.Cal.Evid.Code § 502.

The first is a fair preponderance of the evidence. Some courts interpret the measure as requiring subjective certainty: The jury must actually believe that the fact in dispute exists.[40] Most courts demand less; they interpret the standard as requiring only that the jury believe the fact's existence is more likely than not.[41] Surprisingly, even in criminal cases, juries often use this standard. When a judge rules on an objection to the authenticity of a proffered document, the judge decides only the preliminary question whether there is enough evidence in the record to support a finding that the document is genuine.[42] The judge decides the question of law of the sufficiency of the proponent's evidence to support the finding. Ultimately, the jury decides whether the document is authentic, considering the evidence on both sides and making the final factual determination.[43] The jury uses the preponderance standard to make this determination.

The second measure is clear and convincing evidence. The best explanation of this standard is that it requires a high degree of probability. While civil juries often work with this standard in equity suits, criminal juries almost never use it. However, judges in criminal cases often resort to this measure. Chapter 10 discusses the admissibility of uncharged misconduct evidence.[44] Many courts have held that such evidence is inadmissible unless there is plain, clear, and convincing evidence that the defendant committed the other act.[45] If the prosecutor relies upon consent to validate a search, many courts demand clear and positive evidence of consent.[46] If an unduly suggestive out-of-court lineup has taken place, an in-court identification by the same witness is admissible only if the prosecution establishes an independent basis by clear and convincing evidence.[47]

The third and final measure is proof beyond a reasonable doubt. Chief Justice Shaw furnished the classic definition of this measure: "It is that state of the case, which, after the entire comparison and consideration of all the evidence, leaves the minds of the jurors in that condition that they cannot say they feel an abiding conviction, to a moral certainty, of the truth of the charge."[48] This definition, which is widely employed in common-law jurisdictions, is mandated by some statutes.[49] Judges are reluctant to amplify the pattern instruction, for Chief Justice Shaw's definition is virtually irreducible, and a judge invites reversal by ranging beyond it.

The Supreme Court has used sweeping language to the effect that the reasonable doubt measure applies to "every fact necessary to constitute the crime with which [the defendant] is charged."[50] However, this language is an overstatement. The standard applies only to the ultimate, material facts which either are essential elements of the charged crime or are, in most jurisdictions, elements of affirmative defenses the defendant has properly raised. On the one hand, the prosecution must prove each of charged crime's essential elements beyond a reasonable doubt, and in most jurisdictions the defendant prevails if he or she raises a reason-

---

40. Sargent v. Massachusetts Accident Co., 307 Mass. 246, 29 N.E.2d 825 (1940).

41. Livanovitch v. Livanovitch, 99 Vt. 327, 131 A. 799 (1926).

42. Fed.Evid.Rule 104(b), 28 U.S.C.A.

43. West's Ann.Cal.Evid.Code § 403(c)(1).

44. See Chapter 10, supra.

45. United States v. Urdiales, 523 F.2d 1245 (5th Cir. 1975); United States v. Pollard, 509 F.2d 601 (5th Cir. 1975); United States v. Gocke, 507 F.2d 820 (8th Cir. 1974).

46. People v. Donnell, 52 Cal.App.3d 762, 125 Cal. Rptr. 310 (1975).

47. People v. Carter, 46 Cal.App.3d 260, 120 Cal. Rptr. 181 (1975).

48. Commonwealth v. Webster, 59 Mass. (5 Cush.) 295, 320 (1850).

49. West's Ann.Cal.Penal Code § 1096.

50. In re Winship, 397 U.S. 358, 364, 90 S.Ct. 1068, 1072, 25 L.Ed.2d 368 (1970).

able doubt that an affirmative defense is present. On the other hand, the standard does not apply to evidentiary facts; for example, the prosecution does not have to prove beyond a reasonable doubt the authenticity of every key piece of evidence. Moreover, there is substantial authority that the measure does not apply to preliminary procedural issues such as venue.[51]

CONSTITUTIONAL LIMITATIONS

8. Limitations on the Burden of Going Forward

Limitations on the Creation of Inferences and Presumptions. Both courts and legislatures have the power to create inferences and presumptions. However, like any other governmental power, this power is subject to the limitations stated in the Bill of Rights.[52] One of these limitations is the due process clauses in the fifth and fourteenth amendments,[53] requiring that governmental action be rational. The question thus arises: What is the substantive test for the rationality of an inference or presumption?

The Supreme Court first addressed this question in Tot v. United States.[54] Tot involved a penal statute proscribing an ex-convict's possession of firearms that had been shipped in interstate commerce. The statute provided that "the possession of a firearm . . . by any such person shall be presumptive evidence that such firearm was . . . received by such person in violation of this Act." In invalidating this statutory presumption, the Court announced that "a statutory presumption cannot be sustained if there is no rational connection between the fact proved and the ultimate fact pre-

sumed, if the inference of the one from proof of the other is arbitrary because of lack of connection between the two in common experience."[55]

Unfortunately, the Tot Court did not define "rational connection," leaving open the possibility of two different interpretations. The first was logical relevance: The foundational fact had to be logically relevant to the presumed fact and had to increase the probability of the presumed fact's existence. The second was logical sufficiency: The foundational fact had to have sufficient probative value to support an inference that the presumed fact existed. In Leary v. United States,[56] the Court embraced the second interpretation. Speaking for the Court, Mr. Justice Harlan asserted that "a criminal statutory presumption must be regarded as 'irrational' or 'arbitrary' and hence unconstitutional, unless it can at least be said with substantial assurance that the presumed fact is more likely than not to flow from the proved fact on which it is made to depend."[57] The Court further indicated that except when the subject matter falls within specialized judicial competence or is a matter of common knowledge, it would pay great deference to the legislature's evaluation of the strength of an inference.[58]

In a 1970 decision, Turner v. United States,[59] the Court tested several statutory presumptions in drug prosecutions. In dictum, the Court alluded to "the more exacting reasonable doubt standard normally applicable in criminal cases."[60] The Court's language suggested that in a criminal case, the foundational facts must have sufficient probative value to prove beyond a reasonable doubt the presumed fact's existence. Several

51. United States v. Hopkins, 529 F.2d 775 (8th Cir. 1976).

52. U.S.C.A.Const. Amends. I–VIII.

53. Id. at Amends. V & XIV.

54. 319 U.S. 463, 63 S.Ct. 1241, 87 L.Ed. 1519 (1943).

55. Id. at 467.

56. 395 U.S. 6, 89 S.Ct. 1532, 23 L.Ed.2d 57 (1969).

57. Id. at 36.

58. Id. at 35.

59. 396 U.S. 398, 90 S.Ct. 642, 24 L.Ed.2d 610 (1970).

60. Id. at 416.

lower courts read the dictum as a signal that in the future, the Court would use "beyond a reasonable doubt" as the test for the constitutionality of an inference or presumption.[61]

The last significant case to date in this line of authority is Barnes v. United States.[62] *Barnes* dealt with the decisional rule that the jury may infer guilty knowledge from unexplained possession of stolen goods. The case has two noteworthy aspects. To begin with, the Court for the first time extended the rule for statutory presumptions to a common-law inference. The *Leary* test controls whether the inference is created by the legislature or by the courts. Second, the Court acknowledged that its previous opinions had referred to two different tests, a more-likely-than-not test and a reasonable-doubt test.[63] However, the Court found that the underlying fact of unexplained possession of recently stolen goods had sufficient probative value to establish guilty knowledge beyond a reasonable doubt. For this reason, it was unnecessary for the Court to decide finally whether due process requires the use of the strict reasonable-doubt standard. Thus, although an inference or presumption must now pass muster under the more-likely-than-not standard, soon the Court may opt for the stricter standard, at least if the inference or presumption supplies an essential element of the charged crime.

Tot v. United States, 319 U.S. 463, 63 S.Ct. 1241, 87 L.Ed. 1519 (1943).

Limitations on the Effect of Presumptions. Under the orthodox view, a true presumption is a mandatory inference.[64] Query: Is it constitutional to permit a mandatory inference to operate against a criminal defendant? Can the prosecution actually reach step #3? One of the leading Supreme Court precedents on presumptions is United States v. Gainey.[65] There the Court sustained a statutory presumption but emphasized that in the jury instructions, the judge had described the presumption to the jury as a permissive inference.[66] Some commentators read into *Gainey* a prohibition of the operation of mandatory inferences against a defendant.[67] In 1973, the Court of Appeals for the Ninth Circuit explicitly adopted this view.[68]

Until the Supreme Court's recent decision in Mullaney v. Wilbur,[69] consensus was steadily growing that a court could not permit a true presumption—that is, a mandatory inference—to operate against a criminal defendant. However, in a *Mullaney* footnote [70] Mr. Justice Powell matter-of-factly referred to the possibility that a true presumption requires the jury to draw an inference adverse to the defendant. It remains to be seen whether this passage in *Mullaney* will embolden the lower courts to hold that a mandatory inference may operate against a defendant.

Suggested Reading:

Barnes v. United States, 412 U.S. 837, 93 S.Ct. 2357, 37 L.Ed.2d 380 (1973).

Turner v. United States, 396 U.S. 398, 90 S.Ct. 642, 24 L.Ed.2d 610 (1970).

Leary v. United States, 395 U.S. 6, 89 S.Ct. 1532, 23 L.Ed.2d 57 (1969).

---

61. State v. Cuevas, 53 Hawaii 110, 488 P.2d 322 (1971).

62. 412 U.S. 837, 93 S.Ct. 2357, 37 L.Ed.2d 380 (1973).

63. Id. at 843.

64. See § 3, supra.

65. 380 U.S. 63, 85 S.Ct. 754, 13 L.Ed.2d 658 (1954).

66. Id. at 70.

67. C. McCormick, Handbook of the Law of Evidence § 346 (2d ed. 1972); Note, 2 St. Mary's L.J. 115, 118 (1970).

68. United States v. Lake, 482 F.2d 146 (9th Cir. 1973). See also State v. Hansen, 203 N.W.2d 216 (Iowa 1972).

69. 421 U.S. 684, 95 S.Ct. 1881, 44 L.Ed.2d 508 (1975).

70. Id. at 703 n. 31.

Suggested Reading:

United States v. Gainey, 380 U.S. 63, 85 S.Ct. 754, 13 L.Ed.2d 658 (1954).

United States v. Lake, 482 F.2d 146 (9th Cir. 1973).

9.　Limitations on the Burden of Proof

Suggested Reading:

Patterson v. New York, 432 U.S. 197, 97 S.Ct. 2319, 53 L.Ed.2d 281 (1977).

Mullaney v. Wilbur, 421 U.S. 684, 95 S.Ct. 1881, 44 L.Ed.2d 508 (1975).

Leland v. Oregon, 343 U.S. 790, 72 S.Ct. 1002, 96 L.Ed. 1302 (1952).

Limitations on the Burden's Allocation. As previously stated, the prosecution usually bears the ultimate burden of proof both on the charge offense's essential elements and on affirmative defenses.[71] May a legislature deviate from that norm and allocate to the defendant the ultimate burden at least on affirmative defenses? The first Supreme Court decision to consider the question is Leland v. Oregon.[72] There the Court took the position that a legislature may allocate the defendant the ultimate burden on the issue of insanity. The next decision in point is *Winship*,[73] which states that the government must bear the ultimate burden on the defense's essential elements.

Winship cited *Leland*, thereby indicating that the latter remains good law.[74] The task now is reconciling the two cases. On it face, this is simple enough. *Winship* requires that the government has the burden on the crime's essential elements while *Leland* permits the legislature to shift the burden to the defense on affirmative defenses. The problem is that in the light of the facts of *Leland*, articulating a principled definition of affirmative defense is difficult. The defense in *Leland* was not a true affirmative defense in the nature of confession and avoidance; rather, insanity negatives the essential element of criminal intent. In short, even after *Winship*, a well-settled historical practice of treating a fact as an affirmative defense seems enough to bring that fact within the purview of *Leland*. The recent cases interpreting *Winship* fall into three categories.

In the first category, which includes such defenses as alibi, the government must bear the burden. Although it is common practice to refer to "an alibi defense," alibi is not a true affirmative defense; instead it negatives presence at the crime scene and, consequently, commission of the criminal act. The overwhelming majority of jurisdictions has concluded that due process itself allocates to the prosecution the ultimate burden on alibi.[75]

In the second category, the government may shift the burden to the defendant. This category includes the defenses of insanity and entrapment. Because *Leland* survived *Winship*, the government may assign the defendant the ultimate burden on insanity.[76]

71.　See § 6, supra.

72.　343 U.S. 790, 72 S.Ct. 1002, 96 L.Ed. 1302 (1952).

73.　In re Winship, 397 U.S. 358, 90 S.Ct. 1068, 25 L.Ed.2d 368 (1970).

74.　Id. at 362. United States v. Greene, 489 F.2d 1145, 1154–55 (D.C.Cir. 1973) states: "Reliance by appellant on the proposition that In re Winship has, in effect, overruled Leland v. Oregon is misplaced.

It is noted . . . that the Supreme Court's opinion in Winship cited with approval a group of prior decisions, including Leland v. Oregon."

75.　Smith v. Smith, 454 F.2d 572 (5th Cir. 1971); Stump v. Bennett, 398 F.2d 111 (8th Cir.), cert. denied 393 U.S. 1001, 89 S.Ct. 483, 21 L.Ed.2d 466 (1968); State v. Jewell, 285 A.2d 847 (Me.1972); State v. Grady, 276 Md. 178, 345 A.2d 436 (1975); People v. Pearson, 19 Ill.2d 609, 169 N.E.2d 252 (1960).

76.　People v. Flores, 55 Cal.App.3d 118, 127 Cal. Rptr. 230 (1976); State v. Berry, 324 So.2d 822 (La. 1975).

Entrapment has received similar treatment.[77]

In the third category, dealing with other defenses relating to the criminal state of mind, the courts divide. Much of the confusion is attributable to the Supreme Court's murky opinion in Mullaney v. Wilbur.[78] *Mullaney* dealt with the presumption of malice under Maine homicide law. Under this law, the presence of malice is the distinguishing feature between murder and manslaughter. The Maine courts treat murder and manslaughter as different degrees of felonious homicide rather than as distinct offenses, and the Supreme Court accepted that construction of the state law.[79] The trial judge had instructed the jury that malice could be presumed unless the defendant proved by a preponderance of the evidence that he acted in the heat of passion on sudden provocation.

The State first argued that *Winship* was inapplicable because the fact in question would not "wholly exonerate the defendant."[80] Even if the defendant proved heat of passion, he was nevertheless guilty of a degree of felonious homicide. The Court rejoined that *Winship* applied because substance controlled over form: Even though murder and manslaughter are formally degrees of one offense under Maine law, a person convicted of manslaughter is "subject to substantially less severe penalties" than a person convicted of murder.[81] The State's second argument was that the defendant's superior access to the facts relevant to heat of passion justifies allocating the defendant the ultimate burden. The Court brushed aside this argument, stating

that "nor is the requirement of proving a negative unique in our system of criminal jurisprudence."[82] The Court added that imposing the burden of proof for passion on the prosecution did not visit a "unique hardship on the prosecution."[83]

The Court's opinion is hardly a model of clarity. For that reason, the lower courts understandably disagreed over the opinion's interpretation. Although courts in Maine, New Jersey, and New York sustained malice presumptions, courts in other jurisdictions such as North Carolina felt compelled to direct changes in state homicide instructions.

The Supreme Court attempted to eliminate some of the confusion in the case law when the attack on the New York law reached the Court in 1977. In Patterson v. New York,[84] the Court attempted to clarify the scope of the *Mullaney* doctrine. On the one hand, the Court held that the state may not allocate the burden of proof to the defendant on any fact which would negate an essential element of the crime, an "element included in the definition of the offense of which the defendant is charged."[85] Under the law of Maine, heat of passion operated as a simple defense negativing malice. The Court emphasized that in *Mullaney*, the trial judge instructed the jury that malice was "an essential and indispensable element of the crime of murder" but that "malice aforethought and heat of passion on sudden provocation are two inconsistent things." Because the state of Maine clearly had to bear the burden of proof on malice, the state could not assign the defendant the burden on heat of passion.

On the other hand, the Court declared that the state may allocate the burden of

77. See, e. g., People v. Long, 83 Misc.2d 14, 372 N.Y.S.2d 389 (1975).

78. 421 U.S. 684, 95 S.Ct. 1881, 44 L.Ed.2d 508 (1975).

79. Id. at 690–91.

80. Id. at 697.

81. Id. at 698.

82. Id. at 702.

83. Id.

84. 432 U.S. 197, 97 S.Ct. 2319, 53 L.Ed.2d 281 (1977).

85. Id.

proof to the defendant on facts which "bear no direct relationship to any element" of the charged crime.[86] Patterson had been charged with second-degree murder. Under the law of New York, the only essential elements of that crime are an intent to kill and the killing. New York law recognized the affirmative defense of extreme emotional disturbance. In the Court's words, the fact of disturbance did "not serve to negative any facts of the crime which the State is to prove. It constitutes a separate issue on which the defendant is required to carry the burden of persuasion."[87] Disturbance did not negate any essential element of the charged crime. Rather disturbance was an additional fact mitigating punishment. Thus, the state could allocate the burden of proof on extreme emotional disturbance to the defendant.

The dissenters in *Patterson* charged that the distinction the majority drew between *Mullaney* and *Patterson* was "indefensibly formalistic."[88] It remains to be seen whether *Patterson* will succeed in elim-

inating the confusion among the lower courts over the scope of the *Mullaney* doctrine.

Limitations on the Burden's Measure. The long-standing common-law practice has been to require the prosecution to prove all the crime's essential elements beyond a reasonable doubt. *Winship*[89] now gives this practice constitutional protection, teaching that due process requires that the prosecution present proof beyond a reasonable doubt of every fact necessary to constitute a crime.[90] However, delimiting the scope of *Winship* is important. It does not apply to preliminary procedural issues such as venue. During the trial, it does not apply to mere evidentiary facts; rather it applies only to the ultimate, material facts constituting the crime's essential elements. Finally, it usually does not apply after trial to such procedures as sentencing[91] and probation revocation.[92]

---

86. Id.

87. Id.

88. Id.

---

89. In re Winship, 397 U.S. 358, 90 S.Ct. 1068, 25 L.Ed.2d 368 (1970).

90. United States v. Soria, 519 F.2d 1060 (5th Cir. 1975).

91. United States v. Alvarez, 519 F.2d 1036 (3d Cir. 1975).

92. In re Coughlin, 16 Cal.3d 52, 127 Cal.Rptr. 337, 545 P.2d 249 (1976).

CHAPTER 28

JUDICIAL NOTICE

1. Introduction

As we saw in the last chapter, the party with the burden of production on an issue typically satisfies the burden by introducing testimonial, documentary, or real evidence. If the judge determines that a fact is indisputable, however, the judge may accept the fact as established and dispense with formal evidentiary proof. This process is called judicial notice.[1] Obviously, the process serves to expedite trials and thus conserves both time and expense. In addition, it precludes a jury from reaching an absurd result: "It makes a mockery of a court of justice to permit a jury to accept or reject in accordance with their prejudices a fact capable of exact scientific determination."[2]

Judicial notice is a broad concept.[3] The concept embraces *three distinct types of notice: (1) judicial notice of legislative facts in the court's lawmaking function; (2) judicial notice of adjudicative facts; and (3) judicial notice of law in the court's lawfinding function.*

2. Notice of Legislative Facts

Suggested Reading:

State v. Lawrence, 120 Utah 323, 234 P.2d 600 (1951).

The Distinction Between Legislative and Adjudicative Facts. Facts which judges may judicially notice have been classified as either legislative or adjudicative.[4] Both legislative and adjudicative facts are important in criminal prosecutions. Professor

---

1. The kind of fact referred to in the text has been classified as adjudicative in contradistinction to legislative. See § 2, infra.

2. Keeffe, Landis, and Shaad, Sense and Nonsense About Judicial Notice, 2 Stan.L.Rev. 664, 670 (1950). See also J. Maguire, Evidence, Common Sense and Common Law 167 (1947) ("Both judicial determination to prevent non-sensical verdicts or findings and desire not to waste time litigating about undeniable matters lead to application of judicial notice.").

3. See generally Roberts, Preliminary Notes Toward A Study of Judicial Notice, 52 Cornell L.Q. 210, 236

(1967) ("[J]udicial notice is not a distinct doctrine like the hearsay rule or best evidence; rather, judicial notice *is* the art of thinking as practiced within the legal system. Indeed, the fundamental error lies in teaching judicial notice as an aspect of Evidence.").

4. For example, Federal Rule of Evidence 201(a) provides: "This rule governs only judicial notice of adjudicative facts."

Davis, the originator of these terms,[5] described adjudicative facts as follows: "When a court or an agency finds facts concerning the immediate parties—who did what, where, when, how, and with what motive or intent—the court or agency is performing an adjudicative function, and the facts so determined are conveniently called adjudicative facts. Stated in other terms, the adjudicative facts are those to which the law is applied in the process of adjudication. They are the facts that normally go to the jury in a jury case."[6] If, for example, a defendant is charged with grand larceny of an automobile and under the applicable substantive law, the value of the stolen property must exceed $50 to constitute grand larceny, the value of the automobile is an adjudicative fact.[7] It is the type of fact that would "normally go to the jury in a jury case."

In contrast, when a court "develops law or policy, it is acting legislatively; the courts have created the common law through judicial legislation, and the facts which inform the tribunal's legislative judgment are called legislative facts. Legislative facts are those which help the tribunal to determine the content of law and policy and to exercise its judgment or discretion in determining what course of action to take."[8] Courts could not perform their lawmaking function without resort to facts that are not supported by evidence in the record.[9]

The use of legislative facts in developing constitutional principles, construing statutes, and creating common law is well recognized.[10] For example, in Miranda v. Arizona,[11] the Supreme Court relied extensively on extra-record facts—texts on police interrogation practices[12]—to support its conclusion that the "process of in-custody interrogation of persons suspected or accused of crime contains inherently compelling pressures which work to undermine the individual's will to resist and to compel him to speak where he would not otherwise do so freely."[13] As the Court acknowledged, its factual assumptions about police interrogation played a critical part in its decision.[14]

In Turner v. United States,[15] the Court relied on facts outside the record in deciding whether a criminal presumption of illegal importation from possession of heroin satisfied constitutional standards.[16] The Court upheld the presumption because it concluded that heroin was not produced domestically. To support its conclusion, the Court cited numerous sources that were not part of the trial record.[17] Similarly, in Hawkins v.

---

5. The terms first appeared in Davis, An Approach to Problems of Evidence in the Administrative Process, 55 Harv.L.Rev. 364, 402 (1942). The distinction is more fully developed in Davis, Judicial Notice, 55 Colum.L.Rev. 945 (1955). See also Davis, Administrative Law of the Seventies 349 (1976); Davis, Administrative Law Text 291 (3d ed. 1972); 2 Davis, Administrative Law Treatise Ch. 15 (1958 and Supp. 1970).

6. Davis, Judicial Notice, 55 Colum.L.Rev. 945, 952 (1955).

7. See State v. Lawrence, 120 Utah 323, 234 P.2d 600 (1951).

8. Davis, Judicial Notice, 55 Colum.L.Rev. 945, 952 (1955).

9. Id. at 952–53 ("[F]indings or assumptions of legislative facts need not, frequently are not, and sometimes cannot be supported by evidence.").

10. C. McCormick, Handbook of the Law of Evidence § 331 (2d ed. 1972); Karst, Legislative Facts in Constitutional Litigation, 1960 Supreme Court Review 75; Advisory Committee Note, Fed.Evid.Rule 201, 28 U.S.C.A.; Comment, The Presently Expanding Concept of Judicial Notice, 13 Vill.L.Rev. 528, 533 (1968).

11. 384 U.S. 436, 86 S.Ct. 1602, 16 L.Ed.2d 694 (1966).

12. "A valuable source of information about present police practices . . . may be found in various police manuals and texts." Id. at 448.

13. Id. at 467.

14. "An understanding of the nature and setting of this in-custody interrogation is essential to our decision today." Id. at 445.

15. 396 U.S. 398, 90 S.Ct. 642, 24 L.Ed.2d 610 (1970). See also Leary v. United States, 395 U.S. 6, 89 S.Ct. 1532, 23 L.Ed.2d 57 (1969).

16. See Chapter 27 for a further discussion of Turner and criminal presumptions.

17. The Court relied on previous cases, official reports and other sources. 396 U.S. at 407–19 nn. 7–38. "[T]he massive statistics cited in the Supreme Court's opinion [in Turner] were undoubtedly brought

United States,[18] the Court's decision to retain the testimonial privilege for spouses in criminal cases rested on a factual assumption: "Adverse testimony given in criminal proceedings would, we think, be likely to destroy almost any marriage." [19]

The Relative Informality of Procedures for Judicial Notice of Legislative Facts. As the above examples demonstrate, the use of legislative facts is an integral part of the process of legal reasoning; the Supreme Court could not have decided *Miranda, Turner,* or *Hawkins* without making factual assumptions.[20] However, these facts are far from indisputable. The Federal Rules of Evidence do not attempt to regulate the use of legislative facts; only indisputable adjudicative facts are covered.[21] The Advisory Committee took the view that judicial notice of legislative facts is not properly a subject of the law of evidence.[22] By excluding legislative facts from Rule 201, the Committee limited the formal procedures prescribed in Rule 201 to judicial notice of adjudicative facts. The Federal Rules illustrate the emerging view that judicial notice of legislative facts should be relatively informal but there should be formal, prescribed procedures for judicial notice of adjudicative facts. The Rules codify the existing practice in many jurisdictions; parties informally present legislative facts to the court by including them in briefs and memoranda, but judges often conduct adversary hearings before ruling on requests for judicial notice of adjudicative facts.

3. Notice of Adjudicative Facts

Suggested Reading:

United States v. Wilson, 451 F.2d 209 (5th Cir. 1971).

People v. Donaldson, 36 A.D.2d 37, 319 N.Y.S.2d 172 (1971).

People v. Billon, 266 Cal.App.2d 537, 72 Cal.Rptr. 198 (1968).

State v. Lawrence, 120 Utah 323, 234 P.2d 600 (1951).

The Bases for Judicially Noticing Adjudicative Facts. Judicially noticeable facts include *facts "generally known" within the community and facts "capable of accurate and ready determination."* [23] These two expressions indicate the two separate bases for judicial notice of adjudicative facts. The first basis is that *the fact is "generally known."* Variously described as "matters of common knowledge," [24] "notorious" [25] facts,

---

into the case through appellate briefs or by judicial notice." United States v. Gonzalez, 442 F.2d 698, 707 n. 4 (2d Cir. 1971) (Kaufman, J., dissenting), cert. denied sub nom. Ovalle v. United States, 404 U.S. 845, 92 S.Ct. 146, 30 L.Ed.2d 81 (1971). The presentation of legislative facts in appellate briefs is commonly called the Brandeis-brief technique. See C. McCormick, Handbook of the Law of Evidence § 331 (2d ed. 1972).

18. 358 U.S. 74, 79 S.Ct. 136, 3 L.Ed.2d 125 (1958).

19. Id. at 78.

20. For another example of the use of legislative facts, see Durham v. United States, 214 F.2d 862 (D. C.Cir. 1954) (extra-record writings used in formulating a new test for insanity.).

21. Advisory Committee Note, Fed.Evid.Rule 201, 28 U.S.C.A. ("No rule deals with judicial notice of 'legislative facts.' "). For a criticism of this approach, see Davis, Judicial Notice, 1969 Law & Soc. Order 512, 525–27.

The distinction between legislative and adjudicative facts is not as clear-cut as the text might suggest. Compare Cleary, infra note 22 at 510, with Davis, supra at 521–23.

22. "Thayer also pointed out that the great proportion of the cases on judicial notice do not raise evidence questions, but relate to pleading, construction of writings, meaning of words, interpretation of conduct, the process of reasoning, and the regulation of trials." Cleary, Foreword, Symposium on the Federal Rules of Evidence, 1969 Law & Soc. Order 509, 510.

23. Fed.Evid.Rule 201(b), 28 U.S.C.A.

24. C. McCormick, Handbook of the Law of Evidence § 329 at 76 (2d ed. 1972).

25. J. Maguire, Evidence, Common Sense and Common Law 168 (1947); E. Morgan, Basic Problems in Evidence 4 (1962); 9 Wigmore, Evidence § 2571(1) (3d ed. 1940); Model Code of Evidence Rule 801.

and "universally known" [26] facts, generally known facts have long been regarded as a proper subject of judicial notice. Notwithstanding these labels, facts in this category need be generally known only within the geographic area in which the court sits.[27] The Federal Rules use the phrase, "generally known within the territorial jurisdiction of the trial court."

The following cases illustrate the first basis for judicial notice of adjudicative facts. In Ross v. United States,[28] the court judicially noticed "that a social security check is sent out by first class mail and bears on its envelope not only a return address but a written direction that if the addressee is deceased, it is to be returned to the sender." [29] In United States v. Chadwick,[30] the court took "judicial notice that federal officers do not patrol the interstate highways or the streets en route; there are no federal jails in the states; and committing magistrates are conveniently available." [31]

Facts that are generally known must be distinguished from facts which the judge personally knows; only the former may be judicially noticed. "There is a real but elusive line between the judge's personal knowledge as a private man and the matters of which he takes judicial notice as a judge. The latter does not necessarily include the former; as a judge, indeed, he may have to ignore what he knows as a man, and contrariwise." [32] An illustration of the improper use of private knowledge by a judge is found in Government of Virgin Islands v. Gereau.[33] In Gereau, the appellate court reversed the lower court judgment because the trial judge relied on his "personal subjective belief about the needs and motives" [34] of a witness whose credibility was an issue in a motion for a new trial.

The second category of judicially noticeable adjudicative facts is that of facts "capable of accurate and ready determination by resort to sources whose accuracy cannot be reasonably questioned." [35] The fact's status as a verifiable certainty is a separate basis for judicial notice. Historical, geographic, physical, and scientific facts have all been noticed as verifiably certain. Thus, courts have judicially noticed "that human blood groupings are . . . are not

---

26. Uniform Rule of Evidence 9(1) (1953).

27. E. Morgan, supra note 25 at 6.

28. 374 F.2d 97 (8th Cir. 1967), cert. denied 389 U.S. 882, 88 S.Ct. 130, 19 L.Ed.2d 177.

29. Id. at 103.

30. 415 F.2d 167 (10th Cir. 1969).

31. Id. at 171. Other examples include: United States v. Wilson, 451 F.2d 209, 214 (5th Cir. 1971), cert. denied sub nom. Fairman v. United States, 405 U.S. 1032, 92 S.Ct. 1298, 31 L.Ed.2d 490 (1972) (Court judicially noticed "that 7:30 P.M. in July . . . is daytime in Dallas during Daylight Savings Time."); Mathis v. Superior Court, 28 Cal.App.3d 1038, 1041, 105 Cal.Rptr. 126, 127 (1972) ("it is a fact sufficiently well known to warrant judicial notice that contraband is often smuggled into custodial institutions"); Jones v. United States, 286 A.2d 861, 863 n. 3 (D.C. App.1972) ("Judicial notice may be taken that such items [tapedecks] are often stolen from parked cars.").

32. 9 Wigmore, Evidence § 2569(a) at 539 (3d ed. 1940). See also E. Morgan, supra note 25 at 5.

Judicial notice of generally known facts should also be distinguished from what has been called "jury knowledge"—the common knowledge and experience that juries and judges bring with them and use in deciding cases. See 9 Wigmore, Evidence § 2570 (3d ed. 1940); Morgan, Judicial Notice, 57 Harv.L.Rev. 269, 272 (1944); E. Devitt and C. Blackmar, Federal Jury Practice and Instructions § 15.01 (3d ed. 1977) (instruction informing the jury to consider evidence "in light of [its] common knowledge of natural tendencies and inclinations of human beings.").

33. 523 F.2d 140 (3d Cir. 1975), cert. denied 424 U.S. 917, 96 S.Ct. 1119, 47 L.Ed.2d 323 (1976).

34. Id. at 147. Another finding of the trial judge "was based solely on the judge's personal knowledge of the soundproofing of his chambers." Id. at 148.

35. Fed.Evid.Rule 201(b), 28 U.S.C.A. See also C. McCormick, Handbook of the Law of Evidence § 330 (2d ed. 1972) ("facts capable of certain verification"); E. Morgan, Basic Problems in Evidence 6 (1962) ("facts capable of immediate demonstration"); 9 Wigmore, Evidence § 2571(3) (3d ed. 1940) ("facts capable of such instant and unquestionable demonstration"); Uniform Rule of Evidence 9(2)(c) (1953); Model Code of Evidence Rule 802(c).

subject to change;"[36] "that cocaine is a derivative of coca leaves;"[37] "that the United States was at war" on certain dates;[38] that "according to the national census of 1920 . . . the population of Gold Hill was 442;"[39] "that the moon on that night (when the crime was committed) rose at 10:57 P.M.;"[40] and that "Fort Rucker is a military enclave under Title 18."[41]

Perhaps the most important use of verifiably certain facts in criminal cases involves scientific facts.[42] Courts have judicially noticed the validity of radar,[43] blood typing,[44] fingerprinting,[45] firearms identifi-

cation,[46] intoxication tests,[47] and electronic weapons detectors (airport magnetometer).[48]

The sources a judge may consult to determine whether a fact is verifiably certain need not be admissible in evidence.[49] However, there does not appear to be any definition of an authoritative source for this purpose.[50] Wigmore states that "any source whatever that suffices to satisfy the judge's mind in making a ruling"[51] is acceptable. The Federal Rules require the source be one "whose accuracy cannot reasonably be questioned."[52]

In many instances the source is clearly acceptable—a calendar to identify the day

---

36. Graves v. Beto, 301 F.Supp. 264, 265 (D.C.Tex. 1969), aff'd 424 F.2d 524 (5th Cir. 1970).

37. United States v. Umentum, 401 F.Supp. 746, 748 (E.D.Wis.1975); accord, United States v. Gould, 536 F.2d 216, 220 (8th Cir. 1976).

38. Seebach v. United States, 262 F. 885, 888 (8th Cir. 1919).

39. State v. Kincaid, 133 Or. 95, 103, 285 P. 1105, 1108 (1930).

40. People v. Mayes, 113 Cal. 618, 625, 45 P. 860, 862 (1896).

41. United States v. Benson, 495 F.2d 475, 482 (5th Cir. 1974), cert. denied 419 U.S. 1035, 95 S.Ct. 519, 42 L.Ed.2d 310 (1974). See also United States v. Anderson, 528 F.2d 590, 592 (5th Cir. 1976) (judicial notice that the event occurred on U.S. Government property); United States v. Miller, 499 F.2d 736 (10th Cir. 1974) (judicial notice that U.S. penitentiary at Leavenworth is within the special territorial jurisdiction of United States); United States v. Harris, 331 F.2d 600 (6th Cir. 1964) (district court can take judicial notice of established geographic facts).

42. See Boyce, Judicial Recognition of Scientific Evidence in Criminal Cases, 8 Utah L.Rev. 313 (1964); Kleri, Judicial Notice of Scientific Facts, 15 Clev.-Mar. L.Rev. 140 (1966); Strong, Questions Affecting the Admissibility of Scientific Evidence, 1970, U.Ill.L.F. 1, 6–9. See Chapter 8.

43. E. g., United States v. Dreos, 156 F.Supp. 200 (D.C.Md.1957); People v. MacLaird, 264 Cal.App.2d 972, 71 Cal.Rptr. 191 (1968); State v. Tomanelli, 153 Conn. 365, 216 A.2d 625 (1966); State v. Gerdes, 291 Minn. 353, 191 N.W.2d 428 (1971); State v. Graham, 322 S.W.2d 188, 195 (Mo.App.1959); State v. Dantonio, 18 N.J. 570, 115 A.2d 35 (1955); People v. Magri, 3 N.Y.2d 562, 170 N.Y.S.2d 335, 147 N.E.2d 728 (1958).

44. E. g., State v. Damm, 64 S.D. 309, 266 N.W. 667 (1936). See generally Ross, The Value of Blood Tests

as Evidence in Paternity Cases, 71 Harv.L.Rev. 466 (1958).

45. E. g., Piquett v. United States, 81 F.2d 75 (7th Cir.), cert. denied 298 U.S. 664, 56 S.Ct. 749, 80 L.Ed. 1388 (1936); People v. Jennings, 252 Ill. 534, 96 N.E. 1077 (1911); Lamble v. State, 96 N.J.L. 231, 114 A. 346 (1921); Grice v. State, 142 Tex.Cr. 4, 151 S.W.2d 211 (1941).

46. E. g., State v. Hackett, 215 S.C. 434, 55 S.E.2d 696 (1949).

47. E. g., State v. Johnson, 42 N.J. 146, 199 A.2d 809 (1964) (drunkometer); People v. Donaldson, 36 A.D.2d 37, 319 N.Y.S.2d 172 (1971) (breathalyzer). See generally Slough & Wilson, Alcohol and the Motorist: Practical and Legal Problems of Chemical Testing, 44 Minn.L.Rev. 673 (1960).

48. United States v. Lopez, 328 F.Supp. 1077 (E.D. N.Y.1971).

49. See E. Morgan, supra note 35 at 10 ("If the issue is whether a matter falls within the scope of judicial notice, neither judge nor counsel will be hampered by the rules of evidence."); Uniform Rule of Evidence 10(2)(b) ("no exclusionary rule except a valid claim of privilege shall apply").

50. Note, The Presently Expanding Concept of Judicial Notice, 13 Vill.L.Rev. 528, 545 (1968).

51. 9 Wigmore, Evidence § 2568a (3d ed. 1940) (listing "official records, encyclopedias, any book or articles" as examples). See also People v. Mayes, 113 Cal. 618, 626, 45 P. 860, 862 (1896) ("any source of information which the judge may deem authentic either by inquiring of others, or by the examination of books, or by receiving the testimony of witnesses").

52. Fed.Evid.Rule 201(b), 28 U.S.C.A. See E. Morgan, supra note 35 at 6 ("by resort to sources of indisputable accuracy").

of the week on which a date fell in a particular year, the official census to determine population, or history texts to establish historical facts. Sources relied on to establish scientific facts are more problematical. As one court [53] has noted: "Practically every new scientific discovery has its detractors and unbelievers, but neither unanimity of opinion nor universal infallibility is required for judicial acceptance of generally recognized matters." [54]

Courts have also cited court records to establish facts. In United States v. Alvarado,[55] for example, the Fifth Circuit stated: "The trial judge was warranted in taking judicial notice of immutable geographic and physical facts adjudicated in a previous proceeding." [56] In Government of Virgin Islands v. Testamark,[57] the appellate court upheld the trial court's taking judicial notice of a defendant's prior conviction for purposes of impeachment.

The Formal Procedures for Judicial Notice of Adjudicative Facts. A court may judicially notice an adjudicative fact on a party's request or its own motion.[58] Under the Federal Rules the court has discretion in taking judicial notice unless it is "requested by a party and supplied with the necessary information;" [59] in that circum-

stance, notice is mandatory. Nevertheless the court retains residual discretion with respect to the tenor of the fact to be noticed and whether the information supplied to establish a fact "capable of accurate and ready determination" is sufficient.[60] In addition, the Rules require a party be afforded an "opportunity to be heard as to the propriety of taking judicial notice and the tenor of the matter noticed"[61] if a timely request is made. If judicial notice is taken sua sponte, a party is entitled to be heard after notice has been taken.[62] The hearing should be held outside the jury's presence.[63]

The Supreme Court suggested in Garner v. Louisiana [64] that denial of an opportunity to be heard may violate a defendant's due process rights: "Unless an accused is informed at the trial of the facts of which the court is taking judicial notice, not only does he not know upon what evidence he is being convicted, but, in addition, he is deprived of any opportunity to challenge the deductions drawn from such notice or to dispute the notoriety or truth of the facts allegedly relied upon. Moreover, there is no way by which an appellate court may review the facts and law of a case and intelligently decide whether the findings of the lower court are supported by the evidence where the evidence is unknown. Such an assumption would be denial of due process." [65]

53. State v. Johnson, 42 N.J. 146, 199 A.2d 809 (1964).

54. Id. at 171, 199 A.2d at 823. See also McKay v. State, 155 Tex.Cr.R. 416, 419, 235 S.W.2d 173, 174 (1950) ("This Court may recognize generally accepted scientific conclusions, even though there should be some who disagree with them. In all probability a scientist may be found who will disagree with practically every generally accepted scientific theory.").

55. 519 F.2d 1133, 1135 (5th Cir. 1975), cert. denied 424 U.S. 911, 96 S.Ct. 1107, 47 L.Ed.2d 315 (1976).

56. Id. at 1135.

57. 528 F.2d 742 (3d Cir. 1976).

58. Fed.Evid.Rule 201(c), 28 U.S.C.A.; Uniform Rules of Evidence 9(2) (1953); Model Code of Evidence, Rules 801–02.

59. Fed.Evid.Rule 201(d), 28 U.S.C.A.; see also Uniform Rule of Evidence 9(3) (1953); Model Code

of Evidence Rule 803. Uniform Rule 9(1) and Model Rule 801 require the court to judicially notice certain matters even if not requested by a party.

60. See Morgan, Judicial Notice, 57 Harv.L.Rev. 269, 274–75 (1944) ("Whether or not the truth of a given proposition is disputable may itself be the subject of dispute among reasonable men.").

61. Fed.Evid.Rule 201(e), 28 U.S.C.A.

62. A party may have no advance notice that a fact will be judicially noticed. "In the absence of advance notice, a request for an opportunity to be heard made after the fact could not in fairness be considered untimely." Advisory Committee Note, Fed.Evid.Rule 201(e), 28 U.S.C.A.

63. See Fed.Evid.Rule 103(c), 28 U.S.C.A.

64. 368 U.S. 157, 82 S.Ct. 248, 7 L.Ed.2d 207 (1961).

65. Id. at 173.

There are three pressing questions concerning the formal procedures for judicial notice of adjudicative facts. Is the jury bound to find a judicially noticed fact? May an ultimate fact be judicially noticed in a criminal case? Is evidence controverting the noticed fact admissible? These issues can best be examined by considering the conflicting views on the function of judicial notice held by Professor Morgan and Dean Wigmore.

Professor Morgan argued that only indisputable matters should be judicially noticed. This theory focuses on the judicial function of resolving disputes.[66] A court "cannot adjust legal relations among members of society and thus fulfill the sole purpose of its creation if it permits the parties to take issue on, and thus secure results contrary to, what is so notoriously true as not to be the subject of reasonable dispute, or what is capable of immediate and accurate demonstration by resort to sources of indisputable accuracy easily accessible to men in the situation of members of the court." [67] Under this theory, once a fact has been judicially noticed, the matter is settled; no evidence tending to disprove the fact is admissible, and the jury is instructed that they must find the noticed fact.

In contrast, the Wigmore view,[68] advocated originally by Thayer [69] and current-ly by Davis,[70] is that the doctrine of judicial notice is based on expedience. "Proving facts with evidence takes time and effort. Noticing facts is simple, easier, and more convenient." [71] Consequently, facts which are "probably true" should be judicially noticed even though they may not be indisputable.[72] Under this theory, the opponent is entitled to introduce controverting evidence to persuade the jury to find against the judicially noticed fact.[73] Furthermore, the jury is instructed that they are not bound to find the judicially noticed fact if they are not convinced of its truth. In effect, judicial notice functions as a presumption.

Jury Instructions. The Federal Rules of Evidence purport to follow the Morgan view of judicial notice. Rule 201(b) provides: "A judicially noticed fact must be one not subject to reasonable dispute." The Advisory Committee Note is more explicit: "Within its relatively narrow area of adjudicative facts, the rule contemplates that there is to be no evidence before the jury in disproof. The judge instructs the jury to take judicially noticed facts as established." [74]

However, subsection (g) of the Rule concerning jury instructions in criminal cas-

---

66. See E. Morgan, Basic Problems in Evidence 9–10 (1962); Morgan, Judicial Notice, 57 Harv.L.Rev. 269 (1944); Morgan, The Law of Evidence, 1941–45, 59 Harv.L.Rev. 481, 482–87 (1946). See also C. McCormick, Handbook of the Law of Evidence 710–11 (1954); McNaughton, Judicial Notice—Excerpts Relating to the Morgan-Wigmore Controversy, 14 Vand. L.Rev. 779 (1961).

67. Morgan, Judicial Notice, 57 Harv.L.Rev. 269, 273 (1944). "The obvious policy is that parties shall not be permitted to dispute by proof what the judge has found to be a moot or sham issue, not susceptible of reasonable dispute." C. McCormick, Handbook of the Law of Evidence § 330 at 710–11 (1954).

68. 9 Wigmore, Evidence § 2567 (3d ed. 1940).

69. Thayer, A Preliminary Treatise on Evidence at Common Law 308 (1898).

70. Davis, Judicial Notice, 55 Colum.L.Rev. 945, 948–52 (1955); Davis, Judicial Notice, 1969 Law & Soc. Order 513, 517–19.

71. Davis, Judicial Notice, 1969 Law & Soc. Order 513, 515.

72. "The ultimate principle is that extra-record facts should be assumed whenever it is convenient to assume them, except that convenience should always yield to the requirement of procedural fairness that parties should have an opportunity to meet in the appropriate fashion all facts that influence the disposition of the case." Id.

73. 9 Wigmore, Evidence § 2567 (3d ed. 1940) ("the opponent is not prevented from disputing the matter by evidence.").

74. This provision was taken from a preliminary draft of the Rules which was subsequently deleted by the Supreme Court. See 46 F.R.D. 161, 204 (1969). As promulgated by the Court, subsection (g) required the jury to find a judicially noticed fact in both criminal and civil cases.

es was changed by Congress. It now reads: "In a criminal case the court shall instruct the jury that it may, but is not required to, accept as conclusive any fact judicially noticed." According to the House Judiciary Committee Report, the change resulted from a belief that a "mandatory instruction to a jury in a criminal case to accept as conclusive any fact judicially noticed is inappropriate because contrary to the spirit of the Sixth Amendment right to jury trial." [75]

The leading criminal case regarding jury instructions on judicially noticed facts is State v. Lawrence.[76] In prosecuting the defendant for grand larceny of an automobile, the government failed to introduce evidence to establish that the value of the car exceeded the minimum statutory amount ($50.00) for grand larceny. Instead, at the prosecutor's request, the court judicially noticed the value of the car and instructed the jury that the car had a value in excess of $50. In reversing, the appellate court reasoned: "The provision of our State Constitution which grants accused persons the right to a trial by jury extends to each and all of the facts which must be found to be present to constitute the crime charged, and such right may not be invaded by the presiding judge indicating to the jury that any of such facts are established by the evidence. If a court can take one important element of an offense from the jury and determine the facts for them because such facts seem plain enough to him, then which element cannot be similarly taken away, and where would the process stop?" [77] Lawrence reflects the same policy that supports the rule prohibiting directed verdicts against criminal defendants; it is a recognition of jury nullifi-

cation.[78] The view expressed in Lawrence and in Rule 201(g), however, has not been universally accepted.[79]

Judicial Notice of Ultimate Facts. One commentator [80] reads Lawrence more broadly than a prohibition on binding jury instructions. Instead, it is asserted that the case precludes a trial judge from judicially noticing ultimate facts which are essential elements of the charged offense.[81] Others cite Lawrence only for the narrow proposition that courts are reluctant to judicially notice ultimate facts.[82] The Federal Rules permit the court to judicially notice all adjudicative facts not subject to reasonable dispute, presumably including ultimate facts. However, the trial jury is still not bound to find the noticed fact.

At the appellate level, judicial notice of ultimate facts presents additional problems. It is well-settled that an appellate court may judicially notice a fact for the first time on

---

78. "Under our jury system, it is traditional that in criminal cases juries can, and sometimes do, make findings which are not based on logic, nor even common sense." 120 Utah at 330, 234 P.2d at 603.

79. The Advisors to the Maine Rules of Evidence reached the opposite conclusion: "It would be as absurd in a criminal case as in a civil action to allow jurors to question the accuracy of the court's instruction as to what day of the week December 4, 1972 actually was." Maine Advisors' Note, Me.Evid. Rule 201. See also Advisory Committee Note, Fed. Evid.Rule 201, 28 U.S.C.A. ("the right to jury trial does not extend to matters which are beyond reasonable dispute").

80. 1 J. Weinstein & M. Berger, Weinstein's Evidence 201–48 (1976) ("Lawrence stands only for the proposition that judicial notice of a consequential, material fact cannot be taken against the defendant.").

81. There is some support for this view. See State v. Main, 94 R.I. 338, 346, 180 A.2d 814, 818–19 (1962) ("a trial court may not properly supply essential evidence in a criminal case through an exercise of its power to take judicial notice of matters that are of common knowledge."); State v. Welch, 363 A.2d 1356 (R.I.1976).

82. C. McCormick, Handbook of the Law of Evidence § 320 at 760 n. 19 (2d ed. 1972).

---

75. H.R.Rep. No. 93–650, 93d Cong., 1st Sess. 6–7 (1973), reprinted in 1974 U.S.Code Cong. & Ad.News 7080. See generally E. Devitt & C. Blackmar, Federal Jury Practice and Instructions § 11.11 (3d ed. 1977).

76. 120 Utah 323, 234 P.2d 600 (1951).

77. Id. at 330, 234 P.2d at 603, quoting State v. Estrada, 119 Utah 339, 341, 227 P.2d 247, 248 (1951).

appeal.[83] The question presented is whether an appellate court may judicially notice a fact which the prosecutor failed to establish at trial, either through the introduction of evidence or through judicial notice. In People v. Billon,[84] the defendant was tried for possession of a firearm by a person with a felony conviction which involved a firearm. The appellate court held that admitting the record of a previous conviction for assault with a deadly weapon did not establish that the weapon was a firearm. The court refused to judicially notice the record in the assault case, which showed the use of a firearm, because it "would deny defendant his right to jury trial."[85] In effect, the prosecutor attempted to use judicial notice to cure a defective record. The Supreme Court rejected such a use in *Garner*: "To extend the doctrine of judicial notice to the length pressed by the respondent would require us to allow the prosecution to do through argument to this Court what it is required by due process to do at the trial, and would be 'to turn the doctrine into a pretext for dispensing with a trial.'"[86]

Admissibility of Controverting Evidence. A related problem concerns the criminal defendant's right to introduce evidence controverting a judicially noticed fact. Several courts, citing Wigmore, have held rebuttal evidence admissible: "Judicial notice of the proposition is in no sense conclusive, and the opponent is not prevented from dis-

puting it by evidence if he believes it to be disputable."[87] Federal Rule 201 is unclear on this issue. Rebuttal evidence is inadmissible in civil cases,[88] but it has been argued that the Congressional change in the criminal jury instruction implies a right to offer rebuttal evidence to the jury.[89]

The argument favoring the admissibility of rebuttal evidence can be framed in constitutional terms: The exclusion of evidence rebutting a judicially noticed fact violates the defendant's rights to confrontation and jury trial.[90] The counter argument is that if the fact is indisputable, there is no infringement: "Jury trial does not extend to matters which are beyond reasonable dispute"[91] and "accepting what is plainly true could not abridge any Sixth Amendment right to confront witnesses."[92] As a practical matter, a trial judge should not take judicial notice in the first place if the defense produces evidence controverting the fact, especially if the fact is an element of the offense.

4. Notice of Law

Judges judicially notice law in their law-finding function. At common law a state trial court was assumed to know the statutory and common law of the state. State

83. See, e. g., Fed.Evid.Rule 201(f), 28 U.S.C.A. ("Judicial notice may be taken at any stage of the proceeding."). See 9 Wigmore, Evidence § 2567(c) (3d ed. 1940).

84. 266 Cal.App.2d 537, 72 Cal.Rptr. 198 (1968).

85. Id. at 540, 72 Cal.Rptr. at 201. See also United States v. Sorenson, 504 F.2d 406, 410 (7th Cir. 1974) (Court refused to judicially notice ultimate fact on appeal on double jeopardy grounds); State v. Main, 94 R.I. 338, 180 A.2d 814 (1962) (judicial notice of ultimate fact to save prosecutor from post-trial directed verdict held improper).

86. 368 U.S. at 173, quoting Ohio Bell Telephone Co. v. Public Utilities Comm., 301 U.S. 292, 302, 57 S.Ct. 724, 729, 81 L.Ed. 1093 (1937).

87. State v. Tomanelli, 153 Conn. 365, 369, 216 A. 2d 625, 628–29 (1966); accord, State v. Duranleau, 99 N.H. 30, 33, 104 A.2d 519, 522 (1954) ("It is important that the use of judicial notice should not deprive the defendant of rebutting any matter that is judicially noticed.").

88. Advisory Committee Note, Fed.Evid.Rule 201, 28 U.S.C.A.

89. See K. Redden & S. Saltzburg, Federal Rules of Evidence Manual 30 (1976 Supp.) ("We believe that Rule 201(g) intends to leave the parties in a criminal case free to rebut whatever is noticed.").

90. See Note, The Presently Expanding Concept of Judicial Notice, 13 Vill.L.Rev. 528, 541–50 (1968).

91. Advisory Committee Note, Fed.Evid.Rule 201, 28 U.S.C.A. The provision to which this section of the Note refers was subsequently changed by Congress.

92. United States v. Alvarado, 519 F.2d 1133, 1135 (5th Cir. 1975), cert. denied 424 U.S. 911, 96 S.Ct. 1107, 47 L.Ed.2d 315 (1976).

judges were also assumed to know federal law.[93] Because domestic statewide law was not subject to proof, it became commonplace to speak of judicial knowledge of these laws in judicial notice terms: "A trial judge must take judicial notice of the domestic law of the jurisdiction of which he is a judicial officer."[94] The assumption of judicial knowledge of law, however, generally did not extend to private laws, administrative regulations, or municipal ordinances. These laws as well as the laws of sister states and foreign countries (laws of another forum) were treated as questions of fact to be pleaded and proved like other facts.[95] A split of authority existed concerning whether such a question of fact was more properly one for the judge than the jury.[96]

Treating certain categories of laws as questions of fact was probably justified at an earlier time when access to reliable versions of these laws was a legitimate concern. Foreign law created the further need for assistance in translation and interpretation. Because access to reliable sources has improved, however, these archaic rules have been changed by statute or court decision in most jurisdictions. For example, a majority of states have adopted the Uniform Judicial Notice of Foreign Law Act[97] which requires the laws of sister states to be judicially noticed. In addition, there are statutes requiring judicial notice of administrative regulations.[98] The law of foreign countries, however, is still treated as a question of fact in many jurisdictions. The Federal Rules of Criminal Procedure have adopted a progressive view by treating foreign law as a question of law, not fact. Rule 26.1 provides: "A party who intends to raise an issue concerning the law of a foreign country shall give reasonable written notice. The court, in determining foreign law, may consider any relevant material or source, including testimony, whether or not submitted by a party or admissible under the Federal Rules of Evidence. The court's determination shall be treated as a ruling on a question of law."[99]

The Advisory Committee of the Federal Rules of Evidence took the position that "the manner in which law is fed into the judicial process is never a proper concern of the rules of evidence but rather of the rules of procedure."[1] This approach seems to represent the modern view of judicial notice of law.[2]

93. Federal courts judicially notice the laws of the states. International and maritime law are also subject to judicial notice. See C. McCormick, Handbook of the Law of Evidence § 335 at 776–81 (2d ed. 1972).

94. E. Morgan, Basic Problems of Evidence 1 (1962).

95. See E. Morgan, supra note 94 at 1–4; 9 Wigmore, Evidence §§ 2572–73 (3d ed. 1940); Keeffe, Landis & Shaad, Sense and Nonsense About Judicial Notice, 2 Stan.L.Rev. 664, 672–88 (1950).

96. 9 Wigmore, Evidence § 2558 (3d ed. 1940); Keeffe, Landis & Shaad, supra note 95 at 674–75.

97. 9A Uniform L.Ann. 569 (1965). See also McKinney Consol.Laws of N.Y. CPLR 4511; West's Ann. Cal.Evid.Code § 452; Conn.Gen.Stat.Ann. § 52–163; Mich.Comp.Laws Ann. § 600.2114a; Uniform Rule of Evidence 9(1) (1953).

98. See, e. g., 44 U.S.C.A. § 1507 (judicial notice of contents of Federal Register required).

99. Fed.Cr.Proc.Rule 26.1, 18 U.S.C.A. See generally 2 Wright, Federal Practice and Procedure § 431 (1969); Miller, Federal Rule 44.1 and the "Fact" Approach to Determining Foreign Law: Death Knell for a Die-Hard Doctrine, 65 Mich.L.Rev. 615 (1967).

1. Advisory Committee Note, Fed.Evid.Rule 201, 28 U.S.C.A.

2. C. McCormick, Handbook of the Law of Evidence § 329 at 759–60 (2d ed. 1972).

*

INDEX